International Business

This eagerly awaited update of a popular text has been substantially revised and updated to incorporate developments in the field of International Business. It continues to do so in Alan Sitkin's characteristically direct, lively and accessible style which is ideal for introductory students.

This new edition expands upon issues of growing importance to global businesses, including corporate social responsibility, corporate citizenship and sustainability. It explores topics of great importance to business at the start of the new decade, including digital transformation and digital business, and explores the intersection of technology and pandemic-accelerated change to look to the future of business in a global setting.

Enriched with practitioner examples as well as new, colourful and illustrative cases, and ideally structured to make navigation and learning straightforward, this textbook is an ideal introduction to international business. Tutors are supported with a range of materials including an instructor manual, testbank, suggested assignment questions and resources to offer their students, such as revision tips, additional cases and self-test multiple-choice questions.

Alan Sitkin is Assistant Professor at Regent's University London, UK, following previous careers both in international banking and as a local politician with responsibility for economic development.

T0384009

"At Reuters Group PLC I managed operations in over 100 countries and learned the hard way how to manage across borders. In *International Business: Attitudes and Alternatives*, Alan Sitkin provides a master class in International Business for the aspiring global manager".

—**Tom Glocer,** *former CEO, Reuters*

"By also analysing international business from an economic, political, social and ecological perspective, the book offers a comprehensive overview of this field in all its complexity".

—**Andy Love,** *former MP, Member of the UK Parliamentary Treasury Committee 2005 to 2015*

International Business

Attitudes and Alternatives

Second edition

Alan Sitkin

Routledge
Taylor & Francis Group

LONDON AND NEW YORK

Second edition published 2022
by Routledge
2 Park Square, Milton Park, Abingdon, Oxon, OX14 4RN

and by Routledge
605 Third Avenue, New York, NY 10158

Routledge is an imprint of the Taylor & Francis Group, an informa business

First edition published by Oxford University Press 2013

British Library Cataloguing-in-Publication Data
A catalogue record for this book is available from the British Library

Library of Congress Cataloging-in-Publication Data
Names: Sitkin, Alan, author.
Title: International business / Alan Sitkin.
Description: Second Edition. | New York, NY: Routledge, 2022. |
Includes bibliographical references and index.
Identifiers: LCCN 2021022999 | ISBN 9780367746803 (hardback) |
ISBN 9780367746773 (paperback) | ISBN 9781003159056 (ebook)
Subjects: LCSH: International business enterprises. | International
business enterprises—Management.
Classification: LCC HD2755.5 .S5635 2022 | DDC 658/.049—dc23
LC record available at https://lccn.loc.gov/2021022999

ISBN: 978-0-367-74680-3 (hbk)
ISBN: 978-0-367-74677-3 (pbk)
ISBN: 978-1-003-15905-6 (ebk)

DOI: 10.4324/9781003159056

Typeset in Sabon
by codeMantra

Access the Support Material: www.routledge.com/9780367746803

Contents

Figures

Chapter 3

Chapter 4

Chapter 5

Chapter 6

Chapter 7

Chapter 8

Chapter 9

Chapter 10

Chapter 11

Chapter 12

Chapter 13

Chapter 14

Chapter 15

Credits for the part photos

Tables

Preface

An academic text about international business will always be expected to speak to cross-border exchanges' growing importance to the world economy, the causes and effects of globalisation, and the mechanics by means of which multinational enterprises operate in foreign markets. All these subjects do, of course, feature prominently in this book, which includes both macro-, country-level analyses of the different settings within which international business takes place as well as micro-, company-level analyses of what companies do within such environments – without forgetting the way that these two spheres interact with one another.

On top of this, however, *International Business: Attitudes and Alternatives* works with readers to investigate not only the calculated business strategies that practitioners might pursue in different cross-border situations but also to delve into the psychology of the individuals involved, highlighting human subjectivity and how it affects thought processes. By deconstructing decision-makers as well as decisions, this book provides suitable material both for undergraduate students first discovering this subject area while also enriching the curriculum with more behavioural components and offering in this way a natural progression towards postgraduate programmes. In addition, it leverages the author's 16-year career in international business before he became an academic to help prepare impending graduates for many of the real-life situations they will encounter once they start working in this exhilarating but complicated profession. Notwithstanding the respect due to textbooks aspiring to reveal a "one-best-way" checklist for success, experience teaches that it is much more important that learners be empowered to measure the full range of potential responses to the different circumstances they will face. International business is a social science embedded in the contradictions of human behaviour. Humility dictates that success therefore be defined as optimisation under constraint, a paradigm that constitutes one of this book's guiding principles.

The other is the common humanity of all peoples on Earth and the possibility for international business practitioners to bridge differences in a way that is not only profitable and mutually beneficial but actually very beautiful. The book defies the voices of isolationism who seek to separate communities for demagogic purposes. Even as their cacophony is part of the backdrop against which cross-border interaction takes place – and must therefore be accounted for – the long arc of history has always shown that cooperation, empathy and respect produce infinitely better outcomes for all of humankind than fear and hate. Our differences enrich all of us. International business builds bridges, not walls.

Acknowledgements

This book was written during the second and third UK Covid-19 lockdowns. Before recognising my near and dear ones who have done so much to make my life happy and international, it seems fitting to first acknowledge the epic and selfless work performed this past year by the many citizens who put their lives on the line so the rest of us could survive. First and foremost the stalwart nurses, doctors and other hospital and medical staff; together with the genius scientists and researchers. But also all the frontline workers taking risks day in day out. All heroes we may not know personally but who remind us, as the poet said, that no (hu)man is an island. It is a fitting message for a book on internationalism and where engagement is the seminal value. I thank you from the bottom of my heart.

Heartfulness of course has also been the subtext of a life lived across borders. And I'm deeply grateful. Parents for Watts 65 and Quinto Lingo. Panthers and Gauchos for the stream of warm impermanence. EAP lads for sharing the fascination. Lindens for the liberalism. But mainly Mitchel and Laurel for letting me have my cake and eat it too. You made it easy.

Merci le Sud-Ouest de m'avoir montré d'autres chemins. Je ne connais qu'un devoir – c'est celui d'aimer. Gleichfalls Ihr Hamburger. Es geht nirgends merkwuerdiger zu als auf der Welt.

Brexit heartbreak but I know you agree. We got Haifa in Cambridge, Cork in Aix, Southampton in Wales, Glasgow in Islington, Yanks and Italians in Winchmore Hill. And to top it all, Cypriot-Irish barbecues in Enfield. Without forgetting other good Blighties in Blighty, including the ones we've lost. Always look on the bright side…

Thanks Routledge Amy and Assunta and Alex and Terry. Beer and podcasts, what's not to like? Idem pals past and present from EBS/ Regents Uni, where internationalism is said out loud.

Above all, above all. Utter pride in my loveliest Boo and my admirable Spaniel. DIL, West Wing and Bronte. Ueberhaupt my beautiful Eda. To HH from California with love.

And I think to myself, what a wonderful world.

Glossary

Abatement – Preventing bad outcomes from occurring ex ante

Absolute advantage – Where one country, providing the same quantum of inputs as another, achieves greater outputs and can therefore be said to produce more cheaply

Absorptive capabilities – Speed and facility with which a company integrates feedback from its own experiences and performance

Accountability – Precept that actors must take responsibility for their actions

Acculturate – Where a minority culture assimilates the values or customs of a new culture, usually a dominant one

Affiliate – Foreign unit in which a parent company has a minority stake

Agency – Empowerment to make decisions autonomously

Altruistic – Prioritising the well-being of others rather than oneself

Anecdotal – Conversational, often based on stereotyping. The opposite of scientifically demonstrated

Apatride – Stateless; not associated with any particular nationality

Artificial intelligence – Learning achieved by computer or machine

Autarky – Where an entity operates self-sufficiently and in isolation

Barriers to entry – Regulatory, competitive, financial and other obstacles that make it difficult for a firm to enter a particular market

Basis point – One hundredth of one percent. A common unit in international finance

Beggar-thy-neighbour policies – Where one country manipulates its competitive positioning (often via currency devaluations) to try and gain advantage over its trading partners

Behavioural – Incorporating human agency into explanations of social phenomena

Boundaries of the firm – Scope of the value chain operations that a company performs by itself

Bricks-and-mortars – Tangible physical (as opposed to virtual) operations

Brownfield investment – Where a firm enters a market by buying existing facilities

Bulk purchasing – Companies buying inputs in large quantities have a better chance of negotiating lower per-unit prices with buyers due to the latter's economies of scale

Business cycle – Period during which the economy alternates between boom and bust

Business-to-business (B2B) – Interactions between companies that operate at an intermediary stage of a product's global value chain

Business-to-consumer (B2C) – Interaction between a company operating at the downstream end of the global value chain and a finished product's end user

Cachet – Status due to reputation

Capital flight – Where investors or savers take large sums of money out of a country because of concerns about local risks or disagreements with policy

Capital markets – Virtual but also physical locations where all medium and long-term debt and equity transactions are traded

Cartel – Permanent or ad hoc grouping of producers who collaborate on supply quantity decisions and pricing instead of competing with one another

Catch-up – Term used in development studies in reference to emerging countries' efforts to match their Global North comparators' economic (including technological) performance

Chaebol – South Korean equivalent of Japanese *keiretsu* but where founding family generally retains a majority stake

Clearing – Process of calculating and paying net differences between the amounts due to/owed by system participants

Cluster – Where firms in a similar line of business operate in close physical proximity to one another and build close ties. This can reflect historical factors or strategic intent

Cluster – Where firms in a similar line of business operate in physical proximity to one another and build close ties. This can reflect historical factors or strategic intent

Code of conduct – List of rules detailing accepted behaviour within an organisation

Commitment to internationalisation – Depth of a company's engagement of physical, financial, human and psychic resources in foreign markets

Commoditised – Lacking any particular rarity value

Comparative advantage – Where one country makes all goods more efficiently than another but agrees not to make (hence to import) the good whose production makes the least efficient use of its resources

Competitive intelligence – Compilation and analysis of external information

Complementarity – Where counterparts benefit from association because each offers strengths that other lacks

Configuration – How and where a company locates its various corporate functions such as research, production, marketing and finance

Consolidation – Where producers within a sector acquire or merge with one another in an attempt to reduce over-capacities

Consumer tribes – Communities whose sense of joint identity is based on visible adherence to a particular brand

Corporate governance – Laws and processes regulating a company's executive and accounting practices

Cosmopolitan – Sophisticated, worldly, comfortable in all different environments. The opposite of parochial

Country risk – All the different categories of uncertainty potentially affecting investment in a given country

Coupling – Where countries' economic fortunes are linked due to the inseparability of their economic and financial interests

Credit crunch – Where financial market conditions make it difficult for borrowers to access the funding they need

Critical mass – Minimum threshold beyond which positive, size-related benefits arise

Cultural affinity – Where individuals from different cultural subgroups possess harmonious values and worldviews, notwithstanding their other differences

Cultural flexibility – Willingness and ability to apply the values and customs of a culture other than one's own

Cultural pairing – Specific dynamic between two cultures

Currency squeeze – Where the currencies in which a MNE is long (short) as a result of its international configuration tend to fall (rise) to the point of making international business impossible without some reconfiguration

Currency/capital controls – Where government places administrative restrictions on people's ability to buy/sell the national currency, or to borrow/lend capital across borders

Debt relief – Forgiving debt because the original loan had been misused or embezzled or because reimbursement would be too onerous for the borrower

Decarbonisation – Efforts to reduce an activity's CO_2 emissions

Deferred differentiation – Achieving both economies of scale and product diversity by standardising manufacturing inputs as long as possible and customising outputs as late as possible

Denominate – The specified currency in which a transaction takes place

Design – Activities aimed at defining a product's final shape and attributes

Deskilling – Where lesser competency is required of employees, often because they are being asked to specialise in one or very few value chain operation(s)

Developmental capitalism – Market economy where state often intervenes but primarily to help companies become more competitive

Digitalised – Data converted from physical to digital form for computer processing purposes

Disassembly – Act of breaking a product down into its component parts

Disclosure – Provision of information, often in a specified form to comply with legal requirements

Discretionary spending – Expenditure on non-essential items

Downstream – Late value chain activities undertaken when selling or distributing a product or service

Dumping – Where exporters sell goods at a loss or below the normal price to gain market share and put rivals out of business

Ecological imperative – Precept that restoring environmental sustainability is paramount

Economic patriotism – Where a society or government demonstrates preference for national interests by purchasing domestic products and/or restricting foreign ownership

Economies of scale – Decline in per-unit production costs due to increased output without any increase in assets

Economies of scope – Efficiencies achieved via product portfolio management synergies

Ecosphere – Sum total of living flora or fauna whose interactions with one another enable life on the Earth

Elasticity – Correlation between variables such as income or price and demand for a particular item (or class of items)

Enabling factors – Pre-conditions for an outcome to occur

End users – Final parties consuming a product after it has undergone all intermediary value chain transformations

Endogenous – Inwardly-oriented

Energy-intensity – Energy spend as a proportion of sales, income, etc.

Environmental management system – Accounting and reporting framework used to track and report upon a company's environmental procedures and performance

Environmental footprint – Consumption effects depleting the stock of natural resources; economic activity effects damaging living systems

ESG funding – Investing in companies accredited with certain sustainability qualifications

Ethical premium – Surcharge that consumers pay for a certifiably sustainable item

Ethical reporting group – Associations of companies and other organisations promising to respect certain ethical standards

Ethnologist – Student of cultural differences

Ex post – After the fact. The opposite of "ex ante", or before the fact

Exceptionalism – Sentiment that the attributes of a particular group make it dissimilar – and superior – to any other

Exogenous – Outwardly-oriented

Expatriate – Employee seconded on a long-term or permanent basis to a MNE's foreign office

Exposure – Where assets and liabilities do not match for a given commodity whose price fluctuates. Broader conception of "risk"

Expropriation – Where private property is seized by a government, often without compensation

Externalities – Where the positive or negative consequences of an economic action impact parties not directly involved in it

Extractive industries – Mining and fossil fuel industries that take raw materials out of the ground

Factor endowments – Human, financial and physical capital that an economic entity (often a country) can use in its production process

Factor mobility – Capacity of factor inputs (capital, resources, labour, etc.) to move in time and/or place

Fair trade – Business defined by the equitable distribution of profits up and down the global value chain to ensure that upstream producers receive a decent "living" wage

Fair value – Where the market price for an asset, financial or other, reflects all accurate information regarding its utility

Federative organisation – Entities whose constituent parts work both as autonomous units free to pursue their own goals yet remain members of a unified enterprise

Feed-in tariffs – Public subsidies paid to incentivise private micro-generation selling surplus electricity to the grid

Financial globalisation – Deregulation of global capital markets leading to an acceleration in cross-border capital transfers

Financialisation – View that a company's singular mission is to maximise short-term financial returns

Finite – Non-renewable

Fintech – Technology developed to automate financial services like payments but also credit and market analysis, etc.

First mover advantage – Benefit of being the first to enter a given market in a given location

Follow sourcing – Supplier FDI in locale after prime contractor has done the same

Foreign direct investment (FDI) – Where companies fund a permanent or semi-permanent unit overseas. The OECD defines FDI as a situation where a foreign owner has an equity stake of at least 10 per cent in a company's ordinary shares and aims to establish a "lasting interest" in the host country

Foreign exchange (FX) market – Virtual marketplace(s) where currency prices are set through market supply and demand

Foreignness – Degree to which a national environment varies from the ones to which observer is accustomed

Forward contracts – Deals where price is agreed today for delivery at a specified future date

Franchising – Arrangement where franchiser grants permission to franchisee to run business bearing its name, often using supplies it provides. Franchiser to receive income in return, often based on franchise performance

Free ride – Where a party benefits from an economic activity without contributing to its costs

Free trade zone – "Export processing zones" where companies pay little or no taxes or tariffs on imported items destined for (assembly into) export products

Free trade – Belief that private interests should largely enjoy open access to foreign markets

Frugal – Characterised by thrifty use of inputs and/or pared down functionalities

Functional organisation – Structure focused on cross-border integration of internal capabilities

Functionality – Purpose for which a product is being consumed

Generic – Items not meant for a specific use but serving as the basis for a variety of applications

Geographic organisation – Structure based on idea that the MNE's overriding organisational should be to maximise adaptation to local circumstances

Gig economy – Where employment opportunities made available to workers are predicated on their being classified, often involuntarily, as independent contractors

Global firm – Company designed to serve a single world market instead of a variety of national markets

Global governance – Regulatory and supervisory functions fulfilled by authorities whose oversight transcends national borders

Global North – World's older industrialised nations

Global South – Countries whose industrial base and general level of human welfare is such that many citizens struggle to achieve a decent living standard. This is an umbrella term covering a vast range of economic, social and demographic situations, ranging from "emerging" or "newly industrialised" nations to "heavily indebted poor countries" (HIPC) with very poor growth prospects

Globalisation – Process whereby the world becomes increasingly interconnected socially, economically, politically and commercially

Goodwill – Difference between price at which company can be purchased and break-up value of its assets

Gravity model – Prediction that intensity of international exchanges correlates negatively with geographic and sociocultural distance

Green premium – Surcharge paid for a green product over the equivalent non-green product

Green redemption – Where a company restores a tarnished environmental reputation through positive action

Greenfield investment – Where firm enters market by building new facilities

Gross domestic product (GDP) – National income, defined by aggregate consumption plus/minus investment activity plus/minus government spending plus/minus trade balance

Halo effect – Where a party feels virtuous after transacting with another party deemed to be virtuous

Hedging – Where a party offsets an original risk through a new deal exposing it to the exact opposite risk. The original exposure is called the "underlying" risk. The new exposure is called the "hedge"

Hegemon – Single, supreme power

Heterarchy – Organisation where constituent units are allied and considered of equal value, hence attributed equal leadership roles

Home bias – Preference for domestic counterparts

Home currency – Currency used to calculate a MNE's consolidated global accounts

Home/host countries – People and companies originate from a "home country". When they operate abroad, they are working in a "host country"

Horizontal integration – Where the activities that a company launches in a new market are at a similar stage of the value chain as the one where it operates in its home market

Horizontal *keiretsu* – Japanese corporate network where firms in similar sectors ally with trading companies to ensure widest possible market coverage

Incompressible imports – Items indispensable to a country's economy but which it has no way of producing itself and must therefore import

Industrialisation policies – Concerted efforts by states to increase the role of value-added manufacturing in their national economy or support industrial sectors considered strategic

Infant industry – Sector of activity that has only recently developed in a particular country and whose prospects for survival are uncertain because it lacks the capital and experience to compete with existing (foreign) producers

Insiderisation – Where a person or company has become so integrated into a particular host society that locals forget its foreign origins

Institutional voids – Absence of effective (para-)official bodies that might otherwise exercise jurisdiction over (and regulate) a category of public interactions

Integration – Coordination of different units' activities to the extent that their mission can be defined in light of one another

Intellectual property rights – Exclusive enjoyment of benefits derived from intangible assets like trademarks, patents and copyrights

Intercultural intelligence/adroitness – Understanding of/skill at negotiating complex intercultural situations

Intercultural performance – Success in navigating foreign culture-related hurdles

Intergovernmental organisation – International institution whose membership is comprised of sovereign nations and/or their representatives

Internal market – Where sister units transact with one another on quasi-commercial basis

Internalisation – Where a company decides to run a particular function itself (using its own employees) instead of delegating it to an external party

International division – Structure driven by the idea that all foreign units have in common the fact that they exist outside of the home market and should be managed jointly for this one reason

International marketing mix – Sum total of parameters defining how a commercial item is being positioned in different countries where it is on offer

Internet-of-Things – Web 2.0 where the prime interaction is not between machine and person but between machine and machine

Intersectionality – Recognition of the different ways in which social categories like gender, race or socioeconomic class combine for different people

Interventionism – Belief that the state has a significant role to play in ensuring that market mechanisms are both efficient and lead to a fair and sustainable distribution of income

Intra-firm trade – Where different units within a MNE trade with one another, creating a framework akin to an internal marketplace

Isolationist – Refers in international trade to a policy of minimal interactions with foreign interests

Joint venture – Business entity jointly created by different companies pooling equity capital, knowledge, process and/or human resources

Knowledge economy – Sum total of markets helping agents to gain knowledge

Knowledge management – Systems used to maximise benefits of internal and external knowledge

Knowledge spillovers – Where companies gain knowledge through proximity to specialised institutions like universities, research centres or other companies

Lead-time – Time it takes, once an order has been placed, to deliver a good to the order-giver's premises

Lean production – Production philosophy that emphasizes saving resources through less waste, better inventory management, better quality and shorter industrial cycles

Learning effects – Extra productive efficiency that companies gain after accumulating experience in a given activity

Licensing – Arrangement where licensor grants permission to licensee to use one of its assets, usually intellectual property. Licensor to receive royalties in return

Lifecycle cost – Total cost of an item taking all impacts into account, including acquisition price, running costs, environmental impact and end-of-life disposal

Lightweighting – Engineering products to perform the same function but using fewer materials

Lingua franca – Common language commonly used by people from different linguistic backgrounds

Liquidity – Where sufficient quanta are being traded in a market to allow the transaction of normally sized deals without any major impact on prices

Long position – Owning more of a commodity in the form of assets than the amounts owed in the form of liabilities

Luddite – Deep-seated, almost automatic mistrust of new technology

Market failure – Where markets perform inefficiently by not allocating resources optimally

Market maker – Trader who is always prepared to quote other market participants a price to buy ("bid") and sell ("offer") a given commodity

Matrix organisation – Structure based on the idea that multiple functional reporting lines broaden employees' vision of business and can create synergies

Mergers and acquisitions – Mergers occur when two companies agree to combine their operations into a new company with both wielding more or less equal power. Acquisitions occur when one company takes ownership of another

Mitigation – Compensating for bad outcomes ex post

Modules – Components assembled into a system fulfilling a function in a final product

Modus operandi – Methods customarily applied by individuals or institutions when navigating, respectively, personal or professional situations

Moral hazard – Where actors take potentially dangerous risks because they do not expect to be held accountable if things go wrong

Multidomestic – Management approach eschewing cross-border coordination of units performing different functions and choosing instead to run entire value chain within each national market

Multinational enterprises – Companies whose regular activities cause them to engage with and/or operate in more than one country at a time

Multiplier effect – Where spending by one economic agent creates disposable income for another who can then increase their own spending

Multipolar – Describing a system characterised by a number of different power bases

Neoliberalism – Belief in minimal government intervention in the economy

Net basis – Remaining exposure after a firm's short positions in a given financial category has been subtracted from its long positions in the same category

Non-governmental organisations (NGOs) – Associations created by members of the general public to address specific problems or promote an overall ethos or policy

Non-product ratio – Percentage of inputs that are transformed into waste over the course of a production process

Notoriety – In international marketing, how quickly and spontaneously consumers identify a foreign brand when presented with allusions to it

Obsolescing bargaining – Where a MNE's negotiating position vis-à-vis a host country weakens once it actually owns assets there

Offshore – Transactions or actors over which national regulators have no authority

Offshoring – Where a company undertakes in another country certain value chain functions that it used to perform in its home market

Oligarch – Dominant business figure, often used in Russia to refer to entrepreneurs who took control of formerly state-owned assets following the fall of the communist regime

Oligopoly – Market dominated by few sellers, who might therefore have an incentive to collude and fix prices in a non-competitive manner

Opportunity cost – Cost of doing something in a certain way, thus not receiving the benefits of doing it another way

Organic growth – Where a company leverages internally generated resources to support expansion instead of proceeding via external acquisition

Organisational dilemma – Where employees are confused by the contradictory interests they are asked to represent at different levels within an organisation

Origin control measure – Requirement that production location be certified for items bearing a particular brand name

Otherness strategy – Decision to highlight foreignness. The opposite of "insiderisation"

Outsourcing – Where a company delegates to another company certain functions that it might otherwise undertake itself

Paradigm – Worldview, or vision of how things are and/or should be organised

Paternalistic – Replicating a hierarchical family structure

Peak oil – Idea that at some future point half of all oil will be used up unbeknownst to consumers who will continue buying, causing prices to rise

Per-capita – Where an aggregate sum reflecting an entire population is divided by its size and expressed on an individual basis

Philanthropy – Charitable donations to worthy causes

Pioneering costs – Costs associated with mistakes that companies make when entering an unfamiliar market

Pollution haven – Country characterised by low environmental standards, often in the hope of attracting inwards investment

Polyglots – People who speak two or more languages with a useful level of fluency

Poverty trap – Where high prices and/or actors' low incomes prevent them from amassing sufficient wealth to accumulate capital and/or reimburse debt

Precarity – Absence of job security

Prime contractor – Company at the heart of a corporate network and whose orders trigger supplier tiers' production plans

Procurement – Act of purchasing resources or inputs

Product organisation – Structure where each product division is run autonomously due to an absence of functional overlaps

Protectionist – Where a national government adopts policies benefiting domestic producers and/or restricting foreign interests' access to the domestic market

Psychic distance – People's sense of the degree to which a foreign business culture differs from their own, adding to their sense of its "foreignness"

Purchasing power parity – Theory that currency rate movement reflects the ability of consumers in different economies to buy one and the same basket of goods

Race to the bottom – Where competition among potential host countries forces them to lower their standards

Reciprocity – Precept that the parties to an agreement should both expect to benefit from it

Regime – General system organising interactions between member constituencies. Often refers to a system of regulations and the institutions that formulate and enforce them

Regime shopping/arbitrage – Decision to locate a MNE's activities based on a regime's lax regulations and low taxes

Regional economic group (REG) – Institutional platform created by neighbouring countries to decide issues of mutual interest

Relative pricing – Price of a given category of goods or services expressed in relation to the price of a different category

Renewables obligations – Regulations imposing targets for the percentage of electrical supplies sourced from renewable technologies

Reserve currency – Currency recognised by central banks worldwide as a reliable storage of value

Resilience – Ability to withstand shocks

Resource curse – Temptation for a country possessing significant natural resources to market its commodities without seeking to develop other value-adding industries

Resource productivity – Product output per material input

Responsiveness – Ability and inclination to react quickly to perceived needs of a situation

Reverse logistics – Organised collection of goods that have reached the end of their useful lives and are destined for recycling

Robotics – Use of computer science and engineering to build operational robots

Security issuance – Creation of tradable capital market instruments like stocks and bonds that companies sell to investors to raise capital

Semiotic – Relating to the production of meaning

Shareholder value – Idea that the purpose of a company is to maximise short-term financial returns to shareholders

Short position – Owing more of a commodity in the form of liabilities than the amounts owned in the form of assets

Sister units – Separate corporate entities sharing the same parent company

Small and medium-sized enterprises (SMEs) – "Enterprises which employ fewer than 250 persons and which have an annual turnover not exceeding 50 million euros, and/or an annual balance sheet total not exceeding 43 million euros" (Extract of Article 2 of the Annex of Recommendation 2003/361/EC)

Social affinity – In international marketing, where good relations between countries means that products made by one are attributed premium value by consumers in other

Socialisation – Process by means of which individuals learn to behave and form opinions in a manner acceptable to the social group they are joining

Solvent – Having sufficient funds to pay for goods

Sovereign states – Independent nations whose governments have sole jurisdiction over a defined geographic territory

Sovereign wealth funds – Government-managed pools of national currency reserves. Often invested globally to maximise returns and diversify risk

Specifications – Detailed requirements about how an item should be designed and/or what materials and attributes it should feature

Spread – Difference between market-maker's "bid" and "offer" prices

Stakeholder – Anyone affected by an organisation's actions. Often understood to be comprised of employees, local governments, suppliers, consumers and host communities

State aid – Resources allocated by government entity to provide advantage to local interests

Stereotyping – General expectation that a particular entity – like a national culture – will perform in a specific manner

Stock market capitalisation – Market value of company, calculated by the number of shares issued times the share price

Strategic business unit – Identifiable entity within a corporation, large enough to plan strategy and budget resources on its own

Subsidiary – Foreign unit in which a parent company has a majority stake

Sunk investments – Costs already incurred and that cannot be recovered

Suppliers park – Industrial cluster that suppliers build in immediate proximity to prime contractor operations

Supranational – Where an exercise of political authority transcends national borders

Sustainability – Behaviour comprised of healthy social, environmental and governance practices benefiting both a company and the societies in which it operates

Sustainable development – Emergence model based on respect for social and environmental principles

Sweat shop – Manufacturing facility characterised by particularly harsh working conditions

Syncretisation – Amalgamation of heterogeneous elements from different sources to form a personalised mixture (often of culture-related beliefs)

Tacit – Subliminal and assumed but neither specified nor stated

Tariffs – Levies that governments assess on goods (usually imports) when they cross national borders

Tax avoidance – Use of legal means to avoid paying taxes

Tax competition – Where countries try to attract mobile capital by offering investors lower tax rates than they can find in competitor nations

Tax evasion – Use of illegal means to avoid paying taxes

Tax haven – Country setting egregiously low tax rates specifically to attract financial flows

Technological complementarity – Where the combination of distinct technologies creates new synergies

Technology transfer – Sharing of high-value knowledge with external parties

Teletechnologies – Technologies enabling work over long distances

Terms of trade – Relationship between the value-added of the goods/services that a country imports versus the value-added of its exports

Trade balance – Relationship between the value of a country's exports and imports. When exports exceed imports, the country is running a trade surplus. When imports exceed exports, it runs a trade deficit

Trade diversion – Where imports come from less efficient producers located within an REG instead of from more efficient ones from the outside

Transition – In evolution. Often used in economics to refer to ex-Communist countries shifting towards more market-based economies

Transnational firm – Company whose aim (hence organisation) simultaneously targets global efficiency, local flexibility and shared learning

Trickledown economics – Idea that policy should reward the economically successful because their gains ultimately benefit the rest of society. Often used to justify low tax regimes

Triple bottom line – Precept that companies should not only report financial outcomes but also social and environmental ones

Turnkey projects – Large-scale initiatives where consortium of companies bid to win right to build infrastructure or other physical facilities

Unicorns – Privately-owned technology start-up valued at more than $1 billion

Upgrade – Where a company (or country) improves its terms of trade by intensifying the value-added content of its inputs, processes or outputs

Upgradeability – Product's capacity for integrating newer module versions

Upstream – Early value chain activities undertaken when processing or transforming a product or service

Value chain – Succession of acts adding value to item as it is transformed from raw material or simple input to finished product or service

Value-for-money – Utility associated with ownership or use of an item, qualified by the price paid for it

Vertical integration – Where the activities that a company launches in a new market are further upstream and/or downstream from the value chain stage it operates in its home market

Vertical *keiretsu* – Japanese corporate network based on long-term cooperation between companies with different upstream specialties (often including a bank for funding purposes)

Virtual – Non-physical, intangible

Welfare systems – Provisions made alongside the productive economy to support vulnerable members of society. Usually government-sponsored

Working capital – Excess of long-term liabilities over long-term assets Indicates level of long-term funding available to companies to help fund their operating cycle

Work-life balance – Precept that however hard employees work, they need to also reserve enough time in their schedule to relax and restore their energy levels

Xenophobia – Fear of things that are foreign

Zeitgeist – Dominant mood at a certain point in history

PART I

Economic and political framework

CHAPTER 1

Introduction to international business

Introduction

At its most basic level, international business (IB) encompasses all the different varieties of cross-border entrepreneurialism. The discipline has materialised in many forms ever since various human communities first began interacting with one another. When isolated pre-historic tribes started to exchange commodities like minerals, crops or simple beads, they were in fact engaging in early forms of IB (Watson 2005). Of course, trade has become much more complex since then. Nowadays, IB refers to the exchange not only of physical goods but also of services, capital, technology and human resources. The first point to make about this field of study is that it covers a broad range of economic activities.

Just as important is to recognise both what distinguishes IB from other business disciplines and where it overlaps with them. Many aspects of domestic business can also be found in IB, but the latter's cross-border emphasis means it is generally treated differently here. Similarly, IB covers most of the same topics as international management but goes much further. Whereas the former largely focuses on micro-level

Fig 1.1
Chinese communities were already trading rice up and down the Yangtze River 5,000 years ago.

DOI: 10.4324/9781003159056-2

decisions made by companies and/or the individuals working for them, IB not only incorporates these factors but also analyses the macro-level political, economic, social, technological, philosophical and ecological contexts while also asking to what extent micro-level IB decisions are constrained by external circumstances or, conversely, subject to decision-makers' agency, hence influenced by their subjective and/or psychological profiles.

Agency - Empowerment to make decisions autonomously.

Given the interplay between all these factors, IB students and practitioners must be capable of analysing situations on many levels. In turn, this requires an ability to navigate efficiently between theory, on the one hand, and empirical facts, on the other. The goal in IB studies must therefore be to ascertain whether or not today's reality aligns with the way it is being theorised – a constant confrontation that is crucial to any discipline as dynamic as IB. Reflecting the endless questioning of basic principles, IB students and practitioners tend to be characterised by their inquisitiveness and, associated with this, rich general culture. It is these traits – and the ability and desire to embrace diversity – that give this field of study its distinct philosophy and enduring attraction.

LEARNING OBJECTIVES

After reading this chapter, you will be able to:

- differentiate between international and global business
- explain the importance for international managers of developing a flexible mindset
- understand the main terminology used in IB studies
- connect IB to politics, economics and other relevant disciplines
- analyse the internal and external drivers of IB

Case study 1.1: Foxconn, the apple of Apple's eye

Value chain - Succession of acts adding value to item as it is transformed from raw material or simple input to finished product or service.

Gross domestic product (GDP) - National income, defined by aggregate consumption plus/minus investment activity plus/minus government spending plus/minus trade balance.

Ever since the year 2000 when Taiwanese components maker Foxconn landed its first order with American tech giant Apple to manufacture iMac personal computers (Brightmore 2019), the fate of the two companies has been inextricably linked. Foxconn Technology Group, founded in 1974, epitomises the rise of Southeast Asia's tiger economies, a regional success story that demonstrates how national economies, by nurturing companies capable of carving out a role for themselves in high-tech global value chains, can accelerate the speed at which they grow their gross domestic product. The skills that Foxconn would develop over the years in sectors as diverse as cloud computing, mobile devices, the *Internet-of- Things*, artificial intelligence and robotics – all products that it has learnt to sell to a whole list of top-tier international customers at highly competitive prices – largely explain why it became an essential supplier to Apple. It is not that the

Americans lacked the ability to make the inputs that they have been sourcing from Foxconn. Instead, the real question for Apple is why it would even want to allocate its own resources to generic manufacturing operations when it could generate much greater returns by concentrating on product R&D, design and sales and delegating lower-value activities to someone else. Ultimately the decision seemed straightforward – Apple would mainly focus on the specific activities where it had the greatest competitive advantage and turn to its reliable and cost-effective foreign partner for other key functions.

The partnership has worked like a charm for both companies for many years. Like any relationship, however, it has gone through rough patches. Apple has come under criticism, for instance, from observers decrying what they view as its exploitative capture of the lion's share of the value generated by its products – the idea here being that Foxconn's Chinese workers are insufficiently remunerated for their efforts (Froud et al. 2012). It has also received some very negative coverage for the exhausting schedules the workers are required to put in and the psychological toll this takes on them (Chamberlain 2018). It remains that these critiques – albeit entirely justified – tend to be drowned out by the broader approval of Apple's overall business model, not to mention the occasional argument that by outsourcing some of its functions to China, the American multinational enterprise (MNE) is actually doing an ethical thing by supporting the country's economic emergence.

This status quo was shaken, however, when former US President Donald Trump, a nationalist, entered the White House in January 2017. As part of Mr. Trump's vociferous denunciation of certain American companies that he claimed were importing goods into the country (hence exporting jobs out of it), he met with Apple CEO Tim Cook in late 2018, ostensibly to try and convince the latter that Apple should repatriate to the USA some of the work that Foxconn had been successfully performing on the company's behalf for years. There is a strong case to make that the motive behind this exertion of political pressure had nothing to do with sound business or economic logic: full employment in Apple's home region of Silicon Valley meant there was no real outcry demanding that computer manufacturing jobs be brought back home; and American consumers were delighted to access Apple goods at a lower price than they would have had to pay had its products been entirely produced in the USA.

Using a combination of charm and flattery, Mr. Cook was largely able to pacify the politician, successfully helping Apple avoid paying the brunt of the new tariffs that Mr. Trump had started imposing on many, if not most, imports from China during the course of the multiple trade wars that his administration declared on the USA's long-standing trading partner (Jeakie 2019). As much as anything, Mr. Cook's approach demonstrated the depth of Apple's attachment to its traditional IB model – after all, the company was willing to incur the wrath of a powerful individual to protect its relationship with Foxconn. The same commitment would again become apparent in early 2020, when China's devastating Covid-19 outbreak hampered Foxconn's ability to maintain a steady supply of the parts and products that are so crucial to Apple's market presence. Despite the fragility that the pandemic revealed in its global value chain, at no point did Apple indicate any desire to change its model. Quite the contrary, the only adjustment it made was to develop a backup sourcing relationship with a new foreign supplier – Wistron in India (Mankotia 2020) – basically doubling down on its way of doing IB. For Apple, the idea of abandoning successful overseas partnerships at a time of international turmoil was clearly just plain bananas.

Fig 1.2
Apple headquarters in Cupertino (California) concentrates on higher value-added activities and outsources most, if not all, product manufacturing.

Case study questions

1. What advantages does Apple derive from its supplier relationship with Foxconn?
2. What are the chances that Apple might change its IB model one day?

Section I. The international context

Every discipline has its own vocabulary and it is always helpful to introduce this from the outset. This will be followed by a brief review of some of the trends characterising the shape of IB today. The chapter will then conclude with an introduction to some of the general drivers underpinning companies' participation in cross-border activities.

Terminology and useful concepts

One useful starting point when analysing IB is to differentiate between this discipline's focus on how national settings diverge, versus the convergence themes characterising the neighbouring field of globalisation. The two terms do not denote the same phenomenon and should not be used synonymously. IB's overriding emphasis on variability largely explains this book's seminal principle that the strategies and behaviours which apply in one situation may not be relevant in another, suggesting that, contrary to certain theories (Womack et al. 1991), there is in fact never any "one best way" of doing business. It is an approach that may seem foreign to learners whose culture has taught them to seek optimal solutions to whatever problems they face. On the other hand, students whose culture of origin trains them to prepare multiple responses to any given situation will feel very much at home with this philosophy. Focusing on divergence is also more useful educationally since it accustoms future practitioners to the foreignness of many of the phenomena that they are likely to experience during their careers in IB. Indeed, without this emphasis, there would be little difference between international and domestic business studies.

IB is also associated with a number of specific challenges that practitioners and learners ignore at their peril. As highlighted throughout this book, many of these problems are strategic in nature and relate to the objective obstacles that companies must overcome when seeking to operate across borders. Focusing on these factors is key to understanding IB and therefore constitutes the sort of core curriculum that usually dominates introductory undergraduate studies in this field. However, it is also useful to note other factors that are more psychological in nature. This is because some people find it very difficult when leaving a familiar home country to adjust to the foreignness of a new host country. Others, on the other hand, feel that the world is becoming "flatter" (Friedman 2005), that the psychic distance between societies is diminishing and that it is therefore easier than ever before to operate in a foreign environment. The gap between these two mindsets provides a backdrop to more advanced analyses of how IB practitioners' objective decision-making is affected by their subjective paradigms. It is the way that postgraduate IB studies tend to build upon first-order knowledge within this field.

The textbook also prepares learners to consider the insiderisation strategies that practitioners may wish to apply in order to overcome the barriers that companies often face when operating abroad (Ohmae 1999). In an ideal world, these barriers would never exist. Unfortunately, humankind does not live in such a world. One of the reasons for this is relatively innocuous, namely, the home bias that causes many people to want to support fellow members of their local community. Other factors, however, are much less innocent or palatable. These include the long-standing xenophobia characterising certain cultures, the specific "animosity" expressed by some populations towards others (Barutcu et al. 2016) and the resurgent economic nationalism that has followed the rise of nationalist politicians over the course of the 2010s and even in the wake of the 2020 Covid-19 pandemic (Solis 2020). Of course, these phenomena are being offset to a greater or lesser extent by a sweeping, decades-long

Globalisation - Process whereby the world becomes increasingly interconnected socially, economically, politically and commercially.

Foreignness - Degree to which a national environment varies from the ones to which observer is accustomed.

Home/host countries - People and companies originate from a "home country". When they operate abroad, they are working in a "host country".

Psychic distance - People's sense of the degree to which a foreign business culture differs from their own, adding to their sense of its "foreignness".

Paradigm - Worldview, or vision of how things are and/or should be organised.

Insiderisation - Where a person or company has become so integrated into a particular host society that locals forget its foreign origins.

Home bias - Preference for domestic counterparts.

Xenophobia - Fear of things that are foreign.

Zeitgeist - Dominant mood at a certain point in history.

Multinational enterprises (MNEs) - Companies whose activities cause them to engage with and/or operate in more than one country at a time.

Small and medium-sized enterprises (SMEs) - "Enterprises which employ fewer than 250 persons and which have an annual turnover not exceeding 50 million euros, and/or an annual balance sheet total not exceeding 43 million euros" (European Commission 2003).

Global firm - Company designed to serve a single world market instead of a variety of national markets.

Configuration - How and where a company locates its various corporate functions such as research, production, marketing and finance.

Foreign direct investment (FDI) - Where companies fund a permanent or semi-permanent unit overseas. The Organisation for Economic Co-operation and Development (OECD) defines FDI as a situation where a foreign owner has an equity stake of at least 10 percent in a company's ordinary shares and aims to establish a "lasting interest" in the host country.

generational trend towards greater "cosmopolitanism" (Petriglieri 2016), a zeitgeist that has shifted many individuals' sense of belonging and identity to make them feel more aligned with today's increasingly interconnected world. In reality, globalisation has sparked a wide range of reactions and counter-reactions affecting how people feel about their interactions with foreign populations (Bornman 2010). It is also one of modern society's most contentious debates, exemplified by the extraordinarily strong emotions evoked both when Donald Trump won the US presidential election in 2016 with his "American First" platform, and then in 2020 when he lost to Joe Biden, who would pursue a diametrically opposed policy of international cooperation. Emotivity – political or otherwise – has always been a key element in international business.

Between these different mindsets, it should come as no surprise that IB practitioners overwhelmingly tend to be full-throated advocates of a friendlier, more inclusive approach to international relations. The author of this book is no exception – quite the contrary. At the same time, it is always imperative to keep in mind the existence of constituencies who oppose this mindset, if only to calculate the best way of overcoming the barriers that they will regularly try to erect.

Companies doing business internationally

IB occurs any time that an actor – whether an individual or an institution – engages in a cross-border transaction. Private parties acting on their own behalf have always had an important role to play in the world economy, with examples ranging from individual investors purchasing currencies or shares in foreign companies to chamber of commerce representatives providing foreign interests with information about a local economy. Having said that, the lion's share of IB today is of course transacted by companies, ranging from huge multinational enterprises (MNEs) to small and medium-sized enterprises (SMEs) and even micro-firms.

This textbook will use the term "MNE" when referring to any company (irrespective of its size, thus including SMEs) engaging in any form of IB. Note that other IB textbooks might prefer other terms, including multinational corporations (MNCs), transnational corporations (TNCs) or even global firms. The problem is that each of these expressions refers to a specific kind of company and is therefore slightly loaded. Talking about MNCs, for instance, neglects the fact that not all actors playing a role in IB are corporations or even privately owned enterprises. Similarly, expressions like TNCs and global firms do not sufficiently communicate the connections that continue to tie many, if not most, companies with international interests to their country of origin. MNE is a more neutral term and will therefore form this book's basic unit of analysis.

The first distinction to make is between MNEs whose only interactions with their foreign counterparts occurs on a "trade" (i.e. import/export) basis – and who therefore do not change their configuration when undertaking IB – versus others who engage in foreign direct investment (FDI) and develop a physical presence outside of their home country (see

Figure 1.3). These two categories – trade and FDI – embody, at its most basic level, almost all IB. FDI is often considered the more complicated variant, if only because it involves a company breaking down operations between its head office and the subsidiaries (and/or affiliates) it establishes in foreign markets worldwide. The importance of these latter entities to IB cannot be overstated, with recent accounts estimating that a whopping 64 percent of all global exports and 36 percent of all global output (Backer et al. 2019) are transacted through them. At the same time, MNEs' foreign units are marked by great variability, with some being deeply integrated into their group's global value chain and others merely representing its interests in the particular markets where it is running operations. With the global number of MNE subsidiaries being largely unmeasured but undoubtedly amounting to several hundreds of thousands, it is impossible to generalise about the missions assigned to each.

In a similar vein, it would also be impossible to generalise why companies might even want to set up entities outside of their home market. In very broad terms, earlier operators' main motive for internationalisation was to acquire resources, whereas nowadays it tends to be the development of knowledge and markets (Aharoni and Ramamurti 2008). Dominant IB paradigms vary strongly from one generation to the next, however. As Chapter 7 will demonstrate, history is yet another discipline that has always had much to offer IB learners.

Having said that, there has been a strong tendency in recent decades for MNEs to specialise their foreign units, as far as possible, before moulding them into a coherent whole. This is the IB application of seminal economic theories (see Chapter 2) postulating that economic production be situated in those locations where it can be done most efficiently. It is also a conception that explains the enormous role that intra-firm trade between various MNE subsidiaries has played in IB in recent years – and explains why it is so important to understand the different ways in which MNE head offices organise their relational networks (see Chapter 9).

Subsidiary - Foreign unit in which a parent company has a majority stake.

Affiliate - Foreign unit in which a parent company has a minority stake.

Intra-firm trade - Where different units within a MNE trade with one another, creating a framework akin to an internal marketplace.

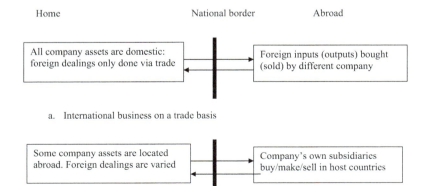

Fig 1.3
Trade and FDI are the two pillars of international business.

Case study 1.2: Fortune favours the brave

Since 2005, *Fortune* magazine, a leading American business magazine, has published an annual list of the world's largest MNEs, ranked by their global revenues (https://fortune.com/global500/). The data are of great interest to IB practitioners and learners alike, particularly because of the year-to-year trends they reveal. One comparison that can be made relates to which sectors are most widely represented at the top of the list (with energy companies having largely displaced banks in recent years). Another possible comparison involves the countries where the 500 largest MNEs are headquartered, with the share of companies from the world's older industrialised countries falling over the period 2005–2021 (in the USA, for instance, from 176 to 122) while those from China skyrocketing (from 16 to 135 over the same period).

Fig 1.4
Today the country where the largest number of Fortune Global 500 MNEs are headquartered is China.

A question might be asked about how important it really is to track where Fortune 500 companies' headquarters (HQ) are located. After all, since MNEs are just as likely to do business out of foreign subsidiaries as out of their home office, there is some sense in assuming that it does not really matter where their headquarters are located (generally the country where the company originated). This assumption, however, would be wrong – MNEs' nationality remains important. On the one hand, it is often the case that many of a company's founders and senior managers come from its country of origin, the end effect being that their cultural tendencies (see Chapter 5) are likely to have a disproportionate effect on the way the group operates in many of the countries where it is present. Having said that, there are also MNEs where the country of origin (and the global headquarters) plays a less important role, with most group decision-makers being hired in foreign subsidiaries and therefore bringing a diverse range of mindsets to the table. These are nuances that cannot be determined by simply reading the Fortune list but require case-by-case scrutiny of the names found there.

Above and beyond headquarters locations, however, many other factors are essential to understanding why MNEs make the strategic choices they do. IB analysis must always be multifaceted, if only because the discipline is not a hard science replete with fixed and deterministic causalities. Instead, it is a social science marked by a great deal of uncertainty about the factors driving different managers' informed yet ultimately subjective assessments of how best to respond to a particular cross-border situation. One example here is the received business wisdom that it generally benefits companies to achieve economies of scale and thereby lower their per-unit production costs. Some might take this to mean that international expansion is a good thing in and of itself, justifying that the Fortune Global 500 list be ranked by revenues. That would neglect a host of other important considerations, however, starting with the way that many shareholders pressure MNEs nowadays to focus more on return on equity (ROE) than on market share. This might explain why *Forbes*, another leading American business magazine, offers its own list of the world's 2,000 largest public companies (https://www.forbes.com/global2000/) based on a weighting of four parameters (market capitalisation, assets, profits and sales). The Forbes 2000 list looks very different from the Fortune Global 500, and it continues, for instance, to feature many banks at the top. Clearly there are different ways of assessing the size of a MNE.

Analysis is further complicated by the argument that the size of a MNE's in-house operations is not a particularly accurate measure of how much power it really wields. Greater significance is sometimes attached to the role that it plays within the broader global value chains that it has built up through its dealings with suppliers and customers worldwide (Kano et al. 2020). This new understanding reflects the fact that many modern products are too complex to be manufactured by a single

Economies of scale - Decline in per-unit production costs due to increased output without any increase in assets.

company working by itself. Instead, there is a growing tendency for the world's leading MNEs to work with a first tier of counterparts, whose own suppliers or customers then become the company's second-tier counterparts, and so on. In the end, studying MNEs without identifying the different components of their power bases and relationships presents an incomplete picture of their strategic possibilities. The *Fortune* and *Forbes* rankings are excellent tools that are well worth monitoring. But they can never replace a more in-depth study of the specific approach that each MNE takes to IB.

Case study analysis

1. Study the Fortune Global 500 rankings over the past decade to determine factors explaining changes in the composition of the top 20 MNEs listed.
2. Study the Forbes Global 2000 rankings over the past decade to determine factors explaining changes in the composition of the top 20 MNEs listed.

Accumulation of value in value chains

The best way of picturing MNEs' value chain is to imagine the production and sale of a good or service as a series of acts that each add value as it is transformed upstream from raw materials into component parts and sub-assemblies before ending up as a finished good or service to be sold downstream (see Figure 1.5). Most stages tend to be run out of different locations, reflecting the economies of scale and other advantages associated with site specialisation. This has led to the fragmentation of most MNEs' value chains today, facilitated by rapid improvements in modern logistics (see Chapter 10). The end effect of this and other historic trends is that more and more companies nowadays are asking specialised foreign partners to assume responsibility for many of the functions that they would once have performed themselves. As a result, the most accurate way of representing global value chains is to depict them as the sum of several intermediate value chains, with the end point for one often being the starting point for another.

Jeans offer a good example of a product best analysed as the sum of many lower-level generic parts and not just as a finished product. One component is the metallic zip, itself the culmination of several intermediary businesses, starting with extraction of minerals and the processing and subsequent transformation of basic metals. Another component is fabric that might be made out of raw cotton fibre, which will then have to be cultivated, harvested, processed and dyed – with each stage representing a sector of activity featuring its own business

Upstream - Early value chain activities undertaken when processing or transforming a product or service.

Downstream - Late value chain activities undertaken when selling or distributing a product or service.

Generic - Items not meant for a specific use but serving as a basis for a variety of applications.

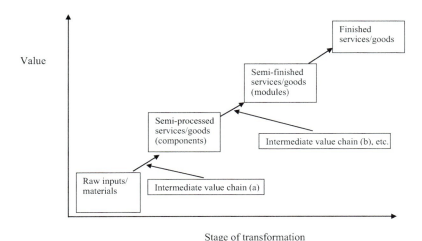

Value

Finished
services/goods

Semi-finished
services/goods
(modules)

Semi-processed
services/goods
(components)

Intermediate value chain (b), etc.

Raw inputs/
materials

Intermediate value chain (a)

Stage of transformation

Fig 1.5
Visualising the
transformation of a good
or service. Each level adds
value and also has its
own intermediate supply
chains.

models, rooted in its own global value chain and reliant on its own
capital equipment, logistics and other processes (each of which will then
also have their own value chains). It would give a very misleading picture
of modern IB to introduce modern MNEs without highlighting how very
deeply most, if not all, are embedded in "interorganisational networks"
(Ghoshal and Bartlett 1990).

This portrayal of IB as a series of cross-border value chains raises
questions about the rate at which value accumulates as a service or
good is transformed into its final form. For presentational purposes,
Figure 1.5 shows value accumulating at a linear rate. This is generally
unrealistic, however. Depending on the sector in question, value
tends to accumulate at different speeds towards either the upstream
or the downstream portion of the global value chain. In the coffee
business, for instance, a tiny percentage of what consumers pay goes
to upstream bean-growers. To some extent, this reflects poor coffee
farmers' lack of bargaining power when dealing with the powerful
MNEs that dominate the value chain at the point where value
accumulates more rapidly – in this case, all the way downstream, close
to the end users. Inversely, in a sellers' market (like oil) marked by less
competition among producers, value tends to accumulate in the hands
of upstream producers. Figure 1.6 offers a more realistic picture of the
curves in global value chains.

Clearly it is more efficient to operate at that portion of the value chain
where value accumulates most rapidly (i.e. where the curve is steepest).
This is just as true for national economies as it is for companies. Those
countries whose firms specialise in high value-added production have a
great advantage over ones that specialise in low value-added goods – as
economists would put it, they enjoy better terms of trade. For example,
if American firms are global champions in computers and companies

Terms of trade -
Relationship between
the value-added of the
goods/services that a
country imports versus
the value-added of its
exports.

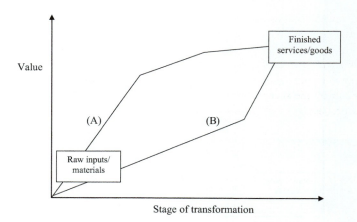

Value

(A)   (B)

Finished services/goods

Raw inputs/ materials

Stage of transformation

Fig 1.6
Value tends not to increase in a straight line. Curve (A) indicates a product or service where greater value accumulates during the early, downstream phases of the value chain. Curve (B) indicates the opposite.

Global North - World's older industrialised nations.

Global South - Countries whose industrial base and general level of human welfare are such that many citizens struggle to achieve a decent living standard. This is an umbrella term covering a vast range of economic, social and demographic situations, ranging from "emerging" or "newly industrialised" nations to "heavily indebted poor countries" (HIPC) with very poor growth prospects.

Offshore - Transactions or actors over which national regulators have no authority.

from Assam, India, lead the world in the tea business, the USA will have a net advantage since the market where it reigns generates greater value than the market where Assam dominates. National governments are very aware of this factor and will often take measures to improve their country's competitive position. Such efforts are part of the political environment within which MNEs operate, as are the measures enacted by global bodies to control their potentially market-distorting effects. This makes certain territories' tendency to specialise in higher – or else, and less advantageously, lower – value-added activities an important aspect of the economic context within which IB occurs, especially given the political effects of the uneven distribution of wealth that results from this. As discussed in Chapter 13 and without underestimating the ongoing strength of MNEs originating from the older industrialised world – generally referred to as the Global North – companies from newly industrialised emerging economies (the Global South) have become major new IB players in recent decades. The question is whether or not their participation in existing global value chains sees them relegated to those segments where value accrues more slowly. MNEs' role in aggravating or reducing income inequalities, on a national but also a global scale, constitutes another major topic of discussion for IB. Out of all the subjects that business school learners will study, IB is very probably the most political and politicised.

When devising their value chain strategies, companies must be aware of all relevant political and legislative frameworks, if only because of the cost implications, not to mention the need to comply with all the laws in the different countries where they operate. That is easier said than done, however. Firstly, there is the fact that much business today is transacted on an offshore basis outside the jurisdiction of any one government – meaning that interactions with national regulatory regimes are sporadic and subject to contradictory interpretations. Further confusion is caused by the fact that even where clear national policies shape the IB environment, they often vary extensively in both time and place – as exemplified by different governments' calls for either greater or lesser trade restrictions in the wake of the 2020 Covid-19 crisis. This inconsistency explains why knowledge gathering has always been such a key capability in IB. It is something that has been facilitated by modern telecommunications (see Chapter 15) – but also made more difficult by the sheer volume of information that MNEs must acquire and process.

Key trends

IB is very much a living subject, rooted in the relationship between actions and outcomes. For this reason, it is crucial that practitioners and learners develop the ability to analyse the seminal concepts within this discipline in light of their real-life applications. Viewing IB in context necessarily involves linking theory to front-page news.

Trade trends

A long period between the early 1980s and 2007 had seen trade volumes increase much more rapidly than total global GDP did – about 5.5 vs. 3.5 percent annually on average. This created a situation where IB would account for a rising share of all economic activity, with the global trade-to-GDP ratio ultimately reaching about 30 percent. Since the 2008 subprime crisis, however, IB growth and GDP growth have progressed at similar rates. This relative slowdown in the rate of trade growth – a phenomenon referred to "slowbalisation" (Economist 2019) – raises questions whether an absolute ceiling exists for the volume of activity that business can and will organise on a cross-border basis (see Case study 1.3).

Within this general trend, regional performances continue to vary widely, reflecting significant differences in economic and/or political orientation. Compared to the composition of global trade in the 1990s, exports from North America and Western Europe have fallen in relative terms (from ca. 75 to 50 percent). This has been mirrored by a rise in the percentage of global exports coming from Africa, the former Soviet Union and the Middle East – largely explained by these regions' greater role in various commodity markets – but above all, from Asia, which has become the centre of global manufacturing over the past 30 years. Variations in economic performance will be better understood by identifying actors' sectoral specialisations, starting with the distinction between primary (raw materials, agriculture), secondary (manufacturing) and tertiary (service and administration) activities. The analysis can then be further deepened by studying the relative pricing of the particular sector(s) in which a country has specialised, in order to determine its current and prospective terms of trade. MNEs play a key role in shaping such pricing, which, in turn, shapes the contexts in which MNEs operate.

On top of this, it is always worth examining IB's relative importance to different national economies, if only to assess its effects on macro-

Relative pricing - Price of a given category of goods or services expressed in relation to the price of a different category.

economic aggregates such as unemployment or inflation as well as the political reactions that these outcomes might provoke. For example, despite the size of its economy, total trade volumes (the sum of total imports and exports) in the USA – the world's second leading exporter behind China – are scarcely higher than for the number three exporter, Germany, which has one-quarter the US population. That translates to total trade only amounting to about 20–25 percent of national GDP in the USA, versus more than 70 percent in Germany. At first glance, this might intimate that American politicians and business leaders pay relatively little attention to IB. Yet because of the country's endemic trade deficit – its propensity to import much more than it exports – the opposite holds true, with protectionist discourse having become increasingly rife in recent years. That international disputes can arise as a result explains why global governance constitutes another major topic in IB today.

Protectionist - Where a national government adopts policies benefitting domestic producers and/ or restricting foreign interests' access to the domestic market.

Lastly, it is also worth commenting upon the growing percentage of world trade accounted for by Global South nations, led by China and other emerging Asian powers. Many observers analyse this as a sign that globalisation offers poorer countries great development prospects, as witnessed by the historic recent decline in the number of people surviving on subsistence-level incomes (often classified as $2 a day). This view is encapsulated in the body of theory supporting the idea that, one way or another, all countries stand to gain from international trade (see Chapter 2). Whether this is true or not, the changing geography of IB – and its impact on the global distribution of capital and markets – is another key feature of the modern era and a further factor affecting MNE managers' decisions at many different levels.

Foreign direct investment (FDI) trends

As indicated above, trade is one of IB's two main pillars. The second, FDI, has risen in importance in recent decades, characterised by a growth rate that has often surpassed trade itself. Being able to analyse the particularities of FDI trends is also key to understanding IB as a whole.

FDI can involve any part of a value chain, from the upstream extraction or industrial transformation of raw materials to the downstream retailing of services or finished goods. Recent FDI data should be handled with care given statistical categorisation problems but also because the long-term uptrend in total FDI volumes has been very inconsistent, characterised by steep annual increases followed by sudden collapses in years beset by international crises – one example being the fall of about 40 percent in global FDI flows that accompanied the outbreak of the Covid-19 pandemic (UNCTAD 2020). Sometimes the explanation lies in events that are external to company life. Funding can dry up when times are hard; MNEs are often pressured by home country governments during times of crisis to support the domestic economy by repatriating certain investments – being, for instance, the condition that ex-French President Nicolas Sarkozy required of national automaker

Renault before consenting a bail-out that the company was seeking in 2008. On other occasions, these sporadic but regular declines in global FDI flows are better explained by MNEs' internal decision-making. There can be psychological factors, like managers' greater hesitation in times of trouble and against a backdrop of falling profits to invest in overseas markets with which they may be unfamiliar (see Chapter 8). Otherwise, there can also be more structural paradigm shifts, starting with the way many managers will respond to recessions by shrinking the size of their firm. This will often lead to a decision to curtail FDI – to stop offshoring one or the other of a company's value chain functions – and to opt instead for greater international outsourcing, effectively replacing FDI with trade. The two pillars of IB may be presented separately from one another for clarity's sake, but they are in fact closely intertwined in MNEs' decision-making processes.

Offshoring - Where a company undertakes in another country certain value chain functions that it used to perform in its home market.

Outsourcing - Where a company delegates to another company certain functions that it might otherwise undertake itself.

All in all, the global stock of FDI has risen considerably since the turn of the 21st century. Unlike international trade in goods and services, however, there has been relatively little variation in the breakdown between different regions' share of global FDI, with the Global North consistently accounting for nearly two-thirds of the total. This has started to even out in recent years, however, as witnessed by rising flows to (and increasingly from) the Global South. Along these lines, it is also useful analysing how the Global South's share of global trade compares with its share of global FDI because of what that reveals about managers' varying levels of comfort in different business environments. It bears repeating that personal psychology and economic action have always been closely interrelated in IB.

Section II. International business drivers

Chapter 8 offers a deeper discussion of the range of motivations explaining why and where companies operate abroad. Some MNEs internationalise systematically, taking advantage of the relationships they have developed to exploit any and all opportunities that arise (Ellis 2011). Others might only venture abroad on specific, ad hoc occasions. The following section offers an overview (see Table 1.1) of general factors driving companies' IB practices.

Strategic drivers

Some of the motives underpinning IB actions are "micro" in nature and revolve around companies' profit-seeking initiatives and strategic intent. Others revolve around their reactions to external "macro" trends, being political, governmental, macro-economic, sociocultural, technological and ecological factors over which they generally have little or no control (Yip 1989). Of course, micro- and macro-level motivations are often interrelated. One example of this linkage can be found in a business concept called internalisation, which is basically the opposite

Internalisation - Where a company decides to run a particular function itself (using its own employees) instead of delegating it to an external party.

Table 1.1
Summary of the main strategic drivers of international business

---

Internal drivers

– Expanding sales
– Leveraging competencies
– Using extra capacities
– Spreading risks
– Avoiding saturation
– Internalising competencies
– Acquiring resources
– Accessing more efficient inputs

External drivers

– Technology
– Greater access to information
– Liberalised regulatory framework
– Free trade-friendly institutions
– Global competitive paradigm
– Availability of finance

---

of the decision to outsource. The idea here is that when markets are functioning poorly (for example, when participants are not being fairly rewarded for their efforts), it is in companies' interest to run their own value chain operations – whether internationally or not – in order to keep in-house control over the knowledge they possess (Buckley and Casson 1976). In this view, firms do not require foreign partners to help them internalise as long as they have top-notch managers capable of assuming responsibilities abroad – and as long as the host countries where they plan to operate are not too different from the ones to which the company and its managers are accustomed. It is yet another situation where IB is shaped by the interface between a company's internal attributes (managers' capabilities) and the characteristics (foreignness and/or market mechanisms) of the host country where it is thinking of moving.

A further example of the interconnection between macro- versus micro-drivers of IB is when a MNE calculates that the cost of going abroad is lower than the potential gains it hopes to achieve by operating in a regulatory, labour or tax system where it is well placed to pressure the local government into offering it certain facilities (Ietto-Gillies 2013). This is because a company's cross-border success depends not only on how suitable its behaviour is to the market(s) where it operates (Porter 1986) but also on how effectively it deals with non-business actors such as politicians or regulators. In short, separating macro and micro-drivers of IB may be a useful categorisation, but it is also a largely artificial one.

Internal drivers of international business
Companies often work outside of their borders because the sector in which they operate is shaped more by international factors than

by domestic ones. Even so, it is rare to find companies that launch as multinationals from the very outset. The vast majority of MNEs throughout history, with the exception of recent "born-globals", have started in their home market and moved abroad at a later date: expanding downstream to increase sales, moving upstream to acquire resources or working in both directions to diversify risk. Each of these actions is based on a different logic that the company will have developed for its own reasons.

Expanding sales

Once a firm has built a system allowing it to manufacture and market a product or service efficiently, it will often seek to leverage this competency by selling the finished good, with or without modification, into a new market. Thus, on the downstream side, the expansion of sales is the main driver of IB. There are countless examples of this rationale being put to use. For instance, Dutch vegetable farmers have developed a greenhouse technology allowing them to grow tomatoes and peppers even during cold North European winters. Because consumer demand for these products from neighbouring countries like Germany and the UK remains strong all year long, doing business across borders is a natural step for Dutch agribusiness companies like The Greenery, which sources fresh produce and sells it to foreign retailers.

A related example is the trade between Australia, which has an abundance of minerals as well as an industrial sector capable of refining ore (like bauxite) into usable production inputs (like aluminium), and Japan, a dynamic but mineral-poor industrial giant whose factories require enormous amounts of raw materials. For Australian mining or refining companies, exporting to Japan is a logical extension of what started out as a domestic activity. It is a trade reflecting the complementarity between the two countries. A third example from the service sector is the way that huge pension funds like Jupiter Asset

Fig 1.7
International sales can be a necessity to ensure the viability of productive facilities sized to achieve economies of scale – one example being Dutch greenhouse exports to the UK.

Management or Allianz Global Investors leverage their large, hence expensive, management infrastructure (often located in international financial centres like London) to sell financial products to customers worldwide. Expanding foreign sales is a quick way of paying for the enormous costs that these companies incurred when they first built their trading rooms. Lastly, cross-border sales can also seem a natural step for small or medium-sized companies operating in sectors that are by their very nature international in scope. German piano-maker Steinway, for instance, is an SME that has been selling to foreign customers for many decades. In all these cases, IB is as relevant to a company's mission as the work that it does in its home market. This is especially true when the company is looking to move into a foreign country that is similar in political, economic and/or cultural terms, not to mention close geographically. Without minimising the real differences that exist between the USA and Canada, when Starbucks first began expanding beyond its home market, setting up outlets a mere 50 miles across its northern border must have seemed a relatively natural thing to do. The skills developed selling in one country can under certain conditions be transplanted seamlessly to another.

There are also more internal strategic reasons why companies organise their commercial functions to embrace international sales as a matter of course. As mentioned above, one basic principle of modern production is that selling large volumes is beneficial because it creates economies of scale. In a similar vein, the greater the experience that a company acquires in producing something, the better it becomes at this activity. This is because it develops knowledge that allows it to generate constant productivity gains. As a result, many companies size their production operations to obtain critical mass. To justify these investments and avoid surplus capacities, they often need to sell more than they would if they were simply serving domestic customers. This is especially true if the firm comes from a small country. For example, Irish discount airliner Ryanair would have been at a disadvantage using its Dublin home as a single hub. With so many more passengers travelling through the UK, it made sense for the company to run its main operations out of London Stansted Airport, which is, after all, a foreign location. Otherwise, finance offers another way of apprehending how market size affects a company's international sales strategies. As a gross rule of thumb, for instance, the cost of building a new automotive plant can be approximated as roughly $1 billion. To have any hope of recovering such a large expenditure, an automaker would have to ensure that any new plant it builds produces enough cars to justify the outlay. This is not possible if the plant is located either in a small country (i.e. Luxemburg, which features no automotive plant serving its domestic market alone) or in one where demand is already saturated due to competition. In both cases, the desired scale of production dictates that sales must be international or else the whole investment becomes unviable.

Critical mass - Minimum threshold beyond which positive, size-related benefits arise.

Acquiring inputs

Another micro-driver of IB is the acquisition of the resources (materials and labour as well as capital and technology) used during a firm's production processes. Sometimes this involves inputs that are unavailable at home. For example, non-oil-producing countries like Japan, Germany and France are necessarily obliged to look abroad to source this essential commodity. At other times, the cost of an input might be so much lower overseas that a company would be at a competitive disadvantage if, unlike its rivals, it did not source it where it can be acquired most cheaply. Here the solar energy business offers a good case in point. Solar installers worldwide seeking to enter this fast-growing sector must procure solar panels at a good price in order to remain competitive. However, few countries can make these items as cheaply as China, where companies such as SunTech Power and Yingli have achieved a critical mass that allows them to compete successfully in world markets. Thus, it is in the interest of panel installers everywhere to import from China if they do not want to pay too much for their most critical input. Lastly, in labour-intensive commodity sectors like off-the-shelf clothing, there has clearly been an advantage for many well-known MNEs to either offshore or else to outsource their manufacturing activities to countries marked by low-wage levels. In short, IB is often driven by firms focusing more on the advantages inherent to a given production location and less on the question of whether this site lies in their country of origin or not.

Diversifying risks

A further strategic driver of IB is the desire to spread risk by working in more than one country at a time. Evidence shows that this kind of "multi-nationality" not only increases flexibility, thereby generating new profit-making opportunities, but also reduces risk by preventing overdependence on any one location or market (Andersen 2011). One way of looking at this is from an upstream, production perspective. If a firm had all its industrial assets in northern Turkey and an earthquake were to hit the region, its chances of continuing its manufacturing operations would be worse than if it also had plants in zones not affected by the earthquake. That is why so many firms have disaster plans allowing them to continue functioning in case a catastrophe affects one of their main production sites. The same logic can be applied on the downstream, sales side. A company that sells into one single market runs the risk that demand there might collapse for whatever reason (recession, natural disaster, war) without it having any other customers to compensate for the lost sales. Any MNE whose entire business revolved around sales to Wuhan (China) when Covid-19 first afflicted that city in late 2019 and shut down its local markets would have experienced a total collapse in revenue. The adversity that a company experiences in one location has less of an impact when it is present in many others.

Spreading risk through international operations can be done in other ways as well. Sales abroad can offset the foreign exchange risk that a company experiences when it accumulates revenues (or liabilities) in just one currency (see Chapter 12). Above all, there is an international marketing construct called "product life cycle" (PLC) which holds that products or services can simultaneously find themselves on an upward trend in some markets while declining in others (see Chapter 11). Clearly, it is advantageous for firms to sell into markets where demand is on the rise since they will be able to command higher prices there. One example from a generation ago is the way that jeans were so much more expensive in Western Europe, where they were new and fashionable, than in California, where they were invented and had long become a commodity product. PLC variations enabled San Francisco MNE Levi Strauss to supplement dwindling per-unit revenues in its home market with lucrative exports to Europe. At a simple level, IB has always been driven by a simple arbitrage between the lower price paid for a good in a country where its supply is abundant and the higher price it can command in a country where it is more rare. The fact that these price differentials often vary over products' lifecycle requires agility on the part of any MNE seeking to take advantage of them. Diversification is the most straightforward way of enabling this agility and therefore a prime driver behind internationalisation.

External drivers of international business

Some of the trends and events affecting a company's decision-making will always escape its direct control. The effects will generally be magnified when they reverberate internationally. A large company operating within a single domestic market may have enough power to influence the turn of events – but this becomes more difficult for MNEs subject to the vagaries of global events with different effects in different national markets.

Fig 1.8
Levi's move to Europe was sparked by the higher prices it could command there.

Technology

It is not always easy to determine which drivers a company can control, and which it cannot. One case in point is technology, a key factor in the modern world. Technology is an umbrella term that refers not only to companies' internal innovation efforts but also to the levels of technological capability characterising the various countries where they might operate. As such, it affects the IB environment in many ways. On the upstream side, for instance, improved telecommunications have allowed companies to stretch their value chains to coordinate operations run out of distant locations offering a competitive advantage in the production of specific items. One example is when hospitals in countries with lower healthcare standards use remote diagnostics facilities to get advice from specialist doctors working out of medically more advanced centres. Leveraging a service that was once completely localised, modern technology creates opportunities for a work organisation that can now be structured along international lines (see Chapter 15). Add to this the positive impact that technology-related transportation improvements have traditionally had on trade and there is an argument that technology is one of the main causes of today's shrinking world. Not only can goods be transported faster and more cheaply than ever before but services can as well, due to the more or less global coverage that Internet connectivity enables nowadays.

Technology has had similar effects on companies' downstream relationships. It is rare that a community chooses to remain completely isolated once the means exist for it to interact with the rest of the world. When modern consumers shop via Amazon instead of through their local retailers, they are often seeing product offers originating from outside of their home market, possibilities that would have been unknown to them in the past. People's outlooks and desires often change when they see not only how foreign societies live but also the prices at which they trade. This expands the battlefields where companies must compete and means that domestic consumers are no longer a captive market that can be price-gouged as easily as they used to be. Cross-border comparison has always been a big driver of IB and technology facilitates this by increasing awareness of opportunities abroad while reducing the costs of distance. The greater market efficiency resulting from the geographically wider vision that technology enables further cements the latter's role as a key IB driver.

Regulatory frameworks

Just because certain conditions exist to enable cross-border activity does not mean that it will actually happen. For IB to take place, there must be a regulatory (hence political) framework that is conducive to foreign-domestic interactions. The main constraint here is the fact that national governments have traditionally viewed their prime regalian responsibility as protecting the domestic population against foreign incursions. The main threat has always been military conflict, of course, but hopefully this is rare. Instead, foreign danger tends to be viewed more often in an economic light, for instance, when domestic companies risk being crowded out of their home market by foreign rivals. In these instances, governments must determine to what extent they want to use their powers to protect local producers against this kind of competition. IB history has run the full gamut of responses.

Chapter 3 will discuss state intervention in greater depth. For the moment, it is worth noting that the dominant paradigm in many if not most countries, from the early 1980s until very recently, has been to accept and indeed encourage two-way cross-border economic activity. The cornerstone of this era of deregulation (also known as "liberalisation") has been a generalised reduction in barriers to entry, making it easier for all companies to operate on an international scale. The big question following the Brexit vote in 2016 – and given certain vulnerabilities in the world economy revealed by the Covid-19 pandemic – is how long political support for IB can be expected to last in some societies.

The openness characterising today's more liberalised era not only affects most countries' trade and FDI regulations but has also culminated in a regime of global governance specifically designed to promote IB. One example has been the proliferation of regional bodies such as the European Union (EU) but also the Association of Southeast Asian Nations (ASEAN), the United States-Mexico-Canada Agreement (USMCA, ex-North American Free Trade Agreement or NAFTA) and Mercosur. These are groups of neighbouring countries that have signed agreements facilitating access to one another's markets. Their degree of integration can vary, but the net effect has been a marked acceleration in trade among members. The same philosophy has underpinned the creation of trade-friendly international institutions such as the World Trade Organization (WTO), bodies whose principles create a framework within which countries are positively discouraged from adopting protectionist policies, much less isolationist ones. The idea in both these instances has been to create a world where IB is the rule, not the exception.

Global competitive paradigms
Before the modern era of liberalised international dealings, most companies would largely position themselves vis-à-vis their domestic rivals, competing for a share of the local market. Given today's increasingly permeable borders, however, rivals can come from anywhere, leveraging all of the experience they have accumulated both home and abroad. This means that some companies that have worked very hard over the years to improve productivity or quality – and who might still reign supreme within a purely domestic framework – risk suddenly losing market share due to the arrival of hyper-efficient foreign competitors. For example, where Bordeaux wineries used to compete successfully with domestic rivals from France's Burgundy region, today

Barriers to entry - Regulatory, competitive, financial and other obstacles that make it difficult for a firm to enter a particular market.

they also have to counter challenges from New World winemakers from Australia, Chile and South Africa. With rivals already achieving economies of scale as a result of their global operations, Bordeaux winemakers can no longer afford to think in domestic terms alone. In part, this is because the profits that more internationalised groups make in one market can be used to fund expansion in another – explaining why it is sometimes just as important to go abroad to undermine a rival as it is to turn a profit oneself. Witness the outcry when companies, like US aircraft-maker Boeing and its European rival Airbus, accuse one another of receiving preferential treatment in their respective domestic markets – with each fearing that their rival's domestic strength will enable it to subsidise lower prices abroad and expand market share in this way. The new competition involves fighting in markets all across the world. It is why business has become so much tougher in many sectors today.

The main consequence of the new competitive paradigm is that many producers can no longer rely on the comfortable positions they used to enjoy domestically. Witness the countless family-run coffee shops that have been muscled out of the marketplace by international chains like Starbucks. Witness the wave of consolidations repeatedly forced on the world's automotive industry as national producers find they have to merge or else be taken over by global rivals whose gigantic size provides them not only with economy of scale advantages but also with much deeper pockets. Add to this the partial convergence of consumer behaviour and demand patterns that has been witnessed worldwide and most companies have come to realise that, irrespective of how directly or indirectly they operate outside of their national borders, IB will affect them in one way or the other. Everyone's playing field has become much bigger today.

International finance

Last but not least, corporate finance has also been affected by the trend towards a more interconnected world. To source the capital needed to run vast multinational empires, MNEs must often rely on different funding sources, many of which operate offshore, thus free from national jurisdictions. The deregulation of banking since the 1980s, part of the overall liberalisation paradigm, has led to an explosion in cross-border capital flows. Much of this money floats freely, meaning that it is no longer directly associated with the production of goods and services. This partial separation of finance from real business activity, one of the causes of the 2008 global credit crunch, has added to the pressures weighing on MNE managers today. On the one hand, financial asset prices are becoming increasingly volatile and difficult to predict, adding to the uncertainty affecting all decision-making, including in relation to FDI. On the other, whereas many MNEs used to be owned by "passive shareholders" mainly interested in the safety of their investments, managers contending with the new shareholder value paradigm are

Shareholder value - Idea that the purpose of a company is to maximise short-term financial returns to shareholders.

under greater pressure than ever to maximise short-term financial returns by taking greater risks, which often means venturing into new markets before the company is fully ready. On top of this, the deregulation and interconnection of the world's capital markets means that financial problems that would have once been ring-fenced within a single national economy are now much more likely to spread (see Chapter 3). A more globalised world has advantages but also creates its own problems.

Attitudes and alternatives

The demanding and constantly evolving nature of modern IB means that the challenges it brings should never be underestimated. Some textbooks adopt what seems at times to be a checklist approach to this discipline, giving readers the false impression that they will necessarily succeed in their international endeavours if they simply tick certain boxes. This is highly misleading in the opinion of this book's author, based both on his professional experience as an IB practitioner and on his research. Firstly, the "situated" nature of international risk management requires a dosage of internal and external knowledge that can vary dramatically from one situation to the next (Ronnback and Holmstrom 2011). Above all, if learners are led to believe that IB is a mere extension of domestic business, they will underestimate the difficulty of acquiring the flexible mindset epitomising almost all successful IB practitioners. Thinking internationally is something new for many people, and the problems they face developing this skill is an integral part of their story. It is less useful to rejoice in the very real opportunities for profit maximisation that IB affords – exemplified by the fact that most, if not all, of the wealthiest companies (and people) in the world operate on a cross-border basis today – than to make prospective practitioners cognisant of the innumerable challenges that they will have never previously faced in their domestic dealings.

One leading example is the way that politics plays out in IB. Despite a decades-long trend towards more internationalist thinking, resistance to foreign competition for markets, resources and jobs remains widespread and has in fact intensified in recent years. Specifically, international economic activities (like technology transfers or global movements of capital) tend to be associated with distinct sets of problems that will regularly come under fire, either because they are perceived as exacerbating the inequalities from which certain populations already suffer or, conversely, because they attack the advantages that a second population has long enjoyed. Otherwise, IB is also increasingly criticised for its environmental consequences, given the way long-distance trade intensifies the consumption of natural resources and adds to the world's pollution problems (Sitkin 2019). Last but not least, and as aforementioned, IB has unmistakable links to the sociocultural phenomenon of xenophobia. Notwithstanding the author's abhorrence, rejection and condemnation of any and all discriminatory attitudes, the academic value of this textbook would be undermined if it underplayed the extent to which some people's fear (or dislike) of foreigners affects IB. Of course, and in an infinitely more positive vein, there is also a case to make that globalisation might stem from (and/or cause) xenophilia, that is, an attraction to foreigners. The hope here is that intensified interactions with people from different origins can create a cosmopolitan mindset that will soon become second nature for most IB practitioners (Badger 2014) and citizens. Indeed, this is already undoubtedly true for some. For others – unfortunately – it would appear that increased contact with foreigners sparks greater dislike of the outside world (Huntingdon 2002; Barber 2003). If an IB book overestimates the cross-border obstacles that managers face, then at worst it is guilty of being overly cautious. If, on the other hand, it underestimates these obstacles, then it is guilty of leaving learners unprepared for situations they might face in the future. The consequences of the latter mistake would be much more severe than the former.

For this reason, the chapters in this book will all end with an "Attitudes and Alternatives" section highlighting different challenges inherent to IB, as well as the different ways that managers might seek to overcome them. Each of these choices – how to allocate resources, how to target markets and customers, how to interact with foreign interests or governments and so forth – is grounded in managers' ability to provide an appropriate response to a specific set of circumstances. The book's fundamental philosophy is that it is more important to help readers learn how to make choices than to dictate to them which choices they should be making.

Chapter summary

This brief introductory chapter set the scene by identifying the differences between global and international approaches, before asking whether it is more effective to undertake a "one-best-way" approach that can be applied in all circumstances or to develop the ability to respond flexibly to different environments. The textbook adopts the second approach. Depending on personal but also corporate and national interests, individuals, companies and governments all respond in various ways to the possibilities afforded by IB – which is therefore best apprehended as a multidisciplinary social science.

The second section studied in greater depth the general factors driving IB today, categorising them either as micro-level strategies that MNEs can choose to adopt or as macro-level variables found in the IB environment. A distinction was made between factors that apply in most circumstances and others that are more case-specific. Lastly, the final section revisited the importance for future practitioners of thinking along paradigmatic lines.

Case study 1.3: Speed kills, or the slowbalisation of international business

Fig 1.9
Even before the Covid-19 pandemic, IB growth rates were no longer exceeding annual increases in global GDP, a trend that *The Economist* magazine would call "slowbalisation".

Following a number of significant social, political and technological changes that took place in the early 1980s, the world economy would enter what came to be known as the "second golden age of globalisation", mirroring a period about 100 years previous that had also witnessed a rapid and widespread reduction in barriers to IB. One manifestation of this resurgence in cross-border economic activity could be seen in the chart published annually by the WTO comparing trade growth with GDP growth. With very few exceptions (mainly accompanying crises like the 2001 and 2008 stock market crashes), the results were the same year in, year out – IB was always expanding much faster than domestic business and therefore accounting for a rising proportion of all economic activity,

During these boom years, few observers were predicting anything but that the trend would extend long into the future. Expectations were that potential IB saturation effects in the world's older industrialised countries (already trading intensively with one another under the aegis of bodies like the WTO and the European Union) would be offset by accelerated trade with their newly industrialised counterparts from the Global South. It is true that starting around 2015, the growth differential between IB and global GDP began to shrink. Even so, the then WTO Director General Roberto Azevedo continued to express optimism, predicting in 2017 that trade volumes would rise by 3.9 percent in 2018 and 3.7 percent in 2019.

However, when the actual numbers came in at only 3.0 and 2.6 percent, respectively, the mood shifted noticeably among IB analysts. A new consensus began to take root, positing that globalisation's decades-long fast growth was finally reversing – a trend that *The Economist* magazine would call "slowbalisation".

A multitude of reasons have been given for this relative slowdown in trade and FDI growth rates, with questions remaining whether the causes are temporary or permanent. Some factors are more political in nature and may therefore disappear once the people responsible for IB-unfriendly policies leave office – one leading example being the dismantlement of Donald Trump's so-called "America First" policies after he was soundly beaten by Joe Biden in the 2020 US presidential election. Having said that, similar attitudes culminating in Britain's departure from the European Union (EU) will have a more lasting effect – it is highly improbable that the UK will be allowed to rejoin the EU before a very long time, hampering cross-Channel trade and FDI for the foreseeable future.

Other explanations for slowbalisation are more structural in nature. Many analysts have started predicting, for instance, that innovations like 3-D printing and robotics will reduce the role that labour performs in global production and therefore diminish MNEs' incentive to continue outsourcing manufacturing operations to Global South countries whose main attraction had been their lower labour costs (Leering 2017). Otherwise, the ongoing rise in Global South households' income levels is not always translating, as had been expected, into greater demand for products made by Global North countries, due in part to some emerging households' preference for national brands with which they are more familiar. Note that whereas Chinese exports had been a major contributor to rising international trade volumes during the second golden age of globalisation, a higher production of the country's output now seems to be targeting domestic customers enjoying a rising standard of living. Thirdly, a certain percentage of economic activity in any country is always destined, by its very nature, to be domestic in scope, that is, there has always been a ceiling on how far global economic integration can advance. This is particularly evident in the Global North whose ageing societies are spending less on goods and more on services – which tend by definition to be much less international in nature. Lastly, there are the effects of the Covid-19 pandemic, which has translated into sporadic border restrictions, if only for disease control reasons. This has caused a number of analysts to predict further negative impacts on international trade volumes – a somewhat irrational forecast, given that the virus is transmitted by human beings and not by packages shipped over long distances. Still, it is yet another thought process speaking to many observers' growing sense that the modern world has become much less borderless than might have been expected just a few short years ago.

This is not to say that certain IB activities are not destined to continue to thrive. FDI is one way that MNEs overcome political resistance to exports and therefore retain a relatively brighter outlook, perhaps becoming the prime mode of market entry in the future. The same applies to cross-border sales of knowledge and other intangibles. Otherwise, the global trade in services has experienced much less of an expansion than the global trade in goods and is therefore less likely to have hit saturation point. Nevertheless, there is little doubt but that the all-conquering optimism that had surrounded IB until very recently has lost some of its lustre. It would be misleading for an IB textbook to underplay – or for that matter, to overplay – the importance of people's expectations of IB.

Case study questions

1. Which social, political and economic events have had the strongest effect on IB confidence in recent years?
2. Looking ahead, which scenarios are likeliest to affect future confidence in IB?
3. Which countries and sectors of activity are mostly likely to experience rapid or slow IB growth in the years to come?

General discussion questions

1   Is globalisation inevitable?
2   How important is nationality to the way people do business?
3   To what extent does international business benefit wealthy versus poor countries?
4   How would international business work if national regulatory environments were stricter?
5   To what extent is international business based on objective science as opposed to human psychology?

References

Aharoni, Y., and Ramamurti, R. (June 2008). "The internationalisation of multinationals", *Research in Global Strategic Management*, Volume 14, pp. 177–201.

Andersen, T. (2011). "The risk implications of multinational enterprise", *International Journal of Organizational Analysis*, Volume 19, Issue 1, pp. 49–70.

Backer, K. et al. (25 September 2019). "Multinational enterprises in the global economy: Heavily discussed, hardly measured", accessed 21 February 2021 at https://voxeu.org/

Badger, K. (2014). "Cosmopolitanism and globalization: A project of collectivity", accessed 16 June 2020 at https://www.dartmouth.edu/

Barber, B. (2003). *Jihad vs. McWorld: Terrorism's Challenge to Democracy*, London: Corgi Books.

Barutcu, S. et al. (September 2016). "Attitudes towards the foreign products from animosity, boycott and ethnocentrism perspectives: The case of Turkish students", *European Scientific Journal*, Special Edition.

Bornman, E. (28 November 2010). "Struggles of identity in the age of globalisation", *South African Journal for Communication Theory and Research*, Volume 29, Issues 1 & 2, pp. 24–47.

Brightmore, D. (10 September 2019). "Manufacturing profile: Foxconn – Apple's premier production partner", accessed 16 June 2020 at https://www.manufacturingglobal.com/

Buckley, P., and Casson, M. (1976). *The Future of the Multinational Enterprise*, New York: Holmes and Meier Publishers.

Chamberlain, G. (2018). "Underpaid and exhausted: the human cost of your kindle", accessed 16 June 2020 at https://www.theguardian.com/

Economist (24 January 2019). "The steam has gone out of globalization", *The Economist*.

Ellis, P. (2011). "Social ties and international entrepreneurship: Opportunities and constraints affecting firm internationalisation", *Journal of International Business Studies*, Volume 42, pp. 99–127.

European Commission (2003). "The new SME definition", accessed 16 June 2020 at http://ec.europa.eu/

Friedman, T. (2005). *The World is Flat: A Brief History of the Twenty-first Century*, London: Penguin Books.

Froud, J. et al. (April 2012). "Apple business model: Financialization across the pacific", *CRESC Working Paper Series*, Number 11.

Ghoshal, S., and Bartlett, G. (October 1990). "The multinational corporation as an interorganizational network", *The Academy of Management Review*, Volume 15, Issue 4, pp. 603–625.

Huntingdon, S. (2002). *The Clash of Civilisations: And the Remaking of World Order*, London: Simon & Schuster.

Ietto-Gillies, G. (2013). "The theory of the transnational corporation at 50+", accessed 8 February 2021 at http://etdiscussion.worldeconomicsassociation.org/

Jeakie, W. (2019). "How apple's Tim Cook mastered Donald Trump", accessed 16 June 2020 at https://www.forbes.com/

Kano, L. et al. (25 February 2020). "Global value chains: A review of the multi-disciplinary literature", *Journal of International Business Studies*, Volume 51, pp. 577–622.

Leering, R. (September 2017). "3D printing: A threat to global trade", *ING Economic and Financial Analysis*, accessed 31 October 2020 at https://www.ingwb.com/

Mankotia, A. (11 May 2020). "Apple may take a bigger bite of India's manufacturing pie", accessed 16 June 2020 at https://tech.economictimes.indiatimes.com/

Ohmae, K. (1999). *The Borderless World: Power and Strategy in the Interlinked Economy*, McKinsey & Company, New York: HarperCollins Publishers.

Petriglieri, G. (December 2016). "In defence of cosmopolitanism", *Harvard Business Review*, accessed 1 November 2020 at https://hbr.org/

Porter, M. (1986). *Competition in Global Industries*, Boston, MA: Harvard Business School Press.

Ronnback, L., and Holmstrom, J. (August 2011). "A case study against the checklist approach: Exploring epistemic strategies in IT risk management", accessed 31 October 2020 at http://umu.diva-portal.org/

Sitkin, A. (2019). *Essentials of Green Business*, Abingdon: Routledge.

Solis, M. (10 July 2020). "The post Covid-19 world: Economic nationalism triumphant?", accessed 30 October 2020 at https://www.brookings.edu/

UNCTAD (2020). "Global foreign direct investment expected to plunge 40% in 2020", accessed 16 June 2020 at https://unctad.org/

Watson, P. (2005). *Ideas: A History of Thought and Invention, from Fire to Freud*, New York: HarperCollins.

Womack, J. et al. (1991). *The Machine that Changed the World: The Story of Lean Production*, New York: Harper Perennial.

Yip, G. (15 October 1989). 'Global strategy ... in a world of nations?' *MIT Sloan Management Review*, Volume 31, Issue 1, pp. 29–41.

CHAPTER 2

Theories of international business

Introduction

> The ideas of economists and political philosophers, both when they are right and when they are wrong, are more powerful than is commonly understood. Indeed, the world is ruled by little else. Practical men, who believe themselves to be quite exempt from intellectual influences, are usually the slaves of some defunct economist …
>
> (Keynes 1936)

To understand the different policy environments within which international business (IB) takes place, it is essential to analyse the trade and investment theories that shape – and in turn, are shaped by – policy-makers and/or practitioners. In turn, given the deep connection between theorists' material circumstances and the worldviews they develop, IB theories can only be fully appreciated against the backdrop of the historical era in which they were formulated. Putting opinions into context will always be a crucial skill in IB.

Fig 2.1
Observers of international business have been trying for centuries to formulate optimal trade theories.

DOI: 10.4324/9781003159056-3

Learning how past theorists reacted to their environment can also provide lessons for today. As expressed in the quote at the beginning of this chapter, the main economic debates tend to recur time and again, with strong ideas being reborn in forms that may differ from their initial expression yet translate a similar vision. This continuum offers consistency but can also become problematic when "zombie" theories reappear even after having been largely invalidated (Krugman 2020). The long-term effect of theorists' attempt to make sense of the world is to create schools of thought that shape people's beliefs, hence their actions. In IB, as in all social sciences, reality and perception influence one another.

LEARNING OBJECTIVES

After reading this chapter, you will be able to:

- situate both international and domestic economic theories in their historical contexts
- determine why certain countries specialise in certain industries
- evaluate the strengths and weaknesses of state intervention in trade and FDI matters
- evaluate the strengths and weaknesses of state intervention in domestic economic matters
- trace historical shifts in the global diffusion of economic policy paradigms

Case study 2.1: South Korea has economic soul

The general image that South Korea exudes today is of a thriving manufacturing economy, home to many successful and even complex products including Hyundai cars, Samsung mobile phones and LG refrigerators. South Korea is a member of the Organisation for Economic Co-operation and Development (OECD), a body representing the world's most advanced economies; its school leavers regularly rank among the top global performers; and its GDP per-capita figures have increased at an above-average rate for decades now. And yet, less than one century ago, Korea was a nation of poor farmers, called the "Hermit Kingdom" due to its limited relations with the outside world. The policies that South Korea has implemented during its industrial ascension offer many lessons about the real-world application of trade theories.

One starting point for studying Korea's development might be the country's early 20th-century occupation by Japan, which oversaw its erstwhile colony's first steps towards industrialisation. After Japan's defeat in the Second World War, two competing powers (China and the USA) stepped into the political vacuum, triggering a war that split the Korean peninsula into

Fig 2.2
South Korea's particular
brand of **developmental
capitalism** has seen its
capital Seoul evolve into
a bustling hyper-modern
city.

half. Following an armistice signed in 1953, North Korea ended up with
a communist regime and closed its borders to international trade. South
Korea, on the other hand, joined the capitalist world's increasingly open
trade regime (Lee 1996).

Throughout the 1950s, the South Korean government followed the
example of many other newly independent countries seeking to improve
their national terms of trade through rapid industrialisation. The preferred
policy during this era was "import substitution", a framework that saw the
state protecting domestic industries from foreign competition in the hope
of helping them to start manufacturing the higher value-added goods
that South Korea had previously had a tendency to import. The idea was
that this would give Korean companies the time they needed to develop
the financial strength and knowledge that would then allow them to
compete successfully with more established rivals.

**Developmental
capitalism** - Market
economy where state
often intervenes,
but primarily to help
companies become
more competitive.

One of the side effects of excluding efficient foreign producers from the South Korean market was high inflation. As a result, the government of Park Chung-Hee decided to change gears in the 1960s by adopting a "strategic trade" policy where, instead of trying to minimise imports, the new priority would be to use preferential-rate loans and direct state subsidies to strengthen the export capabilities of new Korean industries seeking to break through in high value-added sectors like machine tools or electronics. Accompanied by a devaluation of the national currency (the won), the new policy triggered a period of export-driven growth. It also sparked considerable investment in other target sectors like shipbuilding, steel and chemicals. Due to insufficient domestic capital to fund all of these expenditures, however, South Korea also had to increase its foreign borrowings. The debt it accumulated in this way eventually led to a financial crisis – a major factor in the Park regime's 1979 downfall.

Partially in response to this crisis but also mirroring the ideological shifts happening in the rest of the world, South Korea again changed course in the 1980s, opting now for a policy of "trade liberalisation". Key elements of third policy paradigm included the relaxation of existing import restrictions and elimination of many export subsidies. South Korean companies would now be expected to compete with foreign rivals without receiving much state aid at all. Henceforth, governmental interventions would be largely limited to two kinds of indirect action: major investment in workforce education and government coordination of private economic decisions.

South Korea has grown rapidly over the past 30 years, to the extent that this once-poor agrarian society is now a global industrial powerhouse. Still, its continued reliance on Western product markets and its vulnerability to foreign challenges like the 1997 Asian currency crisis or 2020 Covid-19 pandemic mean that it is increasingly dependent on what happens in the rest of the world.

The three paradigms characterising South Korea trade policy since the 1950s (import substitution, strategic export promotion and trade liberalisation) each had their own rationale, strengths and weaknesses. Each also served a purpose in getting South Korea to where it is today. The lesson here is that no trade policy is appropriate in all circumstances and at all times. The same might be said about the theories underlying these policies.

Case study questions

1. To what extent have Korea's economic actions been dictated by circumstances as opposed to ideology?
2. What are the strengths and weaknesses of the three policy regimes that South Korea has pursued since the 1950s?

Section I. International trade and investment theories

For centuries, IB economists and practitioners have tried to develop trade and foreign direction investment (FDI) theories explaining why nations do what they do. An ancillary question has always been which domestic policies should then be implemented to improve trade performance. This linkage explains why the distinction between international and national economic policies is necessarily artificial. Decisions taken in one sphere will almost always affect the other, often intentionally so.

The theories featuring in this chapter will be presented in chronological order of their formulation. The first section will look at theories specifically developed to address trade and FDI concerns. The second will be geared towards domestic economic policy – a topic that is just as relevant to multinational enterprise (MNE) decision-makers due to their frequent need to adapt their actions to the specific political environments they find in each of the national settings where their company operates.

As a general thread running throughout the chapter, readers may find it useful to categorise theories as advocating either a greater or lesser degree of state interventionism – being a much more accurate way of referring to the spectrum of opinions found in this area than the terms "left-wing" or "right-wing", labels whose meaning is always in flux. Otherwise, there are two considerations to remember when applying this "big state vs. small state" filter. Firstly, irrespective of theorists and decision-makers' policy preferences, almost no one ever advocates 0 or 100 percent state interventionism: private enterprise existed in the most communist of regimes, and even the most radical "free market" advocates accept that certain functions (education, infrastructure, policing, etc.) be run by the state. In reality, everyone is somewhere in the middle of the economic interventionism spectrum. The real issue is whether an actor is closer to one end or the other – or indeed, exactly in the middle.

In a similar vein, it should be remembered that whereas some theorists will be consistent in terms of supporting or opposing interventionism both internationally and domestically, others will adopt a hybrid approach. Table 2.1 demonstrates this breakdown for some leading theorists and/or politicians with whom readers may be familiar. Note the possibility of hybrid policy mixes, combined in different ways in different settings. In this as in every aspect of IB, it is crucial to avoid preconceptions about how people think.

Classical country-focused trade theories

Thinkers have long grappled with trade as a topic, with some of the oldest arguments in this field still resonating. Many of Ancient Greece's

Table 2.1
Consistent versus hybrid policy preferences among recent theorists and politicians

	Foreign economic policy	*National economic policy*
Interventionism	DeGaulle/Trump Gandhi/Tito	DeGaulle/Obama Keynes/Merkel
Free market "laissez-faire"	Keynes/Smith Reagan/Thatcher	Smith/Hayek/Friedman Reagan/Thatcher

earliest philosophers, for instance, expressed a negative reaction to foreign merchants (Irwin 1996). This sentiment came to be known as xenophobia (from the Greek *phobia* for "fear", and *xenos* for "foreign"), and to varying degrees it is something that international managers continue to encounter today, along with home bias, its more palatable form. Philosophers Plato and Xenophon did acknowledge the usefulness of establishing an economic division of labour based on the idea that specialisation generates efficiency, but they applied this to individuals rather than to international economics. Aristotle went as far as to accept that imports might occasionally be necessary but also thought that they should be limited to certain categories of goods only – an attitude that anticipated modern "strategic trade" policies. All in all, however, resistance to foreign trade and/or traders was the norm in ancient times.

In the European Middle Ages, trade's image as a fundamentally immoral activity began to evolve under the influence of thinkers like Thomas Aquinas. By the 16th century, legal experts like Spain's Francisco de Vitoria were writing that it was "natural" for countries to trade with foreigners as long as it did not damage their domestic interests. The new vision paved the way for a doctrine that became known as "the right of nations" to trade. Once this was legitimised, it was a short step to mercantilism, the first fully fledged trade theory.

Mercantilism
From the 16th through the 18th centuries, mercantilism was the dominant school of international economics. The main idea here is that national trade policy should aim to maximise exports and minimise imports. This is based on the notion that wealth materialises not in the economic activities that a country hosts but in its accumulation of currency, mainly gold at the time, with trade being the prime vehicle for sourcing this commodity. The doctrine views trade as a zero-sum

proposition where some parties win and others necessarily lose. For this reason, all nations have the right to compete, using almost any means, to improve their trade balance. The main tools to be deployed are import restrictions (starting with taxes on foreign goods) and domestic subsidies – although it is worth noting that this list has evolved over the years to include, in its modern version, other potential actions relating to the appropriation of intellectual property or manipulation of currency rates (Wein et al. 2014).

To some analysts, mercantilism was and remains a logical proposition, largely because it is considered normal behaviour for societies, organised into nation-states, to try and accumulate trade surpluses. Yet the theory has also been widely criticised by others, first and foremost because it incentivises a government to protect inefficient domestic producers who are no longer under pressure to take the steps they should to become competitive. This distorts market mechanisms while harming consumers in two ways: because they must pay higher prices for goods and because financial aid to potentially inefficient local industry drains national resources. Companies that do not receive state aid may also consider the policy unfair and therefore engage in tax evasion and capital flight. This undermines the tax base and further reduces national income – the very problem that mercantilism is supposed to resolve.

Leading mercantilist thinkers like Thomas Mun (1571–1641) recognised the "defensive" problems associated with import taxes and proposed instead more "proactive" solutions where governments would concentrate instead on helping national industry produce better-quality exports. This more constructive version of mercantilism involves greater acceptance of the need for international competitiveness, although it still depends on a government's ability to pick winners. It is also at odds with some modern economists' belief that a country's trade balance does not matter anymore and that it is more important to ensure domestic firms' profitability. Contemporary neo-mercantilists will respond that a policy of facilitating MNE profits does not help an economy if it causes domestic companies to shift work to cheaper foreign locations. All in all, arguments over mercantilism remain highly topical, especially given the recent resurgence of what has come to be known as "anti-globalist" thinking (Economist 2016). Mercantilism is a straightforward philosophy in the sense that it recognises the reality of national interest. But it also has a number of negatives, including the potential for undermining dynamism, obstructing trade and sparking hateful chauvinism.

Classical economics and trade theories

The founder of "classical" economics is the Scotsman Adam Smith (1723–1790), whose seminal work *The Wealth of Nations* (1776) laid the foundations for many of the domestic economic and international trade principles that resonate even today. A keen observer of the changes that Britain was experiencing during the First Industrial Revolution, Smith believed that governments should stay out of markets, which

Trade balance - Relationship between the value of a country's exports and imports. When exports exceed imports, the country is running a trade surplus. When imports exceed exports, it runs a trade deficit.

Capital flight - Where investors or savers take large sums of money out of a country because of concerns about local risks or disagreements with policy.

Fig 2.3
Adam Smith was a seminal
free market theorist
for both domestic and
international economics.

should be steered instead both by the "invisible hand of God" and by individuals' pursuit of self-interest (referred to as "utility"). In this conception, economics has its own laws, irrespective of vested interests. What matters is market performance, not which social partners plead their case the loudest or who has inherited the most wealth.

Such was the power of Smith's "classical-liberal" principles that they continue to dominate economic debate today. Contemporary advocates of his theory like to assert that imposing fewer regulation on companies will spark the kind of entrepreneurship and innovation that they consider key to economic renewal (Paiva et al. 2018). Different theorists would respond, however, by highlighting the dynamism of the Asia's tiger economies and Scandinavia's social democracies, success stories where strong regulation combined with a market economy has produced top economic performance. It is important that IB learners internalise the two sides of this debate since they are likely to encounter both in many professional situations.

Classical economics is driven by the idea that markets left to their own devices will tend towards an optimal allocation of resources, called "equilibrium". One of the main ways that this can be achieved is by allowing uncompetitive industries to die naturally. The resources that are subsequently freed up can then be used to support growth sectors – a process that Austrian economist Joseph Schumpeter would later call "creative destruction". In terms of trade economics, this means that countries should only host those domestic industries that can demonstrate international competitive advantage. Conversely, they should be willing to abandon other productions, even at the price of temporary, "frictional" unemployment for however long it takes those workers who are losing their jobs in the abandoned activities to transition into new, more competitive sectors. At an extreme, this translates into the view that open borders are beneficial because pressure from foreign industry forces national producers and workers to accept the pain of becoming more efficient, viewed here as a good thing in and of itself.

Critics of classical economists often accuse them of overconfidence in market mechanisms and of neglecting the social consequences of their paradigm. In an increasingly globalised world, for instance, there is always a risk that international competition will kill off entire sectors of domestic activity, even ones that are relatively competitive. The marginal improvement in the country's overall economic efficiency is of little consolation to the many workers left behind (Rubin 2018). As British economist John Maynard Keynes once wrote, the weakness of classical economists' precept that markets naturally tend towards an ideal state over time is its failure to recognise that "in the long run, we are all dead".

Classical economists believe that market mechanisms have their own rules that these should reign supreme and that they ultimately lead to an optimum. The problem is – as revealed through the work of mathematicians Henri Poincaré and Edward Lorentz, culminating in what would later come to be known as "chaos theory" – that it is very risky to assume that complex systems are ever capable of achieving lasting equilibrium. If instability is to be a constant, identifying the factors that cause disequilibrium becomes indispensable.

Absolute advantage

One strength of Smith's theory is its premise that having economic protagonists concentrate on specific tasks can be a source of great efficiency. The approach is commonly called a "division of labour" when applied to a work organisation. In the international arena, it means that where two countries both have absolute advantage in different products, it will be in the interest of both to import the speciality product that the other produces instead of making it at home. This is an idealised vision of trade as an activity enabling one country to benefit from the strengths of another. The emphasis here is on a national economy's overall productive capacities, not the amount of currency it earns from a deal (Zhang 2010). By all measures, it is a more sophisticated concept that mercantilism had been.

Smith's argument is substantiated each and every time that a country uses cheap imported components in its domestic production process

Absolute advantage - Where one country, providing the same quantum of inputs as another, achieves greater outputs and can therefore be said to produce more cheaply.

instead of manufacturing the same items locally but at a higher cost. This is particularly important with generic components like steel or micro-conductors that are used at the beginning of a complex production process and which have knock-on effects all the way down the value chain. Manufacturers who are no longer able to access foreign inputs at their lower international price must either accept reduced margins or pass the extra cost of the more expensive domestic replacement on to the consumer, making their offer less competitive.

Having said that, Smith's absolute advantage theory remains insufficient and imperfect, mainly because it does not always correspond to reality. Economic advantage is distributed unevenly worldwide, with some countries enjoying greater factor endowments (land, capital, natural resources and – in the modern conception – knowledge) than others. This might be viewed as a size issue given larger countries' generally greater access to labour (China), natural resources (Russia and Australia) and/or a big home market (the USA). Some countries, however, possess no particular advantage at all – raising the question of why they would even want to open their borders to a trade competition that they are almost certain to lose. Moreover, analysing countries solely in terms of the "natural advantage" that they inherit from their geographic or demographic situation is a static vision neglecting their ability to develop new advantages (like technological know-how). Japan, for example, has few natural advantages yet is an economic powerhouse, thanks in part to its advanced coordination of public and private interests. Smith did not envision this scenario.

Another weakness in Smith's theory is that countries lacking any absolute advantage or suffering from poor terms of trade (a possibility that Smith also did not foresee) will be too poor to buy goods produced by their more competitive counterparts. International trade can only function if sellers find solvent customers. Western Europe, for example, was able to purchase American goods after the Second World War only because the USA used Marshall Plan funding to reinject cash back into the European economies. The same argument is often used today to justify Global North aid to the Global South. To organise a successful market, it is not enough to have efficient producers, as Smith thought; there must also be customers with enough money to buy the goods being offered.

None of this is meant to deny the wealth of statistical evidence that exists to support Smith's basic premise that free trade helps to maximise productivity gains (Ahn et al. 2018), thereby sparking economic development. It has simply always been clear that his theories require greater elaboration. This would be achieved by a student and admirer of Smith, who would go on to formulate what many see today as the epicentre of classical trade theory.

Comparative advantage

David Ricardo's *Principles of Political Economy and Taxation* (1817) presented the idea of comparative advantage, which remains the basis of

Factor endowments - Human, financial and physical capital that an economic entity (often a country) can use in its production process.

Solvent - Having sufficient funds to pay for goods.

Comparative advantage - Where one country makes all goods more efficiently than another but agrees not to make (hence to import) the goods whose production makes the least efficient use of its resources.

most trade models today. Ricardo's insights addressed the basic weakness in Smith's theorems, namely, the fact that countries lacking any absolute advantage whatsoever have no incentive to engage in international trade. The great novelty of Ricardo's work was the idea that trade can also benefit less competitive countries, as long as the workers employed in their less productive activities accept lower wages reflecting their lower productivity levels. This nuance then turns free trade into a "win–win" proposition for all concerned.

Like Smith, Ricardo used a wine versus textiles example to demonstrate his thinking. Unlike Smith, however, he started with the idea that Portugal produces both items more cheaply than England does. Ricardo then set out to prove that England might still have good cause to open its borders to trade with Portugal despite its absence of absolute advantage in either wine or textiles. He began by calculating the price structure if both countries were to work in autarky, with consumers only buying locally produced goods. The domestic prices in this case might be 1 unit of wine and 1 unit of textiles both costing 15 points in England but (as per the conditions of the demonstration) both items being cheaper in Portugal, especially wine, for which 1 unit would cost 5 points, with one 1 unit of textiles costing 10 points.

Autarky - Where an entity operates self-sufficiently and in isolation.

It is at this point that Ricardo had his crucial insight. With Portuguese wine trading domestically at one-half the price of local textiles, it stood to reason that if the country could receive more than one-half unit of textiles for each unit of wine that it sells, there would be an advantage for it to export wine but import textiles, leaving the production of the latter good to its English trading partner. The question then becomes what international price meets this condition. In the present example (see Table 2.2), that happens when 1 unit of wine is priced as the equivalent of 0.75 units of textiles.

The same demonstration can be made from an English perspective. Here, because domestic wine and textiles sell at the same price (15 units), it would only be worth engaging in international trade if consumers can buy 1 unit of wine for less than 1 unit of textile. This condition is also

Table 2.2
A basic Ricardian model

	Wine cost	Textile cost	Domestic price structure (autarky)	At international price of 1 unit of wine = 0.75 units of textile
In Portugal	5	10	1 wine = 0.5 textile (5/10)	Receives an extra 0.25 units of textile when exporting 1 unit of wine
In England	15	15	1 wine = 1 textile (15/15)	Receives an extra 1.33 units of wine (1/0.75) when exporting 1 unit of textile

satisfied at the aforementioned international price, since England only needs to produce 0.75 units of textiles to receive 1 unit of wine. It would therefore save 33 percent (1 unit of wine divided by 0.75 units of wine) by purchasing Portuguese wine, and it could pay for this import by selling to Portugal the item where it has less of a comparative disadvantage, namely, textiles. Thus, despite England not possessing absolute advantage in either product, it would still be in each country's interest to open their borders to one another, with both also having the means to buy the other's output. International trade can exist as long as the international price properly reflects the difference in the two countries' level of efficiency (which Ricardo tended to explain in terms of technology gaps).

A simplified analogy explaining Ricardo's insight has been attributed to US economist Paul Samuelson. The premise here is that an individual, say Alex, is the best solicitor but also the best typist at their firm. Despite being the most productive person at both jobs, it makes more sense to use Alex for lawyering and to hire someone else as secretary. The opportunity cost of not using a comparatively worse typist to do the administrative work is less than the cost of hiring a comparatively worse lawyer to do the legal work.

Opportunity cost - Cost of doing something in a certain way, thus not receiving the benefits of doing it another way.

Ricardo's theory was also imperfect and has been criticised, for instance, because it ignores factors such as capital mobility and technology transfers. These are important because they affect the international distribution of comparative advantage. Yet it remains a very robust construct and one that has been corroborated in countless real-life international trade situations. One example is the agricultural trade between France and Russia. France produces both cereals and farm equipment more efficiently (thus more cheaply) than Russia. Under Smith's theorem, this would mean that Russia must import both items from France. Yet in actual fact it imports tractors but exports grains, since its productivity disadvantage in the former is greater than in the latter. This outcome is perfectly predictable under Ricardo's theorem.

Infant industries

The English philosopher John Stuart Mill (1806–1873) saw three main advantages to free trade. The first two followed on from Smith's and Ricardo's theories regarding the advantages of specialisation and the need for countries to focus on whatever activities increase total productivity. Mill's third construct, however – the "intellectual and moral gains" that a country makes from its contacts with foreigners – was new. It also remains topical today, with analysts continuing to debate to what extent free markets strengthen democracy. One of the ideas associated with this construct is that open borders help to prevent wars, because countries that trade with one another are less likely to fight. This ultimately became one of the drivers behind the foundation of the World Trade Organization (WTO).

Infant industry - Sector of activity that has only recently developed in a particular country and whose prospects for survival are uncertain because it lacks the capital and experience to compete with existing (foreign) producers.

Mill's second significant contribution to international trade theory was the infant industry argument that he developed at the same time as German economist, Friedrich List, with both building on previous work done by an early American politician, Alexander Hamilton. In Mill's opinion, government intervention is justified if and only if a country wants to nurture a new industry in a sector where it might possess a natural advantage. Since the industry is new, it will be at risk from foreign rivals who have a temporary competitive advantage simply because they are already up and running. "The superiority of one country over another in a branch of production often arises only from having begun sooner. There may be no inherent advantage on one part, or disadvantage on the other, but only a present superiority of acquired skill and experience" (Mill 1848). This idea is relevant to modern concerns about the ability of countries, particularly from the Global South, to enter sectors where MNEs are already firmly entrenched. Examples include India's move to develop its own semiconductor manufacturing capabilities, despite the global overcapacities that already exist in this sector.

Trade as exploitation

Underlying Smith's classical theory was his optimistic view that an efficient market economy benefits society as a whole. Ricardo's opposition to England's early-19th-century Corn Laws caused him, on the other hand, to assert that some social classes (industrialists, workers) are more dynamic than others (landowners). This implied the possibility of an uneven and unfair distribution of economic rewards. German philosopher Karl Marx (1818–1883) built on this latter insight, stating that the starting point for all economic analysis should be to view capitalism as a system rooted in the exploitation of one social group by another. Marx's accusations of unfairness resonate even today, for instance, when Global North countries are accused of using open-border globalisation as a smoke screen for "re-colonisation" (Langan 2018). It is a mistake to study capitalism without considering the views of its leading critics.

One Marxian theory with direct relevance to IB today is the "law of diminishing returns", which holds that firms operating in a closed capitalist economy will, for a number of reasons, suffer from falling profit rates. In this view, firms have no choice but to internationalise if they want to survive. The theorem is vulnerable to criticism, however, having been at least partially disproved by Joseph Schumpeter's demonstration in 1912 of the way in which growth within a national economy can be sustained through "technological progress" – a key factor in modern explanations of MNE location (see discussion below on "New Trade Theory"). It remains that many business analysts are unintentionally arguing a Marxist position when they assert that internationalisation is a necessary condition for firms' survival.

Factor proportions (Heckscher–Ohlin)

Renewing with certain Ricardian principles of trade, Scandinavian economists Eli Heckscher (1879–1952) and Bertil Ohlin (1899–1979) devised a model in the 1920s stating that when two countries trade, each should export the goods that make the most intensive use of the particular factor input (labour, capital or material resources) that it possesses in abundance. This is because each can then source the abundant factor more cheaply, thereby raising its (export) competitiveness in those sectors where that factor is key. Conversely, a country should import the goods that make the most intensive use of the factor input that is most scarce locally. The carpet trade can be used to exemplify this construct. In France, for instance, where capital is abundant, industry specialises in factory-manufactured carpets that make intensive use of capital as their prime factor input. In Turkey, on the other hand, labour is abundant so wages are low, making it economically more viable to produce and export handmade rugs. At its simplest level, this elegant so-called "H–O" model is the core of neoclassical trade theory.

H–O's power to explain real data is imperfect, however. The most famous criticism of H–O was formulated in 1953 as Leontief's paradox, which asked why the USA, the world's most capital-intensive country at the time, imported capital-intensive goods and exported labour-intensive goods – the exact opposite of what H–O would have predicted. The theory seems to fully perform only when cross-border differences in productivity and technology are introduced. It ignores the reality of international factor mobility (Zhang 2010).

Factor mobility -
Capacity of factor inputs (capital, resources, labour, etc.) to move in time and/or place.

In actual fact, this is a widespread critique of almost all classical trade theory. It is one thing assuming that countries will differ in terms of their abilities; it is another explaining why this happens. Classical economists generally theorised that national factor inputs would remain constant, since to a large extent this was the world they inhabited. Things have changed in recent decades, however, given the accelerated international mobility of technology and capital. To reflect the new reality, the main trade theories would have to broaden their scope beyond trading nations' characteristics to include the corporate actors who have assumed greater responsibility over time for factor mobility shifts. So this is what the theorists did.

Business-focused modern trade and investment theories

The leading IB theories since the mid-20th century have focused on corporate behaviour more than on national economies. In all probability, this shift in focus translates the greater share of total wealth accruing today to private interests compared to the past when governments possessed an almost monopolistic control over finance and wielded the power that comes with this. It is also a very good example of the notion that economic theorists formulate their ideas within the historical contexts that they know.

Product life cycle
In a seminal article published in 1966, Raymond Vernon linked international manufacturing location decisions to what he called the

Table 2.3
Vernon's product life cycle construct

Phase	Introduction	Growth	Maturity	Decline
Market dynamics	High-priced new good	Demand spreads	Competition intensifies	Demand declines
Key factors of success	R&D, confidentiality	Market coverage	Rejuvenation via marketing	Low prices
Production location	Global North home country	All Global North countries	Mixed Global North and South	Global South only

product life cycle (PLC). Note that the name chosen by Vernon for his theory is the same as the one used in a famous marketing concept developed by the Boston Consulting Group (www.bcg.com). Vernon's version (see Table 2.3) covers four phases.

1   *Introduction.* Goods are manufactured in the technologically advanced country where they are invented (often the USA in Vernon's original model). At this early stage, what matters is the MNE HQ's ability to control the risks involved in the new product launch. Price competition is not an issue yet, especially if a product is innovative. Demand may spread rapidly in the home country and other markets can only access the item via imports.
2   *Growth.* As demand spreads through the rest of the Global North and rivals build factories in their home markets, it becomes worthwhile for the original MNE to do the same, especially since it can leverage the manufacturing experience it gained back home. This international production – based on FDI – reduces the need for exports and the market starts to organise itself on a country-by-country basis.
3   *Maturity.* The technology begins to age and Global North markets saturate. Prices fall and cost becomes paramount. Low-cost manufacturing facilities begin to be built in the Global South.
4   *Decline.* Cost pressures become so severe that all Global North factories shut. The only remaining sites are in the Global South, with output re-exported back to the original markets.

A historical example of PLC is the changing location of the Xerox group's photocopier manufacturing plants. Output began in the USA in the 1940s and 1950s, before moving to Europe within a decade, and finally, as the technology matured, to India in the 1970s and 1980s. The automotive industry offers a similarly useful example, with Ford and GM undertaking their first FDI in Europe in the 1920s, before subsequently opening plants in the Global South and closing sites in their original markets.

Vernon's theory does not work in all cases, however. Products with a short life span (like micro-processors) may not last long enough to experience the entire cycle. Also, products like luxury goods, the perceived value of which can be altered via advertising, may not age in the way that the model predicts. In addition, products can be at different life cycle stages at different times in different countries – a key factor in many international marketing strategies (see Chapter 11). Lastly, the model assumes that product innovation (and most demand) will emanate from an expensive Global North country – an expectation belied by the Global South's recent rapid emergence.

New Trade Theory

The starting point for the New Trade Theory was John Dunning's 1977 proposal of an eclectic paradigm, partially derived from Stephen Hymer's earlier analysis (see Chapter 9) of the advantage that firms gain when they control their internal capabilities. The idea here is that because markets often function imperfectly, foreign MNEs are apt to face higher costs than local firms will. FDI therefore only becomes attractive if internationalisation is accompanied by specific incentives.

Dunning's insights are often referred to as the Ownership, Location and Internalisation (OLI) theory:

- *Ownership advantages*. The foreign MNE must have a special product or production process that it can use to effect against host country rivals. This explains why technologically advanced companies guard their secrets so jealously.
- *Location advantages*. Moving production abroad must offer an advantage, such as economies of scale.
- *Internalisation advantages*. The MNE must be able to exploit any ownership advantages itself – instead of licensing or selling them to another company – controlling in this way a greater proportion of its overall global value chain.

Following on from Dunning, Markusen (2002) discovered that most trade and FDI occur between neighbouring countries operating at a similar stage of industrial development. This finding, contrasting with the classical expectation that countries who differ from one another are more likely to trade, has been conceptualised as the "gravity model" (Krugman 1997). The idea here is that FDI will more often than not involve "horizontal integration" (see Chapter 7) – with companies operating at similar stages of the value chain both home and abroad – rather than "vertical integration", where a MNE's foreign operations are further upstream and/ or downstream than they are at home. In Markusen's view, this means that the key factor in MNE internationalisation is knowledge – a conclusion substantiated by the disproportionate concentration of MNE FDI in high-tech and research-oriented sectors (like computers or pharmaceutical) where intangible, firm-specific assets are key to success.

In both Dunning and Markusen's visions, IB has two main drivers. The first is learning effects, or the idea that because knowledge is easier and cheaper to transfer than other forms of capital, it can be fragmented relatively efficiently between a MNE's research & development (R&D) team, working out of corporate HQs, and its manufacturing teams, working out of its different national subsidiaries. The second driver is first-mover advantage, or the idea that the first firm to enter a new market and leverage its existing experience is well placed to stave off future rivals.

Unlike Heckscher-Ohlin's emphasis on national factor endowments, the New Trade Theory's main explanation for international success is a company's knowledge and ability to apply this worldwide. This introduces the idea that the location of a particular activity may be a simple accident of history and have little to do with a country's absolute or comparative advantage. After all, there is nothing that predestines Seattle or Toulouse (respectively, centres for Boeing and Airbus) to dominate global aircraft manufacturing. New Trade Theory highlights the consequences of international managers' very human decision-making. It is this ability to incorporate personal factors that makes it the most interesting of all post-Second World War theories.

Competitive advantage

Michael Porter's famous 1990 text, *The Competitive Advantage of Nations*, focused less on FDI than on how national factor endowments mesh with MNEs' historical trajectories. Porter's "Diamond" identifies four sources of competitive advantage, some involving actions that companies might choose to implement and others reflecting the national conditions they face.

- *Factor conditions*. Porter considers this to be the main driver of competitive advantage. The distinction here is between basic factors of production (natural resources, climate) and advanced, productivity-enhancing factors associated with the long-term investments that a country has made in technology and education. MNEs operating in locales of this kind have a better chance at benefitting from knowledge spillovers (see Chapter 10).
- *Demand conditions*. The variables here are the size of a company's domestic market as well as buyers' level of sophistication. MNEs that first flourished in large home markets featuring demanding consumers are better placed to succeed abroad. This is because they have already been "battle hardened" before leaving home.
- *Firm strategy, structure and rivalry*. Management orientation (a focus on finance, engineering, etc.) is key to its success.
- *Related and supporting industry*. Firms benefit from proximity to clusters of efficient upstream suppliers offering inexpensive components and up-to-date technology. Some consider this to be Porter's main theoretical contribution, since it opens the door to considerations of

Learning effects - Extra productive efficiency that companies gain after accumulating experience in a given activity.

First-mover advantage - Benefit of being the first to enter a given market in a given location.

Knowledge spillovers - Where companies gain knowledge through proximity to specialised institutions like universities, research centres or other companies. The same mechanism can apply to individuals.

Cluster - Where firms in a similar line of business operate in physical proximity to one another and build close ties. This can reflect historical factors or strategic intent.

firms working within networks instead of in isolation – a model that has become increasingly prevalent in recent years.

Porter's insights are best exemplified by "industrial districts", with one famous case being the cluster of small and medium-sized ceramic roof tile manufacturers located near Sassuolo in Italy's Modena province. This is a high-performance local economy where information is shared vertically up and down the value chain, and whose companies export goods only once they have benefitted from a long apprenticeship in their local market. It is an outcome that fits Porter's model.

Despite specifying the conditions that help companies to succeed internationally, Porter's theory does not explain why failures continue to occur even when these conditions are fulfilled. Clearly other elements are at work as well – with one possibility being the economic, political and social factors that are, at first glance, only indirectly related to management decision-making.

Welfare economists

A final cohort of contemporary economists have gained fame for their efforts to link country- and company-level theories by opining on IB's impact on social well-being. It is a body of work partially rooted in the "marginal utility" school theorised inter alia by Italian economist Vilfredo Pareto (1848–1923), who used an "optimality" construct to determine the equilibrium point beyond which the welfare of one actor can only be enhanced by diminishing the welfare of another. Although Pareto's focus was purely micro-economic and did not consider broader social realities, his work highlighted the risk that actions that are globally positive for some constituencies might be damaging to others. The question then becomes whether the latter parties should be compensated by the former or instead be expected to wait for efficiency benefits to trickle down. One of the best ways of categorising welfare economists – and indeed, political theorists – is by their response to this question.

Two Nobel Prize-winning economists belonging to the welfare school stand out because of the doubts they have expressed about the fair distribution of IB's benefits. Paul Krugman, the 2008 laureate, who in 1997 had justified globalisation's negative impact on less-skilled American workers' wage levels with the argument that "bad jobs at bad wages are better than no jobs at all", would have a change of heart a decade later following massive job losses in the USA and an accelerated rise in the country's trade deficit. Concerned by the disruption to US labour markets, Krugman began to highlight the imbalances caused by the scale of outsourcing to China, where wages were not only a fraction of Global North levels but also much lower than previous destinations such as South Korea or Taiwan. He would ultimately become a critic of globalisation if "winners don't compensate the losers" (Stewart 2007).

Trickle-down economics - Idea that policy should reward the economically successful because their gains ultimately benefit the rest of the society. Often used to justify low-tax regimes.

This aligned with the views of 2001 laureate Joseph Stiglitz, whose earlier work as advisor to US President Bill Clinton (and Chief Economist at the World Bank) had sensitised him to the inequality that modern globalisation can cause. Encapsulated in a 2002 magnus opus titled *Globalisation and Its Discontents*, Stiglitz's premise was that "the market is obviously not efficient" (2012) since it underutilises workers displaced by foreign competition, hence wastes a valuable resource. This focus on market inefficiency built on previous analysis that Stiglitz had done (and which won him the Nobel Prize) decrying the way "informational asymmetry" prevents market participants from possessing all of the price signals that they need to make rational decisions – itself a key assumption in classical economics.

Logically, the practical application of Krugman and Stiglitz's combined thesis is that because the private sector has shown itself incapable of taking responsibility for the re-employment of workers displaced by international trade, the state must do so. It is the epitome of an interventionist stance, the kind of proposition that other, more "small state" welfare economists generally oppose as being counterproductive. One example is Columbia University's Jagdish Bhagwati (2012), who tends to view any state involvement that might undermine private sector dynamism as being ultimately harmful to the world's poorest citizens, hence as fundamentally regressive. Bhagwati's justification for this view is empirical, based on the strikingly rapid rise in the living standards of those emerging economies that have opened up their markets, as opposed to others whose poor performance he attributes to government interference. His is a stance echoed by Peruvian economist Hernando de Soto (2012), whose work has focused on the crucial role that reliable property rights play in giving Global South entrepreneurs (but also Global North MNEs) the confidence they need to invest, and in this way to grow emerging economies in a way that benefits everyone, first and foremost the poor.

Lastly and in a slightly different register, no review of welfare economics would be complete without mentioning the great Indian philosopher (and 1998 Nobel Laureate) Amartya Sen, who famously argued that economic success needs to be measured less quantitatively and more in terms of the real determinants of household well-being in the worlds' poorest countries. The parameters cited by Sen include infant mortality and access to clean drinking water and education. Encapsulated in the Human Development Index that has become one of the United Nations' mostly widely used tools, Sen's work is a reminder that behind the very intelligent theories used to guide economic policy-making, there are populations looking to their representatives for concrete improvements in their standard of living. As American congressman Tip O'Neil once averred, "All politics are local". Achieving a fuller understanding of IB theories therefore requires analysis not only at an international scale (as this chapter has done so far) but also at the local domestic scale where individuals actually live – and where MNEs go to meet them.

Section II. National economic policy theories

One common thread throughout this chapter is the idea that thinkers are children of their time on Earth and that the theories they formulate can be understood only within a given historical context, characterised by specific political, economic, social, ecological and technological factors. It would, for instance, be instructive to ascertain why mercantilism dominated the Age of Exploration; why classical free market economics (but also Marxism) arose during the First Industrial Revolution; and why the New Trade Theory coincided with the contemporary era of globalisation. What remains to be determined is whether economic philosophy determines political action – or vice versa.

Case study 2.2: Dancing la Cochabamba

Fig 2.4
For a period in the early 2000s, the provincial Bolivian Cochabamba was the poster child for international economic policy debates.

After finally gaining independence from Spain in 1825, Bolivia soon fell into crisis due to insufficient agricultural output, scarce investment capital and onerous national debt (Lobina 2000). The economy improved slightly after an import tariff system was implemented to protect Bolivia's infant textile industry but remained desperately poor for most of the 19th century.

The turn of the 20th century saw a brief period of expansion following temporary rises in the global price of tin, one of Bolivia's few natural resources. When this market collapsed in the 1920s, Bolivia began again to run up considerable debt, mainly owed to the USA. There was a growing sense during the 1940s that reform was needed, in part because of the widening gulf between the country's few elites and many poor. Local conservative and socialist parties had very different ideas about how to solve these problems, however, and the country fell victim to decades of political unrest and economic mismanagement. During this time, the USA provided much needed aid but also tightened its grip on the Bolivian economy. This sparked great resentment, with new Bolivian regimes sporadically deciding to renationalise American assets. It also led to an intellectual revolution across Latin America, a rejection of neocolonialism encapsulated in Argentine economist Raul Prebisch's "dependency theory".

When Bolivia turned to the World Bank in the 1990s for loans to fund a much-needed water system near its third largest city, Cochabamba, it was told to structure the project as a private initiative run by a consortium comprised mainly of US and Italian firms (Finnegan 2002). This was agreed by the country's cash-strapped government. However, the ensuing privatisation programme – along with the abandonment of public subsidies – led to a sharp rise in water rates that Cochabamba's impoverished residents could scarcely afford. Tensions rose because the high rates people now had to pay for this staple commodity were not only meant to reimburse the project's construction costs but also pay for foreign shareholders' dividends. Violent riots erupted, a socialist president was elected in 2006 and the Cochabamba water system was ultimately renationalised. The change did not improve the situation, however: construction deadlines were missed, and budgets were not always controlled. A decade later, the municipally owned water system had yet to reach the city's poorer neighbourhoods, with residents still being forced to rely on expensive trucked-in water (Booth 2016). By 2020, the central government was promising that the whole country would enjoy access to clean water by 2025. Much scepticism remained as to whether this would actually happen.

By any measure, the Cochabamba project has been a failure so far, whether in its original market-oriented form or in its subsequent state-driven version. The question now becomes whether Bolivian policy-makers have been wrong to prefer one school of economics over the other. The next step may be to see whether an eclectic hybrid of the two can produce better results.

Case study questions

1. How were Bolivian policies affected by decision-makers' theoretical preconceptions?
2. What other approaches might be used to drive the Cochabamba water project?

Big state versus small state

It is one thing identifying the economic decisions that policy-makers might consider appropriate in different situations. It is another determining their ability to enact them. At the most basic level, the first question for MNEs when entering a country is the respective power of its public and private sectors – a pendulum that can swing wildly in both time and place.

Neoliberalism

The political expression of classical economists' general outlook has gone under many names but is often referred to at present as free market neoliberalism. The idea here is that governments should engage in laisser-faire policies where they "allow people to do as they like" and run few, if any, areas of economic activity themselves. It is a concept grounded in an ideological belief in personal initiative, market efficiency, the sanctity of private property and the state's non-interference in the private domain. For MNEs operating in a country run along these lines, that should normally mean lower taxes and fewer regulatory costs. Of course, non-interference is also neoliberalism's weakness, with governments pursuing this course usually being far too slow to deploy the tools potentially available to them to help companies and people suffering from an economic downturn and/or market failure – problems that have arisen time and again throughout economic history.

It bears repeating that ideological preferences can be easily overshadowed by a country's sense of its immediate interests. There is, for instance, a tendency for some governments to adopt laisser-faire approaches during boom years, confident in the market's ability to enhance general welfare, only to shift course in a time of crisis and intervene actively. A prime example is the plethora of stimulus packages implemented in the wake of the 2020 Covid-19 pandemic by governments that might otherwise define themselves as being more free market-oriented. As Chapter 3 will demonstrate, deciding to wield less state power is not the same thing as wielding none at all.

General support for neoliberalism can also be affected by attitudes towards the countries advocating this philosophy. As the global superpower ("hegemon") since 1945 – not only economically and politically but also in terms of the paradigms it defends – the USA has often influenced other nations' economic policy-making. If global respect for the US were to fade, there is a good chance that its power to set the global paradigm would also wane. Indeed, this appears to have already happened to some extent in the wake of former President Donald Trump's isolationist administration, with the USA's sudden absence from the world stage creating a power vacuum that China, with its much more interventionist traditions, seems highly disposed to fill. At the same time, antipathy in some corners for the Chinese model – and ongoing attachment to free market entrepreneurialism – means that

Neoliberalism - Belief in minimal government intervention in the economy.

Market failure - Where markets perform inefficiently by not allocating resources optimally.

neoliberal economics might also be expected to retain a large number of supporters for years to come. The most likely scenario for the future is the coexistence of different economic paradigms, creating a patchwork of national policy orientations that MNEs must learn how to navigate.

Interventionism

The other end of the spectrum – interventionism – is actually a very diverse category covering two entirely different paradigms. At one extreme, there is communism, with its belief in the state ownership of all means of production. In reality, however, there are extremely few real communists left in the world anymore. An infinitely more dominant variant of interventionism is the kind of "social-democratic" approach that was first formulated by British economist John Maynard Keynes in the 1930s before being successfully implemented by the then US President Franklin Delano Roosevelt in his battle against the Great Depression. Keynesians believe that capitalism is fundamentally prone to alternating periods of expansion and recession, called the business cycle. As a result, policy-makers must always be prepared to implement fiscal and monetary measures, as well as industrial policies, capable of offsetting cyclical volatility and remedying market failure while preventing financial crisis and extreme poverty (Erdogdu 2018). In essence, Keynes's idea is that governments should run budget deficits whenever the economy is weak, using temporary monetary injections to stimulate aggregate demand and reignite growth – and that conversely, during the boom years, governments should take the heat out of the economy by raising taxes to repay the debt incurred during the stimulus phase. This kind of counter-cyclical approach is meant to smooth out the extremes that have historically plagued laisser-faire economies (see Figure 2.5) while providing support for the most vulnerable in society – the constituencies that suffer most when times are hard. Keynesian welfare systems create safety nets preventing the kinds of social tensions that afflict societies where the poor have been historically neglected (and which have historically led to radical outcomes such as Russia's 1917 communist revolution).

Interventionism - Belief that the state has a significant role to play in ensuring that market mechanisms are both efficient and lead to a fair and sustainable distribution of income.

Business cycle - Period during which the economy alternates between boom and bust.

Welfare systems - Provisions made alongside the productive economy to support vulnerable members of society. Usually government-sponsored.

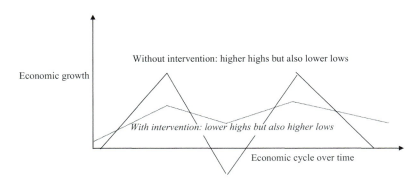

Fig 2.5
Government intervention smooths out the highs and lows of the business cycle.

Free trade - Belief that private interests should largely enjoy open access to foreign markets.

As far as their international policy preferences are concerned (and similarly to numerous neo-liberals), interventionists will often advocate approaches that are diametrically opposed to what they opt for domestically. Keynes himself was a strong supporter of free trade and one of the architects of the Bretton Woods agreement (see Chapter 4). He was a pragmatic man who felt that governments should intervene no more and no less than the circumstances require. The problem is that his counter-cyclical recommendations have not always been followed as he envisioned, given how much easier it is for politicians to lower taxes when the economy needs stimulus than to raise them when it is time to repay government debt. Political leaders advocating a particular economic philosophy will often pick and choose which aspects they apply.

Critics of Keynesianism assert that cheap money causes poor business decisions and therefore wastes capital – something the Austrian neoclassical economist Friedrich Hayek termed "malinvestment". Like any generalisation, this critique will be accurate on some occasions and inaccurate on others. What is clear for MNEs operating in a country run according to Keynesian principles is that they should expect to deal with a government pursuing a much more proactive stance to economic policy-making in all its facets.

All in all, neoliberalism and Keynesianism both have their strengths and weaknesses. In reality, they exist along a continuum, best theorised in British economists David Soskice and Peter Hall's excellent "Varieties of Capitalism" construct (2001), which differentiates between "liberal market economies" where most economic decision-making is price-based, and "coordinated market economies" where institutional negotiation plays a greater role. International managers will want to be familiar with both categories as well as other hybrid forms of capitalism that they are certain to encounter if they travel widely enough (Ong 2006). The reality is that the word "capitalism", when referred to in the singular, covers too many different economic policy combinations to be a useful construct in IB. At most, it should only be used in the plural form.

Historic cycles in economic thinking

The relative popularity of "big state" and "small state" politics also tends to vary over time (see Figure 2.6). The temporary domination of laisser-faire principles from the late 19th through the early 20th centuries came to an abrupt halt following the 1929 Wall Street crash that triggered the Great Depression. It was a crisis calling for a new economic direction due to a new consensus that the old policies had failed. It was against this backdrop – and fears of a communist alternative – that Keynesianism soon became the world's dominant economic policy paradigm, heralding long decades of success that culminated in *Time* magazine's famous 1965 headline announcing that "We're all Keynesians now". The new consensus manifested itself not only in expansive

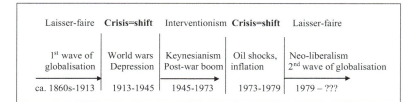

Laisser-faire	**Crisis=shift**	Interventionism	**Crisis=shift**	Laisser-faire
1st wave of globalisation	World wars Depression	Keynesianism Post-war boom	Oil shocks, inflation	Neo-liberalism 2nd wave of globalisation
ca. 1860s-1913	1913-1945	1945-1973	1973-1979	1979 – ???

Fig 2.6
Crisis-related paradigm shifts.

monetary and fiscal policies that ultimately saw full employment replacing the deflation and joblessness that had plagued the 1930s, but also in governments building welfare systems, engaging in structured macro-economic planning and taking ownership of entire industries (including aviation, steel and communications). It is worth noting that these latter actions went far beyond Keynes's original advice. But as long as the economy worked well, criticism was muffled.

Once again, it was an economic crisis that shifted the dominant economic paradigm from the 1970s onwards. The global economy had gone through a bad slump, suffering from high oil prices, budget deficits, inflation, unemployment and market saturation. This caused disenchantment with Keynesianism and revived classical economics' reputation as the alternative. The result was the 1979 and 1980 elections of UK Prime Minister Margaret Thatcher and US President Ronald Reagan, respectively, fans of the neoclassical economist Milton Friedman, whose "monetarist" advice was that governments' only real intervention should be to ensure price stability and that they should leave other outcomes (such as jobs and growth) up to the market. Laisser-faire ideology was back in fashion.

After communism crumbled in Eastern Europe in 1989, neoliberal thinkers floated the idea that nation-states had arrived at the "end of history", with the superiority of free market capitalism supposedly having been proven once and for all (Fukuyama 1993). Associated with this vision was a package of policies that all states were advised to implement, called the "Washington Consensus" (Williamson 2002). The main proposals were that:

– the private sector become the main engine of economic growth, with subsidies slashed and any state-owned enterprises privatised;
– budget deficits, taxes and public spending be minimised;
– price stability become a priority, with interest rates set by the financial markets;
– deregulation and property rights become a priority;
– financial markets be deregulated (with pension provisions privatised);
– currencies be entirely convertible, with prices solely set by the market; and
– trade and foreign direct investment be fully liberalised.

Since paradigms tend to spread more easily in the absence of geopolitical adversaries, the Soviet Union's collapse in 1991 also had the effect of eliminating a major rival to laisser-faire principles. Newfound enthusiasm for market mechanisms was particularly strong in Eastern European transition countries that moved quickly to reject their communist past. The same could be witnessed in a number of Global South nations that had only gained independence a few decades previous. Having initially adopted interventionist (and sometimes isolationist) policies that they saw as providing better protection against the hegemonic oppression from which they had suffered during the colonial years, many would now see merit in reducing the kinds of bureaucratic inefficiencies and even corruption that excessive state interventionism can sometimes generate. Famous examples include Tanzania's once self-defined socialist regime as well as the Indian state of Kerala, which famously had originally prioritised state-run education and health programmes over business-oriented growth policies. The fact that increasing numbers of Global South elites were being educated in Western business schools also explains the at least partial adoption by their home countries of what some began to consider "best practice". The transferability of political and economic paradigms constitutes an important subset of IB studies.

It would be very inaccurate, however, to deduce that neoliberalism's resurgence in the late 20th century signified the end of Keynesianism. When one side of the paradigmatic spectrum is on the rise, the other does not die out – at worst, it goes into temporary hibernation. There remain many countries where Keynesian principles continue to dominate, best exemplified by ongoing support in much of Western Europe for a mixed, social democratic economy. A prime case in point is France, marked by a centuries-old tradition of state intervention in both the domestic and international spheres, embodied in former President Charles De Gaulle's 1966 dictum that *La politique de la France ne se fait pas à la corbeille* ("The stock exchange does not make French policy"). In a French context, there would be nothing noteworthy about this statement except for the fact that De Gaulle identified as a conservative – a political affiliation that has at other times been synonymous with diametrically opposed policy preferences. Indeed, two generations later in France, ideas similar to De Gaulle's about the need for government interventionism (this time to avoid capital interests appropriating an excessive share of national value-added) would again be espoused by a thought leader – but now by one who would self-identify as a progressive, namely, the economist Thomas Piketty. The lesson here for IB practitioners is to ignore the labels that foreign counterparts might give to certain economic policy preferences and to pay attention instead to the substance of their ideas.

In recent years, neoliberalism has suffered a series of crises, raising questions as to whether the world is ready to revert to a more interventionist consensus. The 2008 financial crisis, widely attributed to the kind of radical deregulation associated with extreme free market economics, was expected by many observers to spark a return of the pendulum – especially given the huge debt that many countries would have to assume to surmount the crisis, a burden they would still be carrying more than a decade later, even before the 2020 Covid-19 pandemic required further deficit spending. In the run-up to the 2020 US presidential election, for instance, candidate Joe Biden repeatedly questioned whether the domestic deregulation agenda of his predecessor Donald Trump – as well as the latter's protectionist international stances – was at all relevant to the brave new world of the early 21st century. Biden's victory augured a reversal of these two paradigms in the USA, approximating the policy orientations long applied within the European Union – even as the UK's Brexit-bound Conservative government was careening off in an entirely different direction. Add to this the peculiar international and domestic policy mixes of budding global superpowers like China and India – reflecting the very different historical trajectories that each has followed – and what remains is a potpourri of very different economic frameworks shaping MNEs' IB possibilities. The ability to track relevant policy variations in multiple countries is therefore in and of itself an indispensable skill for practitioners in this field.

Attitudes and alternatives

During the course of their careers, IB practitioners are likely to be introduced to all sorts of political cultures, a number of which will be associated with protectionist attitudes that can ultimately become significant hurdles impeding cross-border activity. The challenge in this area, as in so many others, is learning how to overcome such barriers. Clearly, working in countries that possess a strong tradition of open borders will be less problematic for foreign practitioners. The question then becomes how any one MNE might interact with host country counterparts in such a way as to shift the latter from a defensive mindset to a more welcoming one. All entrepreneurial ventures contain a sales function. In international as opposed to domestic business, however, this is more likely to be imbued with political overtones. This has career implications for new IB practitioners seeking to assume an outwardly facing role.

Chapter summary

Since the dawn of civilisation, theorists have tried to develop ways of explaining trade and, more recently, foreign investment. The chapter began with a brief review of the ongoing debate between protectionist and free trade principles. It then studied classical country-focused trade theories, based on ideas such as absolute or comparative advantage, before covering modern company-focused trade and FDI theories, highlighting constructs such as product life cycle, internalisation and knowledge acquisition. It concluded with a review of welfare economists theorising at the interface between IB and politics. The second section analysed the two main macro-economic paradigms guiding the public policies that shape the different national spaces where MNEs operate: laisser-faire and interventionism. The demonstration was then made that the relative popularity of each of these philosophies varies in time and place (Figure 2.7).

Case study 2.3: The Kremlin rushes in

Fig 2.7
Russia has long been characterised by its centralised political and economic power.

The Union of Soviet Socialist Republics (USSR), of which Russia was the founder state, ran a communist regime from 1917 until 1991. One of the most noteworthy features of this system was its command economy, with bureaucrats making almost all investment, pricing, income and trade decisions. Communism's worthy goal of social equality paled alongside its many economic (and political) defects, including its wasteful and ecologically catastrophic industrialisation policies, as well as a tendency to ration consumer goods. In the end, the system crumbled from within, with Premier Mikhail Gorbachev ultimately overseeing the Soviet Union's official dissolution on 25 December 1991.

The new President Boris Yeltsin, together with his main economic adviser Yegor Gaidar, was strongly influenced by the radical neoliberal attitudes of the early 1990s. Their policy involved the application of a "shock therapy" of market-oriented reforms, including a phase-out of pricing controls and subsidies, a privatisation of national industries and a more welcoming attitude towards market-friendly foreign entities such as the International Monetary Fund (IMF). The IMF provided much needed loans to the new Russian republic but also exerted strong influence over Yeltsin's budgetary and monetary policies. The mid-1990s was a period of extreme inflation and fiscal deficits, with the new regime seemingly incapable of raising enough tax revenue to meet its budgetary needs. Soaring interest rates also made it difficult for Russian industry to fund its ambitious modernisation investments. GDP fell by an estimated 50 percent as the economy restructured. The national currency – the rouble – suffered from volatility, culminating in a 1998 financial crisis where its value was halved. Many financial institutions went bankrupt, destroying the savings of millions of households. Such was the lack of confidence in Russia's future that the country recorded an estimated annual net capital outflow of $20 billion over this period. It is against this backdrop that former KGB agent Vladimir Putin assumed power in 1999.

By 2007, about $35 billion of private capital was flowing into Russia on an annual basis, a phenomenal turnaround. Russia's unique endowment of natural resources such as gas, coal and minerals meant that it had been well placed to benefit from the sharp rise in world commodity prices that began in the late 1990s. Its balance-of-payments surplus rose over the following years to such an extent that when the country experienced net outflows in 2010–2012 and then again in 2016–2017, these were no longer presented as harbingers of a crisis but instead as a sign that Russia had grown wealthy to such an extent that its entrepreneurs could afford to acquire foreign assets without destabilising the mother country.

Like any politician, President Putin took credit for these earlier successes, largely attributing them to a rejection of his predecessor's radical market orientation and his own decision to revive the centralised economic decision-making – and mercantilism – that had typified Russia historically. One example of his approach was greater state control over national energy giants such as Gazprom and Lukoil. Foreign MNEs like BP and Shell were also made to understand that Russia intended to reign supreme over its domestic economy, with both being arm-twisted into selling their stakes in local projects (Parker 2011). Many analysts came to consider the leading Russian energy companies as quasi-nationalised firms run by an inner circle of Kremlin leaders. Clearly, although Russia had adopted many capitalist attributes, it was following a path distinct from the one imagined by the many free market thinkers who had flocked to Moscow at the end of the communist era.

The problem with the Kremlin's resurgent control – asides from the anti-democratic implications of any political centralisation on this scale – is the power imbalance between officials pursuing short-term government (and sometimes personal) interests versus business leaders made to understand that theirs is a secondary role. A good example of the kinds of problems that this would create involves an aspiration first formulated by senior Russian politico Dmitry Medvedev when he temporarily replaced Putin as president from 2008 to 2012. Mr. Medvedev was aware that Russia's economic renewal was being built on the fortunes of a single sector – energy – and that this lack of diversification was inherently dangerous in case commodity prices were to fall durably. He therefore advocated that Russia's prime economic focus in the years to come be on growing other industries. On the face of things, it seems like this succeeded, with oil rents' percentage of Russian GDP falling from 12.5 percent in 2006 to 6.3 percent in 2018. The problem is that this statistic reflected a long-term downtrend in oil prices more than it did any real growth in Russia's non-energy sectors. New business creations stagnated; de-industrialisation continued unabated; and 2020 per-capita income was 73rd in the world, a paltry performance. Some observers would attribute this "illiberal stagnation" to the omnipotence of a Kremlin-aligned oligarchy dominating political society (Stiglitz 2017). Russia may have suffered from free market excesses in the 1990s, but 30 years later it was clearly suffering from the exact opposite. What will be interesting to see is whether future generations will opt for something in between.

Case study questions

1. What were the economic effects of Russia's neoliberal orientation during the 1990s?
2. How sustainable is Russia's currently hyper-centralised economic orientation?
3. What other economic policy directions might Russia pursue in the future?

Chapter discussion questions

1   Adam Smith theorised that an international division of labour is an optimal economic organisation. Does this still hold in the 21st century?
2   To what extent should countries be allowed to protect their infant industries?
3   Economist Paul Krugman disagrees with the idea that "the people who lose from free trade tend to be small, well-organised groups and the winners are more widely spread". He thinks that it may be the other way around. Comment.
4   Philosopher Amartya Sen believes that the best measurements of economic success should be qualitative, not quantitative. Comment.
5   Will interventionism displace laisser-faire principles as the dominant mode of economic organisation in the wake of the 2020 Covid-19 pandemic?

References

Ahn, J. et al. (February 2018). "Reassessing the productivity gains from trade liberalization", *IMF Working Paper no 16/77*, accessed 29 July 2021 at https://www.imf.org/

Bhagwati, J. (1 June 2012). "The broken legs of global trade", accessed 10 February 2021 at https://www.project-syndicate.org/

Booth, A. (9 June 2016). "The communities of Cochabamba taking control of their own water supply", *Guardian*.

De Soto, H. (29 January 2012). "Knowledge lies at the heart of Western capitalism", *Financial Times*.

Economist (1 October 2016). "Anti-globalists: Why they're wrong", accessed 28 July 2021 at https://www.economist.com/

Erdogdu, M. (2018). "Enhanced Keynesian economics for overcoming financial crises", in Mavroudeas, S. et al. (eds.). *Global Economy, Economic Crises and Recession*, London: IJOPEC Publication Ltd.

Finnegan, W. (8 April 2002). "Leasing the rain", *The New Yorker*.

Fukuyama, F. (1993). *The End of History and the Last Man*, New York: Harper Perennial.

Hall, D., and Soskice, P. (2001). *Varieties of Capitalism*, Oxford: Oxford University Press.

Irwin, D. (1996). *Against the Tide: An Intellectual History of Free Trade*, Chichester: Princeton University Press.

Keynes, J. M. (1936). *The General Theory of Employment, Interest and Money*, London: Macmillan.

Krugman, P. (21 March 1997). "In Praise of Cheap Labour", *Slate*.

Krugman, P. (2020). *Arguing with Zombies: Economics, Politics and the Fight for a Better Future*, New York: W.W. Norton.

Langan, M.(2018). *Neo-Colonialism and the Poverty of "Development" in Africa*, London: Palgrave-MacMillan.

Lee, J. (1996). "Economic Growth and Human Development in the Republic of Korea 1945–1992", accessed 10 February 2021 at http://hdr.undp.org

Lobina, E. (2000). "Cochabamba—water war", *University of Greenwich*, accessed 15 October 2008 at www.psiru.org

Markusen, J. (2002). *Multinational Firms and the Theory of International Trade*, London: MIT Press.

Mill, J. S. (1848). *Principles of Political Economy*, London: Prometheus Books.

Ong, A. (2006). *Neo-liberalism as Exception: Mutations in Citizenship and Sovereignty*, Durham, NC: Duke University Press.

Paiva, M. et al. (2018). "Innovation and the effects on market dynamics: A theoretical synthesis of Smith and Schumpeter", *Interacoes*, Volume 19, Issue 1, pp. 155–170.

Parker, L. (31 August 2011). "Trouble Comes Calling for BP Again", accessed 10 February 2021 at https://www.wsj.com/

Porter, M. (1990). *The Competitive Advantage of Nations*, London: Palgrave Macmillan.

Ricardo, D. (1817). *Principles of Political Economy and Taxation*, Oxford World's Classics. Oxford: Oxford University Press

Rubin, J. (February 2018). "Has global trade liberalization left Canadian workers behind?", *CIGI Papers*, Number 163.

Smith, A. (1776). *The Wealth of Nations*, Oxford: Oxford University Press.

Stewart, H. (17 June 2007). "He has an American dream", *The Observer*.

Stiglitz, J. (2012). *The Price of Inequality: How Today's Divided Society Endangers our Future*, London: W.W. Norton & Company.

Stiglitz, J. (3 April 2017). "Putin's illiberal stagnation in Russia offers a lesson", *Guardian*.

Vernon, R. (1966). "International investment and international trade in the product cycle", *Quarterly Journal of Economics*, Volume 80, Issue 2, pp. 190–207.

Wein, M. et al. (8 October 2014). "The global mercantilist index…", *Information Technology and Innovation Foundation*, accessed 22 June 2020 at https://papers.ssrn.com/

Williamson, J. (1 November 2002). "What Washington means by policy reform", accessed 10 February 2021 at https://www.piie.com/

Zhang, W.-B. (2010). *International Trade Theory: Capital, Knowledge, Economic Structure, Money, and Prices over Time*, New York: Springer.

CHAPTER 3

National governments
Powers and tools

Introduction

Multinational enterprises (MNEs) mainly operate in national frameworks
defined by laws, regulations, markets and institutions. Where these
settings have been harmonised through global governance mechanisms,
they can have more or less similar effects. As often as not, however, the
circumstances dictating MNEs' room to manoeuvre in any one country
will be strongly influenced by its national government. To the extent that
sovereign states make divergent political and economic choices – usually
relating, as far as international business (IB) is concerned, to policies
aimed at improving national terms of trade and/or protecting domestic
producers from foreign competition – MNEs must regularly adjust their
strategies, both when entering a market and once they are established
there. The multitude of potential interactions between national
governments and MNEs constitutes a rich subset of IB, often referred to
as "public affairs". The knowledge required to navigate this minefield
is very specific and explains why politics often plays a greater role in IB
than in purely domestic business studies.

Sovereign states -
Independent nations
whose governments have
sole jurisdiction over
a defined geographic
territory.

Fig 3.1
Governments' ability to
intervene in international
business depends both
on the power they
have amassed and the
instruments they decide
to deploy.

DOI: 10.4324/9781003159056-4

It should be remembered that one prime function for any government is to safeguard its local population's interactions with the outside world. Irrespective of a regime's willingness to intervene in domestic or international markets, it is almost impossible to imagine politicians so opposed to the possibility of action that they would willingly abandon all of the powers that they might potentially wield. The question then becomes how to determine how much power they have to affect IB arena, and how they might go about doing this.

LEARNING OBJECTIVES

After reading this chapter, you will be able to:

- ascertain how globalisation affects the power vested in national governments
- evaluate MNE strategies when negotiating market entry conditions
- analyse the power dynamics characterising MNE-politician interactions
- assess the different tools that governments can use to shape trade and FDI (Figure 3.2).

Case study 3.1: India's deregulation takeaway

Fig 3.2
Changes in Indian retail legislation have created new market opportunities for MNEs.

With a need to sustain a population of nearly 1.4 billion citizens, many of whom remain desperately poor, food distribution is a policy area that the Indian government takes very seriously. For ethical reasons but also to avoid social tensions, ensuring the availability of affordable staples is an absolute priority for politicians in the country. Given the many small grocers that are in India, however – and their fear of being crowded out of their home market by huge foreign MNEs – the openness of this sector to IB interests is a politically highly sensitive topic.

Indian population centres are traditionally organised around a vast and fragmented network of family-owned shops that are generally too small to bulk-purchase product at cheap wholesale prices, much less invest in the logistics capabilities (like refrigerated lorries) that make the big global players like Walmart, Carrefour, Tesco, Metro or Shiseido so efficient. This is an acute problem due to India's rapid population growth but also because new middle-class consumers' rising standard of living means they have higher service expectations. The challenge for the Delhi government is to manage this dilemma.

Although Indian policy famously changed course in 1991 when a series of liberalisation reforms led to the partial opening of a sector that had previously been more or less protected from international competition, successive administrations would continue to protect domestic grocers for a number of years, largely to avoid millions of families losing their livelihoods. The end result was a regulatory framework that might best be described as partial globalisation: food retail MNEs would be allowed to invest in India, but they had to do this in partnership with a domestic interest and were not allowed to take majority stakes in local companies.

Several MNEs pursued this option, most notably Walmart, which teamed up with budding local powerhouse Bharti to build a wholesale cash and carry business, replete with the kind of integrated supply chain that the country had previously lacked. India's national logistics and delivery systems were generally slow in modernising, however, with rising global commodity prices sparking high food inflation. Conscious of the social problems this could cause, the government accelerated its liberalisation programme and enacted a new law in late 2011, allowing foreign MNEs to acquire a majority stake in domestic retailers. In less than a decade, retail food volumes had grown by 60 percent to the point of representing more than 10 percent of total national GDP (Singhania and Anand 2018), in part due to the proliferation of online shopping and home delivery services. What was also significant, however, is that these positive outcomes happened despite the government still imposing a number of foreign direct investment (FDI) restrictions that would continue to constrain MNEs' actions in this sector (Dunseith 2017). Within five years of arriving in the country, foreign retailers must demonstrate that they are sourcing at least 30 percent of their product value within India itself (so that their presence can have a positive knock-on effect, benefitting local farmers and wholesalers); multi-brand retailers can take no more than a 51 percent equity stake in Indian companies; and to get approval for this line of business, MNEs are given a maximum of three years to invest a minimum of $100 million in the sort of "backend infrastructure" that the country needs for its broader development objectives. In other words, even as Indian policies vis-à-vis foreign entrants have liberalised, the government has not entirely abandoned the field and still tries to mould MNEs' behaviour to serve its own purposes. In the political arena as in so many other aspects of IB, compromise is often viewed as an optimal way forward.

Case study questions

1. Why did the Indian government protect local retailers' position for so long?
2. Why might MNEs be willing to accept the FDI conditions imposed by the Indian government?

Section I. State power in an era of globalisation

Political discourse about how much power is (and should be) wielded by national governments, both in the abstract and – for the purposes of this book – in their relationships with MNEs, can be highly emotive, if only because of the way it plays on people's deeply held belief systems. Even so, polemics influence policy-makers and therefore have a very real role to play in IB. In this social science as with so many others, it can be just as important to deconstruct protagonists' narratives – the way people talk about things – as to understand the things themselves.

Proposition that national governments are losing the power to shape international business

Over the past few decades, a number of political scientists have taken to arguing that the state is in retreat (Strange 1997) and that the forward march of modern globalisation has both caused this change and been affected by it. The evidence for this view usually comes in the form of new power bases being constituted outside of national governments' reach – the idea being that these new players have turned into rivals for politicians and therefore weakened them.

Increasingly powerful global financial markets

The gigantic sums traded in today's largely deregulated financial markets often dwarf the funds available to national governments. This already puts the latter in a position of seeking favours from the former – especially since the countries with the greatest need of inward investments tend to be those with the lowest aggregate domestic savings, hence the ones who are most reliant on external funding. Given international investors' generally very strong preference for regimes that manage their finances in line with strict (and often deflationary) Washington Consensus principles, many governments can only access the capital they need if they submit to a "Golden Straitjacket" (Friedman 2000). The end result is that they are no longer free to implement the expansionary policies of their choice.

This dependency relationship affects macro-economic policy-making at several levels. A national government may wish, for instance, to increase social spending and be prepared to run a temporary deficit towards this end. When a country lacks the capital to finance the ensuing debt domestically, however, its only choice is to either print money (with all the destabilising consequences this has over time) or to appeal to foreign providers of capital. At best, the latter will then parlay their support into demands that the government pay higher interest rates. In the worst-case scenario, the "herd" of international investors might withdraw their current holdings from the country, in which case a currency crisis can ensue – with the country's worsening exchange rate making incompressible imports even more expensive to purchase. The lesson here is clear: financial globalisation has given investors a more or less free hand to move their funds in and out of countries as they see fit, strengthening their bargaining power vis-à-vis national governments constrained by the limited pool of domestic savings that they can call upon – a situation aggravated in recent times by the enormous public debt that many countries have had to issue in the wake of the Covid-19 pandemic.

Incompressible imports - Items indispensable to a country's economy but which it has no way of producing domestically and must therefore import.

Financial globalisation - Deregulation of global capital markets leading to an acceleration in cross-border capital transfers.

Global governance undermining national sovereignty

Many areas of IB cannot be negotiated within a national framework alone. Examples include regional trading policies, environmental action and currency regimes, all of which involve agreements between states who often pursue divergent goals – requiring, in turn, that some kind of arbitration process be instituted so that a mutually acceptable compromise can be reached. As Chapter 4 will explore in further detail, this understanding has led, over the past century, to the foundation of a number of international institutions that operate on a higher plane than individual national governments. These entities are imbued with powers granted by member-states who are then required to abandon some of their traditional sovereign prerogatives in exchange for the international cooperation they require.

A prime example of this arrangement is the World Trade Organization (WTO), which exists to promote IB and stave off the kinds of protectionist trade wars that have wreaked havoc throughout economic history. The WTO is guided by a principle of non-discrimination, with the idea being that a country should not distort trade to fellow WTO members' detriment. This might make sense given the WTO's free trade mandate – but it also takes away sovereign nations' ability to benefit domestic interests through a mercantilistic manipulation of markets.

Anti-globalists – exemplified by Britain's Brexit campaigners – have long argued that shared sovereignty means less power for national governments simply because they must seek fellow members' agreement before implementing policy. The argument is skewed and incomplete (Volk 2019) insofar as it glosses over the greater powers that national governments wield as members of an international body. But it is true that, by definition, global governance narrows the space where a national government wields sole jurisdiction.

MNEs' technological advantages

Sociology as a discipline speaks to the way that opinion (hence attitudes and subsequent behaviour) is affected by the type and amount of information available to members of a given society – raising questions in turn as to the nature and origins of such information. Before the Internet became a common global medium, information-sharing tended to be dominated by social counterparts (family, friends, teachers) but also by more formal broadcasting channels, often involving trusted local newscasters vetted for their perceived objectivity and integrity. The social media environment that dominates today offers a totally different landscape. It may be easier for citizens to express democratic opinions, but it has also become easier for vested interests to spread misinformation and foment animosity. News has increasingly become a tool that mischievous (often xenophobic) interests can deploy to create artificial discord that national governments must then address. In turn, this wastes limited public resources that might otherwise have been allocated more constructively to actual problems.

Of course, unmediated Internet-based information transfers has also had the effect of empowering domestic consumers to compare global prices for many items and, where advantageous, shop across borders. Consumers' virtual mobility is a positive trend since it means that domestic audiences are less captive than they used to be. At the same time, it also weakens national producers, who are no longer as free to price-gouge a captive audience. In turn, this dilutes the power of national governments, who necessarily have more control over domestic producers than over foreign ones.

Apatride -
Stateless; not associated with any particular nationality.

More broadly, with large firms (generally apatride MNEs) taking a lead in developing the new technologies that define many aspects of the modern world, national governments increasingly find themselves lagging behind the capabilities of the corporate actors who they were traditionally meant to supervise. This gap weakens state power in several ways. One example is when companies use advanced technology to hinder scrutiny of their operations, making it easier for them to manipulate group accounting and reduce the total tax they pay in any one country (see Chapter 12), thereby diminishing the fiscal revenues that are a government's life blood. A second example of this technological imbalance can be witnessed in the ongoing battle that the EU (and Australia) has been waging with American technology companies relating to anti-trust issues or the use of consumer data – with some of the MNEs in question being so dominant in their respective sectors that they can seemingly elude any attempts at regulation. All in all, the asymmetrical technological prowess of governments and MNEs is another factor affecting the balance of power between these two actors.

MNEs' size and mobility advantages

MNEs' growing domination of national governments might also be attributed to two other factors. Firstly, many have grown to a size where they dwarf host country economy. On top of this, MNEs are highly mobile and can move operations between locations worldwide – unlike national governments, who are necessarily bound to the one territory over which they have jurisdiction. Cognisant of this, many MNEs have become adept at pressuring individual politicians into advantageous market entry conditions.

Size

The global networks that large MNEs have amassed in recent decades mean that many have attained a size – measured, for instance, in revenue terms – that surpasses the gross domestic product (GDP) of some of the countries where they operate. By itself, the MNE with the largest global sales in 2020 (Walmart) generated revenues that already more or less match the GDP of Sweden, the world's 23rd largest economy (see Table 3.1). This contrast in economic power is particularly striking when comparing company staff numbers with national population sizes. MNEs concentrate a great deal of wealth among a comparatively small number of people – raising concerns inter alia about the democratic implications of the quasi-monopolistic powers that they might wield (Wu 2020).

Table 3.1
The world's largest MNEs generate revenues matching many nations' GDP

2019–2020 MNE revenues (rounded)	MNE global ranking (and approximate total staff numbers) https://fortune.com/global500/	Closest equivalent GDP ranking (and population size) IMF estimates
$524 billion	nr. 1: Walmart (2.2. million)	23. Sweden (10.2 million)
$282 billion	nr. 8. BP (70,000)	41. South Africa (57.8 million)
$147 billion	nr. 35. Ag. Bk. of China (478,000)	56. Algeria (42.2 million)
$95 billion	nr. 77. General Electric (205,000)	62. Ethiopia (109.2 million)
$81 billion	nr. 106. Hitachi (301,000)	64. Sri Lanka (21.7 million)

MNEs' gigantism cannot help but affect their bargaining position vis-à-vis national governments. This is particularly true when the interaction involves a desperately poor Global South country whose dire need for inward investment is known to the MNE when it first starts negotiating market entry. The idea of bullying a weaker counterpart in a bilateral relationship can be tempting and, according to some critics (Pilger 2002), constitutes a strategy that MNEs avail themselves of far too frequently.

In a similar vein, there are entire categories of economic activity today, including large infrastructure projects or advanced technological research, where corporate input is required, if only because cash-strapped, hence downsized, local governments simply do not have the financial capacity to run such projects by themselves (Sitkin 2019). The crux in these situations is the tenor of the negotiation between government and business, specifically the extent to which the former feels it must accede to the latter's often maximalist demands. In turn, this depends on which side has greater need of the other (Doz and Prahalad 1980) and, more broadly, on participants' general willingness to seek a compromise.

Mobility

Politicians everywhere are acutely aware that getting MNEs to invest in their domestic economy helps to create jobs and prosperity. Thus, with the exception of those rare instances where a host country knows that it possesses uniquely attractive characteristics (i.e. rare natural resources or a particularly dynamic consumer market), MNEs' desirability gives them a strong bargaining chip when lobbying government. This is particularly true before the multinational enters the market since it is still free at that point to engage in regime shopping/arbitrage – that is, to take its business elsewhere – if does not get the deal it wants. Both sides will be aware of this fact – called obsolescing bargaining – which explains why pre-market entry talks tend to be more balanced than subsequent interactions. National governments pressured by mobile MNEs into adopting lower (hence less costly) social, environmental, labour, fiscal and regulatory standards find themselves forced into a race to the bottom where they are competing with other potential destinations. It is a prime example of the way in which globalisation has undermined governments' sovereign power to determine their own destinies.

There are manifold examples of MNE mobility constraining government policy, whether directly or indirectly. Just before the Covid-19 pandemic erupted, for instance, Ireland's accumulated public debt was already third largest in the world on a per-capita basis (Burke-Kennedy 2019). This was unsurprising given that the country had long used a comparatively very low corporate tax rate of 12.5 percent to attract FDI – a policy that had brought jobs to the country but deprived the government of fiscal revenues. The logical policy

Regime shopping/ arbitrage - Decision to locate a MNE's activities based on a regime's lax regulations and low taxes.

Obsolescing bargaining - Where a MNE's negotiating position vis-à-vis a host country weakens once it actually owns assets there.

Race to the bottom - Where competition among potential host countries forces them to lower their standards.

response to this financial predicament – short of welcoming inflation to devalue the debt in current terms, an approach proscribed by Ireland's membership of the Eurozone – would have been to increase corporation tax to raise more fiscal revenue. Yet Irish politicians resisted this option, largely because of their fear that it would further weaken the national economy by inducing MNEs already operating there to move elsewhere, for instance to Bulgaria, Cyprus or Hungary, all fellow EU member-states featuring similarly low or even lower corporation tax rates. Tax competition and the fear of capital flight are major obstacles taking away governments' power to implement the fiscal policies that they might otherwise prefer.

Tax competition - Where countries try to attract mobile capital by offering investors lower tax rates than they can find in competitor nations.

Of course, government negotiations with mobile MNEs do not necessarily have to be adversarial in nature. It is commonplace within an IB setting to see a state-owned investment or marketing agency – or a national chamber of commerce – advertising the relative charms and "ease of doing business" in a country (often based on scores published in an annual World Bank index bearing this name). To the extent that any party to a business deal needs to offer its counterpart some kind of advantage, such actions do not signify any particular loss of state power. Nor should it be forgotten that numerous politicians accommodate MNEs' desires, not because they have been pressured into this but because it reflects their sincerely held ideological beliefs about the role of the state – hence their susceptibility to compromise.

Proposition that national governments have retained the power to shape international business

In reality, it is not difficult to conceive of how relationships between MNEs and host country governments can be more balanced. The first step would be to codify lobbying protocols so that negotiations of this nature are no more lopsided than any other form of advocacy – with transparency ensuring that demands made by one or the other side remain within the realm of decency. Otherwise and more broadly, government officials still exercise control over many, if not most, events transpiring within their territorial jurisdictions. One dramatic recent example is the way governments all across the world appropriated the power – in the name of their public health duties – to dramatically restrict operating conditions for domestic and IB interests alike during 2020 Covid. When an emergency erupts, most societies' first port of call remains the government, whose decisions, even when contested, tend to be widely obeyed. This applies as well in situations that are directly relevant to IB.

Domestic business dealings are still dominant
Despite IB's accelerated progression in recent decades, most business dealings in the world still take place in a domestic setting. Local officials

continue to determine fiscal policy and collect personal and corporate taxes (including levies on MNEs operating locally). They devise macro-economic policy and set labour and environmental standards; operate welfare and education programmes; invest in infrastructure; and determine immigration regulations (El-Ojeili and Hayden 2006). Notwithstanding evidence as to the retreat of the state, a national government's ability to police territorial constituencies remains a powerful tool.

In more purely economic terms, there is also the fact that most global GDP continues to be generated in home market environments. Indeed, despite fantastic growth since the 1980s, IB has never come close to accounting for half of all global GDP. In 2019, for instance – before the Covid-19 pandemic broke out – global trade in merchandise reached $19.1 trillion; trade in services hit $5.9 trillion (WTO 2020); and in a different register, total FDI flows amounted to $1.39 trillion (UNCTAD 2020). Added together, these three pillars of IB amount to $26.39 trillion – a mere 18.6 percent of global GDP that year, estimated by the World Bank at $142 trillion. Even if the value of IB were to be double counted – because every country's exports translate into a partner's imports and because every FDI outflow is another country's inflow – more than 60 percent of global GDP would still be unrelated to cross-border transactions. Domestic business, subject to the jurisdiction of national and/or local government, continues to account for the lion's share of all commerce in the world.

Another way of assessing this is by looking at different economies' relative degree of openness, defined as the sum of a country's total exports and imports of goods and services, expressed as a percentage of GDP. It is an imperfect calculation that does not reflect certain statistical complexities, like how to account for the value of components imported into a country only to be assembled into products that are then re-exported (goods that the WTO classifies as "made in the world"). Nor does it account for the fact that some sectors are inherently more international than others. But it remains an instructive exercise.

As calculated in Table 3.2, in China, USA and Japan – three of the world's leading trading nations – at least 64 percent of all GDP (rising to almost 74 percent in America) is unrelated to the import or export of goods and services. It is true that the opposite holds for Europe's leading trading nations – especially Germany – but it should also be remembered that their membership of the EU means that a great deal of IB here is actually being transacted regionally with a fellow member-state and might therefore be considered as something akin (under European integration principles) to non-EU states' domestic dealings. Now, it is also true that a few very small trading nations (the Netherlands and especially Singapore and Hong Kong) stand out

Table 3.2
Sample of 2019 ratio of total trade (exports plus imports) to GDP in the world's leading trading nations (figures calculated using http://data.worldbank.org/ datasets)

	Total trade (imports+exports) to GDP ratio
Hong Kong	353
Singapore	319.4
The Netherlands	155.2
Germany	88.2
South Korea	83.9
Mexico	78.5
France	66.8
Canada	65
UK	64.3
Italy	60.2
South Africa	59.3
Russia	49.1
Australia	45.4
India	40.2
China	35.7
Japan	33.7
Brazil	28.2
USA	26.2

because their trade volumes far exceed their annual GDP. But more than anything else, this confirms the need to modify classical trade theories to account for country size – not to mention tax incentives causing MNEs to book in these three countries' trade deals that are actually destined for other markets (Klein and Pettis 2020). Asides from that one point, the general lesson from this analysis is that announcements of the decline of purely domestic business are clearly premature.

Economic patriotism remains widespread
A key aspect in many countries' social history has been the "reluctance of people to be ruled by politicians and bureaucrats from the other side of the world over whom they have no democratic or other control" (Friedman 2000). The fact that there are so many examples of this attitude – at a time when globalised mindsets are assumed to be so dominant – indicates how premature it is to infer the insignificance of geography. Borders still count in today's world – and theoretically at least, national governments reign supreme within national borders.

Home bias, first discussed in Chapter 1, has taken a variety of forms over the years. Current references tend to be encapsulated in

Economic patriotism -
Where a society
or government
demonstrates preference
for national interests by
purchasing domestic
products and/or
restricting foreign
ownership.

the idea of economic patriotism, which plays out at several levels. One variant relates to international marketing, involving some consumers' preference for national brands over foreign MNEs' offers. But an even more direct assertion of economic patriotism is when governments restrict non-resident ownership of domestic companies. This has long been a bone of contention in the politics of IB, as witnessed by the uproar caused during the 1990s when the Organisation for Economic Co-operation and Development (OECD) tried to launch a Multilateral Agreement on Investment (MAI) that would have seen signatories commit to a sweeping liberalisation of FDI. Arguing that the accord undermined the basic principle of national sovereignty, a whole array of advocacy groups ran high-profile campaigns opposing it. They had no problems dissuading governments from enacting MAI, proving if need be that as devoted as some politicians may say they are to free trade principles, they will always hesitate before handing away all the powers they have at their disposal.

Indeed, notwithstanding occasional attempts to repackage MAI principles and insert them into regional trading agreements, many governments still continue to keep a tight rein on foreign shareholders. One example from the 2020 Covid-19 pandemic was the way that Germany, along with several other traditionally open economies, suddenly announced measures blocking hostile non-EU takeovers of domestic companies manufacturing the vaccines, protective equipment, ventilators, medicines and other supplies needed for the fight against the virus (Reuters 2020). The Berlin government's concern was that foreign shareholders would want to re-export these life-saving products back to their countries of origin, potentially putting German citizens' lives at risk. Chancellor Angela Merkel began speaking about the need for her country, and more broadly for the whole of the EU, to seek greater self-sufficiency in strategic healthcare sectors. As has so often been the case, when times are good, governments are willing to stay out of the fray, but, conversely, when times are tough, they will want to be involved.

The overarching concern for governments exercising power in this manner is whether foreigners lacking personal ties to a particular society might be less sensitive to its needs (Matelly and Nies 2006). It is a fear largely rooted in social psychology's proximity principle (Festinger et al. 1950), which holds that individuals will feel greater attraction towards (hence solidarity with) the people whom they know best, that is, their fellow citizens. Of course, this supposition stands in contradiction to another modern idea, namely, that people today possess am increasingly fluid sense of global citizenship (Baumunt 2000). The reality is that both attitudes coexist in the modern world, often within one and the same society. If there is one constant in IB, it is the prevalence of inconsistency.

Case study 3.2: Britain closes its channels

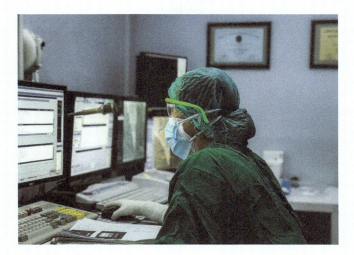

Fig 3.3
Responses to global crises like the Covid-19 pandemic are organised at a national level – whether or not that is optimal.

The UK government has long stood out for its laisser-faire response to foreign interests seeking to acquire British assets. This "Wimbledonisation" of the national economy – in reference to the tennis tournament that the British host but have almost never won – reflect at one level a deeply held belief in the benefits of free markets. Adam Smith was, after all, a Scot. At the same time, political support for a liberalised regime of reciprocal cross-border investment also translates the fact that the UK itself has traditionally been one of the world's leading purchasers of foreign firms – as witnessed by the country's high "cross-border net score", or the number of corporate acquisitions that British interests make abroad versus the number of local firms taken over by foreign shareholders (Kollewe 2011). For several decades, the dividends received from these overseas investments would offset the UK's endemic trade deficit and improve its overall balance-of-payments. It is always easier to advocate a particular policy position when its implementation generates concrete benefits.

Understanding that the UK's positive cross-border net score could only be maintained if overseas shareholders were offered reciprocal arrangements, economic patriotism had never really figured in British politics. In 2018 it was discovered, for instance, that 47 percent of all revenues generated through the UK food industry – a sector considered strategic in most countries because of its role in ensuring a population's basic needs – went to foreign interests, with several famous brands (including Cadbury, Weetabix and Flora) or supermarket chains (Asda) having fallen into the hands of non-UK owners (Chapman 2018). The British public seemingly accepted this state of affairs, so their politicians did as well.

Things have started to change more recently, however, possibly in the wake of certain nationalistic discourses put forward by the UKIP/ Brexit party. On 11 June 2018, for instance, the government passed a law bolstering its ability to scrutinise international mergers and takeovers, especially where they raised national security concerns relating to the development and/or production of military goods but also a number of other technologies, including artificial intelligence and cryptographic authentication (a hacking weapon deployed in cyberwarfare). Then came even bigger changes when the Covid-19 pandemic erupted in spring 2020. One of the early measures taken by the Boris Johnson administration in response to the crisis was to ban the parallel export of many of the therapeutic drugs that the National Health System thought it might need to treat patients inside the country. The decision was not welcome universally, with some critics pointing out that by wilfully blocking certain international supply chains, the UK was creating a boomerang risk that others would do the same – a problematic situation since the country is unable to manufacture by itself all of the medicine that it normally requires. Then in June of that year (Israel and Kelliher 2020), the government altered existing international investment legislation to facilitate further controls over foreign takeovers of domestic companies directly involved in the Covid-19 response. Justifying the change by "public interest considerations" and one minister's argument that "The UK is open for investment, but not for exploitation", the measure stood in stark contrast to Britain's traditional laisser-faire philosophy. This time, however, there was no criticism to be heard, possibly because a number of other countries (including France, Germany, Poland, Spain and Italy) had taken the same steps, but also because, in times of crisis, there is always greater acceptance of the assertion of state power. Like other IB paradigms, economic patriotism is an attitude that ebbs and flows depending on a society's zeitgeist at a given moment in time.

Case study questions

1. How likely is it that the UK would continue to be so nonchalant about foreign ownership of domestic companies when few of its comparator nations felt the same?
2. Has Brexit or the Covid-19 crisis had a greater impact on the British sense of economic patriotism?

Governments often help national companies to compete internationally

There are several ways in which national governments can intervene proactively to increase domestic interests' international competitiveness. These include developing local capabilities in sectors deemed essential for future success, and direct state entrepreneurship.

Encouraging international competitiveness

Notwithstanding classical economics' critique that public monies should not be wasted on "lame duck" firms incapable of surviving in a competitive market without subsidies, there have been many occasions when timely government support has saved companies that subsequently proved themselves more than capable of succeeding internationally. One famous example was when the United States' first Obama administration, under the leadership of then Vice-President Joe Biden, decided to bail out General Motors (GM), which had become basically insolvent in the wake of the 2007–2008 credit crunch. State aid was contingent on the company rethinking its production and sales strategies to prioritise the more fuel-efficient vehicles that were clearly going to be a cornerstone in the automotive market of the future and which were already standard in the international markets, where GM was lagging behind its foreign rivals. GM used the aid to transition successfully, first returning to profitability in 2011 before generating, by the end of the decade, annual earnings of around $2 billion, with more than 60 percent of all sales being realised outside of its home market. Tens of thousands of jobs were saved at the company and throughout its supply chains. Even the most neoliberal of commentators found themselves applauding this textbook example of effective state power.

GM's story exemplifies the kind of ad hoc intervention that the well-resourced government of an already industrialised country might make to help a company it deems either "too big to fail" or which it considers essential to future national strategy. Having said that, there are also many historical examples of governments from less-affluent Global South economies providing domestic industries with strategic aid intended to help them withstand international competition, especially during the country's early industrialisation phases. This type of intervention, which sees public and private sectors working interdependently and pooling resources, is best embodied in the developmental capitalism model that characterised many East Asian Tiger countries during the early years of their exceptionally rapid emergence, before the recipients had grown to the point of no longer requiring any subsidies (Hamilton-Hart and Yeung 2019). Note that similar dynamics could also be witnessed in US economic history, back when the country was first embarking on its own development path. One remarkable study of the American cotton industry (Rivoli 2006) has shown how farmers' ultimate success with this business – the USA being the world's leading exporter of cotton – stemmed not only

Fig 3.4
Early state aid helped
the US cotton industry
ultimately become a world
leader.

from their entrepreneurial spirit and competency but also from more
than 100 years of government support (labour market manipulations
providing cotton growers with a cheap, captive workforce; state-funded
R&D disseminating cutting-edge knowledge). The lesson here is that
an active and/or powerful state is not necessarily incompatible with
a country's pursuit of success in the international markets – quite the
contrary. Note the example of "Japan Incorporated" (Ishinomori 1988),
with most, if not all, of the export industries in this manufacturing
powerhouse still coordinating their efforts under the aegis of its
Ministry for International Trade and Industry. Now, it is true that in
this latter instance, state power tends to be exercised indirectly through
the determination of strategic direction rather than directly through
subsidies. But the effect on companies' IB prospects remains just as
strong.

Public sector entrepreneurship

Governments' most direct exercise of power in the IB arena is when they
themselves assume an entrepreneurial role. The two main forms that
this kind of intervention takes are state-owned enterprises (SOEs) and
sovereign wealth funds (SWFs).

Sovereign wealth funds - Government-managed pools of national currency reserves. Often invested globally to maximise returns and diversify risk.

State-owned MNEs often pursue different objectives than their
privately owned counterparts. MNEs owned by private sector
shareholders – especially where this involves geographically dispersed
institutional investors lacking any deep personal attachment to the
company – tend to be singularly focused on the maximisation of
short-term financial returns. SOEs, on the other hand, will generally
focus not only on viability concerns but also on broader public policy
objectives. These can include job creation (especially at times of high
unemployment), terms of trade improvements, technological progress
(i.e. the seminal US government-funded semiconductors research that
launched Silicon Valley's computer industry), infrastructure

(i.e. China's $4 trillion Belt and Road Initiative) or the acquisition of natural resources (i.e. Chinese extraction ventures in Africa). The main debate here is whether SOEs have an unfair advantage because their shareholder (the state) has deeper pockets. The opposite argument is that their reduced cost of capital allows them to invest in publicly useful activities generating profit margins that are too low to attract private sector interest otherwise. A good example here is the district heating industry, a green business (see Chapter 14) whose high upfront outlays and long payback periods generally repel private investors but are being successfully navigated by SOEs such as Sweden's Vattenfalls or the UK's Energetik, the trailblazing heat-from-waste company that London Borough of Enfield launched in 2016 (Sitkin 2018). By proving that it is possible for a SOE to operate viably in a sector (like energy) that is generally dominated by big, margin-hungry MNEs, these companies are fulfilling their politician founders' vision that government can (and maybe should) assume a more entrepreneurial role in society (Talbot 2018).

Similar debates have been held regarding the role of SWFs, which are state-owned investment vehicles often originating in countries that have amassed large oil surpluses (mainly from the Arabian Gulf but also Norway) and/or where the government has traditionally held the reins of economic power (China and Russia). The main bone of contention here is whether the equity stake that a SWF might take in a privately owned foreign company is merely intended to achieve financial returns or to achieve managerial control. The latter would be tantamount to nationalising another country's industry – an intervention that would be politically highly controversial.

It becomes difficult to argue that the state is in full-blown retreat when governments retain all these different avenues for affecting the shape of IB. A more accurate conclusion would be to say that some IB-related factors undermine state power, whereas others reinforce it. The question then becomes what motives a given government might have to take a more interventionist stance if it is so minded – and in that case, which instruments are available for it to deploy.

Section II. National trade and FDI intervention tools

When governments intervene in IB, the purpose is almost always to defend domestic versus foreign interests. Chapter 2 demonstrated how protectionism can be politically advantageous because it helps local producers retain market share, but economically suboptimal since it diminishes their incentive to modernise and become more efficient. Conversely, deciding not to support home country interests that are exposed to foreign competition, leaving them free to succeed but also to fail, can be politically damaging but economically advantageous. Governments are constantly having to weigh this choice, without forgetting that the way they treat foreign companies will affect how foreign governments treat their country's own firms. It should always be remembered that the decision whether to deploy IB intervention tools, and which ones to deploy, is always made against the backdrop of difficult arbitrages.

Intervention motives

Some interventions by governments in their country's IB landscape are internally oriented and intended to improve the home country population's general well-being. Others are meant to enhance the country's interactions with the outside world.

Interventions for internal purposes
Jobs
Where IB increases the volume of activities conducted within a country's borders, employment levels will tend to rise there (unless automation causes a net replacement of humans by machines; see Chapter 15). Conversely, where IB involves more activities taking place outside of a country, higher national unemployment may well ensue, certainly in the activities that have been offshored or outsourced. The latter situation became a huge political issue in recent decades, resonating mainly in Global North countries that have seen millions of manufacturing jobs shipped to the Global South. It explains, for instance, why politicians in the former group of nations regularly propose fiscal measures to incentivise companies not to offshore labour-intensive activities. Interventions of this kind can become particularly emotive when they involve sectors considered central to a country's cultural identity, like rice in Japan or wine in France.

Foreign investment
Governments generally favour foreign MNE investments aimed at making goods that will subsequently be re-exported because this creates jobs without adding to local competition. It also generates foreign currency for the country while improving its balance-of-payments. Where the FDI involves making goods that are going to be sold domestically, the key issue is whether the MNE's presence is going to displace local interests, in which case, the national government may very well try to get the MNE to commit to compensatory measures.

Terms of trade
A frequent motive for government intervention is the desire to improve the value-added content of national economic activity. Due to the particular emergence trajectories that certain lagging Global South countries have pursued in recent years, they often find themselves in the unfortunate position of specialising in the production of goods that generate relatively little added value. This is not only suboptimal from

a wealth creation and development perspective but also means that the countries in question are likely to suffer endemic trade deficits since, by definition, the goods they import will be of higher value, hence more expensive than the ones they make and export. To improve national terms of trade, governments often formulate industrialisation policies to build up national capabilities.

These efforts are often associated with technology transfer arrangements, where the incoming MNE is required to share part of its knowledge base with domestic partners, sometimes as part of a government-enforced "joint venture" (see Chapter 8). Examples include suppliers being apprised of high-tech components' design specifications, or in-country research centres and institutions of learning helping to train and/or employ home country nationals in science, technology and engineering activities. Note that this was the approach pursued by several Asian Tiger success stories (like Singapore and South Korea), explained in numerous studies revealing a high correlation between technology transfers and host countries' productivity gains (Newman et al. 2015).

Safety/security

Public health is one area where public officials often intervene to ensure local nationals' well-being. This can be exemplified by the many policies enacted worldwide in the wake of the Covid-19 pandemic. Otherwise, governments often fulfil their basic national security duties by keeping a close eye on the defence products but also computer technology that their country trades. This sometimes involves export licensing restrictions, as witnessed by the way that the United States Department of Commerce's Bureau of Industry and Security (www.bis.doc.gov) restricts trade in goods that potentially hostile countries (or individuals) might use for military purposes. On other occasions, a government might even temporarily harass MNEs coming from a country with which it

Industrialisation policies - Concerted efforts by states to increase the role of value-added manufacturing in their national economy or support industrial sectors considered strategic.

Technology transfer - Sharing of high-value knowledge with external parties.

Fig 3.5
Technology transfers have been used by a number of Global South governments to improve their national terms of trade.

entertains a difficult relationship, as exemplified by India's decision in late 2020 to suddenly ban dozens of apps made by Chinese companies, following border hostilities between the two countries earlier that year. Indeed, security restrictions can sometimes lead to foreign MNEs being entirely excluded from certain sectors, with non-American companies rarely, if ever, being allowed to participate in the multiple space, military and energy research projects that Washington organises.

Interventions for external purposes

Reciprocity

Governments (like most commercial interests) are generally not in the business of handing out favours without getting something in return. This means that they will usually expect a foreign market to be as open to domestic producers as their domestic market is to foreign MNEs. Things degenerate when there is a perceived lack of reciprocity. In extreme cases, this can lead to trade wars, exemplified by recurring disputes between China and the USA over issues such as Beijing's unreliable intellectual property regime or the "America First" protectionism that former President Donald Trump tried to impose before he lost the 2020 election. A further example from 2019 is the way that the UK, trying desperately to compensate for the privileged access it was losing to the European Single Market because of Brexit, turned to the USA for a trade deal, which demanded that London agree to import the less healthy chlorinated chicken and hormone-injected beef that American slaughterhouses sell. These products had been proscribed in the UK when it was still a member of the EU, which has the world's highest food hygiene standards. The Americans had always tried to represent the EU's refusal to import lower-quality meat as protectionism and were determined to force the British, weakened by their self-imposed isolation, to fall in line – thereby exemplifying how easy it is to conflate a reasonable demand for normal reciprocity with a more self-interested search for advantage.

Reciprocity - Precept that the parties to an agreement should both expect to benefit from it.

Influence

Trade weapons are used to exercise international influence in a way that can be either defensive or proactive. One example of the former approach happened in the 2000s when a number of Afghanistan's trading partners (including the EU) signed preferential agreements offering Afghan farmers incentives to grow crops other than poppy seeds. The hope here was that by changing the farmers' incentives, they could be cajoled into abandoning the international drug trafficking channels that had been one of their main IB outlets until that point. A more aggressive way of exerting international influence might be exemplified by an idea, mooted by the UK government in 2020, that tariffs be levied on food imports from countries characterised by lower animal welfare standards. The carbon border tax that several Global North governments began conceptualising in summer 2021 can be analysed in a similar way.

Competitive positioning

There is a frequent discussion within the politics of IB about the extent
to which governments can intervene to ensure a level playing field for
the domestic interests that they represent. Sometimes a disadvantage can
stem from stringent hence costly environmental or social standards being
imposed upon companies from one country but not on their competitors
from another. It was in response to this regulatory imbalance that when
former President Bill Clinton negotiated the original North America
Free Trade Agreement (now USMCA) in the 1990s, he made sure that
Mexican manufacturers seeking greater access to US markets were
required to satisfy certain sustainability standards. On other occasions,
the problem may be that politicians in some countries pass legislation
opposing state aid and are therefore neither willing nor allowed to
subsidise domestic firms, which are nevertheless competing with MNEs
that benefit from subsidies in their country of origin. This explains efforts
made in 2020 by Germany and France to convince the EU to tighten its
"trade defence" controls on imports coming from a host of countries,
starting with China, whose government was accused of providing
domestic aid for the sole purpose of distorting trade (Zuleeg 2020).

State aid - Resources
allocated by government
entity to provide
advantage to local
interests.

Sanctions

As aforementioned, governments generally restrict trade and FDI with
governments, investment funds or MNEs from countries with whom
they entertain a hostile relationship. Examples include certain Arab
countries' boycott of Israeli goods due to the tensions in the Middle East,
US blockades of Cuba and sanctions against Iran because of its nuclear
enrichment programme. Note along these lines the possibility that
sanctions ostensibly imposed for political reasons are actually being used
for other, more commercial purposes – something that European tech
companies accused the US government of doing in late 2020, viewing
the latter's blacklisting of certain Chinese companies as a pretext for
preventing European MNEs like Dutch chipmaking equipment specialist
ASML from building up its own Asian business interests and using them
to potentially rival American interests one day.

Intervention tools

Early IB analysts (Doz and Prahalad 1980) used to differentiate between
government actions that limit MNEs' strategic freedom (product/market
specifications, technology conditions, employment requirements and
trade balance effects) as opposed to others that target strategic sectors
and restrict managerial autonomy (joint venture requirements, worker
co-determination regimes). The present textbook makes the choice, on
the other hand, to classify IB intervention tools according to whether
they specifically target trade operations, apply to FDI or modulate the
host country's business cycle. In both cases, it is important to remember

that no list of government IB interventions can be exhaustive. Having
said that, the most commonly applied instruments are listed below.

Trade tools
The main distinction for trade intervention tools is whether a sum of
money is being demanded from a foreign company or if it is being
subjected to bureaucratic controls.

Levies

Tariffs - Levies that
governments assess on
goods (usually imports)
when they cross national
borders.

Tariffs – generally in the form of the "customs duties" that companies
pay to their government when importing foreign goods (categorised
according to the World Intellectual Property Organisation's so-called
"NICE" classification) – are usually assessed as a percentage of a
shipment's value, that is, on an *ad valorem* basis. But they can also
be assessed in "specific" terms, with a lump sum being owed for a
particular quantum of goods. Governments often try to improve a
country's terms of trade by levying higher tariffs on processed goods (i.e.
ones whose transformation has advanced towards the finished product
portion of the value chain) than on raw materials or simple parts. An
example here is the generally lower rates levied on shoe components (like
leather or soles) as opposed to shoes themselves. This is also meant to
avoid penalising domestic industries that might import such inputs for
their own assembly purposes.

By artificially raising the prices of foreign goods, import tariffs affect
consumer preferences. Historically, they have also been the primary
method by means of which governments intervene in trade matters.
This remains the case, as witnessed by the regular flow of tariff-related
complaints adjudicated by the WTO Dispute Settlement Body (see
Chapter 4).

Non-tariff barriers

Higher oil prices in 1973 raised energy import costs worldwide and
sparked a wave of protectionism. Obliged by their General Agreement on
Trade and Tariffs (GATT) commitments to keep import tariffs low, many
countries started looking for other interventionist tools. The end result
has been the formulation of a vast array of non-tariff barriers (NTBs)
that can be a real administrative headache for exporters and
importers alike.

QUANTITATIVE RESTRICTIONS   There are two main variants of this
class of NTB: voluntary export restraints (VERs) and import quotas.
VERs refer to one country's agreement to limit the volume and/or value
of its exports to another country, usually to avoid the kind of hostile
response that can arise when a domestic market is being overwhelmed
by imports. The tool was famously used by the USA during the 1970s to
persuade Japan to reduce its automobile exports. Japanese companies'
growing share of the American market was destroying the domestic
car industry and sparking great resentment. Tokyo's VER policy was

Fig 3.6
What barriers to trade
have in common is that
they all slow down
international business.

one way to prevent Washington from taking more drastic measures. A similar case from 2019 was when the Trump administration requested that the EU and Japan voluntarily restrain their automotive exports to the United States – a politically improbable idea that had little or no basis in law (Chrysolaras and Baschuk 2019). Unsurprisingly, the countries refused.

Otherwise, quotas specify the maximum quantum of a good that a country is prepared to import (or on the odd occasion, export). Volumes are usually agreed in licensing arrangements that, under WTO regulations, must be transparent and non-discriminatory. Note that under the rules that used to apply before the WTO was founded in 1995, Global South countries were allowed to apply quantitative restrictions or other non-tariff measures if they needed to protect their infant industries (Hoekman and Kostecki 2001). The extent of the special and differentiated treatment that can and should be afforded the world's less wealthy countries remains to this day a key debate in the politics of IB.

By restricting the supply of foreign goods, both VERs and import quotas increase the price that consumers pay. Higher prices mean extra revenue for the foreign producer selling the goods. In contrast, where the trade barrier materialises in the form of import tariffs, it is the host country government that collects the surcharge in the form of the levies assessed as the goods enter the country. In this sense, tariffs are a more effective way of protecting national interests than quotas.

STANDARDS   Where consumer health is at stake, governments often require scientific evidence that a product is safe. Problems arise when one country accuses another of misusing controls to disguise a protectionist intent. One example is the debate over whether countries with tough environmental legislation should be allowed to restrict imports of goods produced using a lower standard. An early example of this came in 1998 when the WTO rejected a US import ban on shrimp caught in nets that were harmful to sea turtles – the argument being that the measure was a barrier to trade like any other. Attitudes have changed since then, however, and it is increasingly acceptable to the WTO for countries to prohibit products manufactured in an environmentally unfriendly manner. A major issue for many countries is whether it is appropriate for economic concerns to have greater weightage in policy-making than other, more ethical priorities (see Chapter 6).

Some "phytosanitary" standards exist for health and/or safety reasons. Other technical standards have no real health implications but instead reflect national economic interests. One example is a German law (*Reinheitsgebot*) that had been used to prevent foreign breweries from labelling their exports to Germany as "beer" – that is, until the EU ruled in 2004 that this constituted a disguised form of protectionism. To clarify such situations, the International Organization for Standardization (ISO) tries to harmonise national regimes by providing guidelines that companies worldwide can use for quality audit purposes. It remains that standards-based restrictions on imports continue to this day to be a major stumbling block in many MNE-national government negotiations.

ANTI-DUMPING PROVISIONS   Companies may occasionally try to drive competitors out of the marketplace by dumping goods at artificially low "loss leader" prices. This is considered market-distorting behaviour and generally proscribed. The problem in IB is the difficulty of determining whether imports are cheap because foreign producers have manipulated prices or simply because they are able to manufacture the goods less expensively. Governments that accuse foreign producers of dumping practices will often levy fines to equalise pricing. The problem is that sometimes it is the accusation that is distorting the market, with the politicians who are accusing foreign MNEs of dumping being the parties who are actually committing protectionism.

Lastly, it is important to remember that many NTBs are purely administrative in nature. These include certain product labelling or place-of-origin requirements, as well as assorted bureaucratic controls. Such barriers add to the cost of IB, raising the question of who pays for them: the exporter, the importer or the end user. They also have a negative impact on the speed of international transactions, as UK trading interests learnt to their detriment during the Brexit transition period (and beyond).

Dumping - Where exporters sell goods at a loss or below the normal price to gain market share and put rivals out of business.

FDI tools
An increasing number of intervention tools specifically target MNEs' foreign subsidiaries. This trend reflects FDI's growing importance to IB.

Performance requirements
Governments impose conditions on MNE subsidiaries for various reasons. Sometimes the aim is to monitor how they are using whatever

state aid their mother company may have negotiated when first entering the market. On other occasions, the goal is to control foreign subsidiaries' behaviour, often with an eye towards improving the national balance of trade. The main performance requirements are:

- *Local contents ratios.* The requirement here is that a minimum percentage of the value of the goods being sold within the host country must involve components sourced from domestic manufacturers. To benefit from preferential tariffs, for instance, at least 40 percent of the value of goods being (re-)exported from the Association of Southeast Asian Nations (ASEAN) zone must be manufactured in one of the region's member-states.
- *Dividend repatriation restrictions.* Limits are sometimes placed on how much money a MNE subsidiary can take out of a country in the form of dividends. Similarly, national governments will often have an at least tacit agreement with incoming MNEs that a given percentage of locally generated profits be re-invested locally, and not hoarded as retained earnings.
- *Technology transfers.* As noted above, the goal here is to ensure that a MNE is sharing high-value knowledge within the host country and/or undertaking a modicum of research locally.
- *Employment measures.* These initiatives look to accelerate recruitment schemes, improve pay scales and/or enhance worker training.

Performance requirements are strongly supported by those who argue that without such protections, FDI-related gains would benefit the incoming MNE more than the host country itself. They are often criticised by opponents of government intervention, who view them as vehicles for politicising FDI decisions that they believe should be made by market participants alone. Had the previously discussed Multilateral Agreement on Investment (MAI) not been shelved, for instance, it would have been used to disband a broad swathe of signatory nations' performance requirements. Note that subsequent attempts by the WTO to develop similar regimes – such as the Trade-Related Investment Measures (TRIMs) – have also crumbled in the face of political opposition.

Over the past 30 years, it seems that many governments have shown greater willingness to abandon (or at least make less frequent use of) trade intervention tools than FDI-related instruments. The reasons for these trends are worth discussing and may have something to do with the intimacy of FDI interactions materialising within a country, as opposed to trade, which materialises at the border.

Ownership restrictions
As aforementioned, national governments are often happy to see domestic interests take an equity stake in a foreign MNE's local subsidiary. There are several reasons for this form of economic patriotism, including the contention – long substantiated in academic studies (Marcin 2008) – that having a certain level of domestic ownership helps to ensure that

FDI-related productivity gains spread more widely throughout a local economy. Ownership restrictions can range from limiting foreign stakes in local ventures to the outright seizure of MNE subsidiaries. In many countries, the FDI environment is shaped by competition regulators whose role is to prevent foreign interests from abusing a dominant position. An interesting source of information in this area is the OECD's FDI Regulatory Restrictiveness Index (https://www.oecd.org/investment/fdiindex.htm), which provides an annual update regarding which governments impose the most or the least onerous restrictions (ownership-related or other) on foreign investors. The idea here is that whereas FDI barriers are usually presented as a government's reasonable desire to protect domestic competition, the reality is that they are often intended to protect domestic competitors.

General intervention tools

This category of intervention tools, referring to actions affecting the overall economic environment within a particular host country, is comprised of domestic policies that also have IB repercussions.

Subsidies

The most common variety of IB-related subsidies involves direct payments to domestic exporters and/or producers operating in sectors exposed to foreign competition. Governments' guiding principle here is to ensure that their generosity accrues to home country interests and no one else – as exemplified by the problems that Norwegian Air had when applying for state support during the 2020 Covid-19 pandemic, with several Oslo politicians expressing reservations about subsidising a MNE that may have been flying the national flag but ran many, if not most, of its operations out of foreign locations.

Otherwise, a secondary category of subsidies is comprised of loans or insurance policies offered to exporters at preferential rates, as well as guarantees that can then be used to reduce the cost of doing business. On top of this, many governments have special provisions for subsidies specifically targeting small companies, the goal being to help them maintain what is often a tenuous foothold in the international markets, exemplified by Egypt's 2020 decision to flaunt WTO members' general state aid restrictions by disbursing funds to help national SMEs whose foreign markets had crumbled in the wake of the Covid-19 pandemic.

Where subsidies are viewed as being market-distorting because they enable the survival of grossly uncompetitive companies, opposition to them can be loud and protracted. Witness the treatment meted out in recent years to the European fishing industry, which benefits from EU export subsidies intended to sustain an activity already suffering from the ecological devastation of dwindling fish stocks. In response, the United States has on several occasions imposed extra tariffs on EU fish imports. Penalties of this kind, called "countervailing duties", are meant to restore a semblance of fairness to markets. The complication is that in some cases – for instance, where infant industries are involved – it can be argued that subsidies are what actually restore a level playing field.

Macro-economic policy

A country's trading position is also affected by its general economic policies. Fiscal systems can be used, for instance, to shift domestic demand towards homemade products (for instance, by raising VAT on the categories of goods that a country typically imports). Otherwise, governments might also choose to establish "free trade zones" (see Chapter 10), enabling domestic firms to import, on a tax-free basis, components destined for re-exportation. Interest rates can be raised or lowered, respectively, to reduce demand in a country running a trade deficit and which needs to consume less, or to increase demand in a country running a trade surplus and which can afford to consume more. Governments sometimes keep currency rates artificially low to facilitate exports, or set them artificially high to reduce import prices. Many national economic decisions are taken with an eye towards the IB outcomes that they produce.

It is also commonplace for governments to design targeted IB competitiveness schemes. Examples include state-sponsored workforce training programmes aimed at developing national capabilities in promising export sectors; payroll tax relief schemes targeting export-oriented companies preferential treatment reserved for domestic companies bidding on public procurement contracts; and export assistance packages specifically aimed at SMEs. For all these measures, the border between international and domestic interests is very thin indeed (Table 3.3).

Table 3.3
Recap of main government trade and FDI intervention tools

Trade tools	Levies	Ad valorem tariffs
		Specific tariffs
	Non-tariff barriers	Quantitative restrictions • Import quotas • Voluntary export restraints
		Standards • Environmental • Social • Health and safety/Phytosanitary • Technical
	Anti-dumping provisions	
	Administrative requirements	
FDI tools	Performance requirements	• Local contents ratios • Dividend repatriation restrictions • Technology transfers • Employment measures
	Ownership restrictions	• Maximum equity stakes • Local partnership requirements

Attitudes and alternatives

MNE executives often find it very difficult to calculate how much leeway they have when negotiating market entry with government officials or politicians. The answer largely depends on whether the potential host country has greater need of the MNE or vice versa. Where managers perceive the location as being crucial to their internationalisation strategy, they will be more conciliatory. On those occasions where they are no more attached to this destination than to other potential candidates, they will tend to drive a harder bargain. In turn, this can raise a number of ethical issues. The boundary between a normal and an abusive pursuit of IB interests is often difficult to discern.

Chapter summary

The chapter's first section looked at the issue of whether states have lost the power to control their economic environment. After reviewing arguments that some aspects of modern globalisation – such as global governance, technology, and deregulated finance – have weakened national governments, the counter-arguments were presented, including the continued importance of domestic business dealings, the prevalence of economic patriotism and the rise of state entrepreneurialism.

After detailing some of the main internal and external reasons why governments might intervene in IB, the second section reviewed various instruments that are available for them to deploy if they so choose. The main distinction here was between trade-related tools, divided into tariffs and non-tariff barriers; FDI tools (mainly comprised of ownership restrictions); and general tools implemented through broader macro-economic policy.

Case study 3.3: France's exceptional cultural exception

France's protectionist reputation is not entirely justified, given the long history of openness to trade characterising this key EU member-state. There is also the fact that many of the companies operating in France are foreign-owned, not to mention the power that foreign investors are allowed to wield on the Paris stock exchange.

Yet France's protectionist reputation does exist and is not entirely unjustified. For centuries, French national leaders have pursued what is commonly referred to as a *colbertiste* policy of strong intervention in both domestic and international businesses. In recent years, this has been expressed through opposition by conservative and progressive voices parties alike to what the French commonly refer to as "Anglo-Saxon" capitalism, construed as a neoliberal paradigm where market

Fig 3.7
There is a clear consensus in France that some sectors should be run according to free trade principles, and that others should be exempt.

forces are considered the only legitimate way of determining economic outcomes.

A prime example of this attitude is the way France approaches the global market for cultural goods (film, music, etc.). French authorities began worrying several decades ago that English-language products' world domination would undermine their country's long and proud heritage as a beacon of culture. A long-standing consensus in favour of protecting domestic artists ultimately led in the early 1990s to the then Culture Minister Jack Lang successfully negotiating a "cultural exception"

(*exception culturelle*) waiver, exempting French cinema, music and TV productions from the kinds of restrictions that the WTO normally places on state aid. Instead, France follows a different set of rules ensuring that a share of the receipts from any cultural activity taking place within the country is recycled in the form of subsidies for French artists, whose outlets are further protected by a quota system forcing broadcasters to offer minimum national content thresholds (generally between 40 and 60 percent). The end result is that unlike many other similarly sized or even larger countries, France's cultural production continues, in quantitative terms at least, to punch above its weight.

Recent French business history also abounds with other examples of protectionism, exemplified by country's decades-long refusal to permit major reform of the EU's Common Agricultural Policy, which subsidises many French farmers but places a huge burden on the EU budget. Note along these lines the iconic status accorded to agricultural activities in France's national self-image, explaining why this sector is viewed in more or less the same light as the country's culture industry. It should never be forgotten that in its purest form, the politics of IB is often little more than an expression of national emotion.

In 2003, the French government formally categorised 14 sectors as "strategic", meaning that foreign shareholders would no longer be allowed to take a controlling share of companies working in these areas. Such measures are not unique, with many other countries having adopted similar policies in relation to key industries like energy; however, even in this sector, it was remarkable that France used its new powers to prevent Italian energy company Enel from taking over French consortium Suez only a few short years after Electricité de France had acquired the Italian utility Montedison. What was striking about France's new strategic list was that it also included Danone, a food processing company that the French government prevented from being acquired by PepsiCo, the American soft drinks maker. Most analysts would find it difficult to support the claim that yogurts and soft drinks constitute strategic national activities; yet, in February 2021, another French administration made a similar determination when it rejected Canadian group Couche-Tard's proposed acquisition of French retailer Carrefour, based on claims of the need for "food sovereignty". This decision was all the more telling (and hypocritical) given the fact that just one month previous, French transport engineering giant Alstom had purchased its Montreal-based counterpart and erstwhile rival, Bombardier, one of Canada's leading industrial champions. Non-reciprocal attitudes of this kind reflect the traditional and rather mercantilistic French conception that economics is a war that domestic companies wage on the country's behalf. In this view, it becomes legitimate to adopt almost any means necessary to advance national economic interests, even if this involves bending international trade rules.

Recent years have seen some evolution in French government thinking following the 2017 election of centrist President Emmanuel Macron, who has analysed certain weaknesses in the French economy (starting with an endemic high unemployment) as being at least partially caused by the statist orientations advocated by the country's right- and left-wing parties alike. In Macron's new liberal conception, it behoves France to figure out how to sustain its much-lauded state-managed social protection system while daring to compete more aggressively in the international markets. One of the ways he has envisioned implementing this new hybrid conception is by further developing national capabilities in fast-growing high-tech activities, starting with green business. Macron has designated a greenfield suburb of Paris (Saclay) as the site for the new environmental research and production activities that he hopes to kick-start by luring climate scientists to France from all across the world. It is difficult to determine whether this chess move by the president attests more to France's traditional statist approach to business or to Macron's personal awareness of the power of market mechanisms. The answer is probably a combination of the two.

Case study questions

1. Is it fair to consider France protectionist when it practices open border policies in so many areas?
2. What is the basis for many French politicians' tradition rejection of unadulterated free trade?
3. What are the chances that President Emmanuel Macron will succeed in altering France's approach to international business?

Chapter discussion questions

1   Is the rising power of international business a good or a bad thing for democracy?
2   Musician John Lennon once asked people to "imagine there's no countries". How attractive and/or realistic is this prospect?
3   To what extent can policies that succeed in one country be transferred to another?
4   Buckman (2004) once alleged that globalisation is similar to communism insofar as it concentrates power in few hands. Is this accurate?
5   Which sectors of activity might national governments find harder or easier to control? Why?

References

Baumunt, Z. (2000). *Liquid Modernity*, Cambridge: Polity.

Buckman, G. (2004). *Globalisation: Tame It or Scrap It*, London: Zed Books.

Burke-Kennedy, E. (1 July 2019). "Ireland's €200 bn debt burden: How did we get here", accessed 19 June 2020 at https://www.irishtimes.com/

Chapman, S. (21 May 2018). "Overseas-owned companies make up greater share of UK food sector, research finds", *The Independent*.

Chrysolaras, N., and Baschuk, B. (2019). "EU, Japan reprieve from Trump car tariffs may be short-lived", accesssed 21 June 2020 at https://www.bloomberg.com/

Doz, Y., and Prahalad, C.K. (March 1980). "How MNCs cope with host government intervention", *Harvard Business Review*.

Dunseith, B. (12 July 2017). "India's retail sector: Challenges and opportunities for foreign investors", accessed 19 June 2020 at https://www.india-briefing.com/

El-Ojeili, C., and Hayden, P. (2006). *Critical Theories of Globalisation*, Basingstoke: Palgrave Macmillan.

Festinger, L., Schachter, S., and Bach, K. (1950). *Social Pressures in Informal Groups*, New York: Harper.

Friedman, T. (2000). *The Lexus and the Olive Tree*, New York: Anchor Books.

Hamilton-Hart, N., and Yeung, H. (2019). "Institutions under pressure: East Asian states, global markets and national firms", *Review of International Political Economy*, accessed 21 June 2020 at https://www.tandfonline.com/

Hoekman, B., and Kostecki, M. (2001). *The Political Economy of the World Trading System*, 2nd edition, New York: Oxford University Press.

Ishinomori, S. (1988). *Japan, Inc: Introduction to Japanese Economics*, Berkeley: University of California Press.

Israel, M., and Kelliher, K. (22 June 2020). "UK ushers in new foreign takeover restrictions…", accessed 7 November 2020 at https://www.whitecase.com/

Klein, M., and Pettis, M. (2020). *Trade Wars Are Class Wars*, New Haven, CT: Yale University Press.

Kollewe, J. (13 October 2011). "UK is second-largest buyer of foreign firms", *Guardian*.

Marcin, K. (March 2008). "How does FDI inflow affect productivity of domestic firms? The role of horizontal and vertical spillovers, absorptive capacity and competition", *National Bank of Poland*, Working Paper No. 42, accessed 29 July 2021 at https://papers.ssrn.com/

Matelly, S., and Nies, S. eds. (2006). "La Nationalité des enterprises en Europe", in *La Revue Internationale et stratégique*, Paris: Dalloz, pp. 41–52.

Newman, C. et al. (May 2015). "Technology transfers, foreign investment and productivity spillovers", *European Economic Review*, Volume 76, pp. 168–187.

Pilger, J. (2002). *The New Rulers of the World*, London: Verso.

Reuters (20 May 2020). "Germany approves new powers to block foreign takeovers in healthcare", accessed 7 November 2020 at https://uk.reuters.com/

Rivoli, P. (2006). *The Travels of a Shirt in the Global Economy*, Hoboken, NJ: John Wiley and Sons.

Singhania, R., and Anand, A. (29 April 2018). "FDI in retail trading in India", accessed 7 November 2020 at https://singhania.in/blog/fdi-in-retail-trading-in-india

Sitkin, A. (Spring 2018). "Eight years on the frontlines of regeneration: Ten lessons from the Enfield experiment", *Soundings*, Number 68.

Sitkin, A. (Summer 2019). "Green business and local economies", *Soundings*, Number 72.

Strange, S. (1997). *The Retreat of the State: The Diffusion of Power in the World Economy*, Cambridge: Cambridge University Press.

Talbot, D. (18 December 2018). "Between community and capital: The practice of urban development in UK Labour", accessed 21 February 2021 at https://www.forbes.com/

UNCTAD (20 January 2020). "Global investment flows flat in 2019, moderate increase expected in 2020", accessed 6 November 2020 at https://unctad.org/

Volk, C. (21 February 2019). "The problem of sovereignty in globalized times", accessed 20 June 2020 at https://journals.sagepub.com/

WTO World Trade Organisation (2020). "World trade statistical review", accessed 6 November 2020 at https://www.wto.org/

Wu, T. (2020). *The Curse of Bigness*, London: Atlantic Books.

Zuleeg, F. (1 October 2020). "The end of the level playing field?" accessed 8 November 2020 at https://www.epc.eu/

Global governance and finance

Introduction

Regime - General
system organising
interactions between
member constituencies.
Often refers to a system
of regulations and
the institutions that
formulate and enforce
them.

Global governance -
Regulatory and
supervisory functions
fulfilled by authorities
whose oversight
transcends national
borders.

The impossibility of resolving most international problems within a strictly national setting has made the need for a rules-based regime of global governance patently obvious for many years. This understanding has underpinned the formation of powerful global institutions that create the broader framework within which multinational enterprises (MNEs) make many of their trade and investment decisions. It is a constellation that is all the more striking given the political and regulatory vacuum within which another key international business (IB) activity – finance – operates. The following chapter will review these two very different coordination and oversight mechanisms in turn.

A useful backdrop to this discussion is the ongoing debate in IB about the relative merits of bilateral versus multilateral governance systems. Bilateralism involves isolated dealings between two counterparts, often governments, although it can also include interactions with MNEs. The advantage of bilateral dealings is that they are easier to manage, if only because each side can negotiate as it sees fit. But they also have two sizable disadvantages: the stronger side can bully its weaker counterpart into accepting an unfair, hence unsustainable arrangement, and parties that

Fig 4.1
The United Nations may
be the cornerstone of
today's global governance
regime, but it has few, if
any, enforcement powers.

DOI: 10.4324/9781003159056-5

have negotiated a large number of separate bilateral agreements may find it hard to coordinate and/or enforce them. This explains the growing support from the mid-20th-century onwards for a multilateral regime of global governance, an arrangement whose potential cooperation advantages can be substantiated mathematically through games theory (Jeong et al. 2018). Some analysts also consider multilateralism fairer since it strengthens the bargaining position of smaller and/or less-affluent Global South countries negotiating with bigger and stronger counterparts (Kelly and Grant 2005). Having said that, others believe the opposite is true and see multilateralism as a "Trojan horse", making it easier for big countries to dominate everybody else (Mathews 2005). Above all, multilateral decision-making exercised through a body of global governance is occasionally criticised in some quarters as an infringement on undiluted national sovereignty. That is not the position taken by most IB practitioners, nor by the author of this book – quite the contrary. The reality is that almost every nation in today's multipolar world finds it beneficial to participate in global governance mechanisms and rejects the alternative of a global regime dominated by one or two all-powerful hegemons. Indeed, there is a strong argument to make that existential crises like climate change and recurring global pandemics make multilateralism more necessary than ever (Gurria 2019). The question then is no longer whether multilateral global governance – exercised through sovereign nations' membership in an intergovernmental organisation (IGO) – is a good thing but instead how to maximise its effectiveness.

Multipolar - Describing a system characterised by a number of different power bases.

Hegemon - Single, supreme power.

Intergovernmental organisation (IGO) - International institution whose membership is comprised of sovereign nations and/or their representatives.

LEARNING OBJECTIVES

After reading this chapter, you will be able to:

- compare varying degrees of regional integration
- critique the European Union's methods and performance
- critique the World Trade Organization's methods and performance
- delineate the remits allocated to single purpose IGOs
- debate the effectiveness of today's largely deregulated global financial markets

Case study 4.1: Brexit – a break for Europe?

Much commentary on the UK's 2016 European Union (EU) membership referendum has discussed the event from a British perspective, focusing either on factors explaining the outcome or the expected macro-economic consequences when a once proud trading nation turns its back on the world's largest unified market. But Brexit is also instructive for what it reveals about the European construction process and, more generally, the future of **regional economic groups (REGs)** – a cornerstone of the modern regime of global governance.

Regional economic group (REG) - Institutional platform created by neighbouring countries to decide issues of mutual interest.

Fig 4.2
As members of the EU, countries have a louder voice on the global stage than if they were to operate individually.

Clearly it is never optimal for a REG if one of its largest member-states withdraws. When Brexit occurred, the question for many was to what extent the isolationism advocated by the UK's "Leave" movement would reverberate across the continent, encouraging populist parties like the Lega Nord in Italy, opposed to the EU's humane immigration policies, or Fidesz in Hungary, opposed to the core EU principle of an independent judiciary. It would be problematic for the EU if such radical dissension were to spread too widely. After all, the minimum condition for a REG's survival is that member-states hold fairly similar values. Indeed, the new challenge for the EU was how to continue making strong consensus decisions with such centrifugal forces at work. Scholars even began to wonder something that would have been unthinkable just a few years previous, namely whether the EU might possibly disintegrate (Meyer 2018). These were dark days for Brussels.

By spring 2021, things were already looking very different. The defeat of US President Donald Trump, like the Lega Nord's ejection from the Italian government the year previous, was taken by many to signify that nationalist populism was waning. Across England, polls recorded increased majorities in favour of remaining in the EU – albeit, quite sadly, at the very moment the country's departure was finalised. Other polls in Scotland revealed rising numbers of citizens demanding independence from England, a shift attributed to the Scots' desire to retain their traditionally close relationship with the continent. Neither the sight of huge queues of delivery vehicles stuck in car parks near the Channel Port of Dover nor the woes suffered by British trading companies – including a 68 percent year-on-year fall in exports to the continent as well as new and frighteningly time-consuming hence expensive administrative requirements (like country-of-origin documentation) – gave neutral observers much confidence in the future of self-isolation.

Europe, on the other hand, not only rejected the idea of awarding UK financial institutions any "regulatory equivalence" from 1 January 2021 (the first day of Brexit) onwards – thereby inheriting, inter alia, the country's entire euro currency clearing business – but within a month saw Amsterdam, originally a much smaller financial centre, replace the City of London as the time zone's leading equity trading market. The Netherlands also benefitted from a number of UK interests – ranging from SMEs to large retailers like JD Sports – opening warehouses there, in part to avoid the requirement that non-EU companies exporting to the Continent pay their products' value-added tax upfront. In turn, this sparked a mini-boom in the Dutch logistics industry, capable of rapid transit to all EU destinations without the terrible delays that now afflicted UK-based trade. Northern French ports benefitted similarly, replacing the UK as a hub for maritime traffic with Ireland. And universities all across the continent took advantage of the UK's abandonment of the Erasmus exchange programme to host students who would previously have gone to British institutions.

Leading politicians like French President Emmanuel Macron began opining that the UK's withdrawal actually created an opportunity for the EU to move towards even closer political union, now that the main opponent to the maximalist option had removed itself from the equation. Renewed confidence in the REG's future could also be seen in Germany's decision to abandon its long-standing resistance to bonds being issued in the name of the EU, with Berlin now supporting this vehicle as a means of funding the battle against Covid-19.

Many Brexit supporters had forecast the imminent demise of the EU in the wake of the British referendum. It soon became clear, however, that this self-justifying prediction was inaccurate and that the project would continue, with Commission President Ursula von der Leyen identifying in a September 2020 speech a number of major policy areas (like cloud computing, climate change, labour relations, international conflicts, migration and pandemic response) where the EU was planning major actions for years to come. Global governance requires nuanced thinking, and the path towards greater international cooperation will undoubtedly face other hurdles in the future. But there is so much momentum behind the European project that it would be foolhardy to bet against it.

Case study questions

1. Why might Britain's departure benefit the EU?
2. How does the EU's size affect its ability to achieve its goals?

Section I. The global governance of trade and investment

By any number of measures – whether the fantastic opportunities and rapid improvements in living standards afforded by economic globalisation, the cultural enrichment that has accompanied this or the lesser frequency of military conflict – the global regime born out of the ashes of the Second World War has been an astounding success. This system, consisting of a patchwork of regional economic groups (REGs) and intergovernmental organisations (IGOs) to whom national governments have delegated varying degrees of national sovereignty, embodies the historical lesson that many policy-making capabilities are best performed when they benefit from the collective input of all relevant stakeholders.

Of course, none of this should be taken to mean that today's global governance regime is flawless. As discussed below, there is a good argument to make that some IGOs, for instance, suffer from "mission creep", meaning that they focus more on their own institutional needs than on their original remit (or even member-states' main current interests). Having said that, it is also possible to make the opposite argument that some IGOs have not actually been given sufficient authority to complete the missions for which they were created, a prime example being the lack of enforcement power allocated to the world's leading multi-purpose IGO, the United Nations. On top of this, there are entire areas of international decision-making that are scarcely addressed through global governance mechanisms, starting with the environment (Sitkin 2019) and, as discussed in this chapter's second section, global finance. In short, even as some observers criticise IGOs' rising power, easily as many argue that they should be given even more power than they have today.

Regional economic groups (REGs)

REGs refer to anything from minimal trade and investment agreements to closely integrated entities endowed with extensive policy-making capacities. Whereas simple trade agreements may involve countries that are geographically distant from one another, advanced REGs almost necessarily involve neighbouring countries. This also distinguishes them from IGOs.

From an economic perspective, one of the main arguments for REGs is that they are supposed to protect neighbouring nations against their neighbours' protectionism. Interlinking member-states through a regional division of labour – dividing up the stages of the regional value chain instead of having each country try to do everything by itself – goes a long way towards easing trade tensions. Such openness has other benefits as well, with studies revealing that countries that have joined a REG are much more likely to become foreign direct investment (FDI) destinations and, above all, have greater involvement in international trade (Bruno et al. 2017). Moreover, as long as regional integration does not cause excessive trade diversion, members of a REG will generally experience higher productivity, mainly because the regime forces domestic companies to hone their skills in a larger, hence more competitive, environment. The same applies to learning effects, with MNEs nowadays increasingly innovating on a regional basis since this helps them develop technology on a much larger scale (UNECA 2016).

Trade diversion - Where imports come from less-efficient producers located within a REG instead of from more efficient ones from the outside.

Lastly, IB practitioners also seem to find it much easier to manage internationalisation on a regional as opposed to a global scale, as witnessed by the fact that most MNEs have a much stronger presence in their home region than worldwide. In the abstract, the greater the distance between countries, the more they are likely to differ, hence the greater the complementarity advantage that companies can attain by bridging any gaps. In reality, however, FDI statistics have long revealed managers' much greater tendency to favour investments in

Gravity model -
Prediction that intensity
of international
exchanges correlates
negatively with
geographic and
sociocultural distance.

nearby countries functioning at a stage of socio-economic development similar to their own country of origin. Theorised as the gravity model, this observation translates in IB terms (Mishra and Jena 2019) the foreignness and personal subjectivity concepts that were introduced in Chapter 1 and will be revisited in later chapters. It also raises questions about the extent to which people's patriotism might extend nowadays beyond their country of origin or residence to include the local REG. For some, this is already happening (European Commission 2015).

In terms of policy-making, REGs offer an intermediary level between global and national governance. Widespread recognition of the limitations of undiluted national sovereignty has, as noted in Chapter 3, strengthened the argument for cross-border decision-making mechanisms, even as the global IGOs studied in the section below can often seem quite remote, hence insufficiently representative (or even democratic). Of course, different political cultures will have different feelings about the relative benefits of delegating national power to a nearby regional IGO as opposed to a more distant global one – and about which powers might be shared or indeed kept at home.

This latter arbitrage offers a further way of distinguishing between the REGs that feature on the world stage today. As demonstrated in Box 4.1, REGs vary widely in terms of their level of integration. Clearly, the greater the powers accorded to a REG, the more it can do on members' behalf. At the same time the more integrated a REG is, the greater the risk that some members might bemoan their perceived loss of sovereignty. It is the balancing of these forces that determine the role that REGs will play in the future of IB.

Box 4.1 Regional economic groups range from loose pacts to fully integrated unions. The former tend to focus on trade matters alone, whereas the latter encompass all kinds of policy responsibilities.

Least integrated

- Preferential trading area – Where countries reduce barriers to entry on goods from certain other countries. Implemented via trade pacts (i.e. EU-ACP agreements)
- Free trade area – Where countries eliminate most barriers to trade with one another. There is no common external tariff, however (i.e. USMCA ex-NAFTA)
- Customs union – Free trade area where members have also adopted a common tariff on goods from outside the region (i.e. ASEAN)
- Common market – Customs unions where members have also implemented a free movement of capital and labour (i.e. Mercosur)

> - Single market – Common market whose members have pooled many government functions, including tax and standards. Member-states may or may not pursue a joint monetary policy (i.e. European Union)
> - Currency union – Single market whose members also share single currency (i.e. Eurozone)
>
> **Most integrated**

REGs in Europe

The European Union (EU): https://europa.eu/european-union/index

The world's most politically and economically integrated REG was born in the 1950s at a time when its six founding members – France, Germany, Belgium, Holland, Luxemburg and Italy – were trying to rebuild their postwar economies and counterbalance US and Soviet Russian power. The goal of avoiding future wars explains European nations' drive to form a REG that would be as tightly knit as possible. The EU's philosophy has always been that peace requires regional loyalties above and beyond national patriotism. Its remit is, therefore, much wider than a purely economic grouping and many of its agencies are endowed with supranational competencies. In some corners, this has sparked criticism of the EU as a giant, unaccountable bureaucracy. But that is a minority opinion. It is precisely because so many European citizens support and believe in the EU project that it has become so big.

Supranational - Where an exercise of political authority transcends national borders.

The EU has gone through many phases. One of the most crucial was its transformation from the European Commission's "Common Market" to the European Union's more integrated "Single Market". That happened in 1992 with the signing of the Maastricht Treaty, which paved the way for the 2002 introduction of a single currency throughout most of the region (called the Eurozone). After EU enlargement on 1 January 2007 to ultimately include 28 member-states, the EU became home to around half a billion citizens – falling to 440 million after the UK left in 2021. A huge organisation employing around 55,000 staff members across a wide range of entities (and featuring a 2020 budget of ca. €169 billion), the EU is the biggest and most advanced REG in the world. This size also makes it hard to please all members all the time – one example, above and beyond Brexit of course, being when Germany was asked to bail out Greece in 2012 due to the large budget deficits that the latter had accumulated over time and expected its fellow member-states to help fund. Logically, a close political union characterised by close coordination of member-states' fiscal policies could have prevented this crisis and the moral hazard it embodied. The problem is that maximal integration is not unanimously welcomed throughout the EU. Countries may want the benefits of belonging to a large REG but are less enthusiastic about the restraints that come with this.

Moral hazard - Where actors take potentially dangerous risks because they do not expect to be held accountable if things go wrong.

In addition, the EU represents member-states' interests at a number of levels. This can involve bargaining with fellow Global North nations, like the decades-long dispute with the USA over the subsidies that the two powers have been paying, respectively, to Airbus and Boeing. On other occasions, its negotiations are with emerging powers such as China, repeatedly accused by Brussels of trying to gain European market share by dumping products at below-market prices. In addition, the EU often features at global governance forums like the WTO, presenting a powerful, united front on behalf of its members. Lastly, the EU regularly engages directly with MNEs operating on its territory, as witnessed by its ongoing probe into the market practices of dominant American tech MNEs such as Google and Microsoft, or its anti-trust efforts exemplified by its February 2021 investigation into American technology company Nvidia's proposed acquisition of UK chip designer Arm, a takeover that the EU feared would upset a crucial but finely balanced market. Representing the combined interests of all member-states, the EU is in a better position to bargain with powerful MNEs than each individual government would be.

European Free Trade Association (EFTA): http://www.efta.int/

This loose association was comprised, as of February 2021, of Iceland, Liechtenstein, Norway and Switzerland – European countries that have not sought to join the EU but need a body to organise their relations with it. Since June 1992, the EU and EFTA combined have been referred to as the European Economic Area.

REGs in Asia

Association of Southeast Asian Nations (ASEAN):
http://www.aseansec.org/

When ASEAN was founded in 1967, its original goal – probably representing the specific sensitivities of its founders, Global South nations that had only recently decolonised and were therefore keen to assert their sovereignty – was to encourage national development while preventing member-states from interfering in one another's affairs. This mission has changed radically over the years, with ASEAN increasingly advocating members' full-blown economic integration as well as greater cooperation in security matters, education, human rights and (through its "post-2015 Vision" agenda) climate change.

An early milestone in this transformation was the 1992 launch of the ASEAN Free Trade Area, aimed at enhancing "the region's competitive advantage as a single production unit". This was furthered in a 2007 ASEAN blueprint expressing an intent to approximate "an EU-style community" by ultimately creating a single market capable of serving Southeast Asia's rapidly growing population (622 million in 2020) in the hope that increased intra-regional trade would reduce member-states' dependency on extra-regional exports as their main growth driver.

The question then became how quickly members would implement the economic integration measures associated with this ambition. In fact, progress has been incremental. One key event from 2010 was when the core group of ASEAN-6 countries (Brunei, Indonesia, Malaysia, Philippines, Singapore and Thailand) eliminated internal tariffs on almost all products, with the remaining members (Cambodia Laos, Myanmar and Vietnam) levying tariffs between 0 and 5 percent. Many non-tariff barriers were also eliminated. In 2015, the ASEAN Economic Community was established along with a new Vision 2025 goal of ultimately expanding intra-REG flows beyond trade to include investment, capital, skilled labour and sociocultural exchanges. There has even been talk of developing a single currency one day.

ASEAN also hosts regular summits with Asia's other economic powerhouses, a logical evolution in its scope given that intra-Asian commerce now accounts for more than 50 percent of all trade in this part of the world. ASEAN+3, that is, ASEAN plus China, Japan and South Korea, began meeting in response to the perceived need for a larger body representing local interests following the 1997 currency crisis that had revealed local economies' excessive dependency on speculative Western hot capital. These forums have since been extended to cover a range of other topics, including energy, poverty and financial stability. Otherwise, there are also ASEAN+6 meetings held with Australia, New Zealand and India, again reflecting the intensification of trade within the broader Asian time zone and culminating in a November 2020 Regional Comprehensive Economic Partnership agreement between the aforementioned countries (plus Japan, minus India). With the new agreement including mutual recognition of qualifications and licensing practices, some of the trade barriers that had previously been a cause of regional dispute would now be eliminated.

- Asian Pacific Economic Cooperation (APEC): http://www.apec.org/

This is an informal minimalist forum promoting voluntary economic cooperation among all major Pacific Rim economies (including the USA, China, Russia and Australia). APEC members do not have a common tariff on imports from outside the region, and each can negotiate deals with non-members as it sees fit. As much as anything, this REG has an advocacy function and no real power, as witnessed in 2017 when ex-US President Donald Trump single-handedly cancelled the Trans-Pacific Partnership Pact that several leading APEC nations had proposed.

REGs in the Americas

United States Mexico Canada Agreement (USMCA, ex-NAFTA): https://www.trade.gov/usmca

The NAFTA (North American Free Trade Agreement) – predecessor to the USMCA – was founded on 1 January 1994, partly in reaction to the

European integration process. The pact's main purpose is to eliminate intra-regional tariffs on many types of products, especially consumer durables, textiles and agricultural produce. Other goals include the relaxation of FDI restrictions, protection of intellectual property (like patents and trademarks) and establishment of trade dispute mechanisms. What the USMCA does not seek to achieve is to harmonise the tariffs that its three member-states levy on extra-regional imports. Nor does it allow for a free movement of labour. Above all, it has no aspiration to become a single market, much less a rival to national sovereignty.

The USMCA has been a success if only because it presided over a historic rise in intra-regional trade and FDI. It has also had a few unfavourable outcomes, however. Having opened Mexico's food markets up to highly industrialised (and subsidised) American agribusiness, NAFTA made life very difficult for small Mexican farmers. This had several consequences, one of which was that a greater number of displaced Mexican agricultural workers were forced to seek employment in the USA. More positively, many North American industries' supply chains now stretch south of the border to include low-cost Mexican *maquiladora* plants that import American components, which will then be assembled on goods re-exported to the USA. This has lowered production costs for many American companies (and consumer prices for households) while providing work for people in northern Mexico. However, it has also raised concerns that Mexico might turn into a "pollution haven" for dirtier US industries (Irwin 2020), not to mention the complaint that outsourcing takes work away from specific labour basins within the USA. These concerns explain the relatively minor amendments (strengthened labour and environmental standards, higher intra-regional local contents ratio, etc.) that the US government drafted in 2018 and which led to NAFTA being renamed the USMCA in 2020.

The USMCA is instructive because it contradicts the old consensus that REGs only work if countries have converged towards a similar level of socio-economic development. By combining members from both the Global North and Global South, the USMCA reproduces within a regional framework the kinds of integrated value chains that have come to typify modern globalisation. At a certain level, this is comparable to the hierarchy that now exists within the EU after it incorporated Eastern Europe "transition" nations. Unlike the EU, however, NAFTA does not expect to have a major impact on people's lives. Indeed, political tensions tend to heighten whenever this is perceived to be the case.

Mercosur: http://www.mercosur.int/

In 1991, Brazil, Argentina, Uruguay and Paraguay signed a treaty promoting free trade in goods and currencies as well as the free circulation of persons. One of the main motives had been to counterbalance previous US efforts to open Latin American markets via the so-called Free Trade of the Americas initiative. During its early years,

Mercosur moved quickly to harmonise members' tariffs when transacting with third parties and signed associate agreements with other countries across South America. The sum total of everything that Mercosur does means that it already qualifies as a bona fide common market.

Caribbean Community (CARICOM): http://www.caricom.org/

Replacing an old free trade agreement, CARICOM serves as a forum allowing 15 Caribbean states to harmonise their economic policies and providing them with an agreed mechanism for arbitrating any trade disputes. The REG also pursues few non-economic missions, including actions on sustainability, HIV/AIDS and security. Its ostensible goal is to help create a "viable, internationally competitive and sustainable community, with improved quality of life for all".

REGs in Africa

African Economic Community (AEC): http://www.au.int/

This is an umbrella organisation for the different regional economic groups to which various African countries already belong, sometimes with overlapping memberships. Driven by principles of unity, decolonisation and development, the AEC aspires to ultimately achieve full integration and develop the institutional apparatus associated with this status. It has yet to make significant progress towards that end, however, largely because of frequent conflicts between member-states. The most successful grouping at present is probably the Economic Community of West African States (ECOWAS), a common market characterised by harmonised economic policies, single external tariffs and a joint currency, the Central African franc, recently renamed the eco.

African, Caribbean, Pacific states (ACP): http://www.acp.int/

This is a loose confederation of emerging economies that have signed a joint treaty with the EU (the 2010 Cotonou Agreement) to ensure preferential, low-tariff access to European markets for the agricultural and mining products in which the ACP specialises. It also tries to use development aid to foster price stability in the primary sectors that are crucial to its members.

Intergovernmental organisations

Starting with the United Nations itself, there are literally hundreds of more or less specialised IGOs today, each focused on the global governance of one or several issues that cannot be sufficiently managed within a national framework. Clearly, the most important IGO for IB is the World Trade Organization (WTO), along with the two other

Table 4.1
Overview of the Bretton Woods IGOs (February 2021)

	WTO	*IMF*	*World Bank*
Headquarters	Geneva	Washington DC	Washington DC
Managing director	Ngozi Okonjo-Iweala (Nigeria)	Kristalina Georgieva (Bulgaria)	David Malpass (USA)
Decision-making	Consensus (one country one vote) In reality, agenda set in "Green Room"	24 Directors representing (groups of) countries. Votes weighted by "quota", i.e. % global GDP	Voting powers: USA (15.85%) Japan (6.84%) China (4.42%) Germany (4.00%), etc.
Approximate staff	650	2,700	16,000
Key data (February 2021)	Operating budget CHF 197.2 million	Credit outstanding Ca. $151.5 billion	Outstanding loans (August '20) $161 billion

institutions that came out of the 1944 Bretton Woods conference that fixed the architecture of today's global trade, investment and financial governance regimes (see Table 4.1). There are, however, other IGOs that also affect the IB environment and therefore merit discussion as well.

Bretton Woods institutions

Much research has been done on the motivations underlying the birth of the WTO, the International Monetary Fund (IMF) and the World Bank. Analysts usually speak of a general understanding of the need to develop mechanisms preventing a recurrence of the terrible international conflicts from which the world suffered during the first half of the 20th century, not to mention the "beggar-thy-neighbour" policies enacted in response to the Great Depression of the 1930s, a protectionism that worsened the crisis by placing obstacles in the path of IB. The idea grew that the solution lay in creating coordinating IGOs where cross-border concerns could be discussed and decided in a transparent and friendly manner. It was this mindset that underpinned the Bretton Woods conference held in the US state of New Hampshire from 1944 to 1947, and which would ultimately lay the foundations for today's regime of global governance.

The World Trade Organization (WTO)

The Bretton Woods conference had originally envisioned the creation of a strong International Trade Organization (ITO) with formal links to the IMF, the World Bank and the International Labour Organization (ILO). When the US Congress decided in 1948 not to approve the ITO,

"Beggar-thy-neighbour" policies - Where one country manipulates its competitive positioning (often via currency devaluations) to try and gain advantage over its trading partners.

what remained in the trade arena was the less ambitious GATT (General Agreement on Trade and Tariffs) treaty. Unlike the ITO, the GATT had no links to other IGOs; did not seek to promote full employment (as the ILO does); and had an ineffective dispute settlement mechanism. It did, however, provide a loose framework for a step-by-step reduction in quantitative tariffs on cross-border product flows. Trade ministers from signatory nations would engage in targeted discussions called "rounds" (see Table 4.2). Any problems arising between sessions would be dealt with in ad hoc committees, meaning that the GATT did not have much of a permanent oversight function (Wilkinson 2006). All in all, the regime balanced the need for an open world economy with the sovereignty concerns that many countries still felt at the time – GATT had no supranational mandate to interfere in domestic decision-making (Kelly and Grant 2005).

By the 1990s, it had become apparent that GATT's modest remit limited its effectiveness in several key international sectors, including agriculture and textile – activities of great importance to many Global South countries. Additionally, it had made so much progress in lowering tariffs that little more could be done in this respect. For some, this meant that it was time to move market deregulation on to a wider agenda that would include trade in services, FDI and intellectual property.

Table 4.2
GATT (and since 1995, WTO) trade negotiation rounds

Year(s)	Name of round	Main results
1948	Geneva	45,000 tariff concessions affecting $10 billion worth of goods (around 20% of global trade).
1949	Annecy	5,000 tariff concessions.
1951	Torquay	8,700 tariff concessions, cutting 1948 tariff levels by 25%.
1955–1956	Geneva	$2.5bn in tariff reductions.
1960–1962	Dillon	Tariff concessions worth $4.9bn in global trade. Negotiations following the birth of European Economic Community.
1964–1967	Kennedy	$2.5bn in tariff reductions. Anti-dumping agreement.
1973–1979	Tokyo	$300bn in tariff reductions. Focus on non-tariff barriers.
1986–1994	Uruguay	Agricultural subsidies cut, full access for Global South textiles, intellectual property rights extended. Birth of WTO.
2001–	Doha	Development agenda. Global North-South conflict.

The Uruguay round of GATT negotiations concluded with the
Marrakesh Agreement that gave birth to the WTO on 1 January
1995. On its website, the WTO defines itself as a negotiating forum,
the embodiment of a set of rules and a venue for settling disputes.
Its functions are to administer WTO trade agreements, host trade
negotiations, handle trade disputes, monitor national trade policies, offer
technical assistance and training for developing countries and cooperate
with other international organisations. This is an extremely broad
mandate. The WTO is the cornerstone of today's global trading regime.

In political terms, the WTO fights for free trade, which it equates
with economic progress (see Table 4.3). It is in no way a neutral body
giving equal support to members' free trade and protectionist policies.
On the contrary, it is a single-issue IGO explicitly encouraging the former
and opposing the latter, a divide that causes deep-seated contradictions
in its decision-making processes. On the one hand, the WTO requires
consensual decision-making. On the other, it officially opposes any policies
that run counter to its own free trade inclinations. This means that the
WTO will regularly enter into conflict with its own members, especially
with its requirement that everyone recognise its authority to judge any
trading disputes that may arise. Acting simultaneously as lawmaker, judge
and police, the WTO has more power than any other IGO.

Despite this, almost every country in the world has joined the WTO,
essentially because governments feel it is worth swapping a leading role
in a smaller framework (the nation-state) for a smaller role in a larger
structure (the WTO). It is tempting for politicians to try to get the
best of both worlds, maintaining absolute sovereignty at home while
getting a greater say on the world stage. This is sometimes feasible for
bigger countries, which find it easier to dominate IGOs such as the
WTO. Having said that, it is also true that IGOs all possess mechanisms
ensuring that smaller states have a greater voice than if they stood alone.

Five main principles guide the WTO's actions.

Most-favoured nation (MFN). If a WTO member gives a favourable
treatment (like lower tariffs) to goods made in one member-state, it must
offer the same to all members. There are exceptions to this rule. Firstly,
regional free trade blocs (like the EU Single Market) can favour internal
flows over extra-regional trade, even if the latter involves a fellow WTO

Table 4.3
The WTO's fundamental beliefs

- There should be no discrimination in the world trade system
- A gradual, negotiated move towards open borders is intrinsically
  beneficial
- Trade decisions should be transparent and not arbitrary
- Competition is desirable as long as it is fair
- Trade should be used to encourage development and economic reform

member. Secondly, under certain circumstances, a country can decide to offer Global South producers special market access. Lastly, some discrimination is allowed if the goods in question suffer from unfair competition. On the whole, however, the MFN arrangement facilitates exports by WTO members. It is the main reason why countries want to join this IGO.

National treatment. The WTO also specifies that members should strive to give similar treatment to all goods, regardless of whether they are produced locally or by a fellow member-state. This acceptance of imports is the main price that a country pays to join the WTO and serves as a counterbalance to the MFN provision. Together, the two principles cement reciprocity as a key WTO value, the idea being that any pain caused by WTO membership will be offset by the associated gains. Note that some (mainly Global North) countries have tried to also get the national treatment principle to cover services and copyrights/patents, the two "new issues" that became part of the WTO agenda in the mid-1990s when it started looking at a General Agreement on Trade in Services (GATS) and Trade-Related Aspects of Intellectual Property Rights (TRIPS) – an agenda that would become particularly contentious in the years that followed.

Fairness. A common misunderstanding is that the WTO advocates free trade under all circumstances. In reality, there are situations (balance-of-payments crises, temporary import surges, unfair competition) when it tolerates countries adopting "safeguard" protections. Conversely, the WTO objects when countries adapt barriers to trade that it considers "unfair" or market-distorting.

Special and Differentiated Treatment for LDCs. Various WTO clauses recognise poorer countries' special needs. As discussed in philosopher Robert Nozick's "time slices of history" theory (Singer 2004), applying a single set of rules to everyone neglects the way a country's past problems can handicap its future chances. In this view, it is unfair to poor countries to force them to play by the same rules as wealthier ones because they will never be able to catch up. This can have dire consequences for local populations. When Global North citizens lose their job due to foreign competition, they can often expect help from a social safety network until they find new employment. That is not true in much of the Global South. In a similar vein, very poor countries often cannot afford the capital equipment and technology they need to take advantage of the improved market access that remains their main reason for joining the WTO.

One of the ways in which Special and Differentiated Treatment could help Global South nations is in the diffusion of a General System of Preferences (GSP), exempting them from MFN reciprocity requirements. The system's implementation has been patchy, however, with Global North nations regularly implementing GSP only in the high value-added sectors that they dominate, as opposed to the more commoditised sectors (such as steel, shoes or textile) where Global South countries' cost advantage makes them more competitive. In addition, a distinction needs to be made between countries that are truly "emerging" and those that are not. It would make no sense for China to be treated the same way, for instance, as Somalia. In general, the least straightforward (and most contentious) problems the WTO faces are development related.

Dispute resolution. WTO members who believe that they have suffered from unfair trade practices can make use of a structured complaints process. The hope is that they will turn to this court instead of retaliating unilaterally against trading partners whom they believe have treated them badly. Parties are encouraged to resolve disputes through out-of-court settlements, with only about one-third of all cases completing the Dispute Settlement panel process. For those cases (see Table 4.4) that do come to court, however, the panel's rulings are binding, unless a consensus agreement exists to reject them. Countries are expected to comply with Dispute Settlement rulings by ceasing the practice in question, although some will persist and compensate the plaintiff for damages suffered.

At one level, the WTO is a very useful tool. Its consensual decision-making process (one nation, one vote) should ideally ensure that all participants, from the largest to the smallest, get a fair hearing. Its commitment to transparency should promote good governance, shielding member-states from powerful lobbies. Governments alone are authorised to negotiate at the WTO and they are expected to argue for the interests of the whole of their country. Lastly, the WTO's culture of

Table 4.4
February 2021. Sample of recent WTO Dispute Settlement disputes

Issue	Complainant vs. defendant
Restrictions on palm oil-based products	Malaysia vs. European Union
Measures on certain (food) products	Costa Rica vs. Panama
Anti-dumping/countervailing duties on barley	Australia vs. China
Origin marking requirements	Hong Kong vs. USA
Polyester film anti-dumping measures	Peru vs. Brazil
Steel product safeguard measures	Turkey vs. European Union
Shipbuilder subsidies, funding guarantees, etc.	Japan vs. Korea
Restrictions on palm-oil based biofuels	Indonesia vs. European Union
Export restrictions on steel raw materials	European Union vs. Indonesia

Source: Regular updates at https://www.wto.org/english/tratop_e/dispu_e/dispu_status_e.htm. Reprinted with WTO permission.

multilateralism should translate into less bullying on the part of more powerful nation-states.

At the same time, the WTO remains the most contested of all the major IGOs: by protectionists opposed to its free trade orientation; and by nationalists opposed to its supranational remit. Case study 4.2 takes a closer look at the current state of play in an IGO that is essential to IB.

Case study 4.2: Is the WTO fit for purpose?

Fig 4.3
The WTO has still been unable to implement the services and intellectual property liberalisation plans first formulated at its Doha meeting nearly 20 years ago.

The chief motivation underlying the WTO's foundation in 1995 was to expand the move towards free trade beyond goods alone. IB not only involves physical products but also services, capital and intellectual property. Free trade advocates were looking to subject the three latter elements to global governance in the same way as trade had been. The problem is that each penetrates national economies to a different (and often greater) extent, and therefore provokes a different level of resistance.

One tool that the WTO and other IGOs use to implement their agenda is the "rounds" system. This starts with the identification of a policy goal (i.e. lower trade barriers), with officials then working behind the scenes to agree on a broad framework. Finally, a document is publicly debated and hopefully ratified by political leaders, usually trade ministers where the WTO is concerned. Many Global North countries tried this in 2001 when the WTO organised ministerial-level meetings at Doha in Qatar. Their goal was to introduce three new policy frameworks: a General Agreement for Trade in Services (GATS), a Trade-Related Investment Measures (TRIMs) and an agreement on Trade-Related Aspects of Intellectual Property Rights (TRIPs). The proposals were not entirely new, having been rejected at an earlier meeting in Singapore by the WTO's poorer member-states. When the WTO raised them again and neither side changed position, its entire liberalisation process ground to a halt.

The critique arose that the WTO was turning into a tool for wealthy members alone. This argument was based on the WTO allowing Japan, the United States and Europe to protect domestic agriculture while pushing a Doha agenda that advanced their specific free trade objectives. As a background, note that many Global South countries who had already opened their product markets to international trade were still protecting their banking sectors, considered key to national sovereignty because of finance's cross-sectoral knock-on effects. GATS would have made this control impossible and paved the way for Global North MNEs to acquire Global South banks. TRIMs would have prevented government procurement processes from offering national companies preferential treatment, even though this is an important driver in many emerging economies' development processes. Lastly, TRIPs seemed specifically designed to stop Global South pharmaceutical companies from taking market share from Western MNEs, as witnessed in the HIV retrovirus saga (see Chapter 10).

An IGO that fights for some members but not others is destined to fail (Wilkinson 2006). The WTO organised other meetings to try to repair Doha (Cancun 2003, Hong Kong 2005 and Potsdam 2007), but within a few short years commentators would come to the conclusion that follow-up negotiations had "sharpened divisions, not smoothed them" (Economist 2011). More than a decade later, that remains the case. Titularly, the WTO is still interested in Doha Round goals. The reality is that the deadlock on Doha has basically stopped the WTO from further policy formulation.

As a result, all that really remained for the WTO to do during the 2010s was to administer its Dispute Resolution Mechanism (DRM). This is crucial to the prevention of trade wars and an activity that in and of itself justifies the WTO's existence. Towards the end of the decade, the DRM also came under attack when then US President Donald Trump, ideologically opposed to the concept of shared sovereignty, refused to appoint new judges when it was time to renew their mandates, effectively depriving the court of its ability to function. With Trump's defeat and the arrival of President Joe Biden, a sincere internationalist, the temporary hiccup would be resolved and this key WTO mechanism kept alive.

The lesson from this chronology is that bodies of global governance can only survive on two conditions: that they function in a way that most participants deem fair and that their most powerful member-states remain committed to their survival. There has long been a debate about whether to reform or else eliminate the WTO. This book is very much in favour of the former solution, but it would be unintelligent to ignore the voices advocating the latter. Part of understanding IB is recognising the existence of opposition to IB.

Case study questions

1. Was the WTO right to push its GATS, TRIMs and TRIPs agendas?
2. How important a role might the WTO be expected to play in the future?

The International Monetary Fund and the World Bank

The IMF is an international financial institution (IFI) specialising in crisis lending. Established after the Second World War, it provides temporary funding – often at concessionary, below-market interest rates – to countries suffering from balance-of-payments problems. Its sister organisation, the World Bank, whose original mission was to support European reconstruction, provides long-term funding, mainly to Global South nations seeking to develop their infrastructure. As such, its actions are more strategic in nature, whereas the IMF has a higher profile during times of crisis.

For the first few years of their existence, the two IFIs fulfilled their missions in a flexible manner, adapting their aid packages and technical advice to suit borrowers' various needs. That changed in the late 1980s when they started pushing a "one-size-fits-all" approach that would often require all prospective borrowers, regardless of their particular circumstances, to undertake the same "structural adjustments" as per the Washington Consensus principles. This generally forced potential borrowers to slash spending, including on social programmes, while opening their domestic financial markets up to international investors (Drezner 2007). The reason given for putting so many conditions on the loans was the IFIs' assumption that governments seeking external funding were necessarily guilty of mismanagement and needed to change their modus operandi. The problem was that in many cases, the policies suggested by the IMF and the World Bank would have disastrous effects on recipient countries' poorer populations. This laid them open to the criticism that by imposing capital market liberalisation on Global South nations characterised by immature financial systems, they were contributing to "global instability [and] political chaos" (Stiglitz 2004). By the early 21st century, the IMF and World Bank had become figures of disdain for many reformists.

In response, around 1999 they began to change their philosophy, re-shaping lending packages to turn them into "Poverty Reduction and Growth Facilities". Instead of demanding that borrowers prioritise short-term problems such as negative capital flows or trade deficits, greater focus would henceforth be placed on more structural problems

like financial sector modernisation (Gomel 2002). The World Bank
also began around this time to experiment with what it called a more
"holistic" attitude towards financial intervention, gearing loan conditions
towards borrowers' specific needs. Greater emphasis was also placed on
the two IFIs' advisory role, the aim now being to improve the quality of
debtor nations' monetary policies and banking systems. The high-quality
economic data and forecasts that the IMF and World Bank have always
produced are key inputs in many countries' planning processes. Even
their fiercest critics agree that they are priceless sources of information.

In more recent years, however, a new set of problems have arisen.
Sitting on growing piles of cash following years of rapid export growth
(and hoping to avoid further interference in their domestic policy-
setting), the larger emerging countries have reimbursed most of their
outstanding loans from the IMF and World Bank, whose only remaining
customers therefore tend to be highly indebted poor countries (HIPCs)
struggling to redeem their outstanding debt. Even for this latter category
of borrowers, IMF or World Bank funding today generally pales in
comparison with the amount of capital they can raise through direct
government aid or sovereign wealth fund loans. What has yet to be
seen is what the two Bretton Woods IFIs can do in the future to remain
relevant. In terms of technical advice, there is widespread agreement that
their intellectual firepower is very useful. In pure funding terms, however,
their importance has slipped.

One final discussion about the IMF and World Bank relates to their
evolution in terms of ensuring that all members – not just the Global
North – have a voice in policy-making. Recent years have seen the two
IFIs give greater voice to Global South members, above and beyond their
traditional quota systems that determined voting rights on the basis of
each country's percentage of total global GDP. One materialisation of
this has been the appointment of chief economists hailing from Global
South backgrounds. Even so, the IMF and the World Bank still work out
of Washington DC and traditionally appoint, respectively, European and
US citizens as managing directors. This is out of sync with the changing
geography of IB, especially since it is the cash-rich emerging economies
who are increasingly providing the financial resources that IGOs need to
fulfil their missions, and therefore demanding, quite normally, a greater
say in the way the organisations are run. Seen in this light, reforming
the Bretton Woods IFIs is not just desirable, but also crucial to their
long-term survival.

Other specialist IGOs

One way to categorise single-purpose IGOs is to distinguish between
those that represent specific sector interests and others that promote
general policy frameworks. The former category is typified by producer
entities fighting on behalf of specific sectors. The latter is comprised of
IFIs but also ad hoc government associations, think tanks, lobbyists and
"non-governmental organisations" (see Chapter 6).

Producer IGOs

These entities exist to represent sectoral trade interests. That can be contentious when the IGO in question is accused of representing a cartel, a charge sometimes levied at the Organisation for Petroleum Exporting Countries (OPEC), a key player in the global energy business. Having said that, it is commonplace for countries to try to negotiate higher prices for the good(s) in which they specialise, a strategy that can either involve reducing supply or oligopolistic pricing practices. Nor is this reprehensible when it involves poor countries trying to improve national terms of trade. Note, for instance, widespread support across Africa for the International Cocoa Organisation (ICCO), a producer IGO that tries to ensure that cocoa bean prices remain at a level where farmers get fair remuneration for their work. That OPEC is more powerful (and better-known) than the ICCO is unsurprising, however. Producer IGOs trading essential commodities such as oil will always be in a stronger position than ones trading more discretionary items like chocolate.

Cartel - Permanent or ad hoc grouping of producers who collaborate on supply quantity decisions and pricing instead of competing with one another.

Oligopoly - Market dominated by few sellers, who might therefore have an incentive to collude and fix prices in a non-competitive manner.

Policy IGOs

Alongside the United Nations and regional economic groups, the main multi-purpose IGO is the G8, which is not so much an institution as an ad hoc body that exists to call regular meetings between the leaders of the world's most influential countries. In recent years, topics have ranged from debt relief to terrorism, climate change, energy, financial crises and lately the battle against the Covid-19 pandemic. The G20 is an expanded forum whose 2020 conference, for instance, addressed some of the issues cited above as well as the empowerment of all people (especially women and youth) and the need to share the benefits of innovation and technological advancement.

Debt relief - Forgiving debt because the original loan had been misused or embezzled or because reimbursement would be too onerous for the borrower.

Otherwise, the Organisation for Economic Co-operation and Development (OECD) was created in 1961 to represent the world's industrialised nations and support free markets. Working out of Paris, this IGO uses its enormous data resources to monitor all kinds of economic developments and produce analysis that it hopes will be adopted by policy-makers everywhere, not just member-states. As highlighted throughout this book, the battle for hearts and minds is an important part of the politics of IB. Thus, despite its lack of formal competencies, OECD wields real authority insofar as it influences people in power.

International financial institutions (IFIs)

Whereas the remit given to the IMF and World Bank is global in nature, other IFIs have been organised along regional lines. Examples include the European Bank for Reconstruction and Development (EBRD), the Inter-American Development Bank (IADB) and the Asian Development Bank (ADB). In recent decades, these entities have often been used to funnel aid or loans to emerging or transition economies engaged in an emergence trajectory. Also worthy of note is the Bank for International

Settlements (www.bis.org), which specialises in providing national central banks with information and coordinating transactions.

IFIs are also part of a wider debate about the coordination of the global financial markets (Ikhide 2004). Unlike international trade where a single IGO – the WTO – reigns supreme, there is no equivalent body in the world of finance. Instead, global governance in this key area of IB is largely comprised of the mechanisms set up by market participants themselves, which therefore merit further examination.

Section II. The global governance of finance

In the abstract, global finance exists to provide MNEs and IB practitioners with the capital they need to invest and operate internationally, and with the currency they need to transact with foreign counterparts. Moreover, given IB's rapid expansion in recent decades, there is a good argument to make that global finance has largely fulfilled its mission. Yet numerous dysfunctions have also arisen along the way, manifested in market failures where practitioners either struggle to access the capital they need or where financial assets (like currencies) are valued at prices that do not reflect their fair value, giving market participants wrong information and causing irrational and suboptimal decision-making. This inefficiency also requires analysis, if only to ascertain to what extent finance has served its long validated role of supporting real non-financial IB activities and not hobbled them instead.

Fair value - Where the market price for an asset, financial or other, reflects all accurate information regarding its utility.

International capital markets

A key IB debate for the past 30 years has been whether open capital markets are the best way of providing the liquidity that enables productive IB activity, or whether the deregulation trend characterising the modern era has created a "casino capitalism" (Sinn 2012) culture that harms the real economy while benefiting speculators who are highly remunerated but create little real value.

Deregulation advocates like to say that the best way of improving management performance is to subject MNEs to the scrutiny of the international capital markets, the idea being that investors will withdraw funds from any company that underperforms financially and, conversely, reward any that performs well. This is similar to the argument that politicians also benefit from open financial markets, which will reward or punish them depending on the quality of their economic decision-making (Mazlish and Morss 2005). The logic here is that financial market oversight ensures that neither managers' nor politicians' short-term personal interests conflict with, respectively, their companies or governments' more important long-term objectives. This aligns with a similar argument that pressure from the financial markets will also induce companies originating from a country lacking a tradition of financial rigour to pay closer attention to budgetary constraints. In short, it is the view that being obliged to placate shareholders and other financial interests is a good thing in and of itself.

The opposite view is that unfettered global capital markets are criticisable from at least two perspectives. The first is macro-economic in nature and can be exemplified in three ways. One is the "race to the bottom" dynamic caused by the power imbalance between territorially constrained governments and speculators free to move their money in and out of countries as they see fit. The second relates to a long-term trend that has seen private sector interests growing their share of global wealth to the public sector's detriment, culminating in a situation where certain needs (like healthcare, social housing and old age care) that can be run much more effectively by the state are being privatised due to many governments' currently cash-strapped circumstances. Lastly, the international linkages that are an inevitable consequence of today's open financial markets create a coupling effect where economic mismanagement in one economy spills over to others despite the latter having made no such policy mistakes (Engelen et al. 2011). The cross-border contagion of the 2007 US subprime mortgage crisis is a prime example of this. Indeed, the recurrence of serious global financial market crises over the past few decades (see Table 4.5) argues against global finance's vacuum of governance.

From a business perspective, the criticism of ungoverned global capital markets tends to be that, as aforementioned, finance should

Coupling - Where countries' economic fortunes are linked due to the inseparability of their economic and financial interests.

Table 4.5
Recent examples of global capital market crises

Year	Description
1995	Mexican banking sector requiring bailout after lending spree
1997	Contagion effect leads to capital flight from Southeast Asia
1998	Russia defaults on "GKO" government bonds. US hedge fund LTCR bankruptcy
2001	"Dot.com" stock market bubble bursts. Further panic after September 11 bombings
1999–2003	Argentina balance-of-payment crisis causes government debt repayment default
2007–2008	US subprime mortgage crisis causes global credit crunch and government debt
2011–2012	European sovereign debt crisis
2018	Cryptocurrency crash as bitcoin bubble burst (down 45%)
2020	Covid-19 recession, including Dow Jones 33% fall from peak

exist to support real business activity, not the other way around. It is problematic when managers at non-financial MNEs can no longer confidently predict the present and future value of their international operations or assets, with clarity almost becoming impossible when huge volumes of "hot capital" flow back and forth across borders in seconds, affecting currency and asset prices in unforeseeable ways. This is compounded by the difference between the instantaneous time framework within which financial speculators work and the much longer periods it takes for "stickier" prices to change in the markets for real goods and services. The net effect of this volatility, hence uncertainty, is to dampen entrepreneurs' willingness to engage in IB.

This explains the argument that ungoverned capital markets might actually be less IB-friendly than older, more controlled systems where national authorities had greater oversight of cross-border capital movements. As unexciting as this more administrative model might sound, it is worth recalling that several of today's leading investment destinations, starting with China, have maintained strong capital (and/or currency) controls, specifically because their governments want to reduce financial volatility and maintain greater supervision over financial flows, and have had to organise this themselves in the absence of any global governance of finance. Such restrictions do not prevent China from receiving huge volumes of inward investment, translating a calculation by entrepreneurs and investors alike that the advantages associated with establishing a long-term commercial or industrial presence in the country exceed the disadvantages of not being able to withdraw their funds as quickly as they might otherwise wish.

It remains that one of the main theoretical justifications for deregulating the international capital markets is precisely the idea that investors are only happy to move funds into markets from which they can withdraw them at a moment's notice. Now, it is true that this kind of calculation still applies where riskier markets are concerned. But the real lesson here must be that what counts in international investment decision-making is not the openness of a capital market but the attractiveness of a host economy. Hence the argument that the global capital markets could still perform their prime IB function even if they were partially re-regulated to alleviate the problems caused by erratic short-term capital flows. The question then becomes which global body would have the overview and power to implement this re-regulation. For the moment, there is none.

All in all, there is little doubt that open financial markets have facilitated the international recycling of surplus funds held by cash-rich countries and investors. Since the late 1990s, this has increasingly meant moving capital held by Asian and Middle Eastern interests to MNEs or indebted nations across the world – a function that has clearly been highly useful to IB. At the same time, recurring crises, astronomical private and public debt levels and the general hegemony of global financial capital offer a strong argument that the current regime can and

Currency/capital controls - Where government places administrative restrictions on people's ability to buy/sell the national currency, or to borrow/ lend capital across borders.

must be improved. Over the course of their careers, IB practitioners will regularly meet counterparts who are much more supportive of the idea of free international product and service markets than they are of free global capital markets. The tail is not supposed to wag the dog.

Foreign exchange (FX) regimes and markets

IB has witnessed a number of different currency system over the years. Early on, countries tended to prioritise keeping their national currency stable against an external standard, usually gold. Since the Second World War, however, the global foreign exchange regime has largely revolved around the US dollar, which remains the world's reserve currency, although there are signs that it may one day have to compete with the Chinese renminbi (see Case study 4.3).

There are basically three rival regimes governing the global FX markets today. Where they differ is the extent to which market participants or state authorities set prices. In *fixed* regimes, a country's central bank pegs its national currency to a benchmark – often the US dollar or a basket of currencies – and intervenes to maintain this rate. Examples include the Saudi Arabian riyal or Panamanian balboa. With a *managed float*, a country's central bank sets a target trading range and intervenes when necessary in the market to keep its currency within that range. Prime examples include the Chinese renminbi, Russian rouble and Malaysian ringgit. Lastly, the price for *floating* currencies (most of the world's "major" currencies, including euros, yen, pounds and dollars) is determined solely by supply and demand from private interests. Each of these systems is associated with different levels of *convertibility*, that is, the degree to which the authorities in a country allow their national currency to be traded without prior administrative consent.

In line with the general paradigm that has dominated most economic policy-making since the 1980s, the strong trend in recent decades has been towards free-floating currencies. Many studies view this as a positive outcome, having discovered, for instance, that economic shocks are less likely to damage countries with flexible exchange rate systems than ones whose currencies are fixed (Edwards and Levy Yeyati 2005). Even so, some governments will still prefer fixed FX regimes, often because this corresponds to their view of how public and private interests should interact. Between these extremes, managed float systems have lost much of their attraction (Fischer 2001). This is because since the late-1980s, the resources available to the private sector have been so much greater than the funds available to central banks that it is almost impossible for the latter to control a national currency once it has been made convertible and can be traded freely by investors. Indeed, in the absence of global coordination, central banks find it almost impossible in the early 21st century to impose their will on the FX markets (Ghosh

Reserve currency - Currency recognised by central banks worldwide as a reliable storage of value.

2008). This means that governments today have one less policy weapon at their disposal in times of crisis.

Theoretically, currency markets are supposed to fulfil two main functions: price currencies at their fair value so that people have valid information and can make appropriate IB decisions, and provide liquidity to support international trade and investment. The problem is that neither fixed nor floating currency regimes fulfil these missions perfectly. Fixed regimes can be criticised, for instance, because of the tendency of central banks and/or politicians to price currencies wrongly by allowing non-currency-related considerations to affect their valuations. If national authorities want their economy to export its way out of a slump, for example, they might be tempted to price its currency at an artificially low rate. This might increase goods' price competitiveness over the short run, but it also stokes inflationary pressures due to the greater quantity of local currency needed to pay for incompressible imports. In essence, the economy is hiding behind a weak currency to avoid the hard work of achieving productivity gains. Indeed, many countries have been criticised over the years for this exact behaviour, one example being the United States that has vacillated between its mid-2000s policy of "benign-neglect" and the push at other times to weaken the dollar, exemplified in former President Trump's mercantilist pressure on the Federal Reserve Bank to keep exchange rates low (Szalay 2019). Conversely, if a government's priority is to cut inflation by reducing import costs – as Argentina did in the 1990s – largely under pressure from the IMF – the authorities will try to overvalue their currency. The problem then is that consumers' temporarily inflated purchasing power tempts them to go on a shopping spree for foreign goods, resulting in high trade deficits. These and other mistakes have sustained deregulation advocates in their conviction that politicians should stay out of the FX markets.

Yet markets driven by private interests alone are just as likely to price currencies wrongly. Traders are often motivated by short-term psychological factors like "irrational exuberance" (over-enthusiasm) or "herd mentality" (the tendency of crowds of investors to imitate one another). Such behaviours, which introduce a skew into currency pricing mechanisms, are aggravated by the disproportionate power wielded by just a few leading financial institutions. In 2020, for instance, the world's six leading currency traders (in order, JP Morgan, Union Bank of Switzerland, XTX Markets, Deutsche Bank, Citibank and HSBC) accounted for more than 40 percent of total FX market turnover. Centralising market power on this scale means that the trading decisions of a few very big players will have a disproportionate effect on market outcomes. The end result is that currencies often spend long periods of time trading at prices that do not reflect the true economic situation of the countries they represent. The inevitable corrections are painful for the country affected when it lacks the resources to protect itself from the volatility that inevitably results from the readjustment process; and for MNEs, whose vision of goods and services' cross-border value will be blurred. It bears repeating that non-financial interests only account for 2–3 percent of the total volumes traded in the global FX markets (nominally more than $6.5 trillion a day in 2021). In other words, the FX markets are predominantly run by financial interests pursuing their own financial interest. This was clearly not the original intent behind their design.

Having said that, unfettered FX markets still have their supporters. Sometimes the rationale is the beneficial effect of attracting speculative interests to increase overall market liquidity, the logic being that the sheer volume of counterparts will reduce price volatility. Others find that the repeated currency crises of the 1990s actually had a healthy effect, forcing the countries involved to reform their financial systems and paving the way for renewed growth in the 2000s (Rowe 2007). The argument has also been made that occasional turmoil in the FX markets is a price worth paying for the advantages derived from greater access to foreign currency (Obstfeld 2005). This is a contentious notion, however, given that the parties benefitting from such situations may not be the same as the ones suffering from the associated disruption.

Along these lines, it is worth noting repeated efforts to reduce FX market volatility through a levy that has alternatively been called the Tobin Tax, the Robin Hood Tax and the Financial Transaction Tax (Laurent 2020). The proposal is both economically sensible and ethical. But it does have one problem, namely, that it would have to be implemented by all national governments with an interest in stabilising the FX market, if only because any financial centre levying the tax without its rivals doing the same would necessarily lose market share. Given the very low probability that all politicians will agree this measure, the only other possibility is to have it implemented universally by a centralised global financial market authority. Of course, no such body exists today. The question is whether it ever will!

Attitudes and alternatives

Global governance is clearly a necessity in a world where isolated national policy-making has been proven, at various points in human history, to have disastrous effects. The problem is the ongoing shift in different countries' level of support for these mechanisms of international cooperation. On occasion, they will be contested by a country that has temporarily fallen prey to a bout of economic nationalism, incentivising politicians to sublimate global governance's very real advantages. At other times, it is the imperfect structures of global governance that spark the criticism. The challenge for IB practitioners is to distinguish between the two kinds of criticism, if only because one is much more sustainable (and indeed, valid) than the other.

Chapter summary

Much of the framework within which IB takes place is determined by governance bodies operating outside of sovereign nations' control. The chapter explored the three main categories involved, starting with regional economic groups (REGs) that try to replicate, internationally, some of the functions that national governments perform domestically. This was followed by a section on single-purpose intergovernmental organisations (IGOs), led first and foremost by the three Bretton Woods institutions that have been so important in determining today's IB framework, particularly the WTO, whose political approach has both many supporters and detractors worldwide. The final section debated financial markets' current lack of global governance – a topic that will be further explored in Chapter 12 from the perspective of MNEs' associated FX and funding operations.

Case study 4.3: Running with the renminbi

Fig 4.4
One contemporary debate regarding the governance of international finance is whether the Chinese renminbi might one day replace the US dollar as the world's reserve currency.

Many, if not most, of the consensus rules in the global currency markets are unwritten. That the Swiss franc is deemed a "safe haven" (alongside gold) for parking funds in times of crisis, that the Swedish kroner is so closely correlated to the euro, that the Thai baht is so closely correlated to the Japanese yen – none of these realities is dictated by official authorities anywhere. Instead, they reflect value assessments by private interests, grounded in their analyses and expectations

The same can be said about the US dollar's status as the global reserve currency. Somewhere around 70 percent of all central bank reserves worldwide are constituted in dollars. In reality, however, this reflects little more than a long-standing view of the US Treasury as the "lender of the last resort", i.e. as the authority to whom creditors can ultimately turn should all other sources of liquidity dry up in times of crisis. Of course, having the dollar as the world's reserve currency is also very advantageous to USA, because it ensures that there will always be extra demand for dollars even if the country runs up large trade and/or budget deficits, as it has done for many years now.

It is this advantage and the global financial imbalances which it creates – a state of affairs deemed suboptimal by many economists – that have increasingly raised questions in recent years about how long the dollar should retain its privileged status. After all, nothing predestines any currency to reign supreme forever, as witnessed by the decline of the British pound, which one century ago had performed a function similar to the one the dollar does today. The issue has become all the more poignant given the rising economic power of China, whose manufacturing exports have translated into huge foreign exchange reserves – a good percentage of which are invested in US Treasuries, helping to keep the latter market afloat but also creating a dependency relationship since without this external funding, American taxpayers would have to assume greater responsibility for their own national debt.

In the short run, the main problem for the renminbi is the Beijing government's tight control over its national currency's FX market movements. There has been some loosening in recent years, with the renminbi already being allowed to assume an expanded role in Asian regional trading (Bhat 2013). Also, the mechanical effect of China permitting greater FDI in the country, including by foreign financial institutions, is likely to change market participants' attitudes towards the renminbi. Indeed, some analysts are predicting that it will become the world's third largest reserve currency within a decade (Cheng 2020), with others expecting it to ultimately displace the dollar at some point later in the century. Along these lines, it is worth noting some observers' comments that "Donald Trump's presidency and his toxic politics have taken a toll on the world's trust in America [and] diminished trust in some quarters about the dollar's stability as the global reserve currency", with one consequence being rising consideration of cryptocurrencies such as bitcoin (alongside the renminbi but also the euro) as consensus future stores of value (Foroohar 2021). The deeper lesson here is that modes of governance are never entirely dissociated from modes of government.

One leading factor in the way that global reserve currency arrangements will play out in the future is the question of whether US authorities will want to maintain the status quo, and if they have the power to do this. The lack of any global governance arrangements in the FX markets means that events are likely to unfold organically, dictated by incremental market behaviour rather than by any purposeful policy-making. Whether that is a better way of affecting this key pillar of IB remains to be seen.

Case study questions

1. In the absence of global coordination, on what basis should foreign exchange rates be determined?
2. In the absence of global coordination, on what basis should central banks determine which currencies to use as value reserves?
3. What are the arguments for and against a centralised coordination of the global currency markets?

Chapter discussion questions

1   Why might cause an intergovernmental organisation's mission to change over time?
2   Has regionalisation caused national economic policies to converge?
3   What are the costs and benefits of having a more or less integrated regional economic group?
4   Why might a national government hand power over to an IGO like the WTO?
5   How likely is it that a global governance regime be established for the world's currency and capital markets within the foreseeable future?

References

Bhat, T. (September 2013). "Renminbi: Towards an international reserve currency", *India Quarterly*, Volume 69, Issue 3, pp. 249–263.

Bruno, R. et al. (November 2017). "Economic integration, foreign investment and international trade: The effects of membership of the European Union", *Centre for Economic Performance*, Discussion Paper Number 1518.

Cheng, E. (4 September 2020). "Chinese renminbi could become the world's third largest currency in 10 years, Morgan Stanley predicts", accessed 14 November 2020 at https://www.cnbc.com/

Drezner, D. (2007). "The new world order", accessed 13 February 2020 at https://www.foreignaffairs.com/

Economist (28 April 2011). "Dead man talking", *The Economist*.

Edwards, S., and Levy Yeyati, E. (November 2005). "Flexible exchange rates as shock absorbers", *European Economic Review*, Volume 49, Issue 8, pp. 2079–2105.

Engelen, E. et al. (2011). *After the Great Complacence: Financial Crisis and the Politics of Reform*, Oxford: Oxford University Press.

European Commission (May 2015). "European citizenship", *Standard Eurobarometer*, Number 83, accessed 29 July 2021 at https://data.europa.eu/

Fischer, S. (June 2001). "Exchange rate regimes: Is the bipolar view correct", *IMF Finance and Development*, Volume 38, Issue 2, pp. 3–24.

Foroohar, R. (15 February 2021). "Bitcoin's rise reflects America's decline", *Financial Times*.

Gomel, G. (2002). "Crisis prevention and the role of IMF conditionality", in M. Fratianni et al. (eds.). *Governing Global Finance: New Challenges, G7 and IMF Contributions*. Aldershot: Ashgate, accessed 29 July 2021 at http://www.g8.utoronto.ca/

Ghosh, A. (June 2008). "Turning currencies around", *IMF Finance and Development*, Volume 45, Issue 2.

Gurria, A. (23 January 2019). "What we need is more (and better) multilateralism, not less", accessed 11 November 2020 at https://www.weforum.org/

Ikhide, S. (February 2004). "Reforming the international financial system for effective aid delivery", *World Economy*, Volume 27, Issue 2, pp. 127–152.

Irwin, D. (2020). *Free Trade Under Fire*, 5th edition, Princeton, NJ: Princeton University Press.

Jeong, H. et al. (November 2018). "Games theory-based analysis of decision making for coastal adaptation under multilateral participation", *Journal of Management in Engineering*, Volume 34, Issue 6, accessed 29 July 2021 at https://ascelibrary.org/doi

Kelly, D., and Grant, W. (2005). *The Politics of International Trade in the Twenty-First Century: Actors, Issues and Regional Dynamics*, Basingstoke: Palgrave Macmillan.

Laurent, L. (27 July 2020). "The EU's Tobin tax is being resurrected", accessed 14 November 2020 at https://www.bloomberg.com/

Mathews, R. (8 October 2005). "Free trade and an emerging revolutionary planet", accessed 14 December 2007 at www.vivelecanada.ca

Mazlish, B., and Morss, E. (2005). "A global elite?", in A. Chandler and B. Mazlish (eds.). *Leviathans: Multinational Corporations and the New Global History*, Cambridge: Cambridge University Press.

Meyer, N. (August 2018). "EU break-up? Mapping plausible pathways into alternative futures", *LSE 'Europe in Question' Discussion Paper Series*, Issue 136.

Mishra, B., and Jena, P. (7 January 2019). "Bilateral FDI flows in four major Asian economies; A gravity model analysis", *Journal of Economic Studies*, Volume 46, Issue 1, pp. 71–89.

Obstfeld, M. (August 2005). "Reflections upon re-reading 'The Capital Myth'", accessed 11 June 2008 at http://elsa.berkeley.edu/

Rowe, J. (June 2007). "Countries take stock of financial soundness exercise", *IMF Survey*, Volume 36, Issue 10, accessed 29 July 2021 at https://www.elibrary.imf.org/

Singer, P. (2004). *One World: The Ethics of Globalisation*, London: Yale University Press.

Sinn, H.W. (2012). *Casino Capitalism; How the Financial Crisis Came about and What Needs to be Done Now*, Oxford: Oxford University Press.

Sitkin, A. (2019). *Absolute Essentials of Green Business*, Abingdon: Routledge.

Stiglitz, J. (2004). "The promise of global institutions", in D. Held and A. McGrew (eds.). *The Global Transformations Reader: An Introduction to the Globalisation Debate*. Cambridge: Polity Press, accessed 29 July 2021 at https://sites.middlebury.edu/

Szalay, E. (17 July 2019). "Currency intervention: How would the US do it, and would it work", *Financial Times*.

UNECA (2016). "Regional integration, innovation and competitiveness: A theoretical framework and empirical highlights", accessed 11 November 2020 at https://www.uneca.org/

Wilkinson, R. (2006). *The WTO: Crisis and the Governance of Global Trade*, Abingdon: Routledge.

PART II

International
mindsets and values

CHAPTER 5

Culture in international business

Introduction

By definition, working across borders means interacting with individuals from different countries, and therefore with cultures. By itself, this justifies the important role that culture has always played in international business (IB) studies. Analysis in this area has traditionally looked at the components of cultural identity, which largely tend to be grasped on a national scale. The chapter's first section will also adopt this approach while adding a discussion about its main weakness, namely, the assumption that it is possible to generalise about counterparts' personal culture based on their background. This is, however, risky for two reasons: all humans have at least some agency in specifying how they want to identify; and intersectionality variations have strong effects on people's ultimate sense of who they are or want to be.

The second section offers a more micro-level analysis of how cultural divergence both reflects and affects life in a multinational enterprise (MNE) before concluding with a study of the actions that both companies and individuals might take to overcome any hurdles they encounter in this domain. Given the consensus view that globalisation has sparked a great deal of cultural convergence, some

Intersectionality – Recognition of the different ways in which social categories like gender, race or socio-economic class combine for different people.

Fig 5.1
Cultural interfaces play out at many levels in an international business environment.

DOI: 10.4324/9781003159056-7

IB analysts have recently taken to wondering whether culture matters as much as it once did. That does not seem the right way to frame the question, however. Technology and travel may have increased cultures' exposure to one another (thereby revealing more commonalities than past generations might have suspected), but this does not mean that everyone in the world is the same in every respect. It simply signifies that modern businesspersons are less surprised by the cultural differences they encounter – and hopefully have a greater tendency to cherish them.

LEARNING OBJECTIVES

After reading this chapter, you will be able to:

- recognise the components of culture per se
- assess the components of culture at the different levels where they affect IB practitioners
- compare the strength of cultural convergence trends against the sources of divergence
- analyse companies and individuals' motivations when dealing with cultural challenges
- identify intrapersonal techniques that can be used to reduce cultural barriers

Case study 5.1: Micky grows a moustache

Until recently, if an American of a certain age had been asked which company represented the most wholesome and clean-cut version of their home country culture, Disney Corporation would have come at the top of the list. For many, the "Magic Kingdom" embodies old-fashioned US values, a tidy and unrebellious brand image reflecting the worldviews of its conservative founder, Walt Disney, who was famous for his battles against anything resembling a counterculture. Examples include the way Disney would inaccurately disparage employee trade unions as communist (Harris 2006), or prohibit his amusement parks' "cast members" from adopting the hirsute "beatnik" look adopted by growing numbers of American youth from the 1950s onwards (Tortugapirate 2015). In a similar vein and to preserve this pristine image of American life, Disney parks originally sold no alcohol. The end effect was that most of the paying public would associate Disney's product offer with a very specific mindset, and any criticism, within the USA at least, would be largely muted due to the company's great commercial success.

In 1983, 28 years after the original Disneyland had opened doors in Anaheim (California), the company's first overseas park began

Fig 5.2
Different societies
respond differently to
Disney's very specific
corporate culture.

operations in Japan. Reproducing almost all of the principles guiding its US parks – including a prescribed look for employees and the prohibition of alcohol – Tokyo Disneyland was successful from the outset and gave the company confidence that it could succeed with further international expansion in a similar vein, with Europe coming next on the list. After a long process, it was decided that the Paris region's geographic centrality justified building a park there. In 1992, Euro Disney opened up in Marne-La-Vallée, budgeting for an expected 60,000 visitors.

The actual number at first was closer to 25,000, a disappointment serving as a prelude to years of volatile earnings and other challenges for Disney in France. Problems often reflected a conflict between Disney's strong corporate culture and France's own strong cultural identity. Even before the park opened, voices in the French press began decrying American "cultural imperialism", accusing the company of selling back to

Europeans sanitised versions of their own legends. French society has always been proud of its rich folklore and many citizens viewed Disney's attachment to foreign lifestyles – including initial plans to prohibit on-site sales of wine, a mainstay in French cuisine – as an unwanted encroachment.

Another problem was labour relations. It was more or less unheard of in France for employees to be forced to adopt the kind of conservative dress code that Disney Corporation required (no facial or long hair for men, no leather skirts or high heels for women). Indeed, one ex-park official was actually fined in 1995 for inserting such restrictions into employment contracts instead of negotiating them first with local stakeholders. Euro Disney's early relations with French labour unions were generally fraught, culminating in both protests against restrictions on employees' personal freedoms and strikes against wage settlements.

As the years passed – and partially in response to the problems in France – Disney's corporate culture began to evolve. Alcohol started being served at Euro Disney as early as 1993. In 2000, male staff members could grow a moustache, and in 2012 neat beards were finally allowed. Other branches of the Disney group would move on from a strict adherence to children's products to more adult-oriented themes. It is, however, unclear if the developments were due to generational changes in Disney's executive teams or reflected the company's response to the cultural conflicts it had suffered. The lesson in both instances is clear, however. Corporate cultures – like MNEs themselves – are living entities that cannot help but evolve over time.

Case study questions

1. Why did Disney decide to export its domestic culture abroad?
2. What discussions will Disney executives have had before deciding to change aspects of the culture in their overseas amusement parks?

Section I. Components of culture

Culture has been conceptualised in many excellent (albeit contrasting) ways (Rothman 2014), to such an extent that there is no need to spend much time here reviewing its definitions in any great detail. Suffice it to say that all these characterisations refer to the particular worldviews, social behaviours and customs associated with a given population – the general idea being that groups of people living together can be expected over time to develop common behavioural traits and intellectual orientations that eventually become one of their key identifiers and distinguish them from other groups (Kroeber and Kluckholn 1952).

There is of course a great deal of truth in this kind of stereotyping, if only because of the centripetal socialisation processes that cause newcomers to a social group (infants joining a family and later adult society; new recruits joining a company) to mimic its modus operandi. This provides group members with shared references that help them to interact more harmoniously (Vietze 2019). It is an analysis where culture takes shape precisely because it facilitates understanding between the people sharing that culture – with very success of those relationships being the outcome that keeps the culture alive.

Stereotyping can be useful since it makes it easier to form a quick opinion about a counterpart's expected cultural behaviour. It also contains a serious flaw, however. The very idea of a society possessing a common culture relies on the generalisation that because the individuals in question all come from a certain location, speak a certain language, share a certain religion and so forth, they can then be expected to possess more or less similar worldviews, ideas and customs. This is wrong for several reasons, first and foremost being that it neglects free will, embodied in many individuals' desire to follow a path different from the one laid out for them in their society of origin. On top of this, modern telecommunications have facilitated multiculturalism, helping people gain exposure to (or at least partially identify with) cultures different from their original one (Vora et al. 2018). If they find these foreign cultures attractive and decide to adopt some of their aspects, the syncretisation they create (a hybrid of the foreign and original culture) can translate into a new personalised culture whose dosage will be specific to each individual (Stewart 1999). The argument here is that people also belong to a culture because they think they do and because they have chosen to embrace its "paradigm of analysis" (Omoniyi and Fishman 2006).

Lastly, whereas standard studies of culture in IB tend to focus on aspects such as language and religion (as will be done below), there are countless other aspects of human existence that can have just as strong an effect on a person's cultural self-identification. The list is long but necessarily includes elements as diverse as socioeconomic class, ethnicity, political allegiance and/or "politics of citizenship" (Hall and Held 1989), gender, sexual orientation, profession, hobbies – and even the brands or football teams that a person likes. In addition to these identifiers, there are the stronger opinions that also form part of an individual's culture, including the way they feel about wealth, consumption, ostentation, technology and modernity. As demonstrated in Figure 5.3, it is the sum total of all these subcultural identities that makes a person who s/he is – the point also being that many individuals belong to a culture because they have chosen to adopt it and not because it has adopted them. This has implications for how IB practitioners might navigate the cultural minefields they will encounter throughout their careers (see Section 2 below).

Stereotyping – General expectation that a particular entity – like a national culture – will perform in a specific manner.

Socialisation – Process by means of which individuals learn to behave and form opinions in a manner acceptable to the social group they are joining.

Modus operandi – Methods customarily applied by individuals or institutions when navigating, respectively, personal or professional situations.

Syncretisation – Amalgamation of heterogeneous elements from different sources to form a personalised mixture (often of culture-related beliefs).

Macro-cultural dimensions

The first level of generalisation in culture studies often relates to macro-cultural elements such as language and religion. The general idea here is that customs and values – as well as other manifestations of culture – will often be at least partially framed by these factors.

This is a questionable assumption, however, as demonstrated in the following parable. Imagine three people: an Aboriginal woman living in Australia's Outback, a female Australian international banker living in Sydney and a male French international banker living in Paris. Say on top of this that the two Australian women are Christian and the Frenchman is an atheist. The question becomes which pair within this trio is most likely to enjoy the greatest cultural affinity? The likely answer here is the two international bankers. Yet think what this means: despite the Australians coming from the same country, speaking the same language and having the same religion and gender, they can be reasonably expected to have fewer cultural similarities than a woman in Sydney and a man in Paris, in large part because of the strength of the culture that is inherent to their profession (and the socio-economic status and background with which it is associated). The lesson here is when studying cultural classifications, it is crucial to never view the impact of each element in isolation but instead as part of a puzzle comprised of many pieces that can fit together in varying ways.

Cultural affinity – Where individuals from different cultural subgroups possess harmonious values and worldviews, notwithstanding their other differences.

Language

Several of the world's most widely used languages are spoken by people coming from different countries, explaining why this element is more of a macro-cultural phenomenon rather than a national one. It is an important distinction given the possibility that people speaking one and the same language may experience cultural conflicts with fellow language speakers who are foreign to them – Mexicans, Argentines and Spaniards all speak mutually understandable versions of the same language, but it would be wrong to assume that they therefore share the exact same culture. Having said that, the opposite holds as well, since sharing a native tongue can also make it easier for people from different countries to bridge cultural gaps. The common frame of reference enjoyed by different nationals from the same language group may not be absolute, but it is not insignificant.

There has been a great deal of academic research over the years (Whorf 1940; Gelman and Roberts 2017) speaking to the very real influence that language has on people's sense of self and understanding of the world, hence on their culture. Speaking a language means not only being exposed to its semiotic sense-making but also to its literary traditions (and the philosophical values associated with them); its artwork and music; and even (and maybe above all) its popular culture.

Otherwise, in intercultural situations where two businesspersons with different native tongues meet, the language in which they choose to converse will partially frame each side's cultural expectations of the other. Hence, the recurring debate in IB is whether it is better to try and speak a counterpart's language – to seem less foreign and make the other person feel more comfortable – or one's own language to gain an upper hand in the manipulation of nuances and undertones.

There is a similar debate in numerous MNEs regarding the lingua franca that should be used for exchanges between colleagues from different language groups. For many decades now, much of the IB world has expected English to be the language of interaction, both within MNEs and externally, reflecting the historic hegemony first of the UK and later of the USA. Whereas there are fewer than 450 million people whose native language is English, estimates as to the total number of persons speaking the language run as high as 1.5 billion – a factor of more than three that should be compared with the two languages featuring the greatest number of native speakers (Mandarin Chinese and Spanish, representing, respectively, around 900 million and 500 million persons) but where the total number of speakers is less than 30 percent higher. It is by comparing the multiples between the total and native number of speakers that the linguistic hegemony of English (and to a lesser extent, of French) can be measured.

On the one hand, widespread acceptance of a dominant language has clearly facilitated IB by standardising global communications. On the other, it has also caused resentment in some corners, with voices expressing dismay at the degree to which local nationals are sometimes forced to work in a language that is foreign to them. This includes the strangeness of individuals not coming from an English language background being forced to speak English to fellow nationals because the company they work for has decided that this must be the lingua franca for internal communications – one example being the 2010 decision by Rakuten, Japan's largest online marketplace, to make English the lingua franca, even as Japanese personnel-dominated its Tokyo headquarters (Neeley 2012). To counter the resentment caused by perceptions of

Semiotic – Relating to the production of meaning.

Lingua franca – Common language commonly used by people from different linguistic backgrounds.

linguistic imperialism (Phillipson 1992), some MNEs prefer to hire **polyglots**, particularly for cross-border commercial functions, since professionals with linguistic capabilities are more likely to seem less foreign to foreign counterparts – always an advantage in IB.

Language is not the only core cultural element that cannot be accurately analysed in purely national terms. The same applies to other variables such as social class, exemplified inter alia by a so-called "global elite" (Unruh and Cabrera 2013) whose cultural identities are likely to be better defined by status than by their culture of origin; or even "brand tribes" (Cova 2007), that is, consumers who congregate internationally because they all identify with the values represented by a particular company and/or its products. The difficulty in attributing a cultural category to these and other self-aware and self-defining groupings is the absence of data regarding their numbers. The more formalised nature of religion, on the other hand, means that the influences exercised by this next cultural dimension can be analysed in somewhat greater depth.

Religion

As with language, it would be wrong to assume that just because someone belongs to a religion, s/he will necessarily possess the same values and habits as fellow members. Different branches of one and the same religion may have radically different interpretations of the philosophies and perspectives taught through that particular belief system – not to mention the fact that many atheists share cultural values and habits with believers, due to factors other than religion. At the same time, some common framework of reference probably does exist for almost everyone with a given religion background (Klingenberg and Sjo 2019), meaning that this factor has at least a modicum of intercultural significance. That is particularly true given that many religions overlap with specific parts of the world, so that the values they express often cross over into regional or national values. Inter alia, there is Buddhism (6.9 percent of the 2015 world population), which largely dominates in East Asia and Japan; Hinduism (15.1 percent), a product of India; Islam (24.1 percent), spreading across North Africa through the Middle East to South Asia and Indonesia/Malaysia; Judaism (0.2 percent) divided between Israel and a diaspora population mainly found in Western Europe and North America; and Christianity (31.2 percent), being the majority religion in Europe, the Americas, Oceania and parts of sub-Saharan Africa. Note that these percentages date from a 2015 Pew Research Centre and are bound to change over time to reflect different religions' comparatively higher or lower birth rates. Whether this is a cultural issue or more a question of socioeconomic development is not entirely clear, however.

Having said that, there are other areas where religion clearly affects social and personal culture. These range from values (like the importance of wealth; present vs. future focus; tolerance for non-conformity; and/or reaction to inequality) to personal customs (including **work-life balance**, diet and charity). Navigating religion-based cultural variations is a prime skill for IB practitioners, who will often try over the course of their careers to develop coping strategies in this area. Awareness of a foreign counterpart's religion may reflect the fact that the practitioner shares the same background or can (and/or is willing to) behave in a way that lends itself to good relations. From simply knowing which foreign counterpart should be wished a Happy Vaisakha, Diwali, Eid, Hanukah or Christmas – to being offered which kind of food or drink – religious sensitivity is yet another tool that MNEs and their representatives do well to master. The example of McDonald's having to apologise to its Indian customers in 2001 for initially cooking the French fries it sells in beef fat – given the cow's holy status for that country's majority Hindu religion – stands as a precautionary tale.

National cultural analyses

Having warned against overestimating nationality's impact on culture, it remains that many useful IB culture constructs have been built around people's country of origin. It is in a national setting that most socialisation takes place, ranging from people's formal and informal education to their social relationships and even the information environment that colours the way they process news (Steinwachs 1999). Things may be different for the few *apatride* (stateless) citizens of the world who move incessantly from one country to another. But for the vast majority of humanity, national culture still counts at least somewhat – and often a great deal.

Geert Hofstede

Probably the most successful scholar to theorise – and one of the few to quantify – the different parameters of national culture was the Dutchman Geert Hofstede, who famously worked from 1967 to 1973

Fig 5.4
The Netherlands have been home to some of IB's leading culture analysts.

interviewing IBM staff members employed in different offices worldwide, back at a time when the company had a policy of hiring only local nationals. Hofstede (2010) devised four parameters that he then used to create a scale specifying international cultural variations. These were supplemented in later years by two new categories. All are worth studying in detail.

Power distance (PDI)

Hofstede's first dimension refers to the way that staff view senior management, with the main distinction being between employees who accept an imbalance of power and those who resent or ignore it. This affects the workplace atmosphere in several ways, including management's ability to command obedience, expectations that subordinates will show personal initiative and the ease with which information is volunteered or received.

On the Hofstede scale, countries like Malaysia, Guatemala, Panama and the Philippines (followed closely by Russia, Mexico, the Arab countries and China) score very high on power distance, translating the hierarchical nature of interrelationships within these cultures. The lowest power distance scores (from 11 to 22 on a scale of 100) are for Austria, Israel, Denmark and New Zealand, followed by the other Scandinavian countries. At one level, power distance seems to correlate with the Global North/South divide.

Uncertainty avoidance (UAI)

This dimension distinguishes between risk-averse individuals daunted by unknown situations that they will only address once fairly rigid procedures have been established, versus their more adventurous, spontaneous and even impulsive opposites who tend to jump straight into the water without first dipping in a toe. MNE life can be affected in several ways, often relating to a desire for (or rejection of) the kind of administrative rules that can serve both as a security blanket and as a straitjacket.

There is some correlation between power distance and uncertainty avoidance, since some people will be happy to allocate greater authority to management specifically because that relieves them of the uncertainty of having to make decisions themselves. Examples include Russia, with an extremely high score for both dimensions; some (but not all) Latin American countries like Brazil, which scores 69/100 on power distance and 76/100 on uncertainty avoidance; and France, scoring 68 on power distance and a very high 86/100 on uncertainty avoidance, reflecting the Cartesian traditions of a culture where analysis often focuses more on the framing of a topic than on the topic itself. Conversely and probably for the same but diametrically opposed reasons, Scandinavia tends to score low in both of these dimensions. These are cultures where workers neither accord excessive power to their bosses nor require set rules before showing initiative. Note otherwise the interesting cases of Japan and

Germany, which score, respectively, 92 and 65 on uncertainty avoidance but only 54 and 35 on power distance, indicating that in these two cultures, the responsibility for creating structures (particularly high in Japan) is not passed on to a hierarchical superior but instead something that individuals tend to internalise. Lastly, it is also worth noting that some cultures, especially in the English-speaking countries, score in the middle on both cultures – almost as if an international cultural median actually exists.

Individualism (IDV)

This dimension sits at one end of a spectrum, with collectivism at the other. Hofstede's idea here was that in certain national business cultures, practitioners' main focus will be on how their actions benefit themselves (possibly together with their closest family members), contrasting with more collectivistic individuals' cultural disposition towards creating and supporting a tightly knit social group – including the companies for which they work – whose members can be reasonably expected to look out for one another. Part of this construct is teamwork, a quality that is all the more poignant in IB because the fragmentation and geographic dispersion characterising the world's largest companies can make it hard for employees to feel solidarity with the whole of their MNE. In such large organisations, personal loyalty may extend no further than the subsidiary where an individual is employed; possibly no further than the actual strategic business unit (SBU) – defined by function, product and geography (see Chapter 9) – to which they have been assigned; and possibly no further than their own self-interest, if they are made to feel mere cogs in a machine.

Strategic business unit (SBU) – Identifiable entity within a corporation, large enough to plan strategy and budget resources on its own.

International scores for Hofstede's individualism-collectivism spectrum tend to be less extreme than for his other dimensions. One exception is the United States, which scores a whopping 91/100, reflecting the country's long-standing culture of "rugged individualism". The rest of the English-speaking world also score relatively highly for this dimension. The opposite applies in China but also in Africa-West, where strong group traditions translate into individualism scores of only 20/100. There are clear implications for IB dealings involving US, British or Australian businesspersons as opposed to their Chinese or West Africans counterparts. Appeals to self-interest are more likely to succeed with the former than with the latter.

Masculinity-femininity (MAS)

No one is perfect and Hofstede's choice of words to describe this next dimension probably errs on the side of gender-stereotyping. But as always, his cultural insights are invaluable, proposing here a useful dimension that distinguishes between people whose modus operandi is more assertive and geared towards quantifiable material rewards versus others who tend to behave more cooperatively and prioritise qualitative, affective gratification. A parameter that has sometimes (and probably more appropriately) been referred to as the contrast between "tough vs. tender" cultures, scores here vary widely, ranging from 5/100 in Sweden to 95/100 in Japan. Having said that, many countries are grouped in the mid-range, with relatively few regional patterns appearing, except Scandinavia's very low scores.

It could be interesting to compare the masculinity versus femininity dimension with individualism-collectivism, if only because of the individualistic nature of a "tough" culture's emphasis on personal recognition and the fit between collectivism and a "tender" culture's focus on cooperation. The problem is that once again there is no apparent pattern here, with the cultural pairing between some neighbouring countries seeing both achieve similar scores in relation to the two dimensions (Italy and Germany, for instance), and other pairings (like South Korea and China) seeing them resemble one another as regards one of the two dimensions but not the other. This is one of many lessons that can be drawn from Hofstede's legacy, namely, the inability to generalise about international cultural affinity – just because countries have certain characteristics in common does not mean that they cannot also differ greatly in other ways.

Cultural pairing – Specific dynamic between two cultures.

Long-term orientation (LTO)

In later years, Hofstede added two dimensions to his original model. The first was long-term orientation, which he contrasted with a short-term "normative" approach. Again, the name given to this construct is suboptimal since it intimates a willingness to renounce short-term returns in exchange for long-term rewards, whereas what Hofstede was really talking about here is the difference between an innately and even irrationally conservative culture married to existing paradigms and other cultures that respond more pragmatically to the requirements of a given situation, to the point of being willing to countenance a great deal of disruption. The dimension has some very interesting IB applications in the sense that encounters between practitioners with very different orientations in this respect can often go bad, with the radical innovations that one side is proposing as a logical response to given circumstances running up against the other side's strict adherence to tried and tested approaches (or products). Indeed, it is this kind of cultural disconnect that has led to the break-up of many international partnerships (see Chapter 8).

Some national long-term orientation scores correspond to anecdotal stereotypes, with Germans' famously pragmatic adaptation to a situation's objective realities (*Sachlichkeit*) earning them a very high score of 83/100. Just as noteworthy is Asian cultures' famously multigenerational focus, also earning China and Japan high scores for this dimension. Other outcomes are more surprising, with the United States, so often reputed to be a haven for self-reinvention, coming in at a paltry 26/100. It is an anomaly that raises questions about the validity of this one construct, or else of the way cultures (American or others) are commonly represented.

Anecdotal – Conversational, often based on stereotyping. The opposite of scientifically demonstrated.

Table 5.1
Sample of national Hofstede cultural dimensions scores (Hofstede 2010)

	PDI	IDV	MAS	UAI	LTO	IND
Australia	38	90	61	51	21	71
Japan	54	46	95	92	88	42
China	80	20	66	30	87	24
India	77	48	56	40	51	26
Iran	58	41	43	59	14	40
Israel	13	54	47	81	38	N/A
Turkey	66	37	45	85	46	49
"Arab countries"	80	38	53	68	23	34
"Africa West"	77	20	46	54	9	78
"Africa East"	64	27	41	52	32	40
Russia	93	39	36	95	81	20
Sweden	31	71	5	29	53	78
Germany	35	67	66	65	83	40
Italy	50	76	70	75	61	30
France	68	71	43	86	63	48
UK	35	89	66	35	51	69
USA	40	91	62	46	26	68
Mexico	81	30	69	82	24	97
Brazil	69	38	49	76	44	59

Source: Quoted with permission www.geerthofstede.com. ©Geert Hofstede B.V.

Indulgence (IND)

Hofstede's latest and final dimension referred to the extent to which cultures generate social norms repressing an individual's rapid satisfaction of personal needs or, conversely, tolerating greater hedonism. There is a certain crossover here between pessimistic and optimistic worldviews. Russia and China score very low in this regard (20 and 24/100, respectively), unlike the self-indulgent British, Dutch, Swedish and especially Mexican cultures where individuals apparently have much greater freedom to go out and have fun.

Notwithstanding Hofstede's unassailable status as the seminal IB ethnologist, other scholars have also formulated useful insights in this area. Without pretending to be exhaustive, at least two more deserve to have their theories reproduced here, if only because they cover other national cultural attributes that Hofstede left more or less untouched.

Ethnologist – Student of cultural differences.

Fons Trompenaars

The typology that Trompenaars published in 1997 differed from his fellow Dutchman Hofstede because of its focus on cultural elements with specific relevance to intercultural communications. Trompenaars' dimensions are largely ascribed to national cultures, however, explaining why his work is also very useful for IB studies.

Trompenaars' seven dimensions of natural difference actually do feature one clear crossover with Hofstede's categorisations, even if some of his findings vary. His *individualism vs. communitarianism* parameter is clearly redolent of "Individualism vs. Collectivism", but whereas Hofstede gave Russia a low score on this scale, Trompenaars gave it a high one (along with most, if not all, of Eastern Europe), raising questions about the compatibility of the two Dutchmen's methodologies.

Trompenaars' identified six other dimensions as well:

Universalism vs. particularism. The question here is to what extent individuals coming from a given culture expect their modus operandi – generally the dominant one in their country of origin – to apply everywhere, as opposed to those who believe that the culture governing a given situation depends on the circumstances. Examples of countries in the former category include the USA and much of Western Europe. The opposite applies across East Asia, where few national cultures proclaim their universality.

Specific versus diffuse. With this dimension, Trompenaars refers to the way some people allow relationships to flow easily between their professional and private lives, whereas others keep the two separate. It also includes the formality characterising an intercultural interaction, materialising, for instance, in an employee's willingness to socialise out of work or introduce a business contact to family members. One contrast here is between the British habit of "popping down the pub" with colleagues after work versus French businesspersons' much stricter delineation between their professional and social contacts.

Achievement versus ascription. The distinction here is between cultures where an individual is judged on their material performance as opposed to others where what counts is status (background, title). In an IB context, this has implications for the formality with which people are treated, including in ways redolent of Hofstede's power distance construct. It is a dimension that can be seen, for instance, in the language employed in different business settings (calling people by their first name, use of the informal "you", etc.).

Internal versus external control. Cultures belonging to the former category tend to believe that solutions can be imposed on situations, unlike others that prioritise adaptiveness. One IB adjunct here is the fatalism with which practitioners from some cultures tolerate imperfection as opposed to the German precept that something must be done well or not at all (*Richtig oder gar nicht*).

Neutral versus emotional. This refers to a culture's greater or lesser tolerance for individuals' open expressions of feelings. Misunderstandings here can often lead to accusations of excessive or, conversely, insufficient politeness. In Southern Europe, for instance, long-standing business counterparts (whether colleagues or suppliers-customers) will often greet one another with a kiss. Such acts would not be well received in a Northern European or Asian context.

Sequential versus synchronic. Trompenaars' final dimension refers to time management, an aspect of culture that has frequent repercussions in IB. Conflict can arise between individuals keen to work to defined schedules and others for whom meeting deadlines (or punctuality) is less important. Indeed, there is anecdotal evidence that most contracts which MNEs award culture consultants relate not to commercial misunderstandings with foreign customers – as might be expected – but to intra-firm problems caused by different subsidiaries' time management styles.

Edwin Hall

The model that this pioneering American anthropologist produced in 1959 was, like Trompenaars, also specifically intended to address intercultural communications problems. Far less complete than the work done by his Dutch successors, Hall's basic distinction (1959) between *high-context* and *low-context* cultures still has great value for IB studies.

In high-context cultures (like Japan and France), people believe that their counterparts will share certain understandings even before an interaction begins, and therefore feel less of a need to specify any ground rules. The opposite applies in low-context cultures (like Germany and the USA) where there is little expectation of shared vision, requiring counterparts to spell things out explicitly.

Hall did not consider the two categories to be hermetic and envisioned a more or less fluid spectrum, with cultures fitting to a greater or lesser extent into one or the other dimension. He also noted that people's assumption of operating in a high- or low-context environment applied in national as well as business settings. In turn, this raises questions as to how successfully a MNE can develop value systems and customs fitting the different environments in which it operates and what its people can do to remedy those situations where the fit is less harmonious.

Case study 5.2: Achilleas heals

Note. This case study reproduces the real-life experiences recounted by an international business practitioner, with certain details altered to preserve anonymity.

With a power distance score of 93/100 on the Hofstede scale, the Russian culture is one of the most hierarchical in the world. When combined with centralising political traditions that had more often than not seen the national elite control the circulation of information, the end result has been a business culture frequently characterised by an almost unbreachable gap between executives and front-line operatives. Theoretically, the approach has the advantage of ensuring that everyone in a Russian company adheres to the same guidelines and knows what their precise role is. But it is also a major obstacle impeding

Fig 5.5
Centralised power is a key
facet of Russia's political
and economic culture.

the two-way vertical transmission of information that so many MNEs
consider essential to productivity, extrapolating from the proven success
of Japanese companies where frontline workers – who possess, after all,
the most direct knowledge of what is operationally effective and what is
not – form quality circles to discuss and share the continuous improvement
insights they garner from their daily routines. The trust that Japanese
colleagues place in one another up and down the corporate hierarchy
creates a very specific and positive culture in companies from this country.
In Russia, the atmosphere can be very different.

   This is one of the first things that Achilleas noticed when he first
came to Moscow in the 2000s to evaluate a local manufacturing
company that his British multinational was thinking about acquiring.
Achilleas, whose career in public affairs and communications had seen

him specialise in relations with the host country governments and institutions responsible for many of the more political aspects of his MNE's market entry ventures – starting with labour relations – was struck by what he witnessed at the Russian target company. A senior Russian executive double-locked his office door following their initial meeting – a secretiveness very much at odds with the open floor plan characterising Achilleas' office back in London, an arrangement intended to communicate to all staff members a sense of inclusiveness. Then, when Achilleas joined his hosts for an on-site lunch, he was again surprised to be served by waiters working in the executives' exclusive in-house restaurant – another custom diametrically opposed to his own company, where senior managers ate in the same refectory as workers.

Once Achilleas' MNE finalised the acquisition, he and his colleagues resolved to bring a more egalitarian culture to their new Russian subsidiary. This would involve installing direct communications between managers and workers, in the hope that open two-way communication would not only help disseminate the best practices that the new parent company was bringing in but also imbue Russian staff members with greater trust in management, motivating them to think more about what productivity gains they could mobilise at an operative level.

The new corporate culture was quickly and enthusiastically adopted by Russian staff members, especially since spontaneous process-improving ideas suggested by workers would now be rewarded with a new incentives scheme that Achilleas helped to devise. The response from Russian executives was mixed, however. Some got immediately on board with the new culture and several were subsequently promoted. Others felt that losing control over the management and dissemination of information undermined their position. They therefore tried to manipulate the process and, by so doing, ultimately talked themselves out of a job. In the end, the clash of two very different business approaches benefitted those who displayed enough **cultural flexibility** to accommodate change while penalising anyone set in the old ways. In cultural adaptation like in so many other areas of IB, practitioners are better served by agility than by entrenchment.

Cultural flexibility – Willingness and ability to apply the values and customs of a culture other than one's own.

Case study questions

1. Were Achilleas and his MNE right to try and change the culture in the Russian acquisition?
2. Should Achilleas and his MNE have expended energy teaching recalcitrant managers to resist the new culture, or was it right that they be let go?

Fig 5.6
Three cultural interfaces in
international business.

Section II. Managing cultural differences

Figure 5.6 offers a graphic depiction of how the main categories of
cultural interaction overlap in IB. At first glance, it may seem daunting
to have to contend with three potential sources of incompatibility. But
such negativity would be misplaced. It is much more constructive to
view the need to manage cultural difference as a positive opportunity.
After all, some MNEs and practitioners will be more adept than others
at successfully navigating whatever hurdles they face in this area, turning
their intercultural intelligence and adroitness into yet another exploitable
competitive advantage (Taylor 1994).

**Intercultural
intelligence/
adroitness** –
Understanding of/Skill
at negotiating complex
intercultural situations.

   The problems that arise at these interfaces tend to be managed at two
different levels: the corporate culture that a MNE develops, and through
individual IB practitioners' intrapersonal conduct. There is some overlap
between these levels, but they are largely independent phenomena and
should be studied as such.

Corporate culture

An organic corporate culture can spread across a MNE's different
entities if it successfully reproduces the dominant nationality's values
and customs (usually the original head office's home culture). There are
notable examples of this happening: the BBC replicating throughout
the world its neutral and dispassionate British approach to news-
gathering (as opposed to other more opinionated media companies);
Apple subsidiaries worldwide being staffed by individuals from different
backgrounds but all possessing a similar sense for technological
entrepreneurship; and Tata offices everywhere adhering to the company's
original value system, characterised by the combining of social values
with business objectives.

   In other MNEs, however, there may be less of a desire to disseminate
the original corporate culture and more of a willingness to allow new
cultures to flourish as the company accumulates international experience.
This dichotomy raises questions as to the mindsets of decision-makers
facing the intercultural issues that inevitably arise when they employ
an international workforce and/or interact with foreign suppliers,
customers or even governments. The confidence or, conversely, anxiety

that practitioners feel when broaching the topic of culture is actually an integral part of their own culture. As with so many other aspects of IB, how people deconstruct "the Other" says as much, if not more, about themselves as it does about the objects of their attention (Wood et al. 2010).

Cultural mindsets

In 1969, the American ethnologist Howard Perlmutter published what would become a seminal construct in considerations of IB practitioners' predisposition towards the way cultural differences might be handled. This came to be known as the EPG model, an acronym denoting "ethnocentrism", "polycentrism" and "geocentrism", and which would evolve ten years later into EPRG, with the new initial referring to "regiocentrism". These categorisations are worth studying in greater detail, if only to honour the rare success that Perlmutter enjoyed in developing a concept capable of migrating beyond purely academic circles to become a terminology widely used by IB practitioners themselves (Perlmutter 1969).

Ethnocentric. Individuals possessing this attitude start with the idea that their original culture constitutes ground zero for all other cultures, often because they want to think that it is ethically and/or operationally superior. That being the case, the assumption they make when encountering people from other cultures is that the latter should be the ones making the effort to adapt. Moreover, when this actually happens, the ethnocentric party will feel legitimised in his/her sense of superiority, triggering a hierarchical relationship that becomes difficult to unwind.

When generalised through the whole of a MNE, an ethnocentric mindset tends to spread outwards from global headquarters, especially when the office is located in the founders' country of origin and staffed with home country nationals, who then claim the right to specify the accepted culture for the whole of the group (and often spend a great deal of time and money travelling to impart their dictates to ostensibly subordinate colleagues working in foreign subsidiaries). One example of this was the habit of the First National Bank of Chicago (before it merged with Banc One) of sending American expatriates to assume executive positions in the London trading room despite the abundance of British talent available on-site, with the new managers sometimes demanding that local hires spend time back at the head office in order to acculturate to its particular way of doing business. In situations such as these, the foreign units are being asked to do little more than execute orders from senior management – a centralisation of power typifying certain top-down "push" multinational paradigms, which Chapter 9 analyses in further detail. It is also an approach that can have troublesome international marketing consequences if decision-makers refuse to accommodate foreign customers' diverse demands, insisting instead that the latter be content to purchase the MNE's standardised offer.

Expatriate – Employee seconded on a long-term or permanent basis to a MNE's foreign office.

Acculturate – Where a minority culture assimilates the values or customs of a new culture, usually a dominant one.

Polycentric. This attitude is basically the opposite of ethnocentrism and starts with the idea that it is the culture of the host country being visited by a MNE's representatives that should dictate the intercultural interaction, in line with the precept that "the customer is always right". The emphasis here is not only on respecting foreign cultures but also on adapting to them as far as possible, whether linguistically, operationally, behaviourally or otherwise. From a broader MNE organisational perspective, this tends to translate into head offices devolving strategic decision-making powers to national subsidiaries, manifesting in this way deference to field officers' much greater familiarity with consumer preferences in each of the markets where the company wants to do business. A classic example of this is the way that Nestlé's global headquarters in Vevey (Switzerland) proudly delegates many functional powers to group units worldwide. If pride and arrogance might be appropriate descriptions of an ethnocentric approach, the terms most readily associated with polycentrism must be humility and empathy.

Geocentric. This attitude is somewhere in between the two aforementioned extremes. It is easy to criticise ethnocentricity for its cultural insensitivity (and even apathy), but MNEs and practitioners who become extremely polycentric might also be making the very dangerous mistake of agreeing too readily to the costly adaptations that foreign customers often request – not to mention the fact that they are willingly playing on someone else's cultural terrain, putting themselves at a disadvantage during commercial negotiations. Moreover, whereas ethnocentricity can also be criticised for inflexibility, it helps a MNE to pursue one and same approach everywhere, which at the very least has the merit of clarity. Polycentric MNEs may be much more in tune with different international customers, but that can easily lead to a potpourri of divergent approaches that are not only almost impossible to coordinate (and might confuse co-workers) but can also dilute the company's sense of self.

It is because of the imperfections of the two extremes that Perlmutter formulated the geocentric stance, which seeks to avoid either a home or host country bias and advocates that each cross-border interaction be managed on an ad hoc basis. This is obviously an ideal akin to the Goldilocks solution: MNEs should not be excessively nor insufficiently warm to other cultures, just the right temperature. But geocentrism is actually very difficult to achieve, if only because many MNEs (and practitioners) prefer to either have clear principles guiding their intercultural interactions or, conversely, to not be bound by any rules at all. The geocentric hybrid is a laudable optimum – finding a compromise between being overly global or local – but it is hard to implement.

Regiocentric. The dimension that Perlmutter added later to his original model, regiocentrism, speaks to the need to find an intermediate level of international organisation, conceptualised here in the culture sphere in the same way as other IB theorists have done with respect to market entry (Chapter 8) and MNE structure (Chapter 9). It is the idea that some affinity may be felt with cultures that, although foreign, emanate from neighbouring countries and are therefore less distant from the original culture than if the interaction involved companies or persons from the other side of the world. It is a useful construct that speaks to different gradations of foreignness in people's assessment of international culture.

Notwithstanding Perlmutter's pre-eminence in his chosen area of analysis, other theorists have also made useful contributions categorising practitioners' general attitudes about which approaches are most appropriate when dealing with diverse international cultures. Probably the most famous construct except from the EPG model is the idea that MNEs might try to get employees to internalise a "global mindset" (Aharoni 1966; Govindarajan and Gupta 2001). It is a notion that was very popular in the late 1980s, during the early days of the modern era of globalisation. The idea here was that a MNE might want to foster its own cosmopolitan belief system, ultimately liberating staff members from their culture of origin and getting them to coalesce around the new borderless hybrid culture that management is trying to synthesise.

At first glance, the cultural neutrality that a global mindset can generate seems like a great idea, since the absence of any fixed home country bias should make it easier to accommodate all cultural variations. Having said that, it is not because people are no longer chained to a specific culture that they will necessarily experience a better fit with all foreigners – after all, the barriers preventing good intercultural understanding may have little to do with an individual's origins. Moreover, even as cultural divergence can be off-putting to some practitioners, others actually relish it: either because they have a favourable impression of the different cultures they encounter or, conversely, because they are disconcerted by fully-fledged cosmopolitanism.

Above all, it is very difficult for a MNE to prescribe and especially to impose a global mindset of its own design, explaining why the concept's popularity has waned over time. Many modern MNEs are so big that it is unrealistic to expect them to devise a set of compromise principles to which so many different employees coming from so many different countries will be willing or able to adhere. Instead, it is undoubtedly more realistic to expect a plurality of cultural identities (Backmann et al. 2020). Even taking China's largest MNEs out of the equation (because they work in domestic energy and infrastructure sectors and employ a relatively small percentage of non-Chinese), in 2020, companies like Walmart had approximately 2.2 million employees in 27 countries, Amazon approximately 1 million employees (up sharply from 800,000 pre-Covid) attached to 14 global sites, Volkswagen more than 650,000 employees in 153 countries and Toyota 360,000 employees in at least 170 countries. With such huge workforces and given how geographically (hence culturally) distant employees are from one another, the practical difficulties of getting everyone to align with whatever global

Cosmopolitan –
Sophisticated, worldly, comfortable in all different environments. The opposite of parochial.

values are being specified by the employer – and the wide variation in employee interpretations of whatever guidelines are being formalised – basically precludes any possibility of a unified group culture.

On the other hand, if the culture project is carried out at the smaller scale of the social subunits that form naturally within MNE groups, there is a much greater chance of success – first and foremost because fewer people are involved. Just because building a wider corporate culture presents formidable challenges does not mean there is nothing a MNE can do in this respect.

Culture at a departmental level

The reality for many, if not most, employees of the world's largest MNEs is not communing with all of their colleagues worldwide but instead the work life that they lead within the subsidiary (and actually, within the SBU) to which they have been assigned. In addition to the effects of proximity – employees are more likely to develop a common culture with colleagues they see year in year out on a daily basis – there is also the greater likelihood that people hired in the same office and indeed team will start out with greater cultural similarities than colleagues employed in distant foreign units. This is especially true if the MNE in question has a policy of hiring local nationals rather than importing expensive expatriates from abroad (the latter practice being much less widespread than it used to be due to the extra housing costs that it typically incurs).

Given this reality, the development of a corporate culture in many modern MNEs today involves coordinating the numerous mini corporate cultures that evolve more spontaneously in each of its SBUs. Harmonising these mini-cultures tends to be a big priority for senior management, with all MNEs nowadays regularly producing internal newsletters filled with stories and seminal myths communicating values that are meant to be spread as widely as possible across the group. Also noteworthy are the various social events that some MNEs organise to help colleagues from different SBUs discover commonalities (staff days away, 4th of July picnics in the USA, after-hours karaoke in Japan, etc.). On top of this is many companies' employment of human resource consultants charged with ironing out any intra-departmental culture clashes that may arise. A prime example of this is the way that Volkswagen headquarters in Wolfsburg (Germany) regularly brings in corporate culture psychologists to lead "conflict resolution" seminars. The goal is to nip any potential problems in the bud.

The task of consolidating SBU cultures is a complicated one for several reasons, however. Firstly, unlike the ethical codes of conduct that have proliferated across the MNE sector in recent years (see Chapter 6), many cultural manifestations tend to be more tacit in nature and are therefore harder to codify. It is true that some cultural identifiers are fairly explicit and therefore easier to apprehend, including the language that people speak, their religious habits and even their political affiliation or gendered conduct. Still, in general, there is little that can be done

Tacit – Subliminal and assumed but neither specified nor stated.

to build a culture around these disparate elements, except promoting mutual respect and tolerance among colleagues and/or towards external counterparts – a prescription that is as ethical (and even operational) as it is cultural. It should be remembered that despite the reality of cultural divergence, certain values like equality and helpfulness have just as much a chance of being shared between countries as within countries (Hanel et al. 2018).

A second obstacle impeding the harmonisation of disparate SBU subcultures is the fact that MNEs defined by their dispersed global value chains employ staff in a wide variety of functions, a factor of divergence that can be further complicated when many different sites are involved. One important and often neglected aspect of IB culture is the strong effect that function (production, marketing, finance, logistics, etc.) has on employees' professional culture. In general, downstream staff members tend to have a very different culture than their upstream colleagues. The former will know that it is in their interest to adopt a polycentric attitude that clients worldwide are likely to appreciate. The latter may believe, ethnocentrically, that their success depends on internal factors helping to optimise the processes for which they are responsible. Expecting two SBUs working up and down a MNE's value chain to share the same corporate culture is almost as illogical as expecting, for instance, farmers to share the same corporate culture as food market vendors. Just because both are working in the food business does not mean they share the same values, customs or belief systems.

Similarly, even slight variations in product characteristics can influence SBU subcultures in a multi-divisional MNE. In the London trading rooms

Fig 5.7
Different economic sub-activities will have different working subcultures.

of the erstwhile Republic National Bank of New York (now HSBC), for instance, currency and currency option sales and trading staff sat right next to one another, yet each possessed a very different IB culture, largely reflecting the high-volume/low-margin/low-tech nature of the former business and the low-volume/high-margin/high-tech nature of the latter. It is unclear whether the two departments' cultural divergence developed over time or stemmed from the fact that each SBU had attracted recruits possessing different cultures in the first place. But the point remains that the centrifugal forces hindering cultural harmonisation can be very strong indeed in MNEs.

Of course, even if a MNE's overall corporate culture loses consistency because it struggles to coordinate its different SBU subcultures, that does not mean there is nothing it can do to optimise staff's intercultural performance. There remains one final level where the problems of aggregation and overgeneralisation, referred to throughout this chapter, no longer apply – namely, how employees cope with the intercultural hurdles they face individually.

Intercultural performance – Success in navigating foreign culture-related hurdles.

Culture at an intrapersonal level

This final section is viewed by some as a fun part of IB culture studies, since it brings the object of analysis down to what people can do personally to create greater affinity with their counterparts from other cultures. The tools discussed here are ones that can be applied in a host of international situations, whether dealing with foreign colleagues, relationships with foreign suppliers and customers or acculturation work helping company expatriates to transition as quickly as possible through their early "honeymoon" and "culture shock" phases to a more equanimous and realistic "acceptance and integration" stage of their foreign assignment (Adler 1981).

It would of course be misleading to intimate that there is some checklist or magic wand capable of perfecting practitioners' capabilities in this area under all circumstances. Having said that, a whole subdiscipline has arisen offering tips for cultural rapprochement at a personal level, with actions here largely being divided into verbal and non-verbal categories.

Verbal interplay

Above and beyond straightforward linguistic and translation problems (the fact that words, even when converted accurately into a different language, may not have the same connotation), it is in the style of the conversations held with a foreign national that a number of intrapersonal problems can arise. In addition to the tolerance for (in)formality that Trompenaars introduced in his cultural differences typology – manifested inter alia through the register of language that participants employ (received vs. colloquial discourse, etc.) – different cultures will be more or less receptive to a foreign counterpart, peppering their speech with asides unrelated to the topic at hand, whether comments on broader social or political issues, personal anecdotes, gossip about shared acquaintances or general small talk. Some businesspersons will positively relish such interludes, seeing them as a way of discovering common ground with their interlocutor. Others will view them as an unprofessional waste of time.

Similarly, attempts to ingratiate oneself – a constant in most all business relationships – can spark varying reactions among foreign counterparts. Some will welcome the effort, especially when it involves deference to an older person, which is a key component of certain cultures, particularly in Asia and Africa. They might also view it as a sign of politeness (being a central value in their own culture) or as the kind of recognition that they crave for egotism reasons. Otherwise, they may also feel that overt attempts at ingratiation reduce the overall foreignness of the encounter. Examples of the kinds of topics that can be usefully raised in this respect include references to local politics, geography or cultural output. Sporting allusions also tend to be safe ground. Having said that, some foreign counterparts may be off-put by this kind of chatter, perceiving it as obsequiousness tantamount to phoniness – a posture that their culture of origin might scorn.

Above all, conversational ploys intended to ingratiate oneself with a foreign counterpart can fall flat if they are based on wrongful assumptions of common values. One real life story in this respect saw a London-based customer relationship officer bringing his Chicago-based colleague with him to meet a Parisian customer and offer her US time zone services for the after-hour services she might require once the UK office had closed for the day. Based on the common American habit of businesspersons speaking disparagingly about state interference in the economic sphere, the Chicago colleague took it upon himself to criticise the French government's famously interventionist behaviour. By so doing, he thought he was expressing sympathy for the bureaucratic obstacles that he assumed the French corporate treasurer also resented. What he did not realise was that the large corporation that employed her was in fact state-owned and that in her French political values system, accepting the role of the state was an almost patriotic duty. She was therefore non-plussed by the opinions that the American expressed and turned to her habitual British contact to say – in French – that she would continue working with him but had no intention of entertaining the transatlantic relationship that had been the object of the meeting.

The lesson from this anecdote is that intercultural meetings need to be prepared beforehand, ideally by gathering background information from a MNE colleague with intimate knowledge of the target culture – someone who hails from there or who has accumulated extensive experience of the place. Failing this preparatory work, the second-best idea is to try and get one's foreign counterparts to speak first, so as to detect which topics are of greatest interest to them and, even more importantly, which values they hold most dearly. Intercultural sensitivity

involves, among other skills, the ability to listen intelligently and
respectfully to foreigners.

Non-verbal behaviour

A number of intrapersonal elements are unspoken but remain just as
important to intercultural success as verbal interplays do. One leading
aspect at this level is body language (see Table 5.2), a very rich topic
with a great deal of variability. Examples include the distance at which
foreign counterparts prefer to sit or stand from one another; what, if
any, kinds of physical contact might be made (handshaking, bowing,
waving, etc.); emotional displays that are usually facial but can also
involve body movements (Hareli et al. 2015); and expressivity, which
can involve hand gestures as well as facial movements. The way in
which business cards are exchanged can be viewed as a subset of this
discussion, with different cultures paying (and requiring) more or less
attention to the ritual. Otherwise, there is the real-life anecdote of a
delegation of four Western businesspersons travelling to Beijing and
being sat in the same hierarchical order as their four Chinese hosts, who
had gone to the effort of identifying each participant's exact status before
the meeting. Unfamiliar with this sense of order, the Westerners had
come into the room expecting to grab whichever chairs were available.
They were quickly disabused of this notion by their hosts. One thing that
intercultural sensitivity teaches is that things which are unimportant to
some individuals may be very important to others.

Appearance is another key element of non-verbal interaction. This
includes diverse aspects such as hair length and facial hair – but probably
most importantly, the clothes that someone wears. One aspect of
intrapersonal relationships has always been dress code decisions, ranging
from flashy ostentatious styles preferred by certain national cultures
(and/or business sectors, like high finance) to intentionally simpler
apparel intended to communicate anti-elitism. Each of these and other
choices will elicit various responses depending on the cultural preferences
of the practitioner's interlocutors. Otherwise, there have also been big
changes in different business cultures' clothing habits in recent years,
largely sparked by an American trend that started about 20 years ago of
adopting "casual Friday" wear, an extension of the more relaxed dress
codes characterising successful Silicon Valley high-tech ventures. The
trend has been adopted to varying degrees by different cultures and can
be a source of embarrassment when two sides come to a meeting dressed
in entirely different registers. Again, this is a misunderstanding that can
be avoided beforehand if one or the other side simply seeks clarification
beforehand.

All in all, the enormous variation in behavioural customs means that
no one person can be expected to have full knowledge of everything
needed to optimise global intrapersonal interactions. This reinforces
the need to mobilise all relevant sources of information both inside and
outside of a MNE. It is something that some companies will be better

Table 5.2
Sample of intercultural body language inconsistencies

Signs of approval	• Most cultures: nodding head up and down • Bulgaria/Greece: nodding head sideways (means "no" elsewhere) • Japan: nodding means acknowledgement, not agreement • India: head wobbling expresses understanding
Physical space	• North America/Europe: distance to avoid invasiveness • Latin cultures: proximity to express warmth
Greetings	• English-language cultures: firm handshake to express sincerity • Far Eastern cultures: bowing to express respect
Eye contact	• Middle East: sustained (between same gender) to express interest • Africa, Asia: intermittent to avoid seeming confrontational
Sitting position	• Thailand: showing soles of feet is considered rude • Japan: crossing legs is seen as arrogant

at doing than others – making culture yet another factor of competitive advantage in IB.

Attitudes and alternatives

Some academics will argue that culture is the most important of all IB topics. That may or may not be true, but clearly culture permeates the discipline. The question then becomes practitioners' aptitudes for recognising and managing the variability that they will encounter in this domain – as well as their willingness to engage with it. The cultural intelligence characterising individuals with advanced sensitivities in this domain can, strangely enough, become a source of resentment for others endowed with lesser capabilities – witness the way in which certain nationalistic elements have taken in recent years to attributing negative connotations to other people's "internationalist" worldviews. This textbook and the quasi-unanimity of IB practitioners very much come down on the cosmopolitan side of the culture war, but accept the importance of acknowledging that it is in fact being waged.

Chapter summary

The chapter began by questioning the suppositions underlying many IB culture studies up until now, starting with the idea that nationality suffices for making generalisations about practitioners' cultural identities. After discussing the strengths and weaknesses of this postulate, the leading IB cultural models were reviewed, starting with Geert Hofstede and moving on to Fons Trompenaars and Edwin Hall. This initiated discussion about how well the constructs devised by these and other seminal thinkers apply at the level of a MNE as a whole, followed by the same enquiry on the scale of a strategic business unit. The chapter concluded with consideration of the difficulties of harmonising cultural behaviour throughout an organisation, as well as the various ways in which such efforts can play out through intrapersonal behaviour.

Case study 5.3: International business culture and the sounds of silence

Note. This case study reproduces the real-life experiences recounted by an international business practitioner, with certain details altered to preserve anonymity

Lance had always been fascinated by foreign languages and cultures, so it was no real surprise when he emigrated from his native Toronto to Belgium shortly after earning his initial university degree. Following a fun gap year settling into his new environment, he completed a two-year MBA programme and married his long-standing girlfriend, a Dutch woman whose own European passport meant that Lance now had the right to take up employment in his adopted homeland. He was quickly hired by an American bank, which groomed him to ultimately spearhead its European marketing efforts, reasoning that his own cosmopolitan attitudes would give him an advantage in creating relationships with a broad swathe of continental customers. Lance was delighted with the opportunity and began developing his personal IB profile, largely

Fig 5.8
Intrapersonal skills that succeed with one culture may not work with another.

rooted in the one-to-one professional relationships that he hoped to build up over time.

Like any career, Lance's experienced a number of ups and downs. Because of his customer-facing function, these often involved cultural issues, with certain patterns beginning to emerge over time. The main thing that he learnt was that his particular way of interacting with people worked very well in some cultures but less well in others. As someone raised in a large raucous household where intense communication and philosophical debate were highly prized, Lance found that he got along very well with potential French customers, who not only appreciated the fact that he spoke the language well (as many English-speaking Canadians do) but would also participate fully in the polemic discussions typifying many French business interactions, where counterparts judge one another based not only on the value-for-money aspect of the deal being discussed but also on the general intellectualism of their negotiating counterpart. Often it would only be after sweeping conversations about broader political, economic or social trends that the discussion would turn to the transaction at hand, almost as an afterthought. Visibly enjoying his French counterparts' jousting, Lance seemed less foreign to them and quickly amassed a robust customer list in the country.

In Germany, he found that commercial success depended on a slightly different interactional dynamic. The Germans were always warm and friendly and, like the French, happy to engage in broader discussions with similar expectations of their counterparts' general culture. Contrary to the French, however, they tended to distrust embellishment and preferred *Sachlichkeit*, a more objective focus on hard facts. When dealing with Germans, Lance made sure to reign in the more extravagant tonalities characterising his French interactions – and did well in this country as well.

Other national cultures were more difficult for him, however. On his few visits to Stockholm, he learnt that his Swedish counterparts not only also disliked excessive verbal artistry but also went as far as to tolerate and even expect long silences in the middle of a professional negotiation. This was very different from the greater intensity of the interactions to which Lance had become accustomed to in his dealings with both the French and the Germans, for whom silence seemed to be as much of an uncomfortable experience as it was for him. He struggled to adjust in Scandinavia and ended up having much less commercial success there.

A similar problem arose when Lance went to prospect a large Japanese conglomerate's Belgian subsidiary, presented the products he wanted to sell and noted that his potential customers, albeit not saying much, had smiled warmly and nodded their heads frequently. Lance attributed their silence to linguistic problems and went back to his office to spend a lot of time preparing customer contracts, only to be told by the Japanese upon returning that their warm response to his sale pitch had in no way been a sign of their agreeing to the deal but simply an expression of politeness.

What Lance learnt from his Japanese and Scandinavian failures – along with his French and German successes – was that personal cultural affinities can be very specific in IB. It is why so many MNEs organise their business development staff members into geographic territories, the idea being that commercial representative should all possess a personal competitive advantage in their allocated zones, often relating to a knowledge of (and affinity with) the local culture. International marketing officers may be bridges between the countries where their MNE is currently operating and the ones where it wishes to go next, but this bridging function works better with certain cultural pairings than with others. Lance resolved that in the future he would make better use of his time specialising in customers from cultures that worked better with his own. Of course, this meant that marketing to other cultures would have to done by colleagues, requiring his employer to find qualified recruits. But that seemed a much more efficient approach to the problem, and he spent the rest of his career happy with his specialist destinations.

Case study questions

1. To what extent can someone's family culture predispose them to get along better with certain foreign cultures as opposed to others?
2. What could Lance have done to better prepare the Swedish and Japanese encounters and avoid the failures he experienced there?
3. What are the arguments for and against organising MNEs' customer-facing professionals according to their personal affinities with specific cultures?

Chapter discussion questions

1   What expectations should international business practitioners have that the new markets they are entering will converge with or diverge from the cultures that they know?
2   How essential a concept is intersectionality in understanding culture in an international business context?
3   Which macro-cultural dimensions are the most impactful?
4   Given English's dominance as an international business lingua franca, what is the advantage of continuing to learn other languages?
5   How realistic is it to try and synthesise a hybrid global culture?

References

Adler, N. (September 1981). "Re-entry: Managing cross-cultural transitions", *Group and Organization Management*, Volume 6, Issue 3, pp. 341–356.

Aharoni, Y. (1966). *The Foreign Investment Decision Process*, Boston, MA: Harvard Business School.

Backmann, J. et al. (13 March 2020). "Cultural gap bridging in multinational teams", *Journal of International Business Studies*, Volume 51, Issue 8, pp. 1283–1311.

Cova, B. (2007). *Consumer Tribes*, Abingdon: Routledge.

Gelman, S., and Roberts, S. (25 July 2017). "How language shapes the cultural inheritance of categories", accessed 11 October 2020 at https://www.pnas.org/

Govindarajan, V., and A. K. Gupta. (2001). *The Quest for Global Dominance: Transforming Global Presence into Global Competitive Advantage*, San Francisco, CA: Jossey Bass.

Hall, E. (1959). *The Silent Language*, Waterlooville: Anchor Books.

Hall, S., and Held, D. (June 1989). "Left and Rights", *Marxism Today*, pp. 16–23.

Hanel, P. et al. (29 May 2018). "Intercultural differences and similarities in human value instantiation", accessed 15 February 2021 at https://www.frontiersin.org/

Hareli, S. et al. (2 October 2015). "A cross-cultural study on emotion expression and the learning of social norms", accessed 15 February 2021 at https://www.frontiersin.org/

Harris, P. (26 November 2006). "The cruel reality of Disney's world", accessed 11 October 2020 at https://www.theguardian.com/

Hofstede, G. (2010). *Cultures and Organizations, Software of the Mind*, 3rd revised edition, New York: McGraw-Hill.

Klingenberg, M., and Sjo, S. (2019). "Theorizing religious socialization: A critical assessment", *Religion*, Volume 49, Issue 2, pp. 163–178.

Kroeber, A. L., and Kluckhohn, C. (1952). "Culture: A critical review of concepts and definitions", *Peabody Museum of Archaeology & Ethnology (Harvard University)*, Volume 47, Issue 1, pp. 559–563.

Neeley, T. (May 2012). "Global Business Speaks English", *Harvard Business Review*.

Omoniyi, T., and Fishman J., eds. (2006). *Explorations in the Sociology of Language and Religion*, Philadelphia, PA: John Benjamins.

Perlmutter, H. (January–February 1969). "The tortuous evolution of the multinational corporation", *Columbia Journal of World Business*, pp. 9–18.

Phillipson, R. (1992). *Linguistic Imperialism*, Oxford: Oxford University Press.

Rothman, J. (26 December 2014). "The meaning of 'culture'", *The New Yorker*, accessed 10 October 2020 at https://www.newyorker.com/

Steinwachs, K. (1 June 1999). "Information and culture – the impact of national culture on information processes", *Journal of Information Science*, Volume 25, Issue 3, pp. 193–204.

Stewart, C. (Autumn 1999). "Syncretism and its synonyms: Reflections on cultural mixture", *Diacritics*, Volume 29, Issue 3, pp. 40–62.

Taylor, E. (June 1994). "A learning model for becoming interculturally competent", *International Journal of Intercultural Relations*, Volume 18, Issue 3, pp. 389–408.

Tortugapirate (24 February 2015). "Callie's classroom: A brief history on facial hair at the Disney parks", accessed 11 October 2020 at http://doctordisney.com/

Trompenaars, F., and Hampden-Turner, C. (1997). *Riding the Waves of Culture; Understanding Cultural Diversity in Business*, London: Nicholas Brealey Publishing.

Unruh, G., and Cabrera, A. (May 2013). "Join the global elite", *Harvard Business Review*.

Vietze, J. et al. (30 April 2019). "Peer cultural socialisation: A resource for minority students' cultural identity, life satisfaction, and school values", *Intercultural Education*, Volume 30, Issue 5, pp. 570–598.

Vora, D. et al. (6 December 2018). "Multiculturalism within individuals...", *Journal of International Business Studies*, Volume 50, Issue 4, pp. 499–524.

Whorf, B. (April 1940). "Science and linguistics", *Technology Review*, Volume 42, Issue 6, pp. 229–231.

Wood, D. et al. (July 2010). "Perceiver effects as projective tests: What your perceptions of others say about you", *Journal of Personality and Social Psychology*, Volume 99, Issue 1, pp. 174–190.

CHAPTER 6

Cross-border corporate social responsibility

Introduction

In an international business (IB) setting, corporate social responsibility (CSR) occurs when multinational enterprises (MNEs) behave in a way that produces positive social and environmental outcomes and which can therefore be deemed ethical – with the latter term being used here in traditionally "moral" sense that philosophers associate with it. Having said that, given the variability of contexts and value systems found across the world, it can be very hard at times to determine what actually constitutes ethical behaviour (and positive outcomes) in different national frameworks. The first thing to note about sustainability – the overarching term commonly used nowadays to refer to companies' non-commercial responsibilities – is that different people will have different understandings of what it means.

Analysis of the need for MNEs to demonstrate that they are behaving ethically plays out at several levels. One measures the benefits that host countries derive from a foreign MNE's presence (jobs, capital, etc.) against the harm that it might do: environmentally, socially or as a result of its corporate governance practices. This is particularly important given the way powerful and mobile MNEs capable of regime shopping

Sustainability - Behaviour comprised of healthy social, environmental and governance practices benefitting both a company and the societies in which it operates.

Corporate governance - Laws and processes regulating a company's executive and accounting practices.

Fig 6.1
Moral philosophers have long debated the contours of social responsibility.

DOI: 10.4324/9781003159056-8

Table 6.1
Principal sustainability aspirations that MNEs may address through CSR conduct

Social sustainability	Pay Working conditions and hours Diversity and anti-discrimination Right to association Health/education impacts (inc. child labour) Effects on third parties
Environmental sustainability	Resource depletion Pollution Justice and stewardship
Corporate governance	Accounting (full, honest, transparent disclosure) Anti-corruption Government relations (including lobbying and tax)

can force desperately poor host country governments into a "race to the bottom" – contentious behaviour already addressed in Chapter 3's political discussion of certain less ethical practices within IB.

The question then becomes whether MNEs' behaviour can and should be legislated or if they might be trusted to self-police. It is this topic – discussed in the first section – that speaks to stakeholders' variable expectations of the role of business in society. The chapter's second section then reviews the main sustainability actions by means of which international CSR materialises (see Table 6.1), before concluding with a study of the codes of conduct, institutions and pressure groups that formalise, enforce and advocate MNE sustainability.

Stakeholder – Anyone affected by an organisation's actions. Often understood to be comprised of employees, local governments, suppliers, consumers and host communities.

Code of conduct – List of rules detailing accepted behaviour within an organisation.

LEARNING OBJECTIVES

After reading this chapter, you will be able to:

- put IB ethics into their historical context
- debate the validity of international CSR
- identify the main sustainability issues for MNEs
- analyse problems inherent to the codification and enforcement of international CSR
- appraise the role of international CSR advocacy groups

Case study 6.1: The real cost of cheap food

In Europe's colder northern countries, consumers take for granted the luxury of being able to buy all varieties of produce during the winter months. Every year, billions of euros are spent importing fresh fruit and vegetables from Spanish farms and greenhouses, often located near the

Fig 6.2
Working conditions can
be very harsh in some
countries in some sectors.

southern city of Almeria. This is generally done via cost-effective cross-border supply chains set up by distribution giants like Carrefour, Metro and Sainsbury's who, by providing households with healthy food, are, on the face of things, engaged in an entirely ethical IB.

But there is a problem. The fact that these MNEs pay low wholesale prices makes it possible to keep retail prices affordable but also reduces revenues for Spanish farmers who are already being squeezed by rising fertiliser and fuel costs. Lacking the leverage to negotiate better terms with the food retailers, the farmers only have one way to try and improve margins, namely, by squeezing labour costs. This has a terrible impact on their workers, many of whom are poor migrant Africans.

Investigative publications like *Ethical Consumer* (Carlile 2020) have long written about the working and living conditions suffered by Africans brought to Spain to harvest local produce. Paid less than half the national minimum wage – already one of the lowest in Europe – their jobs are incredibly strenuous, often involving long shifts in temperatures routinely exceeding 40 degrees. It is also dangerous for their health, exposed as they are to the toxic agrichemicals that are regularly sprayed throughout the greenhouses even when they are working there. Nor is there any real hope that the Africans can organise themselves to seek redress; there are numerous accounts of their suffering physical and verbal threats whenever they try to elect union representatives.

Workers' living conditions are just as unsustainable. Many are forced to live in unhygienic, overcrowded shacks lacking modern conveniences such as running water. Moreover, because most have no immigration papers, they run a constant risk of being reported to the police if they complain about the conditions in which they are forced to live. In the end, they often find themselves segregated into unhealthy shanty towns where they are aggressively dissuaded by officials or local residents from mixing with the indigenous Spanish populations or tourists. In some instances, their circumstances have been so dire that the Red Cross had to be called in to distribute food to them.

There is no doubt that the working and living conditions in the poor African countries where many of these workers originate can also be harsh. It seems unethical, however, to view this as a justification for their being similarly mistreated in Europe, a region that has reached a stage of socio-economic well-being such that there is normally zero tolerance for these kinds of labour practices and human rights abuses.

The truth is that the working conditions of the migrants upon whom Europeans rely for their food could be improved quite easily if consumers or supermarkets were willing to, respectively, pay higher prices for winter vegetables or accept lower profit margins on them. The real question is therefore what has the biggest effect on MNE and consumer behaviour: their wallet or their conscience?

Case study questions

1. What are the ethical debates surrounding African farm workers' treatment in Spain?
2. How likely is it that consumers will boycott produce from Spain because of the way workers are treated?

Section I. Principles of international CSR

Moral philosophy, the cornerstone of modern business ethics, is an ancient field of study. One starting point for analysing its application in a corporate context is to look at the factors guiding individual attitudes

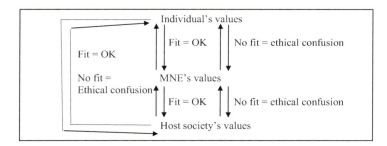

Fig 6.3
The "ethical fit" can vary between personal, corporate and societal values.

at work. The Cambridge theorist Noreena Hertz once asserted that employees bring their personal values to their place of work. Studies have also found that young generation prefers joining companies known as much for their social purpose as for their profitability (Reba 2019). Of course, this is not always possible.

At that point, the question becomes how people can balance their personal values against those of their employer but also, in IB, the values of the country where they are working. Ethical confusion (see Figure 6.3) arises whenever these interfaces clash, for instance, if a company's code of conduct is too vague or enforced inconsistently. It should always be remembered that companies are fictitious persons, staffed by a patchwork of "fragmented identities", each acting in accordance with their own personalised interpretation of the core values proclaimed by their employer (Steinhorst 2019). The ensuing potpourri of expectations is particularly difficult to manage in an IB situation where ethical divergence is much greater than in a purely domestic setting.

International business ethics' variability in time and space

Ethical behaviour must always be analysed in context. For instance, slave traders, "robber barons" and "imperial corporations" are more or less universally condemned in today's world yet were highly respected in many older societies (Schwartz 1999). Practices like child labour and exploitative working conditions that are unanimously criticised in Europe today were widespread before being denounced by reformers such as the UK's Charles Dickens, France's Émile Zola or the American "muckraker" Upton Sinclair. An entire research corpus, embodied in seminal constructs such as Maslow's Hierarchy of Needs or the "Kuznets curve" (see Chapter 13), speaks to the fact that many countries only prioritise social or environmental sustainability once they have achieved a certain level of affluence. Note along these lines the distinction that IB ethics philosopher Thomas Donaldson (1991) makes between situations where conflicts between home and host country values are economic in nature (in which case, less sustainable practices are acceptable if the home country did the same when it was at the same level of socio-economic development), or if they are culture-based (in which case, different ethical practices are only acceptable if they do not violate basic rights).

The difficulty for any of these approaches is that ethical evaluations can also change very quickly over time. One example is the way many analysts who lambasted investment bankers for their role in the 2008 subprime crisis had previously glorified them as wealth creators. Consensus appraisals of business ethics are very dependent on the dominant zeitgeist.

One watershed moment from the early 20th century was the rise of large, multi-divisional firms. This led to a divergence in shareholders and managers' outlooks, with the former's focus on profitability seen as undermining the latter's ostensibly greater concern with community well-being (Vogel 2006). By the 1960s, influential thinkers like the economist J. K. Galbraith were already speaking of a need to formalise social responsibility. Some leading executives at that time, like Chase Manhattan Bank's David Rockefeller, felt that this could best be achieved through philanthropy.

Philanthropy – Charitable donations to worthy causes.

Although charity is a form of ethical behaviour, it is not systematic enough to address major social problems effectively. There is also a debate whether corporate philanthropy is self-serving. It is true that the philanthropic model remains dominant in some Global South business cultures where family traditions, religion and peer pressure (Khan et al. 2020) have seen many business leaders internalise the idea that social harmony is a more meaningful value than material advancement (Hopkins 2007). The problem, however, is the narrow impact that philanthropy-driven CSR has had in the Global South (Yunis et al. 2018). In the world's older industrialised countries, there seems to be greater understanding of the need to systematise business ethics. It is not that philanthropy does not exist in the Global North – witness the activism of the Gates Foundation, started by the family behind Microsoft. But the paradigm here seems to have moved on.

The debate over international CSR

In recent decades, the main way in which companies in general – and MNEs in particular – have signalled their intention to conduct themselves ethically has been through CSR strategy and action. Despite its rising popularity, however, CSR does not enjoy unanimous approval – a seminal debate worth exploring in greater detail.

Supporting international CSR

Externalities – Where the positive or negative consequences of an economic action impact parties not directly involved in it.

From a macro-economic perspective, the argument for international CSR is the need to offset market failure, often exemplified by the externalities (see Figure 6.4) that occur when a transaction between two counterparts has a positive or negative effect on third parties who did not agree the original deal. There are manifold examples of externalities arising in an IB context. They can be positive, for instance, when a MNE pays

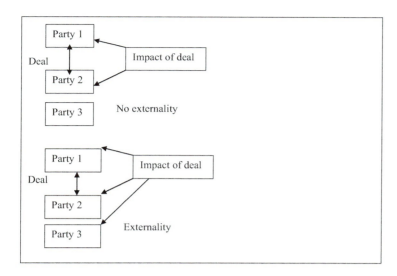

Fig 6.4
Externalities can have a positive or negative effect on someone who is not party to a deal.

higher wages than the national average, allowing employees to increase consumption and sparking greater activity throughout the local economy via a multiplier effect. But externalities can also be negative, for instance, when a MNE offshores its "dirty" industrial activities to a country with low environmental standards, afflicting the local population with concentrated pollution. In the former example, the salutary effects of the MNE's actions means there is little need for compensatory CSR. In the latter, however, without CSR, the MNE's presence will have had a net negative effect on the host country. As formulated by Nobel laureate Joseph Stiglitz (2006), there is a "misalignment of economic incentives when corporations do not bear the downside costs [of their actions]: social welfare is not maximised if corporations single-mindedly maximise profits". Here CSR is viewed as a way of ensuring that the distribution of costs and benefits reflects the actual creation of value – it would be bad economics for a MNE to get a free ride by not paying for the negative outcomes that its activities might generate.

The ethical argument for CSR in IB goes further, however. This is because even if it makes sense from an economic perspective that MNEs offset any damage they inflict upon host country populations, realistically this is not always possible ex post. One seminal case from the year 1985 was when more than 3,000 citizens in the Indian town of Bhopal died because a local plant run by America MNE Union Carbide leaked toxic substances due to a litany of "operating errors, design flaws, maintenance failures, training deficiencies" and, perhaps most reprehensibly of all, "economy measures that endangered safety" (Diamond 1985). A similar case occurred two decades later, when ten Ivory Coast citizens died and a further 9,000 were poisoned, following the careless discharge of chemical waste from a ship chartered by the Dutch firm, Trafigura (Russell 2006). In both these instances, the

Multiplier effect – Where spending by one economic agent creates disposable income for another who can then increase their own spending.

Free ride – Where a party benefits from an economic activity without contributing to its costs.

Ex post – After the fact. The opposite of "ex ante", or before the fact.

companies paid fines subsequently – but the loss of life could never be undone. Moreover, it is ethically highly dubious under any circumstances for ex post settlements to be viewed as satisfactory remedies for harmful behaviour that should never have happened – if only because this can create an incentive to continue behaving unethically if the profits from such conduct exceeds the fines being levied. CSR also exists to lower the probability of bad things ever happening in the first place.

These economic and moral arguments in favour of international CSR are further bolstered by more practical considerations. The first builds on Chapter 3's discussion of the rising power of the private sector. Many governments, especially in the Global South, simply lack the means to attend to all of the social, environmental and other problems besetting their local populations. The net effect is that they are unable to offer constituents satisfactory educational and healthcare provisions. Insofar as having a healthy and well-educated workforce benefits companies operating in these locations, some have argued that most CSR spending in the Global South is actually driven by MNEs' perceived self-interest (Giacomin et al. 2019). Whether or not this is true, there are good examples of educational CSR spending in the Global South: Spanish MNE Telefonica's Educared portal, bringing information technologies to schools worldwide; IBM's KidSmart Learning Program, targeting pre-school children around the world; and British pharmaceutical giant GSK's "Young Physicians and Pharmacists" programmes in Africa. Note that these all companies operate in information-intensive sectors where great competitive advantage can be derived from nurturing human capital wherever it might be found. In such cases, there is no real contradiction between the MNE's selfish or altruistic motives.

Altruistic – Prioritising the well-being of others rather than oneself.

The second practical argument for CSR in an IB context relates to the reputational damage that MNEs incur if they are accused of behaving unethically in a foreign country and, conversely, the advantages for them of being viewed as good citizens. Research has shown, for instance, that some companies operating in hazardous sectors actually go out of their way to move to locations known for tough health and safety standards – despite the higher costs – specifically because this reduces their reputational risks (Maggioni 2019). Depending on the national culture and general expectations of business ethics, "social marketing" teaches that companies can generally expect to benefit from a halo effect if they are seen as behaving ethically and, by so doing, enable potential customers to bathe in an aura of virtuousness when buying their products. The stakes are particularly high when a MNE is involved, if only because home bias can cause consumers to be more suspicious about the motivations of a foreign company than a domestic one. Overt CSR is a tool that many MNEs can and do use to overcome the hurdle of foreignness.

Halo effect – Where a party feels virtuous after transacting with another party deemed to be virtuous.

This kind of marketing-related CSR is sometimes done proactively to pre-empt the negativity that MNEs can suffer due to a host society's unfavourable stereotyping of (or geopolitically driven aversion to) their country of origin. Even more poignant, however, are situations where

MNEs seek to redeem themselves after having been justifiably criticised for bad behaviour in the past. The question in these cases is how long people will remember the misconduct and what the MNE must do to get them to forget – a difficult task in a 24/7 news environment where observers are not only aware of (and feel affected by) dubious actions taking place in their immediate proximity but increasingly of things that MNEs do on the other side of the world.

There are innumerable examples of MNEs using CSR to burnish their damaged reputation. In the 1990s, for instance, some of the world's leading apparel makers (including Gap, Adidas and Nike) came under severe criticism in many Global North markets for purchasing product from Southeast Asian suppliers employing workers in terrible sweat shop conditions. Public disapproval would only abate years later, once the MNEs in question enacted codes of conduct assuming responsibility for working conditions in suppliers' facilities. In a similar vein, the following decade saw mining giant Anglo-American launch an active anti-HIV/AIDS programme, analysed by some as a conscious effort to overcome widespread mistrust of Western mining companies across Africa (Cronin 2006). The same question has been asked about US food giant Chiquita, with observers wondering whether its controversial past collaborations with Central American "banana republics" undermine the credibility of the positive CSR measures (fair wages, social amenities) that the MNE has taken over the past 20 years (Baur 2015). In all probability, MNE misconduct dating from a distant past is likelier to be forgiven and/or forgotten than recent transgressions, especially if the company runs a strong CSR programme today. For MNEs whose misconduct is relatively recent (e.g. Volkswagen' 2015 Dieselgate affair, misrepresenting vehicles' CO_2 emissions) or who are in the midst of an ethical controversy (ongoing allegations of tax avoidance on the part of tech giants Amazon and Google), public opinion may be harsher, with studies in the latter instance showing that companies named and shamed for mobilising tax haven subsidiaries often suffer negative stock price reactions (Rusina 2020). In IB like other social sciences, events viewed retrospectively often seem less dramatic than in real time.

Sweat shop – Manufacturing facility characterised by particularly harsh working conditions.

Criticising international CSR

In the early 1990s, the author of this book was working in the London office of an international bank and, while sharing a lift with the department head, suggested to the latter that the company organise a recycling scheme to manage the huge amount of paper waste being generated. In response, he was sharply rebuked for "wasting time" and "not thinking about what's important – making money". The reality, as witnessed in this example like countless others, is that CSR has not always been universally popular in IB circles.

The theoretical foundation for some business commentators' rejection of CSR is a famous article that neo-classical economist and

Nobel laureate Milton Friedman published in *The New York Times Magazine* in September 1970, opining that sustainability spending is an unjustified imposition on companies. Friedman's argument was that CSR forces shareholders to accept lower dividends and lengthier payback horizons (hence lower returns on investment), workers to accept lower wages and/or customers to pay higher prices – which they may or may not accept, in which case the firm is stuck either with lower margins or forced into a narrow market niche. In Friedman's view, the social responsibility of business is simply to increase profits; as long as it acts legally, it should be left free to do so, if only because it is up to government to achieve the social and environmental sustainability goals to which CSR aspires.

As specified below, there are demonstrable flaws in Friedman's premise. But he is far from having been the only theorist to have condemned CSR as ethical overreach. The main gist of this critique is that CSR proponents unfairly portray companies as free riders instead of giving them credit for the taxes and wages they pay (Marcoux 2000). This supposedly discourages equity investment and risk-taking, brings "interest-group politics into the boardroom" and imposes excessive accountability on managers, especially ones operating in legal systems that make them personally liable for their employer's actions.

Accountability – Precept that actors must take responsibility for their actions.

Lastly and as aforementioned, there is the argument that CSR actually gets in the way of Global South families' more pressing needs. In recent years, for instance, the Mexican government has reversed certain previous stances and committed to the eradication of child labour, which is prevalent among the country's poorer agricultural populations. This has led, however, to the prosecution of adults accused of abetting such practices – an action criticised in turn for its criminalisation of poverty (Deccan Herald 2020). Rebuked internationally for once having tolerated child labour and subsequently for having suppressed it, for Mexican government there is one constant in this saga – the fact they were criticised. That seems unfair.

On the whole, the loudest reproach that one hears today is that CSR does not go far enough and has much less of an effect that companies pretend. This can be either because CSR effects are geographically constrained and only help a small cross-section of the host population (Sitkin 2013), or because verbal commitments (relating, for instance, to healthcare provisions in low-income countries) often fail to materialise as promised (Lamb 2017). International CSR in the Global South tends to come under particular criticism, being accused in some corners of actually providing cover for further unethical practice, for instance, by legitimising "exploitative pricing and procurement practices, which are the key reasons for deplorable [sweat shop] working conditions" (Banerjee and Alamgir 2020). The idea here is that voluntary "CSR tends to be peripheral in most organisations" (Collins and Murphy 2013) and that government policing would be much more effective than CSR is.

The problem with this critique is its assumption that by adhering to government policy, MNEs will necessarily be behaving ethically. In fact, the opposite may be true in countries that are ethnically, hence politically, divided, and where a MNE's cooperation with a ruling faction makes things worse for other communities. One example is Myanmar, where a unit of the French energy multinational Total was criticised for making deals with the country's oppressive military junta through the 2000s, then received absolution from Nobel Peace Prize laureate Aung San Suu Kyi in 2012 when the country democratised before finally coming under renewed criticism in the late 2010s for collaborating with her new regime even as it was being widely condemned for mistreating the country's Rohingya minority. The question here is whether Total's positive CSR programme in the country compensates for its dubious political alliances, past and present. There would also be the question of how it should behave following the February 2021 military coup that deposed Aung San Suu Kyi's government. If a legal system accepts certain unethical behaviour, then acting legally does not necessarily mean acting morally.

This is an important point, since it undermines Friedman's argument that the only thing that companies need to do to act ethically is follow the law. Legislation reflects the balance of power in a society at a given moment in time. "Legality" per se is therefore much too vague a construct, with a better metric probably being "ethicality" (see Figure 6.5) or the proposition that MNEs must respect minimum standards wherever they operate, regardless of local legislation.

In the end, this new understanding – along with new generations' greater sensitivity to the pressing need for all stakeholders (thus including corporate interests) to address the daunting environmental and social challenges that the world faces in the early 2020s – has embedded sustainability as a core function in many, if not most, companies worldwide. Evidence for this can be found, inter alia, in MNEs' skyrocketing membership in bodies such as the World Business Council for Sustainable Development. Nowadays CSR is spoken about less

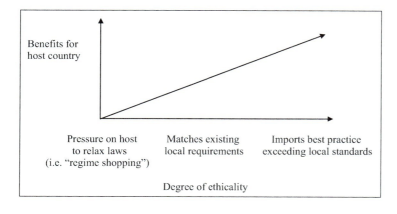

Fig 6.5
Different behaviours can all be legal yet reflect greater or lesser ethicality.

Triple bottom line – Precept that companies should not only report financial outcomes but also social and environmental ones.

ESG funding – Investing in companies accredited with certain sustainability qualifications.

from an ethical perspective and more in terms of the business case. The central idea here, formulated by sustainability advocates such as Andrew Winston, is that "green is gold", that is, having a **triple bottom line** focus is lucrative since it enhances a company's reputation, gives it access to **ESG funding**, maximises recruitment and staff motivation, improves risk management and (maybe first and foremost from some perspectives) attracts customers. Realising this, the vast majority of business schools today provide sustainability training to the future executives. In the early 21st century, international CSR has gone mainstream.

Case study 6.2: Hirdaramani hears the many

In recent decades, Sri Lanka – a densely populated island-nation of 22 million citizens just southeast of the Indian subcontinent – has gone through difficult times. Despite a positive emergence trajectory that saw average per-capita income rise by more than 40 percent from 2010 to 2020, the vast majority of Sri Lankans are anything but affluent, with many households' ongoing poverty adding to the societal tensions inherited from a recent civil war between the country's Tamil and Singhalese populations. Sri Lanka could be a hotbed of constant unrest if its development dynamic is not led responsibly. This is exactly the approach taken by one of the dominant textile industry's leading employers – the Hirdaramani family.

The group has interests throughout South Asia, primarily in its home market but also in Bangladesh and Vietnam. It manufactures clothing on behalf of a number of top-tier European and American retailers. This is a positive situation but also makes Hirdaramani

Fig 6.6
Employers benefit by committing to a green and pleasant working environment.

vulnerable to the kinds of pressures from which many other Global South suppliers have suffered in recent years as competition has intensified and margins shrunk – especially in the wake of the Covid-19 pandemic, with its negative effects on global retail footfall. Under these conditions, Hirdaramani might be expected to batten down the hatches and do everything possible to reduce its own cost base – including by shrinking the very advanced CSR programme that has been this ethical trailblazer's calling card for upwards of 20 years, long before sustainability became as widespread as it is today. But that would be to underestimate the depth of the MNE's commitment to ethical IB.

Several factors explain Hirdaramani's devotion to international CSR. Besides the fact that belonging to an ethical trading group like ETI was a pre-requisite for getting contracts from certain big foreign customers (and/or a competitive advantage with others), family members have long felt a moral obligation to support the company's loyal workforce, largely comprised of female workers, too many of whom have suffered domestic abuse in their private lives and are therefore very much in need of a safe working environment where they feel respected. The group has been repaid over the years with negligible staff turnover and good per-employee productivity in a labour-intensive sector where such metrics are crucial to success. In addition – and again due to their sincere ethical compass but also because the Hirdaramanis are very serious about fulfilling their role as leading citizens in Sri Lankan society – the group has long pursued a very advanced environmental sustainability programme comprised of many admirable elements. These include 14 eco-efficient buildings certified as having attained advanced LEEDS status (many replete with large rooftop solar panel installations), net zero greenhouse gas emissions across all Sri Lankan facilities and an active membership in initiatives such as the Sustainable Apparel Coalition and Make Fashion Circular.

It is an impressive record of international CSR and one that will have entailed significant capital and operational spending over many years. Today, at a time of crisis in the sector, the Hirdaramani group must once again envisage significant capital expenditure, this time to digitise its production operations and lower return costs in this way. How this emerging MNE succeeds in squaring "profit" with "purpose" will be a useful lesson for many other companies worldwide.

Case study questions

1. Why has the Hirdaramani family made such a deep commitment to international CSR?
2. What effect can difficult IB circumstances have on a MNE's CSR actions?

Section II. International CSR in practice

There is a common understanding today of what constitutes the main sustainability issues that MNEs might seek to address through international CSR. Variations persist, however, in the importance attributed to each of these categories in various parts of the world and in how they are codified and potentially enforced.

Categorising international CSR

Human rights

One serious dilemma for MNEs is whether they should do business in countries that violate basic human rights, that is, where they might end up being involved in actions that could easily be characterised as unethical if not criminal. There is a long history of this kind of dilemma in certain extractive industries (i.e. the mining of "blood diamonds") but MNEs from other sectors come under similar scrutiny as well, with recent examples including tobacco giant BAT being accused of profiting from labour abuses on farms in Malawi (Kashyap 2020), or Apple being criticised for its Chinese supplier Foxconn's alleged use of forced Uighur labour (Hamilton 2020). Being even remotely associated with human rights violations of this kind is antithetical to any semblance of ethical IB, and MNEs increasingly publicise the measures they are taking to distance themselves from such behaviour. This can again be exemplified by Apple, which announced in December 2020 that it would be suspending payments to another supplier, Wistron in India, after discovering that the latter was accused of delaying payments to workers at an iPhone plant near Bangalore. The action had the desired effect of Wistron rectifying the situation, raising questions as to how much pressure MNEs might bring to bear in creating a better world.

The easy answer is to threaten to boycott a potential supplier and indeed an entire nation. But this is also ethically complicated since by refusing to do business with a counterpart – hence depriving it of capital, jobs and technology (advantages that many Global South countries are desperate to acquire) – the MNE would cause further harm to a society that is already suffering. According to Kline (2005), MNEs' responsibilities in countries where human rights are being flaunted depend on their intentions, awareness of the situation and proximity to any transgression. In and of itself, business cannot be expected to solve all of the world's problems. However, MNEs might at the very least be expected to not make things worse for victims of human rights abuses. One way to achieve this is by shifting their CSR actions in a given host country away from the populations perpetrating such deeds and towards the ones suffering from it.

Lastly, note one subset of this topic is the treatment of indigenous people in countries where entire communities live according to ancient traditions that have little, if anything, in common with modern industrial civilisation. Where IB involves the destruction of their native habitat, as is currently happening with construction of hydroelectric dams in Brazil's Amazon rainforest, a human rights abuse is arguably being committed. Having said that, as always the debate needs to be balanced, given the benefits that Brazil's poorer citizens would derive from access to affordable clean energy. As happens so often in IB, different parties to a transaction will each have their own interpretation of the benefits thereof.

Labour relations and supply chain management

Labour relations include employee "hiring and firing" practices, wage policies, overtime, health and safety, gender equality, child labour, union relations and fair trade. It is a category that rivals the environment as the main focus of international CSR today.

Fair trade – Business defined by the equitable distribution of profits up and down the global value chain to ensure that upstream producers receive a decent "living" wage.

As discussed throughout this book, one of the main drivers behind modern globalisation is the mass movement of many companies' upstream production activities to low-cost countries, either by outsourcing to local suppliers or by offshoring via foreign direct investment (FDI). These actions all have major political and strategic implications. They also raise a number of CSR issues.

Innumerable households worldwide have benefitted greatly from the internationalisation of production. In MNEs' home countries, consumers enjoy lower prices and shareholders higher profits; in host countries, workers get jobs and governments collect tax revenues. Indeed, the entire development trajectory in countries like South Korea and Singapore was triggered by MNEs' outsourcing contracts or FDI initiatives. Hundreds of millions of people worldwide have been lifted out of abject poverty over the past 20 years due to the globalisation of manufacturing. There are many analysts who view the phenomenon as something highly ethical – an opinion that this textbook shares.

Yet there is no doubt that the internationalisation of production also hurts certain subpopulations and it is here that ethical problems do arise. When MNEs move jobs to low-wage countries, home country workers thrust into a position of job insecurity can easily fall prey to mental health disorders, especially men who, studies have found, are less adept at developing coping strategies (Menendez-Espina et al. 2020). Above all, host countries (increasingly located in the Global South) must often compete with one another to attract the new business. This can exacerbate the race to the bottom, with employment only being created in economies where jobseekers are numerous, poor, lacking in bargaining power (due to an absence of union representation) and therefore vulnerable to exploitation.

Now, it is true that where MNEs enter Global South markets via FDI, they are in a much better position to improve outcomes. And in fact, many do. Studies indicate that foreign ownership of companies operating in emerging markets like China has a positive direct wage effect (Girma

et al. 2019). This clearly constitutes an ethical outcome and should be
lauded accordingly.

That being the case, the greater ethical problem arises when a MNE
outsources production to Global South suppliers and then squeezes
the latter despite (or far too often, because of) their weak bargaining
position. When this happens, the knock-on effect is always to make
life harder for a workforce that is so desperate that it has no choice
but to accept whatever conditions are on offer. There are innumerable
examples of this kind of situation. In South Africa, for instance, Human
Rights Watch (2011) has reported on Western Cape province workers
producing

> "the country's renowned wines and fruit [while] being denied
> adequate housing, proper safety equipment and basic labour rights
> [...living in] conditions that include on-site housing that is unfit
> for living, exposure to pesticides without proper safety equipment,
> lack of access to toilets or drinking water while working".

In Pakistan's Sialkot region, there has long been distress about children
being employed in painfully harsh conditions, sitting in semi-dark
environs for more than ten hours a day, seven days a week, stitching
soccer balls or carving surgical instruments on behalf of major foreign
MNEs. Instances of this nature can be documented all across the globe,
from Bengali sweatshops to Egyptian cotton fields to El Salvadorean
sugar plantations. It is the harsh reality that many hundreds of millions
of labourers face day in day out.

Whereas 20 years ago IB commentators were still wondering to what
extent the Global North MNEs that have been purchasing their inputs
from Global South suppliers should be held responsible for the latter's
labour and human rights practices, today this debate has been largely
settled, with a number of European countries (starting with France)
already moving to enact the so-called "duty of vigilance" laws that
requires MNE to identify the impact that their purchasing behaviour has
on weaker foreign suppliers operating at a more upstream stage of their
global value chain. When times are tough – such as during the Covid-19
pandemic – the easiest option for MNEs had previously been to squeeze
their suppliers for more advantageous conditions (lower prices, faster
deliveries) and/or to simply break their purchasing agreement. What such
behaviour neglected, however, is how devastating these actions' knock-on
effects are for Global South suppliers' already vulnerable workforces. It
is a neglectfulness that international CSR seeks to address.

Now, there is no doubt that some leading MNEs (such as Gap and
Primark in the textile sector) have already started implementing serious
social audit systems aimed at detecting and punishing subcontractors
who abuse workers and/or rely on child labour. The problem for them
and for the other MNEs following in their footsteps is that some
Global South suppliers have proven themselves very adept at preventing

inspectors, representing bodies such as the Fair Labor Association, from monitoring their frontline operations. The end result is that a number of MNEs continue to have their ethics impugned through no fault of their own. It is frustrating situation that has caused some to reconsider their entire IB model.

The ethical dilemma for MNEs then becomes that boycotting a country due to disgust with supplier practices there will cause greater unemployment, worsening the life chances of the very populations that need help (Kline 2005). Hence, the modern conception that it is more ethical for MNEs to work with suppliers to improve working conditions than to abandon them. Of course, cooperation of this kind takes time. By definition, sustainability is always a slow process – especially when it is international in scope.

Discrimination

Sociology teaches that many of the opinions formed (hence policies formulated) by decision-makers are driven by a desire to reproduce social structures mirroring an individual's own identity. In concrete terms, this means that hierarchies tend to be perpetuated, translating into discrimination against anyone dissimilar to the social group constituting the existing power elite. The end result in the world of IB has been the de facto exclusion of broad swathes of the global population from positions of power in MNEs everywhere, based on outsiders' gender, race, sexual orientation, socio-economic and educational background or disability status. Few, if any, theorists can offer a moral justification for such prejudice, making its elimination an ethical aspiration worthy of inclusion in the panoply of core CSR actions. Of course, the ensuing pursuit of diversity is subject, like so many other aspects of IB, to wide global variations in terms of the priority it receives. In general, however, the principle has already risen so far up most MNEs' CSR agenda that it would be anachronistic not to list it alongside other contemporary social sustainability goals.

Corruption

Corruption has long been a major risk management concern within IB because of dubious behaviour that MNEs might encounter in the countries where they are looking to do business, but also because MNE employees may themselves be culpable. It is important to avoid the misconception that MNE encounters with corruption are one-sided. Acts of this nature involve both a purveyor and a recipient, both of whom can be held accountable for the roles they play.

Two examples attest to the bilateral nature of corruption when it happens in a cross-border setting. In one well-known case, the now disbanded US energy company Enron paid a small sum to an official in the Indian state of Maharashtra, who then awarded it a power plant construction contract despite receiving lower bids from rival Deutsche Babcock. The end result was that local residents had to pay much higher utility bills than they should have done. The corrupt transaction may have been done in the name of the state, but it certainly was not a victimless crime. In another example, November 2020 saw US investment bank Goldman Sachs agree to a $2 billion plus settlement with different authorities worldwide following a money laundering and bribery scandal committed by employees working out of one of its Asian subsidiaries. It is important to note that Goldman itself was not blamed for the incident and, on the contrary, received permission to pursue its own activities unabated in recognition of its lack of culpability. Instead, the noteworthy aspect is that the bank had to take responsibility for misconduct occurring in a distant foreign unit, pointing out the importance of CSR not only permeating a MNE's group headquarters but also its subsidiaries (Zhou and Wang 2020). One thing that distinguishes corruption when committed within an IB framework is how hard it is to control behaviour of all the countless individuals working in a global group's many entities.

Large-scale acts of corruption skew market transactions to the benefit of the few and detriment of the many. Note the perception that corruption is negatively correlated with income levels (see Table 6.2), the argument being that once societies reach a certain level of affluence, people no longer get excited at the prospect of making even more money, hence have less interest in partaking in corruption. Whether corruption's link to poverty makes it any more excusable, however, is a topic for debate.

It is also true that outright bribery of the kind that Enron committed is a very different order of magnitude than actions like giving gifts, which may or may not be deemed corrupt, depending on the values of the culture evaluating the case. The Arab custom of *baksheesh* can be analysed, for instance, as a bribe or else as something as harmless as a tip or a finder's fee. The fact is that some practices considered corrupt in some societies may be acceptable in others. An added complication is that firms or individuals who act ethically most of the time may be capable of acting corruptly on a few specific occasions. This inconsistency makes it very hard to audit corruption, either internally by MNEs' compliance departments or externally by national authorities. It also explains why a number of major global initiatives have been devised (notably by the UN or the OECD) to address the problem.

Lastly, it bears repeating that accusations of corruption can themselves be very inconsistent, given wide global variations in "national business ideology" (Baho et al. 2020). No one calls for a boycott of the European Union or the USA, yet extensive political lobbying in Brussels and Washington is by some measures tantamount to corruption. Similarly, some argue that by undermining international tax transparency through their financial secrecy practices, a "pinstripe infrastructure" in countries like Switzerland, Luxemburg or Hong Kong – generally perceived as being among the least corrupt in the world – is in fact culpable of enabling "systemic corruption"

Table 6.2
Selected countries and perceived level of public sector corruption

Ranking (from least corrupt)		Score/100
1	Denmark	87
2	New Zealand	87
3	Finland	86
4	Singapore	85
5	Sweden	85
6	Switzerland	85
12	Germany	80
18	UK	77
22	Japan	73
26	France	69
27	USA	69
42	South Korea	59
55	Italy	53
76	South Africa	44
84	China	41
86	India	41
95	Turkey	39
111	Brazil	35
137	Mexico	29
147	Russia	28
155	Nigeria	26
176	Venezuela	16
177	Yemen	15
178	Syria	13
179	South Sudan	12
180	Somalia	9

(Tax Justice Network 2020). At a certain point, corruption discussions can easily spill over into political ideology debates about public and private bodies' respective roles.

Environmental sustainability
With few exceptions, before the 2010s green issues had been considered less central to international CSR than human rights, labour standards or corruption. Chapter 13 takes an in-depth look at how this has changed in recent years, with the environment fast becoming a paramount issue for most, if not all, MNEs worldwide. For the moment, however, suffice it to say that there is a problem with the disconnect between the national level at which most MNEs implement their CSR programmes and the international level at which the main environmental challenges – resource depletion and pollution – play out. The United Nations has tried to address this gap by holding conferences that codify certain environmental aspirations. However, it possesses insufficient policing power to enforce

its aspirations. A further complication is that whereas environmental sustainability is viewed as an absolute imperative in some countries, this does not apply everywhere, with many Global South countries considering it very unfair that their economic development be hampered due to their Global North counterparts having already disrupted many of the world's ecosystems during their own industrialisation trajectory. Add to this the fact that per-capita consumption of natural resources in the Global North continues to far outpace the Global South – not to mention a greater willingness (and ability) to pay for the green transition in some cultures as opposed to others – and MNEs' application of environmental CSR can be very patchy. Identifying an ethical issue in IB is usually much easier than agreeing how to deal with it.

Codifying international CSR

There have been many attempts over the years to codify ethical behaviour on an international scale. The two main categories here involve work done by the United Nations and the voluntary codes drafted at a MNE level.

The United Nation (UN)

The UN is the closest thing to a world government. It falls short, however, because it lacks policing abilities and because its decisions require consensus agreement from members who often pursue highly divergent interests. This means that UN Declarations tend to be weak compromises or mere statements of intent, unless they are ratified and policed by national governments. It remains that the principles these conventions establish – alongside the 1948 Declaration of Human Rights – have laid the foundations for many aspects of international CSR today.

The issues that the UN typically addresses (environment, corruption, human rights and development) generally call for action from governments and MNEs alike (see Table 6.3). Other issues (such as corporate governance) that are more specific to the business world tend to be addressed by bodies such as the OECD, whose governance ambitions are less extensive than the UN.

In the year 2000, the UN launched its Global Compact. This non-binding pact, featuring 16,592 signatories as of winter 2021, is the most straightforward delineation imaginable of core corporate international CSR principles. MNEs frequently reference its ten principles to validate their own good faith. An abridged version is listed below with the kind permission of the UN.

1 Respect human rights
2 Not be complicit in human rights abuses
3 Recognise freedom of association and right to collective bargaining
4 Eliminate all forced and compulsory labour

Table 6.3
Sample of United Nations conferences relevant to international CSR issues

Name	Year/Location	Comments
Earth Summit	1992: Rio de Janeiro	Declarations on Environment and Development, Forestry, Biodiversity, Climate Change
World Conference on Women	1995: Beijing	Plan to achieve global legal equality
Convention against Corruption	2003: Merida, New York	Legally binding multilateral international treaty, with both preventive and punitive measures
Conference on Sustainable Development	2012: Rio de Janeiro	Formulation of the 17 Sustainable Development Goals (SDGs)
Framework Convention on Climate Change (COP-21)	2015: Paris	Agreement to keep increase in average global temperature to below 2 degrees Celsius
Congress on Crime Prevention and Criminal Justice	2021: Kyoto	Coordination of policies against organised crime, terrorism and corruption

5 Abolish child labour
6 Eliminate discrimination
7 Adopt a precautionary principle to environmental challenges
8 Promote greater environmental responsibility
9 Develop and diffuse environmentally-friendly technology
10 Work against all forms of corruption

In 2015, the UN's General Assembly enriched the organisation's overall body of work with 17 Sustainable Development Goals (SDGs) that the whole of the world would want to achieve by the year 2030. These SDGs may be too aspirational to be fully actionable at the level of any one national government, much less a company. But they do feature widely in MNE sustainability action plans today – either as such or else broken down into more feasible targets – and should therefore be viewed as an important adjunct to discussions about CSR in IB. Again, an abridged version is listed below with the kind permission of the UN.

1 No poverty
2 Zero hunger
3 Good health and well-being
4 Quality education
5 Gender equality

6   Clean water and sanitation
7   Affordable and clear energy
8   Decent work and economic growth
9   Industry, innovation and infrastructure
10 Reduced inequalities
11 Sustainable cities and communities
12 Responsible consumption and production
13 Climate action
14 Life below water
15 Life on land
16 Peace, justice and strong institutions
17 Partnerships for the goals

Voluntary codes

Companies generally like to publicise the fact that they have drafted a
code of conduct or signed up to an existing one for two reasons: this
forces them to engage in an improvement dynamic that they hope will
have salutary effects on their performance over time; and it improves their
ethical reputation hence defuses possible criticism. This is particularly true
for MNEs seeking to achieve "insiderisation" status by demonstrating
their devotion to the well-being of the populations in the various countries
where they operate. Of course, the consistency of these efforts will depend
on how different MNE subsidiaries interact with their local environments
(Beddewela 2019). Unsurprisingly, companies' environmental, social and
ethical reporting activities vary widely across the world. Despite ongoing
efforts to harmonise standards, international CSR tends to materialise on
much more of a national than a global basis.

Ethical report group -
Associations of
companies and other
organisations promising
to respect certain ethical
standards.

After the UN Global Compact, the world's three largest ethical
reporting groups are the Global Reporting Initiative (GRI), the SA8000
and the Ethical Trading Initiative (ETI). The GRI's website calls itself a
large, "multi-stakeholder network" of experts promoting triple bottom
line disclosures through a "Sustainability Reporting Framework". The
purpose is to give the public a full and transparent vision of the actions
taken by member organisations (companies but also public sector bodies
and non-governmental organisations [NGOs]). SA8000, derived from ISO
quality standards, is a "Social Accountability Standard" and verification
system aimed at "assuring humane workplaces". ETI largely exists to
monitor MNEs' international supply chains, building on existing codes of
conduct to ensure enforcement of basic labour standards.

**Non-governmental
organisations (NGOs) -**
Associations created
by members of the
general public to address
specific problems or
promote an overall ethos
or policy.

Other codes of conduct are constructed at a branch level. In some
sectors (like agribusiness), this reflects MNEs' tendency to conceive of
their ethical and other responsibilities not in terms of what each company
in a global value chain does separately but as a reflection of everyone's
behaviour. The joint determination of an ethical code of conduct is a
way to counter the confusion that can arise when partner companies
have different understandings of CSR. Examples of these branch-level
agreements include the International Council of Toy Industries and the

International Code of Conduct on the Distribution and Use of Pesticides. Branch codes often focus on labour practices, product safety and environmental standards. They tend to be used by consumers and other stakeholders as evidence of a MNE's CSR commitment.

The same applies to environmental and social ratings agencies like Environmental Resources Management (ERM) in the USA/UK or BMJ Ratings in France, which fulfil in sustainability matters a function similar to the one performed by financial rating agencies such as Standard and Poor's or Moody's. The reason many MNEs pay for accreditation instead of relying on whatever code of conduct and/or specific CSR plan they have developed in-house is to enhance their credibility – stakeholders (whether customers, counterparts of politicians) tend to have greater faith in a foreign company's good faith when a trusted local evaluator has vouched for this.

Lastly, it should be noted that the growing number of consumers willing to pay an ethical premium for certifiably sustainable goods might incentivise some companies to exaggerate their CSR credentials. This is particularly tempting in IB, where the geographic dispersion of a MNE's operations can make it hard for stakeholders in some parts of the world to monitor its behaviour elsewhere. The issue then becomes whether companies can be trusted not to "greenwash" (over-state) their CSR performance and, if so, what kinds of pressure might be exerted to force them to be as ethical as they say they are.

Ethical premium – Surcharge that consumers pay for a certifiably sustainable item.

Enforcing international CSR

It is one thing to specify the ethical standards that a MNE is supposed to meet. It is another to ensure that it actually does so. Some expectations get formalised in regulations that carry legal weight and can be policed by the authorities. This applies especially in countries characterised by strong institutions of governance. Other expectations are more aspirational and can only be enforced through market behaviour. International CSR enforcement relies to varying degrees on both approaches.

Because everyone operating within a national framework ultimately answers to a single authority (the government), enforcement is always more straightforward at this level. Nor is there any real alternative. Until such time as an intergovernmental organisation is endowed with overarching policing powers – or one country is empowered to prosecute all companies for their behaviour everywhere – CSR can only be fully policed within national borders. This means that enforcement assumes different shapes worldwide.

CSR enforcement in the United States
According to one school of thought (Matten and Moon 2008), due to the comparative vagueness of American liability legislation, firms in the

USA feel great pressure to prove that they are acting ethically even when they are already behaving legally. Before the Sarbanes-Oxley corporate governance laws were enacted in 2002, US executives could often avoid personal responsibility for their behaviour at work by "hiding behind the corporate veil" of limited liability (Stiglitz 2006). It is to overcome the suspicions which this often raises that many US companies take extra steps to reassure their public. Examples include McDonald's publication of ingredient quality standards going well beyond USA Food and Drug Administration minimum requirements, Ben and Jerry's constant reference in advertising to their progressive values and commitment to sustainability and the many American MNEs who have signed up to international sustainability bodies such as the GRI. The end result is that in the USA, CSR tends to be enforced as much, if not more, through the marketplace rather than via legislation.

CSR enforcement in Europe

Characterised by a long social-democratic tradition of cooperation between business and government, European countries have a greater tendency than elsewhere in the world to feature national legislation specifying the social responsibilities that companies are supposed to assume. Epitomised by the German legal construct that *Eigentum verpflichtet* ("ownership implies duties") and materialising, for instance, in France's 2001 *Nouvelles Régulations Economiques* law requiring all companies above a certain size to publish environmental and social accounts alongside their financial statements, the end result is that CSR enforcement in this region tends to revolve more around regulatory compliance than market pressure, all the more so given recent European Union efforts to expand sustainability reporting requirements across all member-states.

CSR enforcement in Asia and the Global South

The CSR approach adopted in Japan and much of East Asia is deeply rooted in a Confucian culture that validates social harmony more than self-interest and relies for this on self-policing. CSR enforcement in this part of the world might therefore be seen as a hybrid of Europe's more collectivist approach and the USA's more market-driven orientation. Having said that, there are significant variations in the way CSR plays out between Asian countries characterised by similar value systems but finding themselves at different stages of socio-economic development. Studies about the relationship between business, government and society in China, for instance, have attributed recurring scandals in the country to the relative absence of independent watchdogs and local advocacy groups, along with the comparative powerlessness of the Chinese media, which makes it harder to expose unethical behaviour here (Wu and Davidson 2011). This exemplifies the "institutional voids" afflicting many countries in the Global South, an issue that Chapter 13 explores in further detail. To compensate, there tends to be the expectation in China that local authorities will step in and police irresponsible companies. The problem is that this mode of enforcement can itself be beset by political calculation and self-interest, if not outright corruption. What remains for MNEs working in China is to try and curry favour with politicians (and protect themselves from arbitrary interventions) through overt manifestations of CSR involving, for instance, support for local MNE workers' unionisation efforts – initiatives that, by the by, the same workers are discouraged from taking in companies owned by domestic interests. Add to this the fact that most unions in China tend to be state-run, and it is clear that stakeholder relations in the country can be both highly political and very different from what MNEs experience in the Global North.

The other salient factor is that CSR, and especially the enforcement thereof, can still seem like a luxury in much of the Global South. Historically, the main priority across these zones has been to create jobs and spark growth by attracting inwards FDI – not to frighten away MNEs by imposing and enforcing costly CSR standards. On top of this, CSR reporting systems are often of poor quality in the Global South; there may be no real obligation for foreign MNEs to implement the relatively fewer regulations that do exist; and even if local populations are aware of CSR, they may not be in a position to pressure a MNE to report on (hence improve) its environmental and social behaviour (Utama 2011). Indeed, the ongoing prevalence of philanthropy in the Indian, Middle Eastern and African business traditions might actually have the unwanted effect of undermining CSR enforcement, given the incentive for MNEs operating in these locales to use charity giving "as a respectable means of buying off stakeholders to accept operating practices" that might not be considered ethical under other circumstances (Hopkins 2007). As for MNEs originating in the Global South themselves, there is some evidence that they view CSR as a "legitimation strategy", particularly vis-à-vis Global North audiences, and decouple this behaviour from the way they behave at home (Tashman et al. 2018). The end result is an unfortunate continuation of certain negative social and environmental outcomes across broad swathes of the planet, specifically besetting the world's poorest populations – the people whose existing vulnerabilities means they are the least capable of withstanding the new problems they face. It is this distress, largely conveyed through images of suffering in the Global South, that explains the passion underpinning many CSR discussions and the advocacy of its main proponents.

Advocating international CSR

Some of the impetus behind international CSR today clearly comes from MNE managers themselves, reflecting their personal ethical compass, sincere goodwill and/or, more cynically, fear of becoming figures of hate for activists or consumers. As MNEs build up their "community affairs" or "sustainability" departments and staff them with Generation Z recruits whose personal ethos may be more "purpose"-oriented and less profit-driven than their predecessors, there is every chance that the current enthusiasm for IB ethics will persist.

At the same time, it is just as evident that much of the push for international CSR will continue to come from external pressure groups – NGOs and consumers themselves – dismayed by IB practices that they bemoan as unethical. Some of this criticism will be based on solid evidence; some will not. The reality is that few, if any, MNEs are entirely ethical or unethical. Most have people capable of doing good or bad, or even both, alternatively. In this respect, like other aspects of IB, the only real rule is that there are no rules.

It is difficult to find a single definition for NGOs, often categorised as bodies representing the views and/or interests of "civil society". The first recognised NGO, founded in the USA in 1839, was the Anti-Slavery Society. At one point, non-profit organisations, starting with small poorly funded charities, were the main protagonists in this sector. Today, however, NGOs are just as likely to be large professionally run organisations with solid revenue streams, employing hundreds of staff members and capable of mobilising thousands of supporters. This is especially true where IB ethics are concerned, perhaps mirroring the huge impact that MNEs can have given how many different countries they can affect (and without forgetting the particular suspicions they often evoke due to their perceived foreignness). It bears remembering that in CSR, like in other matters, mistrust of IB has long been an integral part of IB.

No one knows exactly how many NGOs there are today, but the number runs into the tens of thousands. At a time when the Internet has both broadened awareness of global problems and empowered people to express themselves on all varieties of topics, it is no surprise that reform-minded individuals worldwide have ended up supporting advocacy groups. For many citizens cynical about their national government's ability to control companies – especially footloose foreign MNEs – NGOs offer an alternative vehicle for influencing current affairs, all the more so given the high profile that many have achieved through a savvy use of communications.

NGOs' public exposure campaigns are intended to attract the attention of three targets: politicians, in the hope that they can use legislation (if not sanctions) to get MNEs to change certain behaviours; journalists, in the hope of winning the "battle for hearts and minds"; and/or consumers, in the hope that they will use their spending power discriminately. NGOs' frequent effectiveness at achieving these goals has created a situation where managers are increasingly willing to listen to them, if only to co-opt their message. The logic here is that companies might be able to derive greater reputational benefit from being seen as addressing their failings than from blithely denying them, hence the greater frequency with which most, if not all, trumpet their collaborations with NGOs nowadays.

It remains that like any other commodity, there is a "market for virtue" (Vogel 2006), with boardrooms often making business decisions about how the earnings they generate through certain criticisable actions compare with the legal liabilities they might incur and/or the costs of compensatory CSR. MNEs might choose to ignore protests if the NGOs leading a campaign against them lack credibility or sufficient voice. Where actual customers are being dissuaded, on the other hand, companies are more likely to listen.

Consumer boycotts have sparked changes in MNE policy on several occasions in recent IB history. It remains that such instances are relatively few and far between. Consumers may not monitor a MNE's doings in faraway lands; the lack of proximity might make them feel less concerned even if they are aware of foreign misconduct; their personal values may cause them to not really care about the company's conduct; and/or they may suffer from "sustainability fatigue" in an era when so many companies are promoting their credentials in this domain that the expression can sometimes seem trite.

The question then becomes how consumer demand for MNE sustainability is likely to evolve in the future. In the wake of the Covid-19 pandemic, for instance, there is the possibility that cash-strapped MNEs in particularly hard-hit international sectors (like aviation) will feel that they can no longer afford their current CSR programmes, especially in light of the success that some major companies have been able to achieve during this same period despite being regularly targeted by activists. On the other hand, there is just as strong an argument to make that the greater social solidarity generated by a crisis afflicting all of humankind will increase the number of MNE managers sensing a need to move beyond a shareholder value focus and commit to providing value to all stakeholders, as America's influential Business Roundtable proclaimed in August 2019, just before the pandemic broke out. Notwithstanding the cynicism that often accompanies IB analysis, underestimating the power of MNE CSR in the 21st century would appear to be a very risky career choice.

Attitudes and alternatives

CSR requires real investment, especially when programmes are in their early stages. The challenge for managers is determining whether they are spending enough in the right areas to satisfy their ethical ambitions without wasting company money. Since this cannot be answered objectively, the options they generally face are whether to err by spending too much or else by spending too little on CSR. In IB, this arbitrage will vary from country to country, making the coordination of CSR particularly complicated for MNEs. But despite a few remaining pockets of opposition, ethical expectations have become so widespread nowadays that the safest thing for managers to do is to always integrate them into their core strategic thinking.

Chapter summary

The chapter's first section spoke to the difficulties of defining moral behaviour in cross-border situations characterised by value systems that are not only divergent but which also vary over time. This was followed by a debate on the materiality of MNEs' international CSR efforts, culminating in the verdict that it is a good thing. The second section began by reviewing the contours of the main international CSR issues (human rights, labour standards, discrimination, corruption and environmental sustainability), leading to analysis of efforts to codify MNE conduct in these areas, as well as the challenges inherent to their enforcement. The chapter then concluded with a brief discussion of the kinds of pressure that CSR advocates can exert on MNEs.

Case study 6.3: David takes on the Goliaths

Financial deregulation since the 1980s paved the way to a long period of volatility in the world's currency, bond and stock markets when commercial banks and speculators, largely freed from supervisory oversight, began engaging in mass speculation. Where central banks had once reigned supreme, now herds of investors pushed "hot capital" in and out of national economies, causing financial instability that was particularly problematic when it affected Global South countries unable to afford the sudden stops in funding. For many development advocates, the sight of Western financiers wrecking poor countries' finance was a sign that things had to change in the global currency markets. The question became what and how.

In the 1970s, Nobel laureate James Tobin first floated the idea that a 1 percent tax on foreign exchange (FX) transactions could eliminate virtually all speculation. In the late 1990s, a coterie of reform-minded

Fig 6.7
An electronic herd dominates the world's capital and currency markets.

campaigners revived this proposal and started working on getting governments to implement it.

Across the world, there are many idealistic NGO professionals who devote their lives to remedying the injustices they see. One such individual in London is David Hillman, a veteran of campaigns against apartheid South Africa and the use of landmines. Like many of his peers, David was dismayed by the havoc that currency speculation was wreaking on the global economy, especially in the world's poorer countries. He therefore responded favourably when asked by the anti-poverty NGO War on Want to spearhead a project convincing world leaders to adopt the Tobin tax. The effort would require coordination with like-minded campaigns elsewhere, both in the UK and abroad. Governments can only be convinced of the need to change policy, in the IB arena as in many others, if an idea has widespread support. David Hillman set about marshalling his forces and would spend the next 20 years advancing towards the goal.

The work of an NGO starts with coordinating networks to ensure everyone speaks in a single voice and makes a clear case; many reform campaigns have been lost due to confusing proposals. This definition stage is usually followed by a multipronged communications effort, ranging from participation in conferences and debates worldwide to the production of audiovisual material and, maybe especially, media exposure. There is a dual focus guiding the work at this stage: heightening public awareness of the proposal and educating key players about its technical aspects.

Once a groundswell had built up, David began the long and hard task of influencing the ultimate decision-makers, namely, senior politicians. He also made the decision to lodge the campaign in a standalone NGO called Stamp Out Poverty to avoid being swamped within more diffuse development campaigns. NGOs face tremendous competition for media and political attention, the world's currency regime being only one problem among many.

Painstakingly over the years, David was able to convince more and more politicians of the benefits of advocating what would become known colloquially as the Robin Hood Tax and officially as the Financial Transactions Tax (FTT). The idea began appearing on progressive parties' election manifestoes in several countries, and from 2011, a number of European countries started on the road to implementation. The journey has been painfully slow, with lobbyists hired by the finance industry working hard to oppose the FTT at every turn. Vested interests are a constant obstacle to NGOs' progress agenda.

There were some wins for David, starting with France's adoption of the FTT in 2012, followed by Italy in 2013. But strangely enough, it was the 2020 Covid-19 pandemic that really put the wind back in David's sails. With governments worldwide contracting enormous debt to cope

with Covid-19, the idea of developing a new source of tax revenue –
especially one affecting a small population (financial speculators)
largely unscathed by the same pressures facing other IB practitioners –
suddenly seemed very attractive again. In 2021, Spain joined the ranks
of countries levying the FTT, which today includes the UK and its 0.5
percent stamp duty on share purchases. David still has a long way to
go before seeing universal adoption of the proposal to which he had
devoted 20 years of life, but to paraphrase the philosopher Lao Tzu,
long journeys always start with a single step.

Case study questions

1. What mandate do NGOs have to seek policy changes?
2. How easy is it to coordinate NGO campaigns worldwide?
3. How can NGOs avoid "sustainability fatigue"?

Chapter discussion questions

1   Why might countries respond differently to the call for "purpose
    before profits"?
2   Are critics right to fear that MNEs might use the international
    variability of ethics to avoid their social responsibility?
3   What explains the varying priorities given to different sustainability
    goals across the world?
4   What can MNEs do if CSR puts them at a competitive
    disadvantage?
5   How powerful a voice do NGOs have in international business?

References

Bahoo, S. et al. (August 2020). "Corruption in international business: A
    review and research agenda", *International Business Review*, Volume
    29, Issue 4, accessed 29 July 2021 at https://www.sciencedirect.com/
Banerjee, S., and Alamgir, F. (2020). "Contested compliance regimes
    in global production networks…", *Social and Environmental
    Accountability Journal*, Volume 40, Issue 2.
Baur, D. et al. (May 2015). *The Corporate Social Responsibility Story of
    Chiquita*, Boncourt: Fondation Guilé.
Beddewela, E. (December 2019). "Managing corporate community
    responsibility in multinational corporations: Resolving institutional
    duality", *Long Range Planning*, Volume 52, Issue 6.
Carlile, C. (1 October 2020). "Campaign: The fight for agricultural
    workers' rights in southern Spain", accessed 21 February 2021 at
    https://www.ethicalconsumer.org/

Collins, S., and Murphy, F. (18 July 2013). "Corporations and the fight against hunger: Why CSR wont' do", *Guardian*.

Cronin, J. (4 July 2006). "Let business lift Africa out of poverty", accessed 21 February 2021 at http://news.bbc.co.uk

Deccan Herald (25 August 2020). "Punished for being poor? Mexico child labour case makes poverty a crime, critics say", accessed 20 November 2020 at https://www.deccanherald.com/

Diamond, S. (28 January 1985). "The Bhopal disaster: How it happened", *New York Times*.

Donaldson, T. (1991). *The Ethics of International Business*, Oxford: Oxford University Press.

Giacomin, V. et al. (2019). "Why does business invest in education in emerging markets? Why Does It Matter?" *Harvard Business Review*, Working Paper 20–039.

Girma, S. et al. (8 July 2019). "Which boats are lifted by a foreign tide? Direct and indirect wage effects of foreign ownership", *Journal of International Business Studies*, Volume 50, Issue 6, pp. 923–947.

Hamilton, I. (2 March 2020). "Apple benefits from forced Uighur labour...", accessed 21 February 2021 at https://www.businessinsider.com/

Hopkins, M. (2007). *Corporate Social Responsibility and International Development: Is Business the Solution?* London: Earthscan.

Human Rights Watch (August 2011). "Ripe with abuse: Human rights conditions in South Africa's fruit and wine industries", accessed 29 July 2021 at https://www.hrw.org/

Kashyap, A. (4 February 2020). "UK legal case a wake-up call for garment companies", accessed 21 February 2021 at https://www.hrw.org/

Khan, M. et al. (October 2020). "The institutional analysis of CSR: Learnings from an emerging country", *Emerging Markets Review*, Volume 45.

Kline, J. (2005). *Ethics for International Business*. New York: Routledge.

Lamb, S. et al. (July 2017). "The evolving role of CSR in international development...", *The Extractive Industries and Society*, Volume 4, Issue 3.

Maggioni, D. et al. (10 April 2019). "MNEs' location strategies and labour standards: The role of operating and reputations considerations across industries", *Journal of International Business Studies*, Volume 50, Issue 6, pp. 948–972.

Marcoux, A. (May–June 2000). "Business ethics gone wrong", *Cato Policy Report*, Volume 20, Issue 3.

Matten, D., and Moon, J. (2008). "Implicit and explicit CSR: A conceptual framework for understanding CSR in Europe", *The Academy of Management Review*, Volume 33, Issue 2.

Menendez-Espina, S. et al. (18 February 2020). "Job insecurity and mental health: The moderating role of coping strategies from a gender perspective", accessed 21 February 2021 at https://www.frontiersin.org/

Reba (3 October 2019). "Why social responsibility is now just as important as pay to attract new workers", accessed 21 February 2021 at https://reba.global/

Rusina, A. (28 March 2020). "Name and shame? Evidence from the European Union tax haven blacklist", *International Tax and Public Finance*, Volume 27, pp. 1364–1424.

Russell, J. (12 October 2006). "Ivory coast toxic waste—dumped on", *Ethical Corporation*.

Schwartz, P. (1999). *When Good Companies do Bad Things: Responsibility and Risk in the Age of Gobalisation*. New York: John Wiley & Sons.

Sitkin, A. (December 2013). "Working for the local community: Substantively broader/geographically narrower CSR accounting", *Accounting Forum*, Volume 37, Issue 4, pp. 315–324.

Steinhorst, C. (17 October 2019). "Rethinking the value of core values", accessed 18 November 2020 at https://www.forbes.com/

Stiglitz, J. (2006). *Making Globalisation Work: The Next Steps to Global Justice*. London: Allen Lane.

Tashman, P. et al. (6 August 2018). "Walking the walk or talking the talk? Corporate social responsibility decoupling in emerging market multinationals", *Journal of International Business Studies*, Volume 50, Issue 2, pp. 153–171.

Tax Justice Network (2 November 2020). "Systemic corruption and the oligarchic threat to national security", accessed 17 February 2021 at https://www.taxjustice.net/

Utama, S. (August 2011). "An evaluation of support infrastructures for corporate responsibility reporting in Indonesia", *Asian Business & Management*, Volume 10, Number 3, pp. 405–424.

Vogel, D. (2006). *The Market for Virtue*. Washington, DC: Brookings.

Wu, J., and Davidson, D. (2011). "The business-government-society relationship: A comparison between China and the US", *The Journal of Management Development*, Volume 30, Issue 1, pp. 112–125.

Yunis, M. et al. (19 September 2018). "Corporate social responsibility of foreign multinationals in a development country context", *Sustainability*, Volume 10, Issue 10.

Zhou, N., and Wang, H. (15 July 2020). "Foreign subsidiary CSR as a buffer against parent firm reputation risk", *Journal of International Business Studies*, Volume 51, Issue 8, pp. 1256–1282.

PART III

Internationalisation strategies

CHAPTER 7

Multinational history and configurations

Introduction

The idea that international business (IB) has maintained a great degree of consistency over its thousands of years of existence may seem surprising. After all, the 13th-century example of Marco Polo – a practitioner considered by many as a seminal figure in this field – bears little, if any, resemblance to the way giant multinational enterprises (MNEs) organise today's cross-border ventures. Yet, as discussed in this chapter's first section, the classes of enabling factors that made the famous Italian explorer's fortune during his career are largely the same as the ones that apply today, even if their manifestation is very different. A more instructive filter for analysing the shape of IB across the centuries is therefore to focus on how these drivers have affected the organisational modes that have been implemented by today's Marco Polos – mainly international entrepreneurs working within MNE frameworks – while also considering some of the variables affecting their actions, including the geographic origin and size of the companies for which they work.

The chapter's second section builds upon this initial discussion of configuration paradigms – answering the fundamental IB question of "who does what where" – by studying the specific market entry mode whereby MNEs assume their most material (hence meaningful) presence

Enabling factors - Preconditions for an outcome to occur.

Fig 7.1
Marco Polo, a giant in the history of international business.

DOI: 10.4324/9781003159056-10

at the heart of a foreign country, namely, foreign direct investment (FDI). Given the proximity that FDI creates between a foreign MNE and host country stakeholders, the topic needs to be approached from both a national and a corporate perspective. This then becomes the transition between the textbook's first half, largely focused as it has been on macro-level studies of the IB environment, and its second half, which will give much greater weighting to the micro-level decisions that IB practitioners make in their search for advantage.

LEARNING OBJECTIVES

After reading this chapter, you will be able to:

- track the relative significance over time of different IB enabling factors
- link MNEs' configuration choices to their historical circumstances
- analyse the strengths and weakness of different MNE paradigms
- identify small and medium-sized enterprises' IB-related specificities
- analyse FDI from both a country and a company perspective

Case study 7.1: IBM's Indian summer

Since the country's almost revolutionary liberalisation reforms of 1991, Indian governments have started to adopt a more welcoming attitude to IB. There are still concerns about state interference in tax matters (epitomised by the Delhi regime's 2021 appeals against court rulings that had exonerated multinationals like Vodafone and Cairn Energy of fiscal misconduct). All in all, however, MNEs are taking an increasingly positive view of this continent-sized country, first and foremost because of the millions of world-class mathematicians and

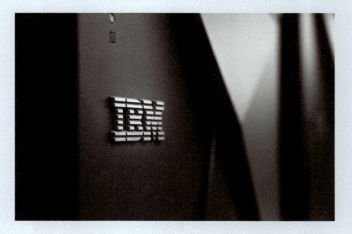

Fig 7.2
IBM has reconfigured its operations many times over the course of its long international history.

engineers that its education system produces. Due to their presence, India has become a global hub for a variety of service sector MNEs, ranging from banks to pharmaceuticals and information technology (IT). The American giant IBM has been part of this wave (Tejaswi 2020).

By 2021, IBM had become one of India's leading private sector employers, with something like one-third of its estimated global staff of around 430,000 working out of the country, more than in the USA itself. The company runs all of its computing and service activities in India, ranging from lower-level business process outsourcing to high value-added research and development, software production and cloud computing.

One of the main reasons behind IBM's decision to expand in India was cost competition from emerging local rivals like Infosys, the software company. With highly competent Indian programmers earning far less than their US counterparts, one obvious response for IBM was to invade Infosys's home market and benefit from its human capital in this way. From an Indian perspective, FDI of this kind, albeit largely positive, has also been a double-edged sword. It brought funding and management knowledge while offering much needed high-quality jobs, but it also drained Indian workers away from domestic companies and distorted national wage structures by widening the gap between workers recruited by MNEs like IBM and domestic employers. Issues relating to the fair distribution of the benefits of globalisation are regular features in the politics of IB, as demonstrated, for instance, by the fact that since 2016, foreign companies operating in India are subject to a 40 percent tax on certain incomes, as opposed to the general rate of 25 percent paid by home-grown firms.

Notwithstanding this disadvantage, MNEs like IBM have continued to delegate greater roles to their Indian-based operations. As ex-CEO Sam Palmisano once famously announced, "Work flows to the places where it will be done best". In its early years, IBM was mainly a domestic US company, but in recent decades it has changed its configuration to access talent from all across the world. In April 2020, Indian-born engineer Arvind Krishna became group CEO, following an early career where he gained widespread recognition for cutting-edge work in fields like artificial intelligence and blockchain technology (see Chapter 15). Under his tutelage, the company now sports a so-called globalisation website touting its ability to both internationalise application components to "enable multicultural support" while also localising them to implement "specific regional conventions". These are the hallmarks of a MNE whose workforce has been diversified specifically with a view towards accommodating the variations in demand that it expects to see in the future across its different markets.

It is true that IBM maintains its headquarters in New York state. Moreover, US nationals still feature widely on its executive committee.

But analysts today would be hard-pressed to say to what extent this deeply internationalised group can still be considered American.

Case study questions

1. At what point do the advantages of reconfiguring a MNE's operations around a country like India outweigh the disadvantages?
2. To what extent does the internationalisation of a MNE's operations require the internationalisation of its executive teams?

Section I. International business paradigms

MNEs come in many forms, ranging from small domestic firms with sporadic foreign interests to huge multi-divisional entities running continuous operations outside their country of origin. This variability in the agents driving IB has been matched over the years by further variability in the organisation of multinational operations. What becomes interesting then is analysing to what extent IB protagonists have had agency in pursuing their preferred internationalisation trajectories; or conversely, if they are largely constrained by circumstances, hence limited in the configurations they can design. It is a fundamental question explored in many IB studies relating to the relative importance of external versus internal factors in MNE decision-making (Tan et al. 2020).

Any determination made at this level will offer lessons about the various ways that MNEs might be expected to configure their operations now and in the future. Path-dependency (hysteresis) teaches that neither the present nor the future materialise on a blank page but build instead on what has come before, that is, contemporary thinking is necessarily grounded in a knowledge of history. It is rare, however, that IB students get hired to look to the past – what matters instead is their ability to look forward. The question then becomes to what extent MNEs can be expected to simply act within the confines of existing paradigms or whether they have the freedom to disrupt the status quo and take quantum leaps in new directions. It is something that IB practitioners will be asked to consider many times over the course of their careers, hence a topic well worth exploring here.

Enabling factors

The main external drivers of international business – politics, finance, technology and paradigms – were briefly introduced in Chapter 1. It is useful, however, to monitor their different manifestations and effects over time. As stressed throughout this book, MNEs always operate within a context.

As discussed in Chapters 2 and 3, *politics* has always been a key determinant of IB, if only because foreign interests like MNEs are, by definition, transacting in spaces regulated by national governments – one of whose traditional tasks, it should be remembered, is to protect domestic interests against potential dangers coming from abroad. Marco Polo, for instance, could only travel the Silk Road to China because he was able to convince Kublai Khan to allow him to cross the Mongolian Empire, which was on the way. Other merchants at the time had been refused entry – or even worse. There is a point to make here that nothing obliges a society to equate foreigners with danger. It is, however, an attitude that has arisen far too many times in history to be ignored.

In truth, the political history of the past two centuries has seen a clear trend towards more IB-friendly mindsets and away from the xenophobia and pure protectionism that had often dominated the more distant past – a change in attitude that has greatly reduced barriers to trade, making it much easier for companies to conceptualise optimal cross-border configurations and try to implement them. Having said that, economic nationalism is still very much alive, best exemplified in recent years by the 2016 Donald Trump and Brexit votes affecting the US and UK, respectively. Probably the best summation of the politics of protectionism is that they will always wax and wane, affecting the impact of this factor at any one point in time.

Certainly, there are still some very extreme examples of political risk to IB, for instance, when a host country government engages in the expropriation of a MNE's local assets. Such actions are no longer as widespread as they once were, although it is still worth noting cases throughout the 2010s of so-called Bolivarian South American regimes seizing foreign entities, like when Venezuela's government expropriated a General Motors plant in 2017. More frequent today are instances of geopolitical tension affecting MNEs' configuration choices. In late 2019, for example, Chinese tech giant Huawei moved its Santa Clara research centre from Silicon Valley, the global centre of computing technology, to Canada for the simple reason that US government's suspicions of the company led to the imposition of restrictions that made it difficult for Huawei's global headquarters to communicate with its Californian subsidiary (AP 2019). Otherwise, it is worth noting how European MNEs like Peugeot and Daimler had upped their operations in Iran in 2015 when Western sanctions on the country were largely lifted, only to have to more or less withdraw again in 2018 when the Trump administration reimposed them. It remains to be seen whether the 2021 advent of a Biden administration – more disposed towards international cooperation, including a normalisation of relations with Iran – will induce these MNEs to return to the country, or if the fear of other bellicose US presidencies in the future will cause them to omit it from their plans. One problem with politics as an

Expropriation - Where private property is seized by a government, often without compensation.

enabling factor is that MNE strategists struggle to predict whether it will be helpful to IB or not.

Political risk can also impact MNEs when the countries involved are allies. One example from 2009 was when the then French President Nicolas Sarkozy told carmaker Renault, suffering from a loss of business in the wake of the previous year's financial crisis, that it would only qualify for domestic state aid if it promised to close a plant it ran in Slovenia – a friendly fellow EU member-state – and moved production back home. In a similar vein, recent European Union investigations into the allegedly oligopolistic practices of two American giants (Google and Amazon) denote no fundamental hostility towards the USA. In both cases, the generally amicable relationships between home and host country governments mean that ad hoc problems of this nature are likely to be resolved relatively easily, following which the MNEs should be able to return to business as usual. Indeed, where there is no tradition of one country negatively stereotyping another, diplomacy – materialising in the liberal global governance regime that Chapter 4 discussed – can turn politics into a catalyst for IB, rather than an obstacle.

The second key driver of MNE activity is *finance*. Logically, delivery systems serving geographically distant markets take longer to set up than domestic businesses. Returning to the Marco Polo analogy, years elapsed between the date the merchant-explorer set forth from Venice and when he was finally able to return from China with silk and spice to sell. To survive all that time, he needed credit to live off (and to pay his suppliers) – funding that he was able to source from medieval Italian sources who were the predecessors to modern banks. This was unusual for the time, however, with the main source for IB finance during its early years being national governments, who tended to conflate trade with imperial expansion. As different European societies' merchant classes started to accumulate more and more wealth, however, they would gradually assume this role, in conjunction with the advent of functioning stock markets in the 17th century and the associated formation of limited liability companies, best exemplified by the British East India Company, recognised as one of the world's first MNEs. Today it would be impossible to analyse IB without reference to the global financial markets where companies access the capital they need to operate internationally. With the exception of disruptive periods like the global credit crunch that followed the 2008 subprime crisis, the reality is that most MNEs today – certainly those of a certain size – find it relatively easy to raise funding. The end result is that finance has become more of an enabling factor in IB than it used to be.

The third constant in IB history is *technology*, which can be broken down for MNEs in terms of how it affects their industrial configurations but also more broadly as regards the impacts on *communications* and *logistics*. The latter factor has always been key to companies' ability to trade abroad and can be exemplified, in a final reference to Marco Polo, by the navigational hardships facing early merchants of his

Credit crunch - Where financial market conditions make it difficult for borrowers to access the funding they need

ilk, always suffering long journeys with uncertain outcomes. It bears repeating that much of the subsequent rise in trade during the Age of Exploration was driven by improvements in naval logistics (i.e. ship designs, longitude calculation methods). Things would improve rapidly after the 18th-century invention of the steam engine, leading, in turn, to faster ships, trains and ultimately motor vehicles and airplanes. The late 19th century also saw major infrastructure projects like the Suez and Panama canals as well as the Trans-Siberian railway, which accelerated the movement of goods and enabled the integration of cross-border value chains, turning trade into a continuous undertaking instead of the discrete and sporadic business that it had been before. The logistics industry will have challenges to face in the coming years, first and foremost its environmental footprint. But few locales today remain inaccessible to the rest of the world, making this factor more of a catalyst for IB activity than ever before.

The same can be said about technology-driving communications, which have always been key to MNEs' identification of external opportunities as well as their ability to link geographically dispersed activities. Note that like the advances in transportation, it was only after the telegraph and telephone had spread in the late 19th century that MNEs were finally able to integrate their operations worldwide. The Internet fulfils a similar function today, helping companies not only to improve market intelligence but also to be effective when delegating, if they so desire, particular stages of their global value chains to foreign subsidiaries or external suppliers. The intra-firm (and inter-firm) transfer of knowledge enabled by Internet technology – quantifiable today in new metrics such as DHL's Global Connectedness Index – may be as important to MNEs as any other IB-enabling factor.

Lastly, the types of knowledge that MNEs typically carry abroad tend to not only relate to products and processes but also to management *paradigms*. Historically, different principles have dominated different business cultures' thinking about the best way to organise their economic activities. With vastly improved and better funded communications and with logistics capabilities enabling infinitely closer cross-border linkages, strategizing internationally is not only easier than ever but also more or less indispensable. After all, if a MNE's foreign rivals are all competing worldwide, it runs great risks by not doing the same. Most of the time, the question is no longer whether or not international factors should figure in managers' configuration thinking. Instead, it is how this should be done.

Organisational modes

MNEs generally develop subsidiaries according to two principles. Much early FDI involved horizontal integration, where companies would open overseas units doing roughly the same things abroad as they did at home,

Integration - Coordination of different units' activities to the extent that their missions can be defined in light of one another.

Horizontal integration - Where the activities that a company launches in a new market are at a similar stage of the value chain as the one where it operates in its home market.

in countries characterised by roughly the same level of industrial and socio-economic development. Some of the earliest examples of this were German engineering group Siemens' launch of UK operations in 1852 and the plant that Scottish thread maker Clark built in New Jersey in 1867. At the time, similarity facilitated internationalisation.

The first MNEs possessed much less information about foreign environments than their successors do today. They also faced greater political and other barriers to entry, while suffering from much slower communication and transport links. All these obstacles impeded inter-subsidiary relationships and meant that foreign units had to be managed autonomously and in isolation. Indeed, given how erratic cross-border deliveries were at the time, it would have been risky for one plant's production to rely on components shipped from distant sister units. Where foreign subsidiaries traded, it usually involved finished products.

From the late 19th century until the 1929 Wall Street Crash, technological progress (and free trade politics) paved the way for what came to be known as the "first golden era of globalisation". Multinationals in this era generally followed two configurational models (see Figure 7.3).

Sister units - Separate corporate entities sharing the same parent company.

- "American" model. MNEs developed competencies at home and either exported or undertook FDI specifically to overcome trade barriers (e.g. Ford and General Motors in Europe)
- "British" model. MNEs set up subsidiaries reflecting local competencies before embedding units into a wider global network (e.g. the Jardine trading company in Hong Kong)

Both models contained the seeds of the HQ-subsidiary configuration typifying modern MNEs. But by accepting that different sites could specialise in different activities reflecting location-specific advantages, the British model came closer to applying Adam Smith's international division of labour principles. As early MNEs became increasingly accustomed to (hence comfortable with) operating in foreign countries – and given the era's growing relaxation of barriers to trade – the costly duplications inherent to horizontal integration seemed less attractive than the idea of organising configurations around the intra-firm trade of intermediary goods, with final products often only being assembled in the

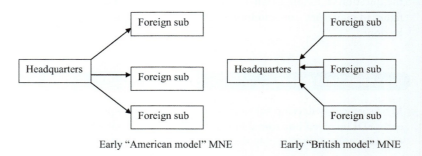

Fig 7.3
MNE configuration models during the first golden era of globalisation (1880–1929). Arrows indicate direction of cross-border knowledge flows (Jones 2005).

Early "American model" MNE   Early "British model" MNE

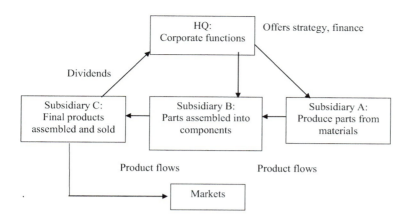

Fig 7.4
Vertically integrated
MNEs characterised by
inter-subsidiary transfer of
components.

country where they would be sold. MNEs seeking maximum value chain control would own all their subsidiaries. The gigantism associated with this vertical integration approach became IB's dominant organisational mode for several decades (Figure 7.4).

The disruptions of the mid-20th century (the Great Depression, Second World War and Decolonisation era) combined to cause a widespread resurgence of trade barriers, undermining one of the main factors that had facilitated earlier MNEs' cross-border configurations. Many responded by adopting a multidomestic approach where they would continue running a series of vertically integrated value chains but this time entirely within the borders of each of the countries where they were operating. That allowed companies to maintain their international presence, but clearly led to costly duplication. The return to free trade politics that picked up pace from the 1970s onwards was therefore a great relief to many IB interests.

A number of MNEs tried at first to revert to a vertically integrated mode, particularly American companies seeking to apply overseas the "big is beautiful" mass production logic that they had long implemented in their huge home market. European MNEs followed suit, in part because the advent of the Common Market lowered the costs of trading intermediary components across the continent – and because they wanted to achieve a critical mass enabling them to serve its increasingly unified consumer markets (and achieve economies of scale by so doing). With the world ostensibly shrinking every day, the new paradigm seemed to demand that companies be big enough to cover all the different value chain stages of their sector's regional (and sometimes even global) markets.

In the 1970s, however, this whole understanding was turned on its head. A major revolution in MNE configurations erupted, sparked by the fantastic success of companies coming out of a country that had suddenly assumed the mantle of a global manufacturing powerhouse – Japan. Not only had Japanese MNEs positioned themselves cleverly in fast-growing high-tech sectors like consumer electronics (Sony and Matsushita) and computing (Fujitsu and Toshiba), but they did this

Vertical integration - Where the activities that a company launches in a new market are further upstream and/ or downstream from the value chain stage it operates in its home market.

Multidomestic - Management approach eschewing cross-border coordination of units performing different functions and choosing instead to run value chain within each national market.

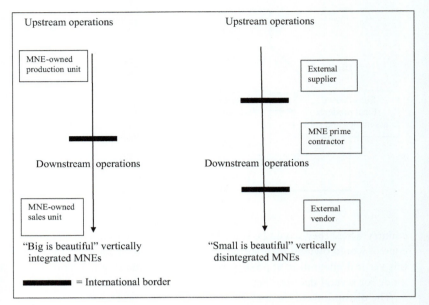

Fig 7.5
A MNE can either cover
the entire international
value chain with in-house
subsidiaries or delegate
certain stages to external
parties.

Prime contractor -
Company at the heart
of a corporate network
and whose orders trigger
supplier tiers' production
plans.

applying a management paradigm and organisational mode that would
become the benchmark for MNEs everywhere.

The main characteristic of the new Japanese model was that
MNEs no longer needed to own all the different units constituting
their global value chains (see Figure 7.5) but should opt instead for a
"vertical disintegration" approach based on maximum outsourcing.
In this configuration, leading MNEs should view themselves as prime
contractors with little direct responsibility for all the upstream (or more
rarely, downstream) operations relevant to their sector and try instead
to build up a network of trusted external partners to whom various
value chain functions could be delegated. In this "small is beautiful"
paradigm, MNEs would no longer conceptualise their configuration
solely in terms of what they do themselves but also incorporate work
done by external suppliers or vendors whose relationships had become
central to their own business models. It remains MNEs' dominant
organisational mode today.

One consequence of the Japanese paradigm is that prime contractors
coordinating a network of companies covering an entire global value
chain will take a very different view of IB than vertically integrated
firms doing everything by themselves. For this latter category, squeezing
costs and/or achieving economies of scale is the priority. For the
new networked MNEs, effective coordination would become just as
important, if not more so, involving not only the prime contractor's
direct first-tier partners but also their own suppliers, who will then
have further tiers of suppliers (see Figure 7.6). These relationships are
conditioned by several factors, including different partners' relative

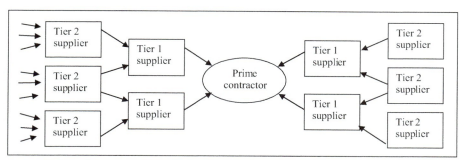

Fig 7.6
Prime contractors at the heart of MNE networks coordinate supplier tiers.

size, who possesses the network's most cutting-edge technology and protagonists' general willingness to share information with the rest of their network.

Although this brief review of the history of MNE configurations has highlighted dominant paradigms at various points in time (as well as the external circumstances creating the contexts within which these worldviews arose), it is necessarily guilty of generalisation. There will always be instances when decision-makers facing the same empirical contexts come to different conclusions as to what constitutes an appropriate response. A number of factors explain this diversity: human agency; but also an often-observed tendency for MNEs originating from a given part of the world to think similarly. This makes the regional scale a useful subset of MNE configuration studies.

MNEs' regional characterisations

Many global authorities, including the Organisation for Economic Co-operation and Development (OECD) and the United Nations, classify MNEs according to their region of origin. This is understandable, given studies showing that most MNEs do in fact configure their operations along regional lines (Verbeke and Asmussen 2016) and, indeed, tend to perform better when they do so (Kim et al. 2019). A number of factors might explain this phenomenon: the fact that so many of the world's leading MNEs realise the lion's share of their international revenues regionally, not globally; the lesser foreignness that many managers feel when working in neighbouring countries rather than the other side of the world; and the IB workday's customary division into three regional time zones (Asia, EMEA [Europe-Middle East-Africa], and the Americas). Now, this does not signify that everyone from a particular region possesses the same mindset nor that MNEs in one part of the world do not imitate companies from elsewhere. There is simply a strong argument supporting the notion that a regional MNE analysis offers as much value as a global or national one.

One way to differentiate MNEs in regional terms is according to their interactions with stakeholders. North American MNEs, for instance,

Financialisation - View that a company's singular mission is to maximise short-term financial returns.

often tend to pursue the financialisation ethos that dominates the business cultures in this part of the world (Froud et al. 2002), embodied in a broad political and cultural consensus that the goal of business is to maximise shareholder value and, therefore, short-term financial returns. This can often only be achieved through greater risk-taking, which can include a constant push to bring new products to market (often following research collaborations with local universities and technology clusters), as well as a constant drive to expand, including across borders. It is a competitive culture that makes it difficult for North American MNEs – especially ones from the USA, with its self-image of exceptionalism – to adopt the sort of harmonious, "vertical disintegration" approach characterising Japan's networked MNEs. Transferring best practice is often a big challenge in IB, and just because a paradigm has been successful in one part of the world does not mean that MNEs elsewhere can or will adopt it.

Within the Asian region, it makes sense to divide MNEs into two paradigm categories. On one hand, there are the networked *keiretsus* and *chaebols* coming out of Japan and Korea, respectively – MNE conglomerates and their suppliers who, unlike their North American counterparts, tend to be very much more focused on long-term survival than on stock market performance. This translates into MNEs from this category spending a great deal of time and money on in-house research and development. They also have a much greater tendency to share the product of these efforts with their tiers of suppliers, working together subsequently to improve current versions of best-selling products. That helps them to consolidate market share, something considered potentially more important than inventing new markets. Competition within this category of companies relates to quality – cost-cutting plays less of a role in configuration choices here than it does elsewhere.

Things are different, however, with MNEs from Asia's Global South nations, whether new manufacturing powerhouses coming out of China and the ASEAN tiger economies, or India's emerging service sector players. Many companies within this category adopt an international positioning defined by their lower cost base, often performing no more than a subordinate role as supplier to Global North prime contractors. Having said that, the dominant paradigm for Far East and South Asia MNEs has started to change given the rapid advance in local technological capabilities (see Chapter 13). The intensification in intra-Asian trade is also bound to cause multiple geographic reconfigurations – and paradigm redefinitions – for the companies in question.

In Europe, finally, one of the most significant trends since the fall of communism and rise of the EU's Single Market has been the drive towards greater sectoral consolidation. Many companies that used to dominate in their home markets have been forced by competitive pressures to reconfigure themselves along trans-continental lines, based on a pan-European division of labour enabling greater

Consolidation - Where producers within a sector acquire or merge with one another in an attempt to reduce over-capacities.

economies of scale. One consequence of this trend has been a rapid rise in intra-regional FDI, often involving cross-border mergers and acquisitions. Even so, many European MNEs remain vulnerable because of their comparatively lesser R&D investment (and performance), reflecting in part a tendency in these societies for research to be the domain of specialist institutes more interested in basic science than in applied technology. There are exceptions, of course, first and foremost being the Swedish-British pharmaceutical MNE AstroZeneca's successful 2020 collaboration with Oxford University to develop one of the world's first Covid-19 vaccinations. But in general, R&D is a function that European MNEs tend to outsource more than their North American or Asian counterparts do.

Of course, regional origin is not the only variable affecting the way MNEs might approach IB configuration decisions. Just as important are the resources that a company can access. As often as not, this reflects its size – a second useful subset of IB configuration studies.

The special case of small and medium-sized enterprises (SMEs)

There are different ways to measure IB's relative importance to any one company. One widespread metric is its penetration of foreign markets versus performance at home (Marshall et al. 2020). Within the SME category, there are significant variations in terms of how frequently companies operate internationally. Some only entertain sporadic dealings, others transact regularly; and recent years have seen a proliferation of tiny, Internet-based "micro-multinational" start-ups that are "born-global" from the outset. By definition, the very smallest and most domestic SMEs account for a minimal proportion of all IB. Others, on the other hand, punch above their weight.

A prime example of the latter category is provided by Germany's *Mittelstand* ("medium-level") SMEs, responsible for around 70 percent of the total exports of one of the world's leading trading nations (Parella and Hernandez 2018). In total, Germany counts upwards of 250 SMEs who are "hidden champions" in their respective sectors and markets. *Mittelstand* firms tend to thrive in niches that are too narrow to be exploited profitably using larger MNEs' heavier (hence more expensive) infrastructure. They often specialise in intermediary goods (i.e. Zeiss glass lenses or Solar-Fabrik photovoltaic cells) that larger companies subsequently incorporate into their own outputs. Having said that, a number of German SMEs (i.e. Neumann microphones or Steinweg pianos) have also had success selling final products worldwide.

Successful *Mittelstand* firms are characterised by narrow product portfolios, if only because their size keeps them from engaging in sweeping diversification strategies (or mass production). Other shared characteristics include an ongoing effort to innovate gradually within

Mergers and acquisitions - Mergers occur when two companies agree to combine their operations into a new company, with both wielding more or less equal power. Acquisitions occur when one company takes ownership of another.

their specialist area, a generalised ambition to dominate the particular markets where they compete and a desire for control that translates into their normally rejecting any configuration requiring them to outsource their sales or production functions, especially not abroad. Quite the contrary, *Mittelstand* SMEs tend to focus instead on nurturing close relationships with their local communities; supporting young recruits' vocational training; and hoping in this way to achieve a level of productivity that will compensate for their having eschewed the benefits of international outsourcing. Their main configuration involves domestic manufacturing and then exporting the output. FDI is rare.

Part of this export focus sees *Mittelstand* SMEs devote a great deal of attention to customers' changing preferences, offsetting their lack of a physical presence in distant local markets through constant communications involving frequent travel and/or assiduous attendance at trade fairs or conferences. Above all, being family-owned, their priority tends to be ensuring the company's long-term survival (so that future generations have something to inherit) rather than maximising short-term financial returns. This explains their incremental focus on increasing market share over time, deemed more reliable than other paradigms requiring a constant renewal of distant foreign customers – always a challenge but one that is even greater for SMEs whose smaller resource base makes it harder for them to run an international network on anything resembling a continuous basis.

The same disadvantage can also turn into an advantage, however. In general, SMEs' smaller size means they benefit from a flexibility that contrasts with the "diseconomies of scale" from which many larger MNEs suffer due to their unwieldy bureaucracies and burdensome procedures. Similarly, it can also be a struggle for larger MNEs to develop the kind of responsiveness they need to keep up with changing trends in fast-moving international environments. For this reason, instead of being rivals, small and large MNEs often complement one another, with each tending to thrive in different settings. SMEs tend to play a greater role in Global South (or Southern European) locations where difficult operating conditions and "institutional voids" make it hard for big MNEs to establish a full-time presence. This is especially true with – as is disproportionately the case – SMEs specialising in knowledge-related services like IT, consulting or legal advice.

It remains that there is no getting around the fact that size severely handicaps smaller companies. This has long been a topic of great concern for many business economists, to the extent that the UN organises regular conferences devoted to SMEs' internationalisation difficulties (UNECE 2001). As demonstrated by Table 7.1, such problems can easily be divided into two categories: objective barriers and human capital deficiencies.

Governments often try to help SMEs overcome the aforementioned handicaps via different mechanisms, including export promotion facilities, financial aid and/or information about foreign markets. Some countries have even restructured their tax systems so that SMEs pay lower marginal rates than larger MNEs. This is because politicians are

Table 7.1
Main barriers undermining SME internationalisation

Objective barriers	
Bureaucracy	Similar amount of paperwork (i.e. customs forms) but spread over smaller volumes
Product range	SMEs' narrower portfolios makes it harder to attack diverse international markets
Commercialisation	SMEs can rarely afford foreign retail outlets. Often dominated in negotiations with foreign distributors
Branding	SMEs' lesser marketing budgets make it harder for them to overcome consumers' home bias
Supply chain pressures	Payment delays, price wars – larger firms (deeper pockets) means they can squeeze SMEs
Scale	SMEs do not have the same size advantages as larger MNEs (bulk purchases/scale output)
Government support	Larger MNEs better than SMEs at lobbying for export assistance, FDI subsidies, etc.
Intellectual property	SMEs have fewer resources to monitor possible infractions
Funding access difficulties	Banks often penalise SME borrowers by charging higher rates and fees
Human capital deficiencies	
Lack of entrepreneurial, managerial, marketing skills	Many top graduates preferring working for the larger, better-known MNEs
Lesser-quality capabilities	SMEs may not have enough staff to implement in-house quality inspections
Trade documents (labelling, packaging requirements, etc.)	SMEs might not be able to afford trade specialists with knowledge of complexities
Lesser investment in technological assets, know-how	SME may not have wherewithal to recruit in-house researchers and must outsource this function
Language, cultural barriers	SMEs employ less internationalised workforce, so have less human capital to master these areas

often happy to recognise SMEs' contribution to the business world, if only because of the vast numbers of people they employ. Taken individually, SMEs may not count for much. But as a whole, they are a force to be reckoned with.

Case study 7.2: Green and Black's is pure gold

In 1991, Josephine Fairley and her husband Craig Sams, founders of a pioneering organic food company named Whole Earth, set out to develop the world's first organic chocolate bar. Working out of small premises on London's Portobello Road, the couple began by launching a new label called Green and Black's for which they developed a whole new supply network. By 1994, they were ready to market "Maya Gold", made from Central American cocoa beans and sold as a fair trade product, with growers receiving 10 percent more than they would have done under normal market conditions. By offering Global South suppliers a "living wage", Green and Black's was positioning itself in the new and fast-growing niche of ethical consumer goods. Along the way, it became the first brand in the UK to receive official fair trade certification. This SME's early history is therefore noteworthy for two reasons: for the sustainability aspect, and because from the very outset, it sought an international dimension, initially on the upstream side of its value chain.

Sainsbury's, a large British supermarket, began selling Green and Black's very early on, but market coverage was patchy. Fairley and Sams started looking to broaden their distribution network, but being both owners and managers of the company, they did not have the resources to finance this. External funding had to be found to achieve the couple's rapid growth targets, so in 1999, they sold 80 percent of the company to an investor group led by a former head of the New Covent Garden Soup Company. This accelerated things, in part because the new partners also had experience in the high-quality foods sector. Carried by all UK supermarkets from 2000 onwards, Green and Black's annual revenues grew by 69 percent on average over the next four years. By the end of 2004, the company was producing revenues of £22.4 million and had 30 employees.

Fig 7.7
Green and Black's original model marketed its fair trade credentials.

Despite this success, Green and Black's size remained a handicap. Firstly, it limited the sums the company could distribute to its Central American supplier communities (a crucial part of its brand image). Beyond this, the lack of financial resources restricted its ability to organise supply chains and scale up across UK retail channels, but even more crucially, to enter foreign markets, starting with Australia and the United States, where Green and Black's realised that it needed to move quickly before better funded rivals could appropriate its concept. Fairley and Sams therefore decided in 2005 to accept a takeover bid from Cadbury a large British MNE with a global reach but different traditions than Green and Black's. The couple received some criticism for this move. They might have felt, however, that they had no choice.

For the first few years after the Cadbury's takeover, Green and Black's would still be run as a separate business and stayed loyal to its original mission, as witnessed by the fact that by 2011 its entire range would qualify and be designated as fair trade. Within a few years, however, things seemed to change, starting with the 2017 launch of the first product line (Velvet Edition) that could neither be labelled fair trade nor organic. A few observers would criticise Green and Black's for this action (Smithers 2017), although the fairness of those attacks is questionable given that it would continue to sell its original organic fair trade products globally, albeit under an in-house label (Cocoa Life) devised by Mondelez International, the new owner. The more accurate analysis is to acknowledge that the SME has had to adapt its original ideal somewhat since being taken over by a large MNE, but that it was also only by aligning with bigger players that it could attain the global success its original idea deserved. It is a predicament that countless SMEs have faced over the years.

Case study questions

1. What other options did Green and Black's have for going international?
2. Is it fair criticising Green and Black's for the changes they were forced to make?

Section II. The special case of foreign direct investment

Whereas the impact of trade is mainly felt at the point when goods or services cross national borders, the impact of FDI is felt at the very heart of a host country's economy. This centrality explains why FDI requires additional analysis when studying MNE interactions with the host countries where they operate, as well as the home countries from whence they come. Of course, because FDI also constitutes such a material change in any MNE's configuration, it is also worth studying from a purely corporate perspective. For clarity's sake, the two emphases will be analysed separately. In reality, however, and as always in IB, they are also very interconnected.

FDI from a country perspective

The macro-economic impact of FDI can be assessed in terms of the benefits but also the disadvantages it creates for home and host country alike. Over the years, a variety of statistical sources including the United Nations Conference on Trade and Development and the World Bank have calculated that somewhere around 10 percent of global GDP and a whopping one-third of total global exports are accounted for by MNE affiliates (De Backer et al. 2019), defined as foreign holdings where a parent company only has a minority share (as opposed to subsidiaries, where it holds a majority stake). Given these enormous volumes, it is clear that FDI is a crucial element within many national economies. The impact is very different, however, depending on whether outflows (from a home country) or inflows (into a host country) are involved.

FDI outflows: beneficial

One frequent argument is that a country benefits when domestic companies offshore low-wage activities, simple business processes or unsophisticated manufacturing operations. The idea is that this helps to refocus the local labour market on higher value-added activities, which is supposed to more than offset the negative effects of losing the lower value jobs. One example from South Korea was the explicit reasoning given when electronics giant Samsung first began offshoring basic mobile phone assembly functions to cheaper locations like Vietnam, Brazil and China. The company hoped to free its domestic units to focus on more strategic design and engineering activities, and ultimately succeeded, increasing the number of high value-added jobs that it offered at home in Korea.

FDI outflows: detrimental

The main critique here is FDI outflows' negative employment effects on home country workers. Most, if not all, Global North economies have suffered severe de-industrialisation (that is, a shrinking industrial base) since the 1980s due to competition from cheaper foreign manufacturers working out of low-wage economies, generally in the Global South. The social consequences can be particularly devastating since factory jobs are often concentrated in specific labour basins. There are ample examples of mass plant closures devastating communities in Britain (Humber and Tyne), France (Lorraine), Germany (Ruhr) and the USA (Ohio/Western Pennsylvania). One reason for this crisis is the difficulty for many of the newly unemployed factory workers to get new jobs offering the same stability as their previous positions. The end result is that they often transition into gig economy arrangements suffering from great precarity (Sitkin 2018). Otherwise, there is also the educational challenge of retraining this population for new jobs that are technologically more challenging. Lastly, there is the sheer improbability that these workers and their families can (or even should) be expected to abandon their existing social capital and move to another part of the country where new jobs might be located. The end result has been a hollowing out of entire swathes of many Global North communities, being the cause for much of the political unrest and extremism that has been a hallmark of the late 2010s – tensions aggravated by the growing disparity within many countries between regions that have integrated the world economy and others that have failed to do so. Add to this the downward pressure on wages in sectors exposed to international competition – as predicted by the Stolper-Samuelson theorem (1941) – plus the tax revenues that national governments lose when domestic companies move profitable units abroad, and it is no surprise to hear so many voices decry outwards FDI as something detrimental to a MNE's country of origin.

Gig economy - Where employment opportunities made available to workers are predicated on their being classified, often involuntarily, as independent contractors.

Precarity - Absence of job security.

FDI inflows: beneficial

One widely held tenet in the economics of IB is that FDI benefits host countries not only because it brings capital and jobs but just as importantly because of the technology and management know-how that accompany them. These two latter variables have been found to have a positive effect on productivity in destination countries: due to the "knowledge spillovers" (see Chapter 10) that occur as the MNE starts collaborating with its new local suppliers, because any inputs that it produces are likely to add value to the final products being assembled by host country manufacturers, or because its presence helps host country nationals to acquire advanced technological skills that they put to good use starting up new companies themselves.

FDI inflows: detrimental

There has long been a small anti-capitalist subset of IB literature that is highly critical of FDI, often starting with the intimation that MNEs enter Global South countries with the specific intention of plundering local resources and exploiting workers (Palast 2003). An ideologically less extreme critique is the observation that inward FDI often exacerbates wage and other inequalities, either because the MNE is working in a knowledge-intensive sector and recruits scarce local talent that is therefore no longer available to home-grown firms (Becker et al. 2020), or because FDI involving horizontal integration not only takes market share away from local companies (Le and Pomfre 2011) but also crowds out domestic investment (Jude 2019). Questions have also been raised regarding the extent to which an incoming MNE's technological know-how actually benefits domestic interests (Chrysovalantou and Sandonis 2020), especially in situations where the FDI involves the relocation of lower value activities, with the new unit being used to import expensive components, thereby worsening the host country's balance of trade. Lastly, there is the observation that where powerful MNEs parlay poor host countries' desperation for inward investment into tax breaks unavailable to domestic firms, they are distorting competition and actually generating economic inefficiency due to their subsidies' high per-job costs (Driffield et al. 2019).

A composite view (Barba Navaretti and Venables 2004) is that FDI's net cost/benefit impact on host countries depends on certain key variables, each of which raises a number of questions.

Capital inflows and outflows. Discussions here include whether the funds used to finance the FDI were sourced from the host country capital market or brought in from elsewhere, how much of the local operation's profits are retained in the country instead of being exported as dividends (i.e. how easy it is for foreign investors to withdraw funds) and the compromises that the government was forced to make in order to attract the FDI in the first place.

Development dynamic. The key points here in terms of the effects on host country infrastructure, industrialisation and terms of trade are whether a particular FDI involves high or low value-added activities (hence how it positions the country within the international division of labour), the extent to which it displaces or discourages local entrepreneurship and how severely it disrupts existing economic (hence social) structures.

Competition effects. Some instances of FDI will enhance domestic productivity over the long run by breaking up existing monopolies and replacing them with new, more efficient producers. On other occasions, the new foreign presence does no more than crowd out local interests. Everything depends on whether incoming MNEs behave like a cartel or compete honestly in the local market.

Flow of goods. From an import perspective, the issue is whether a particular FDI relies on components and finished goods manufactured abroad or else on inputs sourced from (hence benefitting) local suppliers. On the export side, the crux is whether the goods produced as a result of the FDI are to be exported (improving the host country's balance of trade) or sold into the local market.

Labour markets. In addition to concerns like job security, comparative pay and health and safety, topics here include whether the FDI creates new positions or drains human capital currently employed by domestic interests; relies on part-time workers or hires local contractors; entertains harmonious relations with local trade unions; and engages in worker and broader vocational training.

Knowledge spillovers. If the FDI includes technology transfers and an application of new management practices, it may well enhance the destination economy's overall productivity, especially if learning clusters develop. Of course, this is also predicated on the host country being in a position to absorb new knowledge and host high-tech activities.

Sustainability benefits. Referring to an incoming MNE's response to (or influence on) a host government's pollution policies – and more broadly, to local competition for natural resources – the dividing line here is whether the FDI worsens pollution levels or whether the MNE implements best environmental practice, including by using clean technology.

In short, there is no simple answer to the question of how much macro-economic value FDI has for host countries. This is particularly difficult to ascertain given the proven variations between FDI's short- and long-term effects (Dinh et al. 2019). As is so often the case in IB, the most appropriate response is to say that everything depends on the circumstances and on the choices that practitioners make.

FDI from a MNE perspective

The decision to do business in another country via FDI as opposed to another, less capital-intensive entry mode like trading or licensing (see Chapter 8) is one of the most important that a MNE has to make. Because of the extra costs and risks associated with FDI, companies embark upon this path if and only if they can reasonably hope to achieve additional advantage.

As aforementioned, IB analysis commonly distinguishes between horizontal FDI, where the company runs a similar stage of its global value chain in a foreign country, and vertical FDI, where the cross-border move involves a different stage. Horizontal FDI will often be considered "market-seeking" insofar as it is motivated by a desire to sell greater quantities of a company's current product line (potentially with adaptations). Vertical FDI, on the other hand, is generally considered to be "efficiency-seeking" since its main purpose is to help the MNE cover more of (hence gain greater control over) its global value chain. There are two ways of doing this. In case of "backward" vertical integration, the FDI is meant to extend the MNE's total operations further upstream. "Forward" vertical integration, on the other hand, means that it is expanding further downstream. Of course, it is entirely possible that a MNE engages in vertical FDI in both directions, seeking to expand into new inputs as well as outputs (Hofman and Osterwalder 2017). Recent moves have seen Amazon, for instance, both going upstream to produce new in-house brands (like the AmazonBasics batteries or Solimo home goods) while also advancing downstream to operate closer to its end users (e.g. the in-house delivery service that Amazon has built up in consumer markets worldwide). It is a double-edged approach explaining why so much discussion about this giant international player relates to its search for market control.

The other distinction to be made when classifying FDI from a MNE perspective relates to the underlying motive. One common thread permeating sustainability studies is to ask whether companies engaging in

Fig 7.8
MNEs offshoring their production are seeking to avail themselves of the advantages of working out of certain locations while maintaining control over operations.

a particular behaviour are doing so because they are being proactive and "playing to win" or defensive and "playing not to lose". The same filter can be applied to FDI analysis.

Proactive reasons for engaging in FDI

Control

When MNEs open specialist manufacturing units overseas to maximise each site's location-specific advantages, they are putting themselves in a position to accumulate further expertise at the different stages constituting their products' global value chains. As long as intra-firm flows can be coordinated effectively, the end result will be a more rational production organisation. This kind of "internalisation" logic (Narula 2019) helps companies to protect and enhance their competitive knowledge by controlling and even monopolising the intellectual property associated with each value chain operation. One example is Apple's decision to start selling Macs from 2021 onwards using microprocessors that it will design by itself from now on. The chips may still be made by an external supplier (Taiwan Semiconductor Manufacturing Company), but that does not detract from the fact that Apple is bringing back in-house certain design functions that used to be exercised on its behalf by Intel. The net effect is to increase the company's control over product performance while gaining further differentiation from its rivals (Gurman et al. 2020).

Proximity to resources

Over the past 35 years, one of the main drivers behind FDI has been the acquisition of resources, starting with inexpensive manual labour. Countless MNEs in labour-intensive sectors having moved their production facilities to the Global South to take advantage of the often enormous wage differentials. Having said that, the purpose of upstream FDI has shifted somewhat in recent years due to the ongoing rise in emerging economy wages and the way technological progress has reduced the labour intensity of certain types of production. Today, there is a greater focus on access to commodities like oil or minerals, the rationale being that natural resources will become increasingly crucial as depletion leads to future supply shortages. This can be exemplified by metallurgy giant Baosteel's FDI in African mines, one of many cases where MNEs from China have moved to source abroad the inputs that its booming domestic manufacturing sector requires.

Otherwise, it is not only labour or primary resources that companies seek through FDI but also access to knowledge, a crucial input in all sectors but particularly in high-tech industries. When giant German MNE Siemens built medical diagnostic facilities in Berkeley (California), for instance, there was some debate about why the company had chosen this particular locale for an activity that might easily have been exercised elsewhere. The conclusion drawn by several observers was that its real motive was to access the San Francisco Bay Area's concentrated high-tech human capital, comprising all the young talents desirous of working in or around Silicon Valley. A similar dynamic may have been at work, for instance, when Canadian-Britain news giant Thomson-Reuters moved some of its data analysis activities to India, or when Google established a "campus" near London's Silicon Roundabout tech district. By creating physical facilities at the heart of a host country, FDI makes a foreign MNE more accessible to the talents residing there.

Proximity to customers

MNEs will often try to locate distribution facilities in (or near to) fast emerging consumer markets like China or India for the obvious reason that it reduces their time-to-market and increases their chance of gaining a foothold there. This is particularly important where there is a government requirement that the national market be served via FDI rather than imports, due to the still widespread perception that the former is more beneficial to a host country than the latter. A second proximity strategy called "follow sourcing" (see Chapter 10) involves replicating the internationalisation moves of a customer for whom a company has long served as supplier. One example here is the way French automotive parts manufacturer Faurecia built production facilities in South Africa following its automaker customers' decision to build their own assembly plants there.

International economies of scale

The critical mass that companies achieve through FDI can occur on the upstream production side but also on the downstream sales side. For instance, large British banks such as HSBC have opened branches across continental Europe to sell pension products originating in the UK and still serviced out by their administrative teams there. By increasing the number of outlets selling products developed in London, the company reduces its per-unit return costs. Note the particular importance of this factor in sectors of activity where price sensitivity is paramount.

Government incentives

Lastly, FDI can also involve opportunistic behaviour by MNEs taking advantage of government incentives. Chapter 3 detailed some of these measures, which include competitively low corporation tax rates, industrial grants and specific infrastructure outlays maximising new facilities' productivity. Place marketing by governments seeking to dress up their country's image as an investment destination often highlights such incentives.

Defensive reasons for engaging in FDI

Government interference

Because of the aforementioned perception that investment (through the capital, knowledge and jobs that it provides) can be more advantageous to a host country than imports are, governments sometimes establish barriers to trade specifically because they want to induce MNEs to enter their markets via FDI. Such policies, which in the 1970s famously motivated Japanese carmakers' initial decision to build facilities in the USA (or Volkswagen in Brazil), have become somewhat less prevalent in recent years, largely because the WTO sanctions them as a hidden form of protectionism.

Insufficient domestic capacities

Companies originating from smaller countries can be at a disadvantage if their capacities are sized to serve their original market. The prime example here is MNEs originating from the Netherlands, one of the EU's smaller member states with approximately 17 million inhabitants yet which, despite that – or possibly, because of that – usually ranks among the world's top ten countries for inward and especially outward FDI, with Dutch MNEs running, for instance, well over 4,000 subsidiaries in neighbouring Germany (CBS 2020). Were these Dutch interests to configure their operations out of their home country, it is doubtful they would have the capacity to compete internationally. Through FDI, the problem is solved.

Overcoming foreignness

A foreign brand will sometimes be penalised by consumers in a market either because they have a negative stereotype of its country of origin or because they are simply more familiar with domestic alternatives. One way to overcome this obstacle is by engaging in FDI, thereby manifesting greater commitment to the host country and achieving insider status. Foreign MNEs can prove their proximity to a local population in many ways, first and foremost being through employment policies. Local marketing is another tool that MNEs can use to great effect. London's leading football club, Tottenham Hotspur, for instance, was once sponsored by Holsten, a brewery from Hamburg that was able in this way to raise its profile in the already crowded UK beer market.

Diversity risk

As noted in Chapter 1, there are two strategic risks that MNEs can address via FDI. One relates to foreign exchange, that is, the danger of accumulating costs in countries prone to currency upswings and/or revenues in countries prone to currency devaluations. FDI in countries with contrary currency trends can offset this effect. Otherwise, diversity risk can also be an international marketing issue, with some products growing old and unprofitable in one country while remaining young and lucrative in another. Cross-border product life cycle variations can also be counterbalanced through FDI, one frequent example being food sector MNEs that are constantly trying to acquire brands just as they generate positive cash flows within a given national market.

Undermining the competition

Some MNEs engage in FDI without much hope of making any real money. Their aim instead is to undercut a rival in its own home market, preventing it from making profits that could fund price wars elsewhere. This may have been one idea that Opel, the German subsidiary of French automaker Peugeot, had in mind when it entered the Japanese electric vehicle market in 2020.

A few recent FDI trends

As highlighted in UNCTAD's 2020 World Investment Report, Covid-19 had a devastating effect on global FDI, with the annual total expected to come in well below the $1 trillion mark for the first time in over a decade. It is worth noting, however, that FDI's 2019 (hence pre-pandemic) total of $1.5 trillion was already well below its 2015 peak of $2 trillion. The truth is that international trade and FDI volumes stagnated throughout the late 2010s – it would be misguided to attribute 2020's sharp decline to Covid-19 alone.

The question then becomes how to explain this trend and what predictions might be made for the future. Some observers forecast a revival of FDI due to the vulnerabilities that the Covid-19 crisis revealed in certain sectors (e.g. medical equipment, vaccinations but also microprocessors) where MNEs had previously relied on imports. When suppliers' production schedules fell behind demand due to pandemic-related manufacturing problems (and/or because of a sudden increase in demand for these crucial items), many MNEs struggled to access critical inputs. This brought home to them the control benefits that FDI affords a company. It also explained a growing interest in resilience, which may involve MNEs duplicating the number of in-house units they run worldwide fulfilling any one function. Of course, such moves will have cost implications and may therefore be limited in scope. But they will also bolster FDI volumes.

Resilience - Ability to withstand shocks

Besides this one situation, the bigger question is whether there is a ceiling on MNEs' ability to integrate foreign economies. For several decades, FDI has been largely driven by Global North companies either expanding horizontally to extend their commercial reach into similarly industrialised countries, or vertically "backwards" into the Global South for production efficiency or resource acquisition reasons. As income levels rise in emerging economies, it is probable that future FDI inflows will also involve "forward" integration aiming at servicing growing consumer demand in these countries. Above all, as MNEs originating from the Global South build up their own international configurations, South-South and South-North FDIs can also be expected to increase (Economist 2018). Indeed, this has already begun.

Lastly, around three-fifths of total global FDI currently involves services (including finance); one-quarter, manufacturing; and the rest, primary goods. The expectation is that the latter sector is destined to account for a higher share of overall FDI in the future as resource depletion triggers energy and commodity price rises. This view is largely based on accelerating demand for raw materials, mainly driven by rapid industrialisation in the Global South – a trend that has been underway for several decades now in China and across the ASEAN countries but which is also expected to expand throughout South Asia and Africa as these regions are further integrated into the world economy, in no small part as a result of China's gigantic Belt and Road infrastructure project. The question then becomes whether the anticipated rise in commodities' relative price will cause downstream raw material processors worried about rising input costs to use FDI as a means of securing future supplies. This would turn the page on the maximum outsourcing paradigm that has dominated MNE configurations since the Japanese revolution of the 1970s. It is an outcome that seems very plausible in resource-intensive industries and would augur well for FDI volumes in associated sectors.

In more knowledge-intensive sectors, on the other hand, the paramount importance of talent acquisition (plus the ongoing need to protect intellectual property) argues for the continued prevalence of horizontal FDI, further bolstering Big Tech's already formidable international presence. The problem here is the political pushback that these giant MNEs' success has generated, with moves afoot in some countries to break them up (Carbonaro 2020). If friendly politics constitute one of the enabling factors of IB, unfriendly politics must be seen as a disabling factor, revealing once again how crucial it is in IB studies to avoid sweeping generalisations and analyse situations instead on a sector-specific basis.

Attitudes and alternatives

The configuration that a MNE adopts (i.e. which value chain functions it decides to run in which locations) is probably the most difficult decision that executives have to make. Because FDI involves capital investment in foreign operations, it offers MNEs the greatest rewards but also the greatest risks, thereby raising deeper questions about managers' sense of mission, starting with how big they want their company to become. If a MNE stays small, it will struggle to achieve the critical mass required for certain aspects of IB. This may condemn it to remain a niche player, making it vulnerable to the risk that larger rivals might try one day to force their way into its markets. The problem is that for various strategic, financial and human resource reasons, gigantism creates its own risks. Size for size's sake is rarely a reliable internationalisation strategy.

Chapter summary

Chapter 7 serves as an intermediary conclusion to the first half of this book. Focusing on some of the elements shaping the external environment within which MNEs operate, while questioning how much agency decision-makers have to configure their operations in response to their contexts, it sets the table for the transition between a macro-level of analysis (what countries do) and the micro-level (what companies do). The connection between the two resides in a number of enabling factors that have been present throughout IB history, even as their relative importance has waxed and waned over time. MNEs choose their organisational modes depending on the possibilities they see within these factors, their size and, to a lesser extent, the prevailing managerial paradigms within their region of origin. It bears repeating, as has been stressed throughout this book, that IB decision-making never occurs within a vacuum.

The chapter's second section then looked at the special case of FDI, being the IB activity that epitomises, even more than trade does, MNEs' intimate interactions with host countries' frontline realities. FDI produces both advantages and disadvantages that are best analysed in both country and company-level terms. Its evolution in recent years offers few indications regarding the kinds of arbitrages that MNE managers must regularly decide, which will be explored in greater detail in the chapters constituting the second half of this book.

Case study 7.3: Swallowing South African Beer

Founded in 1895, South African Beer (SAB) achieved rapid early success selling its Castle Lager brand to thirsty gold miners. Once the country's relationship with the rest of the British Empire had stabilised following the Boer War, SAB took advantage of its preferential access to the London Stock Exchange to source funds, enabling expansion into

Fig 7.9
The proliferation of beer brands in many markets worldwide has sparked an endless succession of consolidation moves within this industry.

neighbouring Rhodesia (now Zimbabwe), which had no qualms about opening up to a fellow Commonwealth member. The company also worked together with a domestic rival to build up South African hops farming, a vertical integration move that ensured SAB's ability to source what is a key raw material for beer. For the first half of the 20th century, SAB was happy to consolidate its regional presence, but after moving its headquarters to Johannesburg in 1950, management decided to accelerate the company's growth rate. The first step was to acquire a number of local rivals. This helped SAB achieve economies of scale and limit competition in its home market.

From the 1960s onwards, however, further expansion for SAB, like all South African firms, was restricted by the international boycotts that followed global condemnation of the apartheid regime's racist policies. To overcome this obstacle, the company started working together with foreign brands such as Amstel (Amsterdam) and Carling (Cleveland, Ohio) while diversifying into non-beer-related activities. The apartheid regime fell in 1990, and the ensuing cessation of sanctions paved the way for SAB's renewed internationalisation. With the world's former communist bloc also opening up that same year, SAB formulated an opportunistic horizontal integration strategy, negotiating with governments across Eastern Europe, Asia and Central America to purchase a number of local breweries. These moves also reflected SAB's expertise at running operations out of Global South locations, a capability that its main international rivals did not possess.

This unique growth strategy finally gave SAB the size that would allow it to compete directly with some of its more established rivals. This ultimately led in 2002 to the takeover of Miller, the United States' second largest brewer. The following year, the new combined entity, now called SAB Miller, began its move into Western Europe, acquiring a majority stake in leading Italian brand Peroni. Whereas most of today's better known brewing MNEs came out of the Global North and had only recently started expanding into the emerging markets, SAB Miller stood out for having done the opposite. Its success demonstrated that the path to international success is never written in stone but reflects a company's responses to the particular circumstances in which it finds itself at different points in time.

Once SAB Miller had achieved sufficient geographical diversification to avoid being overexposed to any one zone, it returned to its previous pattern of focusing on growth markets, starting with its home region of Africa. This often involved joint ventures with partners like the French company Castel, in order to consolidate its dominant market share in Africa but also because SAB Miller's rapid expansion had stretched its finances. There has long been a consensus within the brewing industry that consolidation is necessary to protect profit margins withered by intense global competition. SAB Miller's management paradigm was fairly typical of its peers, explaining a number of horizontal actions where the company would either launch its own brands in a new market or else acquire existing brands there, most notably Australia's famous Foster's beer in 2011. By the mid-2010s, SAB had reached a size where it could vie with all the other giants in its industry, thereby justifying, in management's eyes, the $100 billion deal it agreed with Belgian-Brazilian AB InBev, a transaction that would for a short while be depicted as a merger between equals (Mickle 2016).

Within a few years, however, the narrative had completely changed. As often happens, one partner in a consolidation transaction ends up dominating the other, to the extent that subsequent analysis would generally refer to the deal as a takeover of SAB Miller by AB InBev (Massoudi and Abboud 2019). This manifested in the way that the new consolidated entity moved quickly to sell off a number of brands that had previously belonged to SAB Miller, for instance by divesting its stake in China's Resource Beer and in parts of its African Coca-Cola bottling franchise, not to mention the striking sell-off in 2019 of major Australian brands Carlton and Great Northern. Some of the Global South and British Commonwealth investments that had defined SAB on its way up were precisely the businesses being hived off as it settled into its new status as a junior partner. The new group still rejoiced in the strengths it maintained in Africa, inherited from SAB's previous efforts. But its interests were now being very much spoken of from AB InBev's perspective, with SAB henceforth being referred to in the past tense.

Case study questions

1. Why did SAB prefer vertical integration at certain moments in history and horizontal integration at others?
2. What advantages and risks were associated with SAB's ambitious FDI programme?
3. Was it a good idea for SAB to merge with AB InBev?

Chapter discussion questions

1 Which of the different factors enabling international business at different times in history (politics, finance, technology and paradigms) will be most problematic in the future? Why?

2 Which MNE configuration is most likely to dominate in the future? Why?

3 Is SMEs' share of international business destined to rise or fall? Why?

4 Is FDI more of a proactive or a defensive action on the part of MNEs?

5 Is there a ceiling on future FDI volumes, and if so, what explains it?

References

AP Associated Press (3 December 2019). "Huawei moving US research center to Canada", accessed 18 February 2021 at https://www.usnews.com/

Becker, B. et al. (5 August 2020). "FDI in hot labour markets: The implications of the war for talent", *Journal of International Business Policy*, Volume 3, pp. 107–133.

CBS (5 November 2020). "Dutch trade in facts and figures 2020", accessed 30 November 2020 at https://www.cbs.nl/

Carbonaro, G. (10 November 2020). "EU takes action against Amazon 'dominance' as regulators get tougher", accessed 18 February 2021 at https://newseu.cgtn.com/

Chrysovalantou, M., and Sandonis, J. (August 2020). "Vertical foreign direct investment: Make, buy, and sell", *Review of International Economics*, Volume 28, Issue 3, pp. 884–912.

De Backer, K. et al. (25 September 2019). "Multinational enterprises in the global economy: Heavily discussed, hardly measured", accessed 18 February 2021 at https://voxeu.org/

Dinh, T. et al. (November 2019). "Foreign direct investment and economic growth in the short run and long run…", *Journal of Risk and Financial Management*, Volume 12, Issue 4, accessed 29 July 2021 at https://www.mdpi.com/

Driffield, N. et al. (June 2019). "FDI and local productivity", *State of the Art Review*, Issue 31, accessed 29 July 2021 at https://www.enterpriseresearch.ac.uk/

Economist (8 February 2018). "South-to-south investment is rising sharply", *Economist*.

Froud. J. et al. (1 October 2002). "Financialisation the coupon pool", *Capital & Class*, Volume 26, Issue 3, pp. 119–151.

Gurman, M. et al. (23 April 2020). "Apple aims to sell Macs with its own chips starting in 2021", accessed 21 February 2021 at https://www.bloomberg.com/

Hofmann, E., and Osterwalder, F. (4 September 2017). "Third party logistics providers in the digital age: Towards a new competitive arena?" *Logistics*, Volume 1, Issue 9, pp. 1–28.

Jones, G. (2005). *Multinationals and Global Capitalism: From the Nineteenth to the Twenty-First Century*, Oxford: Oxford University Press.

Jude, C. (January 2019). "Does FDI crowd out domestic investment in transition countries", *Economics of Transition and Institutional Change*, Volume 27, Issue 1, pp. 163–200.

Kim, H. et al. (9 November 2019). "Chinese multinationals' fast internationalization…", *Journal of International Business Studies*, Volume 51, Issue 7, pp. 1076–1106.

Le, H., and Pomfret, R. (May 2011). "Technology spillovers from direct foreign investment in Vietnam: Horizontal or vertical spillovers?", *Journal of the Asia Pacific Economy*, Volume 16, Issue 2, pp. 183–201.

Marshall, V. et al. (31 March 2020). "RIMS: A new approach to measuring firm internationalization", *Journal of International Business Studies*, Volume 51, Issue 7, pp. 1133–1141.

Massoudi, A., and Abboud, L. (24 July 2019). "How deal for SAB Miller left AB InBev with lasting hangover", *Financial Times*.

Mickle, T. (28 September 2016). "SAB Miller, AB InBev shareholders approve $100 billion-plus merger", *Wall Street Journal*.

Narula, R. et al. (26 August 2019). "Applying and advancing internalization theory: The multinational enterprise in the twenty-first century", *Journal of International Business Studies*, Volume 50, pp. 1231–1253.

Navaretti, G., and Venables, A. (2004). *Multinational Firms in the World Economy*, Princeton, NJ: Princeton University Press.

Palast G. (2003). *The Best Democracy Money Can Buy: The Truth about Corporate Cons, Globalisation and High-Finance Fraudsters*, New York: Plume.

Parella, J., and Hernandez, G. (June 2018). "The German business model: The role of the Mittelstand", *Journal of Management Policies and Practices*, Volume 6, Issue 1, pp. 10–16.

Sitkin, A. (Spring 2018). "Eight years on the frontline of regeneration: Ten lessons from the Enfield experiment", *Soundings*, Number 68, pp. 53–64.

Smithers, R. (3 August 2017). "Green and Black's new UK chocolate bar will be neither organic nor FairTrade", *Guardian*.

Stolper, W., and Samuelson, P. (November 1941). "Protection and real wages", *The Review of Economic Studies*, Volume 9, Issue 1, pp. 58–73.

Tan, D. et al. (12 May 2020). "A review of research on the growth of multinational enterprises: A Penrosean lens". *Journal of International Business Studies*, Volume 51, Issue 4, pp. 498–537.

Tejaswi, M. (28 November 2020). "India key to IBM's pursuit of a $1

trillion hybrid cloud opportunity", accessed 18 February 2021 at
https://www.thehindu.com/

UNCTAD (2020). "World investment report 2020", accessed 30
November 2020 at https://unctad.org/

UNECE (2001). *Entrepreneurship and SME Development*, accessed
1 November 2007 at www.unece.org

Verbeke, A., and Asmussen, C. (September 2016). "Global, local or
regional: The locus of MNE strategies", *Journal of Management
Studies*, Volume 53, Issue 6, pp. 1051–1075.

CHAPTER 8

Market entry

Introduction

Except for a handful of "born-digital" firms (Monaghan et al. 2019) who use the Internet from the very outset as a springboard for their foreign ventures, almost all multinational enterprises (MNEs) began life in their home country before deciding to internationalise. Studying this paramount international business (IB) topic therefore involves a two-step enquiry, starting with the thought processes affecting practitioners' decision to actually venture abroad before looking that at the entry mode choices that a MNE actually makes once it has made the decision to internationalise. These two questions structure the present chapter, which more than any other in the book encapsulates the basic principle that there is no "one-best-way" of engaging in IB, meaning that just as much attention needs to be paid to decision-makers as to their decisions. Human subjectivity and psychology are adjuncts to all social sciences. IB is no different in this respect.

The chapter is also important because it introduces MNEs' thinking about what kind of international presence they want to develop. This is a two-stage process that starts with market entry but then moves on – once the company has established itself outside of its national borders – to

Fig 8.1
In its simplest expression, international business is all about market entry.

DOI: 10.4324/9781003159056-11

include the power relationships that it constructs between its domestic and foreign units. This latter topic will be covered in Chapter 9, which therefore builds upon the present chapter. Altogether, market entry and MNE power structures account for the lion's share of all academic research in the field of IB. This explains their central position in IB modules and in this textbook.

LEARNING OBJECTIVES

After reading this chapter, you should be able to:

- validate the main theories explaining internationalisation moves
- evaluate the trade versus FDI decision in terms of its impact on the boundaries of the firm
- discuss the relative merits of greenfield versus brownfield investments
- assess the risks and rewards of international acquisitions and joint ventures
- assess the risks and rewards of foreign partnerships

Case study 8.1: Bimbo bombs along

Mexican MNE Grupo Bimbo is the world's largest baked packaged-goods maker, generating global revenues of more than $16.5 billion in 2020, up by 10 percent over the year previous. Outside of its home country, which accounts for around one-third of total group sales (down from one-half just a decade before), Bimbo brands have a significant share of markets as widely flung as Latin America, the USA, China and North Africa. It is an unusually successful and rapid internationalisation trajectory for a MNE that began life as a small family-run SME working out of a Global South nation.

Bimbo's internationalisation has been more or less evenly split between **organic growth** and the acquisition of high-profile brands

Organic growth – Where a company leverages internally generated resources to support expansion instead of proceeding via external acquisition.

Fig 8.2
Bimbo has used a broad variety of market entry modes to internationalise.

in target markets. In past interviews, long-serving CEO Daniel Servitje would speak of how Bimbo had learnt in the USA, its first major foreign destination, that it could (and actually had to) enter segments extending well beyond the Spanish-speaking communities with which it was most comfortable. On its website, the company has an entire page devoted to its regular acquisition between 1998 and 2017 of bakeries located in a whole host of countries, often in Latin America but also including Panrico in China in 2006; giant American MNE Sara Lee's North American, Spanish and Portuguese bakery operations in 2011; before going even further afield in the mid-2010s to add Grupo Aghdal in Morocco and Ready Roti in India to its portfolio of companies. The order of these takeovers translates Bimbo's clear-eyed strategy of first moving to countries that it felt were culturally more proximate to its homeland before extending its reach.

Bimbo's early moves in Brazil were a good example of this cautious approach, characterised by a preference for acquiring ongoing concerns instead of growing house brands. To some extent, this was also a response to the fragmentation of the Brazilian market between modern hypermarkets and small grocery stores. At a deeper level, however, it signalled Bimbo's fundamentally incremental approach. In general, Bimbo acts opportunistically when entering new markets. It does not really follow a programmed growth strategy.

Having said that, once embedded in a new market, the company is prepared to take a few risks. One example is what it has done in China where it is creating a whole new product category by challenging an existing gastronomic culture (Chinese pancake wheat flour) with an entirely new starch staple (Mexican tortilla cornflour). This speaks to the way that Bimbo tries to apply lessons from previous internationalisations in new markets, an approach that is particularly effective when the countries involved are at a similar stage of socio-economic development as the ones where Bimbo already operates. CEO Servitje used to say that Bimbo's confidence in its ability to navigate difficult Global South environments removes any fears it might otherwise have had about expanding into economically and culturally different destinations like China. Bimbo's first international successes had been grounded in its ability to gradually nurture localised segments. It is a winning formula that the MNE intends to pursue in the years to come.

Case study questions

1. What are the advantages for Bimbo of moving into countries that resemble its home market?
2. Should Bimbo internationalise in the future via organic growth or by buying going concerns?

Section I. Market entry thinking

Decisions made by IB practitioners, like any social actors, are driven by a whole range of factors, not all of which can be quantified. Classical economics posit that decision-makers are behaving rationally when they seek to optimise their self-interest. The concept is vague and insufficient, however: because different individuals will vary in terms of their assessment of what constitutes optimisation (or self-interest, for that matter); but, above all, because of the myriad of obscure, more psychological factors affecting how humans respond to any given situation. Hence the growing preference for IB analysis that looks at both human objectivity and subjectivity, with the latter filter emphasizing the "influence of affective elements" on MNE decision-makers (Li et al. 2019).

There is insufficient room in this textbook to give full airing to all the theories that have been formulated over many years to try and discern how humans make decisions about foreign environments that are partially unknown to them and therefore uncertain. Readers interested in this topic might find it interesting to explore literature relating to "decision theory": heuristics; and/or loss aversion, also known as prospect theory (Kahneman and Tversky 1979). As far as IB is concerned, the best starting point for conceptualising IB practitioners' market entry psychology is indisputably Uppsala theory, which was first formulated in the 1970s but has undergone several modifications since, because the world of IB has evolved over the past half-century; but also in acknowledgement of the explanatory powers of other more strategic theories, justifying that these be analysed as well.

Uppsala theory

In 1977, Swedish professors Jan Johanson and Jan-Erik Vahlne produced what would become the seminal prism for apprehending the subjectivities underlying MNE managers' market entry decisions, devising a model that has come to be known as Uppsala theory in honour of the university for which the authors worked. The central thesis is that most managers prefer taking an incremental, step-by-step approach to internationalisation. The idea here is that a MNE's first move outside of its home market is likely to be into a neighbouring country that will be less foreign to its culture of origin and therefore psychically less distant. The actual market entry mode that it implements is also likely to be

Commitment to internationalisation – Depth of a company's engagement of physical, financial, human and psychic resources in foreign markets.

more cautious and entail a lesser commitment to internationalisation (see Table 8.1), the assumption being that the less confident a company is in its ability to navigate foreign environments, the more it will prefer internationalising via less committed methods, either trading (importing/exporting) from home or, at best, opening a tiny representative office abroad. Conversely, once it has started accumulating international

Table 8.1
Different modes of market entry require different amounts of funding, knowledge and commitment (bold font indicates internationalisation in conjunction with other interests)

Market entry mode		Level of commitment
Trade from home (import/export)	Firm remains domestic but buys from foreign supplier / sells to foreign buyer	Low
Representative office	Firm employs/hires skeleton staff abroad to broker relationships/gain knowledge	
Licensing/ Franchising	Firm contracts with licensee/franchisee to manufacture/retail on its behalf	
Strategic alliance	Firm shares functions with partner. Often temporary, with no equity investment	
Joint venture/ Merger	Firm makes equity investment abroad, joining/in conjunction with partner	
Wholly owned subsidiary (FDI)	Firm makes standalone equity investment abroad. **Acquisition** or greenfield basis	High

Licensing – Arrangement where licensor grants permission to licensee to use one of its assets, usually intellectual property. Licensor to receive royalties in return.

Franchising – Arrangement where franchiser grants permission to franchisee to run business bearing its name, often using supplies it provides. Franchiser to receive income in return, often based on franchise performance.

Joint venture – Business entity jointly created by different companies pooling equity capital, knowledge, process and/or human resources.

experience, managers will feel more comfortable in foreign environs – at which point they will develop a level of confidence allowing them to enter markets that are more distant and therefore more uncertain, while doing this in a way that commits greater company resources.

In essence, the original Uppsala theory is a "learning cycle" model (Forsgren et al. 2015) predicting that, allegorically, when faced with the choice between jumping into a swimming pool all at once or first dipping in one's toes to check the water temperature, IB practitioners will opt for the latter, more cautious approach. It was an entirely logical thought process at a time when global integration was not as advanced as it is today, hence when objective but also subjective barriers to entry seemed more daunting than they do now. Even so, the original model remains a robust construct, one frequently corroborated by the behaviour of countless companies whose first international forays involve entering countries that are either geographically close or else which seem psychically less distant (e.g. US MNEs like Starbucks first internationalising to Canada; Irish MNEs like Ryanair starting with the UK; French MNEs like St Gobain going to Italy). Uppsala theory's strength resides in the way it ties managers' perceptions of the risks inherent to the uncertainty of foreignness – and their confidence in their company's ability to handle such risks (Tuppura et al. 2008) – to a particular type of market entry mode. All of this explains why Uppsala quickly came to be seen as the embodiment of a behavioural approach to IB studies.

Behavioural – Incorporating human agency into explanations of social phenomena.

Like any theory, however, the original model was a product of its times and bound to be tested by the forward march of history. Globalisation's acceleration from the 1980s onwards led to greater cross-border economic integration and above all to greater cultural convergence, reducing many IB practitioners' fear of foreignness and diminishing their sense of psychic distance. This shift was accompanied – and to some extent, caused – by new MNEs' tendency to internationalise earlier than their predecessors had done, which also meant going further afield (and committing more resources) than Uppsala had forecast. Working faster than previous generations had done to overcome whatever remained of their "domestic mindset" (Nadkarni and Perez 2007), MNEs were now eager to join global "power nodes", markets characterised by their "size, openness, skills levels and institutional stability" (Bolivar et al. 2019) and, being the ones where the battle for global domination was increasingly being fought and won. It was a new modus operandi that corresponded less to Uppsala and more to a construct known as Network theory (Granovetter 1973), originally devised to analyse disciplines other than IB but which could now be applied here as well. For a while, the theoretical question therefore became whether Uppsala or Network theory would do a better job at explaining MNEs' internationalisation behaviour.

To their great credit, Vahlne and Johanson noted this evolution, and updated their original theory in 2009 to account for it. The reformulated model they produced that year spoke less about managers' fears about entering distant countries and more about their desire to link into global networks, replacing the original "liability of foreignness" construct with a "liability of outsidership", being the risk that a MNE which is slow to internationalise might find itself excluded from crucial relational networks. In addition, instead of positing that managers tend to "shy away from radical change and prefer an incremental approach", Uppsala now recognised that this state of mind may apply to some managers but not to all- and that it is therefore more precise to identify the "general psychological characteristics" of managers apt to behave in many different ways (Vahlne and Johanson 2019).

With this honest re-assessment of their original theory's validity, Vahlne and Johanson would ensure Uppsala's ongoing relevance, all the more so because its 2009 version added other interesting insights relating to the entrepreneurial aspects of MNEs' decision whether or not to join a global network. A further refinement came in 2017, with the model now shining greater light on "the importance of evolution in the access and development of knowledge" (Vahlne 2020), something that should be assessed as a dynamic, ongoing process rather than as a snapshot of people's orientations and/or capabilities at a given point in time. The sum total of these addenda would spark, in turn, a whole new wave of studies drilling further down into Uppsala's psychological foundations. These included analyses of how familiarity with a country's language and culture affects perceptions of psychic distance (Ambos et al. 2019) as well as the impact that "leader narcissism" has on foreign direct investment (FDI) decision-making (Fung et al. 2020). All of this new research hovers around the edges of Uppsala, however, without doubting its basic postulates, attesting to a widespread consensus about the robustness of a seminal construct that all IB learners will do well to appropriate.

Strategic theories

It should not be ignored that other, more strategic theories have also arisen to account for MNEs' market entry behaviours. The fact that their explanations reside more in "thinking" and less in "feeling" (Jiang et al. 2018) may explain why none has resonated as widely as Uppsala. It remains that many are built on robust principles, justifying that their applicability also be considered.

The seminal theory for this second grouping is probably Edith Penrose's 1959 masterpiece, "Theory of the Growth of the Firm", offering a "resource-based view" of how the interaction between human and non-human resources affects a company's dynamic capabilities, hence its response to the outside world (Arvidsson and Arvidsson 2019). This was followed by the more IB-specific, company-level theories that Chapter 2 introduced, first and foremost being Dunning's Eclectic Paradigm, itself based on a widely supported school of thought called Internalisation theory (Buckley and Casson 1976). The main assertion in this latter corpus is that companies' internationalisation efforts translate a desire to keep control over the knowledge flows associated with their products' cross-border value chain transformations. It is an insight heralding significant academic interest in knowledge management since the 1990s, with learning starting to be viewed as a (if not the) key factor in international success. Internalisation theory continues to be updated, often – like Uppsala theory – incorporating lessons from Network theory, with one argument here being that the best way to conceptualise the global expansion of Internet-dependent MNEs such as Facebook and Uber is by highlighting how these companies try to combine knowledge they hold internally with whatever external knowledge they might find in the local networks found in the markets that they wish to enter (Zeng et al. 2019). It is an idea redolent of earlier work done by Professor Alan Rugman explaining how a MNE's desire for "country-specific advantage" can induce it to link up with host country partners whenever it struggles to deploy its existing internal advantages across borders. Market entry is equated here with protagonists' efforts to put together the many different pieces of a puzzle.

Another attempt to tie market entry efforts to value chain strategies is Transaction Cost theory, first formulated in the 1930s by British economist Ronald Coase, before being fine-tuned in the 1970s by Nobel laureate Oliver Williamson and ultimately extended to MNEs by

Jean-Francois Hennart in the 1980s. The idea here is that IB decisions are driven by a desire to minimise search and information, bargaining and policing and enforcement costs; that (as posited in Internalisation theory) companies might try to do this in-house; but also that they may well find greater advantage in contracting with external parties. The implication for MNEs is that whereas Internalisation theory might argue for FDI as a preferred market entry mode, Transaction Cost theory leaves open the possibility of internationalising on a trade-only basis. In reality, of course, both of these possibilities can – and do – coexist. Nor should they be considered scientific to the point of dismissing human agency in their application; just because these theories are grounded in sound strategic reasoning does not mean they are entirely devoid of behavioural influences (Elia et al. 2019). Indeed, the same can be said about other recent market entry constructs, like the New Venture theory or the Linkage, Leverage and Learning (LLL) framework that, when applied to Global South MNEs, seeks to advance understanding of internationalisation processes by accounting for factors such as companies' different organisational cultures and/or stages of development – all moderating elements considered crucial to the different ways that MNE decision-makers envision market entry opportunities.

Two other variables feature regularly in theoretical work in this domain. The first relates to the speed with which MNEs internationalise. This can vary greatly, both in terms of how early in a company's life it decides to venture abroad and also how fast it goes once it starts. Many companies (especially SMEs) might begin with an intermediate step, opening small representative offices serving as staging points where managers travelling to a new country can stop to get their bearings. This was a common practice, for instance, among Western banks first entering China in the 1990s. The goal here is to increase organisational learning about a destination before risking greater resources there, thereby avoiding the adverse learning effects that tend to arise when a company undergoes change at a speed exceeding its absorptive capabilities. Along similar lines, note as well a tendency for MNEs to suffer slow growth in markets where the business and/or commercial culture is very dissimilar to the one they grew up in. This is exemplified by the way many otherwise internationally successful American MNEs (including Google, Mattel and eBay) would fail to penetrate the Chinese market, despite growing demand there for the kinds of services and products that they offer. The issue then becomes why these seasoned operators underestimated the problems that they were bound to encounter, highlighting, if need be, the way subjective emotions like overconfidence (if not arrogance) also get in the way of IB rationality.

A final factor moderating market entry theories' applicability is company size. Chapter 7 introduced the particular problems that small and medium-sized enterprises (SMEs) face abroad due to their comparative lack of financial and other resources, a vulnerability that is compounded when their internationalisation decisions are being taken by

Absorptive capabilities – Speed and facility with which a company integrates feedback from its own experiences and performance.

multiple generations of family members whose occasionally conflicting personal interests can create coordination and control problems (Alayo et al. 2019). In general, SME market entry is characterised by modes that are less financially committed and/or slower. They also tend to involve cross-firm alliances because of the need to achieve the kind of critical mass that individual SMEs would otherwise lack, one example being the way that small vineyards in southwest France have banded together in an association called the Conseil Interprofessionnel du Vin de Bordeaux (CIVB) in a bid to optimise their international marketing efforts. Having said that, a few SMEs will opt for a quicker and/or more committed approach, especially if the founder CEO has direct entrepreneurial experience of a particular industry (D'Angelo and Presutti 2019), or, if the company features among its ranks a "bridge maker" employee with deep personal ties to the new target market (Safari and Chetty 2019). At this level, like so many others, the link between the personal and the professional is crucial to understanding IB decision-making.

Section II. Market entry actions

The actual decision to internationalise, and the way this is done, is referred to as the market entry choice. This is best represented as a decision-making ladder (see Figure 8.3). Many of the factors determining which mode a particular MNE is going to choose will be grounded in the subjective variables that were discussed above. Other factors relating to more objective thought processes can be highlighted now.

Trade instead of FDI

Trade is one of the IB's two main pillars for good reason – namely because it is a much easier market entry option than FDI.

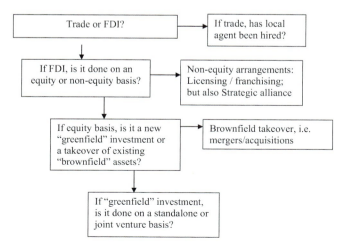

Fig 8.3
Ladder of
internationalisation
choices.

Notwithstanding Michael Porter's contention (see Chapter 2) that firms which have overcome difficult circumstances at home are better prepared to deal with foreign challenges, the fact remains that transferring resources abroad is always problematic. Some of the FDI hurdles that MNEs face will be industrial in nature, as witnessed by the growing supply, logistics and labour shortages that Western manufacturers have started to experience with their Chinese manufacturing units, even before the 2020 Covid-19 pandemic erupted. Others will be more financial in nature, one example being the huge share and cash deal that Japanese pharmaceutical MNE Takeda agreed to fund its 2018 takeover of the British company Shire, and which ultimately caused the acquirer's share price to plummet. Still others will be intellectual property-related, as exemplified by the former joint venture between French food giant Danone and Chinese industrial Wahaha, and where the former accused the latter of appropriating confidential technology that it then used to start a rival company (a claim that Danone, as a foreign MNE, lost – perhaps unsurprisingly – lost in a local court of law). Lastly, some problems are of a more strategic variety, like the pioneering costs that Sweden's giant furniture retailer Ikea suffered when entering Russia before this volatile transition economy had stabilised.

Pioneering costs – Costs associated with mistakes that companies make when entering an unfamiliar market.

MNEs that internationalise without changing their existing domestic configuration – who simply trade from home, importing inputs and/or exporting outputs at their "factory gate" – avoid the aforementioned pitfalls as well as the more cognitive and subjective obstacles outlined in this chapter's first section. This is because they continue to work in the familiar business culture where their company first grew to maturity. Engagements with foreign counterparts (suppliers upstream, distributors or customers downstream) are merely transactional for them, requiring little more than long-distance contract negotiations or sporadic international visits – a remoteness that some high-tech companies will find reassuring if they fear that FDI makes them more vulnerable to security breaches.

Moreover, given the division of labour that has long become a key feature of modern IB, it is hard to think of any minimally complex product nowadays whose value chain has not already been fragmented between different countries based on the location-specific advantages that each possesses. That being the case, a MNE limiting its market entry mode to trade alone, hence continuing to operate solely out of its country of origin, will generally be concentrating on the one value chain activity that is performed most efficiently in its home market, using upstream and downstream outsourcing to maximise the efficiencies afforded by vertical disintegration. In this sense, trade is also easier than FDI because it does not require the MNE to go beyond its current capabilities. On top of that, if the cost of internalising a product's foreign value chain stages is greater than the advantages derived from vertical integration, then it also makes financial sense for the company to externalise certain activities and limit its IB operations to import-export dealings alone.

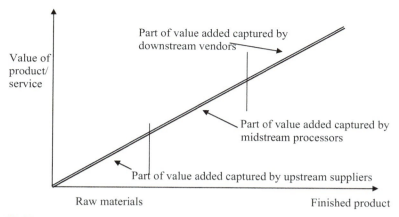

Fig 8.4
Distribution of value-added across a shared global value chain.

FDI instead of trade

Of course, where a MNE outsources entire portions of its value chain to foreign counterparts – where its boundaries have been drawn particularly narrowly (see Figure 8.4) – it is also giving up on the possibility of appropriating a greater share of the total value-added generated throughout its branch. On the upstream side, this means that it must pay foreign suppliers not only their return costs but also the profit margins that come on top of this. On the downstream side, it means that the company will be selling its outputs at lower wholesale prices, again because distributors will have their own margin requirements to satisfy. If the value-added that a trade-only MNE eschews in this way is greater than the cost of running its own upstream or downstream operations in-house, then FDI becomes a more economic proposition.

In addition to these financial considerations, FDI may seem a better market entry option because of the greater control it gives a MNE over the various stages of its global value chain. Companies that limit themselves to one or very few activities run out of their home market are necessarily much more dependent on their foreign counterparts, which can cause serious problems. As Chapter 10 will detail, contracts with foreign suppliers or distributors might be incomplete and not cover certain scenarios; performance can be disappointing (bad quality, unreliable deliveries, late payments); and the frequent need to share crucial know-how often comes with confidentiality risks. There is also the possibility that an opportunistic distributor or supplier will expand its own operations up or down the value chain, respectively, and

Boundaries of the firm –
Scope of the value chain operations that a company performs by itself.

Table 8.2
Trade vs. FDI: strengths and weaknesses

	Advantages	*Disadvantages*
Trade only (import/ export)	– Easier to manage, requires less knowledge – Less capital invested, thus lower risk assumed – Smaller balance sheet, thus more flexible/responsive	– Less opportunity to develop foreign experience – More intermediaries taking share of value added – Dependent on partners, risk of opportunistic behaviour
FDI	– Control/confidentiality – Greater profit potential – Greater foreign capabilities over time	– Harder to manage – Harder to finance – Higher risk of failure

become a direct competitor to the company. These and other issues (see Table 8.2) explain why despite the added difficulty and expense, MNEs often prefer FDI to trade as their prime mode of internationalisation.

It is crucial to remember that the greater risks associated with FDI, starting with the "liability of foreignness" suffered by the subsidiaries that a MNE runs abroad, come with potentially greater rewards, meaning that, to some extent, a company's trade versus FDI arbitrage will also be a reflection of its fundamental attitude towards the volatility of earnings. In addition to this key factor, other considerations weighing upon the FDI decision include whether this involves a riskier but potentially more lucrative new line of business or the simple expansion of an existing commercial activity; the extent to which a potential host country's formal and informal institutions can be relied upon to enforce contracts (Contractor et al. 2020) and protect intellectual property rights (Papageorigiadis et al. 2020); and the country's level of technological advancement, something that correlates positively to its "centrality of position in the global FDI network" (Sultana and Turkina 2020). Where these variables align in a way suiting a MNE's purposes, as happens more often in knowledge-based industries than in low-tech activities, then FDI can seem a better market entry option than trade. The question then becomes what kind of FDI to implement.

Greenfield versus brownfield investments

Greenfield investment – Where a firm enters a market by building new facilities.

Brownfield investment – Where firm enters market by buying existing facilities.

The initial choice whether to enter a foreign market on a FDI basis by either building new greenfield facilities or else by acquiring existing brownfield assets is often referred to as the "build or buy" dilemma. Both modes have their strengths and weaknesses.

Greenfield investments tend to be preferred when the MNE's goal is to attain first-mover advantage by exploiting its knowledge abroad.

Sometimes the reason is because the requisite capabilities do not exist yet in the new locale, which explains why for Silicon Valley MNEs like Google and Intel, greenfield FDI over the past decade has involved their building brand new learning "campuses" in London and Costa Rica, respectively. Otherwise, a greenfield approach makes it easier to preserve confidentiality when transferring in-house technology from existing units to new sites – with intellectual property protection being one of the goals that Tesla, for instance, will have had in mind when it completed Phase 2 of its giant Shanghai Giga factory in winter 2021. Lastly, greenfield FDI means that the MNE does not have to pay the goodwill surcharge that often accompanies equity acquisitions. At times when stock market valuations are high, this can be prohibitively expensive.

Goodwill – Difference between price at which company can be purchased and break-up value of its assets.

Where the market entry move has more of a downstream purpose, on the other hand, a brownfield entry is often deemed more appropriate. One example is the decision made in 2020 by Franco-European educational specialist Galileo to expand in the UK market by acquiring Regent's University London instead of developing organically and building its own facilities. In part, the choice was made to leverage the target entity's existing brand name, viewed by the buyer as a quicker, hence more advantageous, way of building up its own British presence. A second advantage of brownfield FDI is that it avoids the kind of start-up problems that are inherent to any new venture. One example of this was the decision taken in late 2020 by giant US credit rating agency S&P to expand into London's booming financial data provision business by purchasing the UK's IHS Markit instead of building up its own subsidiary as rival Bloomberg had done. S&P Global had already accumulated price benchmarking experience in London (like in other global financial centres) and was therefore painfully aware of the challenges of growing this very niche business from scratch. Thirdly, brownfield FDI on the upstream side involves taking over existing manufacturers instead of creating new supply that adds to a sector's total output and thereby drives down prices – a counterproductive outcome from a producer's perspective. Lastly, the greenfield-brownfield arbitrage also has a sustainability aspect given the environmental footprint of building new industrial facilities on heretofore undeveloped land. As aforementioned, IB has links to many other disciples, including, in this latter instance, to urban planning.

Of course, as always in IB, there is a more subjective side to this decision. MNEs with little foreign experience may prefer to internationalise by acquiring companies that are already up and running and who will therefore require less direction from their new owner. That can be particularly advisable if the new host country in question is psychically very distant from a MNE's country of origin. The greater the perceived difficulties of a given internationalisation move, the more attractive a less risky market entry mode becomes – including where this involves sharing costs and risks with a partner.

Equity partner arrangements

FDI where the MNE takes sole ownership of a new foreign unit, making it a fully owned subsidiary, is the most committed form of internationalisation that exists. It is also the riskiest, in the sense that the company assumes ex ante all market entry costs as well as full responsibility for ex post operations. In response, numerous MNEs prefer sharing FDI risks with equity partners.

Where a FDI is done on a brownfield basis, the main partnership arrangement will involve an incoming MNE – whether by choice or because it is required to do so by the host country government – merging with a target entity's current owner and taking a partial stake in a running concern. Note that even where market entry involves the full-blown acquisition of an existing company, there will still be an ex post partnership aspect until the new owner assimilates the teams currently operating the asset.

The most frequent partnership arrangement with a greenfield FDI is a joint venture – a market entry mode that invokes many of the subjective factors underpinning IB decision-making. These include practitioners' attitude towards risk and uncertainty (hence aversion to loss), confidence in their company's ability to learn by doing and maybe, above all, their inclination to trust foreign actors. This latter factor is actually a very important subset of IB studies, with thinking in this domain often drawing from game theory as formulated in the "beautiful mind" of Nobel laureate John Nash, who posited that alliances can optimise outcomes if actors are able transcend their lack of faith in unfamiliar counterparts' motivations. A construct known as the "prisoner's dilemma" also addresses this interaction, which is clearly of great relevance to a number of international partnership situations.

International mergers and acquisitions

International mergers and acquisitions (M&A) can be driven either by downstream motives (like horizontal market expansion); upstream motives such as the search for efficiency or resources (vertical integration); or strategic motives based on a company's assessment that its sector of activity suffers from overcapacity and is therefore in need of consolidation. International M&A activity tends to occur in waves, often because managers in a given line of business have drawn similar conclusions about which strategies are most appropriate at a particular moment in time. Different waves of international M&A can have different causes but the net effect is often to see entire sectors consolidated in the hands of a few enormous MNEs sometimes achieving quasi-oligopolistic domination in this way. As a result, it is a market entry mode that regularly attracts the attention of national competition agencies, whose interventions often constitute one of the main interfaces between politics and IB.

There are two main advantages for MNEs seeking to acquire a foreign entity (or to merge with one): accelerated market entry (because the target company is already up and running), and complementarity, which can be geographic in nature (because the target is present in parts of the world where the MNE is currently absent), product-related (because it offers a different range of goods or services); or value chain-related (in case of backward or forward vertical integration). Analysis here often relates to the price paid for the foreign target, determined sometimes through private negotiations and on other occasions through stock market operations, some of which become headline IB news stories (especially in case of an unwelcome, "hostile" takeover).

Following the conclusion of an international M&A, managers will still have a great deal of work to do to ensure the new entity's success. Some problems arise in merger situations where one partner begins to dominate the other, despite both having started on an equal footing. Others arise during the post-merger or post-acquisition restructuring phase once the new owner seeks to alter the operational systems of the teams working in the newly consolidated entity, causing counterproductive tensions that can be further aggravated if great psychic distance exists between partners' home and host country cultures. Chapter 9 will discuss this harmonisation challenge in greater detail from a "change management" perspective, but it is already worth noting how hard it can be for companies seeking to internationalise via M&A to screen and choose potential targets that will ultimately turn out to be a good strategic fit. This explains the extreme care with which such operations are always prepared, as well as the frequent engagement of investment bank M&A teams or big consultancy firms like PWC, Deloitte or KPMG, charged with mapping potential scenarios. Headline cases of suboptimal outcomes, such as Microsoft's failure during the 2010s to consolidate the mobile and services businesses it had acquired from Finnish telecoms giant Nokia, stand as precautionary tales of how international M&A can go wrong. Indeed, it is fear of failure that causes many companies to eschew this market entry mode and opt instead for potentially riskier organic growth or even turn down overseas opportunities from which their competitors might then be able to profit.

Of course, there are just as many examples of highly successful international mergers and acquisitions where the synergies created through the deal led to the combined entity's profitability being greater than the sum of the profits previously earned by its constituent parts. One example is French automaker PSA's purchase of originally German brand Opel from General Motors, a deal finalised in late 2017. The new owner realised great efficiencies by having new Opel car models manufactured using Peugeot's existing platforms, a rationalisation measure that along with other cost-cutting steps saw the subsidiary turn a hefty profit for the first time in 20 years. A second success story from the 2010s involves another French MNE, Sanofi, which was able to complement its existing capabilities in the pharmaceutical sector through the hostile takeover of a young American biotech company, Genzyme, offering a pipeline of new products that could be sold more

Complementarity – Where counterparts benefit from association because each offers strengths that other lacks.

Fig 8.5
Nestlé has long been adept at timing its acquisition of foreign brands.

effectively through Sanofi's already established commercial network. Lastly, there is the approach taken by food giant Nestlé, which between 2017 and 2021 engaged in upwards of 75 international M&A deals, notable for the fact that they involved no "big, splashy transactions [but instead] smaller, easily digestible deals" that saw the MNE use its huge commercial profile to accelerate the newly acquired brands' commercialisation in specific national markets (FT Lex 2021).

Whereas many operations of this nature succeed because of the value chain or geographic complementarities that they leverage, other international M&A deals are more opportunistic and often driven by macro-economic considerations. Examples include deals arranged for tax arbitrage purposes: because of expected supply shortages (e.g. commodity super-cycles); because falling stock markets in one country have lowered companies' share prices below their fair value; because crises like the 2020 Covid-19 pandemic have hit specific industries, making them vulnerable to takeover by cash-rich actors from unaffected sectors; or because of a given national economy's role as a nexus of IB. This latter variable is particularly interesting because it speaks to other factors affecting MNE's international M&A decisions: practical ones (like the maturity of a host country's financial market and its FDI regulations) but also the gravity model, referring to managers' level of comfort with the idea of committing resources to an economy that they may perceive as being psychically distant from their home market. Note along these lines a growing tendency in recent years for countries from the Global South to not only be the recipients of inward FDI coming out of the Global North but also to originate their own South-South or South-North flows. Analysis of international M&A cannot be separated from the outlook for the global economy as a whole.

Strategic alliances and international joint ventures
MNEs seeking to enter a foreign market but unwilling (or not allowed) to do so on a standalone basis have only two choices: to abandon the

operation; or to agree a cross-border collaborative arrangement. The
next subsection discusses deals of this nature but where no equity capital
is involved. The current subsection analyses deals where it is.

Collaborations where the original intent is not necessarily to invest
capital in a new entity are generally referred to as strategic alliances.
They tend to involve specific value chain functions where the partners –
who may otherwise be rivals – see good reason to temporarily join
forces, usually to cut costs that would be prohibitive were each company
to assume them separately. A prime example is a strategic alliance that
shares the R&D costs incurred when developing a new technology from
which an entire sector hopes to benefit. One example was the work done
in 2020 by the German specialist BioNTech together with American
pharmaceutical Pfizer to discover a Covid-19 vaccine. Another is the
battery research alliance that BMW and Toyota first launched in 2011,
a strategic collaboration that would blossom over the ensuing decade to
achieve noteworthy advances in hydrogen fuel cell propulsion while also
developing new sports car lines for both brands.

Indeed, it sometimes happens that a strategic alliance becomes a more
or less permanent feature of a MNE's configuration. One example is
the more than two decades-old technical partnership between Japanese
technology giant Fujitsu and German software designer SAP. Several
alliances between airline companies sharing administrative back office
capacities have also been durable. In its broadest sense, strategic alliances
include any kind of international collaboration. For clarity's sake,
however, it is best to apply the term in the more limited sense and specify
different classes within the category.

Collaborations where the original intent is to invest equity capital
and create a more or less permanent structure are referred to as joint
ventures (JVs). They become international JVs (IJVs) either when the
equity partners have different nationalities and/or when the new business
is in a third country. In many, if not most, cases, IJVs involve greenfield
FDI. Owners sometimes hold equal equity stakes in the IJV. On other
occasions, one partner will have a majority share.

IJVs are interesting as a market entry mode largely because of
what they reveal about relationships between international partners.
By putting up equity capital, a MNE entering an IJV is making a
strong commitment to collaboration that may or may not succeed,
depending on the strategic and cultural fit between partners and on
how effectively – and harmoniously – the entity is run. The stakes are
high, with multiple IB commentators asserting that up to 70 percent of
all IJVs fail within five years of their foundation. MNEs must therefore
consider if the benefits of this kind of arrangement are worth the risk
and aggravation.

Sometimes MNEs agree an IJV because they have no other choice
given the host country government's requirements that any incoming
FDI entail a collaboration with a local partner. On occasion, the purpose
of such regulations will be to accelerate technology transfers, especially

where the IJV involves a knowledge-intensive activity that the host country (generally in the Global South) deems crucial to its economic development. At other times, the IJV requirement is because the sector in question is considered "strategic" to national sovereignty. This often relates to defence work, but also to banking, with numerous emerging economies still featuring rules that limit the foreign ownership of domestic banks to minority stakes at best. A prime example is China, where international financial institutions had long been prevented from running standalone operations until a partial liberalisation law was finally enacted in 2018. Even since then, many non-Chinese MNEs still partner with a Chinese interest for the banking and securities work they do in this country, thereby evoking the second (and probably main driver) behind most IJVs, namely, getting help from someone who is more familiar with a challenging new market than the incoming MNE is.

In host countries where operational conditions are difficult (or at least very different from what the MNE is accustomed to), it can be extremely useful working with a local partner who knows how to handle government officials, not to mention suppliers, distributors, logistics, labour unions, workers and other stakeholders. In complicated foreign environments, MNEs may feel that it is impossible to succeed on their own, especially when they are SMEs lacking staff members capable of building bridges to the new market. Add to this the fact that with an IJV, MNEs need to invest less equity capital than they would if they were entering the market alone – plus the possibility of other more technology or production-related synergies with a prospective partner who is no longer acting as a rival – and this entry mode can be very tempting even in the absence of any official requirements.

What becomes critical then is choosing the right partner. This will often be a local interest who can fulfil a specific value chain function within the host country and/or provide broader upstream or downstream knowledge. The incoming MNE will then be expected to offer technological expertise relating to its processes and/or products, provide access to international funding and/or bring a recognisable brand name. The 2018 IJV between Canadian liftgate manufacturer Magna and China's Guangzhou Automotive Group was explicitly justified by the two protagonists in terms of the former's technical competencies and the latter's geographical reach. All in all, the exact breakdown of partners' roles within a new venture, as well as its legal status (usually a partnership or limited liability company), depends on a host of factors, starting with each side's relative bargaining position – often a function of its size – and whether the purpose of the IJV is to sell into the host country or use it as a manufacturing platform for exports elsewhere.

The great weakness of an IJV arrangement is the potential for arguments between partners. Tensions arise for a number of reasons, including one side's sense that the other has performed poorly in operational terms, changes in either partner's strategic goals and problems of culture, communications and above all trust. As noted above, this latter variable is a key topic in IB partnership research, with studies having indicated, for instance, that trust dynamics can be particularly problematic when IJV partners come from very distant business environments and/or commence their collaboration with "over-expectations of partner performance" (Couper et al. 2020). In this case, disappointment is likely to set in as soon as operations begin, especially if the partners are reluctant – possibly due to the distance that separates them – to discuss potential issues before they deteriorate to the point of jeopardising the entire venture. This vicious circle can sometimes be mitigated ex ante by devising an IJV agreement that specifies feedback mechanisms improving information exchanges between partners, as well as potential remedies if and when collaboration issues arise. Unfortunately, it is impossible to strategise in advance all the many things that can possibly go wrong with an IJV, especially since the individuals in charge at the launch of a partnership may be different from the ones in power during its operational phase.

One example of the kinds of strategy-related conflicts that can afflict IJVs is the break-up between US jewellery MNE Tiffany and Swiss watchmaker Swatch, attributed to disagreements about the ultimate design of the products that the new consolidated entity was supposed to manufacture. This was redolent of another famous divorce a few decades previous, when the much-vaunted IJV between top-of-the-range Germany automaker Daimler and its mid-range American counterpart Chrysler fell apart because of the parties' inability to agree a joint strategy (much less adopt a common culture). Complementarity is often a good reason to ally with a company coming from a very different culture, but when the gap is too great, this advantage can easily turn into a liability.

A final example of a culture-related IJV hiccup was a seminal case from the 2000s that saw Mitsubishi engineers refuse to discuss new designs with their Volvo partners because they were put off by the latter's attempts to introduce last-minute changes, a spontaneity that the Japanese found almost disrespectful (Manzoni and Barsoux 2006). Once trust has been lost, it is hard to restore. As argued throughout this chapter and indeed this book, subjectivity is as much a part of IB as rationality. In those many instances when MNE decision-makers end up regarding IJVs as too challenging and standalone FDI as too risky and expensive, they will often start to consider other, less committed modes of internationalisation.

Case study 8.2: The sun rises in the East

Like any infant industry, the renewables sector has experienced a great deal of volatility during its early years, with market participants coming and going as they struggle to achieve the economies of scale

that, by lowering their return costs, would allow them to lower their prices, hence grow demand and trigger a virtuous circle producing further economies of scale. Economists have long understood that when a sector finds itself in this situation, one possibility is government subsidies until such time as self-sustaining scale can be attained. For ideological reasons, many Western governments are reluctant to offer such subsidies. In China, run by a party that is titularly communist, the same inhibition does not exist. This explains Chinese renewables companies' exhilarating growth over the course of the 2010s, ultimately making it far and away into the world's leading solar panel manufacturer.

China's belief in the new sector is matched by countless Global North MNEs who also expect the clean energy business to skyrocket within a few short years and have developed extensive scientific know-how ensuring that this happens. Between the latter companies' technological capabilities and their Chinese counterparts' manufacturing scale and prowess, there is a complementarity that clearly augurs well for cross-border collaboration. Which is what is happening.

One noteworthy 2020 deal was the 37.5 percent stake that France's internationally minded majority state-owned utility, EDF, took in an IJV that it agreed with China Energy Investment Corporation, the purpose being to run several offshore wind projects just north of Shanghai. EDF's aspiration is to build on its existing portfolio of activities in China and increase its share of the domestic market. A similar objective is being followed by another French energy giant, Total, which signed a 50:50 IJV that same year with China's Envision Group, the goal being to further develop the host country's solar infrastructure. Here the fit between the partners is more technical in nature, with Total's capabilities in distributed solar photovoltaic energy systems complementing CEG's expertise in digital solar energy operating systems. What both deals have in common is that they saw Western MNEs exchanging knowledge for market access. It is very doubtful these companies would have been allowed to penetrate the Chinese market to the same extent had they not signed partnership arrangements.

These domestically oriented transactions can be compared with the 2019 joint venture that Chinese solar panel manufacturer GCL agreed with American MNE Powin Energy to sell energy storage solutions throughout Asia-Pacific. Because of solar power's intermittency problems, solar array sales will increasingly combine both PV panels and battery systems. With the two partners each specialising in one of these capabilities, the combined product is deemed technologically advanced enough to be sold all across the region. It is a fully-fledged IJV and therefore ostensibly has a broader scope than the EDF and Total deals, while applying the same seminal principle that the technical and/or geographic synergies created through cross-border rapprochements are more than capable of offsetting whatever foreignness problems might be associated with such arrangements.

Case study questions

1. What risks and rewards do Western renewables MNEs face when agreeing to international joint ventures with Chinese partners?
2. For what reasons might partners in an international joint venture decide that it is better to attack a third market separately instead of together?

Non-equity arrangements

Companies that are hesitant about investing equity capital in a foreign partnership can choose instead to share intangible assets (knowledge, brand name) with a local agent in exchange for the payment of fees and/or royalties. These kinds of non-equity arrangements, called licensing or franchising contracts, are common long-term market entry strategies. Other modes, like turnkey projects or management contracts, tend to happen on a more ad hoc basis.

Turnkey projects – Large-scale initiatives where consortium of companies bid to win right to build infrastructure or other physical facilities.

International licensing

There are two ways for firms to enforce private property rights. Firstly, where they own a particular process or item, they can try to sue any company copying their intellectual property without permission in order to get it to cease such behaviour and, if possible, pay compensation. On the other hand, they might also decide instead to authorise another company to borrow their intellectual property rights, often because this will allow them to enter a foreign market more quickly and less expensively (hence for less risk) than if they were acting on their own. The legal term for this kind of authorisation is licensing, materialising in a contract between one party granting the use of its rights (the "licensor") and another party (the "licensee") receiving them in exchange for the payment of licensing fees and/or royalties.

Licensing contracts typically contain many specific clauses, starting with a precise definition of the product or process covered in the agreement; the geographic territory where it applies; its duration; the licensor's remuneration; and any contract termination/renewal terms. International licensing agreements apply in many different areas but are often manufacturing-related. According to the International Licensing Industry Merchandisers' Association, four leading areas where licensing dominates as a prevailing form of market entry are character and entertainment (replication of figures from movies or television); corporate trademarks and brands (i.e. Coca-Cola's habit of licensing bottlers worldwide to produce and market its products); fashion licensing (often involving globally renowned brands such as Nike, Louis Vuitton or Gap); and sports licensing (satisfying global demand for replications of Tottenham Hotspur football shirts or Lebron James Los Angeles Lakers basketball jerseys). In addition to these headline-grabbing examples, licensing is also used for a number of upstream IB operations. A frequent case is when a pharmaceutical MNE makes a discovery and licenses a rival in another country to market it there, partially because the cost of developing the new product means that the innovator no longer has sufficient capital to fund foreign distribution networks. It is impossible to get an accurate calculation of the total volume of international licensing agreements at a given point in time. For some companies, however, this is clearly an enormous source of income. The world leader in this category, the Disney Corporation, sold approximately $54 billion of global licensed merchandise in 2020, for instance. By offering a quick and relatively low-risk way of entering new markets, licensing overcomes some of the main obstacles facing other modes of internationalisation.

International franchising

Franchising's rationale and contractual aspects are similar to licensing but it tends to focus more on downstream, commercial actions. A "franchisor" signs a contract ("master franchise agreement") with its local agent ("franchisee"), granting the latter the right to operate under the former's trade name and distribute its goods or services in a particular territory. To enable the franchisee to perform this function, the franchisor will typically provide all necessary support, including supplies, training and advertising. The remuneration it receives in return is in the form of royalties, usually calculated as a percentage of the franchisee's gross sales.

Table 8.3
Sample of sectors featuring as "Franchise Opportunities Worldwide"

Advertising	*Gardening*
Assisted living	Handyman services
Automotive	Home improvement
Business advisory	Hotel
Care	Internet-based
Catering	Merchandising
Children	Pet-related
Cleaning	Plumbing
Coffee shop	Property
Courier	Retail
Education	Services
Financial	Sports
Gardening	Travel and leisure
Health and beauty/Health and fitness	Van-based

Source: https://www.franchise-association.org.uk/

Many famous MNEs, often in the retail and fast-food sectors (Starbucks, McDonald's, Burger King), have internationalised via this mode because it is quick and relatively easy. Indeed, as detailed in Table 8.3, franchising is used worldwide in many sectors of activity. The advantage for the franchisor MNE is that it does not need to invest equity capital in overseas commercial outlets and can take advantage of local partners' experience in operating outlets and attracting customers. The advantage for local franchisees is that they can benefit from the brand name and know-how of a company with a tried-and-tested business model.

Running licensing/franchising partnerships

In an ideal scenario, a MNE will sign a licensing or franchising agreement with a local partner and things will run smoothly. Of course, like all foreign ventures, non-equity arrangements have their downsides. The royalties that the MNE receives may offer significant returns (especially since it has been able to enter the foreign market without putting up any equity capital) but are necessarily far lower than potential unshared profits from a wholly owned subsidiary. Secondly, like all collaborations, licensing and franchising entail a set of risks. These include confidentiality (industrial espionage), exclusivity (whether the partner might launch rival operations one day) and maybe, above all, performance (whether the materials that the partner uses or the business practices it applies will end up harming the MNE's reputation).

The question then becomes how to control one's foreign partners. The contracts linking MNEs and their local agents must respect the host country's legal requirements and be enforceable. This is easier to achieve if the MNE has a local presence staffed by individuals with knowledge of the local environment. In the UK, for instance, McDonald's has an office charged with monitoring British franchises' effectiveness. This optimises contract performance but also represents an additional cost for the company.

Above all, the question is how to find a partner that the MNE can trust; who wields useful and compatible business competencies; and who can be counted on to behave loyally and reliably. The first determination here is whether the managers making this particular partnership decision are generally capable of feeling trust, an attitude influenced by a number of factors, including national culture, demography but above all context (Bidault et al. 2018). At a certain point, companies may decide that no trustworthy partners exist. In this case, consideration may revert to the possibility of the company itself taking responsibility for market entry, for example, via greenfield FDI, thereby internalising operations that it had originally hoped to delegate to external partners under a collaborative arrangement. Of course, reversing market entry mode preferences in this way will have a significant effect on a MNE's ultimate configuration.

Ad hoc non-equity arrangements

When a public infrastructure project (like China's Belt and Road Initiative or London's Crossrail train network) is so big that no single company has the financial or technical wherewithal to accomplish it alone, the contractor or order-giver, frequently a governmental authority, will often organise a "call for tender" from groups of companies organised into a consortium, inviting them to bid for the contract. Such consortia will normally be led by a prime contractor responsible for delegating the different sub-projects to each participant. Partners in the consortium are contractually allied in the sense that they work on the same overall project. At the same time, their ties will generally be too provisional to justify a mutual investment of equity capital, meaning that each continues to operate under its own name. Once the project is completed, the consortium will be expected to hand over to the order-giver the keys to a fully functional system and then disband. This explains why such arrangements are known as "turnkey" projects.

By definition, gigantic ventures of this kind are few and far between. There is, however, every chance that as increasing amounts of capital accumulate in the hands of Global South nations – who, almost by definition, require significant infrastructure investment – turnkey projects will become a more prevalent mode of market entry. Indeed, in growth sectors like water systems and public transportation they are already widely practised.

A final category of non-equity arrangements involves "management contracts", where companies receive payment in exchange for seconding competent staff members on temporary work assignments to foreign organisations. This mode of entry is relatively common in certain specialist sectors like healthcare, one example being the way that Johns Hopkins Medicine International, a subsidiary of a major university in the US state of Maryland, enhances its income by running large hospitals throughout the Middle East, starting with Lebanon's Clemenceau Medical Centre. Management contracts are also frequent in the hospitality business, with a number of leading hotels in Asia, for instance, being run under such arrangements. The details (fees, ownership structure) for each of these operations will vary, but in general, all management contracts involve situations where one business partner lacking sector-specific capabilities leases them from another possessing the relevant strengths.

Attitudes and alternatives

MNEs are challenged by market entry more than by any other IB choice. One problem is that many key decisions in this domain must be taken without managers having sufficient understanding of their target market. This might be resolved with help from a partner, often a local company, but it raises in turn a host of new challenges relating to the durability of that relationship. Given the ever-present possibility of failure – regardless of whether the internationalisation is being done on a standalone basis or as part of a partnership – companies will normally always have an exit strategy even as they prepare market entry. This is particularly true with IJVs, where evidence exists that many MNEs only intend to engage with host country environment for as long as it takes to embed themselves there in the before ultimately buying out their partner and reclassifying the IJV as a subsidiary whose local resources can then be transferred to other group units (Fisch and Schmeisser 2020). But market exits can also have other causes, including when the MNE's line of business gains "greater centrality" back in its home market, incentivising it to de-internationalise (Iurkov and Benito 2020). Conversely, there are many other occasions when market exit is followed by re-internationalisation, with MNEs re-entering foreign markets they had previously exited, often by changing their operational mode and incorporating the lessons learnt from their earlier failures to either increase or decrease their level of commitment (Surdu et al. 2019). Market entry is a dynamic process that can and should always be appraised in dynamic terms.

Chapter summary

The chapter started by reviewing the main constructs that have been developed over the years to try and conceptualise MNE decision-makers' mindsets when envisioning the seminal IB action of market entry – first and foremost being Uppsala theory, whose primacy has been further consolidated following its integration of aspects of Network theory. Discussion then went on to consider more strategic theories of IB behaviour as well as moderating elements like company size and internationalisation speed.

The second section looked at the strategic underpinnings of MNEs' different market entry choices. The initial question in this decision-making ladder is whether to internationalise via trade or FDI. For companies choosing the latter option, decisions include whether to proceed on a greenfield or brownfield basis; how to evaluate the strengths and weaknesses of proceeding via international mergers and acquisitions or joint ventures; and how to assess the potential of collaborative arrangements, including non-equity entry modes such as international licensing and franchising. The nature of these kinds of external relationships was then discussed, raising questions in turn as to the kind of internal relations that MNE actors entertain with colleagues working in foreign sister units – topics that Chapter 9 will further address by analysing how and why MNEs structure their international operations in the way that they do.

Case study 8.3: Inditex ups the tempo

Having grown in one generation from a small provincial company to the world's leading clothing manufacturer, Inditex's internationalisation trajectory commands respect. After an initial stage when the company simply manufactured clothes, founder Amancio Ortega Gaona decided on a forward integration strategy in 1975 and opened up the first Zara brand store in La Coruna, Spain. His new "fast fashion" concept of ensuring that changes in consumer preferences translate into quick product line changes was very successful, and within a decade Inditex was running a chain of Zara stores throughout its home market. The next step was to look abroad.

In 1988, Inditex opened its first outlet in Portugal, a choice epitomising Uppsala theory's premise that it can make sense for a budding MNE's first international move to be to a physically and/or culturally proximate country so it can first learn how to operate outside of its borders and gain confidence in its abilities before subsequently going even further afield. Contradictorily, however, Inditex's subsequent moves the following year to Paris and New York – highly visible and potentially profitable retail markets but also extremely competitive ones – epitomised Network theory, a rival concept averring that companies do well to ignore any nervousness about where they might internationalise and should instead head straight for the power centres where fortunes are made or lost. One of the first lessons to glean from Inditex's trajectory is the diversity of filters that can be used to analyse it.

The process accelerated throughout the 1990s, with the company pursuing a variety of market entry modes over the course of the decade. Until 1998, the new countries that Inditex entered were all in the Global North, with one exception, Mexico, which welcomed its first Zara store early on, possibly reflecting the linguistic affinity that a Spanish MNE must feel there. Otherwise, it is worth noting the decision that the

Fig 8.7
Inditex's successful
internationalisation has
been fast and furious.

Group took in 2001 to go public and list its shares on the Madrid Stock
Exchange. Even as the founding Ortega family is said to have maintained
(through 2017 at least) a majority stake in the Group's holding company,
floating shares on the stock market was a clear signal of Inditex's
intention to go fast and far. On some occasions, the company would
grow organically, undertaking downstream FDI in markets characterised
by strong retail demand and no significant barriers to entry. On other
occasions, it would enter markets by acquiring existing brands, some of
which – like Massimo Dutti or Stradivarius – were already fairly well known.
At yet other times, Inditex's international journey would be propelled by

collaborative arrangements, as exemplified by the 2009 IJV that it signed with India's powerful Tata Group before opening stores in that country the following year, reasoning that the challenge of entering this dynamic but complicated emerging market required greater local input. It is rare to find a large and successful MNE that has not pursued a whole variety of market entry approaches, but just as rare to find one as flexible as Inditex has been in adapting its strategy to its circumstances it faces at different times in different places.

Inditex stands out not only for the diversity of its market entry modes but also for the speed with which it has internationalised. By 2004, the Group had opened its 2,000th store (in Hong Kong) across 56 markets; by 2008, it was running 4,000 stores in 73 markets; 2012 saw the opening of outlet number 6,000, a new flagship eco-store in London's Oxford Street (thereby broadcasting Inditex's growing commitment to environmental sustainability); and as of February 2021, the tally had reached 7,199 stores in 202 markets all across the globe. Few, if any, major retail centres anywhere – in the Global North but also in the Global South – are without a clothing store called Zara and/or one of the Group's other successful brand names.

Nor has Inditex stuck to the apparel business alone. Diversification has been an ancillary aspect of the Group's internationalisation, one example being the 2003 opening of the first Zara Homes outlet, followed by an online shop in 2007. This latter action would herald Inditex's wider move into e-commerce over the following decade, with milestones including Zara going fully online in 2010; all other Group brands doing the same the following year; and the work done in 2017 to extend Inditex's integrated store and zara.com online model into a host of new Global South consumer markets including India, Malaysia, Thailand and Vietnam. Inditex may still be family-owned but it it hard to imagine any MNE that is more globalised or has greater geographic and product channel coverage than it does.

Of course, Inditex's enormous scope begs the question of how it supplies product to its countless outlets. Many of the clothing sector's largest MNEs have long been outsourcing most, if not all, of their manufacturing tasks to companies working out of low-cost countries, originally China and more recently Sri Lanka, Bangladesh or Indonesia. Inditex might have been expected to do the same, especially because sourcing from a variety of Global South suppliers would offer the additional benefit of reducing the distance it needs to ship goods to the growing number of outlets that it operates in these regions. Yet once again, the Inditex model differs greatly from customary IB practice. From the very outset, the Group has run the lion's share of its production operations out of Spain or neighbouring Morocco and Portugal. There are several reasons for this seminal choice, first and foremost being that it enables Inditex's world-renowned design centre in Northwest Spain to exercise better quality control than it could if the product were being sourced on the other side of the world. By modernising both its logistics apparatus and its cash register-to-design centre communications systems, the Group has been able to minimise the distance-related problems typically associated with configurations as widely flung as the one it operates. As for the higher costs it incurs by employing a proportionately larger number of Global North-based (hence more expensive) workers, the question today with the acceleration of automation is whether the labour cost differential that had originally caused so many other MNEs to outsource textile production to the Global South matters as much as it used to.

There is also the possibility that Inditex's corporate values preclude cost being viewed as the sole factor dictating the group's configuration choices. After all, the MNE was one of the first anywhere to commit publicly and consequentially to both environmental and social sustainability, an achievement crowned by it being named the global retail sector's group leader in the 2016 Dow Jones Sustainability Index. In this respect as in its other IB dealings, Inditex has a more than 30-year record of seemingly making the right decisions at the right time. No MNE is ever assured of permanent success, but it is very hard indeed to imagine that this upward trajectory is about to cease any time soon.

Case study questions

1. To what extent are the market entry decisions of MNEs like Inditex planned or opportunistic?
2. What are the advantages and disadvantages of the particular value chain configuration that Inditex has organised?
3. What problems might Inditex's sheer size cause it in the future?

Discussion questions

1   What role does subjectivity play in MNEs' internationalisation decisions?
2   What determines the speed at which a company internationalises?
3   At what point might a nascent MNE decide to shift from a trade-based approach to FDI?
4   What is the outlook for greenfield versus brownfield FDI?
5   When do the risks of international partnerships outweigh the advantages?

References

Alayo, M. et al. (February 2019). "Internationalization and entrepreneurial orientation of family SMEs: The influence of the family character", *International Business Review*, Volume 28, Issue 1, pp. 48–59.

Ambos, B. et al. (2019). "Understanding the formation of psychic distance perceptions: Are country-level or individual-level factors more important", *International Business Review*, Volume 28, Issue 4, pp. 660–671.

Arvidsson, H., and Avridsson, R. (2019). "The Uppsala Model of Internationalisation and beyond", accessed 4 December 2020 at https://www.researchgate.net/

Bidault, F. et al. (April 2018). "Willingness to rely on trust in global business collaborations: Context vs. demography", *Journal of World Business*, Volume 53, Issue 3, pp. 373–391.

Bolivar, M. et al. (August 2019). "Global Foreign Direct Investment: A network perspective", *International Business Review*, Volume 28, Issue 4, pp. 696–712.

Buckley, P., and Casson, M. (1976). *The Future of the Multinational Enterprise*, London: MacMillan-Palgrave.

Contractor, F. et al. (April 2020). "How do country regulations and business environment impact foreign direct investment (FDI) inflows?" *International Business Review*, Volume 29, Issue 2, accessed 30 July 2021 at https://www.sciencedirect.com/

Couper, A. et al. (April 2020). "Lost that lovin' feeling: The erosion of trust between small, high-distance partners", *Journal of International Business Studies*, Volume 51, pp. 326–352.

D'Angelo, A., and Presutti, M. (June 2019). "SMEs international growth: The moderating role of experience on entrepreneurial and learning orientations", *International Business Review*, Volume 28, Issue 3, pp. 613–624.

Elia, S. et al. (16 April 2019). "Entry mode deviation: A behavioral approach to internalization theory", *Journal of International Business Studies*, Volume 50, Issue 5, pp. 1359–1371.

Fisch, J., and Schmeisser, B. (13 April 2020). "Phasing the operation mode of foreign subsidiaries...", *Journal of International Business Studies*, Volume 51, Issue 8, pp. 1223–1255.

Forsgren M. et al. (2015). *Knowledge, Networks and Power*, London: Palgrave Macmillan.

FT Lex (18 February 2021). "Nestlé: The water margin", *Financial Times*.

Fung, H. et al. (February 2020). "Leader narcissism and outward foreign direct investment: Evidence from Chinese firms", *International Business Review*, Volume 29, Issue 1, accessed 30 July 2021 at https://www.sciencedirect.com/

Granovetter, M. (May 1973). "The strength of weak ties", *The American Journal of Sociology*, Volume 78, Issue 6, pp. 1360–1380.

Iurkov, V., and Benito, G. (July 2020). "Change in domestic network centrality, uncertainty, and the foreign divestment decisions of firms. *Journal of International Business Studies,* Volume 51, pp. 788–812.

Jiang, F. et al. (10 April 2018). "Global mindset and entry mode decisions: Moderating roles of managers' decision-making style and managerial experience", *Management International Review*, Volume 58, pp. 413–447.

Johanson, J., and Vahlne, J. (1977). "The internationalisation process of the firm – a model of knowledge development and increasing foreign market commitments", *Journal of International Business Studies*, Volume 8, Issue 2, pp. 23–32.

Kahneman, D., and Tversky, A. (1979). "Prospect theory: An analysis of decision under risk", *Econometrica*, Volume 47, Issue 4, pp. 263–291.

Li, M. et al. (October 2019). "Does national sentiment affect foreign direct investment, and if so, how? Additional evidence", *International Business Review*, Volume 8, Issue 5, accessed 30 July 2021 at https://www.sciencedirect.com/

Manzoni, J.-F., and Barsoux, J.-L. (19 October 2006). "Untangling alliances and joint ventures", *Financial Times*.

Monaghan, S. et al. (5 December 2019). "Born digitals: Thoughts on their internationalization and a research agenda", *Journal of International Business Studies*, Volume 51, Issue 1, pp 11–22.

Nadkarni, S., and Perez, P. (January 2007). "Prior conditions and early international commitment: The mediating role of domestic mindset", *Journal of International Business Studies*, Volume 38, Issue 1, pp. 160–176.

Papageorigiadis, N. et al. (February 2020). "The characteristics of intellectual property rights regimes: How formal and informal institutions affect outward FDI location", *International Business Review*, Volume 29, Issue 1, accessed 30 July 2021 at https://www.sciencedirect.com/

Safari, A., and Chetty, S. (2019). "Multilevel psychic distance and its impact on SME internationalization", *International Business Review*, Volume 28, Issue 4, pp. 754–765.

Sultana, N., and Turkina, E. (April 2020). "Foreign direct investment, technological advancement, and absorptive capacity: A network analysis", *International Business Review*, Volume 29, Issue 2, accessed 30 July 2021 at https://www.sciencedirect.com/

Surdu, I. et al. (April 2019). "Once bitten, not necessarily shy? Determinants of foreign market re-entry commitment strategies. *Journal of International Business Studies*, Volume 50, pp. 393–422.

Tuppura, A., et al. (August 2008). "Linking knowledge, entry timing and internationalisation strategy", *International Business Review*, Volume 17, Issue 4, pp. 473–487.

Vahlne, J. (May 2020). "Development of the Uppsala model of internationalization process: From internationalization to evolution", *Global Strategy Journal*, Volume 10, Issue 2, pp. 239–250.

Vahlne, J., and Johanson, J. (9 November 2019). "The Uppsala model: Networks and micro-foundations", *Journal of International Business Studies*, Volume 51, Issue 1, pp. 4–10.

Zeng, J. et al. (December 2019). "The emergence of multi-sided platform MNEs: Internalization theory and networks", *International Business Review*, Volume 28, Issue 6, accessed 30 July 2021 at https://www.sciencedirect.com/

CHAPTER 9

Multinational organisations and structures

Introduction

Following on from Chapter 8's study of market entry modes, the next step is to review the different kinds of relationships that develop within a multinational enterprise (MNE) between its head office and foreign subsidiaries. These two core international business (IB) topics are not entirely unrelated, since many internationalisation decisions are specifically taken because a MNE wants to design a particular structure that it thinks will be conducive to its purposes. Market entry may seem the more dynamic topic because it speaks to a MNE's interfaces with the outside world but that would be to ignore the importance of also understanding a company's internal dynamics, if only because when managers draw an organisational chart's boxes and arrows, what they are really laying out is the basis upon which employees' performance will be assessed, hence rewarded.

MNE structures themselves are a more complicated topic than they first appear, in part because of how hard it can be to coordinate units that are often both geographically and culturally distant from one another. This explains the sheer volume of IB research in this field, generally focusing on the mission assumed by the MNE's headquarters (HQ); the "scope [of its subsidiaries as well as their] practices, knowledge management, engagement with local market and nonmarket actors, performance and individuals" (Meyer et al. 2020); the relationship between these two poles (respectively the "centre" and the "periphery"); and the underlying principles of organisational sociology. The present chapter covers all these topics.

Before starting, however, there must be recognition of the chicken and egg aspect of MNEs' structural choices. As living entities, all organisations evolve and are susceptible to both internal and external pressures. The structures that a group designs to achieve its goals will influence employees' worldviews (hence values and behaviour), but by the same token, their worldviews will also affect how they organise their

DOI: 10.4324/9781003159056-12

collective activity, with feedback mechanisms hopefully ensuring the coherence between these two forces. There is a constant risk that this alignment will not work and that a company's internal processes will be poorly adapted to its circumstances, especially in IB where MNEs must constantly cope with inconsistent and contradictory environments. Sociologists like Talcott Parsons have studied how the efforts that a system (like an organisation) makes to adapt to its environs can be at odds with its need for internal coherency. It bears remembering that in IB, like in other social sciences, contexts, structures and mindsets all influence one another.

LEARNING OBJECTIVES

After reading this chapter, you should be able to:

- trace the evolution of MNEs' organisational paradigms over time
- assess the strengths and weaknesses of different MNE structures
- evaluate the structures MNEs have adopted in response to their variable circumstances
- critique MNE head office-subsidiary power relationships
- apply sociological principles to MNE structures

Case study 9.1: Uniting Unilever

When a company has survived for as long as Unilever has, it knows that new challenges often necessitate new strategies and structures. This grand old name in European consumer goods, the manufacturer of famous household brands like Lipton tea, Knorr soup, Lux soap and Vaseline – and since 2012, Ben and Jerry's ice cream – had traditionally run a decentralised organisation, reflecting in part the duality of its

Fig 9.2
A diverse product range helps Unilever target more markets but is also harder to manage.

Dutch and British origins. This was congruent with Unilever's long-standing conviction, like most companies in the fast-moving consumer goods sector, that it should structure its operations in such a way as to maximise knowledge of consumers' varying preferences. It is a vision that remains central to its business model and speaks to the "multi-local" self-image of a MNE seeking to marry "consensual management style with local autonomy" (Jones and Decker 2017) –
a difficult task for a group coordinating operations across nearly 100 countries worldwide. The problem in today's hyper-competitive environment is that MNEs running localised operations in many different countries risk duplicating a number of functions and running up extra costs.

Having achieved lower operating profits throughout the 2000s than its great rival, Proctor and Gamble, Unilever decided to try and turn things around by embarking on a major streamlining effort that has seen changes throughout the organisation, starting with its upper echelons. After a number of permutations, the current executive management team is actually very lean, comprised of the chair, CEO, CFO, two product line managers, one supply chain officer and four non-executive directors. This compact but diverse committee, pooling competencies in functional, product and geographic areas alike, has paved the way for leaner operational structures, with Unilever's avowed objective now being to "deliver faster decisions", a change felt at all levels within the group.

One example was in 2017 when Unilever's Food R&D units, originally spread across several countries, were combined into a new global Foods Innovation Centre, working out of a single site in the Netherlands. Otherwise, whereas Unilever used to be defined by its geographic focus, its avowed priority in recent years has been to reinforce its product divisions, as exemplified by the new executive management team's own composition. This should improve Unilever's productive efficiency (hence profitability) but also increases the risk that it might pay less attention in the future to variations in consumers' preferences worldwide, this being the type of knowledge that would usually be lodged in the group's foreign subsidiaries, whose managers are more knowledgeable about (and focused on) local markets than about broader international trends. The challenge is determining whether it serves Unilever better to support its subsidiary managers and offer a broader product range that is likelier to appeal to different national markets, or if it should narrow its offer to cut production costs.

Unilever management often speaks nowadays about the best way to simplify its organisation and achieve scale. There is still recognition of the need for "local go-to-market operations" (Dekkers and Pitkethly 2018), but that is now being depicted as something that can come from greater responsiveness and agility – based on improved information and communications technology – rather than from structures organised around demand variations. In 2020, the Group abandoned its dual nationality to consolidate all headquarters operations in the UK alone – a highly symbolic move. The new approach is a far cry from Unilever's formerly decentralised ethos. It will be interesting to see how much of the MNE's strategic heritage can survive in new structures geared towards new objectives.

Case study questions

1. Why have Unilever executives opted for more of a product approach than a geographic focus?
2. What are the risks for Unilever of organising itself around efficiencies instead of customers?

Section I. Theorising MNE structures

Academics have developed a number of prisms to analyse the cross-border interactions that take place between MNE units. Organisational studies, for instance, will ask how a MNE's managerial knowledge and learning might "ensure its administrative coherence" (Tan et al. 2020). Internationalisation studies will use constructs like Uppsala theory's "stages" model to identify how the experience a MNE acquires when entering markets informs subsequent organisational decision-making. Strategy studies will offer perspectives like George Yip's "global transformations" thesis, emphasizing MNEs' need for structures that can unify their pricing, production and account management processes. All these precepts, and many others still, have relevance to discussions about MNE organisations.

In terms of the specific ways that MNEs manage their operations at a given moment in time, however, the theories that stand out most are those that link a company's ambitions to the different power relationships that it establishes within its confines. The spectrum here ranges from "multidomestic" approaches where the MNE runs an entire value chain inside each of the countries where it operates (see Chapter 7) – a configuration awarding each national subsidiary maximum autonomy – to globalised paradigms characterised by fragmented cross-border value chains coordinated by an all-powerful head office. These polar extremes embody the opposition between IB and globalisation.

Stephen Hymer and multinational divisions

Research by a young economist named Stephen Hymer, published posthumously in 1976, is considered the seminal text in this subset of IB studies. One of the many filters used in Hymer's magnus opus involved dividing MNE organisational history into three distinct stages, each characterised by its own logic. It is a good starting point for analysing how MNE structures have been conceptualised over time.

According to Hymer, most companies destined one day to become world leaders began life under the tight control of a few key actors making a single product and working out of a single location in their country of origin. At this early stage, managers would tend to view international ventures as mere adjuncts to their main business in their home market, hiving off foreign activities and grouping them into an international division with responsibility for specifically cross-border tasks like trade documentation and import/export logistics (see Figure 9.3). It was a structure that may have seemed appropriate to young practitioners with a simplistic home-and-away view of the world but it was also deeply flawed, if only because it glossed over the differences between one foreign market and another. The end result is that relatively few MNEs organise themselves in this way anymore.

Hymer's thinking stemmed from his opinion that one of the main drivers behind foreign direct investment (FDI) should be the desire to

International division – Structure driven by the idea that all foreign units have in common the fact that they exist outside of the home market and should be managed jointly for this one reason.

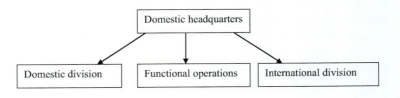

Fig 9.3
International division.

exploit "monopoly advantages", generally materialising in the unique value chain management capabilities that every company develops. As noted in Chapter 7, many multinationals at the time when Hymer was writing were trying to internationalise along vertically integrated lines, largely because the consensus managerial paradigm back then argued that companies should seek maximum control over their global value chains. The inference was that the group executive should take direct responsibility for implementing international strategy, justifying in turn a division-based structure geared towards internal functions. Hymer called this the "Unitary (U-form)" organisation (see Figure 9.4) and made it the second stage that MNEs would attain at a certain stage of growth.

A U-form structure is commonly referred to as a functional organisation, with each division being defined, irrespective of products or locations, in terms of a value chain function such as manufacturing, marketing or finance. Here it is the head office that controls foreign subsidiaries, whose mission is to implement strategies and technologies handed down from the top. For this reason, there is always a risk of fostering an ethnocentric culture within such organisations.

Functional organisations work best for MNEs characterised by narrow product ranges, either because they are at an early stage of their development or due to the narrowness of their product ranges. The first examples date from the early 20th century when this kind of structure was being implemented by MNEs like General Motors, Shell, Standard Oil and Ford, all of whose initial internationalisation tended to involve duplicating abroad the parent company's entire value chain. As such, the main priority with a functional organisation is to ensure headquarters' operational control.

Analysing IB's evolution in the mid-20th century, Hymer detected the advent of a third organisational stage, one he called the "Multi-divisional (M-form)". The idea here was that in response to international consumers' increasingly differentiated demands, MNEs would need structures that were more flexible than the U-form. For some, this meant adopting a product organisation, with each division now becoming its own independent profit centre (see Figure 9.5). Structures of this kind seem to fit MNEs that have a broad product range and where decisions made by one division have little or no effect on sister units, which should therefore be free to pursue their own policies in line with local market conditions. Exemplified by conglomerates such as Westinghouse and Siemens but also some Japanese *keiretsus*, the point here is that where

Functional organisation – Structure focused on cross-border integration of internal capabilities.

Product organisation – Structure where each product division is run autonomously due to an absence of functional overlaps.

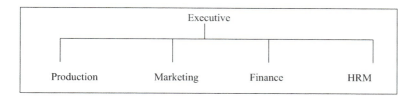

Fig 9.4
Hymer's Unitary "U-form" functional organisation.

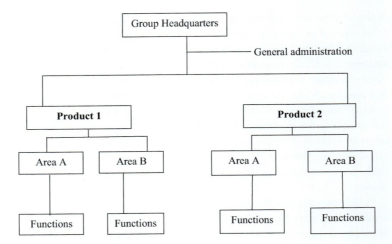

Fig 9.5
Hymer's multi-divisional
"M-form" product
organisation.

no real overlap exists between different product lines, cross-divisional communications are of lesser value.

The second variant of Hymer's multi-divisional M-form –and one that would become very popular among MNEs prioritising **responsiveness** to local specificities – is the **geographic organisation** (see Figure 9.6). Where consumer preferences (or production conditions) vary widely from one country to another, structuring efforts along functional or product lines makes less sense than empowering the front-line units that possess the most knowledge about local circumstances, that is, the MNE's local subsidiaries. This structure emphasizes differentiation instead of a global strategy and therefore usually entails more of a geocentric corporate culture. Power within this kind of MNE shifts from the centre to the periphery, with group headquarters performing little more than resource

Responsiveness – Ability and inclination to react quickly to perceived needs of a situation.

Geographic organisation – Structure based on idea that the MNE's overriding organisational goal should be to maximise adaptation to local circumstances.

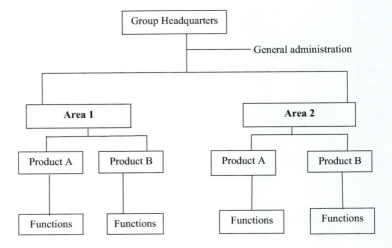

Fig 9.6
Hymer's multi-divisional
"M-form" geographic
organisation.

allocation, performance control and strategic coordination missions. A leading example of a MNE with a geographic organisation is Nestlé, which has traditionally given each of its national subsidiaries great autonomy to make their own product portfolio decisions. In MNEs organised along these lines, being a country manager is a very desirable position, often even more so than working out of headquarters.

By stressing local autonomy over central power, a geographic organisation invokes a multidomestic logic where national subsidiaries are almost run as if they were standalone businesses requiring little coordination. At an extreme, it is a view of the MNE as little more than the sum of its different parts.

Power in geographically organised MNEs tends to be fragmented. Greater responsiveness to local circumstances is a strength but also a weakness, since it can easily translate into wastefulness with functions like R&D or manufacturing being duplicated in several countries. This increases overheads, making it harder to achieve group-wide economies of scale. It is one of the reasons why Unilever and Tata (see Case studies 9.1 and 9.2) would decide after flirting with this approach to ultimately re-centralise some of their group functions. Transferring knowledge from one subsidiary to another can be difficult in geographic organisations that will often induce employees to only communicate information within the confines of their immediate SBU or office. This can be a big problem in a world where the ability to transfer knowledge cultivated by one national subsidiary to another is crucial to creating synergies, hence competitiveness. To make such horizontal transfers effective, they must be formalised in group-wide procedures (Gibson et al. 2019), especially if they involve groundbreaking technologies or innovations. Anything structural that hinders or impoverishes intra-firm communications and coordination is therefore counterproductive, explaining why a pure geographic organisation is also no longer as popular among MNEs as it used to be.

Scope and structure

As Chapter 11 discusses in further detail, at some point in the early 1980s, a number of renowned IB observers, including Harvard University's Theodore Levitt, began proclaiming that international markets (especially for branded consumer goods) had embarked upon an irreversible convergence trajectory. This intimated that organising multinational operations around national borders – the multidomestic paradigm – was no longer advisable. Instead, many now thought that it was time to get ready to service customers globally, especially given the economies of scale advantages being achieved by rivals who were already sizing themselves to do battle all across the world. The new goal of prioritising global reach seemingly called for a new organisational paradigm.

Strengths of global organisations

The main goal for companies pursuing a global strategy is to achieve efficiency by coordinating the actions of subsidiaries from one part of the world with what their sister units are doing elsewhere. There has long been recognition that this can require cross-subsidisation (Hamel and Prahalad 1985), which will only be implemented if the group executive wields sufficient authority over subsidiary managers to compel them to share their surpluses with counterparts in other countries. To this extent, the late 20th-century rise of globally organised MNEs involved a re-assertion of centralised power. Emphasizing standardisation, MNEs of this ilk would seek to coordinate production around a very few specialised factories scattered strategically across the world, while also trying to homogenise their product offer so as to maximise economies of scope, even when this was at odds with their increasingly savvy global customers' preference for product differentiation. The end result would be a jarring contradiction in several sectors between MNEs' desire for integration and customers' call for responsiveness, a conflict embodied in the "push" versus "pull" conundrum that will be studied below in more strategic terms and which Chapter 11 will reprise from more of a marketing perspective. It is a dilemma that drew the main battle lines in IB at the time and which remains IB's most acute debate even today.

The global paradigm that dominated IB thinking throughout the 1980s and 1990s was also based on the hubristic notion that global convergence was unstoppable. The fact that this had become a consensus view is crucial given that a paradigm's adoption is directly related to the publicity it receives. After all, managers risk their careers if they take actions contrary to what everyone else is doing. If the decisions they make correspond to received wisdom at a given point in time and things go wrong, they can always escape blame by pointing out that everyone made the same mistake. It is harder for them to defend themselves, on the other hand, if their decisions counter the consensus view. In IB, as in other disciplines, mavericks are always likely to stand out, for better or for worse.

Critiques of global organisations

Since the turn of the century, a growing number of IB analysts have taken a more negative view of global organisations. From a head office perspective, the problem is that this approach can spread managerial resources thinly, with central units incurring higher overheads due to all the coordination work that is required of them. From a subsidiary perspective, the main criticism is the loss of independence if all group missions are dictated by head office executives solely interested in MNE-wide outcomes, ignoring local employees' greater attachment to the SBU where their own performance is being assessed and rewarded. A secondary effect of subsidiaries' subordination is the de-skilling they suffer as HQ shift competencies from one unit to another in a game of global chess that can often ride roughshod over local ambitions.

Economies of scope – Efficiencies achieved via product portfolio management synergies.

De-skilling – Where lesser competency is required of employees, often because they are being asked to specialise in one or very few value chain operation(s).

In addition, subsidiary employees can resent (and be psychologically confused at) having to follow the orders of bosses working out of distant locations. Note also the risk in a global company that knowledge might only be transmitted vertically, from headquarters to subsidiary or vice versa, undermining potentially fruitful subsidiary–subsidiary communications. Lastly and from a more operational perspective (see Chapter 10), global organisations serving local markets from distant central manufacturing locations inevitably suffer higher logistics and "transit" costs.

The end result is that global organisations are not as popular in the 21st century as they had been during the preceding period. Like other MNE paradigms, the understanding today is that they may be appropriate in some situations, but not in all. A new compromise thinking has taken hold, one asking which functions lend themselves to centralisation and which do not. Running operations out of headquarters seems to make more sense for certain activities: research and development, because this helps to preserve confidentiality; procurement, because this allows for bulk purchasing; manufacturing, because this enables economies of scale; logistics, because this optimises coordination; and finance, because IT platforms can be shared. Conversely, there are other functions where decentralisation seems to make much more sense: design, because of the need for market intelligence; sales, because interpersonal relationships are paramount; and human resources, because of the importance of cultural affinities (and the need to be knowledgeable about national employment laws). One example of this is the way that major international airliners like British Airways (BA) run representative offices in many of the countries they serve. BA could save money by fielding all of the phone calls it gets worldwide out of a single site. However, this kind of centralisation would run counter to the need for human contact that is a key factor of success in most downstream activities.

Broadly speaking, a MNE's decision where to locate its various functions will depend if the priority is internal cohesion or external adaptation. In reality, MNEs must often juggle global and multidomestic considerations simultaneously. Of course, contending with such extremes also hints at the possibility of intermediary solutions, one of which is the regional level.

Debate about regional organisations
Previous chapters already discussed the regional level of IB from a number of perspectives, the operational fact that most MNEs derive their main economies of scope and scale from the services or products that they produce and sell within their home regions (not globally) and the psychological fact that many practitioners feel more comfortable in neighbouring business cultures that, albeit foreign, are still less strange to them than what they might encounter further afield. Add to this the more practical consideration of how time zones affect a MNE's work

organisation – how a unit's regional location defines people's working hours – and what becomes apparent is that regions also have a role to play in the way MNEs' organise their structures.

As different corporate functions lend themselves to greater or lesser centralisation, regionalisation can also be a compromise solution giving practitioners working in different value chain functions a view of the world that is somewhere in the middle of excessive globalism or radical localism. On the upstream side, this can be exemplified by the way that many automotive sector MNEs – having to contend both with high factory construction costs and high delivery costs – use a regional configuration to resolve their scale versus distance dilemma. The same applies when MNEs "near source" supplies (see Chapter 11), that is, when they stop ordering inputs from the very cheapest suppliers located on the other side of the world because long-distance supply chains have greater time-to-market, and turn instead to regional suppliers who, albeit slightly more expensive, still cost less than the domestic alternatives. In both these upstream examples, a regional organisation is seen as a good compromise.

The same can be said about many downstream activities. With the exception of a few high-tech goods like consumer electronics, it is questionable whether Levitt's prediction of mass global convergence has actually come to pass. Instead, most convergence seems to have happened at a regional level. There are countless examples of MNEs who have expanded horizontally throughout their home region precisely because they find it easier to market to populations that are foreign yet whose social, economic and cultural attributes are closer to what they know at home. There is also a greater chance (especially in service sectors like banking or insurance) that regional customers will be more familiar with brands originating from a neighbouring country than one coming from the other side of the world. Add to this the fact that market structures in neighbouring countries have a better chance of featuring some similarities (legal systems, labour relations, distribution networks), particularly in institutionally integrated regional economic groups like the European Union, and it is clear that globalisation is far less widespread than was once argued, with intra-regional transfers of assets and knowledge taking up as much, if not more, of headquarters' staff time as global flows do.

Having said that, note the special case of the so-called "bi-regional MNEs" who are also not truly global in nature – in the sense that neither their upstream nor downstream functions are conducted on a worldwide basis – but for whom IB involves producing in one region and selling in another. This configuration characterises a growing number of internationally competitive MNEs originating from emerging Global South economies. The main issues here are the extent of the manufacturer's dependence on customers in the region where it sells; whether it has the industrial capacity to service other regions beyond this; and if it has any desire to do so. Some bi-regional MNEs will probably never evolve beyond this status. For others, it is transitory until such time as they have grown big enough to service a multiregional (i.e. global) customer base. Static analysis will often reveal different lessons about MNEs than dynamic judgements of their evolution over time.

Glocalisation: juggling global and local perspectives

One of the main lessons from this historical discussion about MNE organisations is that structures are never perfect, if only because the environments in which they are embedded (and in relation to which they are defined) are always changing. IB analysts have long been aware of this problem and often conceptualised it as the risk that an organisation will either have too much of a global or else a local outlook. An entire subset of IB studies exists to find solutions to this dilemma, often by focusing less on structures and more on the individuals working within them.

A variety of concepts have evolved to address the relationship between human agency and the effectiveness of MNE organisations. For instance, Upper Echelons theory posits that executives working out of a MNE's head office may be prone to arrogance (also called "leader narcissism"). Viewing the long-term strategies that they have personally devised as the only way forward for the company, they will try to centralise all planning themselves, considering that subsidiaries' sole role is to carry out whatever instructions they have been given and that they should therefore be assigned a "translator" ensuring obedience with orders (Gutierrez-Huerter 2019). The diametrically opposed argument is that it is much better for subsidiaries to be attributed complete responsibility for their own performance, if only because of how hard it is for the head office in MNEs featuring widely dispersed operations to fully understand everything that their subsidiaries do. Neither perspective is intrinsically right or wrong, with studies revealing better performance by multicultural managers in global environments but also by monocultural managers in less global environments (Szymanski et al. 2019). As demonstrated throughout this book, there is truly no one-best-way of doing IB. The question then becomes how to make MNE structures flexible enough to accommodate this variability.

The risk when companies focus solely on their structures' strategic fit and neglect all other considerations is that they might imprison themselves in a rigid and bureaucratic mindset of their own making. Despite the unifying pressures of globalisation, specific local contexts will also always be important, forcing MNEs to engage in the difficult juggling act of managing subsidiaries' "dual embeddedness" within the group framework but also within their local environment (Cheng and Huang 2020). Both head office and subsidiary decision-makers might feel discouraged if they are being asked to only strategise within the narrow confines of whatever official role they have been assigned. This explains the more advanced argument that MNEs should not actually be forced to choose between global integration and local adaptation since both are essential, but instead be allowed to organise themselves in a way that achieves both these apparently contradictory goals at once. It is a conception that has given birth to the figure of the transnational firm (Bartlett 1986).

Transnational firm – Company whose aim (hence organisation) simultaneously targets global efficiency, local flexibility and shared learning.

Managerial mindsets can be just as important as MNE structures

Transnational theorists argue that attitudes and relationships are just as crucial to a MNE's success as official reporting lines are. They believe that IB practitioners must look beyond their company's "administrative heritage" (Arikan et al. 2019) and give fair weighting to all ideas, even ones originating from other parts of the group. In truth, it does not matter whether a potentially useful idea starts in the centre or the periphery; all that counts is that it be fully communicated. In the transnational view, this is best achieved by encouraging two-way vertical flows between headquarters and subsidiaries, as well as horizontal flows between subsidiaries. It is an insight that has become the cornerstone of a whole subset of modern IB theory, particularly given evidence that the historic assumption that knowledge necessarily starts in the centre and flows to the periphery is inaccurate, since the opposite is just as likely to occur (Da Silva Lopes et al. 2019). IB practitioners' capacity for embracing multiple perspectives all at once needs to be acknowledged and actually nurtured.

One of the primary aims of a transnational approach is to avoid the sorts of problems that can arise when a head office tries to force foreign subsidiaries to reproduce a strong home country culture. An example of this from the early 2000s was when Toyota executives brought Japanese working methods to the plant they had opened in Valenciennes (France). Many staff members reactively negatively to the pressures put on them following HQ's implementation of an ambitious new performance system, a discord that would temporarily upset labour relations. Today, it is rare that a MNE's centre can simply dictate to its periphery. According to Kogut and Zander's "knowledge-based theory of the firm", the main driver of corporate organisation is indeed knowledge, but because this is a commodity deeply embedded in each SBU's own culture and practices, it is almost impossible to replicate it fully across the whole of a group, if only because how hard differences in national (even more than organisational) cultures make it to create synergies (Wang et al. 2020). This explains the need for staff members to develop a wide range of capabilities that they can apply when necessary and depending on the circumstances. MNE structures must also be adapted in such a way as to accelerate and open up innovation processes, facilitating the sharing of best practice across different locations.

In short, the transnational approach is meant to replace the one-way – top-down or bottom-up – information flow that had characterised, respectively, global and multidomestic MNEs. One expression commonly used to describe this new vision is "glocalisation". It is a phrase that many companies apply nowadays, with one of the best-known examples being the advertising campaign that the British banking giant HSBC has run for two decades now, publicising itself as an organisation that is global yet local everywhere. A similar construct calls for so-called "multi-local" MNEs simultaneously managing challenges on a national, regional and global scale, depending on whether a given situation is driven by domestic or international factors. One key variable at this level is the subsidiary CEO's entrepreneurial leadership style and exercise of managerial discretion (Sarabi 2020). Leaders capable of switching between paradigms are said to have reached a more advanced level of transnational flexibility.

Despite the intelligence of this logic, like any paradigm the transnational approach can also create serious organisational dilemmas. One example is the sort of problem that arises when people are asked to assume a leadership role in some situations but not in others. This mixing of assignments raises questions about the permanency of MNE structures and has spawned a body of organisational and human resource literature devoted to concepts like "management by projects" and "flexible working teams". On other occasions, the dilemma is caused by practitioners' excessive pursuit of self-interest. In a structure like a transnational MNE, a modicum of selflessness will always be necessary to advance the common good. Examples include the occasional need to share innovations or to prospect customers that a sister unit will subsequently serve and for which it will ultimately receive credit. Where subsidiary managers focus exclusively on their own SBU's performance, often because they are not being sufficiently rewarded for contributions they make to other teams, their motivation is likely to slacken. Even worse, group and subsidiary interests can sometimes be in direct conflict with one another. Examples include disagreements about the implementation of costly CSR programmes or about a product's pricing and whether it should be endowed with simple or advanced technological attributes, possibly because it is at different stage of its life cycle stage in different subsidiary territories. Conflicts of this nature are a frequent source of discord within transnational MNES. How they are addressed goes a long ways towards defining the roles that subsidiaries might be assigned (Ambos et al. 2020).

Other problems associated with a transnational approach are more cultural in nature. As aforementioned, there is the expectation within such organisations that head office and subsidiary colleagues interact constructively and exchange a great deal of information. This seems especially feasible when the individuals concerned come from similar national, cultural and/or linguistic backgrounds. The problem is that when colleagues come from very different backgrounds, transnational information exchanges might be difficult to achieve. Having said that, it is an obstacle that can be overcome if employees learn to recognise the value of cultural variability. Returning to the Toyota example, the

Organisational dilemma – Where employees are confused by the contradictory interests they are asked to represent at different levels within an organisation.

Japanese business culture is just as foreign to US workers as it is to the French yet employees at the company's plant in Huntsville (Alabama), unlike their Valenciennes counterparts, had relatively few problems adopting Japanese "quality circle" practices where ideas are shared from the bottom-up. In essence, this tolerance for foreign thought processes meant that the company's US workers were closer to a transnational mentality than their French counterparts were. Flexible structures are difficult to implement in the absence of flexible mindsets.

Matrix organisations as the embodiment of a transnational MNE

All in all, the transnational company seeks to maximise vertical (hierarchical) and horizontal (geographical) exchanges between all units – a principle embodied in a relatively recent structure called the matrix organisation (see Figure 9.7). The idea here is that irrespective of employees' unit of origin, there are many occasions when they should be temporarily allocated to mixed ad hoc structures specifically created to fulfil a particular task. Here, everyone should expect to share all their knowledge with their temporary teams, comprised each time of people coming from different departments. The matrix logic was especially popular during the 1990s when it would be applied by a number of leading MNEs, most notably the Swedish–Swiss engineering company Asea Brown Boveri (ABB) following the merger between the constituent companies, each with its own very different corporate (and national) culture. The hope was that by encouraging multiple reporting lines and forums for information sharing, new synergies could arise, benefitting product, function and geographic divisions all at once.

With organisations like this, the main goal is to ensure that the whole of a MNE is in a position to use the "explicit" (open) or "tacit" (unspoken) knowledge held by any one of its units. Indeed, many large MNEs struggle to communicate the data and knowledge stored across their different departments and sites. Getting useful information to the right people at the right time is therefore a priority for international managers. Most MNEs have organised a range of systems and roles towards this end (newsletters, multisite videoconferencing, internal communications specialists and/or peer visits). At a deeper level,

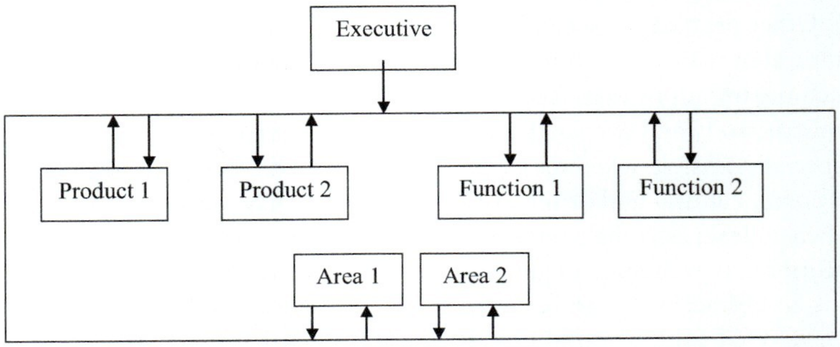

Matrix organisation – Structure based on the idea that multiple functional reporting lines broaden employees' vision of business and can create synergies.

Fig 9.7
Matrix organisation.

however, the decision to share information via these or other methods depends on the amount of trust that a MNE's employees have in foreign colleagues sometimes working on the other side of the world. Much like trust in external partners constitutes a major topic in IB studies, the same can be said about trust in one's own co-workers.

Because of its multiple reporting lines and potential for information overload, a matrix organisation can be confusing to practitioners and will often only truly succeed if there are people within the organisation able and willing to serve as traffic controllers. These key staff members will have the job of identifying and redirecting colleagues' competencies. That is no easy task, as the knowledge that a company holds is often very compartmentalised, especially within national borders. In many cases, this steering role will be played by country managers, who are once again starting to receive the kind of attention that they used to enjoy back in the days when multidomestic structures were dominant. Even so, due to their managerial complexity, matrix organisations have started to lose some of their popularity.

MNEs as alliances of equals

Since national subsidiaries on the one hand, and regional or global headquarters on the other, are all capable of contributing to a MNE's collective performance, there is also a strong argument to make that the only accurate way of conceptualising a group's different power bases is to view all of them as equal partners in a network (Morschett et al. 2015), one where entrepreneurial initiatives are to be designed and communicated both horizontally and vertically (see Figure 9.8). In some instances (i.e. Panasonic, whose website announced in March 2019 that it had given its Design Division "the functions of controlling and supporting design departments inside and outside Japan"), a strong headquarters culture means that the MNE's centre assumes complete responsibility for group strategy. In other cases, it is the periphery that sets the pace. One example of the latter is the way that several of Chinese tech giant Lenovo's business lines are being run today out of its North Carolina subsidiary, the former HQ of the IBM PC division

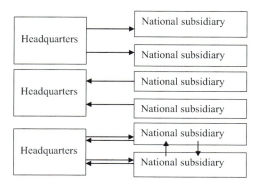

Fig 9.8
Power, strategy and information flows in different types of MNEs.

that Lenovo had acquired. A second example is the programme laid out in German engineering giant Siemens' 2020 Vision announcing that "individual businesses [will be given] more entrepreneurial freedom under the strong Siemens brand in order to sharpen their focus on their respective markets". The broader picture for most MNEs is probably an ongoing readjustment of the centre/periphery relationship. All these arrangements have the potential to succeed or fail at different points in time. To repeat and as always in IB, none is intrinsically right or wrong.

Contrary to the traditional organisational principle of authority being exercised top-down, it appears that it is just as possible today that MNEs will try to establish a more balanced relationship between head offices and subsidiaries, in what Hedlund (1986) had called the heterarchy of an organisation combining diverse but equal power bases. The idea here is that everyone has something to offer. What head office managers provide is big picture thinking, coherence and the ability to coordinate. At the same time, subsidiary managers' awareness of new ideas and opportunities, reflecting their close relationships with suppliers and customers, makes them fertile sources of information, hence useful drivers of change. They possess as much credibility as head office strategists do.

By hypothesising that a company is just as likely to accumulate competency abroad as it is at home, the transnational logic is at odds with Transaction Cost theory, which assumes that most firm-specific advantages are generated in a MNE's home country. It also contradicts resource-based theories rooted in the idea that capabilities develop at the level of the firm as a whole. What it emphasizes instead is that different units contribute in different ways to overall performance. This is an important advancement in general understanding of how MNEs function.

If power is exercised at every level within a MNE, the challenge then becomes determining on what basis each unit should interact with another. A good idea is conceptualising MNEs as internal markets where participants up and down the value chain negotiate their missions – and remuneration – with one another. This incorporates the fact that employees will almost always fight to defend their self-interest whenever it becomes clear, as is usually the case, that their personal appraisal, end-of-year bonus and career prospects are going to be determined by the performance of the particular SBU for which they work, and not by the MNE as a whole. This then translates into frequent competition between sister units for potentially more lucrative assignments that will increase their perceived usefulness to the rest of the group, not to mention constant in-fighting about the prices at which intra-firm asset transfers should be booked (see Chapter 11). Where inter-unit competition becomes too fierce, the centre's main governance role becomes ensuring fair competition among subsidiary managers competing to extend their territories. What remains after this is a vision of the MNEs as something akin to a federative organisation (Papanastassiou and Pearce 2016), one where colleagues engage in "intrapreneurship" within their

Heterarchy – Organisation where constituent units are allied and considered of equal value, hence attributed equal leadership roles.

Internal market – Where sister units transact with one another on quasi-commercial basis.

Federative organisation – Entities whose constituent parts work both as autonomous units free to pursue their own goals yet remain members of a unified enterprise.

broader organisation – a hybrid "semi-globalisation" where MNEs craft "agendas that are both localised and linked across countries" (Ghemawat 2017), avoiding organisational rigidity and incentivising personal initiative at all levels.

Case study 9.2: Tata in its totality

In 1991, when Ratan Tata became the fifth chairman of his namesake company formed more than a century previous, the Group was already a sprawling conglomerate comprised of upwards of 250 constituent firms. Until that point, Tata had been running a relatively modest portfolio of overseas activities, after starting its internationalisation trajectory by almost randomly exporting any product for which it could find an overseas market – ranging from rice, jewellery and castor oil to cars, marine products and pharmaceuticals – before ultimately moving on to a smattering of FDIs. The year 1991 was a watershed year, however, since that was when the Indian government began opening its domestic market up to overseas interests. Foreign countries' reciprocation made it easier for Indian companies to accelerate their own internationalisation, which Tata did extremely quickly, moving over the following 20 years to acquire a host of Global North interests, including major UK names such as Tetley, Corus (ex-British Steel) and Jaguar/Land Rover.

The problem with rapid expansion of this kind is that it made coordination almost impossible, depriving Tata of the much hoped for synergies that would have enhanced its productivity, hence competitiveness. Ratan Tata became keenly aware of this problem, and about ten years into his mandate he started to divest the group's less strategic activities while regrouping the remaining product lines into eight SBUs – leather, steel, minerals, power projects, engineering

Fig 9.9
Tata's restructuring process has seen it concentrate on higher value-added activities like automotive parts.

(including automotive and chemical products), textiles, commodities and information technology.

Finding a common purpose and enhancing inter-unit transfers of knowledge, capital, expertise and products was crucial at a time when Tata was looking to unify its empire. Henceforth, industry experts located in different countries would report not only (as they had done previously) to local country heads but also to global SBU chiefs. These twin reporting lines were specifically set up in recognition of the dual local–global identity that has become a feature of many modern MNEs. For this organisation to be accepted at Tata, however, it was crucial that transnational attitudes take root and that a new culture be developed to accompany the new structures.

Things seemed to evolve quickly, with the total number of group firms falling to around 100 by 2012, the end of Ratan Tata's term. That still represented an enormous coordination challenge, however, all the more so given moves by subsequent chairpersons to add to Tata's portfolio entirely new sectors of activity, including retail, financial services and airlines. These would sometimes be located in Tata's home market of India, but as often as not responded to international opportunities. This explains why after Natarajan Chandrasekaran took office in 2017, he renewed efforts to again restructure the Group by eliminating cross-holdings, consolidating similar businesses and, above all, moving all operations under ten vertical groups in a further attempt to achieve group-wide synergies (Mitra 2019). The new chairman's explicit goal was to unify and scale up previously disparate supply chain and logistics functions, with the ensuing improvements in efficiency (hence profitability) hopefully counteracting a disturbing trend that had seen SBU managers working in isolation across the world frequently losing control over their costs.

With this new structure, the idea became that each vertical division should be run by an individual possessing both sector-specific knowledge and experience in working at scale. On top of this, s/he should be capable of unifying the working cultures associated with such a large group of heterogeneous companies, some of whom had few processes, products or customers in common, especially outside of India. At one level, it made full sense for Tata to try and restructure its operations to attain these goals. On the other, everyone was clear that this extremely complex and challenging task would take years to complete – if indeed it will ever be possible to complete the structural readjustments that a conglomerate MNE of this size must always expect.

Case study questions

1. What are the specific organisational problems facing conglomerate MNE of Tata's size?
2. How can Tata develop corporate unity?

Section II. Human implications of multinational structures

Irrespective of whether a MNE pursues a local, global or transnational approach, its human resources will largely be managed according to a set of sociological principles that are themselves worth studying in greater detail. A century ago, eminent sociologists like Max Weber were already analysing organisations such as bureaucracies in order to gauge employee behaviour in such environments. In a similar vein, group dynamics have long been a focal point in management (hence IB) studies. It is no coincidence that in many languages, a "company" is often referred to by a word translating in English to "society". After all, it almost always constitutes an enterprise undertaken by groups of persons working together, not individually. Business is a highly social profession, as witnessed by the crucial role of non-professional social encounters like the coffee break (Barmeyer et al. 2019), which colleagues use in most, if not all, MNEs to coordinate work processes, share organisational knowledge, build confidence, network, problem-solving – and gossip. As expressed throughout this book, the most accurate way of envisioning IB is as a social phenomenon, not a hard science.

Principles of organisational sociology applies to multinational enterprises

When MNE executives reflect on which structures they think will help them achieve their goals, they are generally being guided by certain overriding principles, mainly derived from the field of organisational sociology. It is yet another example of the multidisciplinary nature of IB studies.

Centralisation

The first question is what are the human effects of the power that a MNE's centre (head office) wields over its periphery (subsidiaries). It is rare that headquarters can unilaterally impose their will throughout a MNE, if only because of the way subsidiary managers learn to manoeuvre politically and "sell" the issues that are of the greatest personal importance to them (Dörrenbächer and Gammelgaard 2016). Having said that, the relationship between these two partners is always imbalanced to at least some extent – the real question being how great an extent. Note that the issue has become particularly acute in the digital age, with HQ executives receiving timelier and better-quality information than ever before, removing from subsidiary managers one of the few weapons still at their disposal (Schmitt et al. 2019).

Companies that centralise power must find a way to motivate subsidiary managers so they feel valued. If the periphery is being asked to solely focus on the centre's needs, it is vital that the latter also seem relevant to the former's aspirations. This raises the issue of whether employees are capable of, and satisfied with, the particular roles that they have been assigned. It is one thing drawing international organisational charts, but another finding people happy to fit into the slots.

Studies have repeatedly detected a link between subsidiary effectiveness and the kinds of coordination mechanisms formalised by their HQ, how it manages cultural distances and the general "atmosphere influence" that it exerts (Lunnan et al. 2019). One example of the way these issues can be addressed came with Kraft Heinz's 2020 announcement that it was hiring Miguel Patricio as new CEO, a Portuguese national who had previously helped lead AB InBev's global marketing efforts. Resulting from a huge 2015 merger, the American MNE had been largely focusing on the integration-related efficiencies that its centre was prioritising, somewhat neglecting its foreign subsidiary–customer interfaces and therefore losing market share outside of its largely saturated home market. Turning to a cosmopolitan leader like Patricio with his greater experience in frontline operations was a way for Kraft Heinz to rebalance. MNEs need not only to optimise the level of (de-)centralisation within their structures but also to hire people who can do the same.

Hierarchy

This principle is rooted in the recognition of authority. Corporate environments are often compared to military organisations in the sense that they tend to be more or less undemocratic, if only because lower-level staff members are not given the opportunity to vote for their senior managers, a hard reality that should make the issue of authority relatively straightforward. In actual fact, however, reporting lines can be very confusing in MNEs. Whereas employees in domestic companies usually work in proximity to their boss and are therefore clear about who determines their objectives and judges their performance, MNE subsidiary employees often have two bosses: one in charge of the local office, and another in charge of their product or functional area. Things can get very complicated when the latter works out of a different time zone, as can often be the case. Having dual reporting lines may be beneficial insofar as it forces people to think along both local and global lines, but if a person has two bosses pursuing two different business philosophies (i.e. in relation to pricing, product adaptation or customer segmentation), it can be impossible knowing whom to please. It is true that this kind of confusion is also quite empowering since it sometimes enables employees to play one boss against another. But even more than that, it runs a risk of aggravating the tensions that already exist between a MNE's different offices.

Specialisation

One solution to practitioners' confusion about their diverse and potentially conflicting roles within a MNE is specialisation. Implementing this can be difficult, however. In SMEs, for instance, defining narrow missions is not always possible given that, by definition, staff numbers are smaller, meaning that each employee must fulfil several roles. Even in larger MNEs, there can be occasions when a manager who, for instance, is in charge of marketing might also be expected to assume responsibility for something totally different, like international contract legalities, a competency that s/he may not possess. The advantage for large MNEs of having enough staff to be able to specialise and develop individuals' expertise in narrow competencies is that this enables administrative economies of scale. This is especially true when there is a critical mass of specialists working in a "shared service" that covers the whole of the MNE.

Having said that, it is much harder in specialised MNEs to ensure that knowledge circulates adequately. The risk here is that employees working in silos will develop tunnel vision and not see how their individual assignment fits the needs of colleagues working on other sites. At a more individual level, unless a MNE guarantees training throughout employees' careers, specialists only get a chance to broaden their horizons once they have changed functions. Generalists, on the other hand, may find it easier to develop a broader, albeit shallower, set of skills.

Coordination

The more specialised employees' missions are within a large organisation like a MNE, the harder it is to coordinate them. A good way to visualise this is by imagining that each employee has to cover a "territory"– a term that is widely used in IB, often in relation to downstream activities. Territory can be defined in product or functional terms (relating, for instance, to a specific stage in the company's global value chain), but it is mainly used to designate commercial responsibility for a particular geographical area. The MNE needs to ensure that all these different kinds of territories fit together in a way that both reduces internal transaction costs and accelerates execution times. One way to achieve this is by getting different territories within a group to develop a common discourse and way of making sense of things (Whittle et al. 2016). The commonality being nurtured in this way can relate to IB paradigms and ethical values, but also (as noted in Chapter 6) to something as simple as language, explaining why a number of MNEs from non-anglophone countries (including Germany's Siemens, Japan's Honda or French food services company Sodexo) use English as their official corporate language.

Problems can arise, however, when boundaries change between individual territories. This can happen following an internal reorganisation in response to changes in external circumstances – but as often as not in MNEs characterised by a competitive culture it happens because colleagues start invading one another's territory when it is perceived to be more lucrative. However carefully a large organisation like a MNE is structured, personal calculations mean that things will not always turn out as planned. Moreover, even as coordination can create efficiency benefits, it also has costs – whether the supervisory time that must be allocated to it or the need to formalise performance monitoring systems. The larger the MNE, the more expensive these costs will be, explaining why there is often a greater tendency to advocate coordination than there is to actually implement it.

Control

Companies spend considerable resources on controlling organisational performance. In widely dispersed MNEs where executives are geographically distant from the teams they supervise, it can be difficult getting feedback on whether performance matches expectations. Senior managers will want to visit foreign staff often, but this may only happen sporadically, especially in times of crisis like the Covid-19 pandemic. MNEs all establish global (or at least regional) reporting systems to compensate for this deficiency. The problem is that information transmitted over long distances does not always paint a full picture of what is really happening in far-off subsidiaries. Firstly, subsidiary managers may have a vested interest in protecting their local teams from head office scrutiny and therefore not communicate all relevant facts (Sarabi 2020). Secondly, where distant headquarters' oversight is exercised by persons with little knowledge of a foreign subsidiary's culture, control becomes much harder to exercise (Giacobbe et al. 2016). Lastly, head office executives suffering from information overload may not have time to cope with anything more than a short and necessarily incomplete rendition of the situation on the ground. It is common, for example, for a manager seeking permission to enter a new market to be asked to write no more than a single-page report on the project. Indeed, this is what happened to the author of this book when, after a prospecting trip to Sweden, he returned with a seven-page report on the local economy, only to be told that this was far too long. One constant in IB today is that people are incredibly busy. The ensuing need for abbreviated communications necessarily undermines managers' oversight and therefore control.

Learning

The difficulties that managers face in communicating information in a busy MNE environment explain why a new element – learning – has been added in recent years to the traditional list of key organisational principles. There have been many studies on this and related phenomena, including "knowledge management", which Chapter 10 covers in some detail. For the moment, it is worth noting that the actual mechanics of learning within a MNE framework depend on many factors above and beyond whatever formal processes have been implemented towards this end. There seems to be a general consensus that maximising two-way knowledge flows between headquarters and subsidiaries is a good way to enhance MNE-wide learning and performance. But this is easier said than done: due to cultural distance (Qin et al. 2017), because a subsidiary may be disincentivised by the passive role it has been assigned (Lee et al. 2020); or simply because it may be hard to know what knowledge is actually beneficial to colleagues working out of geographically distant locations. Hence, MNEs' frequent engagement of corporate communications professionals to publish internal newsletters and run regularly scheduled (video) conferences, not to mention huge investments in systems providing information (about customers, treasury positions, rival technology, etc.) that is meant to be shared across multiple sites. In emerging economies like India, there is even a recent tendency for companies to build in-house universities ensuring that young talents receive the training that will enhance their future usefulness. Otherwise, older MNEs like Nestlé are famous for their traditional willingness to incur substantial travel costs, flying managers to sister units worldwide in an attempt to enhance intra-group information exchanges. Getting colleagues from one time zone to service customers working out of another is a great source of commercial synergy for MNEs, since it extends the number of hours in a day when deals can be done. Of course, employees working in one SBU may not be happy to share lucrative customers with colleagues from another site because of fears that the latter will take credit for the relationship, thus creating a reluctance to collaborate that constitutes yet another obstacle to organisational learning.

Finally, it should also be remembered that MNE employees can also learn through their interactions with external partners. This is a modus operandi frequently pursued, for instance, by Japanese *keiretsus* who have historically been more interested in embedding their global value chain relationships in knowledge exchanges, and less focused on more transient factors like pricing. It is a conception where knowledge flows are elevated to a paramount principle of multinational organisation.

The integration versus responsiveness conundrum, or "push" versus "pull" multinationals

As noted throughout this book, one of the key debates in IB studies is whether a MNE's actions are triggered by the strategic intent it formulates internally or else by its response to external circumstances. Originally designated by scholars as the "integration–responsiveness" dilemma (Prahalad and Doz 1987) – and shortened in this textbook, for clarity's sake, to the contrast between "push" or a "pull" MNEs, respectively – this fundamental duality plays out at many different levels in IB. These include the relative preference for vertical versus horizontal integration as a mode of FDI, the preference for standardisation or for adaptation, the decision where to locate different global value chain sites – and for the purposes of the present chapter's discussion of MNE organisations, the choice between following a top-down approach and investing all power in central structures, or working on a bottom-up basis and decentralising decision-making powers.

"Push" multinationals can be ethnocentric and tend to consider that internationalisation should be an extension – and sometimes even a direct reproduction – of approaches they first developed at home. The greater focus in such companies is on the internal strengths rather than on their fit with different external environments. Foreign subsidiaries are given the relatively simple task of rolling out existing products and processes with as little adaptation as possible. Fully confident in its upstream capabilities and technological prowess, a "push"-oriented MNE will often be less interested in market studies and more animated by the idea that the new and better product or service that it has developed deserves to command a high price everywhere.

If they are right, "push" MNEs can achieve fantastic first-mover advantage, exemplified by the great success of tech companies coming out of Silicon Valley, whose leadership clearly stems more from their ability to innovate than from cultural adaptability. It remains that the potentially higher rewards generated by pushing innovations into foreign markets are also accompanied by much greater risks, mainly because MNEs in this category often commit to internationalisation before receiving confirmation of foreign demand for their brand new product. The approach is always a high-risk, high-reward shot in the dark.

"Pull" MNEs, on the other hand, specifically start by checking demand in foreign markets before working backwards and calculating how they might be able to satisfy it. They will often decentralise power to subsidiaries and empower them to accumulate local knowledge and define strategy. In turn, this helps to determine the product portfolio that the MNE will offer in each location. Using market signals as a starting point is safer, since it gives the company the certainty that the goods it produces are what unknown foreign customers actually want. At the same time, this lesser risk is associated with lower returns. Firstly, to please an international clientele, "pull" companies tend to have wider product ranges and will therefore standardise less and achieve lower economies of scale. Secondly, the market signals to which they are responding will also be heard by their rivals, who might rush in to meet the same demand as they are. Since no one operating in a "pull" market can achieve a radical first-mover advantage, there is no possibility of imposing premium pricing.

Despite these limitations, in sectors such as food or clothing that are deeply embedded in national cultural differences, success will usually require a "pull" orientation. "Pull" MNEs might try to gain a little room to manoeuvre by developing new niches as an adjunct to their core business, as French baker Brioche Dorée did in the USA with its croissant fast-food concept, taking an existing product and finding a novel positioning for it. Ultimately, however, companies operating in "pull" segments rarely have any choice but to be polycentric and give customers by and large what they want. They cannot ignore local particularities in the same way as "push" MNEs can, since the latter have created their own demand and therefore have greater say in how their product should be defined. Having said that, it occurs far too often that a MNE tries to portray, hence price, its offer as something innovative without this actually being the case – a deception that is increasingly difficult to pull off, at least over the long run, in today's interconnected world. Quite the contrary, companies who try to "push" a run-of-the-mill, already commoditised product can do themselves a great deal of reputational damage. Yet mistakes of this kind are surprisingly frequent in IB – and revelatory of the danger for MNEs when their self-image is misaligned with the realities they face.

Attitudes and alternatives

International recruitment is a particularly difficult challenge for MNEs' organisational efforts. If a subsidiary hires people with deep roots in a given host country, it will benefit from their local focus but runs the risk that they will struggle to get along with colleagues hired on other sites (including regional or global headquarters) specifically because theirs is more of a cosmopolitan outlook. Conversely, global strategists taking a broader view of the impacts that certain decisions can have on specific local markets run a risk of treading on their more nationally oriented subsidiary colleagues' toes. It is hard to overstate how often conflicts arise within MNEs due to contrasting opinions regarding the merits of internationalism versus economic patriotism – attitudinal chasms creating great discord between co-workers intentionally thrown together by companies hoping to benefit from the confrontation of their diametrically opposed worldviews. Such encounters do not always culminate in compromise. For most MNEs, the achievement of a generally "glocalised" mindset will always be more of an ideal than a reality.

Chapter summary

The chapter began with a historical analysis of MNE divisional structures as first analysed by Stephen Hymer before moving on to look at the three main business paradigms (multidomestic, global and transnational) driving IB practitioners' more recent organisational thinking. One common thread has been the breakdown between the two extremes of MNEs who prioritise their internal capabilities versus others who emphasize external adaptiveness. Both orientations have imperfections, explaining a long-standing search for hybrid models.

The second section analysed MNEs' structuring initiatives at a more personal level. Five principles derived from organisational sociology – centralisation, hierarchy, coordination, specialisation, control and learning – were applied towards this end. The chapter concluded with a review of the "integration-responsiveness" dilemma, which the book will refer to heretofore, specifically from a production and then a marketing perspective, as the difference between "push" and "pull" MNEs.

Case study 9.3: Duelling dual reporting lines

Note. This case study reproduces the real-life experiences recounted by an international business practitioner, with certain details altered to preserve anonymity.

An educational publishing house, called Democracy Ltd., operates two separate but related product lines: academic texts manufactured and sold by its Books department, and e-learning packages developed by its Education department. The headquarters and main office are in Toronto, but a substantial European operation is run out of Dublin. Both centres have a Books team as well as an Education team. The global Head of Books is an Irish national, and, as the most senior manager in the European subsidiary, she also serves as Country Head. The global Head of Education works out of Toronto and has an office near the CEO, a fellow ethnic Greek with whom her family has a generations-long friendship.

The Education team is widely, and justifiably, seen as possessing greater technical capabilities than the Books department. Education professionals are also better paid, since their high-margin, low-volume e-learning packages can produce greater profits than the books business, which is more of a low-margin, high-volume commodity business. This difference in status has caused some resentment between the two departments. There are other sources of conflict as well.

Because the Books department sells more of a standardised product, it has a wider range of customers than the Education department does. Some customers only purchase books from Democracy, making it clear which of the two departments has responsibility for servicing their account. Having said that, there are also customers who only buy Education's e-learning packages. Above all, there is the complication of

Fig 9.10
In this case study, an education company sells both books and e-learning packages but struggles to disentangle the two product lines' overlapping lines of management.

customers who buy both products because then the two departments will fight over who gets to price such dual deals; how they should be priced; and who gets the credit if they go through. Note that this pricing aspect can be very contentious in dual situations where one department demands that the other reduce its margins in order to get the deal done.

Other disputes have erupted regarding which department should be allowed to make initial contact with prospects, especially when it is unclear if these potential customers buy books and e-learning packages separately or jointly, hence which department should lead the charge. Clearly, because each department is thinking about its own bottom line, it will want to take the lead in developing potentially lucrative relationships without having to share any of the glory (or profits) that the new account might generate. This explains frequent suggestions by salespersons from both departments that they be allowed to make separate visits to the same customers, each marketing their own product. The idea is not very workable, however, since duplicated visits waste customers' time and irritate them. Another solution would be to get a single salesperson working out of one or the other department to sell both products when visiting prospects. In reality, however, Books employees are incapable of selling complicated e-learning packages, and Education employees are not interested in selling books when their annual bonuses are solely determined by the profits their SBU makes on e-learning packages.

The battle over marketing territories has gone on for years. The tensions are particularly acute when Dublin Education professionals do early morning deals before the Head of Education gets to her office at 8 a.m. Toronto time (1 p.m. in Dublin). Above and beyond a certain transaction size, Democracy sales staff must receive executive approval before they can finalise a deal's pricing. In the Irish morning, this means asking the Head of Books, since she is also the local Office Manager. In fact, it is her dual role that is at the heart of this MNE's organisational tug-of-war.

The basic problem is that the Irish Head of Books will often take advantage of situations where Dublin-based Education professionals need to ask for for approval (because their product boss in Toronto is still sleeping) to force them to price dual deals in a way that suits her teams' interests, but not theirs. This generally involves her ordering them to quote loss-leading prices for the e-learning packages, hoping in this way to persuade customers to purchase more books, thereby enhancing the profits of her own department even as the Education team books a loss.

The Head of Books justifies herself with the argument that all of Democracy benefits from her department's increased turnover. But this is both disingenuous (since profits booked in her department will not in fact be shared with other teams) and reflects her low-margin business culture where people tend to think that volume is everything. It is very different from e-learning, a much more high-tech business where every deal comes with specific after-sales service costs and is therefore only worth doing if margins are high enough.

When Dublin Education team members protest to their boss back in Toronto about what is happening to them early in the Irish morning (in the middle of the night in Toronto when she is unreachable), the Head of Books accuses them, somewhat hypocritically, of being selfish and thinking only of their own interest. She also criticises them, somewhat more justifiably, for not agreeing to spend time accompanying Books salespersons on courtesy calls to major book customers whose interest in e-learning packages is vague at best and therefore really not worth their while.

The Head of Education in Toronto is not entirely sure how to deal with these complaints from her team in Dublin. On the one hand, if she goes to the CEO to argue their case, she will be accused of abusing family connections to get special treatment. On the other, there is no doubt that her Dublin team is being exploited by the Head of Books. After lengthy reflection, the Head of Education decides that her best option is to propose alternative forms of organisation to the CEO. The question then is how he will respond to each.

Case study questions

1. What are the strengths and weaknesses of Democracy's current product organisation?
2. What are the organisational alternatives that Democracy's CEO might consider adopting?
3. How would Democracy's different teams react to each of these alternatives?

Chapter discussion questions

1   What are the strengths and weaknesses of Hymer's different divisional structures?
2   Why is a MNE better advised to adopt a global strategy for certain sectors of activity and a local strategy for others?
3   How feasible is it for MNEs to achieve a compromise between a global and local outlook?
4   What are the different ways in which MNEs can coordinate their subsidiaries' actions?
5   What mechanisms can MNEs use to optimise their knowledge flows?

References

Ambos, T. et al. (26 February 2020). "Managing interrelated tensions in headquarters-subsidiary relationships…", *Journal of International Business Studies*, Volume 51, Issue 6, pp. 906–932.

Arikan, I. et al. (October 2019). "Dynamic capabilities and internationalisation of authentic firms: Role of heritage assets, administrative heritage, and signature processes", *Journal of International Business Studies*, accessed 22 February 2021 at https://link.springer.com/

Barmeyer, C. et al. (August 2019). "Informal information flows in organisations: The role of the Italian coffee break", *International Business Review*, Volume 28, Issue 4, pp. 796–801.

Bartlett, C. (1986). "Building and managing the transnational: The new organisational challenge", in M. Porter (ed.). *Competition in Global Industries*. Boston, MA: Harvard Business School Press.

Cheng, H., and Huang, M. (2020). "Does dual embeddedness matter? Mechanisms and patterns of subsidiary ambidexterity that links a subsidiary's dual embeddedness with its learning strategy", *Asia Pacific Journal of Management,* accessed 30 July 2021 at https://link.springer.com/

Da Silva Lopes, T. et al. (October 2019). "Organisational innovation in the multinational enterprise: Internalisation theory and business history", *Journal of International Business Studies*, Volume 50, Issue 8, pp. 1338–1358.

Dekkers, M., and Pitkethly, G. (15 March 2018). "Building the unilever of the future", accessed 22 February 2021 at https://www.unilever.com/

Dörrenbächer, C., and Gammelgaard, J. (May 2016). "Subsidiary initiative taking in multinational corporations: The relationship between power and issue selling", *Organisation Studies*, Volume 37, Issue 9, pp. 1249–1270.

Ghemawat, P. (July–August 2017). "Globalisation in the Age of Trump", *Harvard Business Review.*

Giacobbe, F. et al. (December 2016). "An investigation of wholly-owned foreign subsidiary control through transaction cost economics theory", *Accounting and Finance*, Volume 6, Issue 4, pp. 1041–1070.

Gibson, C. et al. (August 2019). "Managing formalisation to increase global team effectiveness and meaningfulness of work in multinational organisations", *Journal of International Business Studies*, Volume 50, pp. 1021–1052.

Gutierrez-Huerter, G. (April 2019). "Micro-processes of translation in the transfer of practices from MNE headquarters to foreign subsidiaries: The role of subsidiary translators", *Journal of International Business Studies*, Volume 51, Issue 3, pp. 389–413.

Hamel, G., and Prahalad, C. (July–August 1985). "Do you really have a global strategy", *Harvard Business Review.*

Hedlund, G. (1986). "The hypermodern MNC: A heterarchy?" *Human Resource Management*, Volume 25, Issue 1, pp. 9–35

Hymer, S. H. (1976). *The International Operations of National Firms: A Study of Direct Foreign Investment*. Cambridge, MA: MIT Press (originally a Ph.D. thesis, 1960).

Jones, G., and Decker. S. (2017). "Ken Durham and Unilever as a Multi-local Multinational", *Harvard Business Review Store,* accessed 30 July 2021 at https://www.hbs.edu/

Lee, J. et al. (2020). "Subsidiary roles and dual knowledge flows between MNE subsidiaries and headquarters: The moderating effects of organisational governance types," *Journal of Business Research*, Volume 108, pp. 188–200.

Lunnan, R. et al. (June 2019). "Dealing with headquarters in the multinational corporation: A subsidiary perspective on organizing costs", *Journal of Organisation Design*, Volume 8, Issue 12, accessed 30 July 2021 at https://jorgdesign.springeropen.com/

Meyerk, K. et al. (April 2020). "Managing the MNE subsidiary: Advancing a multi-level and dynamic research agenda", *Journal of International Business Studies*, Volume 51, pp. 538–576.

Mitra, P. (5 March 2019). "Tata Group's plan to consolidate its firms, explained", accessed 11 December 2020 at https://qrius.com/

Morschett, D. et al. (2015). "Multinational corporations as networks", chapter in ibid, *Strategic International Management*, Wiesbaden: Springer Gabler.

Papanastassiou, M., and Pearce, R. (2016). "Federative multinational enterprise", in M. Augier and D. Teece (eds). *The Palgrave Encyclopedia of Strategic Management*, London: Palgrave Macmillan.

Prahalad, C., and Doz, Y. (1987). *The Multinational Mission: Balancing Local Demand and Global Vision*, New York: Free Press.

Qin, C. et al. (2017). "The impact of knowledge management on MNC subsidiary performance: does cultural distance matter?" *Knowledge Management Research and Practice*, Volume 15, pp. 78–89.

Sarabi, A. (October 2020). "Shades of silence: Why subsidiary managers remain silent vis-à-vis their headquarters", *Journal of World Business*, Volume 55, Issue 6, accessed 30 July 2021 at https://www.sciencedirect.com/

Sarabi, A. (October 2020). "Shades of silence: Why subsidiary managers remain silent vis-à-vis their headquarters", *Journal of World Business*, Volume 55, Issue 6, accessed 30 July 2021 at https://www.sciencedirect.com/

Schmitt, J. et al. (2019). "How corporate headquarters add value in the digital age", *Journal of Organisational Design*, Volume 8, Issue 9, accessed 30 July 2021 at https://www.springerprofessional.de/

Szymanski, M. et al. (April 2019). "Multicultural managers and competitive advantage: Evidence from elite football teams", *International Business Review*, Volume 28, Issue 2, pp. 305–315.

Tan, D. et al. (2020). "A review of research on the growth of multinational enterprises: A Penrosean lens", *Journal of International Business Studies*, Volume 51, pp. 498–537.

Wang, D. et al. (June 2020). "Cultural differences and synergy realisation in cross-border acquisitions: The moderating effect of acquisition process", *International Business Review*, Volume 28, Issue 3, accessed 30 July 2021 at https://www.sciencedirect.com/

Whittle, A. et al. (2016). "Sensemaking, sense-censoring and strategic inaction: The discursive enactment of power and politics in a multinational corporation", *Organisation Studies*, Volume 37, Issue 9, pp. 1323–1351.

PART IV

Multinational functions

CHAPTER 10

Multinational upstream operations

Introduction

One of the most crucial value chain decisions that international business (IB) practitioners will ever have to make relates to the breadth of their product offer. At one extreme, multinational enterprises (MNEs) might choose to produce large volumes of a narrow range of goods – a standardisation approach that best suits their upstream operatives since it helps them to achieve the economies of scale, efficiency and cost-effectiveness based on which their personal performance will be judged. At the other end of the spectrum, MNEs might opt for a broad, customised product range – an adaptation approach that suits their downstream operatives by making it easier for them to market to a wide range of customers worldwide, increasing the sales volumes based on which they will themselves be appraised. Given the contrasting interests of the operatives working at the two ends of the multinational value chain, internal tension is a permanent fact of life for many IB practitioners – a professional reality that does not get highlighted often enough in IB studies.

Therefore, even though upstream and downstream activities should be presented in separate chapters for clarity, it is crucial never to forget that in the real world, the two functions are interdependent. This explains the importance for all IB learners, even for the many planning to work in a business development capacity, to know what people on the production side are thinking. After all, value chain analysis teaches that the final products which a MNE sells are nothing more than the sum total of their intermediate transformations. This applies to physical items such as computers, made from modules like motherboards or hard drives (themselves built from more basic components), but also to services like education, entailing both a delivery system (classrooms) and an administration (the registry). By remembering that all value chains are the culmination of other value chains, analysts gain a more holistic view equipping them for two of IB's main debates: the merits of adaptation versus standardisation, and who should do what and where.

Modules – Components assembled into a system fulfilling a function in a final product.

DOI: 10.4324/9781003159056-14

Fig 10.1
International production
runs the gamut of
upstream value chain
operations.

LEARNING OBJECTIVES

After reading this chapter, you will be able to:

- evaluate the role that knowledge management plays in international production
- debate the positives and negatives of international outsourcing
- adopt a strategic view of foreign supplier relationships
- compare international manufacturing strategies
- mediate the production scale/logistics distance dilemma

Case study 10.1: Cybersecurity's safety in numbers

Many companies today manage their value chain functions digitally, using all kinds of intranet interfaces to both transfer data between geographic sites and store memory on the cloud. The transition from human instructions to machine-to-machine commands has also led to a marked

Fig 10.2
Cybersecurity risks
are a new frontier in
international knowledge
management.

improvement in connectivity and performance up and down MNEs'
global value chains, whether in relation to R&D; supply, production and
logistics; business processes; financial systems and accounts; or customer
databases. The sum total of this knowledge constitutes, in the modern
conception, one of the most valuable assets that a company possesses.
Protecting it is therefore paramount, especially in an era when hackers
run amok and accusations fly back and forth between governments about
the security risks allegedly associated with some of the global information
technology (IT) industry's top performers – one notorious case in point
being Chinese MNE Huawei, a global leader in both patent registrations
and many cutting-edge technologies (Pearce 2020).

Cyber-criminality and data theft have become major threats in
all business contexts today – but particularly in IB. This is because
the sheer size of the world's largest MNEs makes them a target, and
because their cross-border integration of software and relatively higher
levels of automation increases their vulnerability (Lees et al. 2018).
Add to this the unequal protection afforded to intellectual property
rights in different countries, variable sanctions in case of infractions
and above all national governments' interest in appropriating rival

technologies (while protecting their own) and it's easy to see why few MNEs today are dissuaded by the high cost of cybersecurity. Quite the contrary, they almost always pay up in the hope that interventions by trusted industrial control system (ICS) operators will help them to withstand any incidents and/or recover more quickly in case of breaches. In the 2020s, cybersecurity has become a big business.

The sector had tended to be segmented along domestic lines in its early years, largely due to its national defence aspects. It has, however, become more internationalised in recent times, both to reflect its customers' needs and because of a frequent need to go offshore to find the young talents possessing the requisite computing skills. Many of the companies leading the charge in this field are big names, such as American IT players like Cisco, IBM and Microsoft, all of whom view cybersecurity as a logical extension of their existing global presence. Other interested parties are smaller sector-specific players such as Crowdstrike or Gigamon, several of whom also work out of Silicon Valley and are seemingly trying to replicate the same start-up model that their predecessors had used to launch the global IT market in the 1980s. One problem for these new companies is the stringent foreign worker visa restrictions that the USA's former Trump administration had imposed in late 2017. This is one of the reasons for the booming number of cybersecurity companies now working out of Japan and increasingly the European Union. Taking the example of just one new name, Manchester's NCC Group, having already achieved a size that justified its being listed on the London Stock Exchange, has opened a slew of foreign offices all across Europe (8 as of early 2021), the USA (7), Canada, Asia-Pacific (4) and the United Arab Emirates. National interest may have been a key factor in kick-starting the cybersecurity industry, but it has taken very little time for players to understand that the business is actually best managed on an international basis.

Case study questions

1. List all the different capabilities and kinds of knowledge that MNEs might digitise.
2. How does the national security element of cybersecurity mesh with the sector's natural tendency to internationalise?

Section I. International knowledge management

As discussed in Chapter 2, classical economics tended to view capital, labour and physical resources as the three factor inputs defining national production capabilities. In recent years, however, the importance of a fourth factor has become increasingly apparent, that is, knowledge, which is the sum total of the experiences, ability to handle complexity, judgement, intuition, values and beliefs held by individuals but also by organisations like MNEs (Davenport and Prusak 1998). Much work has been done in recent years looking both on a micro-scale at how knowledge management (KM) increases "organisational learning" (Nonaka and Takeuchi 1995) and on a more macro-level at the factors explaining KM's rising importance, including advances in IT, the rise of the knowledge economy and the growing share of global wealth produced by knowledge-intensive service sectors such as computing and biotechnology.

KM is not only an upstream phenomenon. Marketing specialists will have their own knowledge to manage (product specifications, customer lists), as will financial professionals (market pricing, back office), trade specialists (routing optimisation, customs clearance) and so forth. Nevertheless, many, if not most, of the world's best-known MNEs have built their success on production advantages specifically based on the transformation of knowledge into new products or services, particularly where these outputs are conceptualised as value "bundles" comprised not only of tangible materials but also of intangible inputs like technology and know-how (Ietto-Gillies 2012). Stated simply, some products are more knowledge-intensive than others.

It is important to remember that knowledge management not only involves final outputs but also includes a company's process needs, relating, for instance, to the compilation and transfer of data, information and management practices. Having said that, most MNEs would view product research and development (R&D) as the cornerstone of their KM efforts and as the spark triggering their entire upstream operation.

Knowledge management – Systems used to maximise benefits of internal and external knowledge.

Knowledge economy – Sum total of markets helping agents to gain knowledge.

National research efforts

Of course, KM like all IB processes occurs within a context, often referred to as the national R&D environment. There are several ways to analyse this factor. One is to monitor variations over time in "R&D intensity". This indicator, measuring the percentage of a country's GDP spent on R&D, is imperfect insofar as it does not incorporate the research that a company from a particular country performs outside of its home market. On the other hand, it has also been used frequently going back at least as far as the original NASA space programmes, when many observers would tie the plethora of new core business technologies (e.g. the Internet, GPS) that the USA was developing to the country's comparatively high R&D intensity levels (Slaughter 2020). Also noteworthy is how global rankings changed over the first two decades of the 21st century, during which time Chinese R&D intensity rose by more than a factor of three, signalling that country's transition from a low- to a mid-level value-added economy. Monitoring international R&D

Table 10.1
2018 ranking of R&D spending as percentage of GDP

Rank	Country	R&D spending as percent GDP
1	Israel	4.94
2	Korea	4.53
5	Japan	3.28
7	Germany	3.13
9	USA	2.83
12	France	2.19
13	Netherlands	2.16
14	China	2.14
17	European Union average	2.03
20	Singapore	1.84
21	UK	1.73
24	Italy	1.43
27	Spain	1.24
33	Russia	0.98
39	Mexico	0.31

Source: Copyright OECD (2021), gross domestic spending on R&D (indicator). doi : 10.1787/d8b068b4-en (accessed 24 February 2021)

intensity rankings (see Table 10.1) helps detect to what extent a given economy is tilting towards knowledge-intensive production.

Above and beyond the quantum of funding that a country invests in R&D, it is also useful to monitor how effective different "national innovation system" are at stimulating R&D-related knowledge spillovers. MNEs generally fund their own R&D efforts but often look to gain further advantage by working in proximity to other knowledge producers in the markets they have entered. Some companies even set up operations in places like Silicon Valley in California or Bangalore in India specifically because they want to move closer to a high-tech cluster. Host governments generally view such actions favourably, that is, as long as they coincide with the foreign MNE bringing some of its own technology into the country. This is often achieved by getting it to enter a strategic alliance with local interests or else to join a quasi-official body like the European Research Area. Indeed, it is a policy mechanism seen as having been a key factor in several Asian countries' rapid rise to become centres of global technology (Clarke and Lee 2018).

Multinational research

Corporate research can be so expensive that it leaves companies without enough spare cash to fund the commercial networks they would normally need to distribute whatever new products are being developed despite the fact that global sales are their only hope of recouping hefty upfront R&D outlays. Cost is a hurdle for large MNEs but especially for small and medium-sized enterprises (SMEs), whose smaller size means that by themselves they can rarely achieve the sales volumes justifying R&D spending (Jalali 2017). This explains a number of international mergers and acquisitions such as Anglo-Swedish drug company AstroZeneca's 2020 acquisition of US immunology specialist Alexion, with the bigger MNE's expansive sales networks (in markets like China, for instance) becoming a way for the SME to achieve a global reach that would otherwise have been beyond its means. It is worth noting the high level of "corporate R&D intensity" (percentage of value-added spent on research) that characterises the pharmaceutical sector, averaging 11.6 percent across the Global North in the mid-2010s, preceded only by electronics (16.6 percent) and aerospace (14.6 percent). Sectoral averages can vary over time as can individual leaders in R&D intensity, with Amazon skyrocketing to the top of this list in the late 2010s. But the rule of thumb remains that industries where knowledge is key to international competitiveness tend to have the highest R&D spend.

To derive maximum advantage from their efforts in this domain, MNEs are always very interested in protecting their intellectual property rights (IPR). This is particularly challenging in IB where variations in the amount of protection afforded under different legal regimes can become a real risk factor. Sometimes the fight over IPR turns into a public welfare debate, one famous example being Global North pharmaceutical companies' efforts during the 1990s and 2000s to control the production of AIDS medicine and prevent Global South competitors from selling cheaper generic substitutes. On other occasions, it can involve more ad hoc commercial and/or geopolitical interests exemplified by attempts witnessed in 2021 to hack pharmaceutical MNEs' Covid-19 vaccine discoveries. IPR theft is a growing bone of contention in IB today.

Having said that, MNEs are also very aware of the beneficial "relationship learning" effects of sharing knowledge with foreign value chain partners (Bhatti et al. 2020). The question then becomes how to balance the benefits of disclosure with the need for confidentiality (Contractor 2019). To some extent, this will reflect a company's pursuit of a "push" versus "pull" orientation (see Chapter 9). Most MNEs centralise R&D near global headquarters because this makes it possible to assemble a critical mass of scientists, facilitate confidentiality and reduce overheads. Moreover, in high value-added sectors like computing, there is little need to account for consumer preferences – science counts more than responsiveness to demand variability.

On the other hand, teams of isolated MNE researchers will also be less aware of what distant foreign consumers are looking for, a problem in certain low-tech, culturally embedded ancestral sectors (such as food and clothing) where local knowledge is a key factor of success. Partially because of this (but also due to the tendential clustering of knowledge production and the globalised nature of talent searches today), a number of MNEs have started to decentralise their R&D function, seeking proximity to global hotspots (Murphy and Siedschlag 2018), especially locales where the institutional environment is conducive to knowledge

Intellectual property rights – Exclusive enjoyment of benefits derived from intangible assets like trademarks, patents and copyrights.

Fig 10.3
MNEs operating in the
"learning economy" view
R&D as their main success
factor.

networks (Zhao et al. 2020) and alliances. The global proliferation
of purpose-built research parks encouraging business and academic
collaboration bears witness to this trend, with examples ranging from
Sweden's Research Park Ideon to Brazil's Technopark Campinas, Seoul's
incipient biomedical cluster and, of course, Silicon Valley near Stanford
(California).

Design

Design – Activities
aimed at defining a
product's final shape and
attributes.

A similar "push" versus "pull" filter applies to international design,
defined as the stage at which an idea materialises physically. Some MNEs
configure their operations specifically with a view towards increasing
design staff's exposure to different consumer preferences worldwide. One
seminal IB example of this "pull" approach in design, dating from the
late 1980s, was when US toolmaker Black and Decker used to run design
centres in almost 30 countries – a commercially successful but extremely
expensive configuration that the MNE would abandon a decade later.
Conversely, other MNEs will push design standardisation, in large
part because if this succeeds, they can achieve economies of scale. One
example from the 1990s was when Ford spent $6 billion designing a
so-called world car (known in its first version as the Mondeo in Europe
and the Contour in North America) but lost a great deal of money
doing so. Having said that, Swedish furniture retailer Ikea has enjoyed
great success selling its standard Scandinavian designs worldwide, as
has Apple with its various versions of the i-Phone. At this value chain
level like others, there is no fixed rule about whether a global standard
or local adaptation works best. What counts is that MNEs receive quick
and accurate information whether customers worldwide are willing to
pay for an existing design or instead if customisation will be necessary,

explaining the importance of information systems like the one set up by giant clothing retailer Inditex, instantaneously linking all store cash registers worldwide to the group's centralised design office back home in Spain. Inditex's goal has been to ensure that its Zara designers can transcend the culture and fashion in the city where they live and work – a very human temptation – yet continue to cluster on a single site to reduce overheads and optimise team dynamics. It is a prime example, this time within the international design subfunction, of how technology can be used to address IB's fundamental global–local conundrum.

Lastly, the coherence between product design and definition is also a key factor shaping a MNE's upstream activities. This can be exemplified, for instance, by the early decision taken by Dell to offer IBM PCs instead of Apple Macbooks. The impact on the company's value chain was fundamental, affecting its supply relationships (given certain components' incompatibility with particular standards) as well as in-house production operations (assembly work, in Dell's case). Upstream decisions are almost never taken without consideration for their knock-on effects.

Section II. International supply chain management

Supply chain management (SCM) refers to all the operations involved in sourcing, producing, transporting, assembling and finalising a product or service. Global SCM occurs when companies are in a position to purchase and take delivery of raw materials, components and modules anywhere in the world. As noted in Chapter 1, it is a topic that can be analysed in either macro-level political, economic, social and ecological terms or else from a more micro-level corporate and business perspective. The section below adopts the latter focus.

The first dividing line in global SCM is whether a MNE sources raw materials and components from a domestic source, from its own offshored facilities (i.e. a supplier plant that it owns in a foreign country) or from a foreign supplier. The latter option is called international outsourcing and has been the main driver behind skyrocketing IB volumes in recent decades.

International outsourcing

There is a large body of academic work addressing MNEs' growing tendency to focus on their own core competencies and outsource the other value chain functions to external partners. The basic idea is that by using outsourcing as a means of acquiring foreign resources and knowledge, companies can improve their international competitiveness (Lagunes et al. 2016). This has been an extremely popular strategy over the past 30 years, with inputs for some products involving so many parts coming from so many countries that the World Trade Organization now argues that the concept of country of origin is itself outdated and should be replaced by a "made in the world" classification.

Of course, because outsourcing is based on a company entertaining functional relationships with external partners, it also comes with risks. Like any IB subtopic, strategic benefits will always be accompanied by costs. Nor is international outsourcing inevitable. The things that practitioners do always reflect the particular paradigms that they are applying at a given moment in time, and these can always change.

The positives of international outsourcing

For simpler goods, international outsourcing generally involves companies trying to take advantage of foreign suppliers' cost advantages. For more complex goods, there is the added advantage of being able to access suppliers' technology, at least indirectly. In both cases, by outsourcing non-essential functions, MNEs are freeing themselves to concentrate on those activities where they feel they can be most productive. Moreover, even after paying large specialist suppliers' profit margins, it is almost always cheaper to access an input made by someone who has many customers and therefore enjoys economies of scale than to manufacture the items oneself in necessarily smaller quantities.

Such advantages are particularly crucial in an international context, where performance differentials are even more acute than in purely domestic competitions. In addition, MNEs that run fewer functions in-house, and which therefore have a smaller balance sheet to fund, are in a position to improve their return on equity (ROE). Lastly, because it is easier and cheaper during economic downturns (like the 2020 Covid-19 pandemic) to renegotiate supplier contracts than to shut down factories, outsourcing enhances productive flexibility.

Procurement – Act of purchasing resources or inputs.

International outsourcing has also evolved over time. The main driver in the 1990s was the procurement of labour-intensive components or finished products manufactured in the world's low-wage regions, mainly Southeast Asia, which tended at the time to specialise in textiles and basic semiconductors; as well as Latin America, particularly after US automakers began buying parts, under NAFTA provisions, from North Mexican *maquiladora* factories. Protests against manufacturing job losses in the industrialised world would be met with the argument that the new international division of labour enabled the Global North to specialise in higher value-added activities and leave the rest to the Global South. This turned out to be inaccurate, however, given emerging market firms' increasingly sophisticated capabilities, to the extent that all sorts of service-related functions are being outsourced today, not just product manufacturing. Indeed, the dynamics underlying these two categories of international outsourcing are quite distinct.

Product outsourcing

Modern technology means that MNEs are much less daunted nowadays by the kinds of physical and informational coordination problems that often arise when distant foreign suppliers are brought into their production system. It is easier than ever to monitor all kinds of the various parameters that are relevant to this process. These includes foreign suppliers' delivery times and adherence to global standards as well as the inventory levels in a company's own warehouses. The consequences for MNE value chain strategies have been enormous. Today, many of the world's best-known names (whether carmakers like Volkswagen, airplane manufacturers like Boeing or electronics companies like Samsung) produce in-house no more than a very small percentage of the final products that they sell. Indeed, for some "hollow firms" like Nike, outsourcing has become so significant that they run almost no physical production activities internally (and few, if any, retail outlets). The only functions that MNEs in this category perform themselves are branding and, above all, the coordination of contracts with all the different companies constituting their global value chains. It is the epitome of a virtual approach to IB.

Virtual – Non-physical, intangible.

Even as the strategic principles of MNE product outsourcing remain constant, received wisdom about the best way to organise such activities can vary. Companies that are just starting to outsource internationally may prefer at first to purchase large quantities from a single supplier but then decide over time to organise a shortlist of potential providers who will be asked to compete on price and innovation (called "multi-sourcing"). Such diversification might also protect against the kinds of disruptive supply shocks witnessed during the 2020 Covid-19 pandemic. Otherwise, MNEs might also seek to improve their bargaining position by centralising procurement for all of their subsidiaries worldwide in the hope of benefiting from bulk purchasing rates. Of course, coordinated outsourcing of this kind is complex and requires high-performance communications and logistics systems.

Bulk purchasing – Companies buying inputs in large quantities have a better chance of negotiating lower per-unit prices with buyers due to the latter's economies of scale.

Service outsourcing

Recent years have seen a sharp rise in international service outsourcing volumes, often relating to MNEs' own administrative processes. The trend reflects work done by many Global South employers to enhance workers' professional training, certifications and performance standards (Randolph and Dewan 2017), thereby ensuring their competence in more intellectual (thus more lucrative) service activities. The end result is that for some Global South interests, services are a more important IB activity than manufacturing. For instance, whereas China remains the world's leading destination for product outsourcing, the top of the list for service contracts features, in order, India, with its strong computing skills; the Philippines, dominating the global market for medical transcriptions; and the ex-Soviet Union (Russia and Ukraine), accounting for a rising share of global software development. Service outsourcing includes technology work (e.g. telecommunications infrastructure and data networks); business processes, ranging from invoicing to payroll, human resource management and customer contacts; and knowledge processes, starting with R&D and patent development geared towards the customer's processing needs but also, increasingly, towards actual product development.

Studies have shown that more and more MNEs are selecting providers based on factors such as the relative complexity of the services that they are looking to outsource (Žitkienė and Dudė 2018); institutional stability in the host country; and cultural proximity. This means that suppliers bidding for such contracts will not only highlight their lower costs but also service quality and possibilities for collaboration. Since having a common language facilitates information exchanges, there is evidence of particularly intense service linkages between, for instance, UK MNEs and Anglosphere suppliers working out of India; French MNEs and North Africa; and Spanish MNEs and Latin America. Clearly, physical proximity is more important in the outsourcing of products than it is for services, where more qualitative factors also weigh on the decision.

The negatives of international outsourcing

Like any IB activity, outsourcing also has certain shortcomings. A MNE that does not produce its own inputs in-house but relies instead on foreign suppliers becomes dependent since it loses the knowledge and capacity to manufacture the items in question. Dependency creates vulnerability at several levels: if prices rise suddenly due to sudden wage increase in the countries where the MNE has its main outsourcing relationships (as has happened in China where rapid industrialisation is causing labour shortages in several provinces); if adverse currency or raw material price movements increase the input's cost without any substitute becoming available (as happened when the British pound fell following the 2016 Brexit referendum, raising the cost of the jars that food maker Marmite imported from continental Europe to the point of endangering its entire business model); or if the supplier pursues a forward integration strategy, threatening to bypass its customer and become a direct rival to it (epitomised by the burgeoning online direct-to-consumer market). In the worst-case scenario where suppliers go bankrupt and shut down, a fully dependent MNE might be forced to cease operations until it finds alternative channels, a situation experienced in numerous sectors during the 2020 Covid-19 pandemic. Otherwise, there is a more indirect kind of dependency linked to today's ambient vision of multi-stakeholder supply chains (Gurzawska 2020) in which all participants are assumed to be responsible for one another's behaviour. In recent IB history, a number of MNEs have suffered serious reputational damage, not because of anything they did themselves but due to social or environmental misconduct by their suppliers. It is a situation that is particularly difficult to manage with distant foreign suppliers about whom a MNE knows little and which it has no way of controlling.

Lastly, long-distance international outsourcing can run afoul of the lean production principles that countless MNEs have adopted in recent

Lean production – Production philosophy that emphasizes saving resources through less waste, better inventory management, better quality and shorter industrial cycles.

decades. The main idea behind this paradigm is that companies should reduce inventory costs by getting inputs delivered "just-in-time", that is, right before they are to be assembled into a final product. It is a robust idea but one that can create risks for MNEs who are sourcing inputs from the other side of the world, insofar as long-distance deliveries infer long lead times and therefore a greater likelihood of arriving late and upending production schedules. To counter the risk of "black swan" events (Pisch 2020) like strikes, shipping delays or natural disasters, some MNEs find themselves obliged to hold larger inventories than they would otherwise want to, defeating the very purpose of a just-in-time organisation (Banker 2016).

Solutions do exist for many of these distance-related problems, however. For example, a widely used real-time tracking and inventory management software called radio frequency identification (RFID) technology allows contractors to monitor components' location on an almost permanent basis, improving their oversight (hence management) of deliveries and inventories. At a more structural level, many component-makers have taken to building supplier parks immediately adjacent to prime contractors' foreign plants, in a phenomenon often referred to as follow sourcing. Such initiatives strengthen the argument that the most accurate way of analysing MNEs' upstream operations is not in terms of what each company does by itself but instead by encompassing the entirety of the supply chain network to which it belongs, comprised of direct "first-tier" suppliers but also the latter's own suppliers and so on. It is further proof that the Japanese vertical disintegration paradigm discussed in Chapter 7 has taken root in IB today.

Future trends in international outsourcing

In recent times, some MNEs have started to take a more nuanced view of the benefits of outsourcing from certain locations, increasingly weighing the cost advantages of long-distance procurement against its inherent delay, quality and control problems. The reality is that outsourcing is no longer a default strategy in IB. Most MNEs have had time to reflect upon their experience in this domain, especially where the factors explaining a destination country's original advantages (like wage, productivity or currency differentials, not to mention IPR protections) have evolved unfavourably. There is never any guarantee in IB that the conditions that made a strategy viable in the past will still apply in the future.

In truth, much of the current reassessment does not involve an outright rejection of international outsourcing, but instead a geographic shift. In sectors like "fast fashion" that are increasingly constrained by time-to-market considerations, for instance, working with the absolute cheapest supplier is no longer a singular priority if distance-related delivery delays mean that a MNE will struggle to keep abreast of market changes. Thus, whereas the first externalisation efforts for global clothing giants like GAP or Nike translated into mass

Lead-time – Time it takes, once an order has been placed, to deliver a good to the order-giver's premises.

Suppliers park – Industrial cluster that suppliers build in immediate proximity to prime contractor operations.

Follow sourcing – Supplier FDI in locale after prime contractor has done the same.

outsourcing to countries like Indonesia, Bangladesh and Sri Lanka, by the mid-2000s major European names like Mango were turning to slightly more expensive alternatives like Tunisia and Turkey, specifically because they are geographically closer to Europe's consumer markets. Calculations in this area are very complicated, however, as apparel manufacturing requires the coordination of many different supply chains, whether fabric made from processed raw materials, zippers made from mined metals or stitching, which is itself a very labour-intensive activity. Achieving an optimal balance between logistics and manufacturing can be a challenge.

This "near-sourcing" phenomenon would also become topical in the wake of the 2020 Covid-19 pandemic, given the brittleness that the crisis revealed in fragmented, long-distance supply chains characterised by many intermediaries, hence vulnerable to many risks of disruption. The debate here is whether the world's dire need to maximise value generation in the wake of a deep recession argues for a continuation of the outsourcing paradigm that has proven so efficient over the past 30 years of IB history, or if multinational prime contractors are likelier to want to secure their supply chains by shortening them – an expensive proposition if no alternate supplier exists near their assembly plants, potentially forcing them to invest in bringing the functions in question back in-house ("in-sourcing"). The likelihood is that both approaches will be seen in the future, with greater re-shoring of some items considered "strategic" (such as healthcare and medical equipment) but not of others whose complex nature means that relevant supply chain decisions are dictated by the location-specific advantages of the countries where they are currently being made.

Carrying on from this debate, there are other considerations that potentially portend a stark reduction in the volume of international outsourcing. Chapter 15 will take a closer look at the impact that technological progress, specifically in the guise of automation and robotisation, is having on MNE manufacturing configurations. Suffice it to say for the moment that if machines increasingly replace humans in labour-intensive upstream activities, the lower wages paid to distant foreign workers will no longer be as powerful a catalyst for outsourcing as they once were. Otherwise, with growing attention paid to the ecological crisis that the Earth faces – and given the heavy "footprint" of transportation, which accounts for between one-quarter and one-third of total global energy consumption and CO_2 emissions – there is growing recognition that environmental constraints may also lead to the re-shoring of some previously outsourced activities. Whether or not these activities will be undertaken in the future by a MNE's domestic suppliers or in-sourced by the company itself remains to be seen. The only thing that seems clear is that international outsourcing models (see Figure 10.4) will continue to diversify as time passes.

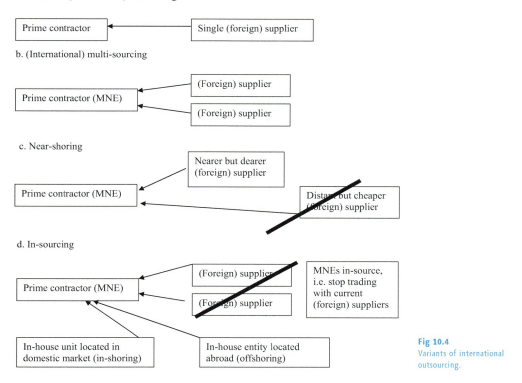

a. Exclusive (international) outsourcing

Prime contractor ← Single (foreign) supplier

b. (International) multi-sourcing

Prime contractor (MNE) ← (Foreign) supplier
← (Foreign) supplier

c. Near-shoring

Prime contractor (MNE) ← Nearer but dearer (foreign) supplier
← Distant but cheaper (foreign) supplier

d. In-sourcing

Prime contractor (MNE) ← (Foreign) supplier
← (Foreign) supplier

MNEs in-source, i.e. stop trading with current (foreign) suppliers

In-house unit located in domestic market (in-shoring)

In-house entity located abroad (offshoring)

Fig 10.4
Variants of international outsourcing.

Case study 10.2: Dellism, a new model value chain

When a customer buys a personal computer from a Dell salesperson, the order is transmitted immediately to one of the company's "factories" as soon as payment has been verified. The decision as to which facility should fill the order depends on geographic proximity and the particular product in question. For example, most of the laptop notebooks that Dell sells globally are made in Asia.

The first thing to note about this system is that the term "factory" is a misnomer since the production facilities that Dell runs are in actual fact assembly plants. The company makes almost none of the components used in its computers. When notification of a laptop notebook purchased in the USA reaches Dell's Malaysian plant, for instance, the parts will be immediately ordered from a "supplier logistics centre" comprised of the many value chain partners who will have set up operations immediately adjacent to Dell's facilities. Each supplier is in constant contact with the company, booking future deliveries and tracking current orders. More than any other factor, Dell's production system relies on effective intra- and inter-firm communications (see Figure 10.6).

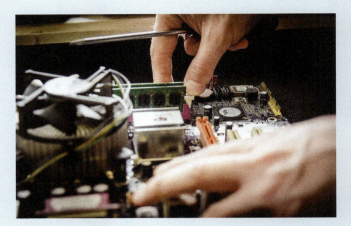

Fig 10.5
Dell computers are best analysed as the culmination of innumerable global supply chains.

Dellism has evolved to allow the company to meet the three commitments it makes. The first is to provide a product customised to different consumer preferences. This is feasible because of Dell's ability to vary the subsystems it orders from suppliers. The second is quick delivery, something it can achieve because of the direct links it has established between different participants in its upstream networks. Lastly, Dell promises low prices, thanks to the volume discounts it negotiates with suppliers but also because its just-in-time delivery system reduces inventory costs.

The arrangement shifts many manufacturing and inventory pressures to Dell's suppliers, all the more so because Dell's policy of multi-sourcing certain products means suppliers can never be entirely sure of the exact volume of orders that they are going to receive. Having said that, the mere fact of being on the shortlist of suppliers to one the world's biggest computer retailers generally promises them economies of scale that they would otherwise struggle to achieve. To that extent, Dellism works for both the prime contractor and its upstream partners.

Fig 10.6
Dell's model fully integrates communications, manufacturing, supply, assembly and logistics functions.

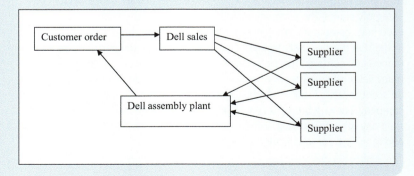

Dell's own industrial competencies involve relatively straightforward assembly operations. This is actually a potential weakness since the company always faces the risk that its biggest suppliers might try to bypass it one day and trade directly with end users. It is unlikely that they would succeed, however, given how hard it would be to replicate Dell's exceptional prowess in using modern communications and logistics to interlink the various threads comprising its complex global value chain. Excellence today is defined not only by what a MNE does by itself but also by the quality of its relationships.

Case study questions

1. What are Dellism's strengths and weaknesses?
2. How replicable is the Dell system?

International supplier relationships

Depending on their market power and the codifiability of the information being exchanged (Strange and Humphrey 2019), prime contractors will establish different kinds of relationships with foreign suppliers. This includes the "integrated hierarchy" of single product companies which rely heavily on specific counterparts; the "semi-hierarchy" of relatively autonomous multi-divisional MNEs; the "coordinated revenue links" typifying licensing/franchising arrangements; and the "medium-term trading commitments" of companies working with supplier shortlists (Harland et al. 2004). All these relationships will evolve over time if the balance of power shifts between a prime contractor and its suppliers, with one example being what has happened in the sports shoe industry as Global South suppliers increasingly compete with (and even acquire) former customers (Lechner et al. 2020). Much depends as well on whether the relationship between supplier and contractor is based on competition or cooperation, with the former mode seemingly superior at improving delivery, quality and innovation, and the latter better at reducing costs (Terpend and Krause, 2015).

A simple way of categorising the various types of international supplier relationships is to differentiate between the short-term, so-called American model, the longer-term Asian model and the compromise "flagship" model.

Short-term supply relationships

In this model, subcontractors are asked to bid anew every time their MNE customer replenishes inputs. This means that they are at a constant risk of losing the business if they slip on quality and/or price. There is little room for loyalty or joint planning in such arrangements, but they

do force suppliers to remain competitive. One interesting example is
the Covisint online auction platform that General Motors, Ford and
Daimler Chrysler originally created to get global suppliers to compete on
price day in day out, translating the transactional nature of this kind of
relationship.

Long-term supply relationships

The focus here is on collaboration up and down the supply chain.
Encapsulated in Japanese vertical or horizontal *keiretsus* but also in
Korean *chaebols* (and less formally in Chinese *guanxi* networks), these
supply systems are prime examples of the cultural embeddedness of IB.
Reflecting Asian emphasis on social harmony over individual success, in
a *keiretsu*, for instance, a prime contractor like Mitsubishi or Mitsui will
lend its name to a network of companies that work together to cover
all of the upstream operations needed to bring a good to market. Firms
typically take an equity stake in one another and collaborate on research,
product design and even FDI. Supply contracts tend to be renewed
without non-*keiretsu* members having much opportunity to compete,
thereby stabilising the volumes hence the market share that a supplier
can expect to achieve (Kosaka et al. 2019). Predictability of this kind
is priceless, since it helps industrial planners avoid the difficult choice
of opting for smaller capacities that cost less but cannot accommodate
demand spikes, as opposed to larger capacities that can cope with big
orders but cost more to maintain and amortise. Being able to size plant
capacities correctly is an advantage resulting in lower costs that the
supplier can then pass on to the prime contractor.

Asian supply networks are not without their faults, of course. For
instance, the long recession that Japan suffered during the 1990s has
often been blamed on *keiretsu* members' tolerance for partners' poor
investment decisions. Overdependence on local partners can also be
dangerous, as Toyota discovered when the 2011 Fukuyama earthquake
flattened many of its suppliers' facilities, disrupting its just-in-time
delivery systems. At the same time, there is no doubt that Asia's rise to
become a global manufacturing powerhouse is partially rooted in the
success of its supply chain organisation. This has drawn the attention of
many Western MNEs. In manufacturing, as in other IB functions, success
breeds imitation.

Compromise "flagship model"

A number of Western MNEs have moved over the years to establish
a more collaborative "flagship" arrangement (Rugman and D'Cruz
2000) where prime contractors compete in markets under their own
names while also acting as figureheads for networks of dedicated
suppliers organised into clusters. The benefits for the network leader
are reliable sourcing, a lesser risk of price-gouging and ultimately
faster internationalisation because it does not have to build its own
input manufacturing facilities. It is a system that Italian clothing giant

Vertical *keiretsu* – Japanese corporate network based on long-term cooperation between companies with different upstream specialties (often including a bank for funding purposes)

Horizontal *keiretsu* – Japanese corporate network where firms in similar sectors ally with trading companies to ensure widest possible market coverage.

Chaebol – South Korean equivalent of Japanese *keiretsu* but where founding family generally retains a majority stake.

Bennetton, for instance, has put to good use with its raw wool suppliers. Confident that centralised control over subcontractors' product design and quality standards will guarantee sourcing while protecting its brand name, the MNE has been free to focus resources on opening stores in Europe and elsewhere. The extra management costs it has incurred because of the need to supervise suppliers have been more than offset by the savings achieved by sticking to its core competencies. In a sense, the flagship arrangement is a microcosm of the division of labour concept.

As for flagship suppliers, they benefit from their prime contractor's expertise in production and materials planning, quality control and technical assistance. On occasion, suppliers can piggyback the leader's ability to buy raw materials in bulk, thus cheaply. Above all, flagship suppliers benefit from greater stability, with more or less guaranteed sales volumes allowing them to size their production capacities more accurately.

It remains that flagship suppliers will also incur extra costs. New members of a network are often forced to build expensive, capital-intensive facilities to manufacture the inputs they are expected to provide. Indeed, one analysis of the flagship arrangement is that it involves prime contractors passing on to their suppliers some of the performance pressures that they would otherwise have to shoulder themselves. This is particularly true in sectors like mass retail and fast food characterised by highly demanding and somewhat volatile customers, although it could also be applied to the Dell case study.

Not all pressures are cost-related, however. For many suppliers, it is just as important to offer technological competencies like the ability to share information. Some flagship leaders are also interested in "concurrent engineering", with value chain partners designing in parallel the different stages for which each is responsible. Today, industrial collaboration often starts as early as a product's pre-production phase, with suppliers and prime contractors cooperating openly on basic component designs to ensure that they fit seamlessly into useful sub-assemblies while reducing product development times and costs (Rihar et al. 2020). The priority in this kind of "fractal production" is coherence in the way that each network participant draws the boundaries between its own operations and what its partners do. Like most aspects of IB, production can only be accurately analysed in conjunction with managers' strategic intent.

Section III. International manufacturing

It is only by having an efficient manufacturing and logistics network that MNEs can satisfy global consumers' demand that different goods be delivered to different destinations at different times. Dominant thinking about the most efficient way of building such networks has varied over time. As much as anything, this justifies the present textbook's seminal principle that there is no one best way of doing IB.

Industrial models

Grosso modo, industrial models refer to not only the various ways in which companies can organise their production activities but also how this affects the distribution of power and wealth within society as a whole. From a corporate perspective, a good place to start is the mass production system that Henry Ford implemented in the early 20th century. This model offered the advantage of standardisation and efficiency, featuring specialised workers stationed along an assembly line and completing a succession of tasks creating parts that would then be assembled into a final product. By enabling economies of scale, Ford's system cut costs, leading to lower retail prices and higher sales. For several decades, it was the starting point for most industrialists' manufacturing efforts.

As powerful as Fordism was, however, it had several flaws, starting with its emphasis on uniformity. This may be acceptable in the early stages of a new product but as markets mature or internationalise, greater diversity becomes necessary. This was problematic for Fordist manufacturers. Offering a broad product range is expensive, both because it takes time to switch factory equipment from one production line to another and because as production runs shorten, so do their economies of scale.

To solve this problem while continuing to reap the benefits of standardisation, Ford's great rival at General Motors, Alfred Sloan, devised in the 1920s a so-called "volume and diversity" strategy (Boyer and Freyssenet 2002) where manufacturers would achieve economies of scale by using the same invisible sub-assemblies on all products even as they bolted visibly different parts on at the end of the process to give consumers a greater sense of customisation. Car buyers can see whether or not a particular vehicle comes with a sunroof, for instance, but are unlikely to know if the carburettor is a Holley or an Edelbrock. The practice of standardising for as long as possible before customising as late as possible (see Figure 10.7) is known alternatively as deferred differentiation, "platform strategy" and/or "postponement" (Saghiri and Barnes 2016). Not only does it allow manufacturers to combine scale with diversity, but it also reduces inventory costs given that generic modules are cheaper to store than expensive sub-assemblies that are specific to one model only (Christopher 2005). Indeed, the only real problem with postponement is the difficulty of balancing factory workloads when product differentiation occurs at different times on different lines (Ko and Hu 2008). The engineers who overcome such mathematical challenges are the quiet heroes of international production.

Sloan's ideas would become the driving force behind many of the sectoral consolidations that have marked IB over the past century. His platform strategy would spread throughout the automotive industry, with famous takeovers such as Volkswagen's purchase of Spain's SEAT Motor Company in the 1970s or Renault's more recent M&A with

Deferred differentiation – Achieving both economies of scale and product diversity by standardising manufacturing inputs as long as possible, and customising outputs as late as possible.

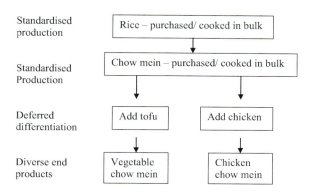

Standardised
production — Rice – purchased/ cooked in bulk

Standardised
Production — Chow mein – purchased/ cooked in bulk

Deferred
differentiation — Add tofu | Add chicken

Diverse end
products — Vegetable chow mein | Chicken chow mein

Fig 10.7
Deferred differentiation
in a Chinese restaurant
kitchen. Customers get
different dishes but the
restaurant owner also
achieves economies of
scale.

Nissan being specifically designed to rationalise factories that had
previously manufactured different chassis (platforms). On the surface,
VW and SEAT models, like Renaults and Nissans, still look different,
satisfying consumers' desire for choice. Most today share the same
platform, however, enabling manufacturers to achieve economies of scale.

The Fordist mass production model also had problems because of its
assembly line organisation. Disruptions to operations anywhere along
the line (for example, if a workstation runs out of parts) shut down the
whole process. To offset this risk, Fordist manufacturers tend to carry
large inventories of parts, which is an expensive undertaking. Secondly, a
Fordist factory's lack of flexibility meant that it is not particularly suited
to a world where MNEs are expected to service highly diverse markets.
It is largely in reaction to these two challenges that a new industrial
model, called "Toyotaism", would become the dominant international
manufacturing paradigm from the 1970s onwards.

A Japanese manufacturing model

The Toyota Production System is built on the idea that, contrary to
received wisdom, volume manufacturing can coincide with product
flexibility as long as uncertainty about the level and timing of factory
flows ("throughput") is minimised. This is achieved by getting
staff members to adopt what the Japanese call *kaizen* (continuous
improvement) attitudes aspiring to a "permanent reduction in costs"
(Boyer and Freyssenet 2002). The Toyotaist bottom-up approach is
based on the precept that frontline operatives are the best placed to form
"quality circles" and identify potential efficiency improvements. Given
today's increasingly knowledgeable consumers, quality has become a
key factor in all industrial models, but none more so than in Toyotaism,
dominated by a total quality management (TQM) ethos targeting zero
defects.

TQM is an ambitious goal that firms usually achieve only through
a combination of approaches. Contractors need to audit not only their
own operations but also their suppliers. One of the leading processes
in this field is the "Six Sigma" model that Motorola developed in the

1980s, asking managers to improve business processes by establishing thresholds for quantitative defects and compiling performance statistics. Corporate controls of this kind can be relatively difficult to implement, however. For reasons pertaining to culture but also to self-interest, not all workers cooperate with quality control inspectors as readily, for instance, as Japanese employees traditionally do. Inspections are also expensive to run, especially in IB where it is unclear whether the prime contractor or supplier is supposed to bear the cost.

One response has been the creation of autonomous international quality assessment organisations. The leader in this field is the Geneva-based International Organization for Standardization, often referred to as the ISO. As of 2021, this body had developed more than 21,500 standards covering all aspects of quality, relating notably to management systems (covered in ISO 9001) but also to environmental performance (ISO 14001). Most MNEs are prepared to enact the changes they need to receive certification because they want to demonstrate their commitment to quality, if only because ISO is recognised worldwide and can therefore be used to enhance companies' marketing credibility.

Aside from quality and in addition to the aforementioned "just-in-time" and "lean" principles, the Toyota Production System also stands out because of its revolutionary throughput determination process. Instead of ordering supplies based on managers' ex ante predictions, a Toyotaist prime contractor asks subcontractors to replenish stocks at a rate defined by actual customer demand. In this *kanban* (automatic signalling) approach, supplies to each level of the value chain are "pulled" backwards by the next level downstream, and ultimately by orders from end users. The system contrasts with a Fordist one where replenishment is "pushed" by pre-established factory schedules, which are poor predictors of future flows, especially in MNEs serving volatile global markets. *Kanban* prevents the distortions ("bullwhip effects") that Fordist supply chains suffer when factory production volumes are misjudged. By stopping surplus production from piling up, *kanban* keeps inventory costs down. Conversely, when supplies run short, *kanban* reduces bottlenecks. Much of Japanese MNEs' international success can be attributed to the lean manufacturing systems that they run.

Despite Toyotaism's ongoing popularity since the 1980s, it would be wrong to assume that this is the only industrial model capable of succeeding in IB today. The Dell case study talks about a MNE that has been extremely successful in replacing a traditional manufacturing function with an assembly/logistics focus. Also noteworthy is the white label model, exemplified by multiple European retailers selling, as house brands, generic products actually manufactured by specialist MNEs, often from the Global South (but also by companies like McBride from the UK). Notwithstanding these and other interesting models (like service activities' de-materialised production systems), the fact remains that where physical goods are involved, someone still needs to be making them somewhere in the world.

Physical operations

A host of factors determine where MNEs locate their production units as well as the missions assigned to each. Some analyses tend to highlight purely upstream considerations, like the cost and availability of labour, raw materials or knowledge (without forgetting host country government attitudes). Others focus more on downstream elements like the size and importance of the market(s) that a plant is being asked to service, a given item's life cycle stage and where the outputs are being sold (locally, regionally or globally; to sister units or to customers). But there is one aspect that observers generally overlook, despite how crucial it is to MNEs' physical operations, namely, the dissimilarity between manufacturing and assembly plants.

It happens far too often that the two terms are conflated under the expression "production". The reality is that they have very different IB implications. Manufacturing plants make things and generally require very expensive capital equipment to do this. MNEs try to overcome this cost in two ways: by sizing plants so they are big enough to achieve economies of scale, and by building fewer plants worldwide in order to reduce FDI outlays. Of course, having fewer plants creates its own distribution problems, ones that an industrial MNE is more likely than not to delegate to a logistics specialist.

Conversely, where a company's production function is solely comprised of assembly operations, it makes nothing itself and therefore does not need the same heavy equipment as a manufacturer does. Moreover, with lower capital expenditure for each plant, it can build more units worldwide for the same overall cost. Alongside these advantages, however, assembly plants of course have their own challenges – namely, the advanced (hence expensive) logistics capabilities they need to receive, stock and assemble all the parts needed for the assembly work they do before warehousing and then shipping the finished products – with the latter stage being the ones where inventory costs are the most expensive (Christopher 2005). The only thing that these very different production logics have in common is that both are inextricably linked with logistics, justifying in turn that the chapter's final subsection address this topic as well.

Manufacturing paradigms

Where MNEs' market entry actions involve a transfer of technologically advanced knowledge, they may find value in "bundling" different production stages together on one foreign site, if only because this helps to preserve confidentiality. It is an approach that many Japanese high-tech companies have put to good use over the years. On the other hand, huge multi-stage investments of this kind are necessarily very expensive, which can be particularly daunting to companies who are also entering what they view as a very foreign business environment. As a result, mammoth bundled manufacturing FDI is relatively rare. What happens more often is that MNEs seeking vertical integration advantages will disperse the different stages of their overseas production operations in such a way as to optimise sites' location-specific advantages. This often culminates in "focused factories" that are both large enough to achieve plant-level economies of scale and specialised enough to maximise learning effects.

The consequence of having foreign factories focused on a single global value chain activity is that each will then produce and/or export a larger quantity of the one or few item(s) for which it is responsible. Swiss–Swedish MNE ABB, for instance, concentrates on its Ludvika site the manufacturing of many of the electrical modules (like current transformers or voltage transformers) that it either sells directly to customers or transfers to sister units who will then fit the part on to a more complex final product being assembled elsewhere. Examples of focused factories of this kind being built outside of a MNE's home country (and where the output is being exported intra-firm) attest to the somewhat artificial distinction made between MNEs' FDI or trade practices. The two are often complementary.

Of course and as always, the benefits of a focused factory approach (like any other) come with certain disadvantages, first and foremost being high internal "trade costs" (packaging, freight, tariffs, delays and communications systems) due to the need to ship large volumes of semi-finished goods between sites. These issues can be particularly problematic for MNEs if customers require, for instance, delivery to various sites of the different items that the company is making in each of its focused factories (see Figure 10.8). In such cases, factory location rationale must be weighed against the logistics problems caused by the poor fit between the MNE's configuration and its customers' locations.

Some MNEs try to overcome this barrier by running manufacturing operations on a very few sites only, often located near their final assembly plants. Examples include the *maquiladora* components factories that US industrials have established in north Mexico near the Texas

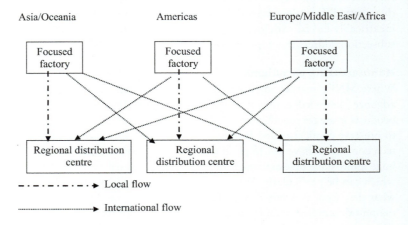

Fig 10.8
Focused factories'
complicated cross-flows.

border, or the automotive parts plants that German carmakers have helped build in neighbouring Eastern European countries like Hungary and the Czech Republic. Other MNEs have come up with ideas like the "dual shore" model that Indian automotive parts maker Bharat Forge uses, based on an international division of labour where focused factories in low-wage India specialise in labour-intensive activities, while higher value-added production is done in plants situated in more expensive countries. The problem with these solutions, however, is that each requires further FDI which may be even more expensive than the intra-firm trade costs incurred with focused factories, explaining why some MNEs are still attracted by the idea of organising their international manufacturing according to a more horizontal logic.

Having said that, horizontal FDI – where a MNE duplicates one value chain function in different countries – costs a great deal. It can be particularly expensive when each site is designed to only serve its local market instead of customers or sister units elsewhere – especially when this displaces exports from existing units, diminishing everybody's economies of scale. On the other hand, these are losses felt at an individual plant-level. On a broader plane, it is also possible to achieve firm-level economies of scale through horizontal FDI since some of the intangible assets involved (like scientific know-how, patents and brand reputation) can be duplicated – a boon for MNEs that market worldwide. Above all, the main advantage of horizontal manufacturing is that locating sites in proximity to foreign markets necessarily reduces plant-level transport costs on the downstream side, and potentially on the upstream side as well if local suppliers can be found – further evidence, if need be, of the central role that logistics play in MNEs' international production choices.

International logistics

Growing pressure for rapid yet flexible global delivery execution puts enormous pressure on every stage of the MNE value chain. Logistics management applies to raw materials, parts and sub-assemblies, finished goods and even used products and packaging destined for recycling. On some occasions the pressure will be commercial in nature, coming from retailers requiring suppliers to replenish outlets that may be centralised or, conversely, scattered worldwide. On other occasions, it is savvy online shoppers who will be asking companies to compete on delivery performance. And of course, logistics solutions also apply to MNEs' internal needs, be it the replenishment of globally dispersed assembly operations, the temporary storage in free trade zones of parts destined for assembly and re-export or the warehousing in regional distribution centres of "centralised inventories" of semi-finished or finished goods until such time as the MNE has gauged national demand variations – the latter solution being one that increases flexibility but also adds to the distance between a MNE's storage facilities and its ultimate end users, potentially slowing delivery times. Note that to address this problem,

Free trade zone – "Export processing zones" where companies pay little or no taxes or tariffs on imported items destined for (assembly into) export products.

many companies have organised with customers joint information systems similar to the ones they operate with suppliers. It should always be remembered that communications are a key component of modern international logistics, including (and maybe especially) for service activities transferring intangibles across borders via web-based technologies. In this sense, the Internet is necessarily as much a mode of international transportation as any other.

The broader question, of course, is if current global logistic capabilities can meet MNEs' future needs. The background to this analysis is skyrocketing IB transport volumes over the past 40 years, exacerbated by the fragmentation of cross-border supply chains and prevalence of focused factories. The main effects have been twofold. Firstly, the rise in long-distance deliveries has placed global transportation infrastructure under tremendous strain, as witnessed by the recurring saturation of ports ill-equipped to handle the ever-bigger vessels needed to carry the sheer tonnage of IB volumes today. In response, governments have invested heavily to refurbish ageing infrastructure and avoid the delays regularly witnessed, for instance, at some Chinese ports or US–Mexico border crossings. Transportation companies engage in similar infrastructure productivity and capacity investments by purchasing bigger and better cranes to roll containers on and off ocean freighters as quickly as possible. The logistics sector may exist to service its professional customers but it also has its own needs, exemplified by shipping and haulage firms' huge vehicle orders and, even more poignantly, by China's $4 trillion Belt and Road Initiative that will extend the country's reach across South Asia into the Middle East and Africa. This is the largest infrastructure project in history. In and of itself, logistics is very big business.

Rising international trade volumes also affect the vehicle modes being used to actually carry freight. As aforementioned, one key aspect here is the transport sector's enormous environmental footprint, a topic that Chapter 14 will discuss in further detail from a sustainability perspective. For the moment, suffice it to say that fuel-efficiency and pollution standards have become increasingly important factors affecting MNEs' predilection for using one or the other mode of transportation. Another is the arbitrage between cost, speed and flexibility. Shipping, for instance, accounts for around 80 percent of world trade in volume (and 60–65 percent in value) not because it is flexible or fast but due to its comparatively low per-kilogram cost of transporting either freight in containers or commodities like oil or grains in bulk. Indeed, to maximise their economies of scale, in the early 2000s, the three alliances dominating the world's shipping markets began ordering mega-vessels capable of carrying up to 12,000 containers. This was four times greater than the standard just half a generation previous, and a choice that, like any in IB, carries its own risks. Some are strategic, such as the potential for over-capacity if slowbalisation continues to dampen trade volumes. Others are more practical, like the inability of such huge "slow-streamers" to travel as fast as their smaller predecessors; the fact that they are often too big to dock in shallower harbours l and the complications that their size causes in the ports where they do unload.

Of course, once freight carried by ship has been unloaded, it needs to be forwarded onwards, almost always via a different mode of transportation. Trains resemble ships insofar as they are cheap but also slow and inflexible, although there is also a possibility for big companies to build their own train spurs connecting their facilities to the rail network, thereby reducing the need for further intermodal transfers. Planes are the fastest mode, but they are inflexible, bureaucratic and above all very expensive on a per-kilogram basis. Road haulage is not cheap due to the fact that trucks cannot carry loads above two containers (and also because of taxes and driver salaries), but its great flexibility means that it is often the only way of satisfying the demand for integrated, end-to-end solutions.

A few very large MNEs might run transportation operations in-house if their delivery volumes and frequencies justify investment in a large multimodal fleet. This is rare, however, given the cost (and wastefulness) of commissioning a less than full-load shipment. That explains why the vast majority of MNEs outsource the function to third-party logistics providers (3PLs) such as Germany's DHL, Japan's DB Schenker or the USA's UPS, who will then do the complicated work of negotiating on their behalf freight contracts full of performance and size (hence price) contingencies. The sheer scope of these 3PLs, resulting from the recurring waves of international consolidation witnessed within this sector, means they can achieve coordinational economies of scale that they can then pass on to customers. Having said that, because of the peculiar logistics needs of some of the world's more atypical and/or remote regions, there is still room within the sector for smaller companies. It is yet another example about the coexistence in modern IB between the global and the local.

Attitudes and alternatives

A major challenge for IB practitioners is determining to what extent their value chain focus should skew to support internal priorities like standardisation and efficiency rather than external demands for adaptation and responsiveness. More than any other IB conundrum, this is one that preoccupies MNE decision-makers, if only because of upstream and downstream colleagues' very different perspectives and interests, often culminating in great tension within a company. Arbitration is especially difficult because people's supposedly objective arguments are often underpinned by their psychological predispositions. Developing an optimal response under these conditions is further complicated by the fact that senior managers will also have their own preferences. It is yet another example of the linkage within IB between the personal and the professional.

Chapter summary

The chapter divided the global value chain's upstream portion into three sections. The first is knowledge management, generally viewed in recent years as having become an increasingly crucial factor of success. The second section looked at supply chain management, specifically highlighting the trend towards international outsourcing that has played such a key role in expanding IB volumes. This discussion was divided between analysis of outsourcing arguments and scrutiny of the various relationships that MNEs might entertain with foreign suppliers. The chapter concluded with an exploration of international manufacturing, starting with industrial models, each characterised by its own underlying principles (specialisation for Fordism, quality for Toyotaism). A connection was also noted between companies' plant location paradigms and their logistics needs.

Case study 10.3: Trade operations are the nuts and bolts of international business

The physical side of logistics is only one of several aspects of this function that MNEs often decide to outsource. Trade operations also include financial and administrative tasks that can be just as cumbersome for companies whose main IB focus lies elsewhere. The knowledge required for these activities involves very specific competencies and is therefore a topic worth further exploration, all the more so because of all the career opportunities IB learners might find in these professions.

Fig 10.9
International business would be impossible without effective cross-border administration.

Trade finance generally refers to the services provided by banks mediating between exporters and importers to ensure that an international transaction runs smoothly. The risk for exporters selling to an unknown customer is that they will not receive payment. The obverse risk for a buyer importing goods from foreign suppliers, especially unfamiliar ones, is that it will have paid for goods that are of poor quality and/or defective, delivered late or potentially do not come at all. To overcome these potential barriers, most major banks have trade finance departments offering, for a fee, a variety of problem-solving services. One involves a "letter of credit" (also known as a documentary credit or letter of understanding) where the seller is reassured by the bank that it will be paid fully and in a timely fashion. Payment will come either from the buyer or its agent upon receipt of documents transferring ownership of the goods in question as long as the terms specified for the deal have been met l or by the bank itself in case of a default. Note that the specification that payment for documents will only be made if the exporter has satisfied the contract conditions also serves to protect the importer, who can otherwise benefit from another trade finance service that most banks offer, namely, the possibility of buying insurance for performance. Exporters can also buy insurance or arrange with their bank the possibility of "factoring" the invoices they have issued. This accelerates the receipt of funds, albeit at a discounted rate. All these instruments have been in place for centuries and attest to trade finance's central role within the IB system.

The same can be said about the administrative side of logistics, a task generally performed by dedicated freight forwarders responsible for compiling all relevant international trade documents, first and foremost being a "bill of lading", the transferable document that carriers issue upon receipt of cargo and which specifies a whole range of important information, including the quantity and classification of the goods being transported; the conditions of their carriage (vessels, estimated time of arrival); and, above all, transfer of ownership stipulations. Processing bills of lading, alongside a shipment's commercial invoices, phytosanitary certifications when relevant and customs clearances (a key brokerage activity that forwarders also perform), can be very time-consuming. That is one reason why most MNEs prefer outsourcing this task. Another is because they want to access the specialist knowledge that freight forwarders possess in a variety of trade-related areas, starting with the relative price (and availability) of different modes of transport. Depending on the fit between global trade volumes and available shipping capacities at a given moment in time, vessel charter rates (what it costs to rent space on a ship) will rise or fall at Shanghai's Shipping Exchange or London's Baltic Exchange, which are the main markets where global bulk freight future prices are traded (unlike spot prices negotiated by the shipping lines themselves, led by

Denmark's AP-Moeller/Maersk, the Swiss-Italian giant MSC or China's COSCO). Forwarders track this and other relevant data that they then use to advise customers about transport alternatives, much in the same way as they provide advice about organising cargo transshipments from points of origin to ports of departure, and ultimately from ports of arrival to final destinations. This latter category of advice is particularly useful given the patchy infrastructure found in some regions of the world (particularly Western China and Eastern Europe) that are currently experiencing a rapid growth in trade. Few companies possess the knowledge and political contacts that big forwarders have in these locales (Mohr et al. 2019). That puts the latter in a very strong position.

Last but not least, freight forwarders can advise MNEs on the terms under which they may wish to trade. A standardised international system called Incoterms exists to delineate – between exporters, carriers and buyers – who has responsibility for cargo at different junctures in a shipment. There are many variants, but broadly speaking, an importer may decide that it wants to buy goods on a cost, insurance and freight (CIF) basis and let other parties take responsibility for the shipment, in which case ownership is transferred when the goods get to the port of arrival. Otherwise, it may decide to buy goods on a cheaper free on board (FOB) basis and assume responsibility for the shipment at an earlier point. MNEs' choice between CIF versus FOB is instructive because it reflects how confident they are in their ability to organise logistics internally, a capability that mostly only develops when frequent shipments of large quantities are integral to their particular business model. It remains that this is the exception rather than the rule, meaning that for most MNEs, IB at its most basic level would be impossible without the armies of trade intermediaries exercising their profession worldwide.

Case study questions

1. When is it worthwhile for a MNE to pay trade finance fees to a bank instead of assuming its own counterpart risks?
2. At what point should a MNE consider insourcing freight forwarding functions?
3. What is the argument for trading on a CIF as opposed to a FOB basis?

Discussion questions

1   To what extent should MNEs engage in R&D on their own or via alliances?
2   What forms might international outsourcing assume in the future?
3   Can Japanese *keiretsu* networks be replicated in other business cultures?
4   How different is the production function in a MNE that manufactures goods as opposed to one that assembles goods?

5   What are the arguments for insourcing or outsourcing a MNE's logistics activities?

References

Banker, S. (July 2016). "The costs of excess inventory can be huge", accessed 16 December 2020 at https://www.forbes.com/

Bhatti, W. et al. (June 2020). "Relationship learning: A conduit for internationalisation", *International Business Review*, Volume 29, Issue 3, accessed 30 July 2021 at https://www.sciencedirect.com/

Boyer, R., and Freyssenet, M. (2002). *Productive Models: The Conditions of Profitability*, Basingstoke: Palgrave Macmillan.

Christopher, M. (2005). *Logistics and Supply Chain Management: Creating Value-Added Networks*, 3rd edition, Harlow: Prentice-Hall.

Clarke, T., and Lee. K. (2018). *Innovation in the Asia Pacific: From Manufacturing to the Knowledge Economy*, Singapore: Springer.

Contractor, F. (March 2019). "Can a firm find the balance between openness and secrecy? Towards a theory of an optimum level of disclosure", *Journal of International Business Studies*, Volume 50, pp. 261–274.

Davenport, T., and Prusak, L. (1998). *Working Knowledge: How Organisations Manage What They Know*, Boston, MA: Harvard Business School.

Gurzawska, A. (2020). "Towards responsible and sustainable supply chains – innovation, multi-stakeholder approach and governance", *Philosophy of Management*, Volume 19, pp. 267–295.

Harland, C. et al. (2004). "Supply chain relationships", in S. New and R. Westbrook (eds.). *Understanding Supply Chains: Concepts, Critiques and Futures*. London: Oxford University Press.

Ietto-Gillies, G. (2012). *Transnational Corporations and International Production: Concepts, Theories and Effects*, 2nd edition, Cheltenham: Edward Elgar.

Jalali, S. (January 2017). "Partner Capabilities and Alliance Time Frame: An Analysis of International Strategic Alliances from the CEE", *Journal of Entrepreneurship, Management and Innovation*, Volume 13, Issue 2, pp. 59–76.

Ko, J., and Hu, S. (August 2008). "Balancing of manufacturing systems with complex configurations for delayed product differentiation", *International Journal of Production Research*, Volume 46, Issue 15, pp. 4285–4308.

Kosaka, G. et al. (June 2019). "The vertical keiretsu advantage in the era of Westernisation in the Japanese automobile industry…", *Asian Business and Management*, Volume 19, Issue 2, pp. 36–61.

Lagunes, S. et al. (June 2016). "Moderating effects of the relationship between offshore outsourcing and the export capability of firms", *South African Journal of Business Management*, Volume 47, Issue 2, pp. 33–42.

Lechner, C. et al. (August 2020). "Supplier evolution in global value chains and the new brand game from an attention-based view", *Global Strategy Journal*, Volume 10, Issue 3, pp. 520–555.

Lees, M. et al. (2018). "Towards industrial cybersecurity: resilience of multinational corporations", *IFAC Papers Online*, Volume 51, Issue 30, pp. 756–761.

Murphy, G., and Siedschlag, I. (August 2018). "Determinants of R&D offshoring: firm-level evidence from a small open economy", *Economia Politica*, Volume 35, Issue 2, pp. 529–553.

Mohr, D. et al. (September 2019). "Fast and furious: Riding the new growth wave of logistics in India and China", accessed 15 December 2020 at https://www.mckinsey.com/

Nonaka, I., and Takeuchi, H. (1995). *The Knowledge Creating Company*, New York: Oxford University Press.

Pearce, J. (17 March 2020). "Huawei slowly overcomes 5G challenges yet the cyber-security debate rages on", accessed 24 February 2021 at https://www.ibc.org/

Pisch, F. (30 June 2020). "Just-in-time supply chains after the Covid-19 crisis", accessed 24 February 2021 at https://voxeu.org/

Randolph, G., and Dewan, S. (2017). "Skills, social protection and empowerment in the platform economy: A research and policy agenda for the global South", pp. 53–56, in The Future of Work in the Global South, ed. Galperin, H. and Alarcon, A. (International Development Research Centre).

Rihar, L. et al. (November 2020). "How to successfully introduce concurrent engineering into new product development", *Concurrent Engineering*, accessed 24 February 2021 at https://journals.sagepub.com/

Rugman, A., and D'Cruz, J. (2000). *Multinationals as Flagship Firms: Regional Business Networks*, London: Oxford University Press.

Saghiri, S., and Barnes, S. (2016). "Supplier flexibility and postponement implementation: An empirical analysis", *International Journal of Production Economics*, Volume 173, pp. 170–183.

Slaughter, M. (14 December 2020). "To the moon and back, Chinese R&D is leaving the US behind", *Financial Times*.

Strange, R., and Humphrey, J. (October 2019). "What lies between market and hierarchy? Insights from internalisation theory and global value chain theory", *Journal of International Business Studies*, Volume 50, pp. 1401–1413.

Terpend, R., and Krause, D. (May 2015). "Competition or cooperation? Promoting supplier performance with incentives under varying conditions df Dependence", *Journal of Supply Chain Management*, Volume 51, Issue 4, pp. 29–53.

Zhao, S. et al. (January 2020). "MNE R&D internationalisation in developing Asia", *Asia Pacific Journal of Management*, accessed 30 July 2021 at https://link.springer.com/

Žitkienė, R., and Dudė, U. (2018). "The impact of outsourcing implementation on service companies", *Entrepreneurship and Sustainability Issues, Entrepreneurship and Sustainability Center*, Volume 6, Issue 1, pp. 342–355.

CHAPTER 11

Multinational downstream activities

Introduction

In a text intended for learners who have reached an advanced stage of their business education, it can be assumed that everyone possesses good basic understanding of the principles of marketing. Thus, many of the topics broached in this chapter will be ones with which readers are already familiar, with one major difference – here, they will be treated from a specifically international business (IB) perspective, with emphasis on how they are handled within the framework of a multinational enterprise (MNE). Before that, however, and in line with this book's ambition to not only study the decisions that IB practitioners make but also the motives behind their choices, the first section will speak very specifically to the relationship between a MNE's overall approach to IB (its position on the "push" vs. "pull" spectrum) and the constraints placed on its marketing teams. This latter aspect carries on from Chapter 10's discussion about the tension existing within all companies, and particularly within MNEs, between colleagues working at upstream versus downstream stages of the value chain. To repeat, international production and marketing may need to be studied in isolation from one another: for clarity's sake; and to highlight the stark opposition

Fig 11.1
Global and local brands mix in most major international retail markets.

DOI: 10.4324/9781003159056-15

between their guiding principles (standardisation for the former, adaptation for the latter). In fact, however, decisions made in one of these areas have a direct impact on the other. To really grasp how much room to manoeuvre international marketing professionals enjoy in the performance of their functions, it is therefore essential to remember the lessons from the preceding chapter while reading the present one.

Having said that, international marketing also has its own precepts, best encapsulated in the standard "4 Ps" (product, price, place and promotion) framework that structures this chapter's second section, again, partially altered to focus on how these factors play out in specifically cross-border situations. Lastly, because of the frequent confusion within international marketing between adaptations in the way that products are physically designed versus adaptations in the way they are advertised, the final section takes a separate look at this latter aspect to analyse the thought process underlying MNEs' cross-border messaging efforts, itself a key subset of general IB studies.

LEARNING OBJECTIVES

After reading this chapter, you should be able to:

- assess the tensions between a MNE's upstream and downstream interests
- judge how a MNE's "push" or "pull" orientations affect its marketing behaviour
- draw lessons from common international marketing mistakes
- apply a standard "4 Ps" marketing framework to IB situations
- evaluate the factors shaping MNEs' cross-border messaging and advertising efforts

Case study 11.1: No logo, no thought control

It is rare for books on globalisation to become international bestsellers – and even rarer for this to happen with works whose main purpose is to deride globalisation. Yet that is what Canadian journalist Naomi Klein achieved with her 1999 publication *No Logo*, a critique of the international marketing approaches that she accused MNEs of pursuing in their efforts to resolve the inherent tension that exists between upstream and downstream value chain functions. There is no need to agree with all of Klein's politics to respect the strength of many of her arguments. IB, like any system, benefits from robust scrutiny, and bona fide critics like Klein have a valuable role to play in that respect.

No Logo started with Klein's observation of young Norwegian consumers' habit one generation ago of tearing brand labels off their clothing. Upon enquiry, she discovered that this translated their fear of being manipulated by large apparel multinationals whom they

Fig 11.2
Globalisation critics see logos as way for brands to colonise consumers' minds.

accused of trying to turn them into walking billboards. Pushing her investigation further, Klein believed that some of the world's biggest MNEs were trying to use the so-called Madeleine effect to instil lifelong brand loyalty in impressionable youngsters. This was in reference to a French pastry that one of novelist Marcel Proust's protagonists had been lovingly served by his mother as an infant, which he again smelled while walking down a street one day as a grown man, whereupon he immediately found himself transported back to the happy emotions of his childhood. The idea here is that if someone can be inculcated with a positive association when they are too young to make a reasoned judgement, it should be easy to pull on their heartstrings for the rest of their lives, thereby turning them into loyal brand consumers - an action some consider highly dubious.

According to Klein, savvy marketing departments working for well-known MNEs like Nike or Tommy Hilfiger were trying something along these lines when they would hand out free samples to school children as young as 11, in Norway and elsewhere. In her view, such attempts to create **consumer tribes** (Cova 2007) before the targets were old enough to think for themselves are morally reprehensible. An ancillary analysis was that by accustoming children worldwide to adopt the same brand,

Consumer tribes – Communities whose sense of joint identity is based on visible adherence to a particular brand.

MNEs were trying to engineer a situation where consumer preferences everywhere would converge even further than they already have done, making it easier for companies to sell their standardised product lines without having to incur the added costs of national variation. It would be tantamount to using the marketing function to resolve the age-old upstream versus downstream battle in favour of the former, at the cost of impoverishing society as a whole by eliminating cultural sovereignty and variability.

If Klein's analysis is correct, this would be a social psychology experiment conducted on a monstrous scale. It would also mean that MNEs are using their powers of persuasion to get societies everywhere to adapt to the companies' own value chain management needs, rather than the other way around. Note that Klein was not the only voice of her era to comment on MNEs' alleged use of a Madeleine effect. A very popular 2004 documentary called *Super Size Me* saw film-maker Morgan Spurlock make the same point about McDonald's invention of Ronald the Clown to breed brand loyalty in susceptible children. The question for international marketing analysts is whether Klein, Spurlock and others of their ilk were right to condemn such behaviour. On the one hand, they are far from having been the only social observers in modern history to condemn efforts to homogenise the experience of childhood in order to manufacture passive, acquiescent adults – the very same idea had been evoked, for instance, in prog rock group Pink Floyd's iconic 1979 album, *The Wall*, which among other verses rejected "thought control" and called upon "teachers [to] leave them kids alone". Having said that, there is also the opposing argument that children constitute a bona fide international marketing target, that this can be done ethically (Grad 2015) and that the credibility of Klein's critique needs to be assessed in light of her general antipathy to MNEs.

Above and beyond the moral debates that Naomi Klein's magnus opus would trigger, the IB implications of her insights are fairly monumental. By making MNEs' drive for standardisation the heart of the debate, Klein asked an interesting question about how far companies are willing to go to avoid the costly adaptation that is taught far too often in business schools as if it were an inevitable aspect of international marketing. She was right to do so. In that respect at least, this renowned critic is unlikely to attract much criticism.

Case study questions

1. Are MNEs really trying to mould consumers worldwide to get them to accept standardised product lines?
2. If indeed this were happening, what would be the chances of success?

Section I. International marketing preconceptions

Commercialising a company's products or services across borders is tantamount to forming a bridge between the home country where a MNE originates and the host markets that it wants to enter. The architecture of this bridge goes far beyond pure marketing actions to span, inter alia, the entry mode alternatives analysed in Chapter 8 and the globalisation versus localisation choices discussed in Chapter 9. Each of these aspects has a direct impact on MNEs' downstream activities, justifying that this work be framed more broadly as business development function rather than as simple marketing per se.

International marketing in "push"-oriented MNEs

There are several reasons why some MNEs might decide to impose a standardisation logic on their marketing department. One relates to the general corporate culture, reflecting the strategic priorities of senior managers who may, for instance, have a background in upstream operations and expect their marketing teams to cohere to the inwardly focused efficiency logic that generally dominates at that part of the value chain. The sector of activity can also be determinant, given that the main success factors for many high-tech products are their intrinsic attributes, not their international adaptation. Thirdly, there are cultural and/or psychological factors, starting with decision-makers' own ethnocentricity, if not arrogance (Cowan et al. 2019) – attitudes which, it bears repeating, can be a constant issue in IB. As posited in Upper Echelons theory, mindsets of this kind often reflect successful senior managers' pride in their own success in ascending the corporate ladder, which, at an extreme, can trigger a quasi-messianic self-image leading to the expectation that foreign customers should be happy to accept whatever goods or services the manager in question – and the company that s/he represents – deigns to offer. Otherwise and in a similar vein, there is the possibility of a MNE's executives coming from a national culture characterised by its sense of exceptionalism, spawning a superiority complex that also diminishes practitioners' willingness to validate potential foreign customers' desires. One real-life example of this atmosphere was when the author of this book was instructed to sell financial products to a top French institution at above-market prices, based on a prejudiced opinion expressed by his boss – a Eurosceptic British elitist without any real academic (much less mathematical) background – that "the French won't understand the maths". This reasoning was all the more absurd given that the customers in question were all graduates of l'Ecole Polytechnique, one of the world's leading engineering (and mathematics) universities. That kind of snobbery, much more common in the real world than in IB textbooks, will always be

Exceptionalism – Sentiment that the attributes of a particular group make it dissimilar – and superior – to any other.

problematic since it prevents an accurate vision of foreign customers, spawning the illusion that they will have more respect for (and greater need of) the MNE and its products than is really the case – a clear hurdle to realistic hence productive international marketing relationships. Now, it is also true that other, less ethnocentric MNEs will insist on product standardisation purely based on the financial calculation that the cost of adaptation exceeds the expected marginal increase in international sales. This is a perfectly reasonable thought process and one that should not be conflated with the aforementioned arrogance bias. In the end, however, the effect is generally the same.

Downstream professionals working in any kind of "push"-oriented MNE will typically be constrained and even demoted to the subordinated position of being expected to simply execute whatever instructions they receive. Usually they will be asked to try and find foreign customers willing to accept the company's standard offer as is, that is, without requesting any modifications. It should be said that in some cases this is entirely feasible and can even become a constructive international marketing strategy if companies' products are truly exceptional and stand out from the competition because, for instance, they offer advanced technology and/or markedly superior **value-for-money**. Where a "push" marketing drive falls short, however, is when the product offer is not unusual yet the MNE's representatives are under orders to present it as if it were. This is a regular occurrence not only in "push" MNEs that bathe in the aforementioned culture of arrogance but also in ones subject to extreme profit maximisation pressures, and where the assumption is that the only hope is finding uninformed foreign customers willing to pay more for products than they are really worth.

Overpricing may have been somewhat easier back in the pre-Internet days when it was harder to know how a given product was being valued elsewhere. Nowadays, however, it is almost impossible to charge "premium pricing" (see Table 11.2) for **commoditised** goods. Moreover, it is risky to even try since foreign prospects can resent being taken for fools, lessening the MNE's credibility even if it subsequently offers the item at its fair value.

One example of this is the different ways that the beer sold by Belgian MNE Stella Artois, a product commonly viewed as being of mid-range quality on the European continent, has been marketed in Great Britain. Until 2007, the company's UK advertisement carried the strapline "Refreshingly expensive", seemingly to justify its commanding a high price. One of the reasons why Stella Artois adopted this positioning may have included its need to amortise the cost of the brewery that it was operating at Magor in Wales. Potentially, however, it also included a calculation that because UK customers were less accustomed to European lager than to traditional local bitter, they would be willing to pay up for it. As time passed and as British lager drinkers acquired more points of comparison, however, it was no longer possible for Stella Artois to position itself in this way, so that by the year 2020, the company was

Value for money – Utility associated with ownership or use of an item, qualified by the price paid for it.

Commoditised – Lacking any particular rarity value.

advertising artistic lifestyles and no longer portraying its product as being top-of-the-range. Paraphrasing something the American circus entrepreneur P.T. Barnum once famously said, it may be possible to fool some of the people all the time and all of the people some of the time, but not all the people all the time. Today's hyper-efficient global communications networks make price ignorance less of a factor than it has ever been before. The convergence trends in today's markets have not only changed people's tastes but also increased their acumen.

What mainly remains for push-oriented MNEs is positive national stereotyping or the hope that customers will be willing to pay extra for a foreign product, as sometimes happens, simply because of the status associated with its country of origin (German cars, French wine, Swiss chocolate, Japanese electronics, etc.). Failing that, there is the alternative of trying to find in different markets worldwide those customers who are all buying the same global product, so that standardisation is no longer being imposed upon them but instead becomes something that they actually want. Such customers are always the most attractive to MNEs since servicing them requires no more than extending existing delivery systems geographically.

Having said that, this latter strategy also has its challenges. The desirability of these global customers is such that they will be heavily courted by all of a company's competitors. That only leaves a few options for a MNE to stand out from the pack. Either its downstream staff members are able to quickly build an unusually good personal rapport with the prospect (always a challenge with new contacts) or the company has to compete on price and/or ancillary services and therefore accept lower margins. This latter strategy is coherent in light of the fact that these global customers are cheaper to serve, but it is also at odds with the widespread assumption among certain "push"-oriented executives, especially ones working out of a centralised MNE's head

Fig 11.3
All Swiss chocolates benefit from positive stereotyping yet not all are equal in quality.

office, that IB can only be justified if it is more lucrative than its domestic counterpart.

International marketing in a "pull"-oriented MNE

It might seem self-evident that the best antidote to the handicaps that international marketing staff face in upstream-oriented MNEs is to decentralise the power to make commercial decisions and let strategy be determined by local subsidiaries working at the customer interface in each of the national markets where the company wants to compete. After all, these are probably the MNE employees with the greatest knowledge about what prospective customers really want. They are also probably in the best position to play on any social affinity that may be felt for the country from whence the MNE originates (Siganos and Tabner 2020). More generally, a MNE's marketing professionals can be counted on to have accumulated experiences throughout their careers, attuning them to the specific sales arguments that might convince potential customers in the territories to which they have been assigned. This is, after all, what they will have been hired and paid to do.

Social affinity – In international marketing, where good relations between countries mean that products made by one are attributed premium value by consumers in the other.

Having said that, a MNE's decision to devolve international marketing decision-making to its local subsidiaries will cause its own problems. The tendency in many multidomestic MNEs to hire staff characterised by a polycentric mindset (Lakshman et al. 2017) creates a major risk that each team will be largely focused on local market conditions alone, with little or no regard for the kind of cross-border integration that ensures the efficiency of more standardised rivals' product offer. At that point, the MNE is sacrificing its overall competitiveness in order to adapt to the very diverse preferences of different consumer populations whose needs may not only bear little resemblance to one another but who will necessarily also trade smaller quantities of each product line. The company therefore runs the risk that the greater sales it is hoping to generate through customisation may not cover the economies of scale advantages that it loses. This can be particularly problematic when a product's locally adapted version is already being offered by smaller domestic competitors who might be unable to compete with the MNE in more commoditised global markets but will have developed a local specialty, much in the way that SMEs can sometimes rival bigger companies in the niche sectors that the latter struggle to enter.

One real-life example of this dilemma occurred when the European marketing manager of a London currency options department visited top-tier Stockholm industrials to sell her team's trading capabilities in the so-called "major" currencies, only to be told by the Swedes that they were already well-served in these commoditised products and would only envision new relationships with counterparts willing to trade in their domestic currency, the Swedish kroner, which, by its very nature, involves much smaller volumes. This counterproposal seemed encouraging to the manager, who returned to her home office with what she felt was the good news that the bank would be able to add these new customers as long as it agreed to service their very particular demand – only to be told by her upstream colleagues, supported by the department's efficiency-oriented director, that creating a new product portfolio would require too much work. Subsequent analysis revealed the validity of this response, since the volume of business needed from the new customers to amortise the cost of setting up a new production line on their behalf exceeded the turnover that could be reasonably expected from them. It was a harsh reality ignored by the commercial specialist, singularly focused as she was on increasing sales volumes, possibly because this was the basis upon which her own performance would be appraised. International marketing is always taught with the supposedly obvious principle that adaptation is a good thing because it increases sales opportunities. But adaptation always comes with a cost, something downstream professionals find very easy to forget.

Add to this polycentric marketeers' greater tendency to allow themselves to be convinced by a wily foreign customer that their product is nothing special – hence that it should be offered for cheap, irrespective of the seller's cross-border delivery costs – and it becomes apparent that international marketing mistakes can be committed just as readily in pull-oriented as in push-oriented MNEs. What then behoves MNE marketing officers is to have the humility to recognise that they can be just as biased as their upstream counterparts'- as well as the confidence to affirm that they have just as much a right to plead their case. The balanced view is that the best chance for success is when a company's international marketing mix is coherent both with its broader orientation (Kraft et al. 2012) and with its target market requirements. Unfortunately, this does not happen all the time.

International marketing mix – Sum total of parameters defining how a commercial item is being positioned in different countries where it is on offer.

Learning from international marketing mistakes

Like other social sciences, there has long been an awareness in IB of the great benefits of learning from mistakes. Of course, the willingness to self-criticise is largely a cultural phenomenon (Harteis et al. 2008) since companies (and indeed individuals) who self-define by their responsiveness to external circumstances, are likelier to implement feedback mechanisms informing them of the need to change course. As much as any other MNE function, international marketing benefits from self-reflective practitioners, humbled by the complications in their profession, which obliges them to juggle day in day out a host of potentially very different contexts, many of which will be unfamiliar to them.

It would be impossible to inventory all the different international marketing mistakes that a MNE can potentially make. It could, however, be useful to start with empirical examples of successes and failures (see Table 11.1) and then work backwards to try and ascertain the reasons why

Table 11.1
Neither standardisation nor adaptation is inherently effective internationally

	Successful	*Unsuccessful*
Standardisation	Foreign market accepts same products as those sold elsewhere Ex. Uniqlo's narrow but high-quality "Made for all" range eschews fast fashion	Foreign market would have preferred being offered customised products Ex. Spanish MNE Montaditos' tapas format struggled in US due to small portions
Adaptation	Foreign sales more than offset cost of production system alterations Ex. McDonald's changes menus to suit national tastes, but system is the same	Foreign market would have preferred being offered MNE's original product Ex. M&S selling French shirts to French, who were more interested in English design

seasoned and assumedly otherwise successful professionals got things so wrong. It should always be remembered that there is as much, if not more, to learn from what IB practitioners do poorly as from what they do well.

Overconfidence in the brand name

Uppsala theory (see Chapter 8) posits the value of gradual internationalisation, in part because practitioners' may feel daunted by their psychic distance to a particular foreign market but, even more importantly, because it can take time for a company not only to learn how to operate outside of its home market but also to develop the capabilities that will ensure its success when doing so – starting, as far as international marketing is concerned, with foreigners' awareness of a brand as well as the existence of a sufficient number and variety of distribution channels (San Emeterio et al. 2020). Conversely, where a company internationalises too quickly because managers extrapolate excessively from the success that their brand had previously experienced in its home market, the risk is that they will position it abroad as if the name conferred greater status and/or commanded a higher price than foreign consumers think it deserves. There are manifold cases of this happening in IB history. One old example from the years immediately following the Second World War was when Eastman Kodak, assuming that potential Japanese consumers would be as familiar with its trademark orange packaging as the company's American customers had been back home, set up an extensive distribution channel marketing its film canisters in Japan – where customers were already more than satisfied with a good domestic brand, Fuji – without even deigning to translate the contents into Japanese. Sales were terrible, yet it took years for Kodak to realise that it needed to do much more to build up a brand recognition in Asia that came anywhere close to the notoriety it enjoyed in the USA. Otherwise, there is the more recent example of Starbucks' episodic failures in countries like Israel, Italy and Australia to deploy its famous brand and displace its target foreign customers' long-standing loyalty to independent local coffee shops. Globalisation may have sparked much wider support for world's leading brands, but there are still many exceptions to this rule and it is always dangerous for MNEs to assume that the popularity their brands enjoy in some countries will necessarily be duplicated in others.

Notoriety - In international marketing, how quickly and spontaneously consumers identify a foreign brand when presented with allusions to it.

Failure to undertake market studies

One obvious safeguard against the pitfall of overconfidence is that international marketing departments get into the habit of commissioning a market study each and every time they consider entering a foreign market. In reality, this occurs much less frequently than might be expected, often for the very simple reason that international market studies can be extremely expensive, with leading consultancy firms regularly charging more than US$100,000 even for very narrow analyses. Now, it is true that such sums may seem modest at a MNE-wide level, especially when compared to the risk of losing a great deal more money if the market entry effort fails. In actual fact, however, the decision whether or not to commission a market study is almost never taken at a group-wide level but instead by the strategic business unit (SBU), with functional and/or product and/or geographic responsibility for the proposed initiative. The SBU in question will often look at the market study's hefty price tag, calculate that this will diminish its end-of-year profits (hence bonus pool) and find reason to rely on staff member intuitions when making an international marketing decision, all the more so because the employees involved will often have been hired specifically because they supposedly possess deep knowledge about the target territories. The end result is that MNEs follow much less frequently than might be expected the standard academic suggestion that foreign markets be systematically studied before any entry it attempted, further increasing the importance of IB practitioners' personal preconceptions to international marketing decisions.

(Mis)Interpretations of market signals

The question then becomes how to maximise the accuracy of MNE decision-makers' marketing forecasts. Clearly, it is helpful in this respect to have employed individuals who possess an in-depth understanding of conditions in a given target market, but also who have been trained not to extrapolate excessively from any unrelated previous experiences. There are several levels where this latter factor can play out.

One market signal that is frequently misinterpreted relates to a particular culture's interest in (hence willingness to pay for) the latest, technologically most advanced variant of a given item. In any society, there will always be some people who get excited by product updates and are willing to pay extra for the latest version replete with all "bells and whistles", as opposed to other, technologically more conservative and even Luddite individuals who mistrust novelty items they deride as gadgets and prefer tried and tested "plain vanilla" variants that usually have the added benefit of being cheaper. To diversify their offer, MNEs in most, if not all, sectors possess both categories within their product portfolios, meaning that their marketing teams theoretically have a choice of which to highlight in their sales pitches.

Luddite - Deep-seated, almost automatic mistrust of new technology.

For instance, French banks Société Générale and BNP-Paribas are not the biggest in the world in terms of their market share for standard financial market trading services but have both carved out a successful niche for themselves with certain sophisticated solutions that they have developed in recent years (equity and interest rate derivatives, respectively). The opposite applies to Google, which has had enormous success with its entry-level products (browser, Gmail and calendar services) but somewhat less with the more advanced smart-home networking technologies that it also offers.

Of course, it is also possible in the abstract for MNE marketing teams to offer both their most and least high-tech products all at once. The problem with a multipronged approach of this nature is that it also runs a strong risk of blurring the company's brand image and confusing customers. Add to this the potential for customers from one country to stereotype the strengths and weaknesses of MNEs coming from another, and it is often better for marketing professionals to project one clear technological identity when representing their offer – a positioning that they will, of course, sometimes get right and sometimes wrong.

A second way in which foreign market signals can be misinterpreted involves a misunderstanding of how changes in prospective customers' income levels will affect their demand for a particular class of products, that is, the elasticity of their demand. Thinking in this area is often rooted in Maslow's famous hierarchy of needs (1954), which teaches inter alia that the human desire for self-actualisation – which in international marketing terms translates into demand for foreign goods whose subjective value is greater than their functional utility – only really kicks in once people have satisfied their more basic needs (see Figure 11.4). An old example of how this principle can go wrong in an IB setting goes back nearly a century ago when expensive fountain pens were being widely used in Europe, only to see demand plummet in the aftermath of the Second World War as devastated societies turned to the cheaper ballpoint pens that France's Baron Marcel Bich had invented. American MNE Parker Pens, predicting resurgent demand for fountain pens in Europe once its economies had recovered, invested heavily in these markets, only to lose substantial sums as the continent remained loyal to Bic pens, which were cheaper and easier to handle. More recently, there are the problems that American retailer Home Depot has

Elasticity – Correlation between variables such as income or price and demand for a particular item (or class of items).

faced in China, where the company had invested heavily based on the expectation that as consumers here became wealthier, they would become increasingly interested in Home Depot's do-it-yourself (DIY) product ranges – only to be forced to shut down in 2012 largely due to the fact that irrespective of their income levels, Chinese households remain relatively unattracted to DIY. The problem in both these cases was that the MNE's international marketing teams projected the way a product was being valued at a given point in time onto the way they expected it to be received in a later, more affluent era. Entrepreneurship always requires that assumptions be made about the future, but due to the large number of variables involved in international as opposed to domestic marketing, there is also a greater chance of getting things wrong here.

Section II. The 4 Ps in international marketing

Traditional marketing instruction tends to revolve around the "4 Ps" (product, price, place and promotion) that altogether constitute what is called the marketing mix. An international marketing chapter benefits by exploring these topics but will necessarily do it differently, namely, by highlighting the various ways in which MNEs can apply such parameters in cross-border situations. To some extent, this will depend on a company's preferred strategic orientation. It should be noted, however, that other IB factors will also have an effect on the relative importance of one or the other of these marketing mix parameters. Studies have revealed, for instance: that distribution tends to be crucial for sales into Global South markets, that pricing tends to have a greater marginal effect in the Global North; and that product innovation and advertising have a much greater impact on the former than the latter (Bahadir et al. 2015). In marketing, like in all of IB, geography is paramount.

Received marketing wisdom holds that the sales argument embodied within a product – the reason why people might see value in purchasing it – is the most important of all marketing mix factors. In an IB context, understanding different populations' sense of the value they receive from a product can be broken down into several levels, including whether the product is generic in nature or has been adapted to their specific needs and preferences; the different functions it may be seen as performing in one culture as opposed to another; and the impact of irrational, non-market variables affecting general attitudes towards the MNE selling the product (such as its country of origin). Note that the two latter factors speak more to people's subjectivity when evaluating a foreign product. This is the emotional side of the purchasing decision, something that be affected as strongly – if not more so – by the way an item is advertised as opposed to its innate qualities. It is important to distinguish between the more objective nature of the first three elements in the marketing mix (product, price and place) as opposed to the more emotional nature of the final element (promotion), which therefore merits special analysis (see Section III). After all, the decision to standardise or adapt the physical aspects of a product, its pricing and delivery may or may not be matched by a similar decision as to how it should be advertised (see Figure 11.5). All sorts of international marketing combinations are possible in this respect.

Product

Business-to-business (B2B) – Interactions between companies that both operate at an intermediary stage of a product's global value chain.

Specifications – Detailed requirements about how an item should be designed and/or what materials and attributes it should feature.

In some instances, MNEs have no choice but to adapt the physical attributes of their product to local market requirements, at which point their decision how and indeed whether to adapt will be largely based on upstream considerations. Mandatory adaptation might involve factors that are technical (i.e. whether cars are supposed to have left-hand or right-hand-side drive), regulatory (i.e. Germany's *Reinheitsgebot* requirement that a beverage can only be labelled "beer" if brewed according to specified time tested processes) or practical (i.e. Canadian cars' need for powerful heating systems, unlike cars sold in Brazil). As noted in Chapter 10, there are also business-to-business (B2B) situations where a company supplies an upstream component to a foreign customer according to the specifications that the latter has determined. In countless

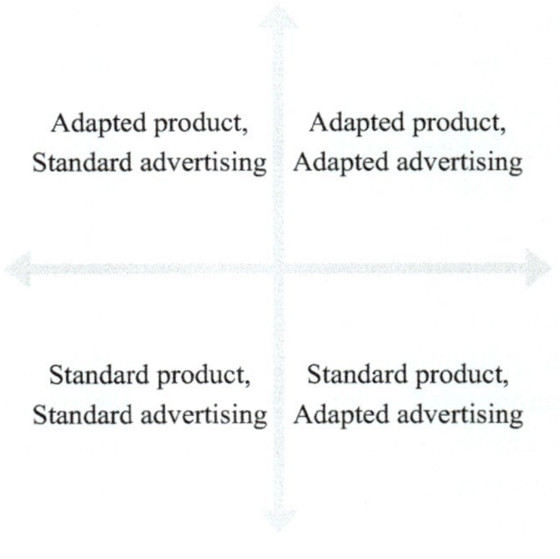

Fig 11.5
International adaptation can be either both tangible and presentational or just one or the other.

Adapted product, Standard advertising	Adapted product, Adapted advertising
Standard product, Standard advertising	Standard product, Adapted advertising

other cases, however, it is the MNE itself that chooses whether or not to physically adapt its products to assumed consumer preferences.

The criteria used to make this decision will be more or less objective in nature. Variables include a comparison of production system alteration costs and the marginal profits expected from the adapted product. The sector is also important, given the generally greater need to adapt products influenced by deep-seated personal factors such as food and drink as opposed to products like consumer electronics that are more technological in nature, hence less culturally embedded. Note that producers will also sometimes offer product adaptability simply because this enhances their sales argument, as exemplified by Germany's Leica microscopes, recognised (alongside its Japanese rival, Nikon) as a top-quality producer yet which offers a wider product range than might be expected because it sees this as a way of consolidating long-term market share, in part by locking out potential rivals.

Otherwise, the decision to adapt a product can also reflect decision-makers' subjectivity. This can translate their general worldview and/or stem from their position within a MNE's configuration (see the discussion in Chapter 9 on the power relationships between head offices and national subsidiaries). Along these lines, it is worth noting studies indicating that another key factor in a MNE's decision whether or not to standardise its products (and indeed its brand names and main labels) is internal corporate strategy, whereas decisions about parameters like distribution channels, prices and communications tend to be driven by factors that are more external in nature (Jimenez-Asenjo and Filipescu 2019).

One such factor is consumers' general receptiveness to the product in its standardised foreign version, hence the demand that it be adapted. Sometimes this has little to do with an item's objective utility. The country of origin of the foreign MNE selling the product might, for instance, enjoy a positive stereotype, adding perceived value to the product in its original, non-adapted form. Conversely, a product or MNE can suffer from the negative stereotyping of the country of origin in the event of geopolitical tensions (viz. the recurring trade and other disputes between China and the USA, not to mention ongoing hostilities in the Middle East). In the worst-case scenario, this can create a "clash of civilisations" (Huntington 1997) causing the target market to sense greater animosity towards (hence reluctance to buy) certain foreign offers (Khan 2019) and/or to perceive them as being of lesser quality than they really are. MNEs can only really overcome such hurdles if they detach the product offer from its geographic origins (Antonetti 2019), usually by altering its features and presentation to make it appear more local. In addition, the sentiment of economic patriotism alluded to in Chapter 3, epitomised in "buy local" campaigns but also in the greater fondness that some consumers feel for domestic brands that are more familiar (hence credible) to them, can also harm products whose foreignness might otherwise have been an advantage. Here, additional efforts of localisation will once again be required.

Case study 11.2: Lululemon looking lively locally

In 1998, Chip Wilson, an apparel entrepreneur transplanted from his native Southern California up the Pacific Coast to the Canadian city of Vancouver, founded a yoga-wear retailer called Lululemon. From the very outset, Wilson was looking for different ways of marketing internationally, having apparently decided, for instance, to insert the letter "l" as many times as possible into his new brand's name specifically because he thought this would signal its "innately North American and authentic" origins to the Japanese customers he hoped to reach one day (Edwards 2015). Alongside of this, he was also quoted as saying that watching future Japanese customers try to pronounce a name that is phonetically difficult in their language would be "funny" – a remark some might deem ill-deem. Indeed, the very fact that Lululemon has succeeded internationally against this backdrop is instructive and raises the possibility that host country consumers do not always know (or care) as much as social or ethical marketing analysts contend about the people behind a given foreign brand – a further example of the importance of distance in IB.

After 15 years honing its vertically integrated operations in North America, Lululemon opened its first stores in Europe in 2013, followed a year later in Asia. Subsequent international expansion proceeded at a breakneck pace so that by early 2019 – the year before the Covid-19 pandemic devastated retail outlets worldwide – 95 of the MNE's total 440 stores were located outside of its home market, with plans in place for a quadrupling of international sales by the year 2023 (Hensel 2019). Now, normally a company internationalising that quickly might be expected to market standard global product lines in order to maximise

Fig 11.6
Yoga practice is similar worldwide, but different populations approach it with different sensitivities.

operational efficiencies offsetting the cost of growth. But Lululemon was also surprising in this regard, having adopted a hybrid approach where its strong global brand would be marketed in a myriad of localised forms. Some adaptations are specific to the different places where it engages with customers; alongside its retail spaces, Lululemon maintains a strong e-commerce presence in most of the countries where it operates, while also participating in major sector events and trade fairs that can help publicise its identity as a lifestyle brand. Other localisation efforts involved advertising. The company tries to maintain ongoing two-way communications with the different communities it targets, a decentralised approach where it invites creatives to intervene in the product definition process and help it tailor a "brand experience [that] celebrates the quirks and qualities" of its potential customers (Legault 2016). In short, Lululemon has purposefully rejected a global marketing approach, despite all the efficiencies that this could create, to pursue instead a differentiation strategy based instead on ensuring the linguistic and cultural translation of its brand's core selling points even as it continues to identify new elements that are specific to each target market.

As always, there are risks associated with this marketing philosophy, first and foremost being that Lululemon's global brand image will be diluted if there is too great a divergence in its local versions. On top of this, localisation is expensive, and given the havoc that the Covid-19 pandemic has wreaked on the global retail sector (and the possibility that future recovery will be slow and limited), Lululemon, like most of its rivals, undoubtedly needs to find cost-cutting efficiency savings somewhere. The company's international profile had skyrocketed in the years preceding the crisis, with marketing playing a big role in this success. It will be instructive to see how this turns out in the future in an IB environment that may well be more challenging than it was before.

Case study questions

1. How important are MNE managers' persona to their marketing success?
2. What are the chances that Lululemon may resort to a more globalised marketing approach in the future, and what would be the costs/benefits of doing so?

Price

Price is often represented as the most flexible parameter in the marketing mix, if only because companies are free to decide what they are going to ask for their products. The problem, of course, is the many contradictory variables they must take into consideration, especially in

IB dealings, given the added complications of manufacturing, delivering and promoting products in multiple markets all at once. Add to this the more psychological influences signalled throughout this textbook relating to the different ways that the individuals responsible for such decisions interact with all their internal and external counterparts both home and abroad, and it becomes clear that MNE pricing policies cover a wide spectrum of possibilities.

At one level, the simple ambition here is to set prices that satisfy as many international marketing aspirations as possible. In general, this means attaining target profit margins without dissuading customers by being too expensive. In a few cases, the opposite logic prevails, with the goal being to price foreign sales competitively enough to increase market share, if only to avoid the kinds of problems suffered, for instance, by retail giants Carrefour and Walmart when they failed to penetrate the Japanese market because high local procurement costs prevented them from offering customers their usual discounts.

In theory, there exists an objective basis for price-setting in foreign (like domestic) markets, being the full cost of delivery plus the gross margin. Things can go wrong at both these stages, however: either because the MNE's analytical accounting system does a poor job at assessing the cost of getting an item to its international point-of-sale or because the expected mark-up does not correspond to the foreign customers' own assessment of how the product should be positioned. It bears remembering that, very broadly speaking, there are two marketing classifications: rare and/or novel low-volume/high-margin goods offering substantial per-unit value-added; and widely traded and/or commoditised high-volume/low-margin goods sold at scale. The problem is when MNE decision-makers get this wrong, almost always by trying to position plain vanilla products as being more special than they really are in the hope that their foreign customers will not notice the difference.

This tendency to over-price products sold abroad can reflect subjective factors (like arrogance) but also objective pressures such as the need to cover the added cost of marketing internationally. If the MNE has entered a foreign market on a foreign direct investment (FDI) basis, then its prices must amortise the full cost of this investment. Where the market entry has been done on a trade basis, then the price will need to cover items like international logistics, the likelihood of the MNE being in a weaker position when bargaining with host country distributors than it is back home, any regulatory and/or fiscal barriers that the host country government might impose (along with customs duties), foreign exchange risk and the possibility that the item in question will have to be segmented differently because the target population is unfamiliar with the brand and assigns it lesser utility. Add to this the fact that the same item can very easily find itself at a different stage of its product life cycle in different countries and it is clear why pricing can be such a difficult and contentious topic of discussion for MNEs, especially ones where

Table 11.2
Main international pricing policy options

Pricing strategy	Application in an international marketing context
Premium	Where product is priced above the competition to signal its extra quality or the rarity value associated with its foreignness
Penetration	Where product is priced low when it first enters a market in order to overcome foreignness barriers and trigger brand loyalty
Competition	Where product pricing is pegged to competition, irrespective of MNE's specific IB costs
Product life cycle	Where pricing depends on whether product demand is growing or declining in a particular foreign market
Skimming	Where MNE lowers product prices incrementally as foreign customer volumes rise, increasing IB-related economies of scale
Cost-based	Where product pricing solely based on specific IB costs of delivering it abroad, plus fixed margin

headquarters and national subsidiaries dispute the right to make the ultimate determinations in this area.

Having said that, experience has taught that a few pricing philosophies tend to be replicated time and again (see Table 11.2). They are interesting to learn, if only to spark reflection about what each represents in terms of how MNEs arbitrate between internal aims and external constraints – an ongoing theme in IB.

From a foreign customer perspective, the value-for-money status accredited to a foreign product – hence the receptiveness to the way it has been priced – can vary significantly from one country to another. In part, this is because the functionality attributed to products often varies, particularly where the MNE is engaged in direct business-to-consumer (B2C) dealings involving end users. A product as simple as a bottle of red wine will, for instance, fulfil a different function in a French household, where it is part of the normal culinary culture, than in a Japanese household, where the foreignness of this comparatively rarer product (associated with a positive stereotyping of France) adds to its mystique and makes it more exotic, hence something that is more valuable and can therefore be sold at a higher price. This is lucky for French wine exporters to Asia, of course, because the hefty logistics costs of shipping bottles to the other side of the world means that they must find a way to justify selling their wares at a higher gross price. Above all, this cross-border variability in product functionality underlines the importance for international marketing professionals of being able to ascertain to what extent consumers in one country reproduce the consumption practices witnessed elsewhere – a phenomenon sometimes

Functionality – Purpose for which a product is being consumed.

Business-to-consumer (B2C) – Interaction between a company operating at the downstream end of the global value chain and a finished product's end user.

End users – Final parties consuming a product after it has undergone all intermediary value chain transformations.

referred to within a subset of IB studies, called consumer culture theory, as "cultural appropriation" (Bardhi et al. 2020). Where there has been significant convergence between international markets – the vision of future globalisation that Harvard's Theodore Levitt had famously proposed in 1983 – there is every chance that a product will serve a similar functionality both home and away, and can therefore be priced with similar gross margins. Where divergence persists, however, marketing specialists are well advised to explore whether the product serves a different functionality in both markets, hence whether it needs to be priced differently.

Place

The third marketing mix parameter – the place where the foreign sale is made – entails fewer subjective considerations than the others and involves instead more straightforward logistic and distribution factors. Variables in this area start with the nature of the product, one aspect of which is how quickly it has to be delivered (for instance, if it is perishable), a consideration affected in turn by the accessibility of its destination. Coca-Cola, for instance, is sold in easy-to-access urban centres worldwide but also in remote mountain-top villages from Peru to Thailand, with the greater difficulty of delivering to the latter locations clearly affecting the product's cost and hence positioning. The practicality of distribution plays out at another level as well, being the proportionate cost of delivery compared to the product's total price. Cement, for instance, is a low value-added item that weighs a lot, meaning that shipping it long distances can be uneconomic on a per-kilogram cost basis. This explains why the world's leading cement companies, such as France's LafargeHolcim or China's Anhui Conch Cement, are more likely to engage in IB through FDI (building production plants near customers) rather than via long-distance trade operations.

Place is also important because it speaks to the nature of a MNE's management of its global value chain. There is a big difference, for instance, between a vertically integrated company distributing product (either directly or after in-house warehousing) to its own foreign outlets – as is the case with certain big brand clothing labels like Uniqlo or Levi Strauss – and a vertically disintegrated MNE delivering to an external distributor with its own logistics needs. This emphasizes once again the crucial difference between international marketing on a B2B versus a B2C basis. Because the latter involves direct dealings with end users, it means that the MNE is selling at a higher retail price but must also incur the costs of bringing the goods to their final place-of-sale. This can be either done directly, using the company's own fleet; or indirectly, hiring a "last mile" delivery service. B2B IB interacting with fellow professionals, on the other hand, is easier because the counterpart will share similar technical understandings (facilitating communication while reducing psychic distance) and because it is probably also configured to receive deliveries. Having said that, B2B international sales are done at lower wholesale prices and therefore offer smaller margins. They present less risk, so unsurprisingly offer less reward.

Promotions

This final marketing mix parameter would normally involve a discussion of all the processes involved in the international messaging that helps to nurture foreign demand, and hence sales. But it constitutes such a rich IB topic that it deserves a deeper dive, as Section III will do.

For the moment, suffice it to say that promotions also have a "place" component, relating to the debate about where advertising should be located in the different markets where a MNE operates. This largely depends on where customers make their purchasing decisions. In B2B interactions, this may be in the office but also at conferences and trade fairs, explaining the major role that travel plays in international marketing. For B2C interactions, the breakdown tends to be between fragmented retail markets such as France – explaining the prevalence of point-of-sales promotions in supermarkets like Centre Leclerc and Carrefour – and mass markets like the USA, where consumers are likely to have already decided which brands they wish to purchase before visiting an outlet, justifying the greater use of pre-sales advertising (on TV or online) in this country. The question then becomes what messages these promotions should actually convey.

Section III. International advertising

As a theoretical background to discussions about MNEs' promotional communications, some readers may find it useful to briefly explore an academic discipline called semiotics (Zakia and Nadin 1987), which is the study of the different ways in which meaning can be created and shared. In an IB context, this discussion is particularly important, given how hard it can often be to transfer to a host market culture the actual meaning that a MNE is trying to convey. Those interested in this subject may wish to investigate a seminal construct known as Peirce's theory of signs, which speaks to the triad interactions between a sign, its object and its interpretant. More than mastering the specifics of semiotics, what is useful to international marketing specialists is to gain awarenss of the cognitive obstacles that can make it so hard to get cross-border messaging right.

IB commentaries are full of often humorous anecdotes about the dangers of inaccurate translations of advertising straplines and/or indelicate visual branding. Frequently cited examples of the former include Ford having once advertised in Belgium that "Every car has a high-quality body" but rendering this in French as "Every car has a high-quality corpse"; Electrolux advertising its vacuum cleaners by saying that "Nothing sucks" like them, equivalent in English-language slang

Fig 11.7
Traditional fairy tales
in one culture may be
incomprehensible to
another.

to admitting that they perform terribly; and HSBC's 2009 strapline, "Assume nothing", which mistranslated in several languages as "Do nothing". Examples of poor brand renditions include an insignia on Nike's Air Max 270 that offended some in the Muslim world because it resembled the word for God in Arabic; Dolce & Gabbana appearing to make fun of Chinese consumers by showing them eating Italian food with chopsticks; or less obnoxiously, but just as ineffectively, Pampers diapers being sold in Japan with the image of a stork carrying a baby, a fairy tale familiar to Western cultures but which had zero meaning in the target market. What is important to consider about all these mishaps is that they were committed by intelligent and experienced international marketing operatives. The question then becomes how this could have happened.

The causes of international advertising mistakes are often similar to the ones evoked above for international marketing in general, including overconfidence in a brand name (and/or insufficient knowledge of target markets); decisions based on assumptions rather than in-depth (hence expensive) ex ante market studies; and a misinterpretation of signals. Normally MNE staff working in a national (or regional) subsidiary, hence in greater proximity to the target market with whom the company wants to interface, might be expected to make fewer errors along these lines. But, of course, decentralising MNE advertising decisions causes its own problems, first and foremost being the much greater probability that brand identity will be blurred if different subsidiaries emit contradictory messages, which is a much bigger issue today than it was in the past, when the absence of Internet communications made it harder for potential consumers to discover that a brand they were being sold, for instance, as representing top-of-the-range value in one market is positioned in neighbouring countries as only being of mid-range quality.

Decentralised advertising also has major financial implications. MNEs spend enormous sums in this area, with the biggest multimedia campaigns easily exceeding $20 million. As a result, many will do almost anything they can to cut spending on the item, often running huge global campaigns instead of differentiated local efforts that would each incur its own hefty agency costs. In 2019, for instance, the global advertising media reported a whopping $587 billion in revenue, up 44 percent in just seven years (Guttman 2020). It is true that this total would plummet in 2020 due to the Covid-19 pandemic, and that MNE-specific cross-border messaging only accounts for part of the global total, alongside other sponsors such as domestic firms and public sector actors. It remains that the biggest advertisers in the world are all MNEs, with Amazon, Proctor & Gamble and L'Oréal – all consumer goods companies, it is worth noting – leading the charge in 2019, spending a staggering $11 billion, $10.7 billion and $10.3 billion, respectively (Brownfield 2020). With such large sums at stake, it is unsurprising that a MNE's global headquarters will often keep a close eye on this activity, supervising MNE subsidiary marketing teams who might normally be expected to have sole responsibility for it: because they know more about local audiences; but also because theirs is the one SBU within a MNE that can warehouse all relevant information in this area (i.e. legalities like the possibility of engaging in comparative advertising, relative importance of digital vs. print media, up-to-date cultural references, etc.).

Assuming that an international marketing campaign run out of global headquarters will be more standardised, the debate then becomes whether this can be culturally effective. The main issue here is whether the images, connotations and references in a given advertisement are sufficiently universal to ensure that it provokes the desired emotional response. For years, for instance, Coca-Cola would advertise its products in Thailand, a warm weather Buddhist country, by showing Santa Claus, a non-Buddhist character, in snow – something that does not at all speak to the Thai experience. It is possible that by creating a contrast with the target culture's everyday life, Coke was seeking to stand out more than it would have done otherwise. Indeed, some MNEs' efforts to highlight rather than underplay their foreignness can be very effective. The example that springs to mind is when US clothing maker GAP used to run its "United Colors" campaign in the UK, employing a spelling that the company's downstream teams would have undoubtedly known differed from the British variant ("colours") yet maintaining the foreign version, precisely because they felt that highlighting the product's American-ness would help sales.

At the same time, an otherness strategy of this kind also carries the risk that part of the host country population will not relate to the advertisement. This can be particularly problematic when the advertiser's credibility has yet to be established, as exemplified by the problems that German winemakers have had marketing their wares across Europe, where consumers typically associate this product with other countries. Note along these lines the origin control measures that certain regions have put in place to protect products they are famous for having developed – Parmesan cheese from Italy, Champagne wine from

Otherness strategy – Decision to highlight foreignness. The opposite of "insiderisation".

Origin control measure – Requirement that production location be certified for items bearing a particular brand name.

France – but which are increasingly being copied by foreign rivals. The purpose here is specifically not to seem local and generic but, quite the contrary, to emphasize specialness.

Above all, standardised international advertising carries a risk of insufficient equivalence between the home and host markets, with the MNE making the mistake of assuming that the connotations and subtexts associated with certain images or themes in one will be understood and/or tolerated in the other. There are several ways that cultural faux pas of this kind can arise. The first involves an insensitive mishandling of topical issues, exemplified by a 2017 Facebook advertisement by Dove, the Unilever brand, purporting to publicise "the diversity of real beauty" but showing pictures of a Black woman pulling a sweater over her head to reveal that she was actually White – at a time when the egregious disrespect of Black citizens in many countries was finally rising to top of the social agenda. In a similar vein and over the same period, the German personal care brand Nivea thought it appropriate to release in the Middle East a skin cream advertisement proclaiming that "White is purity" – a reprehensible statement under any circumstances but particularly given the problems experienced at the time with overtly racist movements in several Western countries. Both advertisements were quickly withdrawn by the MNEs in question, and there is no indication whatsoever that either had the slightest racist intent (and every indication that they did not). But it still needs to be analysed why the international marketing professionals who had approved these campaigns were so unaware of the zeitgeist and sensitivities in the different national markets they were targeting as to believe that the advertisements might ever be acceptable.

Note that there are occasions when a MNE will court notoriety by purposefully being controversial. The most famous example of this approach was the series of advertisements produced by Italian clothing company Bennetton in the 1990s, offering images (a nun and a priest kissing; a Jesus-like figure dying of AIDS) specifically chosen for their shock value, ostensibly doing this to associate the brand with liberation from social conventions, including religion. The exact opposite approach was taken about a decade later by a diamond company De Beers, then owned by South African interests, offering three very different (albeit graphically similarly) visions of a man giving a ring to a woman. In Britain, the De Beers advertisement showed a sedate couple on their 50th wedding anniversary; Saudi Arabians saw a prim and proper image of a middle-aged husband and wife; but Spaniards got highly sexualised images of passionate young fiancés. The decision to shock (or not to shock) potential foreign consumers through advertising is another judgement that international marketing specialists are often called to make.

Further challenges associated with standardised advertising are subtler in nature and involve a more semiotic communication of meaning. One is the use of colours given the different responses they evoke in different cultures; mourning, for instance, is represented by black in many Western societies, but by purple in Italy and white in Japan. In a similar vein, tonality can also vary internationally, with some consumer cultures seemingly preferring serious fact-based infomercials detailing a product's technical qualities, and others leaning more towards humorous advertisements evoking the joyous sentiments associated with its purchase and consumption. The question here is whether the MNE's purpose is to inform foreign customers or to entice them, a dichotomy also affected by the split between B2B and B2C marketing, with the former tending to be more serious and factual in nature and the latter more emotive.

Lastly, there is the challenge for an international advertising campaign of finding a register that will induce different cultures to respond in a similar fashion to one and the same linguistic stimulus. Even with translations that have been done accurately – as is increasingly the case given the growing proficiency of translators worldwide – there is always a possibility that the message will go astray simply because it does not have the same resonance in the target culture as in the original one. This explains why so many international advertisements downplay verbal exchanges and replace them with music – frequently classical music, deemed to be less culture-specific, hence to travel better.

In the end, international advertising often sees MNEs trying to address all these challenges through a hybrid glocalisation compromise where certain elements such as product concept and colour are adapted, while others – like promotions and, above all, the branding – are standardised (Akgun et al. 2014). It is intriguing that notwithstanding ongoing evidence of clear affection for local brands in many domestic markets, there is even greater evidence today of a growing "xenocentric" favouritism in many countries for foreign brands (Balabanis et al. 2019), especially in high-profile sectors like technology where a number of big American names such as Apple, Google, Microsoft, Amazon and Facebook have been very successful at monetising their brand value all across the world (Swant 2020). Stereotyping has a role to play at this level as well, with studies indicating that international branding can be particularly effective when it is congruent with the image that the target audience already has of a MNE's home country (Magnusson et al. 2019). It is further evidence that for marketing, like all other value chain functions, IB is affected as strongly by the way people represent things as by the things themselves.

Attitudes and alternatives

The rise of social marketing as a new approach aligned with today's increasingly widespread sustainability agenda has dominated IB headlines and analyses in recent years. But as always in this field, there is the question whether a given trend represents all customer segments worldwide or just a few small niches. As Chapter 14 will explore in greater detail, the Kuznets curve intimates that it is only when a population has surpassed a certain threshold of affluence that it starts to prioritise social and/or environmental sustainability. This would indicate that MNEs' social marketing efforts should be more extensive in the Global North than in the South. At the same time, that may well be a highly prejudicial preconception, especially given the desperate sustainability challenges that many emerging market populations are currently experiencing. As is so often the case in IB, the real debate for a MNE is whether it wants to be ahead of the pack and "push" certain ideas or if it should instead by "pulled" into certain approaches based on demand emanating from potential customers.

Chapter summary

To differentiate international marketing studies from their domestic variant, the chapter began with an empirical and experiential discussion of the way MNEs' "push" versus "pull" orientations affect this key downstream function, with a particular focus on the kinds of errors that arise most frequently when organisational and/or personal factors skew a MNE's marketing attitudes. It then went on to engage in a more traditional analysis of the traditional marketing mix framework, examining how these parameters materialise in a specifically international environment. The final section delved more deeply into the challenges inherent to cross-border messaging, with special attention paid to the problems associated with international advertising and branding.

Case study 11.3: Volkswagen gets folksy

Volkswagen's international empire expanded at breakneck speed throughout the 20th century and into the early 2000s. This made it increasingly difficult for the Group to control either its operations or its

Fig 11.8
VW's new marketing approach highlights common humanity more than superior technology.

image in the four corners of the world where it has a market presence. An initial response in 2007 was to centralise global management, but that was largely reversed in 2018 when VW decided instead to adopt a somewhat more decentralised structure that assigned to each of its lead brands responsibility for the Group's regional markets: VW itself for the Americas and sub-Saharan Africa; SEAT for North Africa; Audi for the Middle East and Asia-Pacific (asides from China, run by the Group as a whole); and Skoda for Russia and India. The idea, according to group CEO Herbert Diess, was to "to tailor the model range to the relevant market requirements and customers' needs rapidly and effectively on the basis of regional knowledge" and to do this by putting local entities in charge of "coordinating brand activities, partnerships and the exploitation of synergy effects" within each geographic zone without having to get prior approval from global headquarters (Volkswagen 2018). VW's overarching aim was to ensure that the cross-border product adaptation decisions that are at the heart of any MNEs' marketing mix would henceforth be made by people with greater knowledge of the realities on the ground.

Although this change was partially made for operational reasons, it coincided with VW reducing the number of advertising agencies it employed from 40 to 3, seeking to achieve within a few years a 30 percent improvement in the efficiency of its €1.5 billion global marketing budget (Harman 2018). Although the new downstream strategy might appear to have been at odds with its upstream counterpart – with the former instituting less localisation and the latter more – the two approaches were in fact congruent insofar as they established the regional level as the new basis for organising VW's production and marketing thinking. This is in line with the premise formulated in consumer culture theory that it is at the regional level that the global homogenisation of demand preferences is taking place. From now on, VW would assign teams of up to 200 marketing employees to four so-called "powerhouse" centres (Berlin, New York, São Paulo and Beijing), with each bearing full responsibility for producing all communications and advertising within their allotted territory. Digital platforms would also be used to personalise customer contacts where beneficial, but also, and somewhat contradictorily, to lay the foundations for global campaigns whenever the four powerhouses identified brand arguments that had overlapping features and could therefore be shared. In essence, VW was now hoping that it could use technology and restructuring to help its marketing activities overcome the same global versus local dilemma that MNEs face in all other aspects of IB.

The net effect of these moves was to shift power away from global headquarters in Wolfsburg (Germany), raising questions in turn as to why VW felt the need to make such a radical change. Explanations included the critique that VW had been too slow in taking new product design decisions (due to managers' fear of being second-guessed by headquarters), had struggled to adapt to changing consumer preferences in major markets like the USA and/or that its high-quality but upstream-oriented engineering culture had caused it to design models that were too expensive for the new Global South consumers whom they were supposed to target (Cremer 2017). Otherwise, there was also a widespread sense that VW was in desperate need of restoring its brand following the reputational damage it incurred in the wake of the 2015 "Dieselgate" scandal. From 2019 onwards, the "New Volkswagen" would be associated with a lighter and digitally friendlier logo, backed everywhere now with audio advertising featuring a "softer, warmer and pleasant" female voice, the idea being to make the brand appear more relatable. This included increasing the number of advertising images of people with whom potential customers might find it easier to identify. Instead of communicating the (justifiably) positive stereotype of German engineering that had traditionally been one of the hallmarks of this proud MNE's international marketing efforts, VW was now issuing press releases saying that it wanted to reveal a more human face, or as Chief Marketing Officer Jochen Sengpiehl put it, "A new holistic global brand experience [adopting] the customer's perspective to a greater extent". This would include, for instance, plans to market VW's wholesale move into the e-mobility market with a series of films issued in different markets and across different channels: first getting influencers to talk about the need for greater sustainability; then addressing any barriers that might impede potential buyers' migration to electric vehicles; before finally advertising VW's actual products. In the past, Volkswagen might have gone straight to this final message and expected its products to speak for themselves, despite the inherent challenge of attempting the new approach in foreign markets where the MNE would always enjoy less brand loyalty than it did back home. Adversity has taught the Group well, however, and there is every chance that appealing to customers' common humanity will be a more effective way of marketing itself internationally in the future.

Case study questions

1. Is Volkswagen right to organise its marketing efforts along regional lines?
2. How can Volkswagen use technology to optimise its international marketing?
3. Has the generally positive stereotyping of German cars helped or harmed Volkswagen's international marketing efforts?

Chapter discussion questions

1   How much power do MNE marketing specialists wield vis-à-vis their upstream colleagues?

2   To what extent does the dictum "The customer is always right" apply in international business?

3   How effective can adapted international advertising be if the underlying product remains unadapted?

4   Must products sold internationally necessarily come with a higher price than ones sold domestically?

5   How can a MNE headquarters improve its knowledge of distant countries' marketing peculiarities?

References

Akgun, A. et al. (15 September 2014). "Standardization and adaptation of international marketing mix activities: A case study", *Procedia – Social and Behavioral Sciences*, Volume 150, pp. 609–618.

Antonetti, P. (August 2019). "Why consumer animosity reduces product quality perceptions: The role of extreme emotions in international crises", *International Business Review*, Volume 28, Issue 4, pp. 739–753.

Bahadir, S. et al. (2015). "Marketing mix and brand sales in global markets: Examining the contingent role of country-market characteristics", *Journal of International Business Studies*, Volume 46, Issue 5, pp. 596–619.

Balabanis, G. et al. (24 April 2019). "Favouritism towards foreign and domestic brands", *Journal of International Marketing*, Volume 27, Issue 2, pp. 38–55.

Bardhi, F. et al. (26 February 2020). "The effect of globalisation on consumers", accessed 1 January 2021 at https://www.cass.city.ac.uk/

Brownfield, A. (7 December 2020). "P&G dethroned as the world's largest advertiser", accessed 2 January 2021 at https://www.bizjournals.com/

Cova, B. (2007). *Consumer Tribes*, Abingdon: Routledge.

Cowan, N. et al. (December 2019). "Foundations of arrogance: A broad survey and foundations for research", accessed 28 December 2020 at https://journals.sagepub.com/

Cremer, A. (12 July 2017). "After dieselgate, Volkswagen loosens reins on empire", *Reuters*.

Edwards, J. (4 September 2015). "The long, strange history of Lululemon: North America's weirdest clothing brand", accessed 1 January 2021 at https://www.businessinsider.com/

Grad, I. (December 2015). "Ethical considerations on advertising to children", *Postmodern Openings*, Volume 6, Issue, 2, pp. 43–57.

Guttmann, A. (2020). "Global advertising revenue 2012–2024", accessed
    2 January 2021 at https://www.statista.com/

Harman, A. (6 December 2018). "Volkswagen shakes up global
    marketing structure", accessed 31 December 2020 at https://www.
    wardsauto.com/

Harteis, C. et al. (October 2008). "The culture of learning from
    mistakes: How employees handle mistakes in everyday work",
    International Journal of Educational Research, Volume 47, Issue 4,
    pp. 223–231.

Hensel, A. (9 September 2019). "To quadruple its international business
    by 2023, Lululemon takes a local approach", accessed 1 January 2021
    at https://www.modernretail.co/

Huntington, S. (1997). *The Clash of Civilisations and the Remaking of
    World Order*, New York: Simon & Schuster.

Jimenez-Asenjo, N., and Filipescu, D. (August 2019). "Cheers in
    China! International marketing strategies of Spanish wine exporters",
    International Business Review, Volume 28, Issue 4, pp. 647–659.

Khan, H. (April 2019). "How anticipated regret influences the effect
    of economic animosity on consumers' reaction towards a foreign
    product", *International Business Review*, Volume 28, Issue 2,
    pp. 405–414.

Klein, N. (1999). *No Logo*, New York: Picador.

Kraft, P. et al. (January 2012). "International orientation, marketing mix
    and the performance of international German Mittelstand companies",
    International Journal of Business and Globalisation, Volume 8, Issue
    3, pp. 293–315.

Lakshman, S. et al. (May 2017). "The relationship between MNCs'
    strategies and executive staffing", *International Journal of
    Organizational Analysis*, Volume 25, Issue 2, accessed 31 July 2021 at
    https://www.emerald.com/

Legault, M.-J. (February 2016). "Local vs. global marketing with
    Lululemon", accessed 1 January 2021 at https://www.originoutside.
    com/

Levitt, T. (1983). "The globalization of markets", *Harvard Business
    Review Magazine*.

Magnusson, P. et al. (April 2019). "Beyond country image favorability:
    How brand positioning via country personality stereotypes enhances
    brand evaluations", *Journal of International Business Studies*, Volume
    50, pp. 318–338.

Maslow, A. (1954). *Motivation and Personality*, New York: Harper.

San Emeterio, M. et al. (January 2020). "Influence of relationship
    networks on the internationalization process: The moderating effect
    of born-global", *Heliyon*, Volume 6, Issue 1, accessed 31 July 2021 at
    https://www.sciencedirect.com/

Siganos, A., and Tabner, I. (March 2020). "Capturing the role of societal affinity in cross-border mergers...", *Journal of International Business Studies*, Volume 51, pp. 263–273.

Swant, M. (27 July 2020). "Apple, Microsoft and other tech giants top Forbes' 2020 most valuable brands list", accessed 4 January 2021 at https://www.forbes.com/

Volkswagen (22 June 2018). "Volkswagen defines new group structure more precisely: brands assume responsibility for regions", accessed 31 December 2020 at https://www.volkswagenag.com/

Zakia, R., and Nadin, M. (1987). "Semiotics, advertising and marketing", *Journal of Consumer Marketing*, Volume 4, Number 2, pp. 5–12.

CHAPTER 12

Multinational treasury

Introduction

At its most elementary expression, business is comprised of production and sales, being the two main pillars of any company's value chain. International business (IB) occurs when a multinational enterprise (MNE) crosses borders during the execution of one and/or the other of these functions. Finance is often viewed by IB learners as a mere adjunct to a MNE's more material operations – a way of funding them and calculating their viability – possibly explaining why a relatively small percentage of business school graduates envision a career for themselves in multinational treasury, imagining that it is a profession that can be left to specialists and therefore something that they do not need to learn in any great detail.

This preconception is wrong and even dangerous, given how important financial considerations are to the discussions that IB practitioners are bound to have throughout their careers with counterparts both inside and outside of their companies. After all, business requires, among other skills, the ability to count money, if only to assess the viability of a given action. For that reason alone, it is crucial that all IB students possess at least a basic understanding of how MNE treasury operations work. This chapter tries to make that easy.

The two main financial challenges that MNEs face – and the two sections comprising this chapter – relate to the management of foreign exchange (FX)-related risks and to funding needs. Both require companies to develop detailed knowledge at all times of their current and prospective positions, as well as the risks associated with them. This can be a difficult and expensive undertaking, explaining why the vast majority of MNEs spend considerable sums structuring a centralised treasury function capable of providing decision-makers with a snapshot of the group's financial circumstances at any moment in time. The advantage of this approach is that it generates administrative economies of scale and concentrates treasury operatives in just a few locations so that they can share information more easily (Bartsch 2019). There is a small downside to treasury centralisation, however, insofar as it focuses greater attention on group-wide interests to the detriment of those (admittedly relatively few) financial issues that play out at a purely local level, potentially demotivating and even deskilling staff working in a MNE's subsidiaries. It remains that the global

DOI: 10.4324/9781003159056-16

Fig 12.1
Finance permeates all MNE value chain functions.

digitisation of real-time information minimises this risk and maximises centralisation's advantages, at the very least on a regional scale. The end result is that unlike other MNE functions, there is a clear hierarchy in finance between the global and the local perspectives. Out of all the operations that MNEs run, finance is probably the most supranational.

LEARNING OBJECTIVES

After reading this chapter, you will be able to:

- identify the origins of MNEs' foreign exchange risks
- implement FX risk management strategies
- compare MNE funding modalities
- evaluate MNEs' internal movements of funds
- judge MNEs' tax behaviour

Case study 12.1: Foreign exchange is no small beer for Heineken

Transacting in multiple currencies with its network of 165 breweries and countless distributors in more than 70 countries worldwide, giant Dutch brewer Heineken needs to manage its FX positions on a daily basis. Its avowed policy is to minimise risks relating to the changing values of the currencies in which Group units trade. More specifically, Heineken uses **forward contracts** to try and eliminate up to 90 percent of the FX **exposure** that it routinely forecasts, more or less divided between Group revenues (often represented in dollars) versus the production costs that it incurs in different local currencies but largely calculates in euros, being this MNE's **home currency** (i.e. the one in which it books

Forward contracts – Deals where price is agreed today for delivery at a specified future date.

Exposure – Where assets and liabilities do not match for a given commodity whose price fluctuates. Broader conception of "risk".

Home currency – Currency used to calculate a MNE's consolidated global accounts.

Fig 12.2
Heineken's global operations see it managing a host of both "major" and "minor" currencies.

its consolidated annual financial statement). The end result is that Heineken runs minimal risk in most of the world's so-called "major" currencies, that is, the ones for which a liquid market exists. At year-end 2019, for instance, it had been estimated (Heineken 2020) that a 10 percent fall in the value of the dollar against the euro would have reduced the Group's overall equity position by a mere €18 million (vs. €7 million the year before). Given Heineken's €2.5 billion consolidated 2019 profits, this was a very small residual exposure.

Having said that, the major currencies are not the only ones that Heineken trades. Early 2021 results indicated, for instance, that negative FX translations the previous fiscal year had had a negative impact of 5.3 percent on the Group's "top-line" revenues, "mainly driven by the Brazilian real, Mexican peso, Nigerian naira, Russian rouble and South African rand". This was a substantial hit and begs the question of why the MNE fell short in terms of its goal of minimising FX risk.

The response largely resides in the fact that even as Heineken eliminates most of its exposure to variations in the world's major currencies, it still runs positions in the minor (also called "exotic") currencies in which its subsidiaries transact, including the ones listed above, the Vietnamese dong and the currencies of the many African countries where it has generated surprisingly high margins by selling beer at European-level prices despite much lower labour and other operational costs (van Beemen 2019). One reason for this approach may be that exotic currencies are harder to trade due to lesser **liquidity** in these markets, that is, the fact that they have fewer and/or smaller participants. Because Heineken's positions here largely result from the profits it generates in the Global South, it runs a risk that this sector of the FX market will devalue as a whole, which is precisely what happened in early 2020 when traders initially assessed the Covid-19 pandemic as having a particularly bad effect on emerging economies and sold their currencies en masse. It was a worst-case scenario for Heineken's treasury team, an adverse price movement that had occurred suddenly and for entirely unpredictable reasons.

The big question then became what Heineken should do after the value of its portfolio of exotic currencies had already fallen. The MNE could have decided to limit further losses and join the general sell-off, albeit at worse (i.e. lower) prices. In hindsight, however, that would have caused another problem, given the way certain emerging market currencies (like the Chinese yuan) recovered from summer 2020 onwards. Had Heineken decided to sell off its exotic positions when they were at their lowest, it would have not only locked in its losses but also incurred a significant opportunity cost compared to any rivals who might have held on to these currencies and generated windfall profits as they recovered. The problem is that no one has a crystal ball allowing them to predict with certainty when a market move is going to persist or else reverse. For MNE treasury teams managing a FX position, covering risk can be as risky as not covering it.

> **Liquidity** – Where sufficient quanta are being traded in a market to allow the transaction of normally sized deals without any major impact on prices.

Case study questions

1. What factors determine Heineken's foreign exchange risk management policies?
2. What should Heineken have done when its portfolio of exotic currencies devalued?

Section I. Foreign exchange

The first task when identifying a MNE's foreign exchange exposures is to clarify why companies operating in multi-currency environments are at risk when market prices move. After this, analysis will explore the main value chain operations that generate FX risk.

Variable exposures

There are many occasions when a MNE will deal in a currency other than the one traded in its home market. The US dollar, for example, is the standard currency of transaction in commodity markets such as oil or rubber but also for many complex goods like airplanes. For non-dollar-based companies, doing IB in these sectors of activity necessarily generates FX exposures. The opposite applies to companies whose entire value chain involves transactions in a single currency, although they still face an indirect risk given the possibility that rivals' competitiveness could be enhanced by a fortuitous movement in their own currencies.

Managing FX exposure is a costly and difficult process that most MNEs like to avoid if at all possible. For this reason, one key aspect of international contract negotiations tends to be the currency of transaction. The party that is in the stronger position (usually the one that is larger in size, technologically more advanced and/or enjoys a more dominant market position) will generally require that the deal be denominated in its own currency, forcing upon its counterpart the bother of having to manage any FX risk.

A firm is exposed to FX risk if the three following conditions are met:

1   Its assets and/or liabilities (respectively, what it owns and owes) are denominated in different currencies. This is the case for almost all MNEs worldwide.
2   It suffers an "asset-liability gap", that is, its assets in any one currency do not match its liabilities in that same currency. An example here would be German discount airline Eurowings selling to both European and UK customers, thus accumulating assets in both pounds and euros, even as many of its liabilities are in dollars (the currency it uses to buy planes and fuel).
3   The market price of the currency in question varies – as is always the case, unless the price has been "fixed" by government and cannot move.

FX management is based on two fundamental risks. Where a MNE has a long position and owns more assets in a given currency than the liabilities it owes in that same currency, the risk is that the value of this currency will fall before the assets can be sold – meaning that when they are ultimately sold, this will happen at a lower rate. Where a MNE has a short position and owes more liabilities than the assets it owns in a given currency, the risk is that the value of this currency will rise before the liabilities can be acquired, meaning that when they are ultimately purchased, this will happen at a higher rate. Thus, regardless of a MNE's currency of origin, it will be exposed to FX price variations as long as its different currency positions are not equal to zero at all times.

Once the existence of a foreign exchange exposure has been quantified, the next step is to identify the multitude of factors that caused it. These will tend to revolve around the nature of the MNE's international operations (whether it goes abroad via trade or FDI); its configuration (i.e. the locations where it produces and sells goods or services); and how substantial the FX risk is compared to

Denominate – The specified currency in which a transaction takes place.

Long position – Owning more of a commodity in the form of assets than the amounts owed in the form of liabilities.

Short position– Owing more of a commodity in the form of liabilities than the amounts owned in the form of assets.

the company's other financial flows (reflecting its "commitment to internationalisation"). It is only after these evaluations have been done that it can then decide what, if anything, to do about a position.

Types of FX exposure

The main source of MNEs' FX risk is the "transactional" exposure that they incur through their daily value chain activities. For the companies that are the most internationalised (like many of the biggest names in the fast-moving consumer goods sector) and who therefore transact in foreign currencies all the time, such exposures are a daily fact of life. Of course, the opposite can be said about other companies (i.e. in the construction sector) for whom FX transactions tend to be more sporadic.

Transactional FX risks

The first category is *commercial risk*, which happens when a MNE exports goods or services to a customer and receives foreign currency in payment. Sales of this kind increase the seller's "long" exposure. As shown in Figure 12.3, one example would be a euro-based German SME selling beer in the UK and receiving payment in the customer's domestic currency, the pound. Given that the currency in which the German accrues its export revenues differs from the domestic currency in which it incurs costs, it is exposed to the risk that the pound will fall in value against the euro before the company has had enough time to sell its receipts. Note that from the perspective of the British importer, on the other hand – buying foreign goods in pounds and selling them on in the same currency – the deal would not create any FX exposure (unless the supply contract stipulates that future prices be adjusted to account for currency variations).

Operational risk is the opposite of commercial risk and arises when a firm buys goods or services from a supplier and pays in foreign currency. These purchases increase the importer's "short" exposure. Returning to the Germany-UK example, if the British firm were to pay its German supplier in euros, it would be exposed to the risk that this

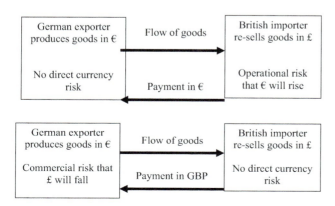

Fig 12.3
FX risk for a German export to the UK depends on the currency of transaction.

Table 12.1
Hypothetical long versus short currency exposures. Net calculations

	Position subsidiary A	Position subsidiary B	Net group exposure	Risk
In dollars ($)	+10	−5	Long $: +5	$ will fall
In yen (¥)	−20	+10	Short ¥: −10	¥ will rise
In euros (€)	+5	−20	Short €: −15	€ will rise
In sterling (£)	0	+5	Long £: +5	£ will fall

foreign currency will rise in value against its home currency, the pound, increasing its import costs. The German exporter, on the other hand, would have no direct FX exposure since it would be transacting in its home currency – attesting again to the fact that it is the currency of transaction that determines whether it is the exporter who is going to be assuming a commercial risk or the importer an operational risk.

This example represents a simple situation where one firm faces a single exposure as a result of one cross-border deal. Things are very different for many, if not most, MNEs insofar as they operate day in, day out in a multi-currency environment, incurring costs and accumulating revenues in many currencies worldwide. It is commonplace for a MNE subsidiary in one country (i.e. in Switzerland) to accumulate assets and liabilities denominated in euro, USD, yen and other currencies alongside the Swiss franc, while a sister unit (i.e. in Japan) has its own exposure to these very same currencies and to others as well. That is why MNEs tend as a matter of course to calculate their transactional FX risks on a **net basis**, not only within each unit but consolidating all units worldwide. Thus, as demonstrated in Table 12.1, a multinational group will not calculate its exposure to each of the four currencies represented here based on the risks that subsidiary A or B faces separately but only after combining the two units' positions.

Net basis – Remaining exposure after a firm's short positions in a given financial category has been subtracted from its long positions in the same category.

Non-transactional FX risks

A third category of FX exposure is called *translational* risk and occurs when FX variations have an impact on a company's efforts to convert foreign assets or liabilities back into its home currency. This includes the profits that a MNE's foreign subsidiaries send back to headquarters in the form of dividends, foreign currency loans that a MNE makes or receives and, above all, the value of foreign assets. Take a Japanese firm that owns a factory in the USA. Table 12.2 shows how currency variations could affect its year-end results without the company having engaged in further international dealings. In this example, the value of the firm's overseas assets does not change in host country terms, but it does when translated back into the home currency.

Analysts have long wondered whether it is desirable for companies to protect themselves against translational risk (Bonini et al. 2016). The question arises because some companies configure their international

Table 12.2
Translational risk. MNEs' foreign assets are automatically exposed to FX variations

	Year 1	Year 2
Current valuation of US factory in dollars	$100 million	$100 million (unchanged)
Dollar/yen exchange rate	$1 = ¥110	$1 = ¥100
Current valuation of US factory in yen	¥11 billion (100 million X 110)	¥10 billion (100 million X 100)
Book loss between year 1 and year 2	¥1 billion	

operations in such a way as to diversify exposures so that the risks encountered in one currency zone are almost always offset by the risks faced elsewhere. In this case, hedging any component of the group's FX risk would disturb the overall balance and create new exposures.

A fourth source of FX exposure is *speculative* risk. MNEs are free to decide what percentage of their currency risk they want to offset. A company might reason that its treasury specialists are as competent at currency trading as the bank with whom they currently offload their positions and authorise their teams to trade directly in the FX markets. Of course, this creates a greater volatility of earnings, since the treasury team is just as likely to lose money as to make money with the currency exposures that it leaves uncovered. Interesting academic research exists indicating a connection between a company's tendency to speculate in the financial markets and the value systems epitomising its senior managers (Beber and Fabbri 2011), encapsulated, for instance, in different practitioners' vision of a company's purpose. This includes their inclination to succumb to financialisation pressures from so-called active shareholders requiring that everything possible be done to maximise short-term returns – including by speculating on currencies, even when this was not part of the company's original mission. The debate "to hedge or not to hedge" – hence, conversely, how much FX speculation risk a MNE might be willing to assume – raises issues that go beyond pure financial analysis.

Lastly, it is worth noting that the different FX exposures discussed above involve risks that can be identified (hence attended to) more or less immediately. This differs from *economic risk*, which relates to long-term movements in the currencies of the countries where a MNE has interests. An interesting example of economic risk is the Japanese yen's decades-long rise from a 1949 rate of 360 per US dollar to an August 2021 rate of around 109 (and as high as 80 several years previous). Back in the 1950s and 1960s, when the yen was much weaker than it is today, Japanese companies manufacturing at home (and therefore incurring costs in yen) could embark on a long-term development path centred on massive exports to the USA of consumer durables like automobiles and electronics. The substantial receipts that they accumulated sparked the

Hedging – Where a party offsets an original risk through a new deal exposing it to the exact opposite risk. The original exposure is called the "underlying" risk. The new exposure is called the "hedge".

US dollar's decades-long downtrend against the yen. This had the effect of making their exports more expensive in the American market and put pressure on Japanese exporters to cut their dollar retail prices (hence their profit margins) to maintain market share. Because Japan's strategy at the time was to consolidate its new role as a global player, most of its exporters accepted lower margins, compensating through greater productivity measures. Fortunately for them, they already had the Toyota Production System (see Chapter 10) to deploy towards that end.

At a certain point, however, the yen had risen so high, and the dollar fallen so low, that it was no longer possible for Japan-based manufacturers to compete profitably. This currency squeeze, in conjunction with the quotas that US authorities decided to levy on Japanese car imports, was one of the main reasons given for the famous decision taken by major Japanese carmakers such as Toyota and Honda to engage in massive foreign direct investment (FDI) in the United States from the 1970s onwards. Once these and other Japanese MNEs had diversified their production locations, the negative effect of further dollar weakness on their US revenues would be largely offset by the concomitant positive effect of lowering their new US production costs. In this way, FDI became a prime vehicle for managing FX-related economic risk.

Of course, FDI is a demanding structural action that will only be undertaken once a MNE is convinced that the FX problem requiring resolution is just as fundamental in nature. The big challenge here is predicting when a currency price trend is going to continue over the long term or if it is likely to revert to its mean value over time. No one has perfect knowledge of the future, so decisions made in this respect will always be judgement calls. Nor is FDI a panacea. A MNE can also suffer indirect economic risk, for instance, if it has a rival whose manufacturing operations are run out of a country with a weak currency, and which exports from this cheap locale. The MNE may then rush to build up its own productive capacity in the same location to match its competitor's lower cost base – as several Western European carmakers did in Eastern Europe in the years immediately following the region's abandonment of communism – but this can create other problems, starting with the operational difficulties that the company might encounter in certain environments (see Chapter 13). As important as FX is to MNE decision-making about market entry possibilities like FDI, like almost everything else in IB, it needs to be assessed in conjunction with a multitude of other factors.

Managing FX risk

As exemplified by Japanese exporters' historic response to the long-term rise in the yen, whenever a company fears that an adverse currency movement is destined to have lasting effects, reconfiguring its entire global value chain may be the only viable response. Immediate exposures, on the other hand, can be dealt with through simpler

Currency squeeze – Where the currencies in which a MNE is long (or, conversely, short) as a result of its international configuration tend to fall (or, conversely, rise) to the point of making IB impossible without some structural reconfiguration.

mechanisms, first and foremost being short-term financial hedging. Understanding how MNEs manage their FX risk means studying both these time horizons.

Long-term "natural" hedging

Where a MNE suffers durably from a FX squeeze – that is, when its configuration tends to accumulate assets in a tendentially weakening currency and/or liabilities in a tendentially strengthening currency – the only possible responses are to either change the currencies in which it denominates assets and liabilities and/or to change the locations where it does business so that its assets and liabilities are more evenly matched. Configurational adaptations of this kind are referred to as "natural hedging".

In terms of long-term upstream ("buy-side") actions, there are two ways of increasing liabilities (i.e. developing a cost base) in currencies that are expected to fall over the long term. The quickest and easiest is to source greater quantities of components from suppliers invoicing in that currency – being one of the leading explanations for skyrocketing international outsourcing volumes since the 1980s. A costlier and less flexible (but more structural) way is through upstream FDI, which involves the MNE manufacturing more either out of countries whose currencies it predicts will weaken over time or – less speculatively – starting to produce more in the same countries where it already sells. The difference between these two approaches is that the latter diminishes the MNE's overall exposure; a further weakening of the currency in question may reduce the relative value of sales in that locale but will do the same to any costs incurred there. In this way, upstream FDI can help a company to offset its long-term "long" exposures.

Notwithstanding the robustness of this mechanism, there remains some uncertainty as to how managers' expectations of a currency's future prospects affect their willingness to undertake FDI (Veeramani et al. 2020). One view is that MNEs will be reluctant to invest in a country with a currency that they predict will weaken, if only because the assets they accumulate there will ultimately be devalued when they are consolidated back into the MNE's global accounts at the lower future exchange rate (Morrissey and Udomkerdmongkol 2008). Similarly, other studies find that countries with currencies currently trading higher than they are expected to in the future are likely to receive less inward investment, probably because MNEs are daunted by the higher greenfield or brownfield outlays that they have to make in the short run (Nayak and Sahoo 2020). As always in IB, decisions in the FX realm are necessarily made in a context of uncertainty.

Otherwise and in terms of long-term downstream ("sell-side") actions, MNEs can try to increase revenues denominated in the currencies in which they currently pay suppliers and/or where they already incur manufacturing costs. A case in point is the situation facing many Western MNEs who source product from China. Given the country's massive export surplus, its currency (the renminbi) is widely expected to appreciate over the decades to come. Until now, most MNEs have used China solely as a manufacturing base, but the prospect of a higher renminbi, combined with Chinese consumers' rising purchasing power, means that many are now looking to sell more into this market, partially motivated by their hope that the expected rise in renminbi-denominated production costs can be offset by higher revenues in the same currency. Of course, it is rarely clear whether a company's motive for increasing sales in one country stems from a desire to offset currency risk or to simply take advantage of market growth, since the two often go hand in hand (with countries where incomes are rising theoretically supposed to have stronger currencies). As so often, the goal is to achieve the virtuous circle of aligning internal strategy with fortuitous external circumstances.

Short-term financial hedging

Where MNEs have no vision of a currency's long-term strength, they will often cover any exposure they have to it by hedging in the foreign exchange market. By creating new exposures diametrically opposed to the original risks associated with their normal IB transactions, hedging protects companies against adverse future price movements for however long the hedge lasts. The FX market offers a wide variety of relatively cheap and accessible instruments that can be used towards this end. One is a forward contract, where counterparts establish today at what price an exchange will take place at a specified date in the future – with the forward price varying from today's "spot" rate after adjustments have been made for the two currencies' interest rate differential. Otherwise, companies have the possibility of trading FX options, a kind of insurance policy where the purchaser pays a premium in order to own the right (but not the obligation) to sell or buy a given quantity of a given currency at a given "strike" price on a specified date. Lastly, of course, there is the spot rate at which an immediate transaction can be made. Fundamentally, however, the long/short approaches described above will always apply, regardless of the trading instrument being used.

Unlike structural reconfigurations of a company's value chain through natural hedging, however, with short-term hedges the initial exposure will reappear once the deal arrives at maturity – creating a possibility that any new hedge will be transacted at a less favourable rate. Moreover, recurring short-term hedges increase the transaction costs that a MNE pays every time a deal is done: the market-maker (usually a bank) will always monetise the service it provides in assuming its counterpart's FX risk by buying currency at one price and selling it at a higher price, with the spread between the two rates working to the disadvantage of the "price-taker". Of course, it is always possible that when one hedge matures, the next might be done at a more advantageous rate. This adds a speculative component to the hedging decision itself, which is somewhat ironic, considering that hedging is

Foreign exchange (FX) market – Virtual marketplace(s) where currency prices are set through market supply and demand.

Market-maker – Trader who is always prepared to quote other market participants a price to buy ("bid") and sell ("offer") a given commodity.

Spread – Difference between market-maker's "bid" and "offer" prices.

used precisely because non-financial MNEs are trying to reduce their speculative risk.

Tables 12.3a and 12.3b demonstrate the successive steps taken by MNE treasurers when they call a market-maker to hedge either a long or a short FX risk, exemplified here by the US dollar versus the Korean won. The sequence is the same in both cases: the MNE assesses its underlying transactional exposure, and then does a new deal with its counterpart to create the opposite risk. In so doing, it fixes the exchange rate irrespective of subsequent price movements in the currency market, and irrespective of the instrument used to do the deal.

Because hedging provides companies with an advantage (risk reduction), it necessarily has a cost. After all, as business economists so often say, there is no such thing as a free lunch. This complicates decisions about how much of a MNE's FX exposure it should actually hedge. Some variables affecting that decision are more strategic in nature. Firm size is one such factor, since SMEs generally find it harder to manage systematic hedging programmes (and are likely to get wider, hence worse, bid-offer spreads than big MNEs). Otherwise, there is the question of whether a company views its treasury department as a profit

Table 12.3a
Korean exporter offsetting long ($) exposure with a short hedge

	Step 1. Exporter notes long exposure, i.e. risk that $ will fall vs. won	*Step 2. It therefore shorts (sells) $ against won to hedge against this (long) risk*	*Net effect*
Scenario (a). If $ then falls. . .	Underlying position loses money as feared (−)	Hedge makes money (+)	Zero: profit on hedge offsets underlying loss
Scenario (b). If $ then rises. . .	Underlying position makes unexpected "windfall" profit (+)	Hedge loses money (−)	Zero: loss on hedge offsets windfall profit

Table 12.3b
Korean importer offsetting short ($) exposure with a long hedge

	Step 1. Importer notes short exposure, i.e. risk that $ will rise vs. won	*Step 2. It therefore goes long (buys) $ against won to hedge this (short) risk*	*Net effect*
Scenario (a). If $ then rises...	Underlying position loses money as feared (−)	Hedge makes money (+)	Zero: profit on hedge offsets underlying loss
Scenario (b). If $ then falls...	Underlying position makes unexpected "windfall" profit (+)	Hedge loses money (−)	Zero: loss on hedge offsets windfall profit

or cost centre, how big a currency risk is involved compared to the company's total volumes and the ancillary consideration that hedging stabilises earnings by reducing FX-related uncertainty, something that creditors might find reassuring and therefore be more willing to lend the company funds at a lower interest rate.

As aforementioned, however, other factors affecting the "hedge or not to hedge" decision are more subjective in nature. Depending on the business culture, most non-financial MNEs do not see FX speculation as a part of their mission, meaning they will hedge at least 90 percent of any exposure they have. After all, not hedging can lose a company a great deal of money. Given the loss-aversion psychology characterising many MNE treasurers, this may not seem a risk worth taking, that is, unless they have supreme confidence in their ability to predict the likelihood of adverse currency movements hitting any unhedged positions that they may be running. This kind of self-belief will depend on factors like general market volatility but also on the trust treasury operatives place in their internal forecasting models, which tend to be split between chart-based "technical" analysis aimed at discerning short-term market sentiment ("bullish" optimism vs. "bearish" pessimism) as opposed to a more long-term "fundamental" analysis of macro-economic aggregates (i.e. GDP growth, trade or budget deficits, inflation, estimated purchasing power parity) where currency predictions are based on the economic performance of the countries whose currencies are being traded.

Purchasing power parity – Theory that currency rate movement reflects the ability of consumers in different economies to buy one and the same basket of goods.

A MNE's decision to manage its own currency risk rather than hedging it away will also be affected by its attitudes towards the transaction costs associated with all FX deals, comprised, as noted above, of the market maker's bid-offer spread, which will be more competitive in calm and/or liquid markets than in volatile and/or illiquid conditions (Skillman 2013). On top of this, companies that lock in prices through systematic hedging exclude any possibility of windfall profits, unlike their unprotected rivals. Lastly, there is a notion in portfolio theory that investors may hold an equity stake in a MNE specifically because the currency risk that is associated with it offsets the other risks to which its shareholders are exposed through the other assets comprising their portfolio (Markowitz 1959). In short, there are just as many arguments against over-hedging as for under-hedging. In treasury operations as in other MNE functions, there truly is no one-best-way of doing IB.

Section II. Multinational funding

Working capital – Excess of long-term liabilities over long-term assets. Indicates level of long-term funding available to companies to help fund their operating cycle.

MNE treasurers' second crucial mission is securing the capital that is vital to their company's survival: working capital for short-term operational purposes, and long-term resources enabling the acquisition of assets when desired while also providing a margin of security when times get tough. Besides certain exceptionally cash-rich companies, it is hard to imagine a MNE generating all the cash it needs internally. This means that MNE treasury officers usually entertain relationships with external fund providers.

External funding sources

Where the funds that a MNE raises through its internal operations do not suffice for its needs, it must source them externally. Generally, there are two categories: debt (borrowings) and equity (shares).

Debt finance

MNE debt tends to be divided between loans from banks or borrowings in the financial markets.

Bank lending

The banking industry has developed a wide range of products tailored to the many different situations that MNEs face when transacting IB. The list is too long to be detailed here but suffice it to say that terms can be very competitive for the largest, most desirable MNE borrowers – most of whose deals will therefore be transacted with the largest financial counterparts. Having said that, there are still a few country-specific financial products that can only be sourced from national banks. For that reason, MNEs generally tend to work with shortlists of global banks while maintaining relations with a few smaller ones providing specialised local services and information.

The traditional "transformation" model of bank lending involves savers depositing short-term funds with banks, which then lend them on to corporate (and other) borrowers, often for a longer period of time. In this system, the bank serves as a screen between providers and users of capital. Its gross margin is the difference between the interest it pays on deposits versus what it receives on loans.

The model revealed its shortcomings during the 1980s when several large debtor nations, such as Peru and Brazil, defaulted on their debt repayments, raising fears about the solvency of some of the world's biggest banks. To reinforce the global financial system, in 1988 the Bank for International Settlements (BIS) sponsored a capital adequacy agreement called Basel I (extended over the years by Basel II and Basel III) specifying that banks should hold equity capital equal to at least 8 percent of their assets (mainly their outstanding loans). To meet this so-called Cooke ratio, many banks reduced their direct lending volumes and began acting instead as intermediaries between investors and borrowers, receiving fees for facilitating and underwriting companies' security issuance in both domestic and global capital markets. It is this "securitisation" focus that explains the explosion in international financial volumes since the 1980s.

Security issuance – Creation of tradable capital market instruments like stocks and bonds that companies sell to investors to raise capital.

Capital markets – Virtual but also physical locations where all medium- and long-term debt and equity transactions are traded.

Greater securitisation does not mean that banks no longer lend directly to corporate borrowers. Indeed, for SMEs too small to issue securities, banks remain crucial partners. All that has happened is that bank lending now constitutes one funding source among several others.

Debt markets

The two main considerations when MNEs issue debt (called "bonds" when they extend beyond a certain maturity) are whether investors are attracted by the general interest rates that the corporate sector is paying as a whole and how a specific borrower's creditworthiness is perceived. Investors confident of recovering the funds they lend will demand lower interest rates than ones worried whether they will be reimbursed. The standard way of representing this is the "risk premium" that creditors require a company to pay before agreeing to lend to it. Expressed in basis points, the risk premium can be envisioned as the "credit spread" that exists between the yields which creditors require from potential borrowers characterised by a certain level of risk as opposed to what they would ask from a zero-risk borrower (usually the government). Clearly, the more worried people are about a MNE's ability to repay its debts, the higher the risk premium that it will be asked to pay.

The same applies to the duration of borrowings. Because the distant future is more uncertain than the near term, generally there will be a lower credit spread on short-term "money market" loans, which tend to be priced in line with recognised benchmarks such as the London Interbank Offered Rate (LIBOR). MNE treasurers seeking to fund their companies at the lowest possible cost will therefore generally pay very close attention to the difference between short- and long-term interest rates (called the "yield curve") when deciding the duration of the debt that they want to issue, but also to detect market sentiment about an economy's future growth and/or inflation prospects.

The problem with credit spreads, however, is that they can widen rapidly if investors have cause to downgrade weaker borrowers. The 2011–2012 European sovereign debt crisis, for instance, saw money pouring out of bank securities (or debt issued by countries running large deficits such as Greece, Spain or Italy) into bonds issued by reputedly safer governments like the USA or Germany. Effectively, this raised the cost of capital for the borrowers whose bonds were being sold off. The same happened early on in the 2020 Covid-19 pandemic when investors shifted from emerging market bonds to debt issued by so-called "safe haven" borrowers. Perceptions of creditworthiness are influenced by the scores awarded by "ratings" agencies such as Standard and Poor's or Moody's. A highly rated (i.e. "Triple A") borrower will be asked to pay a much lower interest rate than one with a lower rating (i.e. "Triple B"), explaining why being upgraded or downgraded is such a big event in a MNE's life. The downgrading of famous household names (such

Basis point – 100th of 1 percent. A common unit in international finance.

as Citigroup or Bank of America) in late 2011, and indeed of the UK government in 2020 (beset by the double whammy of Covid-19 and Brexit), caused creditors to withdraw funds at the very moment when they were most needed.

A second topic when analysing a MNE's debt market funding possibilities is whether the company wants to sell its bonds to domestic interests or to offshore parties – so-called euro-investors – operating outside of a national government's jurisdiction. This is largely a question of who has the greatest appetite for the bonds that the MNE is issuing. A number of technical considerations also play out at this level. Offshore markets often feature lower transaction costs and tax advantages; domestic exchanges offer greater transparency and regulation. These latter benefits are often seen as outweighing the former, both in markets where home-country investors are afforded higher levels of protection (Huang et al. 2020) and, more generally, where institutional investors (usually fund managers) have been required by their internal statutes to only purchase securities traded on a domestic exchange. Despite much press coverage about the globalisation of finance, most people continue to invest the lion's share of their savings in their home markets. The end result is a very uneven distribution of capital worldwide, a situation exacerbated by wide variations in national savings rates.

Financial markets worldwide are generally very keen to get foreign companies to list their bonds (and shares) locally, particularly given evidence of the crucial role that MNE issuers can play in getting investors limited to trading on "imperfect" local exchanges to diversify their portfolios, thereby increasing their willingness to invest more and by so doing lowering the general cost of capital (Mihav and Naranjo 2019). One element in the competition between financial centres is the cost of listing securities. A key factor here is the different levels of disclosure that companies are required to make in different countries. Providing in-depth information on group activities is expensive and therefore something that some MNEs will try to minimise. A further consideration is the level of security afforded to different classes of investors worldwide, with some countries (like Germany) offering greater protection to creditors and others (like Australia) favouring shareholders (Anderson et al. 2012). Note along these lines an ongoing concern whether relatively immature Global South exchanges offer investor protection to an international standard (Deakin et al. 2018). MNEs need to take all these variables into account when deciding where to list their securities. As a result, their external funding efforts often end up by resembling a patchwork of distinct channels.

One final way that credit considerations affect corporate borrowings relates to the guarantees they might be required to provide. MNEs often record debt in the name of a small subsidiary, sometimes an offshore vehicle specifically set up for this purpose. The practice, known as "ring-fencing", ensures that when times are tough and loan reimbursements

Disclosure – Provision of information, often in a specified form to comply with legal requirements.

become problematic, creditors can only make claims against assets held by this one subsidiary. From lenders' perspective, of course, it is safer to have loans secured against the assets of the whole group. One surprising aspect of an IB career is how much time will be spent negotiating which entity has responsibility for a particular liability.

Equity finance

The second external source of funding is equity capital. Here, investors purchase shares in the hope that their price will rise in the future. Share price changes reflect not only general economic conditions but also expectations of a company's future profitability, something influenced by many variables.

One factor that is specifically under the control of a MNE's treasury operation is the extent to which it might seek to improve the return on equity (ROE) by increasing the amount of debt the company issues in proportion to its equity capital. This "leverage" strategy, also called "gearing", has a high risk/reward profile. If things go well, the company can achieve a greater return on equity by funding its operations using money borrowed from other people. If things go poorly, however, it must still reimburse its debt, increasing the risk of bankruptcy. Generally, leverage is more typical of American MNEs, which have historically had higher debt-to-equity ratios than their European and Japanese counterparts. This means that US companies often achieve higher returns but also tend to experience greater earnings volatility. That might make them more attractive to some international investors but less so to others who prefer a more conservatively managed balance sheet.

A second distinction in international equity finance exists between "passive" and "active" approaches. The former involves situations where foreign investors do not get directly involved in managing a company whose shares they acquire. Active shareholders, on the other hand, do intervene. Note that this latter category, increasingly comprised of foreign institutional investors desirous of maximising short-term financial returns and therefore ready to pressurise CEOs into adopting strategies which serve that purpose (Fontana et al. 2019), has been on the rise since the 1980s. There are mixed feelings about this development. In some societies (generally ones marked by attitudes of economic patriotism), the presence of active foreign shareholders can be resented, especially if they are accused of ignoring local stakeholders' aspirations. On the other hand, having international institutional investors on a national company's board of directors has also been shown to improve the general level of financial monitoring (Lei 2019), particularly in countries otherwise characterised by weak investor protections – a positive contribution by any measure. It is difficult when discussing multinational equity finance, like almost every other IB topic, to determine to what extent analysis of a situation is neutral or skewed by the analyst's personal politics.

Case study 12.2: It's up to you,
Hong Kong, Hong Kong

Given the costs associated with rights issues, most MNEs seeking to raise equity capital might theoretically prefer to list their shares on a single exchange and hope that investors worldwide will flock to buy them there. The problem is that a sizable proportion of all long-term stock market trading is done by institutional investors, many of whose funds are obliged by their own statutes of incorporation to only invest domestically: because they are more familiar with local disclosure provisions; or because the national government prefers to see the savings amassed in a country staying there. Having said that, if a MNE were to issue all its shares on a single exchange, it would soon create a glut. That would ultimately have the effect of driving down investor demand, forcing the company to eventually sell even more shares in order to raise the same amount of capital, thereby diluting existing shareholders' ownership prerogatives. Keenly aware of this limitation, MNEs are long accustomed to "cross-listing" their shares on several exchanges worldwide, thereby broadening the investor pools that they can tap into.

Certain stock exchanges dominate globally, if only because they represent big equity players' favourite hunting grounds. At the top of the list comes the New York Stock Exchange (NYSE), due to the sheer size of the national economy it represents and because of American savers' traditional preference for equity investments. It was therefore no surprise that many of the Chinese MNEs who expanded so rapidly over the course of the 2010s would list their stock inter alia on the NYSE. This general trend eventually turned into something akin to a tidal wave,

Fig 12.4
Several Chinese tech companies have repatriated their share listings back to Hong Kong.

Stock market capitalisation – Market value of company, calculated by number of shares issued times the share price.

amounting by February 2019 to 156 Chinese companies representing a total **stock market capitalisation** of $1.2 trillion (USCC 2020). On the face of things, it was a trend that had been beneficial both to Chinese interests seeking equity capital and to American investors seeking diversification.

The relationship was never seamless, in part due to long-standing doubts in the US market about the accuracy of Chinese accounting methods. However, in and of itself this one obstacle never seemed insurmountable, as witnessed by the steady rise in the volume of capital that the Chinese were able to access in the US. Things began to change, however, as political tensions between Beijing and Washington spilled over into the financial arena. In 2020, after more than three years of the USA's former Trump administration constantly criticising Chinese trade surpluses (and making wild accusations regarding its role in the Covid-19 outbreak, something Beijing bitterly resented), the US Senate began preparing legislation that would culminate in Chinese companies being de-listed in the US if they did not start complying with American accounting standards (Lockett et al. 2020). US index provider MSCI made a similar move by removing from its index Chinese companies with links to the country's military, including giant chipmaker SMIC. In response, many of these MNEs took a new look at Hong Kong, one of Asia's leading financial centres and a market whose deep investor pools made it attractive despite certain ongoing political and social unrest (Ruehl and Riordan 2020).

This potential "homecoming" – actively courted by Hong Kong-based bankers seeking to burnish their local pipeline of high-quality Chinese technology stocks – would constitute a huge step towards financial deglobalisation, similar to the repatriation of funding channels that the world last witnessed during the international credit crunch accompanying the USA's 2008 subprime mortgage crisis. Having Chinese companies delist from a foreign stock exchange to move back to Hong Kong would bolster the city's status as a domestic financial centre, but also potentially as a regional one. After all, the huge Regional Comprehensive Economic Partnership (RCEP) trade deal that 14 Asian countries (including China) signed in 2020 included a very strong financial services liberalisation chapter. This augurs well for cross-border funding flows within Asia at least, raising in turn the question of whether the future of international finance will play out on more of a regional scale than a global one.

Case study questions

1. What effects can politics have on international equity finance?
2. What chance is there that equity finance will be done in the future on more of a regional than a global basis?

A MNE will often organise an international "road show" to convince foreign investors of its shares' attractiveness. The question then becomes where they might be found. The big institutional investors working out of the world's major financial centres are, as aforementioned, very well known. They can range from huge pension funds such as CALPERS (representing California state employees) to speculative "hedge funds", investment groups (called mutual funds in the US and unit trusts in the UK) and increasingly sovereign wealth funds like China's State Administration of Foreign Exchange, UAE's ADIA or Norway's Government Pension Fund, a sector that, according to the giant consultancy PWC, had around $15 trillion of assets under management in 2020. But the big-name investors are not the only international equity funding sources that MNEs can try to tap, especially the small and medium-sized enterprises (SMEs) who tend to be excluded from the larger stock exchanges due to minimum size and longevity thresholds. SMEs have the possibility of turning to the small exchanges that many countries have created to try and incentivise high-tech entrepreneurship. Examples include Nasdaq in the USA, JASDAQ in Japan and the UK's Alternative Investment Market. Otherwise, during their start-up phases, they might also seek venture capitalists interested in their long-term prospects – a historically domestic funding source that has become more international in recent years as "dragons" (professional fund managers) spread their wings to seek opportunities beyond their local shores.

Beyond this, there is a broader category of equity finance called "private equity", in reference to non-public dealings where small groups of professional investors converse directly with budding entrepreneurs (and on occasion, with large concerns). Private equity was the main funding vehicle used to launch the companies that drove the information technology revolution that swept out of California's Silicon Valley in the 1980s to create some of the world's largest MNEs today. Lastly, a more recent equity finance innovation is the rise of SPACs (special purpose acquisition companies), entities created to acquire heretofore private (i.e. unlisted) companies and make them public without having to go through certain unwieldy processes. First launched in the USA in the 1990s, these vehicles have also internationalised in recent years to intervene on different stock exchanges worldwide, attesting once again to the key role that imitation plays in the launch of new IB ventures.

Internal funding sources and uses

In addition to managing a MNE's foreign exchange and external funding needs, multinational treasury teams also have a number of more internally oriented responsibilities. Examples include investment planning, simulation, budgeting, management control, accounting, reporting, cash management, insurance and tax management. The end effect of centralising all these activities is to make treasury officers, as much if not more than anyone else, the people with the widest overview of everything that is actually happening in the group, thereby, arguably, turning finance into the most strategic of all value chain functions.

Treasurers complement their control over a MNE's external funding relationships with their supervision of the way cash is distributed among group units. This is crucial for several reasons. Due to the specialist role that is being increasingly performed by MNE subsidiaries operating under a fragmented, vertically disintegrated logic, cash tends to be distributed very unevenly. Some units will be "long" and have more cash than they need, often because they have a sales function. Others are "short" and have less than they need, often because they have a production function. Such imbalances require close monitoring: because they have tax implications (see below); because they have FX implications; but also because as MNEs do more business in Global South nations characterised by comparatively underdeveloped financial markets, they may find it harder to fund subsidiaries there, hence will need to rely more on cash sourced from elsewhere within the group (Islam and Mozumdar 2007). It is a vision where treasurers serve as bankers to the whole of the MNE.

Netting

Like FX, banks will usually quote debt instruments with a bid-offer spread. On other occasions, they will charge fees for this service. Thus, every time a company trades with a bank, it incurs a cost: lending any surplus funds it has at a below-market interest rate, or borrowing the funds it needs at an above-market interest rate. It is therefore in companies' interest to transact as few external deals as possible. Towards this end, many MNEs create a "netting" department that recycles long units' surplus cash to fund short units' deficits. By internalising this clearing process, they can reduce the number of operations they do with the outside world.

Clearing – Process of calculating and paying net differences between the amounts due to/owed by system participants.

To perform this function, MNE treasurers will take a snapshot of the different cash positions that each SBU is running in each of the currencies that it trades. This can be a challenge for firms running widely flung global operations, one requiring a high-performance information system, the backbone of all global finance. Indeed, with their Reuters and Bloomberg screens, spreadsheets, cash-flow simulation models and economic research papers, MNE treasury departments often resemble bank trading rooms.

MNE subsidiaries may have their own accounting and cash teams, but to get a full view of group needs, save on overhead and maximise innovation (Sarkanova and Kristofik 2018), many, if not most, companies will run their strategic financial operations out of a regional treasury centre (rather than a global one, due to time zone factors). Such offices are often located in tax jurisdictions that treat MNEs' internal flows favourably: Belgium for Europe, Singapore for Asia (see Case study 12.3) and Delaware for the United States.

Fig 12.5
Brussels tends to attract MNEs' EMEA time zone treasury centres.

To demonstrate the principle of netting, take a MNE whose internal currency is the US dollar and where unit A has a cash surplus of $10 million that it wants to leave on deposit for a period of three months in order to earn interest – with its sister unit B needing to borrow $20 million, also for three months. If a bank quoted three-month dollar deposits with an annual rate of 1.75–2.00 percent (a realistic level and bid-offer spread in December 2019 before the Covid-19 pandemic erupted and skewed interest rates) and if the two units were to trade separately, unit A would lend its $10 million surplus for three months at the bank's 1.75 percent borrowing rate (receiving $43,750 in interest), whereas unit B would borrow $20 million from the bank at its three-month, 2.00 percent lending rate (paying $100,000 in interest). In total, the group would pay the difference between these two sums, or $56,450. If, on the other hand, a netting procedure were in place, unit A could deposit its $10 million surplus in an in-house clearing account, which would then shift the funds to unit B, whose only external transaction would then involve borrowing the remaining $10 million it needs at the bank's 2.00 percent lending rate, for a total three-month cost of $50,000. By having subsidiaries grant one another internal loans at a neutral "mid-market" interest rate—and in the absence of any tax considerations—the group would save $6,450 just by netting.

As is the case with all intra-MNE fund movements, the price that one unit pays its sister unit will translate into one site declaring higher profits at the end of the year and the other site lower ones. Unsurprisingly, this mechanism is of deep interest to MNEs and a source of frequent and bitter disputes between colleagues.

Transfer pricing and tax implications

MNE subsidiaries and headquarters trade a wide range of assets with one another. This can include tangible items such as raw materials, parts and finished goods; but also intangible items like capital, loans, fees, royalties, trademarks and dividends. MNEs are obliged to put a price on all such deals because they involve an exchange of value between entities that are supposedly independent of one another (if only because each might file separate tax returns within its local jurisdiction). Given the huge proportion of contemporary IB conducted on this intra-firm basis, transfer prices have become a topic of great importance.

Although international standards vary in this area, most authorities (including the US Internal Revenue Service and the OECD) favour transfer prices being calculated as so-called "arm's length" dealings, with a MNE's various units pricing any and all trading with one another as if each entity were unrelated and subject to a perfect state of market competition. In reality, these concepts are vague enough to leave MNEs a great deal of freedom to set their own transfer prices, often due to the fact that for many goods (intangible assets, company-specific modules), there is nothing comparable in the outside world that can serve as a pricing benchmark.

The three main transfer price categories are:

- "Cost pricing": where an item is transferred without any mark-up;
- "Cost plus pricing": where a defined margin is added to the item's return price (often applied to finished products); and
- "Profit split" pricing: where the ultimate operating profit realised on an item after it has been sold is split between the MNE's manufacturing and sales subsidiaries following an objective measurement of the contribution that each has made.

Because such dealings occur between sister units, there are two main goals guiding the ultimate decision about how to price the intra-firm transfer: arriving at a more or less objective assessment of each unit's actual performance and minimising the group's overall tax bill. In terms of the former, transferring assets at a high price will leave more money in the hands of the unit making the transfer, whereas a transfer made at a lower price will favour the receiver. The end result is that one unit will declare higher profits at year-end and therefore expect a higher bonus, and the other lower profits, with all the adverse effects this has for the team there.

Colleagues in multisite MNEs spend much time negotiating transfer prices. Understandably, practitioners' greatest loyalty may be to the particular SBU employing them rather than to the MNE as a whole, since as often as not it is at the more immediate level that their personal remuneration and career prospects will be determined. Some companies actually engage in double accounting practices, quantifying employees' contribution to sister units so as to incentivise them to think beyond what is simply necessary to increase their own team's bonus pool. Interdepartmental competition, whether vertical or horizontal, can be fierce in many MNEs.

In terms of transfer pricing's second aspect (tax minimisation), the starting point for any discussion here must be numerous MNEs' habit of declaring losses in countries where taxes are high and profits in countries where they are low. MNE treasurers tend to be keenly aware of the wide international variation in corporation tax rates (see Table 12.4), as well as other fiscal provisions relating, for instance, to foreign tax credits, value-added taxes, double taxation measures and even customs duties. This is because many view tax reduction as an integral part of their job, especially in industries like pharmaceuticals characterised by complex value chains and large transferable profits (Ernst and Young 2019).

In turn, this creates an incentive for them to use transfer prices as a way of lowering their group's global tax bill, including by playing on the vagueness of many international transfer pricing protocols. One consequence has been some MNEs' ethically dubious habit of setting up artificial billing offices in low-tax jurisdictions. These units only exist to re-invoice internal flows (of capital but also goods, services, etc.) to group units operating in higher tax jurdisdictions in order that losses be declared in the latter locales and profits elsewhere. This "base erosion and profit shifting" (BEPS) manoeuvre, where MNEs intentionally exploit mismatches and gaps in tax and transfer pricing regulations to reduce the total amount of tax they pay, has had a tremendously

Table 12.4
Sample 2020 corporation tax rates (figures rounded)

DR Congo/India	35
Brazil/France	34
Cameroon/Colombia	33
Argentina/Germany/Mexico	30
South Africa	28
Canada	26.5
Bangladesh/Chile/China/Indonesia/Spain	25
Italy/Malaysia	24
Israel/Japan	23
Denmark/Norway/Sweden	22
USA	21
Russia/ Saudi Arabia/Thailand	20
UK	19
Cyprus/Ireland	12.5
Andorra/Bulgaria	10
Hungary	9
Switzerland	7.8
Barbados	5.5
Bahamas/Bahrain/Bermuda/Guernsey etc.	0

Sources include KPMG, Deloitte, PWC, Tax Foundation and relevant government websites.

negative effect on public finances in many countries over the past few decades, contributing to a huge rise in cumulative state debt and creating financial instability that could wreak havoc on future generations' fortunes. It is a prime example of the link between the micro- and the macro-levels of IB behaviour, and of the relevance of applying ethical filters to analysis in this domain.

Tax avoidance – Use of legal means to avoid paying taxes.

Tax evasion – Use of illegal means to avoid paying taxes.

Where a MNE's accounting principles comply with national legislation, actions taken to minimise taxable income are called tax avoidance. If not, the talk is of tax evasion, an illegal and often criminal offence. Even where a tax avoidance tactic has been found legal, many observers consider such behaviour at odds with good corporate governance. Recent years have seen growing concern about the quality and transparency of accounting in many MNEs. Part of this simply reflects the difficulties that some companies have had in navigating differences between the world's two main accounting standards: the Generally Accepted Accounting Principles (c.f., www.fasb.org), which apply in the USA, and the International Financial Reporting Standards (www.ifrs.org), which apply elsewhere. But the bigger problem is how easy, hence tempting, it can be for MNEs operating across borders to use the inconsistency between different standards as a way of masking their real dealings.

Tax haven – Country setting egregiously low tax rates specifically to attract financial flows.

One current debate in this area relates to the huge gap between the historically normal corporation tax rates being practised in many countries worldwide versus levels elsewhere that can go as low as 10 percent, or even less in a tax haven like Bermuda, which levies no income tax on foreign earnings, not to mention the British Virgin Islands, which levies no corporation or capital gains tax at all. Booking transactions in these latter locations can seem very attractive to MNE treasurers attending to their fiduciary responsibility of maximising shareholder returns. But they can hardly be construed as an honest and accurate way of representing their company's real activities. It is to reduce such temptations that the USA's Biden administration proposed in summer 2021 that a minimum corporate tax be applied worldwide. Whether or not this will ever be fully implemented remains to be seen, however.

A second debate that is more technical in nature relates to whether the arm's length principle remains an appropriate mechanism for normalising MNE tax behaviour (Collier and Andrus 2017). There is a growing sense that it makes little sense to continue to book MNE subsidiary earnings at a national level given the intensity of cross-border intra-firm dealings in today's highly digitised world (McGaughey and Raimondos 2019). The idea now is that MNEs should be taxed on their global income, with fiscal liabilities being apportioned to each of the countries where they operate. Some argue that even if this change will have the effect of reducing MNEs' net global earnings, they might benefit as well since the current system incentivises them to move activities to particular locations, not because these are the best places to operate but for tax reasons. Taking tax out of the equation may have the effect of making MNE value chains more efficient economically, if not financially (Foss et al. 2019). Financial returns will always be a dominant aspiration in IB – but whether it should override all other considerations is very much up for debate.

Attitudes and alternatives

MNEs require real-time information on their current and prospective currency and funding positions to gain an accurate understanding of their potential risks. Once this is achieved, the question becomes whether the company should cover its financial exposures systematically or instead only do this sporadically to try and generate extra profits. The answer depends on how MNE treasurers conceptualise their role. If they are given a personal incentive to maximise profits, they may tend to behave like market speculators trading proprietary positions. If, on the other hand, they are incentivised to minimise costs, the job becomes much less lucrative. The jury is still out on how these two behaviours might be balanced within a multinational treasury department.

Chapter summary

The chapter began with an analysis of FX exposures before identifying the different activities engendering this kind of risk: transactional (commercial and operational), translational, speculative and economic. A distinction was made between FX risks that can be identified and managed immediately and those that materialise over the long run and require more of a structural adjustment. The second section started with a brief comparison of debt versus equity as sources of external funding, with the former largely depending on borrowers' perceived creditworthiness and the latter focusing more on MNEs' ability to tap different investor pools. The chapter's final section reviewed internal funding sources, primarily the way MNEs can try to shift cash from sites running a surplus to sister units running deficits to both achieve wider group objectives and reduce financial transaction costs. It concluded by scrutinising the fiscal (but also ethical) implications of the prices applied to these internal transfers.

Case study 12.3: Singapore slings

Finance tends to be one of many MNEs' most centralised functions given the administrative economies of scale that can be achieved in this way. Not only is it cheaper to run a single global team working out of one site than many local units spread worldwide, but large, streamlined

Fig 12.6
Singapore is a hotspot
for multinational treasury
operations in the Asia
region.

multinational treasury operations generally benefit from knowledge spillover effects, particularly where this involves the management of "market-facing exposures" (Albovias 2019).

Even so, staffing a single global treasury office on a 24/7 basis is very challenging. Firstly, it requires people willing to work all through the night in order to cover the three main time zones that structure IB life – Asia; Europe-Middle East-Africa (EMEA); and the Americas. It is also questionable whether people employed out of a central site will possess (or be able to access) all the knowledge needed for the occasional specialist deals that a MNE has to do in certain local markets. This explains the decision taken by most MNEs to spread their treasurers across a few key regional financial centres, organising them into two or three offices across the world, each of which is responsible for coordinating units in its own time zone and for supporting all regional foreign exchange, funding, financial risk management and tax activities.

The Asian locale that has attracted the greatest number of MNE regional treasury centres in recent years is Singapore. This small but dynamic city-state has moved ahead of neighbouring financial hotspots: Tokyo, deemed too expensive and Japan-centric; and Hong Kong, where recurring unrest has recently translated into a wave of financial specialists moving to Singapore to avail themselves of the latter locale's comparatively greater political stability and lesser government interference (Lewis 2020). To some extent, a city's success in being acknowledged as a cluster is a self-fulfilling prophecy. Becoming a financial centre necessitates the presence of a large workforce of experienced professionals trained in this highly technical field, but once specialists have invested a particular location, they tend to stay there and attract others of their ilk. On top of this, Singapore offers

MNEs additional benefits, including a competitive flat tax rate of 17 percent on chargeable income, low withholding taxes (referring to the sums that governments deduct at source on investment payouts) and numerous double taxation treaties (Thakur 2019). Moreover, MNEs that receive certification as having located a bona fide global or regional "Finance & Treasury Centre" in Singapore receive both further income tax concessions and withholding tax exemptions lasting anywhere from five to ten years. The net effect of all these measures has been to entice a very long list of famous MNEs from many different countries to move their Asian regional treasury operations to Singapore. Amazon, for instance, is expanding its operations there in recognition of the city's positioning as Asia's tech hub but also because it seems a good launchpad for expanding operations into fast-growing ASEAN neighbours like Indonesia (Ruehl 2020). Indeed, there is a long list of other big name MNEs that have taken similar steps to bolster their Singapore treasury operations, including Bosch, Sony, Phillips, Bayer, Pfizer, Google and Cargill. Clearly Singapore is benefitting from the virtuous circle that all clusters enjoy – as posited in Network theory, success breeds success and the "power nodes" of treasury centres that are already up and running in the city augur well for others to want to come and join them.

One remaining doubt does hang over this success story, however, namely that Singapore is very small. This means that despite having experienced fantastic development over the past half-century, its domestic economy only accounts for a tiny percentage of total growth in what has become the world's most dynamic economic zone. At a certain point, it is likely that its neighbours will become jealous of Singapore's success and try to lure some businesses away, much as the City of London would lose some equity trading business to Amsterdam in the wake of the Brexit debacle. The question then becomes whether those MNEs who had helped Singapore to accumulate its financial expertise in the first place will remain loyal to it, or if they will decide that their future interest resides in currying favours with other, more powerful Asian governments by moving their treasury centres there. In multinational finance as in MNE product markets, international competition can be very fierce indeed.

Case study questions

1. What are the different tasks that a multinational treasury department performs?
2. What problems might a MNE face when covering a large and diverse region out of a single treasury centre?
3. To what extent can Singapore use tax incentives to permanently lock in MNE treasury business?

Discussion questions

1 What kinds of MNEs are more or less likely to be exposed to FX risk? Why?
2 When does a short-term transactional risk turn into a long-term economic one?
3 To what extent should a MNE hedge all, some or none of its FX exposures?
4 Which factors determine whether MNEs should fund themselves through debt or equity?
5 To what extent is transfer pricing a techncial, strategic or ethical topic?

References

Albovias, V. (25 November 2019). "The centralized treasury: Different paths to improved control", accessed 1 March 2021 at https://www.jpmorgan.com/

Anderson, H. et al. (January 2012). "The evolution of shareholder and creditor protection in Australia: An international comparison", *International and Comparative Law Quarterly*, Volume 61, pp. 171–207.

Bartsch, C. (10 September 2019). "Factors to consider when centralising cash management", accessed 1 March 2021 at https://www.theglobaltreasurer.com/

Beber, A., and Fabbri, D. (2011). "Who times the foreign exchange market? Corporate speculation and CEO characteristics", accessed 1 March 2021 at http://www1.fee.uva.nl

Bonini, S. et al. (December 2016). "Do firms hedge translation risks?" *Journal of Financial Management*, Issue 2, accessed 31 July 2021 at https://papers.ssrn.com/

Collier, R., and Andrus, J. (2017). *Transfer Pricing and the Arm's Length Principle after BEPS*, Oxford: Oxford University Press.

Deakin, S. et al. (2018). "Is there a relationship between shareholder protection and stock market development", accessed 1 March 2021 at https://www.law.ox.ac.uk/business-law-blog

Ernst and Young (2019). "Transfer pricing and international tax survey 2019", accessed 22 June 2020 at www.ey.com/

Fontana, G. et al. (July 2019). "Financialisation and the new capitalism", *Cambridge Journal of Economics,* Volume 43, Issue 4, pp. 799–804.

Foss, N. et al. (December 2019). "Taxing the multinational enterprise: On the forced redesign of global value chains and other inefficiencies", *Journal of International Business Studies*, Volume 50, pp. 1644–1655.

Heineken (2020). *2019 Annual Report*, accessed 21 June 2020 at https://www.theheinekencompany.com/

Heineken (2021). "Heineken N.V. reports 2020 full year results…", accessed 3 March 2021 at https://www.globenewswire.com/news-release/

Huang, T. et al. (February 2020). "Investor protection and the value impact of stock liquidity", *Journal of International Business Studies*, Volume 51, pp. 72–94.

Islam, S., and Mozumdar, A. (March 2007). "Financial market development and the importance of internal cash: Evidence from international data", *Journal of Bank and Finance*, Volume 31, Issue 3, pp. 641–658.

Lei, U. (August 2019). "The role of foreign institutional investors in restrained earnings management activities across countries", *Journal of International Business Studies*, Volume 50, pp. 895–922.

Lewis, L. (22 November 2020). "Rivals spy weakness in HK's status as Asia's prime financial centre", *Financial Times*.

Lockett, H. et al. (18 June 2020). "Bankers hunt for NY listed Chinese companies to bring home to HK", *Financial Times*.

Markowitz, H. (1959). *Portfolio Selection: Efficient Diversification of Investments*, New Haven, CT: Wiley & Sons

McGaughey, S., and Raimondos, P. (December 2019). "Shifting MNE taxation from national to global profits: A radical reform long overdue", *Journal of International Business Studies*, Volume 50, pp. 1668–1683.

Mihav, A., and Naranjo, A. (December 2019). "Corporate internationalization, subsidiary locations, and the cost of equity capital", *Journal of International Business Studies*, Volume 50, pp. 1544–1565.

Morrissey, O., and Udomkerdmongkol, M. (2008). "Foreign direct investment and exchange rates: A case study of US FDI in emerging market countries", accessed 1 March 2021 at https://www.nottingham.ac.uk/

Nayak, S., and Sahoo, D. (June 2020). "Dimensions of foreign direct investment inflow in India after 1991", *FIIB Business Review*, Volume 9, Issue 2, pp. 106–117.

Ruehl, M. (30 September 2020). "Amazon to expand presence in Singapore", *Financial Times*.

Ruehl, M., and Riordan, P. (20 December 2020). "Global banks boost Singapore hiring to mitigate Hong Kong risk", *Financial Times*.

Sarkanova, B., and Kristofik, P. (January 2018). "Innovation through treasury centralization…", accessed 3 March 2021 at https://www.researchgate.net/publication/

Skillman, S. (December 2013). "How to get FX hedging costs under control", accessed 22 June 2020 at https://www.euromoney.com/

Thakur, P. (1 August 2019). "Challenges for treasurers and corporates in the Asian market", accessed 3 March 2021 at https://www.bloomberg.com/

USCC US-China Economic and Security Review Commission (regularly updated), accessed 2 March 2021 at https://www.uscc.gov/

Van Beemen, O. (2019). *Heineken in Africa: A Multinational Unleashed*, London: C. Hurst & Co.

Veeramani, S. et al. (June 2020). "Financial theories of foreign direct investment: A review of literature", *Journal of Industrial and Business Economics*, Volume 47, pp. 185–217.

The future of international business

CHAPTER 13

The changing geography of international business

Introduction

Until the mid-2010s, McKinsey & Company – one of the world's leading consultancy groups – would conduct a survey every few years of around 10,000 international business (IB) practitioners, seeking their views as to which trends were likeliest to have the greatest impact on multinational enterprises (MNEs) for the foreseeable future. The publications have changed somewhat, with the earlier predictive focus being replaced by the still excellent but more specific global reports that McKinsey continues to generate on a regular basis. What remains from the earlier surveys is the noteworthy fact that they generally tended to list the same three items as possessing the greatest strategic significance for MNEs' future: the emergence of the Global South, the ecological imperative and technological progress. Since business school graduates are always recruited for their ability to create new value – and because they can only do this by developing a capacity for

Fig 13.1
The Global North no longer has a monopoly on international business.

DOI: 10.4324/9781003159056-18

dynamic analysis – futurology should always be an integral part of IB studies. The most relevant way of structuring this is around the three mega-topics identified by IB practitioners themselves, which therefore become the basis for this textbook's final three chapters.

The reason why the Global South's emergence can also be referred to as the changing geography of IB is that until a generation ago, the vast majority of all IB transactions (hence analysis) revolved around Global North interests. That is no longer the case, and the implications are so radical that a whole new subset of IB studies has taken shape, evoking new skills that tomorrow's practitioners will need to develop, to wit, knowing how to interact with counterparts who come from countries that are at very different stages of socio-economic development, and whose business experiences (hence paradigms) are therefore also very different. Studying the relatively specific trajectory typifying most, if not all, of the companies and countries involved in this emergence process is a good way to understand these new players on the IB scene – a three-part chronological analysis that can be used to structure the present chapter.

Before starting, however, it is important to note that the very term "Global South" – while superior to the prejudicial overtones of its predecessor, "developing nations" – remains inadequate given the huge variety of countries it is meant to cover. Global South nations range from highly indebted poor countries (HIPCs) struggling to survive financially, to the emerging powerhouses expected to dominate the global economy within a few short decades. Even within the latter category, there is a clear distinction between continent-sized nations that ex-Goldman Sachs economist Jim O'Neil famously called the BRICs (Brazil, Russia, India and China) and others that he would later call the "Next 11" (Bangladesh, Egypt, Indonesia, Iran, Mexico, Nigeria, Pakistan, Philippines, South Korea, Turkey and Vietnam; O'Neill 2013). Of course, this new categorisation was also incomplete, ignoring further emerging success stories like South Africa, Malaysia, Taiwan, Thailand, Poland and the Czech Republic. This is in no way meant to criticise O'Neill's groundbreaking work. It is just that generalisations of this kind will never be able to account for all of the differences in national geography (resource endowment, proximity to trade routes), level of industrialisation (Eastern Europe's ex-communist transition states vs. most other emerging economies) or policy preferences (e.g. traditionally interventionist regimes like Malaysia vs. others like Chile that have more of a free market inclination).

Transition - In evolution. Often used in economics to refer to ex-communist countries shifting towards more market-based economies.

For all these reasons, terms like the "Global South" or "emerging economies" will always be too broad to be considered scientific. But they do offer a useful shorthand when referring to all the new nations that have recently started emerging on the IB scene. Readers should therefore be comfortable applying them as long as they remember their limitations.

LEARNING OBJECTIVES

After reading this chapter, you will be able to:

- situate the changing geography of international business in a historical context
- differentiate between various Global South emergence trajectories
- pinpoint the role that international business has played in accelerating development
- evaluate the particularities of selling into emerging economies
- forecast growth prospects for MNEs emanating from the Global South

Case study 13.1: Ghana is going places

Fig 13.2
Improvements in the standard of living in Ghana makes it an exemplar for Africa.

In his 2003 masterpiece *The End of Poverty*, development expert Jeffrey Sachs gave thought to the reasons why GDP growth over the past 200 years has been so much slower in Africa, the world's poorest region, than in the countries constituting today's Global North. Sachs found, inter alia, that the institutional and political instability afflicting many African nations – both during the long decades they suffered from colonialism but also afterwards – had created a difficult environment for entrepreneurship and technological progress, being key factors in any country's long-term economic success. Of course, Africa is a huge continent with more than 50 countries, meaning that Sach's generalisation will always be contradicted by exceptions, starting with Ghana.

It is not that this relatively small West African nation, with its current population of around 30 million, did not endure problems similar to its neighbours in the years following independence in 1957. Like many others, Ghana suffered from a **resource curse**, relying on very few natural resources and therefore being vulnerable to declines in their relative pricing. It also experienced, at least initially, its own share of arbitrary

Resource curse - Temptation for a country possessing significant natural resources to market its commodities without seeking to develop other value-adding industries.

governance and corrupt politicians. But for a host of reasons (many relating to the life work of Jerry Rawlings, a figure viewed negatively by some historians but very positively by many others), the country today features one of Africa's most stable and democratic governments and, not coincidentally, one of its fastest growing economies.

Ghanaian GDP (hence per-capita income) had suffered greatly before the early-1980s due to declining world prices for the country's main exports (cocoa and a few minerals). Instead of maintaining its underperforming economic structures, however, successive regimes have worked since that time to implement a number of reforms intended to equip Ghana's poor (mainly rural) communities with the means and incentives to start new businesses. These measures were complemented by others aimed at building the different kinds of infrastructure (agricultural, transport and electrification) that are a prerequisite for macro-economic efficiency. Democracy reforms have also been implemented, giving budding entrepreneurs a sense that they have a personal stake in advancing the country's fortunes – another one of Sach's preconditions for development.

It is true that commodities still account for a large share of Ghana's economy, and that it therefore remains subject to a resource curse. On the other hand, with citizens achieving an average per-capita income of around $1,500 (five times the sub-Saharan average), it also seems clear that profits from these natural resource activities are being distributed much more widely than elsewhere, ensuring social harmony and spawning the kind of service sector activities that are the hallmark of more advanced economies. Services account for around 60 percent of Ghana's GDP, a very high number in Africa and one that helps to explain why the country has a sub-5 percent unemployment rate, less than half its comparators.

This relative economic stability – reinforced by solid educational provisions and by a functioning legal system where contracts are largely enforceable and enforced (and where IFRS global accounting standards are applied) – makes Ghana a solid partner for IB interests as well. In-depth work is being done to digitise the banking sector in an attempt to further secure national financial transactions. Now, it is true that Ghanaian funding channels can be difficult, given the high real interest rates being practised largely in an effort to reduce an inflation rate that is around 10 percent, reflecting the country's bulging budget deficit but also, and more positively, its very fast growth (with GDP up by 6.7 percent in 2019 for instance, about twice the sub-Saharan average).

Ghana remains a Global South economy and much work must still be done to further diversify its economy, including by building up a processing industry that will allow it to improve its terms of trade (and ultimately to become less dependent on raw material exports). It remains that the same nickname that Ghana gives its increasingly impressive national football team – the Black Stars – could very well be applied to the country's emergence prospects as a whole.

Case study questions

1. Why does Ghana's political stability enhance its emergence prospects?
2. What secondary or tertiary sector actions should Ghana's economic planners prioritise?

Section I. Stage 1: using manufacturing as a launchpad

Despite all their many differences, the cohort of countries referred to today alternatively as the emerging economies or as the Global South do have one thing in common – until a few short decades ago, they were much poorer (in both national and per-capita GDP terms) than their Global North counterparts, the older industrialised nations. At some point between 1980 and 2000, however, things began changing all across the Global South. That makes it useful, when trying to understand the trajectories of the countries involved, to start by asking what happened, and why.

Per-capita - Where an aggregate sum reflecting an entire population is divided by its size and expressed on an individual basis.

The decision to open up

Throughout most of the 20th century, most (and maybe all) of today's emerging economies had taken a fairly negative view of the IB system such as it was at the time. There were two main reasons for this isolationist reluctance to integrate the world trading system. Firstly, those regimes that defined themselves as communist felt an ideological reluctance to open up to private IB interests, either opting for autarky (e.g. Tito's Yugoslavia but also Maoist China) or to only trade with one another (e.g. Eastern Europe's COMECON association). One consequence of the changes that these regimes experienced in the late 20th century, due to the disenchantment with (and ultimate fall of) communism in Europe and because of the reforms introduced in China after Mao's death, was an infinitely greater willingness to engage in IB with Western counterparts that had previously been depicted as Cold War adversaries. The West's much higher standard of living will also have been a factor in this new attitude.

Isolationist - Refers in international trade to a policy of minimal interactions with foreign interests.

The rest of the Global South, however, followed a very different path. With most countries having only gained their independence in the mid-20th century (except for Latin America, largely liberated a century before), early political leaders all had painful personal memories of colonial subjugation. Aspiring as a result to greater self-sufficiency, many adopted import substitution policies, rejecting the interconnectedness that is an essential condition for IB. It was only decades later once these countries felt sufficiently confident in their ability to compete internationally (and were being led by a new generation of political leaders, many of whom had been educated in IB-friendly Global North universities) that attitudes would evolve. The paradigm shift would then become fairly radical, however, exemplified by the priority that many Global South countries have given since the late 20th century to their integration of global value chains, often by easing earlier restrictions on trade and FDI.

Of course, liberalisation would assume different forms in different places. Brazil, for example, has few nationalised companies anymore and features a relatively unregulated financial system that more or less authorises the free flow of capital. India has also loosened many financial controls but kept other IB restrictions, particularly in the retail sector where the government has maintained a set of regulations designed to protect "rural cottage industries and other micro, small and medium enterprises, or even artisans and craftsmen" from the incursion of MNEs (Rout 2020). This focus on how IB might affect the less privileged in Indian society contrasts, in turn, with Russia, where IB tends to revolve around the interests of a cadre of oligarchs working hand-in-hand with the state, particularly in the natural resources sector. In turn, Russia's ongoing centralisation of power contrasts with other emerging nations like Peru or Mexico where there has been greater emphasis on devolution. The diverse nature of the countries classified as being part of the Global South is also reflected in the diverse nature of the policies they pursue.

Despite these variations, however, there is no doubt that all these countries possess one feature in common, namely the radical difference between their more or less IB-friendly policies today and their previous reticence in this area. The most striking sign of the new consensus is the fact that almost every country in the world today has joined the World Trade Organization and therefore largely accepts the requirement that it minimise barriers to trade and FDI, hence that it allow foreign MNEs to enter the domestic marketplace. As China's reformist ex-leader Deng Xiaoping once said to justify his country's decision to open up, "It doesn't matter if a cat is black or white as long as it catches mice". In most, if not all, of the Global South, political sensitivities and/or ideology can, of course, hamper IB, but they rarely prevent it anymore.

Oligarch - Dominant business figure, often used in Russia to refer to entrepreneurs who took control of formerly state-owned assets following the fall of the communist regime.

An emergence dynamic largely driven by upstream factors

Exogenous - Outwardly oriented.

Endogenous - Inwardly oriented.

Economists with an interest in development studies tend to differentiate between two categories of growth drivers: exogenous, revolving around foreign dealings (exports, inward investment); and endogenous, emphasizing domestic consumption and investment. When today's emerging economies were in their earlier, less IB-friendly phase, they had largely hoped that endogenous growth would free them from foreign dependence. The ensuing move towards greater market liberalisation was partially based on their realisation that until such time as a poor country amasses a critical mass of capital, growth driven by purely domestic factors is likely to be much slower than exogenous growth – a lesson that would become all the more apparent as those countries that had moved early to adopt a trade focus (led by Southeast Asian "tigers" like Taiwan and Singapore) performed markedly better than other, more closed economies (like Kenya, to use a famous academic example). Desperately poor Global South nations may have had understandable misgivings about their ability to negotiate good deals with all-conquering MNEs – a power imbalance widely decried at the time by pundits like John Pilger, Greg Palast and George Monbiot, who would become quite famous on the IB scene. But it soon became apparent that it was only by striking deals with Global North counterparts that their economic emergency would accelerate.

The question then became how they might fit into an international division of labour. For most of today's emerging economies, the answer was more or less the same – they would invite Global North business interests to avail themselves of the Global South's comparatively inexpensive factor inputs: natural resources; and, above all, labour. The former activity was actually nothing new and involved the same extractive industries that had been a key feature of IB during the bad old colonial days, the only difference being that this time, hopefully, trade would be done on a fairer, less exploitative basis. What was novel – and even revolutionary, given the change it has affected in the overall geography of IB – is that within a few short decades, countless big-name Global North companies from innumerable sectors would shift most, if not all, of their upstream operations to the South. Whether this involved FDI that would see a MNE build its own production facilities in a low-income country or (and especially) outsourcing that saw it give Global South-owned interests orders to manufacture their inputs or even finished products, it is impossible to overstate the scale and significance of this phenomenon. It has radically changed IB in both the Global North and South and has been the launchpad for many formerly destitute countries' entire emergence process.

Analysis of this historical phenomenon has also changed over time. The initial prediction that many economists (starting with Nobel laureate Paul Krugman) were making in the 1990s was that Global North MNEs were likely to move only basic operations to the South and would continue to locate high value-added design and engineering activities in their home countries. In some sectors, this is what actually happened, with one famous (and frequently cited) example being the Apple business model that sees less than one-third of the retail price paid for high-value goods such as mobile phones allocated to the remuneration of the

Extractive industries - Mining and fossil fuel industries that take raw materials out of the ground.

upstream operations outsourced to Global South suppliers, with the rest used to remunerate the intellectual and marketing work done out of the group's California offices. One way of debating this distribution of value is from a macro-economic perspective, focusing on the terms of trade effects for the various countries involved in Apple's global value chain. But the most noteworthy aspect from an IB perspective is how beneficial the model has been: for the prime contractor, of course, as well as consumers; but also for the emerging market suppliers who have been getting orders (hence lucrative workflows) that they would not have won otherwise. It is one thing to argue, quite understandably, that MNEs should pay their Global South employees an even greater premium over average national wages than they already tend to do. It is another to dispute the wealth creation effects that their outsourcing orders have had in some of the world's poorest societies. Since the 1980s, there has been a vertiginous decline in the percentage of households worldwide living in absolute poverty (see Figure 13.3). Part of this trend can be attributed to technological progress, but it would be very wrong to ignore the part played by MNEs' mass displacement of industrial employment to the Global South.

The second debate relating to the Global South's manufacturing launchpad is whether the upstream operations being outsourced or offshored are destined to always involve low value-added activities. At first glance, it is true that the first years of international openness for many, if not most, of these countries were dominated by cheap outputs. Indeed, in less technologically advanced sectors like textiles – a huge IB employing millions of people worldwide – that remains the case, especially in countries like Sri Lanka and Bangladesh.

In others like China, however, internationalisation also began with the production of textiles and other simple outputs, but has complexified since then to an awe-inspiring extent. Almost as impressive has been the slightly different path followed by India, which has leveraged

Fig 13.3
Absolute poverty has plummeted across the world at the same time as Global South countries have hosted a rising proportion of global upstream operations. World Bank. 2018. Poverty headcount ratio at $1.90 a day (2011 PPP) (% of population). Washington, DC: World Bank. © World Bank. https://data. worldbank.org/indicator/ SI.POV.DDAYLicense: CC BY 3.0 IGO. Downloaded 12 January 2021.

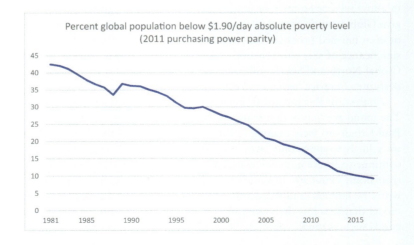

"inwards-outwards linkages" (Chittoor 2015) to help knowledge-intensive domestic firms transition from an early specialisation in low-value services into the production of software, pharmaceuticals and other technologically demanding products. Add to this the rapid integration into global value chains of a cohort of small emerging nations like Singapore and Taiwan that have from the very outset geared their development around technologically advanced components like micro-processors and other computer components, and it soon became clear that a positive correlation exists between "exposure to foreign competition through inward FDI and exporting activity and innovative innovation" (Nuruzzaman et al. 2019).

During the early years of many Global South countries' transformation process, maximising incoming MNEs' technology transfers clearly became important, if only to kick-start the kinds of intellectual spillovers that are a precondition for the creation of a knowledge economy. Embodied in requirements such as the sharing of technical specifications or the organisation of vocational training, technology transfers would increasingly be mediated by host country governments, who would either drive a hard bargain when negotiating a MNE's inward FDI or, to the contrary, tighten up the local legal and regulatory framework to reassure the foreign MNE that its patents would be protected, hence that it could take the risk of transferring to its new Global South partners whatever technology needed to be shared for value chain coordination purposes. Lastly, arrangements would also be made to maximise joint ventures between Global North and South interests, again with a view towards making the former more willing to collaborate with the latter and help upgrade its technological capabilities.

Upgrade - Where a company (or country) improves its terms of trade by intensifying the value-added content of its inputs, processes or outputs.

The end result of these cooperation initiatives – alongside, of course, many countries' internal efforts to advance the level of science, technology, engineering and mathematics (STEM) training disseminated through their institutions of higher education or lifelong learning – is that the upstream capabilities in most Global South economies would quickly surpass the simplicity that had characterised their initial emergence phase. Of course, a clear distinction should be made between production based on the implementation of advanced knowledge that was first developed elsewhere before being brought to the Global South, as opposed to production based on innovative research actually conducted in this part of the world. Here it is worth noting the huge gap that exists between the three leading emerging economies – China (far and away the world's biggest patents holder) followed by India and then further back by Russia – versus the rest of the Global South. These three countries already host cutting-edge domestic research activities in a number of sectors, including pharmaceuticals, aerospace and quantum computing. This has impacted their manufacturing profiles, all the more so because the higher wages they now pay domestic workers make it increasingly difficult for them to compete in simpler activities where cost is a key success factor. The end result is that most emerging market

firms with significant research need no longer look to the Global North
for guidance (Cohle 2019) – with only one of India's big pharmaceutical
MNEs (Dr Reddy) currently running any major research centres outside
the country. Altogether, the picture is clear – there is no truth to the
old adage that the Global South is necessarily condemned to low-tech
operations.

Having said that, behind the three aforementioned standouts the
rest of the emerging world is largely split between mid-level producers
seeking to catch up with technologies that already exist elsewhere and
other players limited to low-value manufacturing for the time being. The
former cohort is at some risk because of the costs and difficulties they face
in importing the knowledge they use, although many may soon benefit
from a process known as "frugal" innovation, which is when product
designs offer a minimal but satisfactory level of performance for minimal
cost (Gandenberger and Walz 2020). This "mid-tech" approach may be
enough to advance these players' emergence trajectory, especially if their
commercial targets are fellow Global South markets (see Section II).

Catch-up - Term used
in development studies
in reference to emerging
countries' efforts to
match their Global North
comparators' economic
(including technological)
performance.

However, serious concerns do remain about the prospects of the
subset of Global South countries that are still struggling to import
(much less implement) any advanced technology. This cohort does
fit the original vision of low-value global offshoring and outsourcing
insofar as the IB they attract is based on the cheapness of the inputs
they provide rather than any value-added. It is a positioning that is very
undesirable from their perspective, first and foremost because the main
purpose of development must be a rise in poor people's standards of
living, hence pay, reflecting the extra value they are given an opportunity
to create. The problem is that when wages finally do rise in a low-tech
Global South country, footloose MNEs may shift their business to other
locales where wages continue to stagnate, creating a race to the bottom
that has been deplored in so many ethical critiques of IB. In addition,
there is also the danger that in the years to come, automation (and
specifically, robotisation) will increasingly offer a viable alternative to
low value-added manufacturing, with MNEs no longer seeing any real
cost advantage in outsourcing this activity. As helpful a growth driver

as manufacturing has been for some Global South countries' emergence trajectories, this does not fully apply across the board. As always in IB, it depends.

Operating conditions that often remain difficult

Enthusiasm about manufacturing as a first-stage development catalyst must also be tempered by the fact that operating conditions in the Global South are often more problematic than in the North. That may be a gross generalisation – something which is normally proscribed in IB analysis – but a great deal of evidence exists to substantiate it. Notwithstanding many newly industrialised countries' rapid emergence, it must be remembered that all had been characterised until recently by widespread and sometimes abject poverty. Indeed, for many, that remains the case to a greater or lesser extent, creating and/or reflecting social and political phenomena that can make IB very difficult indeed.

Firstly, political governance and civil liberties, both factors identified by Sachs as key development drivers, generally tend to be less advanced in the Global South than in the North (Filippaios et al. 2019). The institutional voids characterising many of these societies – arbitrary judicial decisions (including unilateral renunciations of investment treaties), inefficient tax collection systems, opaque policy-making and immature and illiquid currency or capital markets – can be very discomfiting to MNEs possessing little experience in such "non-market" factors. This then has a negative effect on their commitment to internationalisation (hence to invest) in countries where such risks are widespread. A similar effect is caused by corruption, which, according to the Transparency International indexes discussed in Chapter 6, is widely perceived to be much more rampant in the Global South than in the North.

Similarly, ongoing problems with the protection of MNEs' intellectual property rights in several Global South regimes also dampen some IB practitioners' enthusiasm for running operations in these locales, most famously in China, which has been repeatedly criticised by the USA and the European Union for transgressions in this area. Add to this the less frequent but even more draconian threat of expropriation (considered an ongoing risk in regimes like Venezuela and Russia), and it is little surprise that country risk remains such an important component of MNEs' strategic planning. Despite recent improvements in this respect, the fact remains the "ease of doing business" – specifically the "ease of trading internationally" – is still higher in the Global North than in the South (see Figure 13.5).

Of course and as is often the case, political problems of this nature tend to go hand-in-hand with social problems. Poverty, overpopulation and fragile public finances combine in many Global South nations in a way that negatively impacts their educational system, which is often only free for pre-teens, with girls especially being disadvantaged in terms of

Institutional voids - Absence of effective (para-)official bodies that might otherwise exercise jurisdiction over (and regulate) a category of public interactions.

Country risk - All the different categories of uncertainty potentially affecting investment in a given country.

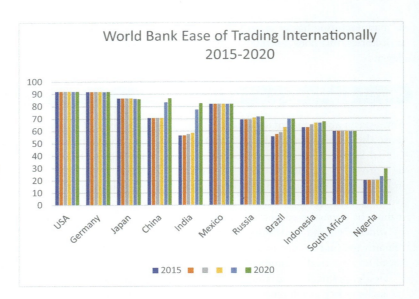

Fig 13.5
Despite improvements, Global South economies still lag behind in terms of their ease of trading internationally. World Bank. 2020. Doing Business 2020: Comparing Business Regulation in 190 Economies. Washington, DC: World Bank. © World Bank. https://openknowledge.worldbank.org/handle/10986/32436 License: CC BY 3.0 IGO. Downloaded 12 January 2021.

Poverty trap - Where high prices and/or actors' low incomes prevent them from amassing sufficient wealth to accumulate capital and/or reimburse debt.

access to schooling. This clearly has a negative impact on human capital and therefore on economic development. The same can be said in some countries about recurring inter-community ethnic and/or religious strife, exemplified in recent years by the terrible conflicts witnessed in Syria, Yemen, Myanmar and the Congo. Crime also tends to be higher in places like South Africa or Honduras, creating concerns for everyone's physical safety, including expatriate or locally hired MNE managers. These are all consequences, at least in part, of the vast income disparities that continue to plague many Global South societies, exacerbating the resentment felt by very poor populations often caught (much like the country itself) in a poverty trap that is exceedingly difficult to escape – a situation that will be further exacerbated by the Covid-19 pandemic, which has increased total emerging market debt from 170 percent of aggregate GDP in 2010 to over 240 percent (Wheatley 2020) and worsened the plight of hundreds of millions of precariously employed Global South workers lacking any safety net.

These harsh realities may temper the enthusiasm that some MNEs feel about the positive economic developments taking place in the Global South. Other IB practitioners, however, may view such problems as nothing more than the cost of doing business in a new environment. The optimal (and most balanced) response is, as always, to try and maximise the benefits of a situation while minimising the costs. And as always in IB, there are a number of ways to do this.

Section II. Stage 2: emerging consumer markets

Notwithstanding the operational problems that MNEs face in the Global South, there is no doubt that the emergence trajectories

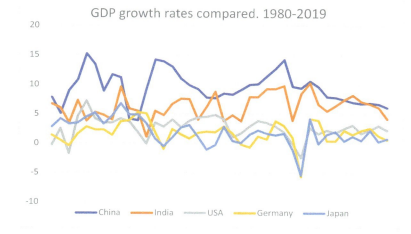

GDP growth rates compared. 1980-2019

China — India — USA — Germany — Japan

Fig 13.6
For decades, Global South
GDP growth outpaced
the Global North. World
Bank. 2020. GDP growth
(annual %). Washington,
DC: World Bank. © World
Bank. https://data.
worldbank.org/indicator/
NY.GDP.MKTP.KD.ZG.
License: CC BY 3.0 IGO.
Downloaded 12 January
2021.

characterising this cohort of nations has translated in recent decades
into their achieving GDP growth rate far exceeding their Global North
counterparts (see Figure 13.6). The consensus view is that this gap is
bound to widen further in the years to come, with several of today's
top performing emerging economies often predicted to dominate
global rankings within a few short decades. Consulting firm PWC
has forecast, for instance (2017), that by 2050 China will easily have
become the world's largest economy, followed by India in second place,
then Indonesia fourth, Brazil fifth, Russia sixth and Mexico seventh.
Secondary emerging economies like Vietnam, the Philippines and Nigeria
are also expected to ascend the rankings rapidly and figure among the
global top 20. This new accumulation of national wealth will inevitably
have a huge impact on the IB conducted in these places, first and
foremost because of the solvency effects it will engender.

Greater solvency will cause emerging market demand to skyrocket...

Analysis in this area often starts with how hard it is to identify which
emerging consumers can be considered sufficiently "middle class" to
afford new discretionary spending, being a pre-condition for the kinds of
growth rates that the Global South is expected to attain. There is little
doubt that for the foreseeable future, both average and median income
levels in these countries will remain lower than in the Global North. Of
course, prices are also lower, explaining the usefulness of thinking in
purchasing power parity terms. A daily income of $10 to $100 might
be akin to severe poverty in the older industrialised world, but in many
emerging economies it qualifies as middle class.

By some calculations, the number of middle-class consumers in
the world rose from 2 billion to 3.6 billion over the 2010s, with 700

**Discretionary
spending** -
Expenditure on
non-essential items.

million of these newly solvent households being located in China and
a further 300 million in India (Canals 2019). Of course, this is a very
heterogeneous grouping, with the per-capita expenditure of China's new
middle class being 30 percent higher, for instance, than in India, which,
in turn, sports higher numbers than some other emerging economies,
say Bangladesh or Algeria. Altogether, the aggregate consumption of
this emerging middle class accounts for about one-sixth of total global
consumption. It is already equal in size to middle class consumption in
the Global North (comprised of individually wealthier but many fewer
households) and will surely race far ahead within a few
short years.

That is actually very good news for IB because it translates into new
demand emanating from people who have only recently been able to
afford the kinds of goods and services that Global North households
have long enjoyed. A more conceptual way of framing this is by
distinguishing between markets in their "product renewal" or their "first
equipment" phases. The former involves products (i.e. refrigerators)
that most people in Global North markets already own and which are
therefore more or less saturated since replacement purchases will only be
made when existing stock becomes obsolete. Contrast this with societies
where millions of households always wanted refrigerators; previously
found them too expensive; but can now afford them. Demand growth
here is bound to be immensely higher.

The same can be said about other categories of demand. A lack of
infrastructure is the first sign of economic underdevelopment, but as
public administrations in the emerging world acquire the resources
enabling them to finally engage in the kinds of public works that their
populations require, this will also translate into huge contracts. The net
effect of these two new sources of demand alone makes it clear why the
prospect of serving newly solvent Global South markets has become so
critical in so many global sectors today.

Construction and infrastructure

In the late 1970s, more than 80 percent of China's population lived in
rural environments. By 2020, more than 60 percent lived in metropolises,
with vast numbers of ex-agricultural workers swarming into the cities in
search of better paid industrial employment. To accommodate this huge
internal migration, the equivalent of 10 to 15 Manhattans are having
to be built from scratch each and every year in this one country alone –
an accelerated urbanisation that can be observed all across the Global
South. The knock-on effect is tremendous demand for all the systems
required to build a functioning city – materials, of course, but also water
and energy infrastructure, public transport networks, road works and so
forth. Much of this business will be satisfied by domestic interests given
the general governmental principle of localising public expenditure as far
as possible. But the knock-on effects for foreign MNEs, particularly in
niche engineering activities, will also be substantial.

Telecommunications

Paradoxically, it is the emerging economies' lack of infrastructure that gives them an advantage in the telecoms market since they are free to purchase up-to-date technology instead of having to force modern systems onto old ones. An example is the technological leapfrogging (Ho 2008) currently happening in Southeast Africa, where countries like Angola that, until a few short decades ago, were lacking in basic landlines are skipping the old telephone mast rollout stage and jumping immediately to fibre optic networks with the help of MNEs coming from right across the Indian Ocean. Otherwise, the sheer size of these emerging market populations has also made them an epicentre for global smart phone sales.

Automotive

Given many emerging nations' vast expanses, large populations and lower levels of car ownership, it is no surprise that the global automotive sector is targeting these markets. Goldman Sachs economist O'Neill had predicted in the early 2000s, for instance, that the Chinese car market would soon become the largest in the world, projecting 200 million owners by the year 2025. In actual fact, it had already hit the 225 million mark by 2019. Around the same time, the Indian automotive market was on the verge of becoming the world's third largest market, after attracting a whopping $24.5 billion in automotive FDI over the previous two decades, with a particular focus recently on the electric vehicles segment that is predicted to dominate this sector for decades to come (IBEF 2020).

Faster current and future growth in the emerging world raises a question as to which MNEs will be best placed to satisfy this demand – and the cost of doing so. Section III will speak to the competitive strengths of the new MNEs coming out of the Global South, being the third stage of these locales' emergence. But for the older, more established MNEs operating in sectors like the ones listed above, geographical reorientation presents not only positives but negatives. The first risk relates to an over-dependency on markets that are not only distant but also prone to political interference, often exacerbated by geopolitical tensions. China currently accounts for 30 percent of Daimler's Mercedes sales and more than one-fifth of all sales by other German MNEs like semiconductor maker Infineon and plastics manufacturer Covestro (without forgetting BMW), yet all these investments must now be considered at risk given the ongoing trade disputes between Beijing and the European Union (Hall 2020). Plus, adaptation can be a major issue. It is clearly less costly for established MNEs to sell the same products in the new markets as they already do elsewhere. This is entirely feasible in sectors like luxury where a Global North cachet has appeal for conspicuous consumption reasons; indeed, China accounted in 2021 for an estimated 20 percent of global luxury demand, helping UK and French MNEs like Burberry and Richemont,

Cachet - Status due to reputation.

respectively, to survive the Covid-19 recession. The problem is that the
rise in income, hence in demand emanating from the Global South, does
not apply equally across all economies, creating a real need to segment
between potential customers susceptible to purchasing MNEs' existing
offer and the much larger population that cannot afford this.

…but many consumers still require different treatment

Notwithstanding the growing number of relatively affluent Global South
households, it bears repeating that there are many more "bottom-of-the-
pyramid" (BOP) citizens whose consumption possibilities still suffer from
a host of factors. First and foremost is a level of disposable income that,
albeit improving, remains very low. On top of this, many consumers
in this category lack easy access to efficient distribution outlets and are
therefore over-dependent on inefficient (hence expensive) intermediaries.
Unlike their emerging counterparts, these kinds of challenges are new
for many Global North MNEs, requiring a paradigm shift that some are
better at navigating than others.

Frugal - Characterised
by thrifty use of inputs
and/or pared down
functionalities.

The main adaptation that most MNEs must make when catering to
these huge BOP markets involves frugal products, that is, "plain vanilla"
items that can be afforded by customers who have only recently become
solvent. MNEs in several sectors have downsized and simplified their
products to make this change. One prime example is European consumer
goods conglomerate Unilever when it decided, after entering Africa, that
the only way to address poorer populations' demand there was to sell
smaller detergent packages at much lower prices, in the hope that the
long-term brand loyalty it would build in this way might compensate for
lower per-unit margins. Unilever went on to pursue this same low-cost,
single-use approach in other Global South locales, like the Philippines,
where, after discovering that potential customers struggled to pay 35
cents for its Rexona mini-stick deodorants, it created a single-use cream
version that sold well at 10 cents per packet (Mahajan 2016). This
frugal adaptation was accompanied by new distribution systems across
low-income Asian and African nations, reflecting the fact that most poor
rural consumers in these regions shop for small quantities at local "mom
and pop" grocery stores. Unilever's general marketing approach also
changed. It started training women to become rural sales agents (and
run beauty salon businesses out of their homes), subcontracted product
distribution to big local stores and offered ancillary services (ATMs,
community washing machines) at points-of-sale. It is only by engaging in
all of these different adjustments that the MNE felt apt to address BOP
Global South demand.

Similarly but in a different product sector, Signify (the new name that
venerable Dutch MNE Phillips Lighting adopted in 2018) has for several
years now been selling low-cost solar-powered lighting products to Africans
who live off-grid. On the one hand, actions of this kind teach MNEs a
great deal about accessing low-income consumers, with studies having

revealed the possibility for companies adept at small step "bricolage" innovation strategies to perform well despite the BOP constraints they face (Zhu et al. 2019). On the other hand, many of these businesses currently break even at best, raising questions about the feasibility for MNEs whose traditional Global North models revolve around high-tech (hence expensive) innovations of suddenly moving into low-cost markets where they must compete with local firms that have a lot of experience in these practices. To some extent, the answer depends on how cheaply goods must be priced to attract BOP demand. Up until about 2010, IB analysts used to talk about the "China price" being so low as to be prohibitive for any company with anything but a minimal cost base. This has changed somewhat over the past decade as Global South emergence dynamics have increased local prices – not to mention the fact that as emerging consumers become accustomed to quality goods, their tolerance for cheaper versions (or counterfeits) diminishes. But gross margins over the cost of goods sold remain tight with frugal products, intimating that Global North MNEs must have other reasons to pursue this approach.

One rationale may be the possibility for companies to apply here certain lessons that they first learnt back home. Renault's acquisition of Dacia's Romanian plants, which the French carmaker is using to produce low-cost electric vehicles that it hopes to sell across Europe, exemplifies this idea. Some might consider the strategy dangerous since Renault's cheaper versions could cannibalise its existing range. Of course, there is also a possibility that if Global North MNEs do not start offering frugal products in their home markets, their new emerging rivals will.

It remains that the main aspiration for most MNEs considering frugality is to build brand loyalty among the billions of consumers who are too poor today to purchase any other product class, but who will hopefully become much more solvent in the future. Above and beyond margin considerations, the factors that come into play here relate to the tensions that might arise between this population's attraction to Global North brands versus any loyalty that they feel for local companies. On the one hand, many Global South consumers remain "tired of daily life struggle and are [therefore] passionate for those brands which can help them escape from reality" (Sarkar 2014). This association of foreign brands with a lifestyle and standard of living which almost no Global South citizen could afford in the past (and relatively few can today) explains repeated findings that ethnocentrism is often less of a factor in purchasing decisions here than it is in the Global North (Karoui and Khemakhem 2019). The question going forward is to what extent the status currently conferred by having a Global North country of brand origin will dissipate in the future as people realise that more and more of the products being consumed in the emerging markets are actually being manufactured locally, irrespective of the nationality of the company selling them. Evidence that Global South consumers' love of local brands can readily coincide with a demand for global brands offers hope to foreign MNEs (Van den Berg et al. 2017), but also to their local rivals.

Case study 13.2: Diageo digs in

Fig 13.7
Africa's alcoholic
drinks market is highly
segmented.

As the product of a 1997 merger between two mega-multinationals,
it is no surprise that UK drinks giant Diageo – until recently, the
world's largest company in this sector – has always had an enormous
international presence. Having been invented out of thin air by
communications experts, the company name may not resonate among
the wider public, but many of its lead products (like Johnnie Walker
whisky and Gordon's gin) are long established global brands ensuring the
group's notoriety. After divesting its non-drinks (and wine) businesses,
by the mid-2010s, Diageo was running a coherent portfolio of alcoholic
products that (aside from its remaining beer lines, starting with its legacy
Guinness brand) placed it squarely in the hard liquor bracket.

This was actually a big decision, since unlike wine (consumed in
numerous cultures as a mealtime staple), hard alcohol is more of a niche
product that, in certain markets, conveys luxury connotations (and prices)
that under normal circumstances might be expected to restrict demand
to more affluent consumers alone. Now, Diageo, like all global leaders,
has long been aware of (and preparing) for the mass arrival of new
middle-class consumers from the Global South. And it could easily have
calculated that this newly solvent market would be happy to increase
its discretionary spending on high-status Western liquor brands; target
these segments by only pushing its liquor products (which generate
substantially higher margins than beer); and consider that by so doing it
had maximised its penetration of the Global South.

That is not what Diageo did, however, and it is useful to ask why.
Statistics show that even if the new Global South middle classes

count anywhere up to 2 billion members (a liberal estimate), there remain at least 3 billion other people whose income puts them below that classification, that is, at the bottom-of-the-pyramid. For these populations, expensive hard liquor is more or less out of the question. Indeed, the very poorest generally find beer too expensive, explaining why in countries like Kenya, it happens far too often that consumers are illegally served a cheap home-grown brew that makes them sick.

Instead of ignoring this cohort, Diageo intervened. Its decision-makers would have been motivated by a multitude of factors, potentially including a commitment to sustainability as well a desire to enhance the brand's reputation with governments and/or build brand loyalty with future consumers. It remains that Diageo has not only addressed Kenya's predicament by developing a good-quality beer specifically for that country – Senator Keg, made from local barley and sold at unprofitably low prices – but it also replicated this BOP strategy in a number of other African nations, in essence reinvesting in the local economies some of the profits it makes elsewhere on its liquor products (the one exception being Nigeria, where Guinness beer has been widely sold for more than 60 years).

Questions remain whether Diageo might consider extending this BOP marketing orientation to its liquor range in order to generate demand from consumers for whom such products are normally too expensive. This would be more problematic, however, if only because there is a greater quality risk with the distillation of cheap liquor than with beer brewing. The likelihood is that Diageo will cross-subsidise and continue to differentiate its marketing between various Global South segments. If someone is convinced that the geography of IB is going to change forever, it is best to dig in for the long haul.

Case study questions

1. What are the costs/benefits for Diageo of selling liquor as opposed to beer products to the new Global South middle classes?
2. How long should Diageo continue to subsidise its BOP marketing efforts?

Section III. Phase 3: emerging MNEs

The discussion so far about the changing geography of IB has highlighted the great opportunities afforded by the Global South's rapid emergence as well as the associated challenges, be it the difficult operating conditions often encountered in these locales or the tight margins associated with frugal products. As always in IB, a company able to overcome hurdles that others find daunting can achieve great competitive advantage. As noted by Columbia University's Karl Sauvant, the first scholar to really try to classify Global South MNEs' particularities, there is every chance that these new players' long experience in managing the aforementioned problems gives them real competitive advantage over their more established rivals – at home in the emerging markets but also potentially in the Global North. This then becomes the third and final stage in the Global South's emergence trajectory – and one that could have very significant implications for business school graduates, in terms of both the paradigms applied by the MNEs where they may decide to work and where this is likely to happen.

Emerging MNE paradigms

Although generalisations are always imperfect, certain patterns detected in the behaviour and mindsets of the first major MNEs to have emerged out of the Global South might argue for an adjustment in current IB thinking. The first observation here questions Uppsala theory's inference that internationalisation is likely to be incremental until managers get accustomed to working outside of their home market. The opposite appears to apply to emerging market MNEs, especially ones unaffiliated with home country institutions, since they seem to "springboard into their first cross-border acquisition at an earlier age than their Global North counterparts had done at a similar stage of development" (Kumar et al. 2020). There could also be some contradiction of Uppsala's psychic distance construct given the number of emerging MNEs whose internationalisation preferences privilege "well-developed institutionally distant host-country environments" (James et al. 2020) over fellow Global South countries that one would assume are more familiar to them. Having said that, Latin American MNEs' "multilatina" attraction to fellow Spanish-speaking countries (much like China's massive Belt and Road Initiative) indicate that at least some Global South IB interests are looking to develop a presence in other countries at a similar stage of socioeconomic development, as Uppsala does predict. The compromise analysis would be to view the new players as pursuing both cautious and adventurous internationalisation: the former because they want to leverage the capabilities they have developed at home and use them to navigate similarly difficult conditions in other Global South countries, and the latter because after honing their skills surmounting the volatile conditions in their home markets, they will have full confidence in their ability to overcome any competition they might face in the Global North (Samlee and Chirapanda 2019).

The second way that emerging MNEs differ is their basic philosophy. Whereas much business in the Global North involves single-minded pursuit of profitability, companies from the South are also expected to fulfil a significant social and political mission. In part, this may be due to the generally greater politicisation of most, if not all, enterprises in the emerging world, exemplified by the fact that China's second biggest food manufacturing multinational, Bright Food, is wholly owned by a municipal administration (Shanghai), something that would be unheard of in the older industrialised world. Otherwise, representing very poor populations as they do, emerging MNE decision-makers are likelier to realise the wider role that their companies are supposed to play serving the interests of a home country that possesses few other actors upon which it can rely to drive development. This sensitivity manifests in various ways, which IB analysis breaks down, as so often, along regional lines.

African MNEs

The vast diversity of this continent, along with its checkered colonial (and/or apartheid) past, makes it hard to generalise about the character of the MNEs originating here. Many began as state-owned enterprises and, despite recent privatisation measures, retain traces of their original public mission. Otherwise and with the exception of a few South African names or energy and mining interests working out of North Africa, internationalisation has tended to take place within the continent itself, reflecting the fact that most companies here are still at a relatively early stage of development and may therefore feel more comfortable in neighbouring environments. Few cross-border actions have been vertical in nature, however, translating into a dearth of trans-African supply chains (Bavier 2021) – something that planners are hoping to address through the African Continental Free Trade Area that came into existence on 1 January 2021 and which is intended to loosen the high barriers to trade that have hampered the continent's integration. For the moment, investment in Africa continues to be dominated by agreements where local authorities license foreign interests to extract natural resources. What follows is a permanent debate about the extent to which these dealings benefit local populations – a goal that is often evoked but not always achieved.

Asian MNEs

Unlike its comparators, the emergence of Global South Asian MNEs has caused an absolute revolution in IB. Enormous variations between the continent's subregions make it hard to generalise about business cultures here, but two notable ideal-types do stand out (in addition to a third Global North Asian model already discussed in Chapter 10 and involving Japanese *keiretsus* and Korean *chaebols*).

The first ideal-type is a well-documented phenomenon that has come to be known as the "Indian way of doing business" (Cappelli et al. 2010), based on the idea that companies originating in this massive national business culture are much more focused on long-term results and/or sustainability than on shareholder value. This can be witnessed in the prevalence of philanthropic activities among this cohort but also in the way that Indian managers famously engage with employees, encouraging them (even as they are supposed to show respect for seniority) to be intuitive and imaginative, thereby finding "creative advantage where no one is looking" in the hope that ensuing innovations will enhance the company's value-added over the long run.

Springboarding into foreign markets via early cross-border acquisitions is also prevalent among Indian MNEs, conceivably because they want to compensate for their status as latecomers to the world of IB. Some Indian companies have shown a willingness to assume major international risks, funding expansion via debt rather than equity. This reveals a self-confidence that would appear to be based on the success many have had pursuing frugal engineering and BOP segmentation strategies back home. Similar self-belief has also been revealed in the willingness by big names such as Tata Motors, Hindalco and Mahindra & Mahindra to engage in vertical cross-border acquisitions, an ambitious approach but one that is also risker – as witnessed by the major losses that Dr Reddy's Labs suffered when it bought Germany's Betapharm, or Tata Steel when it bought Corus in the UK (Chittoor 2015).

The second Global South Asian ideal-type involves "yang" multinationals (Rugman and Doh 2008) whose internationalisation broadly began with the export of commoditised components or generic products under outsourcing arrangements, followed by upgraded high-tech joint ventures with foreign partners, before culminating in these companies undertaking their own outwards FDI (Larçon 2009). Certainly, this was the pattern followed by two of China's earliest MNEs, TCL and Haier, which only differed from one another insofar as the former internationalised incrementally (starting with FDI in neighbouring Vietnam and the Philippines), whereas the latter went straight to the USA and Europe. Otherwise, given East Asian regimes' developmental capitalism tendencies (not to mention the prevalence of state-owned enterprise in China), yang MNEs have historically worked hand-in-hand with their home country governments when managing international risk, one early example being Beijing's use of its old "863 program" to funnel enormous subsidies over several decades to help national telecommunications companies like Huawei and ZTE catch up with their Western rivals and become the behemoths they are today.

Latin American MNEs

Early studies on the internationalisation of this cohort had highlighted the paternalistic attitudes of companies that often began either as state-owned concerns or entertained close dealings with their home country governments, and which therefore felt well-equipped for the public–private interfaces that are an integral part of IB (Cassanova 2009). Having experienced recurring political and economic crises throughout their history, many executives from this part of the world became adept at advancing on long-term objectives even as they would continue to navigate choppy waters over the short run. This has given these "puma" MNEs the confidence to engage in IB at a relatively early stage of development, with the acquisition of foreign assets being viewed as a hedge against the many problems they face in their home markets.

Paternalistic - Replicating a hierarchical family structure.

Puma MNEs' internationalisation results have been mixed, however. On the one hand, several leading Latin American names (like Brazil's Vale) famously embarked in the late 2000s on billions of dollars of acquisitions all across the Global North, only to incur enormous debt on the way, culminating in a dramatic reduction in capital expenditures (hence outward FDI) over the ensuing decade. Cost competition from China also seems to be a recurring problem for Latin American MNEs in many of the mid-tech sectors where they operate. Having said that, a few have internationalised very successfully, like Chilean winegrower Vina Concha Y Toro, which has done well adopting a more incremental rate of overseas expansion and consolidating market share in the Global North. Otherwise, there have also been noteworthy successes by several "multilatinas" (led by Mexican stalwarts like Mexichem, Cemex, Bimbo Grupo Alfa and America Movil) who have largely stayed within the Spanish-speaking Americas and maximised their linguistic and cultural affinities in this way (Pasquali 2020). It bears repeating that success in IB occurs just as often at a regional level than at a global one.

Transition MNEs (Eastern Europe)

Puma MNEs' slower approach contrasts with the FDI behaviour of their counterparts from Russia, which is the only country in transitional Eastern European whose companies have invested internationally to any notable degree (although it is also worth noting the export successes of top Czech brands Budvar Budweiser beer and Skoda cars). Leading names in Russia's resource-driven economy, led by Gazprom, Lukoil and Rosneft, all moved at an early stage of their development to build a presence outside their home country. The deals were either horizontal in nature, involving other energy and mining interests, or vertical, with the Russians purchasing downstream distribution channels for the commodities they produce. What is particularly noteworthy here is the sheer magnitude of these investments, especially at such an early stage, as well as the intimate relationships that these MNEs entertain, like their Latin American counterparts, with national politicians, possibly explaining (at least in part) their ability to fund such substantial FDI programmes so early on.

The changing geography of international competition

Where emerging market countries and companies once required Global North technology to improve their terms of trade, that is rarely the case anymore. Indeed, Global South companies set the pace for many cutting-edge products and services today. Examples include a 2020 partnership between Brazilian avionics company Embraer and Uber to explore vertical take-off and landing vehicles for short urban journeys; or the astounding number of product and invention patents – counted in the many hundreds apiece – registered by a slew of Global South MNEs, ranging from Chinese appliance maker Haier to South African coal-to-liquid conversion and syngas specialist Sasol.

Similar technological leadership is also being shown in service activities, exemplified by the smart and multilingual ATMs that a Bolivian financial services company called Prodem FFP was already pioneering at the very beginning of the digital era; or the more recent example of Bangkok's Bumrungrad International Hospital, which in 2020 become one of the first microbiology laboratories in the world to fully digitise its end-to-end processes. The era when the older industrialised world was expected to be the location of all basic or applied R&D – as Vernon had famously posited in his Product Life Cycle theory – is truly gone.

That being the case, the question becomes what sort of configurations these emerging MNEs are likely to build overseas as they seek to catch up with (and even surpass) their older Global North rivals. As demonstrated above, many have evolved far past the initial stages when their only cross-border role was to fit into other MNEs' global value chains, simply exporting intermediary components (or finished goods that would then be branded under a prime contractor's name). Instead, they now have the confidence to intensify their own commitment to internationalisation, as witnessed in the sharp rise in the percentage of global FDI emanating from the Global South today (see Figure 13.8). In part, this confidence is based on emerging MNEs' greater access to the financial resources they need to expand: their home country currencies have often strengthened and, maybe even more importantly, their domestic capital markets have deepened significantly – trends that have had the additional benefit of empowering Global South governments politically, enabling them to be more assertive when negotiating trade and FDI deals with their Global North counterparts. This more level playing field, exemplified by a recent European Union–China investment treaty that the Beijing government was able to agree despite offering few

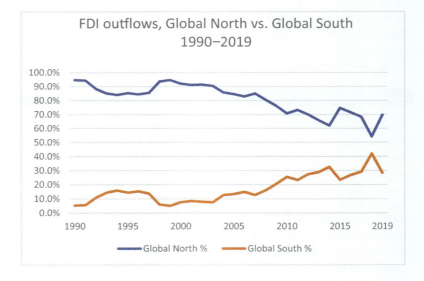

Fig 13.8
Breakdown in global FDI outflows (Global North vs. South). Derived from 2020 UNCTAD World Investment Report ©(2020) United Nations. Used with the permission of the United Nations. Accessed 11 January 2021 at https://worldinvestmentreport.unctad.org/annex-tables/

concessions on subsidies or labour standards (Rachman 2021), puts paid to the notion that powerful Global North MNEs and governments will always be able to force their Global South counterparts into a race to the bottom. That can still happen with struggling highly indebted poor countries (HIPC), but no longer with the emerging powerhouses.

These developments have also affected the locations where IB, and specifically FDI, is being done today. Through the first few stages of the Global South's emergence, that is, into the early 2000s, dealings in this part of the world were either largely done on a trade basis or, if FDI was involved, often saw the North extract natural resources from the South. In recent years, however – and as emerging MNEs have bolstered both their technological capabilities and financial resources – Global South destinations have accounted for a rising share of global FDI inflows (see Figure 13.9). Some of this still has to do with resource extraction, the difference being that much of this business today is conducted on a South-South basis (e.g. China's entry into Africa's primary sector). Indeed, South-South IB is widely predicted to skyrocket over the next few decades, enhanced by factors like the astronomical rise expected in intra-Asian trade (Dotiwala 2020), without forgetting China's earth-shattering Belt and Road Initiative, the biggest infrastructure project in history (costing well above $4 trillion) and a venture that will increase the ability of vast swathes of East and South Asia, the Mideast and Africa to trade without any need for Global North intermediation.

This is not to say that FDI between the Global North and South will not intensify as well, just that a higher proportion than before will be on a South-North basis rather than the other way around. To some extent, the degree of variation can be expected to depend on the type of IB involved. Resource-seeking South-North FDI is likely to fade: the South has almost never turned to the North for raw materials, and as noted above, even the North's undisputed technological prowess is increasingly being matched by Southern (especially Chinese and Indian) strengths. On

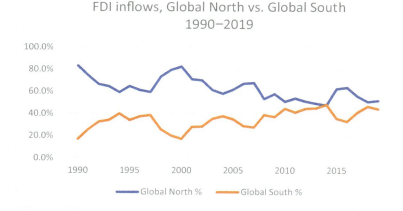

Fig 13.9
Breakdown in global FDI inflows (Global North vs. South). Derived from 2020 UNCTAD World Investment Report ©(2020) United Nations. Used with the permission of the United Nations. Accessed 11 January 2021 at https://worldinvestmentreport.unctad.org/annex-tables/

the other hand, asset-seeking South-North FDI, sometimes for backwards integration purposes but increasingly to access end user markets, is likely to skyrocket. Emerging MNEs (exemplified in the white goods sector, for instance, by Turkey's Beko or China's Haier) will increasingly sell to the Global North in their own name instead of working through host country intermediaries. Global South brands that were totally ignored in the North until recently will become household names. The world is changing indeed.

It is a turn of events that also offers today's business school graduates fantastic new career opportunities. Until recently, the main demand for ambassadors across the North-South divide targeted IB practitioners skilled at building bridges from the former to the latter. Today, with a whole host of emerging market MNEs such as China's Lenovo actively broadcasting their intention to hire Global North citizens capable of helping them enter the older established markets (Holstein 2014), international bridging has truly become a bilateral affair.

Attitudes and alternatives

The emergence of the Global South countries may be a major opportunity for MNEs originating in the Global North, but it also challenges their long-standing domination. For political and cultural reasons, they often feel uncomfortable when entering emerging markets without a local partner. Yet where a MNE chooses to form a partnership, there is always the risk that it is arming a future rival. Where a company has a head start in a given market, it can be difficult deciding whether the benefits of the occasional alliances that are a normal part of IB, especially when entering an unfamiliar locale, justify the risks.

Chapter summary

The chapter starts by speaking to the decision made by most, if not all, Global South governments over the past 30 years to open up to the world of IB. This has generally involved a three-stage process where these countries would first integrate existing global value chains by assuming a number of upstream responsibilities, often starting with low value-added manufacturing but increasingly moving towards technologically more advanced productions. The net effect was to increase the aggregate income of Global South households and public administrations, sparking the second stage of the process, with the emerging world now being targeted for its commercial potential. Part of this new demand might be addressed by selling established MNEs' existing product lines to the South's rapidly expanding middle classes, but frugal innovation is also necessary if these countries' numerous BOP consumers are to be brought into the market as well. The capabilities that some emerging MNEs have developed in addressing demand in their home markets and in navigating the difficult operating conditions that can prevail there explain the third and final phase in this development chronology, that is, the Global South companies' rapid expansion not only in other emerging markets but also and increasingly in the Global North. The net effect of this sequence is a radical change in the geography of IB.

Case study 13.3: Morocco rocks with OCP

Fig 13.10
Morocco's beautiful desert also contains mineral riches.

With a 2021 per-capita GDP of around $3,500, Morocco might be classified as a lower middle-income nation positioned about halfway up the Global South rankings. The Cherifan Kingdom is a constitutional monarchy with a comparatively stable political environment; rigorous fiscal management has helped to keep inflation low (and enabled, before the Covid-19 pandemic at least, a rapid fall in public debt); plus the country's cultural affinity with (and physical proximity to) Spain and France, combined with the rising cost of doing business in transition Eastern Europe, has translated into a wave of foreign investment inflows. On the other hand, official unemployment has hovered around 9 percent since 2010 (with a disproportionately high proportion of the workforce still employed in poorly paid agricultural activities); income inequality, as measured by the Gini coefficient, remains high compared to other African nations; and Morocco only ranks 80th on Transparency International's Corruption Perceptions Index. As with any country, but maybe especially with a Global South country, economic performances can be mixed.

At the same time – and again, like most of its comparators – there has also been a concerted effort on the part of the authorities in Rabat to accelerate national emergence by means of a developmental capitalist approach that combines market liberalisation with programmed industrialisation. The year 2008 saw one example of this shift when Morocco's leading state-owned enterprise, l'Office Chérifien des Phosphates (OCP), converted to a limited liability company. OCP would remain nationalised, notwithstanding talk in early 2020 at the Casablanca stock exchange that several of its affiliates could be privatised one day soon. This maintenance of state ownership reflects both the dominant business culture in Morocco (influenced by French centralising traditions) and also concern about the need to stop foreign interests gaining control of a company responsible for one of the country's most strategic exports – phosphates. About 72 percent of total global reserves of this mineral are found in Morocco, and given an almost endemic national trade deficit, it seems crucial that the country's leading exporter continues to prioritise the public interest. Having said that, the 2008 change in OCP's status materialised a very specific intention, one expressed in a book written in the early 2010s by the company's visionary CEO, Moustafa Terrab and relating what he described as "a lesson in management from the South". Underlining his goal of transforming OCP's business culture, Terrab called for a new entrepreneurial spirit where voices throughout the group – regardless of their position in the managerial hierarchy and irrespective of whether they were working out of headquarters or on the operational frontlines – felt empowered to offer creative thinking and indeed criticism where necessary. The goal was to inject private sector sensitivities and feedback mechanisms into a company that remained in public sector hands. It is a hybrid mentality characteristic of many emerging market MNEs today.

OCP's efforts to increase its value-added also represents received wisdom among development economists. Phosphate is crucial to many of the functions that plants undertake to sustain life on Earth, starting with the transformation of starches and sugars, nutrient transfers, genetics and even photosynthesis. For example, phosphoric acid is a key ingredient in the fertilisers that global agriculture has been using intensively ever since the Green Revolution of the late 1940s, meaning that a sizable global trade exists in raw phosphates and its more advanced (and higher value-added) forms: phosphoric acid and fertilisers themselves. Like many Global South manufacturers who have yet to move up their global value chain, OCP could have confined its international activity to merely shipping raw phosphate rocks abroad, but it hasn't. Recognising relatively early on the terms of trade implications for Morocco, the company has been operating its own intermediary transformation facilities for many decades, the end result being that fertilisers account today for around half of global group revenues.

For the first few decades, a large proportion of OCP's exports went to fellow African nations, in part because this was easier logistically but probably also because managers felt more comfortable not straying too far from home with their first internationalisation exercise. This has changed markedly since 2016, however, with the Group now running international sales and distribution (and occasionally processing) operations out of New York, São Paulo, India, Singapore and Beijing, without forgetting its ongoing presence across Africa. Expansion has not gone without hiccups, as exemplified in late 2020 by a decision taken by the USA's former Trump administration – inclined as it was towards protectionism – to assess countervailing duties on OCP, allegedly because of the export subsidies that the company had enjoyed. The year previous, OCP's North American business had also suffered declining orders from a struggling Canadian client. The upwards trajectory that saw the Group more than double its global revenues over the 2010s has not been seamless. History, whether IB-related or not, may trend in a given direction, but there are always bumps along the way.

It remains that OCP's new role as a globally significant emerging MNE is one that it seems happy to embrace. Market volatility will, by definition, come and go, but the company seems confident that the long-term outlook for global food (hence agricultural) demand – particularly in Africa, OCP's home region – puts it in a good position to consolidate its positive early international performance. In which case, Morocco's economic future will be a lot less rocky than its phosphate mines.

Case study questions

1. What effect might OCP's state ownership have on its international business strategies?
2. What are the costs and benefits of OCP's decision to move up its global value chain?
3. Which factors might determine OCP's future internationalisation trajectory?

Chapter discussion questions

1   What other development models might exist besides the manufacturing-for-export trajectory that kick-started most Global South economies' emergence?
2   Which countries might be added or subtracted from Jim O'Neill's Next 11 emerging markets lists?
3   How feasible is it for Global North MNEs to adapt their product ranges to bottom-of-the-pyramid consumers' specific demands?
4   How relevant is the experience that emerging MNEs have accumulated in their home markets to their target Global North markets?
5   What new IB opportunities will arise as a result of China's Road and Belt Initiative?

References

Bavier, J. (5 January 2021). "African free trade bloc opens for business, but challenges remain", accessed 8 January 2021 at https://www.weforum.org/

Canals, C. (16 September 2019). "The emergence of the middle class: an emerging-country phenomenon", accessed 9 January 2021 at https://www.caixabankresearch.com/

Cappelli P., Singh, H. Singh, J., and Useem, M. (2010). *India Way: How India's Top Business Leaders are Revolutionizing Management*, Cambridge, MA: Harvard Business School Press.

Cassanova, L. (2009). *Global Latinas: Latin America's Emerging Multinationals: The New Latin American Jaguars*, Palgrave Macmillan.

Chittoor, R. (27 February 2015). "Why the rapid emergence of MNCs from India intrigued international business pundits", accessed 13 January 2021 at https://economictimes.indiatimes.com/

Cohle, Z. (June 2019). "Explaining the current innovative R&D outsourcing to developing countries", *Journal of Industry Competition and Trade*, Volume 19, Issue 4, pp. 211–234.

Dotiwala, F. (17 December 2020). "Emerging stronger, fitter, faster: The rise of the Asian Corporation", *McKinsey & Company*.

Filippaios, F. et al. (September 2019). "Political governance, civil liberties, and human capital…", *Journal of International Business Studies*, Volume 50, pp. 1103–1129.

Gandenberger, C., and Walz, R. (January 2020). "The role of frugal innovation in the global diffusion of green technologies", *International Journal of Technology Management*, Volume 83, Issues 1/2/3, p. 97.

Hall, B. (25 November 2020). "Germany frets over its corporate dependency on China", *Financial Times*.

Ho, P. (2008). *Leapfrogging Development in Emerging Asia: Caught between Greening and Pollution*, New York: Nova Science Publishers Inc.

Holstein. W. (8 August 2014). "Lenovo goes global", accessed 8 January 2021 at https://www.strategy-business.com/

IBEF Indian Brand Equity Foundation (December 2020). "Automobile Industry in India", accessed 8 January 2021 at https://www.ibef.org/

James, B. et al. (October 2020). "Emerging market multinationals' firm-specific advantages, institutional distance, and foreign acquisition location decision", *International Business Review*, Volume 29, Issue 5, accessed 31 July 2021 at https://www.sciencedirect.com/

Karoui, S., and Khemakhem, R. (May–August 2019). "Consumer ethnocentrism in developing countries", *European Research on Management and Business Economics*, Volume 25, Issue 2, pp. 63–71.

Kumar, V. et al. (March 2020). "Springboard internationalization by emerging market firms: Speed of first cross-border acquistion", *Journal of International Business Studies*, Volume 51, pp. 172–193.

Larçon, J. ed. (2009). *Chinese Multinationals*, Hackensack, NJ: World Scientific.

Mahajan, V. (14 December 2016). "How unilever reaches rural consumers in emerging markets", *Harvard Business Review*.

Nuruzzaman, N. et al. (October 2019). "Competing to be innovative: Foreign competition and imitative innovation of emerging economy firms", *International Business Review*, Volume 28, Issue 5, accessed 31 July 2021 at https://www.sciencedirect.com/

O'Neill, J. (2013). *The Growth Map: Economic Opportunity in the BRICs and Beyond*, Kindle: Penguin.

Pasquali, M. (8 September 2020). "Latin America: Multilatinas by index score 2019", accessed 8 January 2020 at https://www.statista.com/

PWC (2017). "The World in 2050", accessed 8 January 2021 at https://www.pwc.com/

Rachman, G. (4 January 2021). "Europe has handed China a strategic victory", *Financial Times*.

Rout, S. (19 January 2020). "FDI policy for Indian retail sector – major implications", accessed 8 January 2021 at https://www.indianfolk.com/

Rugman, A., and Doh, J. (2008). *Multinationals and Development*, New Haven, CT: Yale University Press.

Samlee, S., and Chirapanda, S. (March 2019). "International marketing strategy in emerging-market exporting firms", *Journal of International Marketing*, Volume 27, Issue 1, pp. 20–37.

Sarkar, A. (September 2014). "Brand love in emerging market: A qualitative investigation", *Qualitative Market Research*, Volume 17, Issue 4, pp. 481–494.

Van den Berg, A., et al. (2017). "Ethnocentrism and local brand love: What are the consequences for global brands? The case of fashion brands in South Africa", accessed 8 January 2021 at https://www.researchgate.net/

Wheatley, J. (20 December 2020). "Debt dilemma: How to avoid a crisis in emerging nations", *Financial Times*.

Zhu, F. et al. (December 2019). "Base-of-the-Pyramid (BOP) orientation and firm performance: A strategy tripod view and evidence from China", *International Business Review*, Volume 28, Issue 6, accessed 31 July 2021 at https://www.sciencedirect.com/

CHAPTER 14

International business and the natural environment

Introduction

The second of the three priorities that practitioners would usually identify in McKinsey's erstwhile international business (IB) surveys was the ecological imperative – an existential crisis that the world of commerce, disturbingly, took a very long time to acknowledge. Having said that, things have changed rapidly in recent years, with environmental sustainability rapidly becoming a priority for many, if not most, companies worldwide, starting with multinational enterprises (MNEs). It is a new agenda, and the new academic discipline that it has spawned, widely referred to as green business (Sitkin 2019), is one that it behoves all IB learners to study today.

This chapter takes a specifically cross-border view of green business topics, analysing how the natural environment affects IB and vice versa. It is an approach that transcends pure ethics to highlight practical (and profitability) considerations. Ecological challenges like resource depletion and pollution, as well as the inconsistency of the international regulatory

Ecological imperative - Precept that restoring environmental sustainability is paramount.

Fig 14.1
Trade may be beneficial, but it also has a heavy environmental footprint.

DOI: 10.4324/9781003159056–19

framework, clearly interact with multinational operations, a problematic relationship addressed in the first section below. In response to these challenges, MNEs can and do undertake a series of value chain actions, as discussed in the chapter's second section. The chapter then concludes by looking at the green sectors offering the greatest IB opportunities today, with the final case study delving into an IB sub-sector (battery technology) that supports what is probably the most exciting green growth opportunity of all, namely, clean energy.

LEARNING OBJECTIVES

After reading this chapter, you will be able to:

- categorise MNEs' environmental problems
- assess the processes by means of which MNEs gain awareness of these issues
- analyse MNEs' greening process from an operational perspective
- evaluate different cross-border green marketing approaches
- determine various green sectors' international growth prospects

Case study 14.1: Siemens sees seams

The environmental expectations placed on MNEs from Germany are as demanding as anywhere else in the world. The German Green Party was the first to become a major political force, consistently winning office in state elections and becoming a key partner in Gerhardt Schroeder's 1998–2005 federal government. Environmental movements in most countries tend to only partner with other progressive parties, but ecology is so mainstream in Germany that ad hoc coalitions between Greens and the centre-right are also commonplace. Indeed, it was CDU Chancellor Angela Merkel who first introduced the groundbreaking *Wende* policy of transitioning out of nuclear power and accelerating renewables investment. The ecological imperative is deeply ingrained in German consciousness.

It was therefore surprising when one of the country's major engineering MNEs – Siemens, a world leader in its field for more than 100 years – announced in early 2020 that notwithstanding loud international protests, it would build the infrastructure for a huge coal project that Indian MNE Kadani was planning in Australia's Queensland state. It has long been demonstrated that coal is one of the "dirtiest" fuel sources imaginable, emitting high quantities of carbon dioxide (CO_2) when burned. Climate science has proven indisputably that the emission of greenhouse gases such as CO_2 causes the global warming that is wreaking havoc on the Earth's living systems, as brutally exemplified by the horrific forest fires that Australia suffered in early 2020 or the "heat domes" experienced in British Columbia in summer 2021. Governments worldwide have committed to finding alternatives to dirty fuel sources,

Decarbonisation -
Efforts to reduce an
activity's CO2 emissions.

as have most MNEs, starting with Siemens itself, which proclaims support
for the principles of environmental sustainability and actually has a good
track record to back this up, including a strong commitment to become
entirely carbon-neutral by the year 2030.

Siemens' participation in the coal project is also inconsistent with
recent positive green actions it has taken, setting aside over €100 million
for decarbonisation, agreeing to a wholesale adoption of renewables,

transitioning to electric vehicles and implementing eco-efficient distributed energy systems. In the words of CEO Joe Kaeser, Siemens clearly has enormous "empathy" for environmentalism. But it is also under pressure to satisfy its other stakeholders, in this case, the shareholders. The difficulty of juggling planet and profits is a constant in IB greening discussions.

Case study questions

1. What effect does the culture of a MNE's home country have on its environmental attitudes?
2. In Siemens' internal debates, how were the pros and cons of doing the Australian deal likely to have been framed?

Section I. International business and environmental deterioration

It would not be an exaggeration to say that until recently, many IB practitioners were apathetic about environmentalism and even hostile towards environmentalists, dismissing both as irrelevant, utopian (Monbiot 2007) and anti-capitalist. This estrangement would sometimes be justified for philosophical reasons, often based on Friedman's argument (see Chapter 6) that business should focus on profitability, not sustainability. Of course, receptiveness to corporate environmentalism would also vary internationally. In markets where competition prevented companies from passing onto customers the costs they would incur when reducing their environmental footprint, going green meant internalising costs that used to be externalised – a step that managers in less collectivistic cultures would reject because they felt it gave others a free ride. Otherwise, because greening generally involves upfront costs that companies hope to recoup through future eco-efficiency, short-term national business cultures were always tempted to delay their green transition. Against this backdrop, it is not surprising that IB was so slow in responding to scientists' long-standing warnings about environmental deterioration.

Things shifted rapidly in the 2010s, however. Whether this can be attributed to the changing values of a new generation of managers or simply to overwhelming evidence of the clear and present danger of environmental deterioration, few, if any, companies today ignore the need for major and immediate action. That holds particularly true for IB: because the global depletion of finite natural resources raises the spectre of higher future input costs (increasing the cost of inaction); and because it is no longer as easy for MNEs to pollute distant ecospheres without this damaging their reputation with customers elsewhere. Indeed, there is an argument that MNEs bear a particular responsibility for

Environmental footprint - Consumption effects depleting the stock of natural resources; economic activity effects damaging living systems.

Finite - Non-renewable.

Ecosphere - Sum total of living flora or fauna whose interactions with one another enable life on Earth.

environmental deterioration given the intensified transportation (hence greater fuel consumption) caused by their decades-long implementation of fragmented, long-distance supply chains. This justifies further exploration of the two main environmental challenges that IB faces – resource depletion and pollution – as well as a look at how MNEs' incentives to improve their environmental performance are affected (and sometimes hampered) by the international regulatory framework.

Resource depletion

All economic activity involves consuming raw materials, transforming them into products and running the processes enabling this transformation. Materials' availability at an affordable price is therefore an indispensable condition of business. The problem is planet Earth's stock of finite resources is, by definition, limited. A 2019 World Wildlife Fund report announced that at current rates of resource consumption, 2.8 Earths would be needed to satisfy global demand – up from 2 just ten years before. This is clearly impossible and explains the relevance of resource productivity scenarios, especially to MNEs that, by virtue of their needs as the biggest companies in the world, are most vulnerable to resource depletion.

Resource productivity - Product output per material input.

Energy resources

There is a strong argument that the main interface between the natural and business worlds is the energy required to run corporate operations. The problem, as per King Hubbert's 1955 Peak Oil construct, is that non-renewable sources run out. Research including BP's excellent annual Statistical Review of World Energy calculates that at current consumption and production rates, and given probable reserves, the Earth only has about 50 years of oil or natural gas left, about 120 years of coal and 90 years of uranium. Supply may be extended a few years by sporadic discoveries of new sources like shale gas or deep-sea oil. But the picture is clear – before students reading this book finish their careers, the MNEs employing them will all suffer a supply-side energy crunch. It is a terrifying prospect for IB.

Peak Oil - Idea that at some future point half of all oil will be used up unbeknownst to consumers who will continue buying, causing prices to rise.

Today's global energy consumption patterns are no more reassuring. Over the course of the 2010s and despite widespread communication of the need for energy savings, demand rose by an annual average of 1.6 percent. In part, this reflects the energy-intensity of different economies, affected by factors like disposable income, the relative preponderance of industrial versus service activities and the breakdown between user sectors (residential, commercial, industrial and transportation) – each with its own footprint, electrification levels and environmental consciousness. World Bank data show an enormous variation between per-capita energy consumption in the USA (ca, 13,000 kilowatt hours per-capita); France, Germany and Japan (from 6,900 to 7,900); China (ca, 4,000); India (805); and Nigeria (145). The Global North economies

Energy-intensity - Energy spend as a proportion of sales, income, etc.

may benefit from advanced energy-savings technology, but this has had little effect on their overall demand due to the Jevon's Paradox, where consumers take advantage of energy efficiency to consume more than they would otherwise. As for the Global South, energy-intensity here is skyrocketing in lockstep with these countries' rapid industrialisation, with China itself accounting for well over half of the recent increase in energy demand. Unless things change, there is little prospect of energy demand not continuing to rise, further accelerating the depletion of conventional fuel sources. Even as per-capita consumption is due to decline because of energy-efficiency measures, expected population growth means that total use will rise (McKinsey & Company 2021a). As is so often the case with environmental matters, demographic influences are preponderant.

This scenario is of course at odds with classical economics' assumption that demand falls as prices rise. Quite the contrary, energy consumption seems inelastic, although there is evidence of a positive correlation in some countries between price rises and renewables investment. This inertia may be due to sunk investments calculations that incentivise companies to get as much value as possible out of their current energy-specific infrastructures before replacing them. Moreover, some managers have a cultural, ostrich-like inability to process frightening data. The first step towards addressing a crisis is to acknowledge its existence.

Sunk investments - Costs already incurred and that cannot be recovered.

Mineral resources

IB also consumes large quantities of minerals. Unlike fossil fuels, however, global reserves of the main minerals used in industrial processes and products are counted in centuries, not in decades. Moreover, most minerals can be at least partially recycled, although this adds to their cost and can cause performance problems. Whereas elements like gold and copper largely retain their properties after recycling, others like chromium lose strength in this process, which also requires chemical additives that can be highly polluting.

A further problem is minerals' uneven global distribution. The sites where ore is mined are often distant from where they are processed or used. This complicates availability, hence inventory calculations, sparking price volatility. To some extent, MNEs' access to mineral resources reflects their value chain coverage, as exemplified by many industrialists' historic tendency to secure inputs by acquiring mining companies in Africa and Brazil.

Also noteworthy are "rare earths" like dysprosium, terbium and neodymium that are used for wind turbine generators or hybrid automobile engine parts; or lanthanum, which enhances battery performance. More than 60 percent of global rare earth reserves are in China, which can therefore dictate global supply and create bottlenecks if it so chooses, as happened in February 2021 when Beijing announced it would limit the export of certain rare earths that are crucial to US weaponry systems. Having said that, just as important is another mineral – lithium – that is often classified as rare because it is always found in small concentrations but which is actually widespread, especially across Argentina, Bolivia and Chile. Lithium is a key element in batteries, which have become an essential green business because of the need to store ever-greater quantities of energy between the places where it is sourced and where it is used. In this like in other respects, distance and geography are crucial factors in IB flows.

Biological resources

A further depletion worry involves the plant and animal systems that (along with water) sustain life on Earth. The culprit here is overly intensive economic activity. It is not so much that forest and soil cannot renew themselves but instead, as formulated in Garret Hardin's famous "Tragedy of the Commons" construct, they are being consumed at a rate surpassing their ability to regenerate. The consequences are devastating, as witnessed by the way rapid deforestation is disrupting the natural carbon cycle, thereby exacerbating the climate change crisis. Stewardship policies vary widely internationally, with spending on reforestation (and biodiversity) being one key way that MNEs signal their green credentials to governments and consumers in certain countries. In others, however, mainly in the Global South, including Brazil and Indonesia, wood harvesting is considered a key development driver. How MNEs balance the frequent disconnect that exists between environmental and social sustainability is another subset of green IB studies.

As regards soil management, agriculture is of course a key IB activity, albeit more significant in employment than in GDP terms. Section III speaks to the prospects for this sector. For the moment, suffice it to note rising food prices' knock-on effects. As an everyday staple, food inflation propagates throughout an economy, epitomising the link between the natural and the IB worlds.

Lastly, water also does not deplete per se, but a similar effect is created when it becomes inaccessible (due to increasing droughts in hot zones), or when pollution causes clean water to be in short supply. The urgent need to address these problems makes this sub-sector another developing IB topic.

Pollution

Non-product ratio -
Percentage of inputs that are transformed into waste over the course of a production process.

Converting raw materials into final goods generates two outputs: products and waste. This latter output, resulting from the fact that matter is never destroyed, is called the **non-product ratio** (NPO) and almost always represents a much greater proportion of the original raw materials than the amount found in final products themselves. Because NPO is an undesired by-product of industrial processes, it counts as waste. Where waste has toxic effects because it is comprised of synthetic compounds that harm the natural environment when it is returned there in quantities too great to be diluted, it constitutes pollution.

Categorising pollution

The harm caused by noxious substances created through common industrial activities (see Table 14.1) depends on their nature and concentration. The topic is therefore intrinsically international in nature: because pollutants disperse geographically without regard for national borders but also given the difficulty of addressing this problem in the absence of full information about its origins.

Moreover, with some recent studies (Lopez et al. 2019) indicating that MNEs' foreign affiliates often have a greater carbon footprint than other units (often because they have been assigned the group's dirtier manufacturing operations), analysing pollution in national terms provides an incomplete picture of the reasons for its global distribution, especially given the way poor countries can feel pressured to become a pollution haven to attract desperately needed inward investment. Categorising pollutants by their physical characteristics neutralises these attribution of responsibility issues and is therefore a better way to broach the topic.

Pollution haven - Country characterised by low environmental standards, often in the hope of attracting inward investment.

Air pollution

Although climate change materialises in different ways worldwide, the causes – and potential remedies – are necessarily planetary, if only

Table 14.1
Examples of industrial pollutants

Type	Sources include
Gaseous pollutants	
- Solid particles (inc. asbestos)	Mineral extraction, cement/steel/glass works
- SO_2 (sulphur dioxide)	Power stations, refineries, large combustion plants
- NO_x (Nitrogen oxides)	International combustion engines, forest fires
- CO (carbon monoxide)	Motor vehicle exhaust fumes
- CO2 (carbon dioxide)	Fossil energy
- CH_4 (methane)	Coal mine, landfill sites, livestock
Heavy metals	
- As (arsenic)	Glassmaking, metalworking
- Cd (cadmium)	Burning solid mineral fuels, heavy fuel oil
- Cr (chromium)	Production of glass, cement, ferrous metals
- Hg (mercury)	Chlorine production, waste incineration
- Pb (lead)	Fusion of lead, manufacture of batteries
- Se (selenium)	Glass production, use of heavy fuel oil
Other pollutants	
- NH_3 (ammonia)	Agricultural activities
- PCDD-F Dioxins	Incineration, fuel combustion

Source: http://www.citepa.org/pollution/sources.htm

because greenhouse gases like CO2 emitted in one country affect global warming patterns elsewhere. The dangers of climate change play out at several levels, affecting, for instance, liveability and workability, global food systems and the maintenance of physical assets – without forgetting the general erosion of natural capital (Woetzel 2020). It is a phenomenon with a frightening potential to devastate modern civilisation, epitomised in the spectre of melting polar ice caps raising sea levels to the point of endangering coastal populations everywhere; flooding farmlands in countries like Bangladesh or the Netherlands; and endangering drinking water systems in many great metropolises (ranging from Shanghai, Mumbai and Buenos Aires to New York, Amsterdam and Tokyo). Add to this food supply concerns about recurring droughts, and it is easy to see why decarbonisation has become a priority green business objective for most MNEs today.

Having said that, there is another air pollution problem – one recognised long before climate change science was confirmed – to which many MNEs pay great attention, namely the toxic pollutant particles emitted through localised industrial activities. Smog may have less of a planetary effect than greenhouse gas-induced climate change, although as demonstrated by acid rain, it can also damage neighbouring eco-systems. It is, however, a serious health risk for populations residing near a polluting factory and therefore one of the main ways industrial MNEs interface with green business.

Liquid pollution

International industry pollutes the world's water systems in several ways. Liquid effluents from factories operating in countries lacking sufficient regulations or controls often contain toxic residues that pollute the local water table. A similar effect is produced when the gigantic agricultural exploitations that have become necessary to feed burgeoning global populations overuse fertiliser to hit their yield targets, causing toxic residues to run off. Lastly, the (sometimes unlawfully) inadequate disposal of waste products and/or used packaging – especially plastics –translates into an accumulation of solid pollutants that become highly toxic as they degrade into their aquatic environment. The example of the Great Pacific Garbage Patch, an estimated 1.5 million square kilometre patch of plastic waste in an ocean vortex between Hawaii and California, offers a precautionary tale. Where pollution comes from too many national and corporate sources, it becomes very difficult to incentivise clean-up, given a generalised reluctance to remedy problems that someone else has helped cause. In many instances, international cooperation is a precondition to green business.

Solid pollution

This is a diverse category that is easiest to apprehend in the mountains of finished products that have come to the end of their useful lives, are taken to waste facilities but cannot be recycled. Examples include

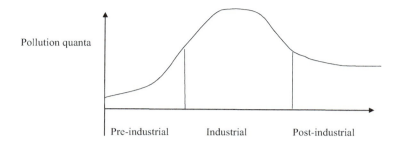

Fig 14.3
The Kuznets curve links
willingness and ability to
invest in pollution control
to a society's level of
industrialisation, hence
affluence.

non-biodegradable plastics and other materials used in discarded packaging, or consumer durables ranging from cars and old household appliances to electronic waste like outdated computers and mobile telephones.

Most Global North countries have the means and policies to process solid waste in a way that minimise pollutants seeping into the environment. As posited by the Kuznets curve, however (see Figure 14.3), poorer Global South countries that have yet to reach a certain threshold of affluence will often view development as a greater short-term priority than pollution control. The end result is that they tend to suffer from a greater concentration of unprocessed solid waste: because they have already industrialised but are yet unable to dispose of the by-products, and/or because they augment national income by importing end-of-life items discarded by the Global North. It is a reminder that green business does not occur in a vacuum but in a context partially defined by international variations in wealth.

Depollution responsibilities

This is not to say that Global South governments bear no responsibilities in this regard. There are countless examples of their populations suffering from environmental deterioration: killer smog in Beijing; epidemics or dysentery outbreaks in South Asia or Africa; or huge smoke clouds hanging over Southeast Asia. The problem is that many poor countries lack the resources to address pollution, which is one of the reasons that sustainable development has become such an important topic in recent international conferences. The idea here is that the Global North should help fund environmentally friendly growth in the South. The justification is that many of today's ecological problems can be attributed to the wealthy world's "dirty" growth trajectory during its own development process. Similarly, today's international division of labour has translated into NPO pollutants accumulating in Global South countries even as the products they manufacture are largely enjoyed by Global North consumers (see Figure 14.4). Add to this the fact that pollution generated in one part of the world moves to others, and it seems clear that the older industrialised nations have common cause with their emerging counterparts.

The political problem is convincing cash-strapped Global North governments to subsidise foreign countries they sometimes view as trade

Sustainable development - Emergence model based on respect for social and environmental principles.

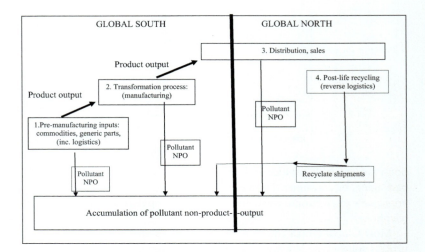

Fig 14.4
Global value chain inflicting greater NPO, hence pollution on the Global South.

rivals. Like all green business, depollution costs money, if only because of the need for manufacturers to install higher-quality, hence more expensive, eco-efficient equipment. Global North politicians will only be prepared to subsidise their Southern counterparts if they believe they share common environmental interests.

Just as difficult is discerning who in the private sector has most responsibility for depollution. Automakers make cars that pollute but individuals drive them excessively; builders install inefficient heating or ventilation systems but households overuse them; industrialists manufacture goods using environmentally unfriendly methods but consumers buy them because they are cheaper. Add to this the variations in national environmental standards and regulations and it becomes hard to say which stakeholders are supposed to lead on the green transition. The best answer is that there are that steps everyone can take if they are so minded (and indeed must take if they want to prevent Earth's destruction). The problem is the great variability in green consciousness worldwide.

Due to MNEs' concentrated power and potentially centralised decision-making, there is a strong argument that they should lead on international depollution efforts, internalising costs that they had previously externalised. MNEs alone can coordinate the environmental behaviour of both upstream suppliers and downstream end users, harmonise global environmental standards through their operations and wield the financial resources required for the green transition. What remains is the question of how committed different MNEs are to this goal. Some are only willing to undertake an ex post mitigation of the pollution they generate (often because the penalties for ongoing bad behaviour are lower than the operational restructuring costs). Others are prepared to engage in expensive ex ante abatement efforts in the hope of generating little (and possibly zero) pollution. In environmental behaviour as in all areas of IB, it is one thing to establish an external context but quite another to determine how MNEs will respond.

Mitigation - Compensating for bad outcomes ex post.

Abatement - Preventing bad outcomes from occurring ex ante.

Case study 14.2: Steeling South Africa against pollution

Fig 14.5
Steel foundries provide
work but are also a
health risk.

Having emerged from India to become world leader in steel, Mittal
exemplifies modern globalisation in several ways. Pursuing a volume
strategy based on maximum geographic coverage, Mittal tends to
internationalise via brownfield FDI, acquiring rivals and integrating them
into its network. Economies of scale and capacity use are crucial to a
product like steel, which is very sensitive to variations in global demand.
In short, Mittal needs its factories to be running at all times.

In 2002, Mittal purchased Iscor's 5,683 acre Saldanha Steel Mill at
Vanderbijlpark in South Africa. For as long as local residents could
remember, the plant's chimneys had produced heavy smoke and
poisonous black dust. The hope was that the new owners would have the
means and desire to cut emissions.

After an initial lapse of time, concerns arose that Mittla was not doing
enough. The company had rehabilitated Vanderbijlpark's waste disposal
sites and planned to cover its slag heaps of spent materials. Yet residents
still suffered from pollution-related health disorders, livestock was often
born deformed and metal surfaces would often rust uncontrollably (SAPA
2009).

The issue came to a head in January 2010 when Mittal South Africa
was shortlisted for the Public Eye Global prize awarded alongside the
Davos World Economic Forum to firms accused of lacking corporate
responsibility. Vanderbijlpark was nominated for dumping toxic waste,
failing to clean up contamination, opposing air quality controls and
lacking transparency (GAAM 2010). The company's website at the

time contained an environmental responsibility section portraying sustainability as a core value, which makes it all the more surprising that it was still being accused of more or less the same negligence a decade later (King 2019).

The chiding that ArcelorMittal (as the company is now known) had received from Davos's Global North NGOs does not appear to have had enormous effect on its Global South operations. What remains to be seen, however, is the impact of a 2020 South African order fining ArcelorMittal 3.64 million rands for emissions violations. Note that in dollars this was only about $240,000, a paltry disincentive possibly reflecting the fact that the Vanderbijlpark plant had been losing money and the South African government feared a loss of jobs if it shut down. Note also that ArcelorMittal's 2020 website featured much more specific sustainability news than ever before, speaking to "global leadership on climate action", a 2050 group target of net zero emissions and plans to use hydrogen technologies to produce "green steel" in Europe. These developments are laudable but also very expensive. And Europe is not South Africa. So the question remains when the environmental progress that the MNE is planning in some parts of its network will reach the others.

Case study questions

1. What cost/benefit analysis would ArcelorMittal have done regarding the depollution of its South African plant?
2. What would it take for ArcelorMittal to apply its European green technology to its South African plant?

Section II. MNEs' green transition

IB practitioners respond to the ecological imperative in different ways. Some may feign to ignore its urgency: either because they are daunted by the difficulty (and cost) of adapting their productive systems; and space or because they lack environmental education. Others will respond entrepreneurially, viewing the problem either as an opportunity to become a "green giant" value creator (Williams 2018) or else a "green swan" staving off potentially cataclysmic black swan events (Elkington 2020). Variations in attitude are partially explained by national business culture differences, like the arbitrage between long-term goals (e.g. sustainability and group-interest) versus short-term goals (e.g. profit maximisation and self-interest) – competing orientations that can be difficult to reconcile (Sheffi and Blanco 2018). Material circumstances also play a role, given the variable urgency attributed across the world to different ecological challenges (i.e. drought, water quality, climate change). Add to this the countless factors affecting each individual's own path towards environmentalism – motivated inter alia by personal value systems; the influence of family or friends; political, business or science news; and/or pressure from stakeholders like government or customers – and it becomes impossible to generalise why so many MNEs have started announcing their intention of making environmental sustainability as much of a core corporate function as production, finance or marketing have always been (Bresciani and Oliveira 2007). And yet, it is happening.

Implementation frameworks

In some situations, human agency plays little or no role in MNEs' greening processes and it is the authorities who set the pace. National governments that ratify United Nation-sponsored treaties (generally relating to climate change in recent years) usually follow-up by enacting local regulations like renewables obligations or CO_2 reduction targets, forcing companies operating under their jurisdiction, including foreign MNEs, to perform to specified standards. Domestic interests may complicate implementation but given the absence of any global environmental authority, national regulation is really the only avenue for state-imposed change. Indeed, the one body with potentially relevant transnational powers, the World Trade Organization, sometimes attacks domestic environmental regulations it considers antithetical to free trade.

On occasion, national regulation can actually be a powerful driver for multinational greening as well. The state of California, for instance, has determined that by 2030 all new vehicles sold locally must produce zero emissions. This establishes clear guidelines for the many companies worldwide who want to sell into this lucrative market. Indeed, those managers who view eco-efficiency as a competitive advantage tend to welcome stringent green regulation since it reduces the uncertainty surrounding future process investments. Others fall in line simply because they want to keep up with the competition.

Where regulations are lax, on the other hand, any green transition will necessarily be the doing of the companies themselves – often involving, in centralised MNEs at least, a top-down push by the group executive. As aforementioned, a variety of motives explain such efforts: the personal motives discussed above, but also business calculations. The latter can be divided into two categories: "playing to win" (increasing revenues by selling green products and/or burnishing a company's CSR reputation with customers); or "playing not to lose" (avoiding pollution-related liabilities and/or reducing exposure to resource costs). In both cases, the transition becomes an integral part of the company's "green to gold" strategy (Esty and Winston 2006). That makes it easier to explain to shareholders, who are, after all, a MNE executive's chief constituency, especially in more financialised business cultures.

Some of the changes that greening might cause to a MNE's configuration are so fundamental that executives alone have the authority to enact them. One example might be a company deciding to adopt a near-sourcing policy in order to shorten its international

Renewables obligations - Regulations imposing targets for the percentage of electrical supplies sourced from renewable technologies.

supply chains and reduce fuel consumption. Indeed, many corporate greening efforts today focus specifically on logistics (McKinnon et al. 2016). Pushed to an extreme, this could see MNEs revert one day to a more localised, multidomestic approach to IB (Xu et al. 2020) and place greater emphasis henceforth on trading intangibles as opposed to tangibles – two of the more revolutionary ideas evoked by IB observers in the wake of the Covid-19 pandemic.

Other greening measures are best initiated and guided by workforce operatives, in part due to their greater frontline knowledge. A prime example, especially in the wake of the Covid-19 pandemic, has been the replacement of commuting and business travel with home-working and videoconferencing. Of course, in the absence of a participative working culture (of the kind epitomised by Japanese MNEs), there is always a possibility that such actions will meet resistance from senior management or even fellow workers. People can be complacent and/or reluctant to change their routines, and the green agenda may be poorly communicated, especially to remote subsidiaries distant from where a decision is being made. This explains increasing efforts by numerous MNEs to communicate their best green practices internationally (Byrne 2020) and design programmes (i.e. training, personal sustainability budgets) encouraging staff to get on board with the green agenda, Whether monitoring is done by a sustainability manager lodged within each SBU or a cross-departmental task force created for this purpose, the narrative surrounding environmentalism is an essential part of its implementation. To paraphrase business guru Peter Drucker, "What gets measured get managed", which explains a subset of green business literature focusing on the contents of green accounting scorecards (Hedstrom 2018).

Some countries require triple bottom line accounting (Elkington 1994) – one of the first being France, which for two decades has had *Nouvelles Régulations Economiques* legislation specifying that companies above a certain size must file annual reports on a number of environmental (but also social) indicators. In most other countries, such reporting is voluntary, although for many MNEs it may feel mandatory, either because their rivals are doing it or because they see a commercial benefit in communicating the seriousness of their intent. Even so, there tend to be certain categories of information (like toxic releases) that companies do not like publicising. A MNE's real commitment to environmentalism is signified as much by what it does not disclose as what it does.

Lastly, more and more MNEs today commission green ratings from specialist agencies like France's EcoVadis or MSCI in the USA; order green audits from global bodies like the GRI (Global Reporting Initiative) or the ISO (International Organization for Standardization); and buy or build environmental management systems to monitor green performance and trigger an improvement dynamic. Note an ongoing debate whether it is more effective to run such green monitoring processes out of a MNE's global headquarters or its local subsidiaries, a

Environmental management systems – Accounting and reporting framework used to track and report upon a company's environmental procedures and performance.

further sign that environmental management increasingly involves MNEs facing similar organisational choices as they do with other IB decisions.

Operational greening

Ever since the Industrial Revolution, manufacturing stands accused of "commoditising nature" (Braungart and McDonough 2009), that is, of forcing harsh synthetic processes on the natural world instead of working within "planetary boundaries" (Rockstroem et al. 2015). "Industrial ecology" would see this traditional approach replaced with a "cradle-to-cradle" design (see Figure 14.6) that restructures value chains in such a way as to minimise resource consumption and waste. Thinking here is analogous to self-sufficient forests requiring no new inputs (asides from renewable sources like sunlight and water) because all end-of-life materials become nutrients for future life. With cradle-to-cradle, products are designed to differentiate between "biological nutrients" whose return to the environment is harmless versus "technical nutrients" comprised of synthetic chemical compounds and/or materials whose disposal would be toxic and which must therefore be recycled. Adopting these principles would force companies to restructure their entire production system – clearly an expensive undertaking that some IB practitioners may resist. The environmental benefits are, however, undeniable.

An example of this "closed loop" logic is Denmark's Kallenborg industrial cluster, where waste outputs from one plant become inputs for another. Proximity to suppliers can be helpful in this respect and is another argument that environmentalists use to advocate shorter global value chains. The same applies to information exchanges. The only companies that can confidently affirm their green credentials are ones possessing full knowledge of their suppliers' footprint, something

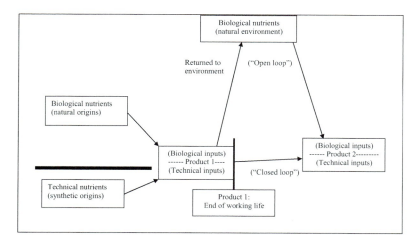

Fig 14.6
McDonough's "cradle-to-cradle" industrial process design.

that is difficult for MNEs sourcing inputs from the other side of the world. In the absence of comprehensive "environmentally preferable purchasing" specifications with suppliers agreeing full disclosure, there is a risk that as green as a company's own operations have become, it cannot guarantee the same for its products. A major recent study (Meinrenken et al. 2020) showed that as much as 45 percent of all product-related CO_2 emissions come from upstream suppliers, with only 23 percent arising during a prime contractor's own manufacturing operations (and 32 percent resulting from downstream activities like deliveries). Add to this the legal liability arising if imported inputs contain toxic substances – as toys giant Mattel infamously experienced in the 2000s with certain supplies from China – and it is clear that supplier monitoring is a crucial part of a MNE's greening process.

Of course, operational greening is also driven by what MNEs do themselves. Some actions in this area (like heating and lighting systems) relate to facilities management, others to the eco-efficiency of capital equipment and others to energy supply (affected by global variations in access to renewable energy sources). Note along these lines the significant environmental footprint of the world's leading tech companies, largely due to their intensive use of data centres. It explains why MNEs like Amazon, Google, Microsoft and Tesla have all become leading consumers of green energy, as well as their many collaborations in the countries where they operate with parties capable of providing this commodity.

Further operational greening actions pertain to product design. Above and beyond general principles like "biomimicry" and "biomorphism" – where products are designed to replicate "intelligent patterns" found in natural engineering (the aerodynamism of birds, the strength of snail shells) – noteworthy industrial practices today include the lightweighting of materials, the extension of products' useful lives via upgradeability and enhanced end-of-life disassembly. The main IB question here is different customers' receptiveness to such innovations.

Lastly, operational greening also applies to product delivery. The topic has become important in IB, as consumers everywhere go online to order items that are increasingly being shipped directly from foreign suppliers. The packaging and transportation this requires has a significant environmental footprint that some but not all MNEs have started to address. Efforts in this area include "rightsizing" smaller packages (and making them sturdier or reusable); using recycled, biodegradable or bio-based materials; developing reverse logistics schemes to accelerate recycling; re-manufacturing goods using identifiable and interchangeable modules; and rationalising transportation routes (with this latter aim being particularly problematic in MNEs characterised by globally dispersed value chains). All these measures serve a dual purpose: they save money; and they burnish a MNE's environmental reputation.

Lightweighting - Engineering products to perform the same function but using fewer materials.

Upgradeability - Product's capacity for integrating newer module versions.

Disassembly - Act of breaking a product down into its component parts.

Reverse logistics - Organised collection of goods that have reached the end of their useful lives and are destined for recycling.

Green marketing

It bears repeating that environmentalism is not a priority for many consumers making a purchasing decision, especially in societies where less attention is paid to this topic. Green marketing may be intended to spark greater interest, but it also suffers from the fundamental contradiction of asking people to behave in a way that might not correspond to what they perceive as their immediate material interest. This conflict between self-interest and group-interest (Sitkin 2019) becomes particularly problematic during economic downturns, with demand for green products often falling during recessions. Add to this the fact that green consumers do not represent a unified whole but constitute an accumulation of segments characterised by contrasting needs and perceptions, and the challenges associated with green international marketing can seem very daunting indeed.

All of which makes it important to understand why so many MNEs have decided to add a green component to their marketing mix in recent years. Logically, this represents their general opinion that sustainable brands can outperform conventional ones (Grant 2020).

MNEs targeting populations who are already sensitive to green issues obviously have it easier since they are merely responding to existing demand, either laying out green products' objective lifecycle cost benefits or cementing a particular brand's halo effects (see Table 14.2). Things are much harder in markets where consumers ignore (or are apathetic towards) the ecological imperative. The first step here is to proactively educate potential consumers either about green products' value-for-money compared to non-green products, or about the trustworthiness of the brand promise, both difficult tasks given evidence that a product's eco-benefits rarely suffice in and of themselves to attract

Lifecycle cost - Total cost of an item taking all impacts into account, including acquisition price, running costs, environmental impact and end-of-life disposal.

Table 14.2
Proactive vs. responsive green marketing matrix

	Green product marketing	Green brand marketing
Consumers already sensitised to environmental problems: responsive approach	Long-term argument focused on benefits like "life cycle" costs	Emotional argument to cement "halo effect"
Consumers not yet sensitised to environmental problems: proactive approach	Competition argument, i.e. value-for-money vs. non-green products	Psychological argument reassuring customers that company is trustworthy

buyers (Delmas 2018). The degree of resistance that MNEs encounter in these situations depends on whether consumers are being primed to accept a green product for its objective qualities, or a green brand for its aura. The company's own credibility also comes into play, with trusted local brands having an advantage over unknown foreign offers, unless the latter hail from a country stereotypically reputed for its high green standards. Add to this the international variations in consumers' receptiveness to novel products, and there is a good argument that green marketing is a function best run out of MNEs' local subsidiaries.

Green products

There are various ways to categorise green products. One is to distinguish between items that generate no environmental benefits themselves but are made according to environmental principles. A second is to highlight the green benefits that end users realise upon consumption. Otherwise, a distinction also exists between B2B and B2C green products.

Professional goods

One leading example of an industrial MNE that has transitioned into green B2B products is France's Schneider Electric. In 2010, this venerable old electrical engineering conglomerate signaled its intent to transition by co-launching a venture capital fund aimed at supporting start-ups advancing new energy and environmental technologies. Building up its knowledge base in this way, and after its 2012 acquisition of UK energy optimisation specialist M&C, Schneider has enjoyed international success with green B2B products since 2016, when it expanded its product portfolio to include "EcoStruxure", an Internet-of-Things-based digital architecture offering customers worldwide a wide range of power, IT, building, machine, plant and grid-related solutions.

Consumer goods

An early example of the greening of a B2C product came from a decision taken at UN's 1987 Montreal Conference to reduce the global production of ozone-depleting CFC chemicals. Following this directive, companies worldwide, led by the giant American conglomerate Westinghouse and European white goods specialist Electrolux, designed a new range of refrigerators featuring coolant systems using a safer chemical compound called HCFC. Within a few short years, HCFC refrigerators became the sector standard.

Today, the number of innovative green consumer products being offered to consumers worldwide has increased so rapidly that any list purporting to be comprehensive would soon be outdated. Suffice it to say that a useful distinction can be made between consumer durables (like energy-efficient cars, telecommunications devises or household appliances) versus perishables or health and beauty products. The appeal of the former category tends to be based on more rational, quantitative indicators (like life cycle costing) that are easier to standardise, with the main constraint here being a generally higher price tag. Products in the latter category are, on the other hand, more intimate in nature and therefore require greater adaptation to consumers' varying sensitivities, calling for an altogether more subjective kind of marketing.

Green pricing

There are several reasons why green products are more expensive. Companies may take advantage of their novelty value to charge more, especially in affluent societies where households can afford more discretionary spending. Also, green products' return costs are generally higher because they are made with better quality equipment and materials, because many have yet to attain economies of scale and because of the cost of organising end-of-life recycling. The net effect of these factors is to put green products at a price disadvantage vis-à-vis their non-green rivals and condemn them to a niche positioning, targeting customers willing and capable of paying a green premium. It is a market segment that varies greatly in size from one country to another.

Green premium - Surcharge paid for a green product over the equivalent non-green product.

Green places

Green marketing originally started with its own distribution channels, often involving small stores or cooperatives staffed by environmental devotees eschewing a more corporate image. Even today, specialist outlets continue to account for a relatively larger share of green product sales, although this is less true than before, with most of the world's leading retail chains now offering some green product ranges. Whether these are mixed with non-green goods in store sections defined by product category or sold separately in dedicated sections, depends if management's priority is to normalise customers' transition to green consumption or burnish the store's reputation as a green provider – again, the kind of decision that tends to vary from one market to another.

Green promotions

Green advertising signals that a company is not only aware of stakeholders' ecological concerns but also proactive about protecting the environment. It is intended to produce a halo effect, something that is particularly important to MNEs that have been accused of environmental mismanagement in the past and seek green redemption. One example is McDonald's. Sometimes criticised for meat procurement policies that some feel have indirectly helped to destroy the Amazon rainforest, the MNE now works with an NGO called Rainforest Alliance on a variety of food procurement issues. Similarly, oil giants like BP, Shell or Exxon Mobil, all criticised for oil spills, produce advertisements highlighting their work on renewable energies. Such messages will be received differently across the world, depending on a particular culture's instinct to doubt or else to trust the advertising messages it receives from a big-name foreign MNE. Evidence of "greenwashing", or the tendency

Green redemption - Where a company restores a tarnished environmental reputation through positive action.

to overstate a company's environmental commitment or performance, can exacerbate resistance, a hurdle that some MNEs try to overcome by participating in an international eco-labelling system that has arisen to certify product authenticity. The problem is the lack of standardisation in labelling standards. International green business can only take off once markets believe in its basic proposition.

Green finance

It would not be relevant in an IB textbook to go into any great detail regarding the particularities of green finance. There are, however, two points that can be made to introduce readers to the topic. One pertains to the funding schemes habitually associated with "ecopreneurship" (Schneider 2020). The other speaks to the different ways governments might choose to intervene in this domain.

The main dividing line when funding green ventures is between start-ups – maturing similarly to the way that Silicon Valley's IT superstars did a generation ago – versus diversification efforts by large MNEs. The former stream tends to rely on a combination of state support and venture capital, sprinkled with a small dose of asset financing as creditor banks seek to collateralise their loans to new customers who are small and innovative, hence risky. Access to capital will be less problematic for large ongoing concerns, especially MNEs who can tap into investor pools worldwide. There can be an issue with their perceived cost of capital, however, especially where shareholders within a particular national business culture have become accustomed to fast returns and expect quicker payback than is normally possible with green investments, which tend to be characterised by front-loaded outlays. Indeed, this may be one of the reasons why companies have increasingly turned in recent years to long-dated "green bonds" as a prime funding vehicle. These instruments offer a good alternative to tapping impatient shareholders, who have an unfortunate track record of pressuring big companies to abandon their green ventures even as the technologies involved start coming online. In opposition to this, note the growing number of socially responsible investment funds, but also mainstream funds like the American Black Rock, threatening to divest from firms showing insufficient commitment to environmentalism. These are some of the battle lines being drawn in the global market for green capital.

Timing is another part of the problem here. Sectors like solar energy, for instance, have experienced more than their fair share of false dawns, explaining why potential investors in this field tend to demand significant reassurances. In turn, this is one reason why so many green projects benefit from state backing in the form of direct guarantees. It is an undertaking that governments in some political cultures can be particularly susceptible to agreeing because environmentalism is a top priority for them and/or because they are comfortable with the prospect of economic intervention.

Public financial support for green projects can assume various forms. At one level there are the subsidies, production tax credits, co-investment arrangements or cheap loans that some governments are willing to offer, along with the feed-in tariffs that more aspirational countries like Germany grant to incentivise private investment in renewables. At a deeper level, there are government authorities in some parts of the world who are prepared to launch state-owned green enterprises. China's success in the global market for solar panels bears testament to the fact that this can be done viably, with public capital essentially helping an infant industry to survive until its sales reached a level enabling economies of scale. Green business is yet another subset of IB where governments regularly assume a greater role than they might do elsewhere.

Feed-in tariffs - Public subsidies paid to incentivise private micro-generation selling surplus electricity to the grid.

Section III. International green business sectors

Green business is widely expected to account for a growing share of all IB in the years to come. The United Nations, for instance, predicted in 2019 that the green economy would create 24 million new jobs globally within a decade. The big question for today's job-seeking graduates therefore becomes which specific sectors are likely to experience the fastest growth, and where this will happen.

In the years to come, green business will create so many international opportunities that it is impossible to analyse them all here. At the very least, however, some consideration should be given to "foundational" sectors like food and habitat (construction and transportation), so named because they are always in demand, regardless of the economic cycle. These businesses are worth detailing first and foremost because they are expected to account for large numbers of future green jobs. Beyond that, however, there is the prediction by visionaries like Bill Gates that clean energy is destined to become a leading driver of future international green business growth. Given Mr. Gates' track record, future IB practitioners would be very well-advised to respect his opinion.

Agriculture

Following the Green Revolution of the 1960s, populations worldwide (with the notable exception of certain highly indebted poor countries) experienced nearly half a century of abundant food. Benefitting from technological progress and government support, the Global North's agricultural output soon exceeded global consumption needs, despite the world population jumping from 3 billion in 1970 to nearly 8 billion by 2021. The ensuing food surpluses flooded many markets, putting downward pressure on prices and forcing farmers to restore profit margins by implementing increasingly intensive agricultural methods.

Fig 14.7
One green aspiration
is to shorten today's
long-distance food chains.

The ensuing overuse of fertilisers and pesticides impoverished arable land everywhere, however. Add to this the water stresses resulting from population growth, over-irrigation and recurring drought, and it became clear that the conditions of agriculture's economic success were also the ones endangering its ecological health.

The early 21st century saw a historic reversal in the food markets' long-standing trend towards higher surpluses and lower prices. The explanation for this is simply that demand outpaced supply – always a promising situation for producers. Of course, rapid population growth was always likely to drive food prices higher in the absence of a concomitant rise in productivity. The effects have been amplified, however, by "food globalisation", reflecting the changing preferences of many Global South consumers once their living standards improves sufficiently to allow them to enjoy a meat and dairy diet. The problem is that this wastes primary food since a great deal of edible grain must be fed to livestock for them to produce the same amount of energy as people can get from plants directly. Also (and possibly more) wasteful is the food culture that has long reigned in the Global North, reflecting well-to-do consumers' rich diet and habit of buying (or having supermarkets stock) more food than is needed, with surpluses being thrown away.

On the supply side, one of the main factors coming into play is the way growing amounts of farmland have been taken out of production either due to nutrient depletion caused by overuse or because climate conditions have deteriorated to the point of turning previously fertile fields into quasi-arid deserts. These effects are compounded by the ever-increasing competition for land, exemplified by the destruction of farmland through urban sprawl, not to mention of the use of some crops for biofuel production. Then there are the supply-side effects of applying international division of labour principles to global agriculture. Pursuing a specialisation logic, many countries (especially in the Global South) have made a proactive choice to produce just a few cash crops and import everything else. This has further fragmented the food sector's global value chains, adding to the power of big retailers who amortise their expensive delivery systems by ignoring traditional seasonality and offering the same products everywhere all year long. It is a system that not only racks up environmentally damaging "food miles" but adds to the sector's overall dependence on transport (hence energy) costs, thus affecting the prices farmers pay for fertilisers.

One remedy commonly proposed is a better integration between rural agriculture and urban consumption, embodied in the development of new "transition towns" characterised by seamless land use. Shortening production-consumption channels would have the additional ecological benefit of promoting biodiversity. It will be detrimental, however, to the sector's current international architecture, explaining the hope that big agricultural interests are currently placing in locales such as South Russia and above all Africa, where technological progress and land reform could see rapid rises in productivity and yields. The territorial scales involved also mean that big MNEs will probably be the only players able to take advantage of these opportunities.

As always in green business, the main determinant will be cost. A partial relocalisation of food supply chains could have an environmentally beneficial effect, but this may entail some farming activities returning to the Global North, where costs are much higher. On top of this, localisation creates diseconomies of scale compared to the current system where agricultural production is increasingly focused on a few mega-sites that are often very distant from where produce is consumed. The irony is that small farmers who might be interested in positioning themselves in sustainable local niches may not have the resources to make the transition, whereas big MNEs who can afford to do so may lack the motivation.

Habitat

The word "ecology", coined by German zoologist Ernst Haeckel in the 1860, translates broadly from Greek as the way people think about where they live, that is, their habitat. This is a broad construct that can be largely apprehended from a green business perspective in terms of the opportunities currently arising in the construction and transportation sectors. Readers should remember, however, that innumerable other IB activities (ranging from utilities to infrastructure to smart technology) will also benefit from the greening of humankind's living environment.

Construction

The construction industry is comprised of myriad sub-sectors, each with its own environmental interests. An example is the lighting sector, accounting in some countries for around one-third of all electricity used in buildings. Another is building materials. Few companies are in a position to specialise in all these competencies, meaning that construction projects tend to be driven by consortia of partners, often MNEs if a large infrastructure project is involved and/or if materials are being shipped across borders. One question this raises is to what extent partners in such ventures have similar environmental expectations or performance.

Otherwise, it is also important in green construction to distinguish between existing build and new build. Many developers nowadays are compelled by state authorities to use green materials or technologies either directly in the structures that they are building and/or in the surrounding infrastructure (i.e. CHP combined heat and power systems). These principles are relatively straightforward in new projects. On the other hand, retrofitting older units built to pre-ecological specifications is much more difficult, hence expensive. In this sector as in others, the more a green solution is applied ex post facto instead of being incorporated into the design from the very outset, the harder it is to implement. That may explain why larger business interests like MNEs tend to specialise in new construction and leave retrofitting to smaller, local concerns.

Lastly, it is also worth noting the growing emphasis placed today on empowering building occupants to control their micro-environments via thermostats, smart meters and other tools and energy management systems. All these technologies replaced the heavy-handed old practice of blasting vast quantities of heated or cooled air indiscriminately through buildings. And all involve products that MNEs are already selling internationally.

Transportation

The outlook for this sector can only be fully analysed in the context of broader trends like population dispersion, migration patterns (including commuting) and general economic flows. Geographers tend to apply a "hinterland" concept when assessing the relationship between a population centre and the regions with which it entertains regular economic relations. Clearly, the lengthier a supply chain, the greater its transportation needs (and the more it uses resources and generates pollution). The same applies when commuters face long daily journeys due to a locale's "extensive" spatial organisation. Macro-level responses at these levels involve public mass transit systems and urban infill policies directing further development to intra-mural brownfield sites instead of distant suburbs. Focusing on transportation modes exclusively without bearing in mind the sector's more contextual factors necessarily skews understanding of this business. Cross-border trade in new, energy-efficient vehicles is already well-established, but the products involved will necessarily have to fit the local infrastructure.

Aviation

Flying is the mode of transportation that has been most criticised for its environmental footprint. Although it only accounts for a small proportion of all greenhouse gases (and despite the design of new energy-efficient aircraft), the problem is expected to worsen, in part because the gases that planes emit in the upper atmosphere have stronger effects. The commoditisation of flying for both business and leisure travellers means that passenger numbers have skyrocketed in recent years despite higher ticket prices resulting from fuel inflation and the generalisation of airport taxes. Airline sector profitability does not entirely reflect this trend, since in addition to rising fuel costs, operators must also fund costly fixed assets and regularly struggle to adjust their capacities to demand variability. Add to this the extreme competition affecting the sector since its general deregulation, the rise of discount airlines and the after-effects of the Covid-19 crisis – and the global airline industry (including manufacturers like Boeing and Airbus) has good reason to worry.

Railroads

Like aviation, railways require significant upfront investment. Train itineraries are just as inflexible as planes, since they only offer "port-to-port" links and require users to organise further connections to their final destination. On the other hand, trains perform astronomically better in fuel-efficiency and carbon emissions terms, which may explain why the outlook for this sector is so much more positive.

Countries where the rail network is relatively underdeveloped are experiencing a small boom, translating into a constant flow of orders for leading MNEs like France's Alstom. There is a general consensus that many travellers will stop flying or driving if there is a rail alternative, possibly involving a hub system connecting intra-urban transport systems with inter-city fast train networks, the latter being a sector dominated by MNEs from countries already featuring integrated systems of this kind.

Note as well the strong move afoot to transfer freight traffic from road to rail, despite the latter's relative inflexibility. The shift would lead to a big reduction in fuel consumption and carbon emissions, although provisions would still have to be made to transfer goods from freight depots to final destinations. Trains, the earliest mode of motorised transportation, also appear to have the brightest future.

Road

The automotive sector can be subdivided into two categories. The first is freight trucking, an activity responsible for a sizeable proportion of total global transport emissions, despite recent technological improvements achieved by leading truck manufacturers like Daimler from Germany. But above all, there is the passenger car industry, a key green business sector given the many all-electric or hybrid vehicles that are already selling internationally, led, respectively, by MNEs such as Tesla and Renault-Nissan, or else Toyota and Hyundai. The background to technological transition in this area has been a fear of future fuel price raises and of the huge emissions of $CO2$ (and carcinogenic particulates) that traditional petrol-based vehicles cause. Governments in many countries have implemented regulatory and financial incentives steering future demand towards electric vehicles (EVs). Many automotive MNEs have announced plans to only produce EVs within a few short years. Under these conditions, it is surprising that consumers' global take-up remains so slow.

Some of this hesitation can be attributed to EVs' limited driving range (and a relative dearth of charging points). But the main factor is obviously their higher price tag, caused by factors like the cost of batteries and, more broadly, because many models have yet to reach economies of scale. This price differential is expected to last either until battery technologies become cheaper and more efficient, or until oil prices skyrocket to such a point that petrol-based cars become prohibitively expensive. Now, it is true that like many other green products, international demand for EVs remains more or less dominated by more affluent consumer segments in the world's wealthier countries. The big question is when it might spread to a wider global population and to what extent new entrants (like BYD in China) will be able to benefit from the fact that the market has yet to really launch.

There are many reasons to hope, however, that EVs are about to skyrocket globally. Access to charging points is improving rapidly, with new moves afoot to install devices not only at petrol stations but in buildings everywhere (Hoover et al. 2021). As for the economies of scale (hence profitability) aspect – indispensable to lowering EVs' price tag and therefore to expanding sales and creating a virtuous circle of further economies of scale – there are signs that some companies have reached this point. Renault, for instance, is already making as much profit from its electric Zoe model as from petrol equivalents and hopes that this will apply across all of its range within a few short years, especially given imminent plans to convert existing French factories to EV facilities and indeed to exit combustion engine vehicle manufacturing entirely within a decade (Campbell and Keohane 2021). Add to this the growing realisation in Asia, the world's fastest-growing market for automobiles, that environmental deterioration hampers regional development dynamics (McKinsey & Company 2021b) – and that future vehicle fleets must therefore be comprised of non-polluting EVs – and the outlook for the sector is rosy.

Clean energy

In the absence of a mass global geo-engineering/reforestation programme capable of dramatically decreasing the amount of CO_2 already in the Earth's atmosphere, there is widespread awareness that the only hope of slowing global warming is by quickly replacing fossil fuels – which currently account for around 80 percent of total primary energy supplies – with renewables. This imperative is translating all across the world into transition agendas that are breathtakingly ambitious. In India, for instance, two-thirds of the rise in future electricity capacity, which is set to double over the next 20 years, will come from renewable sources (Khera and Li 2021). China aspires to be totally carbon-neutral by the year 2060. Similar road maps exist in countries across the world. The question then becomes how this enormous demand will translate in IB terms.

As a rule of thumb, renewables industries are split between upstream operations that can be as internationalised as any other physical item, versus downstream installation activities that are necessarily localised (although there is a recent trend towards manufacturing MNEs engaging in forward vertical integration to expand their geographic coverage). An IB example of the former activity is China Molybdenum's acquisition from the USA's Freeport-McMoran of mines in Congo producing the copper and cobalt that are essential materials both for, respectively, wind turbines and electric cables (increasingly important as more energy is consumed in an electric instead of hydrocarbon form) on the one hand, and EV batteries on the other, Broadly speaking, companies with control over the raw materials or components essential to clean-tech supply chains are set to become increasingly important to IB flows over the next few years as the world economy transitions away from fossil fuels.

It is also worth noting that the clean energy manufacturing sub-sector with the greatest cross-border growth potential at present seems to be solar, which can be broken down into:

panel manufacturing (dominated by Chinese interests that are already producing at scale);
utility-scale operations (power plants and grids; also German utility RWE's intriguing plan to connect concentrated solar arrays in the Sahara desert to the European network);

distributed generation, a business selling smaller systems to non-utility
   interests (with more and more MNEs producing their own power
   on-site using equipment supplied by companies ranging from small
   start-ups to electrical engineering giants like the Swiss ABB, the
   Japanese Mitsubishi and the American General Electric); and
cell research, diversification for many of the world's largest computer
   chip makers.

Other renewables sectors are also worth consideration, however,
starting with wind. Unlike the solar sector, global value chains are less
fragmented in this business, with the world's leading wind company –
Denmark's Vestas – running both upstream and downstream activities.
Note otherwise the conversion of MNE interests in the fast-depleting
North Sea oil fields from hydrocarbons to offshore wind energy. Last
but not least, it is also worth keeping an eye on hydrogen power, with
a great deal of research currently being done on how renewables can
be used to split water into its component molecules to generate clean
electricity – the basis of a huge new international joint venture proposed
by Australian and Singaporean interests – and/or to create new hydrogen
fuel cells that can, under certain circumstances, be a more convenient
way of carrying energy (Smyth and Harding 2020). In green business like
in IB, bridging distance creates value.

Attitudes and alternatives

There is broad international consensus that the environmental challenge
is one of the greatest problems that the world has ever faced. What is less
certain is the role that MNEs will play in addressing the issue. Companies
that invest heavily in the environment should be able to improve their
operational efficiency and brand image. Yet transition is costly and will
be hard to justify in financial terms until the cost of inaction becomes
prohibitive. The real question is to what extent IB practitioners are
beholden to the status quo or, conversely, impatient to embrace the
future. Like most decisions, change is a matter of temperament.

Chapter summary

The chapter started with a review of the main environmental problems
facing MNEs: the depletion of natural resources (leading to higher
future input costs) and pollution. It then assessed factors determining
companies' recognition of the ecological imperative as well as their
options for operational greening (design measures, adapted international
supply chains and production processes), green marketing and finance.
The final section reviewed prospects for key international green business
sectors (agriculture, habitat [construction and transportation] and clean
energy). The key message throughout has been that the future is bright
for IB learners with green business capabilities.

Case study 14.3: Invinity seeking invincibility

Fig 14.8
Better batteries are
a prerequisite for
accelerating clean
energy's roll-out.

Renewable energy sources like the sun, the wind and the tides are without a shadow of a doubt excellent ways of powering IB in the future. But like any opportunity, they come with a downside that needs to be managed, namely, the fact that they are intermittent. The sun doesn't always shine, the wind doesn't always blow and even tides vary in their strength. There needs to be a way of capturing whatever energy these sources produce so that it can be consumed when needed. Add to this the many occasions when electricity users are off-grid yet still require power, and it becomes obvious why so many IB voices today consider energy storage to be such an exciting growth opportunity.

Until such time as a high-voltage "internet of energy" network has been developed (Hook and Sanderson 2021) and given the limitations of the currently predominant method used to store energy (pumped hydro in dams), batteries offer the only real solution to this problem (Sanderson 2020). They are a product that can be useful to a myriad range of customers: utilities seeking to integrate renewables into their power sources; electric vehicle users l and any person or company who relies on portable telecommunication or computing devices for their private or professional needs. It is therefore no surprise that so many battery plants are being built across the world today, often by large MNEs from the automotive industry (starting with Tesla and Nissan). Nor is it any surprise that IB ecopreneurs have also started to invest in this technology.

The main raw material that batteries use today is lithium. Until recently, this was primarily mined in brine form in the Congo and in South America (although Australian hard rock mines have also expanded in recent years). No real global supply problems are expected in the short run, although skyrocketing demand and the global supply chain's domination by one country (China) are causing some observers to question lithium's long-term availability and therefore seek new sources. One innovative idea is being pushed by a young company called Invinity Energy Systems, headquartered on the British island of Jersey. Invinity differentiates itself from bigger MNEs by banking on vanadium as an alternative to lithium. There are two reasons for this strategy: Invinity's belief that vanadium has superior properties (and a better safety record); but also because as a smaller company and relative newcomer, it may need to follow a different path than its more established rivals who already enjoy a global reach.

Invinity itself is the product of a merger between two small flow battery companies (redT from the USA and Avalon from the UK). The explicit reasoning given for this operation had been participants' recognition of the fact that attacking the global battery market required a scale that neither SME possessed separately, especially because the technology involved is new and would therefore require a great deal of support at first. The website for the consolidated group – now a MNE itself – expresses an ambition to "compete head-to-head against incumbent lithium-ion giants" in Europe, North America, Asia, Australasia and sub-Saharan Africa. It may be more precise to say that Invinity is actually seeking to carve out a new niche for itself rather than engaging in direct competition with bigger competitors like China's CATL, which is already operating at scale. Invinity's website expects the flow battery market to reach £3.5 billion by 2028, while predicting that the global storage market will receive £55 billion in new investments by 2024. Even within its chosen niche, Invinity may need to hurry to sign international contracts, given news coming out of China that another new player, Rongke Power, is now looking to build the world's largest vanadium battery – a feat that it could then use as its own IB launchpad. All of which proves, to no one's surprise, that even as IB practitioners can be delighted by the great growth prospects afforded by the burgeoning green business sector, it is an opportunity that their competitors will have also noticed. The cat is truly out of the bag.

Case study questions

1. Does a company need a certain size to impose a new technology internationally?
2. How quickly can a new player like Invinity move to attack markets worldwide?
3. What can Invinity do to further accelerate its international presence?

Chapter discussion questions

1. How will natural resource depletion affect MNE configurations?
2. How should MNEs cost their anti-pollution efforts?
3. What are the different ways of adapting green marketing to local circumstances?
4. How might cultural variations affect MNEs' willingness to go green?
5. At what point will the cost of environmental inaction signal to MNEs a need to assume the costs of environmental action?

References

Braungart, M., and McDonough, W. (2009). *Cradle to Cradle: Re-Making the Way We Make Things*, London: Vintage Books.

Bresciani, S., and Oliveira, N. (2007). "Corporate environmental strategy: A must in the new millennium", *International Journal of Business Environment*, Volume 1, Issue 4, accessed 31 July 2021 at https://www.researchgate.net/

Byrne, J. (2020). *Green Your Business Now!...*, independently published.

Campbell, P., and Keohane, D. (18 January 2021). "Renault boss hails EV supremacy on road back 'from hell'", *Financial Times*.

Delmas, M. (2018). *The Green Bundle: Pairing the Market with the Planet*, Palo Alto, CA: Stanford University Press.

Elkington, J. (1994). "Towards the sustainable corporation: Win-win-win strategies for sustainable development", *California Management Review*, Volume 36, pp. 90–100.

Elkington, J. (2020). *Green Swans*, New York: First Company Press.

Esty, D., and Winston, A. (2006). *Green to Gold: How Smart Companies Use Environmental Strategy to Innovate, Create Value and Build Competitive Advantage*, Hoboken, NJ: John Wiley & Sons.

GAAM (19 January 2010). "ArcelorMittal's polluting South African plant shortlisted for Public Eye Global Award…", accessed 2 February 2010 at www.globalaction-arcelormittal.org/

Grant, J. (2020). *Greener Marketing*, Chichester: John Wiley & Sons.

Hedstrom, G. (2018). *Sustainability: What Is It and How to Measure It*, Boston, MA: DejG Press.

Hook, L., and Sanderson, K. (4 February 2021). "How the race for renewable energy is shaping global politics", *Financial Times*.

Hoover, Z. et al. (5 January 2021). "How charging in buildings can power up the electric-vehicle industry", accessed 16 January 2021 at https://www.mckinsey.com/

Khera, A., and Li. J (14 January 2021). "Asia at the speed of light: An interview with the head of ReNew power", accessed 22 January 2021 at https://www.mckinsey.com/

King, S. (22 March 2019). "No end to Arcelor's toxic practices", accessed 16 January 2021 at https://mg.co.za/

Lopez, L.-A. et al. (April 2019). "The carbon footprint of the US multinationals' foreign affiliates", *Nature Communications*, Volume 10, Article number 1672.

McKinnon, A. et al. eds. (2016). *Green Logistics: Improving the Environmental Sustainability of Logistics*, London: Kogan.

McKinsey & Company (January 2021a). "Global energy perspective", accessed 16 January 2021 at https://www.mckinsey.com/

McKinsey & Company (12 January 2021b). "Future of sustainability. Asia's climate change imperative", accessed 22 January 2021 at https://www.mckinsey.com/

Meinrenken, C. et al. (April 2020). "Carbon emissions embodied in product value chains and the role of life cycle assessment in curbing them", *Scientific Reports*, Volume 10, Article number 6184.

Monbiot, G. (2007). *Heat: How We Can Stop the Planet Burning*, London: Penguin.

Rockstroem, J. et al. (2015). *Big World, Small Planet: Abundance Within Planetary Boundaries*, Stockholm: Bokfoerlaget Max Stroem.

Sanderson, H. (22 November 2020). "Battery life: The race to find a storage solution for a green energy future", *Financial Times*.

Sapa-AP (25 September 2009). "Arcelor Mittal South Africa dismisses pollution claims", accessed 2 February 2010 at www.corpwatch.org/

Schneider, N. (2020). *Ecopreneurship: Business Practices for a Sustainable Future*, Berlin: De Gruyter.

Sheffi, Y., and Blanco, E (2018). *Balancing Green: When to Embrace Sustainability in a Business (and When Not To)*. Cambridge, MA: MIT Press.

Sitkin, A. (2019). *Absolute Essentials of Green Business*, Abingdon: Routledge.

Smyth, J., and Harding, R. (29 November 2020). "Will Australia's 'hydrogen road' to Japan cut emissions?" *Financial Times*.

Williams, E. (2018). *Green Giants: How Smart Companies Turn Sustainability into Billion-Dollar Businesses*, Hertogenbosch (NL): Amacom.

Woetzel, J. et al. (16 January 2020). "Climate risk and response: Physical hazards and socioeconomic impacts", accessed 16 January 2021 at https://www.mckinsey.com/

Xu, Z. et al. (September 2020). "Impacts of Covid-19 on global supply chains: Facts and perspectives", *IEEE Engineering Management Review*, Volume 48, Issue 3, accessed 31 July 2021 at https://ieeexplore.ieee.org/

CHAPTER 15

Multinational technology and talent

Introduction

Learning is an essential skill in any field of human endeavour. International business (IB) professionals, with their culture of openness and intellectual curiosity, will always be expected to have one eye turned to the future, accumulating competitive intelligence by scanning their environment to detect which developments are likeliest to have the greatest impact on their future fortunes. Historically, one such trend has always been technology, explaining why this would usually be the third and final theme cited in McKinsey's erstwhile IB practitioner surveys. It is a topic that that this book has already broached with Chapter 10's discussion of the knowledge development policies that multinational enterprises (MNEs) try to implement – and traditionally a key element in any analysis of business economics.

Where observers pinpoint external trends that are economic, political or social in nature, there will always be a question whether the impact is apt to be felt worldwide or within the confines of a single country. This is less of a factor with technology, however, given the inherent

Competitive intelligence - Compilation and analysis of external information.

Fig 15.1
New technologies have interconnected the world more than ever before.

DOI: 10.4324/9781003159056-20

universality of hard science and engineering. A better starting point here is asking whether a MNE's trend-spotters are themselves technology specialists (often working out of a centralised R&D unit) or commercial generalists whose main strength is interfacing with the outside world. Depending on the answer – and on a MNE's "push" versus "pull" orientation or headquarter versus subsidiary power relationship – there can be a huge difference in the speed with which new technologies will be adopted, hence on their potential for disrupting existing work organisations. As always in IB analysis, first-order discussions of strategic capability are enriched when more human elements are added to the equation. On the one hand, there is technology; on the other, there are the people implementing it.

The first section starts by reviewing some of the newer technologies that are widely expected to have the greatest effect on MNE processes and/or products over the next decade or so: artificial intelligence (AI); and robotics. Note that this list is necessarily contingent on the particular moment in history when the determination is being made. Around the year 2000, for instance, online "dot.com" enterprises were considered novel, but that is no longer the case today. Then, in the early to mid-2010s, analysis of new IB technologies would often revolve around 4G and 5G broadband connectivity, usually framed in terms of their operational effects (improved coordination of remote upstream partners) and potential for helping companies to reach a wider customer base, including the world's more rural populations, who had been operating up until that point at 2G or less. A great deal of discussion also began at the time about cloud computing and the way it would help MNEs store (hence process) immensely greater quantities of useful data. Both these technological advances remain highly relevant today, but they are no longer novel per se. By definition, IB practitioners with competitive "watch" responsibilities must always be aware of whatever technology is cutting-edge at a given point in time. Tomorrow's future is almost necessarily different from today's.

All of this heralds the overview provided within this final chapter regarding the relationship between multinational technology and IB careers. Note that instead of offering a generalised study of human resource management (HRM) within MNEs – a topic better explored in a dedicated HRM text – the focus here will be on the specific challenges facing this book's readers as business school graduates starting their IB careers in the early 2020s. It is a time-specific approach chosen in recognition of the fact that a future edition of this book published, for instance, in the year 2030 would almost certainly discuss technology, HRM and skills in a different light. After all, if indeed there is no one-best-way of teaching IB, education in this area must always be relevant to the real-life situations that readers are likely to encounter imminently. It bears repeating that for all its theoretical and conceptual aspects, IB will always be first and foremost a living discipline.

Artificial intelligence (AI) - Learning achieved by computer or machine.

Robotics - Use of computer science and engineering to build operational robots.

Case study 15.1: Teva's troubled trails

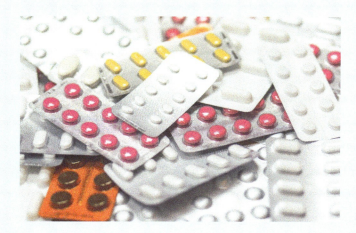

Fig 15.2
Generic products arbitrage market share versus per-unit margins.

The word "technology", when applied to a business activity, covers a wide spectrum of knowledge-intensive activities and outputs. Some are disruptive and revolutionise a market's manufacturing methods or product designs. Others, however, are more generic in nature and simply apply existing knowledge. MNEs can decide to opt for one or the other approach, or else for a combination of the two. Their choices in this respect can also vary over time, the end effect being that they might find themselves more or less in sync with the prevailing conditions in the various international markets where they choose to compete – as the nearly centennial Israeli pharmaceuticals company Teva has discovered on several occasions over its long history.

Pushing a new high-tech product can be risky, especially when this involves targeting unfamiliar foreign customers. A MNE can never be entirely certain of a given population's receptiveness to its new concepts, especially since their novelty aspect (and initial lack of economies of scale) means they will often be more expensive. This explains some companies compromise solution of offsetting the greater risk of IB with the lesser risk of selling a tried and tested technology, sold at an affordable price to try and ensure market penetration. For many years, Teva succeeded in making a name for itself by offering generic medicines, often pain management-related, all across the world. A low-risk approach intended to generate steady (if unspectacular) returns, the strategy would be successful for as long as volumes remained high and margins satisfactory.

Because generic technology is easier to operationalise than scientific innovation, it is also easier for new market entrants to appropriate – as has happened in the global pharmaceuticals industry, which recently welcomed a host of emerging MNEs competing as much, if not more, on price than on R&D capabilities. Perhaps conscious of this threat to its traditional model, Teva undertook over the course of the 2010s a series of cross-border acquisitions, partially to increase its generics volumes but also to diversify into potentially higher-margin branded drugs (culminating in these two product lines ultimately accounting for an equal share of total group revenues). The expansion programme produced very mixed results for Teva, however. On the one hand, the MNE could rejoice in the top three leadership position that it had achieved by 2019 in more than 25 national markets worldwide, led by its top ten or better ranking in the USA, UK and Germany. On the other hand, having acquired so many foreign interests (and running 65 production sites worlds), Teva found itself carrying very high levels of debt that become especially onerous in the late 2010s as margins began to be squeezed in many generic markets, without the company's new branded drugs experiencing sufficient success to offset these pressures.

Teva's situation actually became quite dramatic, with shares plummeting from a high of nearly 27,000 shekels in 2015 to a low of just above 2,500 in mid-2019. To reduce debt levels, it decided to divest assets, including a number of abbreviated new drug applications – never good news for a pharmaceutical company's growth prospects. Following these moves, however, the share price would stabilise in 2020 between 3,000 and 4,000 shekels, with some market commentators opining that Teva now looked likely to regain its financial equilibrium over time, albeit with a narrower product range. What remains to be seen is how the company's future product portfolio will break down between new and old technologies. Neither is intrinsically good or bad – in IB, like so much else in life, timing is everything.

Case study questions

1. What are the costs and benefits for Teva of concentrating on generic technologies?
2. What are the costs and benefits for Teva of concentrating on new technologies?

LEARNING OBJECTIVES

After reading this chapter, you will be able to:

- assess the main technologies apt to affect IB over the next few years
- evaluate technology development processes in different contexts worldwide
- identify how the new technologies will affect MNE value chain functions
- ascertain which technological skills IB practitioners will need in the future
- critique different IB career pathways

Section I. Technology in an international business context

Notwithstanding historical variations in technology's impact on the shape of IB, it is always in practitioners' interest to calculate to what extent the new technologies being rolled out at any given moment in time are likely to affect their future careers – and how this might happen. People develop tools that allow them to act upon the world in which they find themselves. Yet it is also that world which shapes the tools they will have at their disposal. The section below explores both topics in turn.

MNEs and today's new technologies

Observers will often try to inventory all the technologies that are apt to alter the course of IB at a given moment in history (see Table 15.1), but such lists are necessarily subjective. Having said that, text analysis in the early 2020s reveals a strong consensus around five topical "platforms of innovation", many of which relate in some way or another to information technology (IT): blockchain technology, energy storage, DNA sequencing, automation (especially robotics), and artificial intelligence (Wood 2020). The first item is relevant to the nascent cybersecurity industry (see Case study 10.1) and discussions about future "crypto-currencies". The second – energy storage – was covered at great length in Chapter 14, although there is value in giving additional thought to the potential of energy efficiency-related technological complementarities, epitomised by the new distributed energy capabilities that Korean manufacturer LG is building into its new refrigerators, enabling any excess power that these appliances generate to be fed into the electric grid. The lesson here is that the full

Technological complementarity - Where the combination of distinct technologies creates new synergies.

Table 15.1
Sample of IT-related technologies broadly predicted to have a significant impact on international business over the course of the 2020s

Accelerator chips	*Mobile applications*
Artificial (general) intelligence	Nanotechnology
Augmented reality	Natural language generation
Biometrics inc. facial recognition	Near-field communications
Blockchain/cybersecurity technology/ SASE	Predictive analytics
Edge computing (for containers)	Robotic process automation
Energy management systems	Smart technology/sensors
5G/superfast broadband	3-D printing
Geolocation/geotargeting	Virtual reality
Internet-of-Things	Wearable technology

benefits of any one technology might only be realised in conjunction with another. Complementarity often translates into synergies, a principle also exemplified in an idea currently being mooted by Apple and Nissan that twinning the former's AI capabilities with the latter's automotive technology might spawn the world's first viable driverless car. To the extent that different countries specialise in different technologies – and where these are allowed to cross borders – complementarity-related considerations can already make technology an IB topic in and of itself.

The third item in the list above, DNA sequencing, also has a rosy future, despite being largely limited at present to one or two sectors (biopharmaceuticals, and agriculture, to a lesser extent). Strong recent cross-border activity in the healthcare sector – whether on a M&A basis (e.g. takeover of Belgian viral-vector manufacturer Novasep by the American Thermo Fisher Scientific; of the UK's Kymab drug and vaccine developer by France's Sanofi) or via alliances (between the German BioNTech and the American Pfizer) – is a direct translation of the vulnerabilities that the Covid-19 pandemic has revealed in the world economy. It is one thing for companies to possess basic science patents but quite another for them to parlay this into concrete product designs and then sales – two additional steps that often require collaboration with other actors, especially when commercialisation must be international in scale in order to recoup sizable upfront R&D outlays. Otherwise, it is also worth noting the hope that biotechnology can ultimately surpass the healthcare sector to interact with the rest of the global economy, with some observers having mooted the possibility that up to 60 percent of all physical inputs could be made in the future using biological materials or processes (Chui et al. 2020). Indeed, by some estimates, upwards of $4 trillion in additional GDP growth can be generated in this way over the next 10 or 20 years. If or when that happens, biotechnology will become a core enabling factor for all MNEs, irrespective of the sectors where they are currently operating.

This essential and universal status is something that the final two technologies listed above – automation (in the form of robotics) and artificial intelligence (AI) – have already attained, however. That is probably the reason why so much attention is being paid to them in IB literature nowadays – not to mention the fact that they are both IT-related and indeed partially interlinked already, much in the same way as the Internet-of-Things (IoT) is often studied alongside 5G broadband. For both these tandems, the actions taken by one technology depend on data being digitalised by the other (WEF 2020b). A good example is the way that e-retailers' digitalised enterprise resource planning, combined with their 5G connections, allowed them to perform much better during the Covid-19 pandemic that their bricks-and-mortars counterparts did wielding just one or the other technology (Weldon 2020). Having said that, it is better for clarity's sake to introduce AI and robotics separately, before delving more deeply into the conditions under which each has arisen, plus the role that each might perform in the technological transition of today's MNEs.

Internet-of-Things - Web 2.0 where the prime interaction is not between machine and person but between machine and machine.

Digitalised - Data converted from physical to digital form for computer processing purposes.

Bricks-and-mortars - Tangible physical (as opposed to virtual) operations.

Artificial intelligence (AI)

AI is a broad term referring to the replacement of human cognition with mechanised systems designed to leverage experience into more evolved reasoning. In concrete terms, this often involves machine learning where algorithms are prepared enabling computers to process large quantities of data in the hope that they will then be able to detect patterns imperceptible to human analysts and come up with predictions and prescriptions that can be useful to business. Deep learning takes this one step further by interconnecting layers of software-based calculators known as neural networks in the hope that they can process even larger quantities of complex data with less need for pre-programming than machine learning has. In both instances, the goal is to produce new knowledge about heretofore unknown social realities – an aspiration that is especially relevant in IB contexts where practitioners' distance from (and lack of familiarity with) foreign environments can have a negative effect on the quality of their understanding, hence on decision-making. This incomprehension risk can be problematic for MNEs working both at the upstream portion of their global value chain (i.e. when determining throughput volumes for a production unit serving volatile global markets) and on the downstream side (i.e. when trying to compute foreign consumers' diverse price sensitivities). Indeed, some AI-based applications –- like GPT-3, a language-generation model capable of generating tailored browser search advertisements that reflect the habits and profiles of diverse categories of users – go a long way towards replacing the need for human marketing intelligence (Thornhill 2020a). In turn, this could mean that some MNEs will view the ability to interpret such models (like several other AI applications) as a more important capability than downstream operatives' international intuitions.

By 2021, nearly half of all companies worldwide had already applied AI to their processes or products in some form or the other, although it is worth noting the gap that exists at this level between Global North MNEs and their Global South (particularly Latin American) counterparts (Balakrishnan et al. 2020). Unsurprisingly, high-tech and telecommunications sectors have been global leaders in the implementation of AI, with automotive and other assembly activities – plus fintech – coming right behind. The main functions being performed using the new technology tend to relate either to product development or service operations, materialising in tasks such as inventory and parts optimisation, pricing and promotions, customer services analytics and sales and demand forecasting. The sheer scope of these interventions highlights the advantage that MNEs endowed with AI capabilities have over smaller and/or poorer rivals who have yet to make a similar technological transition. The fact that American tech groups (the big Silicon Valley names but also dynamic newcomers) dominate the development of artificial intelligence is clearly beneficial to the USA's IB profile.

Fintech - Technology developed to automate financial services like payments but also credit and market analysis, etc.

Robotics

Automation is a centuries-old business strategy mainly embodied today in companies' growing use of robots to perform physical tasks (manufacturing, logistics, warehousing, handling, etc.) that were once done by humans. From a specifically international perspective, the first aspects to discuss here include the various speeds at which robots are being rolled out in different countries, as well as the factors affecting the way in which MNEs are implementing this technology. Similarly, important issues like robotisation's impact on international value chains, hence on national workforces and economies, can then be addressed later in this chapter.

According to the International Federation of Robotics, whereas Western and Nordic Europe are the parts of the world where production has been automated to the greatest extent, the country with the highest "robot density" – or number of operational robots per worker – is Singapore, which had 9.18 units per 100 workers in 2019, three-quarters of which were being used by the electronics industry (especially for semiconductors and computer peripherals). South Korea came a close second with score of 8.68, mainly involving LCD and memory chip manufacturing, without forgetting automotive (including electric battery) applications. A long way behind this leading pair came Japan, then Germany and then the others. The first observation is that the leadership which Asia shows in many aspects of modern industry can also be witnessed in relation to robotics technology, with two of the sector's three leading manufacturers (Mitsubishi and Fanuc) originating from Japan. A second observation is that the global stock of robots is actually concentrated in a few countries and manufacturing industries (see Figure 15.3), usually specialised in the more knowledge-intensive global value chain operations that produce the more technologically advanced goods that tend to be sold in Global North automotive or electronics markets (Seric and Winkler 2020). Robots continue to be rarely if ever used in low value-added activities, especially if a business has access to low-cost labour. Indeed, even in advanced manufacturing nations such as Germany, there is evidence that robot use is highly skewed towards a sector's biggest and most highly skilled exporters (Deng et al. 2021). It is important to reiterate that this is a relatively new technology which is just beginning to proliferate.

Having said that, global robot growth numbers are already very impressive. In the year preceding the Covid-19 outbreak, total year-on-year sales were up by 32 percent. Even during the pandemic and contrary to the rest of the world economy, the robotics sector continued to expand (Romei 2020). Not only do robots help companies achieve their long-term productivity objectives, but they are also immune to pandemic-related social distancing requirements and, in one sense, already embody a remote working logic. On top of this, robots performing factory work and supply chain and logistics handling tasks make it easier for MNEs to operate further upstream if they so desire, but also and maybe especially further downstream, as witnessed by

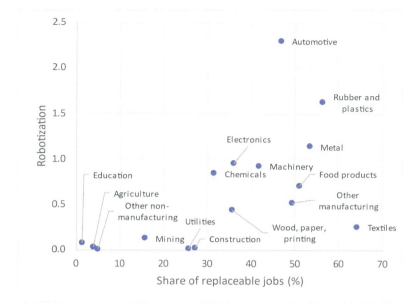

Fig 15.3
"Robot adoption and
feasibility of automation
across sectors". World
Bank. 2020. World
Development Report
2020: Washington, DC:
World Bank. © World
Bank. Artuc, Erhan;
Bastos, Paulo; Rijkers,
Bob. 2018. Robots,
Tasks and Trade. Policy
Research Working Paper;
No. 8674. World Bank,
Washington, DC.

the accelerating digitalisation of retail customer interactions in many countries, first and foremost in Asia (Sneader and Singhai 2021).

Digitalisation is a subset of both AI and robotics, being a process innovation that modern MNEs commonly apply throughout their value chains, mainly in white collar functions ranging from R&D to back office administration and on to commercial representation. It is a parallel development to robotics, in the sense that it also involves the replacement of humans by machine functions (albeit in this case, by software). Indeed, to the extent that data accumulated via digitalisation can be treated with AI, it also complements this latter technology. The net effect of these linkages is that robot and AI manufacturers – along with digitalisation system providers – are struggling to keep up with current demand, explaining ongoing waves of consolidation within these industries today. These tend to involve either mergers and acquisitions twinning users with producers, or else major investments by MNEs in AI and/or in automation start-ups (Dekhne et al. 2019). Such actions are the materialisation of a growing consensus among IB practitioners today that the new technologies should be accounted for much in the same way as labour, raw materials and generic components always have been. They are indispensable inputs for most all multinational production processes, making it useful, in turn, to examine the conditions in which they might be nurtured.

Technology contexts

At one level, the significant capital and/or R&D expenditure required to develop and implement technologies like AI and robotics tend to limit actions in these areas to those countries and companies with sufficient means to undertake such investments. This means there is a strong risk that access to the new IT-related technologies will become yet another factor exacerbating current international disparities. Cognisant of this possibility, governments worldwide try proactively to either promote or prevent access to them, depending on where their interests lie. The sum total of these forces combines to create the contexts within which AI and robotics can be developed and applied by MNEs to their value chain operations.

The first observation to make about today's cutting-edge technologies is that they vary considerably in terms of their region of origin. As aforementioned, despite ongoing problems relating to intellectual property protection, most Asian economies have been remarkably fast in building up their digital and mobile technological capabilities and infrastructure, to the point that this one region now accounts for nearly half of all global tech company growth and R&D spending, and an even greater percentage of total patent applications (see Table 15.2). The hope is that this leadership will also help Asia's Global South economies to leapfrog traditional stages of development and catch up as quickly as possible with their more advanced neighbours like Japan and Korea. Certainly, this is the path upon which China and India have already embarked, even if both nations still feature entire sectors of activity that lack key technical capabilities. Other Asian countries do lag behind these leaders, however, painting a picture of multiple technological tiers within a single continent and inferring a possible future intra-regional division of labour. Having said that, efforts are also being made by these so-called laggards to catch up, as exemplified by the digital free trade zone that Malaysia has recently created to accelerate its own integration into the higher tech tranches of the manufacturing value chains in which Asia continues to specialise.

Table 15.2
Global top ten countries for 2019 patent applications by resident entities

China	1,400,000
USA	621,453
Japan	307,969
Korea	218,975
European Patent Office	181,479
Germany	67,434
India	53,627
Canada	36,488
Russia	35,511
Australia	29,758

Source: WIPO. 2021. WIPO Facts and Figures 2020. Geneva: World Intellectual Property Organisation. © WIPO https://www.wipo.int/edocs/pubdocs/en/wipo_pub_943_2020.pdf License: CC BY 3.0 IGO. Downloaded 30 January 2021.

This picture contrasts with the technological progress witnessed in North America (and to a lesser extent, Europe), where there tends to be a greater focus on non-manufacturing global value chains. Exemplified by Silicon Valley's aforementioned prowess in artificial intelligence, Western technology today seems to revolve more around intangible applications, exemplified a decade ago by cloud computing and today by the IoT. When viewed in this light, the contemporary intellectual international division of labour seems to be replicating its material counterpart, with the West focusing to a greater extent on service-related applications and the East having more of a tangible focus. Of course, it is an arrangement that will displease some participants in the technology world, first and foremost in Europe, which finds itself once again squeezed between American concept leaders and Asian industrial powerhouses. This explains debates within the European Union about what steps might be taken to challenge other regions' growing technological dominance (Sandbu 2020). At one level, policy discussions in this domain highlight the comparative dearth of risk-taking equity capital in Europe, as well as the continent's fragmented intellectual property and licensing regimes. At another level, much airing is also being given today to critiques about the way in which different tech interests conduct their IB.

The first bone of contention relates to tax behaviour, and specifically to a perception in parts of Europe that some (mainly American) Big Tech interests have been using creative accounting to avoid paying sufficient tax in the different countries where they operate. In early 2021, the OECD ran international consultations on this topic, with France already announcing that it wanted to see the EU levy a continent-wide tax on digital services in case more conciliatory talks failed to produce concrete outcomes. Along these lines, it is worth noting that the USA's new Biden administration gave signs of supporting the same proposal a few months later. Otherwise, a second kind of dispute pertains to more regulatory issues, often relating to variable tolerance worldwide for the private technology interests have been using and/or protecting privileged customer data. Lastly, technology dispersion issues can also overlap with general political tensions. Sometimes, this happens domestically, with national governments trying to claw power back from home-grown technology oligarchs (Thornhill 2020b). On other occasions, the problem is more international in nature, reflecting rivalries between superpowers who try to avoid sharing technology because they see this as a way of expressing their disapproval of a counterpart's domestic policies, reducing the incidence of cyber-attacks and/or protecting domestic intellectual property that the other country is suspected of stealing.

At first glance, restrictions of this kind may seem quite reasonable. The problem is when trade-related international tensions transcend legitimate security concerns and turn into "techno-nationalism" (WEF 2020b). Given how crucial technology is to development dynamics and the deflationary effects it can have on the global economy as a whole (Booth 2020), protectionism in this area risks exacerbating the terms of trade disadvantages from which poorer countries and smaller companies already suffer. Add to this more circumstantial factors like the need following the Covid-19 pandemic to use technology to redesign urban lifestyles in rich and poor countries alike, and there is a strong argument to make that this is yet another domain where cooperation serves international interests infinitely better than conflict.

Technology and MNE functions

To the extent that MNEs are capable of developing disruptive technologies (and/or purchasing them from a third party), the next step is to determine the effects such tools might have on their global value chains. This is of course likely to vary from company to company, if only because each will have its own way of processing the new inter- and intra-firm interactions that are an integral part of any digital transformation process. It remains that certain generalisations are possible and indeed crucial to understanding the future of IB from a work organisation perspective.

Upstream

The new technologies are changing how IB practitioners view their upstream supply arrangements, especially given the vulnerability to disruption that the Covid-19 pandemic has revealed in today's fragmented global value chains. This is particularly problematic when a MNE's business model is built around a just-in-time logic, as is so often the case nowadays. The global shortage in semiconductor components that leading carmakers (like Volkswagen and Nissan) and automotive suppliers (like Bosch and Valeo) suffered in 2020 attests to the fragility of a system where long-distance outsourcing is a quasi-default IB strategy (Miller et al. 2021).

The end result has been a radical reassessment of possible MNE configurations. Because "Industry 4.0 principles (involving an application of data analytics, human-machine interactions, advanced robotics and 3-D printing) can offset almost half the labour-cost differential between China and the USA"; because AI makes it easier for prime contractors to monitor their lower-tier suppliers (Sneader and Singhai 2021); and given the opportunity for greater flexibility when advanced automation is combined with re-shoring (Seric and Winkler 2020), some would argue that the new technologies make a stronger case than ever for shortening MNEs' global value chains and in-sourcing many of the activities that are currently being outsourced. Of course, there is also the opposite view that MNEs should continue to outsource as much as they have been doing but simply use "end-to-end" digitalisation to tie foreign suppliers into their in-house platforms and improve process coordination in this way. The fact is that the new technologies enable both strategies.

The second noteworthy change to MNEs' production organisation involves the possibility of substituting robots for human workers.

Logically, companies predicting that labour costs will rise in the future
– due, for instance, to changes in national minimum wage levels – are
more likely to consider robotisation. Certainly, recent evidence from
China indicates a correlation between these two factors (Fan et al.
2020). Further research has uncovered, however, a much more nuanced
relationship than might otherwise be expected. There are questions, for
instance, about where the jobs that a MNE replaces with robots are
likely to be situated. The displacement could either occur abroad, if that
is where the company is already running its manufacturing operations,
or at home, if not. Otherwise, there is also the possibility that a MNE
will use its automation-related savings not to lower production costs
but instead to hire more people for those jobs that cannot be automated
(Stapleton and Webb 2020) After all, as apt as robotisation is to
displace a certain percentage of current manufacturing jobs, it does
not necessarily have to translate into MNEs employing a smaller total
workforce. According to some estimates, even if machines are likely to
displace up 85 million upstream and other human jobs globally during
the first half of the 2020s, expectations are that as many as 97 million
other positions will be created during the same period (WEF 2020a).
Most of the new jobs will be technologically much more advanced,
making the real question whether they will be filled by workers who
lost their old positions but have recently retrained, external contractors
hired for task-specialised work or individuals who were already working
in highly skilled positions and are simply evolving into the latest
technology. Over the past few years, the answer has tended to be the
latter two groups, raising concerns about the fate of the former and the
risk of seeing an exacerbation of social and geographic inequalities.

Lastly, it is also worth considering the future of "cobots". These are
robots that only operate in collaboration with humans, meaning they are
tools used to enhance workers' productivity, not replace them. Cobots'
proliferation points to the fact that under certain circumstances and with
an upskilled workforce, there may be less of a substitution effect between
human and non-human manufacturing labour than some had originally
predicted (Marin 2014). Clearly there are situations where the two
workforces can complement one another.

Logistics

Rapid automation and/or digitalisation is also affecting many cross-
border logistics tasks (components' arrival in factories; finished product
deliveries to warehouses, distributors and customers; picking and sorting
operations, etc.). The problem is that implementing new technologies in
these functional areas requires significant, hence expensive, changes to a
company's handling processes, excluding most SMEs from the equation,
with the exception of a very few "lighthouse" cases (exemplified by
Indonesian mining company, Petrosea, widely lauded for its predictive
maintenance of vehicles using AI and detection of mineral seams using
smart sensors). In general, it is only the world's biggest MNEs – the

ones like Amazon and Alibaba that are most committed to cutting-edge
technology – who possess the financial and technical wherewithal to fully
revolutionise their logistics function. Route optimisation software can
be incredibly complicated, and substantial capital outlays are required
to build the special warehouses needed for the "last mile delivery"
services that have become such an essential part of modern e-commerce.
Notwithstanding the ambient enthusiasm for the industry of tomorrow,
not every MNE (much less company) is in a position to implement the
new technologies, explaining why the value chain functions most closely
associated with them tend so often to be outsourced to specialists.

In actual fact, most technological progress in the field of logistics
has been the doing of 3PLs (third-party logistics providers). Motivated
by a number of factors (labour shortages, online retailers' skyrocketing
demand, complicated omni-channel delivery orders – without forgetting
many practitioners' spontaneous enthusiasm for the new technologies'
inherent promise), the global "transportation-and-warehousing" industry
has pivoted sharply in automation's direction (Dekhne et al. 2019). To
some extent, the new orientation is being financed by 3PLs' increased
profitability, itself resulting from skyrocketing growth in e-commerce
transactions, a business that more than offsets stagnating revenues from
traditional retailers. The fact that certain lifestyle changes are happening
worldwide is also helpful because it means that the successful new
technology-based business models being established in some countries
stand a good chance of working elsewhere as well.

3PLs like DHL, Fedex or Ocado are also leading the charge because
they and a few other specialists of their ilk are the only MNEs who
actually know how to run efficient but complex modern warehouses,
if only because that is their full-time business. Whether this relates to
automated pallet-handling systems that shorten shipment processing
times, parcel-sorting robots, driverless goods movers, robotic arms fitted
with picking sensors or scanner-equipped conveyor belts – technological
know-how in this sector has advanced to the point of making it almost
impossible for MNEs who do not possess the relevant capabilities to
compete with those that do.

The main problem for the big 3PLs is when their e-commerce
customers play them off against one another to squeeze margins. This
makes it harder for the 3PLs to accumulate the capital they need to
acquire the most up-to-date technology. Even worse, because their
production organisation is often built to external specifications and
cannot be altered as quickly as contracts can be cancelled, they risk
spending enormous sums on technology only to see the customers on
whose behalf they made a technological investment disappear before
it can be amortised. The end result is that despite the generally very
positive effects that technological progress has had on the logistics
business, it also gives players in this sector the headache of having to
figure out how to size their capacities – a factor input dilemma that has
plagued MNE upstream operatives for countless years.

Case study 15.2: Amazon continues to amaze

Fig 15.4
Amazon has become the indispensable e-retailer in much of the world.

One good way of ascertaining the dynamism of an economic activity is to track changes in the companies comprising its top tier. Various IB sectors are characterised by a host of highly successful MNEs that have been global champions for a very long time. But new names always make it to the top periodically, often as a result of technological progress. Amazon is a prime example. Founded in 1994 by Jeff Bezos, by 2021 this retail (and warehousing) giant already figured among the world's ten largest MNEs in revenue terms, top five in workforce terms and was number one in R&D expenditures, spending almost twice as much as the number two in this category (Samsung). The first performance (revenue) is an outcome, the second and third (staff and technology) are inputs. It is impossible to achieve the former without the latter.

Technology has been key to Amazon's rise from the very outset. Some advances in this area were started outside of the company, shaping an external environment in which it was then able to nurture its own trademark specialties. For instance, the excess fibre optic infrastructure and capacity remaining after the dot.com boom and bust period of the early 2000s left more than enough spare bandwidth for Amazon to develop its incredibly high-traffic business model – first in its home market (the USA), then internationally – based on a centralised and real-time communication of offers and orders. A decade and a half later, the Covid-19 pandemic would induce new global consumer habits reliant on the very same technologies as the ones in which Amazon had built up its strengths. One example is the ease with which consumers who were locked down at home could both order goods and track courier and driver movements using Amazon's own website. It is a service enabled by the "dark store" mini-urban warehouses that the company has built in innumerable locales worldwide (Bradshaw 2021) – last mile logistics hubs that are increasingly being robotised to further improve stock picking and handling operations. Similarly, Amazon has also been using technology to exert greater control over the downstream portions of its value chain, increasingly in-sourcing its front-door delivery function worldwide and even trialing new drone-based delivery modalities. Add to this the Amazon Prime film and TV service plus the successful Alexa technology – which, in its own way, also constitutes a delivery system (of on-line vocal commands, this time) – and Amazon seems perfectly placed for tomorrow's increasingly high-tech world.

Of course, and as often happens in IB, it is a MNE's success that makes it a target. One problem for Amazon is the devastation that the online shopping sector which it spearheads has wreaked upon traditional retailing, a big source of employment in many countries and a key component of the social fabric in most cities. Questions have been raised, for instance, about whether Amazon uses its size (and the masses of customer data it accumulates and processes via AI) to boost the house brands it has been developing and selling to the detriment of customer merchants who have no other choice today but to advertise through its website due to the lack of viable alternatives (Espinoza 2020). The European Union, for instance – already irritated both by rumours of difficult labour relations within Amazon – launched an investigation of this giant MNE in winter 2021, ostensibly under the auspices of an anti-trust enquiry. It is significant that Amazon responded in a highly conciliatory manner, demonstrating a willingness to cooperate that lowered the tone on all sides and bodes well for a consolidation of its status. Of course, the fact that technological services which this giant MNE provides are appreciated by hundreds of millions of daily consumers all across the world should also help to settle matters.

Case study questions

1. To what extent is Amazon's international success based on technological as opposed to other aspects of its business model?
2. Should the EU try to restrain Amazon's use of artificial intelligence?

Marketing

It would be difficult to overstate the positive impact that AI is having on MNEs' understanding of distant (hence initially unfamiliar) foreign populations, or the secondary effects that these changes are bound to have on the way that international marketing will be performed the future. Add to this the mass migration of consumers worldwide to online shopping (the global rise of e-commerce) and there is an argument that the new technologies' greatest impact will in fact be on MNEs' downstream functions.

With respect to the first point, the basic principle of AI – that machines supplied with huge quantities of behavioural data can be engineered to process all this information in such a way as to reveal heretofore unperceived social realities – goes to the heart of what has always been the key factor of success in international marketing, namely knowledge of foreign customers (Jain and Aggarwal 2020). With AI, it becomes much easier for MNEs – at least those who have access to sufficiently large data sets (a whole topic in and of itself) – to identify consumer preference segmentations much more accurately and quickly. In turn, this will help decision-makers tailor product ranges, adaptations and promotions more closely to what their different target markets really want. There are already manifold examples of this technology being put to good use by the world's largest MNEs, with one noteworthy case being the way that US apparel maker Levi Strauss was able to increase its 2020 year-on-year European revenues by a factor of five simply through a savvy use of marketing-focused AI.

The new technology turns on its head the traditional marketing view that proximity improves knowledge. AI-derived market data give practitioners working out of distant regional or global headquarters greater insight into local market conditions, intimating that MNEs' national subsidiaries may in the future need fewer downstream professionals and more data analysts – a function that can be performed almost anywhere, with potentially very significant implications for the long-standing IB debate about the optimal (de)centralisation of power within MNEs.

Otherwise, it will also take time to gauge the implications of the explosion in digital shopping, another deep global trend that, it should be remembered, started well before the Covid-19 pandemic erupted. In addition to the aforementioned effects on retailer delivery systems, there is likely to be a sea change in the very nature of customer interactions, including promotions. Much greater attention will have to be paid to the various ways that different national cultures process pre-purchase digital advertising in general, transition from a vague interest to an actual click and develop brand loyalty online. Moreover, it remains to be seen whether the quality of analysis in these various domains correlates or not to a given analyst's personal familiarity with a particular market.

As always in IB, certain trends apply more to some populations than to others. What is currently known about e-commerce is that Asia is far and away the biggest market in the world, with 2020 revenues triple the number two region, the USA (Tonby et al. 2020). Asia also stands out because of the high proportion of e-spending being done on a mobile basis, speaking to the relative lack of fixed digital infrastructure in several of the Global South countries (here but also in Latin America) that have recently witnessed a sharp rise in mobile e-commerce, albeit from a very low starting point. This contrasts with the situation in much of the European Union, characterised by a slower rise in digital shopping rates despite the region's generally good Wi-Fi coverage. The lesson is that above and beyond the physical and technological factors shaping different international marketing environments, culture still counts.

Finance

Even if some IB analysts do not view finance as a MNE value chain stage, the impact that artificial intelligence is also having on this activity merits a brief review. First of all, AI is changing the basis on which many companies determine their pricing models (Hudelson 2021). Micro-segmenting global consumer data creates a more rational basis for the discounting practices that up until now often tended to be decided independently by national subsidiaries focused solely on local circumstances, culminating in erratic cross-border pricing. Where MNE sister units used to vary widely in terms of how objectively or subjectively they would assess product mark-ups, if an entire multinational group does its calculations using the same technology, it becomes easier both to rationalise the way products are positioned in different markets and to track the contribution that each makes to total costs.

Lastly, it should be remembered that finance is not only a MNE function but also an IB activity in and of itself. The application of AI (and more broadly, digitalisation) to this business is also reshaping the landscape for banks and other fund providers worldwide. There is a growing realisation today – drawing from insights developed by Jack Ma, the founder of Alibaba, China's answer to Amazon – that "big data" can be useful in both making customer credit decisions and offering more targeted financial products (Tett 2020). The hope here – underpinning a recent AI collaboration between Amazon and Barclays Bank in Germany – is that by using data to improve the quality of credit decisions, lenders will be comfortable offering good borrowers lower rates. It is yet further proof that however important technology and other objective factors are to IB decision-making, consideration must always be given to the human element.

Section II. Technology and MNE careers

The topics discussed in the previous section will all have a big impact on IB practitioners, not only in terms of the way the way that the MNE employing them is bound to conduct business in the future but also because of the implications for their own careers. Readers aspiring one day to higher echelon positions will want to reflect upon the skill sets that they need to acquire, where they might be asked to apply such skills and the different ways of developing them. It is an analysis that opens the door to final reflections on life working for a MNE.

Future IB skill sets

Although future practitioners should be able to transfer many of the skills they hone using the new technologies from one job to another, there is

Fig 15.5
Technology is changing
MNE working habits and
job specifications.

of course some correlation between the prospects for different economic
sectors and the particular aptitudes that will be required of people
working in them. A good starting point here is the quasi-consensus that
exists today about the variable outlook for sectors (like healthcare, data
analytics, cybersecurity and even education) where the implementation
of teletechnologies will lead to job growth, as opposed to other sectors
(like face-to-face retail, hospitality, local and personal services, assembly
lines and warehousing operations) where automation will necessarily
result in jobs being destroyed. There is little doubt that global demand
for manual labour or for positions requiring little more than basic
cognitive skills will plummet over the next few years, certainly in the
Global North but increasingly in the Global South as well. For the many
hundreds of millions of workers currently employed in such capacities,
the big question is how to transition to higher-level activities with better
prospects. The problem in many countries is the lack of mobility between
workers' three main career pathways, each of which future-proofs
employment to a greater or lesser degree (see Table 15.3). On top of this,
it must also be remembered that the cumulative micro-consequences of
workers' personal fortunes will always product effects at a macro-societal
level as well. Clearly, the countries that do better at transitioning their
workforce to higher value-added employment will fare better on the
whole, affecting in turn the IB framework in which MNEs evolve.

The World Economic Forum recently asserted that half of today's
global workforce will be in desperate need of upskilling or reskilling
within a few short years. In a similar vein, Finnish telecoms MNE
Nokia has specifically predicted that by the year 2030, almost 70
percent of all positions will be in so-called "new-collar jobs", divided
between traditional blue-collar workers supported by robots and
white collar jobs. The latter functions will differ from the way they
are currently being performed insofar as much more work is going to
be done remotely (using 5G-powered automation) and because of the

Teletechnologies -
Technologies
enabling work over
long distances.

Table 15.3
Variable outlooks for future IB career trajectories

Value-added intensity of activity	High	Medium	Low
Professional mindset	Conceptual	Technical	Repetitive
Requisite skills	Blue-sky thinking	Problem-solving	Basic cognitive
Autonomy	High	Medium	Low
Vulnerability to technological displacement	Low	Medium	High
Vulnerability to international displacement	Low	Low	High
Initial education	Higher	Further	Secondary
Initial career training	Internships	Apprenticeships	On the job
Ongoing training	Bespoken seminars	Short courses	On the job
Reporting lines	Executive	Middle management	Site supervisor

greater creativity that AI and machine learning are expected to foster (Weldon 2020). The challenge for IB practitioners aspiring to senior responsibilities then becomes how they might develop the skill set enabling them to fulfil such expectations.

Almost without exception, the aptitudes being described today as desirable and even indispensable include a capacity for critical thinking, self-management, "active learning, resilience, stress tolerance and flexibility" (WEF 2020a) as well as "a collaborative mindset and an ability to deal with ambiguity and complexity" (Kumar and George 2020). Crucially, this means that above and beyond the task-oriented technical skills that people acquire through formal academic education and/or vocational training, future professionals will also want to demonstrate their capacity to acquire soft skills on the job, some of which they can "learn-by-doing" either when participating in company-organised innovation programmes or, in the case of frontline operatives, via apprenticeships.

These new skills expectations do not mean that more formal educational pathways – like universities or further education colleges – have less value than before. Indeed, there is a strong thread of commentary speaking to graduates' potentially superior capacity for benefitting from the lifelong learning that is an adjunct of a more holistic approach to professional qualifications. The common thread, however, is that personal skills are enhanced when employee mindsets are flexible – the kind of worldview that this book has already suggested is a precondition for succeeding in IB in general. "In the automated future, workers [who] will be able to acquire new skills by using tools and systems that augment human abilities [will find it] easier to change jobs across industries. This will make employment and the overall economy more adaptive and resilient to change" (Weldon 2020). Again, it is a vision that emphasizes a dynamic over a static understanding of competitive advantage.

Career geographies

As always in IB, the question of what should be done is inextricably linked to asking where this should be done. The technological changes affecting today's IB environment have certain geographic implications that are also important to future practitioners. After all, as focused as people are on what they want to do in their careers, they are likely to be just as interested in where they are going to do this.

The first thing to note is the conjunction of a clustering effect – where high value-added activities amass in specific locales as MNEs seek to maximise knowledge spillovers – and the spread of remote "teleworking", a work organisation that has accelerated in response to the Covid-19 pandemic and which is enabled by a number of new digitalisation technologies including superfast 5G broadband. Local labour markets that have already started to decline after failing to transition into advanced technological activities might shrink further if clustering accelerates. With future jobs growth even more concentrated than it is today, regional wealth disparities will be exacerbated, widening the gap that already exists between skilled and unskilled labour, between rural and urban societies and – indeed – unless fairer, more inclusive HRM policies are implemented – between men and women.

The focus in this scenario would have to be on mobility, with employees prepared to move to the world's centres of growth, either to be hired locally or to work on an expatriate basis. Some forecasters expect this to translate into more jobs in the Global South: due to the emerging markets' dynamism and because, notwithstanding teletechnologies, it might still be helpful to keep some people deployed "on the ground" (PWC 2020). Such assignments could either occur at the behest of Global North MNEs entering what they consider new markets (via foreign direct investment, for instance) or, increasingly, they might involve people getting hired by an emerging MNE working in its home country. Note, however, a body of research indicating that Western managers' willingness to move to certain environments depends largely on subjective factors like their familiarity with the conditions there and the country-of-origin image of the Global South company they are considering (Zhang et al. 2020). More broadly, there are also more objective factors that might limit future global flows of skilled workers, as exemplified by the very negative effects that the travel restrictions introduced in the wake of the Covid-19 pandemic have had on the cross-border recruitment of talent. IB practitioners are not robots, after all. Notwithstanding the rational decision-making processes that Network theory asserts – positing that the main motive for a company (or indeed, a businessperson) moving somewhere is to gain proximity to a centre of power – career choices will also always be tinged by personal preferences or practicalities.

The opposite view is that the remote working arrangements that countless MNEs have implemented in the wake of the Covid-19 pandemic will become deeply ingrained, the end result being that many managers will no longer live in proximity to the office with which they are titularly associated but instead work mainly from their home, situated in a community that they have chosen for personal reasons. The idea here is that the abandonment of office work is not only desirable for social distancing reasons but also because decades of wealth accumulation in a few concentrated locales (financial centres, technology hubs) have made living there very expensive and difficult. An example is the recent "Techodus" of companies and workers from Silicon Valley, due to skyrocketing house prices in the San Francisco Bay Area, and because the former Trump administration's hostile attitudes towards international talents caused them to take their skills to countries other than the USA (Thornhill 2020b). The end result has been a kind of e-globalisation characterised by a greater geographic dispersion of tech unicorns, each using cloud computing technologies to provide their services all across the world.

Unicorns - Privately owned technology start-ups valued at more than $1 billion.

The new model global tech economy has certain advantages for employees, including greater flexibility in people's personal schedules, less time lost to commuting, the lesser environmental footprint of the smaller office spaces that are now required and the greater possibility today of recruiting talented individuals who would have otherwise refused to move to the locale where a company has its offices. Of course, remote working also has its downsides. Office interactions are crucial to creating a sense of belonging and social cohesion within a workforce, something that is particularly important in MNEs whose typically more internationalised and dispersed personnel stand to benefit most from physical proximity because this makes it easier for them to integrate their diverse knowledge bases and cultures (Seo et al. 2020). Hybrid workforces – with some people working in the office and others at home – can also create problems with hierarchisation, atomisation and isolation (because some people may struggle to bond with colleagues via videoconferencing). On top of this, the idea of working from home will be less welcome in some countries than it is in others: for culture-related status reasons; because Wi-fi connectivity and cybersecurity is not always guaranteed; due to fears that employees working on-site will have a higher status than their off-site colleagues; and/or simply because less-affluent workers may have fewer home computers and/or live in smaller, more cramped conditions. For all these reasons, the idea of technologically enabled remote working seems to have progressed more in the Global North than South, although contradictorily enough, there is also an argument that teleworking could accelerate offshoring to the Global South, given the fact that once an employment connection is broken, it becomes easier for a company to either rehire staff abroad (O'Connor 2020) and/or to replace full-time on-site staff with skilled foreign contractors awarded time-limited assignments. Of course, reallocating work to offshore sites has its own risks for a MNE (teletechnology problems, localised pandemic-related shutdowns), the severity of which will vary depending if the tasks involved are simple and commoditised or complex and strategic. MNEs can, however, remedy these problems with hybrid solutions such as multi-sourcing "white-collar platform work" from an international shortlist of freelance suppliers. This could enhance resilience, which is always a good idea in an era of rapid technological change - and pandemics.

Fig 15.6
Teleworking may lead to further offshoring.

Acquiring useful future IB skills

Of course, discussions about the kinds of skills required for the technologically more advanced IB jobs of the future – and about where such skills might be deployed – are both predicated on workers acquiring them in the first place. This then raises questions about the various approaches that companies and governments are taking worldwide to try and raise the skills levels of their citizens currently in employment and, more broadly, of their general populations.

One starting point here is the revelation in recent studies that companies from different parts of the world have different ways of trying to close the technological and other skills gaps that they have detected (Agrawal et al. 2020). In Europe, for instance, there seems to be a greater focus on schemes that further the skills levels of currently employed workers. This contrasts with North America, where there is more of an expectation that workers take responsibility for their own capabilities, failing which they stand a greater chance of being released. It is an opposition similar to the one found in Asia, between India, where company-organised skills-building activities are common, versus Korea and Japan, where such programmes are less widespread (albeit with much less risk of less-skilled employees getting fired in the two latter countries than in the USA). Note as well the international variations in the degree to which public and private sectors cooperate when establishing skill enhancement programmes. Some countries like Germany stand out for the considerable funding (from government and corporate sources alike) supporting a vocational system that specifically targets school leavers predicted to pursue a mid-tech career pathway. In Korea and Singapore, on the other hand, STEM education is an integral part of the government's standard secondary school offer, with funding contributions from leading MNEs like Samsung being more or less voluntary in nature and largely provided in the name of social sustainability. This is different again from the USA, where secondary schools are largely left to their own devices (and mostly under-funded), as opposed to the country's university sector, which often receives significant contributions from companies seeking to develop graduate skills in the technologies of the future – an approach not dissimilar to the one observed in France, where close ties can be observed between leading corporations and the more technologicallyoriented *Grandes Ecoles*. Lastly, it is worth noting the problems experienced in the UK, where a once thriving industrial apprenticeships system has been more or less discarded, with school leavers often forced nowadays to take responsibility for their own skills training, frequenting further education colleges that are generally very under-funded. Under these circumstances, it is not really surprising that British industrial productivity has plummeted over the years, with the country's technological performance being concentrated at the elite levels of new discovery (like the Oxford Covid-19 vaccine) instead of being spread throughout the wider working population. It is an outcome that reflects the main differences in the way skills sets are distributed in different national business cultures: elite but narrowly spread l versus standardised and widespread. Once again, it shows the primacy of context and comparison in IB studies.

Of course, human agency will also have an impact in this domain like it does in so many others. A recent World Economic Forum study (2020a) has revealed a strong global uptick in the number of individuals seeking to participate in private or government-sponsored online learning programmes (without forgetting a similarly growing interest in employer-sponsored initiatives). Just as instructive is the growing popularity among contemporary learners (students but also the recently unemployed) in subjects like information technology, computer sciences and data analysis. Clearly the message has gone out that if people want to (re-) enter the workforce, this is the training that they need to acquire. It is an opinion shared by the employers surveyed in the same study, most of whom want to reskill and upskill their existing workforce over the next few years in the hope of re-deploying half of those destined to be displaced by automation instead of letting them go. The question then becomes the willingness and ability of current employees to acquire the new skills that will allow such redeployment– and whether a new generation might step into the breach if they fail to do so.

Final reflections on life in a multinational enterprise

In the end, the brightest future IB careers will accrue to those individuals who embody a modern, more technological version of the same qualities and values that have always prevailed in this field, namely openness to new and diverse experiences; intellectual curiosity about models and their universality (or lack thereof); and the ability to simultaneously juggle big-picture contextualisation and finite knowledge (technological but also, of course, commercial and financial, without forgetting economic, political, social and ecological). In short, it is the ability to learn that is the characteristic trademark of a successful IB practitioner and, indeed, the quality that MNEs seek most from the candidates they recruit.

It bears repeating that the ability to learn needs to be demonstrated not only when recent graduates are interviewing at the beginning of their careers but all the way throughout as well. Students reading this textbook need to know that they will have as much, if not more, reading to do once they have joined a MNE as they had during their years of study. The wide general (but also specific technical) culture required of an IB practitioner makes learning not only desirable but also indispensable. MNE employees will almost always know which of their colleagues are coasting on past knowledge as opposed to others that are continuing to develop themselves, with the prospects of promotion being far superior for the latter than for the former. A real-life example of this involves the story of a Europe region marketing manager who used to only concentrate on her commercial responsibilities and let someone else within her strategic business unit take responsibility for the team's information technology needs. Her career progression during the years when she only focused on her official job had been good but not outstanding. When the colleague in charge of coordinating with the company's IT deparment left and she volunteered to assume this responsibility on her teammates' behalf, however, she suddenly found herself being offered promotion after promotion. Whereas senior management had previously identified her as someone who fit into their designated slot – competently but without going beyond her official role - their appraisal of her potential changed once she demonstrated a willingness to leave her comfort zone and acquire technological skills that would not only be helpful to everyone else but which also trained her in the kind of advanced data analytics that improves decision-making in complicated international environments. As much as for the learning she undertook, she was rewarded for wanting to undertake learning. Promoting her under these conditions was a very IB thing for her MNE to do.

All in all, the final word in IB studies is that there can never be a final word. The diversity that lies at the very heart of this discipline is the one real constant over the years. Moreover, the dynamism that marks a career in IB is bound to be reinforced in the years to come as the ranks of senior management are enriched by new contributions from new categories of decision-makers mobilising heretofore underused talents that they will bring to the table, drawing from new experiences rooted in race, ethnicity and/or gender – and indeed, from their heightened technological knowledge. Finishing a textbook with three chapters speaking to three of the phenomena expected to shape IB over the next decade merely re-states the overwhelming likelihood that a similar textbook published in a decade's time will have its own future scenarios to enumerate. In the meantime, the best thing that readers can do is to keep reading.

Attitudes and alternatives

Technological progress and workforce upskilling seem uniquely positive strategies for companies insofar as they increase productivity hence competitiveness. There is a problem, however, with the cost of technological investment, which is sometimes so onerous that it can only be recouped by increasing output – including and maybe especially by increasing international sales. This then forces the company to rival other MNEs that are already technologically advanced. Competing in the higher tiers of a global sector can generate greater gains but automatically entails greater risks as well. Everyone's playing field gets bigger.

Otherwise and from a national government's more macro-perspective, there is evidence that many of the lower-skilled workers currently being displaced by automation have no choice but to transfer to other declining professions due to problems they have in accessing (or internalising) the training required to undertake higher value-added activities. This conundrum infers a need for government to support the expansion of vocational training – but that is also contentious, since it involves using taxpayers' money to improve an input factor (labour) from which the private sector is going to benefit and which it should therefore logically be asked to help finance. This makes the funding of national technology training programmes yet another IB debate that can and should be politicised – like so many other topics in this discipline.

Chapter summary

Out of all the IT-related new technologies, AI and robotics are widely predicted to have the greatest effect on IB over the next few years. The chapter began by reviewing the nature of these technologies and the conditions affecting their implementation in different countries before going on to analyse the impacts that they are likely to have on MNE configurations and value chain operations. The second section then analysed the effects that current technological innovations are apt to have on the IB careers of business school graduates with the imminent intention of working for a MNE. More specifically, it looked at the professional and personal skills that future IB practitioners will want to develop, where they might be expected to deploy these new aptitudes and how they might acquire them. The book then concluded with final reflections on the importance of learning to an IB career.

Case study 15.3: Generation regeneration

Fig 15.7
Many national education systems are starting STEM curriculum earlier.

Note. This case study recounts the real-life experiences recounted by an IB practitioner, with certain details altered to preserve anonymity.

One manifestation of the globalisation trend that relaunched in the 1980s was the mass displacement of manufacturing from the world's older industrialised nations to newly emerging economies, largely in response to the latter's much lower labour costs. This deep trend benefitted Global North consumers by keeping prices low while helping many companies increase profits. It also accelerated the Global South's economic development, alleviating poverty and turning these populations into newly solvent customers for Global North companies facing saturation back home.

Of course, not everyone welcomed these developments, with the main downside being the displacement of many factory jobs that had once been run out of proud manufacturing powerhouses like the United Kingdom. A real fear arose that vast swathes of ex-British factory workers could be condemned to long-term unemployment or poorly paid work in the "gig economy" – a critique sometimes countered by the argument that it was in the UK's interest to outsource simple manufacturing because the local population could then transition into higher-value precision engineering or service activities. Ensuring a successful transition –materialised through UK-based companies offering higher value-added jobs to workers possessing the requisite skills – was therefore seen as key to successful regeneration.

In the UK, much of the work done to achieve such aspirations is organised at a local government level. Certainly, that was the agenda set by an elected official named Jonathan after he was given cabinet responsibility for economic development in London Borough of Marike – a once dynamic manufacturing basin that had, over the years, lost numerous multinational industries to cheaper foreign locations. The challenge became how to reverse Marike's 30-year decline in a way that could benefit the local population and economy.

To entice new MNEs to move back to Marike, Jonathan had his officers put together a high-profile place marketing programme extolling the borough's advantages, specifically its proximity to Central London, good transport links, plentiful industrial land, cooperative government and willing and available workforce. He himself prospected candidates for inward investment and had some small success in convincing a few to move to Marike, in sectors ranging from telecommunications to urban infrastructure and even beer. Jonathan also brokered a relationship between local companies and the British-Indian Chamber of Commerce, in the hope that Marike industrialists could leverage new international contracts to both increase exports and sharpen their know-how.

Alongside this international effort, Jonathan implemented several schemes intended to equip the local population with the skills they needed to take on higher value-added assignments. All age ranges were targeted for professional development, starting with secondary school pupils encouraged to enroll in the new STEM (science, technology, engineering and mathematics) curriculum that Marike schools were asked to formulate. Note that for this latter initiative, a special effort was made to encourage women learners so as to offset men's traditional predominance in STEM careers. Jonathan then went to an American computer giant renowned for its willingness to hunt worldwide for raw talents capable of being moulded into tomorrow's coding and programming geniuses. He persuaded this MNE, in the name of social sustainability, to contribute to a local training provider specialising in BAME (Black and Minority Ethnic) youth and helped to publicise this offer in the local community. Lastly, he brokered meetings between the three foreign MNEs that were still running light engineering activities in Marike, on the one hand, and the district's further education colleges, on the other, to discuss the development of technological training programmes where the companies would provide funding, and the colleges, teachers, equipment and premises. This vocational scheme welcomed school leavers but also older learners, many of whom already had a job but could benefit from an introduction to digitalisation software, smart sensors and even AI technologies – the hope being that their new technical know-how would equip them for the disruptive innovations that employers were planning on introducing within a few short years.

Although it will take decades to fully evaluate the success of these measures, the first signs were good, with the gap between Marike's high manufacturing unemployment rate and the lower average for the rest of London shrinking rapidly over the course of the 2010s. In the middle of this period, Jonathan and his team of officers were awarded a national prize by a UK-wide local government body in recognition of the "entrepreneurial" approach they had taken to regeneration. When asked by an interviewer which key ideas had triggered his programmes, Jonathan referred to the examples of Germany and Sweden: the former because of its *Fachhochschule* system where educators and businesses work together to ensure that school leaver apprentices who are not going to university possess the technical skills that will maximise their productivity once they enter the workforce; the latter because of a commitment to "lifelong learning" shared by government, companies and unions alike. In Jonathan's view, these approaches had proven their value in helping German and Swedish companies fend off the outsourcing and offshoring waves that had devastated the manufacturing sector in most other European countries. IB succeeds not only when practitioners develop their own good ideas but also when they recognise the validity of good ideas coming from elsewhere.

Case study questions

1. To what extent can the technical upskilling of a comparatively more expensive workforce prevent its jobs from being moved to a lower-wage economy?
2. What role should the public sector play in upskilling a country's private sector workforce? What policies have various countries developed in this respect over time?
3. How easy is it to transfer best practice from one country to another?

Discussion questions

1 Which technologies would you add or subtract from the two highlighted in this chapter as being most likely to affect IB over the next decade?
2 What explains Asia's advance in the implementation of today's new technologies?
3 Which cross-border value chain functions are likely to be most affected by robotics?
4 What challenges do MNEs face in upskilling/reskilling current and future workers?
5 How are IB practitioners similar to or different from domestic businesspersons?

References

Agrawal, S. et al. (February 2020). "Beyond hiring: How companies are reskilling to address talent gaps", accessed 31 January 2021 at https://www.mckinsey.com/

Balakrishnan, T. et al. (17 November 2020). "The state of AI in 2020", accessed 24 January 2021 at https://www.mckinsey.com/

Booth, J. (2020). *The Price of Tomorrow: Why Deflation Is Key to an Abundant Future*, Stanley Press, at https://www.amazon.co.uk/dp/B08334WFSQ/ref=dp-kindle-redirect?_encoding=UTF8&btkr=1&asin=1999257405&revisionId=&format=4&depth=2

Bradshaw, T. (12 January 2021). "The pandemic tech boom is reshaping our cities", *Financial Times*.

Chui, M. et al. (13 May 2020). "The bio revolution: Innovations transforming economies, societies, and our lives", accessed 24 January 2021 at https://www.mckinsey.com/

Dekhne, A. et al. (24 April 2019). "Automation in logistics: Big opportunity, bigger uncertainty", accessed 24 January 2021 at https://www.mckinsey.com/

Deng, L. et al. (16 January 2021). "Robot adoption at German plants", accessed 24 January 2021 at https://voxeu.org/

Espinoza, J. (10 November 2020). "EU accuses Amazon of breaching antitrust rules", *Financial Times*.

Fan, H. et al. (30 November 2020). "Labor costs and the adoption of robots in China", *Journal of Economic Behavior and Organization*, accessed 28 January 2021 at https://www.sciencedirect.com/

Hudelson, P. (15 January 2021). "Digital pricing tranformations: The key to better margins", accessed 24 January 2021 at https://www.mckinsey.com/

Jain, P. and Aggarwal, K. (July 2020). "Transforming marketing with artificial intelligence", *International Research Journal of Engineering and Technology*, Volume 7, Issue 7, pp. 291–297.

Kumar, R. and George, S. (21 September 2020). "Why skills – not degrees – will shape the future of work", accessed 24 January 2021 at https://www.weforum.org/

Marin, D. (15 November 2014). "Globalisation and the rise of robots", accessed 24 January 2021at https://voxeu.org/

Miller, J. et al. (8 January 2021). "Car manufacturing hit by global semiconductor shortage". *Financial Times*.

O'Connor, S. (23 November 2020). "The shift to remote work carries an inherent risk". *Financial Times*.

PWC PriceWaterhouseCooper (2020). "Talent Mobility 2020", accessed 4 January 2021 at https://www.pwc.com/

Romei, V. (20 October 2020). "Pandemic boosts automation and robotics", *Financial Times*.

Sandbu, M. (20 December 2020). "Regulation alone will not strengthen Europe's digital sector", *Financial Times*.

Seo, E. et al. (2020). "Blending talents for innovation: Team composition for cross-border R&D collaboration within multinational corporations", *Journal of International Business Studies*, Volume 51, pp. 851–885.

Seric, A. and Winkler, D. (28 April 2020). "Covid-19 could spur automation and reverse globalisation – to some extent", accessed 24 January 2021 at https://voxeu.org/

Sneader, K. and Singhai, S. (4 January 2021). "The next normal arrives: Trends that will define 2021 – and beyond", accessed 23 January 2021 at https://www.mckinsey.com/

Stapleton, K. and Webb, M. (2020)., "Automation, trade and multinational activity: Micro evidence from Spain", accessed 28 January 2021 at https://voxeu.org/

Tett, G. (19 November 2020). "Artificial intelligence is reshaping finance", *Financial Times*.

Thornhill, J. (12 November 2020a). "Is AI finally closing in on human intelligence?" *Financial Times*.

Thornhill, J. (31 December 2020b). "The big questions for Big Tech in 2021", *Financial Times*.

Tonby, O. et al. (2 December 2020). "How Asia can boost growth through technological leapfrogging", accessed 24 January 2020 at https://www.mckinsey.com/

WEF World Economic Forum (October 2020a). "The future of jobs report", accessed 24 January 2021 at http://www3.weforum.org/

WEF World Economic Forum (December 2020b). "Mapping TradeTech: Trade in the fourth industrial revolution", accessed 24 January 2021 at http://www3.weforum.org/

Weldon, M. (14 October 2020). "5G-powered automation will transform work for the better", *Financial Times*.

Wood, C. (23 December 2020). "Stand ready for the big five technology convulsions reshaping markets", *Financial Times*.

Zhang, J. et al. (October 2020). "Willingness to work for multinational enterprises from emerging countries: The case of Chinese multinational enterprises in the Netherlands", *International Business Review*, Volume 29, Issue 3, accessed 31 July 2021 at https://www.sciencedirect.com/

Index